Unemployment

Unemployment

*Macroeconomic Performance
and the Labour Market*

RICHARD LAYARD   STEPHEN NICKELL

RICHARD JACKMAN

OXFORD UNIVERSITY PRESS
1991

Oxford University Press, Walton Street, Oxford OX2 6DP

Oxford New York Toronto
Delhi Bombay Calcutta Madras Karachi
Petaling Jaya Singapore Hong Kong Tokyo
Nairobi Dar es Salaam Cape Town
Melbourne Auckland

and associated companies in
Berlin Ibadan

Oxford is a trade mark of Oxford University Press

Published in the United States
by Oxford University Press, New York

British Library Cataloguing in Publication Data
Data available
ISBN 0–19–828433–0
ISBN 0–19–828434–9 (pbk.)

Library of Congress Cataloging in Publication Data
Layard, P. R. G. (P. Richard G.)
Unemployment : macroeconomic performance and the labour market /
Richard Layard, Stephen Nickell, Richard Jackman.
P.   cm.
Includes bibliographical references and index.
1. Unemployment.   2. Inflation—Effect of Unemployment on
3. Labor market.   I. Nickell, S. J.   II. Jackman, Richard, 1945–.
III. Title.
HD5707.5.L393 1991   331.13'7—dc20   91-605
ISBN 0–19–828433–0
ISBN 0–19–828434–9 (pbk.)

Typeset by Latimer Trend & Company Ltd, Plymouth
Printed in Great Britain by
the Alden Press, Oxford

**To the millions who suffer
through want of work**

CONTENTS

Preface   xiii

1. Overview   1

The Microfoundations

2. Wage-Bargaining and Unions   83
3. Efficiency Wages   150
4. Wage Behaviour: the Evidence   173
5. Job Search: the Duration of Unemployment   216
6. Mismatch: the Structure of Unemployment   285
7. The Pricing and Employment Behaviour of Firms   336

The Macroeconomic Outcome

8. The Macroeconomics of Unemployment   361
9. Explaining Post-war Unemployment in OECD Countries   397

Policy Implications

10. Policies to Cut Unemployment   471

Annexes   512
Discussion Questions   556
List of Symbols   560
List of Tables   562
List of Figures   565
References   568
Index   593

Detailed Contents

Preface   xiii

1. Overview   1

1. Facts to be explained   1
2. Our broad approach   8
3. What determines equilibrium unemployment?   12
4. Why does unemployment fluctuate?   16
5. How do real wages relate to unemployment?   19
6. If labour markets don't clear, why don't wages fall?   22
7. How do import prices, taxes, and productivity affect unemployment?   31
8. How does job-search behaviour affect unemployment?   34
9. Is unemployment voluntary or involuntary?   41
10. Why are some groups more unemployed than others?   44
11. Why has unemployment differed between countries?   48
12. How can unemployment be reduced?   61
13. Summary   75
    Notes   77

MICROFOUNDATIONS

2. Wage Bargaining and Unions   83

1. Basic facts and bargaining theory   86
2. How unions affect unemployment   100
3. Bargaining over employment? A digression   112
4. Does featherbedding create jobs?   118
5. A world with good and bad jobs   125
6. Corporatism: centralized versus decentralized bargaining   129
7. Trade unions and nominal inertia   138
8. Summary   143
    Notes   144

3. Efficiency Wages   150

1. 'Recruit, retain, and motivate': basic theory   151
2. Underlying mechanisms   157
3. Evidence   164
4. Efficiency wages and the persistence of unemployment   168
5. Summary   170
   Notes   172

4. Wage Behaviour: The Evidence   173

1. Is the labour market competitive? Inter-industry evidence   174
2. The effect of outside and inside factors   181
3. The effect of the characteristics of the firm   189
4. The effect of unions   193
5. The effect of unemployment   199
6. The effect of productivity   204
7. Real wage resistance and benefit effects   209
8. Nominal inertia   211
9. Summary   212
   Notes   214

5. Job Search: The Duration of Unemployment   216

1. Unemployment duration: the facts   220
2. Job search: theory   230
3. Job search: the facts   235
4. Determinants of duration: cross-section evidence   250
5. Determinants of duration: time-series evidence   256
6. Unemployment inflow and the U/V curve   266
7. Determinants of vacancies   272
8. Summary   276
   Appendix: Job search of unemployed people in Britain, 1987   277
   Notes   282

6. Mismatch: The Structure of Unemployment   285

1. The structure of unemployment: some facts   286
2. How the structure of unemployment is determined   299
3. How mismatch is related to the NAIRU   307
4. Evidence on sectoral wage behaviour and on mobility   313
5. Policy implications   317
6. Mismatch and the unemployment–vacancy relationship   324
7. Summary   331
   Notes   333

7. The Pricing and Employment Behaviour of Firms   336

1. A static model of price and employment behaviour   338
2. Dynamic models of prices and employment with convex adjustment costs   342
3. Time delays and staggered price-setting   351
4. Optimal pricing with fixed costs of adjustment   354
5. Summary   356
    Notes   358

THE MACROECONOMIC OUTCOME

8. The Macroeconomics of Unemployment   361

1. A closed-economy model   362
2. The dynamics of the model   370
3. The unemployment–inflation trade-off and the NAIRU   377
4. The open-economy model   384
5. The behaviour of the open economy   389
6. Summary   393
    Notes   395

9. Explaining Post-war Unemployment in OECD Countries   397

1 The model   401
2. Evidence on the parameters   402
3. Explaining changes in unemployment   408
4. Explaining the key parameters   413
5. A common multi-country equation for unemployment dynamics   430
6. Unemployment in Britain: a case-study of the open economy   437
7. Summary   448
    Appendix: The derivation of model parameters   449
    Notes   467

POLICY IMPLICATIONS

10. Policies to Cut Unemployment   471

1. Policies for the unemployed: benefits and active manpower policy   472
2. Policies on mismatch: employment subsidies and training   482
3. The reform of wage-bargaining and incomes policy   483
4. Marginal employment subsidies   490
5. Non-targeted public employment   492
6. Profit-sharing   493
7. Work-sharing and early retirement   502
8. Deregulation   508
9. Summary   508
    Notes   510

Annexes   512

1.1   The 'intertemporal substitution' theory of fluctuations   512
1.2   A model of the OECD economy with endogenous commodity prices   513
1.3   Unemployment benefit systems in OECD countries   514
1.4   Wage-bargaining systems in OECD countries   517
1.5   Optimal disinflation policy with hysteresis in wage-setting   524
1.6   Unemployment and inflation series for each OECD country   526

2.1   A brief note on implicit contract theory   533
2.2   Bargaining theory   533
2.3   Properties of the survival function   537
2.4   Effect of employment measures upon wage-bargaining in corporatist
      economies   538

3.1   Efficiency wages and bargaining combined   539

4.1   Wage determination in a turnover model   541
4.2   A model of wages and employment in a two-stage bargaining
      framework   541

5.1   Unemployment stocks and flows: selected countries   544
5.2   The reservation wage: the dynamic programming approach   547
5.3   Allowing for employed job-seekers   549

6.1   Mismatch and substitution between types of labour   550

8.1   A 'disequilibrium' framework   551
      Notes   554

Discussion Questions   556
List of Symbols   560
List of Tables   562
List of Figures   565
References   568
Index of Names   593
Index of Subjects   598

Preface

UNEMPLOYMENT is a major source of human misery. Despite economic growth, it is a bigger problem now than in most of the last fifty years. In Western Europe three times more people are out of work than in the 1960s, and the numbers in Eastern Europe are rising rapidly. The US job market has been more resilient, but in many sections of the community unemployment remains a source of dread.

No economy can function well without some unemployment. But do we really need this much, and, if not, how can it be reduced?

To answer these questions, we must first understand how unemployment comes about and why it changes. This is the prime purpose of this book. We develop a general framework of analysis, and then use it to explain the history of our times. Unemployment depends on so many different factors that it is not easy to find a single coherent framework for analysing how they interact. Yet without such a framework, it is difficult to refute the apparent plausibility of a thousand quack remedies.

An adequate framework requires a new combination of macroeconomics with a detailed micro analysis of the labour market. Traditionally, macroeconomics has concerned itself with how temporary shocks make unemployment fluctuate in the short term around its average level, while labour economics has focused on what determines that average level—factors such as unemployment insurance, labour mobility, and the like. But it has become more and more obvious that the average level itself varies greatly between decades, with previous unemployment exerting a persistent effect on subsequent unemployment. To explain this persistence requires new micro foundations of macroeconomics, going far beyond the influences considered in the 1970s.

A key issue is the role of the employed 'insiders' and the unemployed 'outsiders' in the labour market. How do they affect wage pressure and thus set limits to non-inflationary growth? The employed insiders want to have wages set in their own interest, with little regard to the interests of the unemployed outsiders. But the outsiders still have a role. If they search less hard for work or

xiii

are unsuited to the jobs available, this reduces the effective supply of labour and thus increases wage pressure. Through these mechanisms it becomes quite easy for a relatively small shock, like an oil price rise, to have long-lasting effects.

But there are many other issues. To fit them all in, we develop a single integrated view of the labour market, which explains both the stock of unemployed people and the flows into and out of unemployment, as well as the evolution of wage and price inflation. It allows for union bargaining, efficiency wages, unemployment insurance, labour mobility, and many other influences. It draws on microeconomic and macroeconomic evidence, and provides a convincing explanation of the astonishing movements of unemployment and inflation that have occurred in the post-war world.

The analysis we present is in many ways original. This is bound to be the case, since recent events have so often been inconsistent with old explanations, and since many basic issues still lack an adequate analytical framework. But we have also aimed to incorporate the best of existing knowledge. In this sense we have tried to write a book that is simultaneously a contribution to new social thought and a textbook.

Using the book

We have written the book so that it can be used at many levels. The overview in Chapter 1 is much simpler than the rest, and can, we hope, be followed by any general reader with knowledge of elementary economics. We have tried to write it so that the argument can be followed while skipping the maths. For what ultimately matters is what is in the minds of politicians, administrators, and voters. We would not have written the book unless we hoped that it would affect how they think.

Much of the rest of the book is also widely accessible. It aims to link theory and evidence throughout. None of it requires more than intermediate economics, and each chapter has a succinct summary.

For teaching purposes, a macro-oriented course could consist of Chapters 1, 2 (Sections 2 and 7), 3 (Section 4), 5 (Section 5), 6 (Section 3), 7, 8, and 9, while a labour-oriented course could consist of Chapters 1, 2, 3, 4, 5, 6, 9, and 10. As a stimulus to thought, we include at the end a series of possible discussion/ essay questions.

Our thanks

We have learned so much from our colleagues that it is difficult to distinguish our own thoughts from theirs. Nearly every idea and piece of evidence in the book has been discussed with Christopher Pissarides and Sushil Wadhwani; and Sushil Wadhwani has generously allowed us to use his draft as the basis for Chapter 4. We have also had constant help from our other colleagues in the Centre for Labour Economics (now incorporated in the Centre for Economic Performance), and especially from Charles Bean, David Grubb, Andrew Oswald, and James Symons. In some ways the authors of this book should be 'the Centre'.

But we owe almost as much to our friends in the USA. Olivier Blanchard has taught us so much on so many issues, as has George Johnson. Rudi Dornbusch has been a constant source of encouragement.

Orley Ashenfelter generously proposed holding a conference near Princeton, NJ, to discuss an early draft of the book. The John M. Olin Conference on Unemployment was organized by Alan Krueger, and we learned much from the comments of the discussants: Robert Solow, Lawrence Katz, Peter Diamond, George Johnson, Alan Krueger, Gregory Mankiw, Larry Summers, Martin Weitzman, David Card and Richard Freeman. They caused us much rewriting! We also organized our own conference in Sussex, England, and have learned much from the contributions of our colleagues here: James Malcomson, Alan Manning, David Stanton, Richard Blundell, Patrick Minford, Andrew Britton, Gavyn Davies, George Alogoskoufis, Peter Sinclair, Michael Hoel, and, above all, David Soskice.

We have received invaluable research support from Savvas Savouri, who played a major role in Chapter 6, and from Paul Kong and Mark Walsh, who did the same in Chapter 9. The whole manuscript received comments from Mark Armstrong; and Bob Gross, Hartmut Lehmann, Marcus Rubin, Mike Sadler, and, especially, John Schmitt were key figures in helping us with the final draft.

The number of drafts has been uncountable. Only three wonderful people could have coped with the typing: Joanne Putterford, Phyllis Gamble, and Caroline Wise.

Andrew Schuller has been a patient and helpful publisher, and Gary Fethke organized an enjoyable stay for two of us at the University of Iowa, where some key chapters were drafted. Throughout the long process of this work, the Centre has been financed by the Economic and Social Research Council, the Department of Employment, and the Esmee Fairbairn Charitable Trust. Their support has been invaluable. But the chief support has been from our families.

Thank you all.

London and Oxford

R. L.
S. N.

December 1990

R. J.

1

Overview

UNEMPLOYMENT matters. It generally reduces output and aggregate income. It increases inequality, since the unemployed lose more than the employed. It erodes human capital. And, finally, it involves psychic costs. People need to be needed. Though unemployment increases leisure, the value of this is largely offset by the pain of rejection.

So we have to explain why unemployment occurs, how it changes over time, and why it affects some kinds of people and not others. We can then suggest policies that will make things better.

1. Facts to be explained

Let us begin with some of the key facts that need to be explained.

1. Unemployment fluctuates over time. Some of these fluctuations are short-term changes which get reversed quite quickly. But there are also big secular changes (see Fig. 1). The 1960s were a period of very low unemployment. Since then unemployment has risen in most countries. The rise has been much worse in the European Community (EC) than anywhere else, with unemployment increasing in every year between 1973 and 1986 (from 3 to 11 per cent). After 1986 European unemployment fell—but very slowly. The major falls were in Britain and Spain.

2. Unemployment varies much more between business cycles than within business cycles. This is true of almost all countries. For example, unemployment rose hugely between the 1920s and 1930s, and then fell to very low levels in most countries during and after the Second World War.

This is illustrated for the USA and Britain in Fig. 2, which shows how much average unemployment varies between business cycles. To summarize this variation, we can divide the twentieth century into half-decades and take the average unemployment for each half-decade. For Britain the standard deviation of these averages is 3.16. This is hardly any less than the standard deviation of the *annual* unemployment rates, which is 3.36. The corresponding figures for the USA are 4.29 and 4.88. Thus, most of the annual variation 'comes from' the long-frequency fluctuations between half-decades rather than from the short-frequency fluctuations within half-decades.[1] Conventional business cycles account for relatively little of the history of unemployment.

The reasons for this are a central issue of this book. In our view they stem

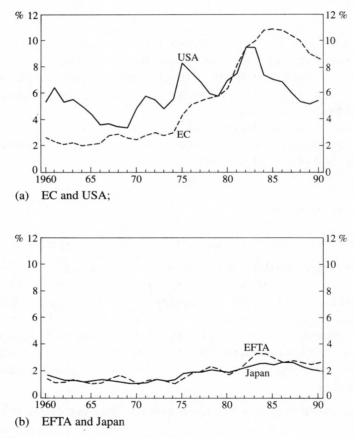

(a)   EC and USA;

(b)   EFTA and Japan

Fig. 1.   *Unemployment, 1960–1990.*

EFTA (the European Free Trade Area) includes Norway, Sweden, Finland, Austria, and Switzerland. Detailed annual data for each country are in Annex 1.6.

Sources: see Annex 1.6.

from two sources: first, there are long-period changes in social institutions; and, second, big shocks to the system (such as oil price rises or major wars) have long-lasting effects.

The main social institutions that affect unemployment are the unemployment benefit system and the system of wage determination. In Europe unemployment benefit systems generally became more generous financially and more readily available up to around 1980. This did not happen in the USA. In addition, the position of the unions became increasingly strong in Europe up to around 1980. Union membership grew in many countries, while

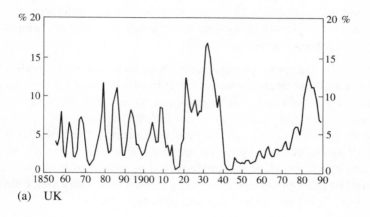

(a) UK

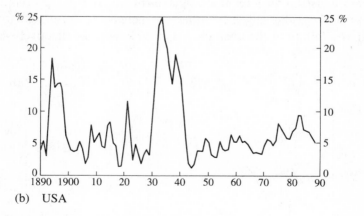

(b) USA

Fig. 2. *Unemployment since the nineteenth century*:

Sources: *UK*: Feinstein (1972), chained to data in Annex 1.6, OECD series. *USA*: 1890–1954: U.S. Census, *Historical Statistics of the United States* (1976), Series D85–86, chained to 1955–1990 series in Annex 1.6.

it was falling in the USA. On most indices, militancy grew. For example, from 1968 onwards (the year of the Paris riots) the number of industrial conflicts rose sharply (see Fig. 3). Even before the oil shocks, increased militancy was making it difficult to contain inflation without rising unemployment.

However, it was the big commodity price shocks of 1973–4 and 1979–80, shown in Fig. 4, that gave the sharpest impulse to inflation. And the ensuing efforts of governments to disinflate then led to the further rises in unemployment. Europe, as a major importer of raw materials, suffered much more from the commodity price rises than did the USA, which is much more self-sufficient. But what surprised everybody was the extraordinary persistence of European unemployment in the 1980s, and the fact that inflation fell so slowly despite mass unemployment. In our view, a key to understanding this is the emergence of long-term unemployment.

3. The rise in European unemployment has been associated with a massive increase in long-term unemployment (see Table 1). In most European countries the proportion of workers entering unemployment is quite small: it is much lower than in the USA and has risen little. The huge difference is in the duration of unemployment: nearly half of Europe's unemployed have now been out of work for over a year. As we shall show, long-term unemployment reduces the effectiveness of the unemployed as potential fillers of vacancies. Once long-term unemployment has taken root, it has a very weak tendency to correct itself. This helps to explain our next fact.

4. In many countries the level of unemployment has risen sharply relative to the level of vacancies. This suggests either an increase in mismatch (which we question) or a failure of the unemployed to seek work as effectively as before.

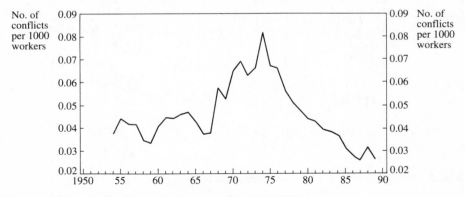

Fig. 3. *Industrial conflicts in the OECD, 1954–1989.*

Sources: ILO, *Yearbook of Labour Statistics*; OECD, *Labour Force Statistics*.

5. Despite all this, unemployment is untrended over the very long term (see Fig. 2). This is a key point. It suggests that ultimately there are very powerful mechanisms at work which have forced the number of jobs to respond to huge changes that have occurred in the numbers of people wanting work. It also suggests that in the long term productivity and taxes have no impact on unemployment.

These are the main time-series facts about unemployment. We turn now to cross-sectional differences.

6. Unemployment differs greatly between countries (see Table 1). Among industrial countries it is worst in the countries of the EC, while the other Western European (EFTA) countries (Norway, Sweden, Finland, Austria, and Switzerland) and Japan have been remarkably unaffected (see Fig. 1). This appears to be due to differences in social institutions, with the latter countries having highly corporatist wage-setting arrangements and/or shorter entitlements to benefits (combined in Sweden with major training and employment programmes for the unemployed). These arrangements both inhibited unemployment's original rise and ensured that unemployment did not persist. In the USA there was by contrast a big rise in unemployment in the early 1980s, but, with unemployment benefits running out after six months, this could not persist.

The differences in unemployment rates in Table 1 are quite genuine. People are defined as unemployed if they are not working but are available for work and have taken specific steps to find work within the last month. This is the

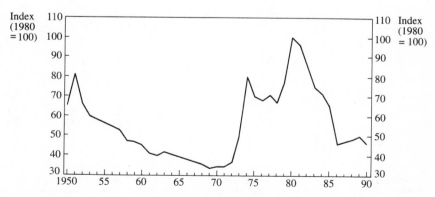

Fig. 4. *Real commodity prices (including oil), 1950–1990.*

Sources: UN, *Statistical Papers* Series M, no. 82, and *Monthly Bulletin*; IMF, *International Financial Statistics*; OECD, *Main Economic Indicators*.

standard OECD definition, and the data are generally got by household surveys such as the EC Labour Force Survey or the US Current Population Survey. Unemployed people do of course differ in the intensity with which they seek work and in the type of work they are willing to accept. We shall discuss this issue at length. But it in no way invalidates the concept of unemployment, any more than the concept of tallness is invalidated by the fact that, if we defined tall as 'over 6 feet', some people are even taller.

7. Few unemployed people have deliberately chosen to become unemployed. In the USA about a half have lost their last job, a quarter have re-entered the

Table 1 *Percentage of labour force unemployed, 1979 and 1990*

	1990			1979		
	All	*Under 1 year*	*Over 1 year*	*All*	*Under 1 year*	*Over 1 year*
Belgium	8.7	1.9	6.8	8.2	3.4	4.8
Denmark	9.6	6.8	2.8	6.2	—	—
France	8.9	5.4	3.5	5.9	4.1	1.8
Germany	5.0	2.6	2.4	3.2	2.6	0.6
Ireland	14.0	4.8	9.2	7.1	4.8	2.3
Italy	7.9	2.4	5.5	5.2	3.3	1.9
Netherlands	7.6	3.8	3.8	5.4	3.9	1.5
Portugal	5.1	2.5	2.6	4.8	—	—
Spain	16.2	6.7	9.5	8.5	6.1	2.4
UK	6.5	3.6	2.9	5.0	3.8	1.3
Australia	6.8	5.2	1.6	6.2	5.1	1.1
New Zealand	7.6	—	—	1.9	—	—
Canada	8.1	7.6	0.5	7.4	7.1	0.3
USA	5.5	5.2	0.3	5.8	5.6	0.2
Japan	2.1	1.7	0.4	2.1	1.7	0.4
Austria	3.3	2.9	0.4	1.7	1.5	0.2
Finland	3.4	2.8	0.6	5.9	4.8	1.1
Norway	5.3	4.7	0.6	2.0	1.9	0.1
Sweden	1.6	1.5	0.1	1.7	1.6	0.1
Switzerland	1.8	—	—	0.9	—	—

Source: Unemployment rates have so far as possible been standardized, as described on page 529. Percentage of unemployed who are unemployed over one year is from OECD, *Employment Outlook*, 1985, Table H (for 1979) and 1990, Table M (which refers to 1988 or 1989).

Notes: Detailed country series for unemployment and inflation are given on pp. 526–32.

Throughout this book, 'Germany' refers to 'West Germany'.

labour force after an interval, and over 10 per cent are looking for their first job. Figures for the UK are similar. Only a small minority become unemployed by quitting their last job. Thus, the issue of whether unemployment is in any sense voluntary arises mainly in relation to the duration of unemployment rather than the inflow into it.

8.   Unemployment differs greatly between age-groups, occupations, regions, and races. As Table 2 shows, young people are much more likely to be unemployed than older people. In some countries like Italy and Spain the differences are truly astounding. And it is clear that countries differ less in the 'core'

Table 2   *Percentage of labour force unemployed, 1987*

	All workers (1)	Over 25		Under 25	
		Men (2)	Women (3)	Men (4)	Women (5)
Belgium	11.0	5.6	15.3	16.0	27.1
Denmark	7.8	5.2	9.4	9.3	11.9
France	10.5	6.4	10.1	19.6	27.9
Germany	6.2	5.1	7.5	6.1	8.5
Greece	7.4	3.8	6.7	15.5	35.1
Ireland	17.5	13.5	18.5	27.2	22.6
Italy	7.9	2.3	6.5	21.0	30.1
Netherlands	9.6	6.8	11.7	14.2	14.3
Portugal	7.0	3.3	5.6	13.1	21.5
Spain	20.1	11.9	16.8	39.9	50.1
UK	10.2	8.8	8.0	16.9	14.6
Australia	8.0	5.6	6.1	15.0	14.5
New Zealand	4.1	1.9	2.4	6.1	5.5
Canada	8.8	7.0	8.4	14.9	12.5
USA	6.1	4.8	4.8	12.6	11.7
Japan	2.8	2.6	2.4	5.4	5.0
Austria	3.8	3.4	3.7	4.4	4.7
Finland	5.0	5.0	3.8	9.7	8.1
Norway	2.1	1.8	1.5	3.8	3.9
Sweden	1.9	1.4	1.5	4.4	4.0
Switzerland	2.4	—	—	—	—

Sources: For total unemployment see p. 526. Age analysis is: *EC*, Eurostat, Series 3C, *Employment and Unemployment*, 1988, Table IV/1, all figures being multiplied by ratio of col. (1) to the Eurostat total; *Others*: ILO, *Yearbook of Labour Statistics*, 1988, Tables 1 and 9B, multiplied by ratio of col. (1) to ILO total.

unemployment of adult males than in youth unemployment or female unemployment.

The most important difference in unemployment rates is between occupations. The rate for semi- and unskilled workers is four to five times higher than that for professional and managerial workers. Over three-quarters of unemployed men are manual workers. Thus, the theory of unemployment has to focus on the labour market for manual workers. The labour market experiences of economists will not throw much light on the subject.

The challenge is to find a consistent and plausible framework which explains the facts. Needless to say, the most plausible framework is one in which the actions of firms and individuals are described in terms that they would themselves recognize.

2. Our broad approach

In developing a framework, we start from the fact that, when buoyant demand reduces unemployment (at least relative to recently experienced levels), inflationary pressure develops. Firms start bidding against each other for labour, and workers feel more confident in pressing wage claims. If the inflationary pressure is too great, inflation starts spiralling upwards: higher wage rises lead to higher price rises, leading to still higher wage rises, and so on. This is the wage–price spiral.

The outcome is illustrated for the OECD as a whole in Fig. 5. Panel (*a*) shows the level of economic activity measured by the (detrended) proportion of the labour force in work—in other words, the (detrended) employment rate. It shows clearly the pattern of boom and slump over the last quarter-century. Panel (*b*) shows the inflation rate (GDP deflator). In each boom inflation rose and in each slump it fell. Panel (*c*) therefore shows the relation between the change in the inflation rate and the level of employment. The association between the two is clear.[2]

But increasing inflation can be sustained only by continued monetary and/or fiscal injections. If financial policy is stable, with nominal income growing at a constant rate, rising inflation will in due course lead to rising unemployment. Eventually the higher unemployment will stop inflation rising, and both unemployment and inflation will stabilize.

The level of unemployment at which inflation stabilizes is the *equilibrium* level of unemployment. This concept of equilibrium has nothing to do with the concept of 'market-clearing', any more than the equilibrium of a system of

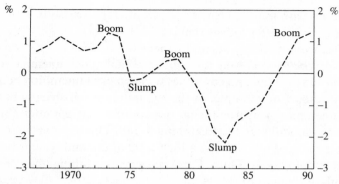

(a)   Employment rate (minus trend)

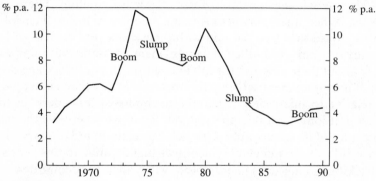

(b)   Inflation rate

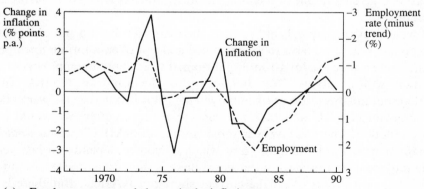

(c)   Employment rate and change in the inflation rate

Fig. 5.   *Unemployment–inflation trade-off in the OECD.*

For trend see note 2. Inflation is change in GDP deflator.
Source: OECD.

pulleys has to do with market-clearing. It simply represents the state to which the system will return after a disturbance.

However, as we have seen, unemployment often takes a very long time to return to its original level. And it is not true that, once unemployment has risen, inflation starts to fall and continues to do so until unemployment returns to its original level. For example, in the EC inflation fell sharply in the early 1980s while unemployment was rising, but stabilized in the later 1980s when unemployment was still high but beginning to fall. This suggests that inflationary pressure is reduced not only by a high *level* of unemployment but also by *increases* in unemployment. Thus, if unemployment is falling (even though it is still high), inflation may not fall at all.

It is easy to see why inflation is affected not only by the level of unemployment but also by whether unemployment is rising or falling. There are two main reasons. When unemployment is rising, people are losing their jobs, and when the employed 'insiders' bargain with their employers the fear of job loss induces wage restraint. But when unemployment is falling, very few workers need worry about their jobs and the fall in unemployment fuels wage pressure.

Second, if unemployment is rising, this means that last year's unemployment was low relative to this year's. Thus, the unemployed 'outsiders' include no large backlog of long-term unemployed, and employers perceive the majority of the unemployed as employable. This helps to restrain inflationary pressure. By contrast, if last year's unemployment was high relative to this year's, there will be a backlog of long-term unemployed, who will have become demoralized and deskilled and will not be perceived as desirable by employers. In this situation a given amount of unemployment will be less effective in restraining inflation.

If wage pressure depends not only on this year's level of unemployment but also on last year's, we have to augment our concept of equilibrium unemployment. There is indeed a long-run equilibrium at which both unemployment and inflation will be stable. We shall call this the long-run NAIRU (non-accelerating-inflation rate of unemployment).[3] But if last year we were above the long-run NAIRU and then fell back to it immediately, we would have rising inflation. There is however some 'short-run NAIRU', which *would* be consistent with stable inflation, and which of course depends on last year's unemployment. In this view of the world there is short-term 'hysteresis', in the sense that past events affect the current short-run NAIRU. But there is no long-term 'hysteresis': there is a unique long-run NAIRU. In the end, the unemployment rate always reverts. And employment always adjusts to the size of the labour force.

Thus, the theory of unemployment goes as follows.

1. There is a long-run NAIRU which depends on social and economic variables. It is of course subject to long-term change (e.g. from different benefit systems or wage-bargaining arrangements) and to temporary change (e.g. from changes in oil prices).
2. Nominal demand shocks move employment away from the NAIRU and move inflation in the same direction as employment.
3. Supply shocks move employment by moving the NAIRU, and move inflation in the opposite direction to employment.
4. Once unemployment is away from the NAIRU, it takes some time to return even if inflation is stable.

There is no point trying to label this theory as Keynesian or classical. It has classical elements (the NAIRU) and it has Keynesian elements (the role of demand and the role of persistence). So it is best to avoid the use of those terms, which mean something different to every reader.

The issue of market-clearing

As we have said, our concept of equilibrium does not imply market-clearing. Everyone knows that some people fail to get jobs, while others who are just like them succeed. What explains this process of job rationing? Why do firms not drop their wages, so that it becomes worthwhile for them to employ the extra workers? There are two main explanations. First, every personnel director will tell his board that this will reduce morale and cause trained workers to quit; the losses from this would outweigh the savings made on the lower wages. This is the 'efficiency wage' explanation. Second, the union may prevent the firm paying less.

But we have to be careful here. Even when unemployment is high, there are not queues for all vacancies. There is a secondary sector of the labour market that does more or less clear (e.g. in catering, cleaning, maintenance and repairs, and some retailing and construction). If people are unemployed, it is generally because they have decided against these jobs. They are however willing to work in a range of good 'primary' sector jobs, but they cannot get them. In this sense unemployment is both voluntary and involuntary.

Outline

Our task now is to develop this framework in more detail, and to use it to explain the facts. When we have done this, we should have a good idea about how unemployment can be reduced.

Thus we shall proceed in this Overview chapter by asking (and answering) the following ten questions:

- What determines equilibrium unemployment?
- Why does unemployment fluctuate?
- How do real wages relate to unemployment?
- If labour markets don't clear, why don't wages fall?
- How do import prices, taxes, and productivity affect unemployment?
- How does job-search behaviour affect unemployment?
- Is unemployment voluntary or involuntary?
- Why are some groups more unemployed than others?
- Why has unemployment differed between countries?
- How can unemployment be reduced?

The questions follow the sequence of the book (except for the first three). The answers that we give in this chapter will inevitably be somewhat terse and dogmatic, but we use the rest of the book to substantiate them at leisure.[4]

3. What determines equilibrium unemployment?

When buoyant demand reduces unemployment (at least, relative to recent average values) inflationary pressure develops, and when unemployment is high the reverse happens. In a sequence of years when the average price level is stable, inflationary pressure means rising prices; in a sequence of years when the average inflation rate is stable, inflationary pressure means rising inflation. Since around 1970 the latter case is the most relevant, and, as we have seen in Fig. 5(*c*), there is a clear positive relation between changes in inflation and the (detrended) employment rate. In each case high employment applies an impulse to the inertial process by which prices are evolving, and a wage–price spiral develops with wages and prices chasing each other upwards.

Wage-setting and price-setting

Why exactly does a wage–price spiral develop? The answer is that stable inflation requires consistency between

(*a*) the way in which wage-setters set wages (W) relative to prices (P), and
(*b*) the way in which price-setters set prices (P) relative to wages (W).

Only if the real wage (W/P) desired by wage-setters is the same as that desired by price-setters will inflation be stable. *And the variable which brings about this*

12

consistency is the level of unemployment. This affects the wage mark-up and also (probably) the price mark-up. Thus, inflation will be stable only if unemployment is at the appropriate equilibrium level. By the same token, if financial policy ensures that inflation *is* stable, then unemployment will adjust to its equilibrium level.

Thus, unemployment is the mechanism which ensures that the claims on the national output are compatible. If a worker produces 100 units of output priced at $1 and wage-setters set his wage at $60, then the worker gets 60 units of output and profit-receivers get 40 units per worker. If this is what wage-setters and price-setters intended, we have an equilibrium. But if wage-setters aim at 61 units ($W/P = 61$) and price-setters aim to provide profits per worker equal to 41 units ($W/P = 59$), we have an inconsistency. This leads to a wage–price spiral, as wage-setters try to recoup the losses imposed on them by price-setters, and vice versa. In the long run, unemployment will have to be higher in order to reduce both sets of claims until they are equal with each other. Only in this way is the wage–price spiral eliminated.

There is another equally important spiral which unemployment eliminates. This is the wage–wage spiral. If unemployment is too low, wage-setters will try to raise their relative wage. Only if the labour market is slack enough will this leapfrogging be eliminated. In equilibrium, unemployment must be high enough to induce each particular wage-bargain to equal the bargain expected to prevail elsewhere.

We can illustrate all this with the following stripped-down model, in which (as throughout the book) parameter symbols are generally written as positive. We look first at price-setting, then at wage-setting. Prices (of value added) are set as a mark-up on expected wages. The mark-up tends to rise with the level of activity although this effect may not be very strong. (And if it is non-existent we have 'normal-cost' pricing.) Thus,

$$p - w^e = \beta_0 - \beta_1 u \qquad (\beta_1 \geqslant 0), \qquad (1)$$

where p is log prices, w^e log expected wages, and u the unemployment rate. This is graphed in Fig. 6(a) as the intended real wage set by price-setting. It can, if one likes, be thought of as the 'feasible' real wage—that real wage which (for given productivity) price-setters are willing to concede.

We turn now to wage-setting. Wages are set as a mark-up on expected prices, with the mark-up tending to rise as the employment rate rises and unemployment falls. Hence

$$w - p^e = \gamma_0 - \gamma_1 u \qquad (\gamma_1 > 0). \qquad (2)$$

13

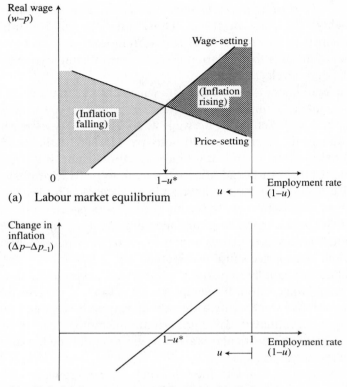

(a)   Labour market equilibrium

(b)   Relation between unemployment and inflation

Fig. 6.   *Unemployment and inflation.*

This is graphed in Fig. 6(*a*) as the intended real wage set by wage-setting. It is, if you like, the 'target' real wage which wage-setters intend.

If actual wages and prices are at their 'expected' values ($p = p^e$, $w = w^e$), the equilibrium unemployment rate is given by adding (1) and (2) to obtain

$$u^* = \frac{\beta_0 + \gamma_0}{\beta_1 + \gamma_1}. \tag{3}$$

This is illustrated in Fig. 6(*a*). The wage-setting and price-setting lines are drawn for $p - p^e = w - w^e = 0$, and their intersection determines equilibrium unemployment and real wages. Any factor that exogenously raises wage push (γ_0) or price push (β_0) raises the equilibrium rate. Any factor that raises real wage flexibility (γ_1) or price flexibility (β_1) reduces the equilibrium rate.

14

Unemployment and changes in inflation

If expected values of prices and wages are *not* realized, we have

$$u = \frac{\beta_0 + \gamma_0 - (p - p^e) - (w - w^e)}{\beta_1 + \gamma_1}$$

or

$$u = u^* - \frac{(p - p^e) + (w - w^e)}{\beta_1 + \gamma_1}.$$

Assuming that the 'surprises' on wages and prices are similar,

$$u - u^* = -\frac{1}{\theta_1}(p - p^e), \tag{3'}$$

where $\theta_1 = (\beta_1 + \gamma_1)/2$, which is a measure of real wage and price flexibility. Thus, low unemployment is associated with positive price surprises.

Suppose that we are in a period when inflation (Δp) has no long-run trend, and inflation is perceived as a random walk with

$$\Delta p = \Delta p_{-1} + \varepsilon,$$

where ε is white noise, Δ means the change since the previous period, and -1 means one period earlier. Then the rational forecast of inflation is

$$p^e - p_{-1} = \Delta p_{-1}.$$

In consequence, the price 'surprise', $p - p^e$, is

$$p - p^e = p - p_{-1} - \Delta p_{-1} = \Delta p - \Delta p_{-1} = \text{change in inflation.}$$

Price surprises are equivalent to increases in inflation. The same is true of wages.

Thus, equation (3') implies that

$$\Delta p - \Delta p_{-1} = -\theta_1 (u - u^*). \tag{3''}$$

This is a standard Phillips curve relation and is shown in Fig. 6(*b*). When unemployment is lower than u^*, inflation is increasing; and vice versa. Thus u^* can be thought of as the non-accelerating inflation rate of unemployment (NAIRU).[5]

Notice that inflation in one year is influenced by previous inflation. There is thus an element of 'nominal inertia' in the system: nominal prices are influenced by past history, and not only by forces at work today. The explanation of nominal inertia which we have just given is that the past influences expectations (so that unemployment can fluctuate only if expec-

15

tations turn out to be wrong). But in fact, as we shall explain later, nominal inertia arises also from staggered wage- and price-setting, and from the cost of changing wages and prices.

4. Why does unemployment fluctuate?

In the long run, unemployment is determined entirely by long-run supply factors and equals the NAIRU (u^*). But in the short run, unemployment is determined by the interaction of aggregate demand and short-run aggregate supply. Short-run aggregate supply is given by

$$\Delta p - \Delta p_{-1} = -\theta_1 (u - u^*). \tag{3''}$$

Aggregate demand is (with suitable choice of units) given by

$$u = -\frac{1}{\lambda} (m - p),$$

where m is the log of nominal GDP (adjusted for trend real growth). This aggregate demand relation implies that

$$\Delta p = \Delta m + \lambda(u - u_{-1}). \tag{4}$$

This demand curve (D) is drawn together with the short-run aggregate supply curve (SRS) in Fig. 7(a). Together they determine the current levels of unemployment and inflation.

This framework brings out two key points. First, a 'demand shock', associated with a rise in Δm, will shift D outwards and thus raise both inflation and employment. By contrast, a 'supply shock', associated with a rise in u^*, will also raise inflation but will reduce employment (see Fig. 7(b)).

The general expression for the level of unemployment is, from combining (3'') and (4),

$$u = \frac{1}{\theta_1 + \lambda} [\theta_1 u^* + \lambda u_{-1} - (\Delta m - \Delta p_{-1})] \tag{5}$$

If Δm is constant for long enough and u^* is constant, Δp_{-1} converges on Δm and unemployment converges on u^*.

This provides an adequate framework for analysing the history of our times.

Demand and supply shocks

In the late 1960s and early 1970s demand was stoked up, partly because of the

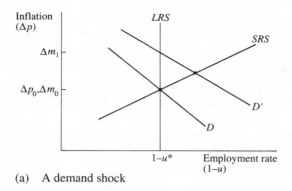

(a) A demand shock

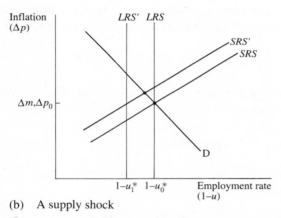

(b) A supply shock

Fig. 7. *Aggregate supply and demand:* (a) *a demand shock;* (b) *a supply shock.*

Vietnam War. Δm rose, dragging up inflation and driving down unemployment (see Fig. 7(*a*)).

But, partly as a result, there followed in 1973–4 the huge rise in the price of commodities, including oil, mostly supplied from outside the OECD. This (together with greater union militancy) raised the NAIRU in the OECD, at least for a time—from u_0^* to u_1^*. The short-run aggregate supply curve therefore shifted leftward (see Fig. 7(*b*)). In consequence inflation rose, but this time unemployment rose also. Many analysts at the time were baffled, since they had been educated to believe that inflation and unemployment always moved in opposite directions, as in Fig. 6(*b*). But this is true only when the shock is a demand shock: with a supply shock, inflation and unemployment move together.

17

Following on the first oil shock there was little demand deflation, so inflation fell little. But then followed the second oil shock in 1979–80, which again raised inflation and also unemployment. At this point the electors in most countries declared that enough was enough: inflation must be reduced. There followed massive demand deflation in all countries, and by 1985 OECD inflation had been reduced to the same level as existed in 1969. At the same time, OECD unemployment had risen by over a half.

It was already evident by the middle 1980s that European inflation was coming down much more slowly than might have been expected, given the high level of unemployment. Since then performance has been even more disappointing. In 1985–6 we had a beneficial oil shock, and real commodity prices fell to the same level as around 1960. One would have expected this to produce a major fall in inflation and unemployment. There has indeed been some fall in unemployment, but OECD inflation by the end of the 1980s was the same as in 1985.

Persistence

These disappointing experiences have raised in sharp form the issue of hysteresis in unemployment. Clearly, we have to modify our model to allow for this. If wage and price behaviour depends on the change in unemployment as well as on its level, the aggregate supply curve (3″) becomes

$$\Delta p = \Delta p_{-1} - \theta_1(u - u^*) - \theta_{11}(u - u_{-1}).\tag{3‴}$$

Thus the short-run NAIRU (u_s^*) is given by

$$u_s^* = \frac{\theta_1}{\theta_1 + \theta_{11}}u^* + \frac{\theta_{11}}{\theta_1 + \theta_{11}}u_{-1}.$$

It lies between last period's unemployment and the long-run NAIRU.[6] The higher the effect (θ_{11}) of the change in unemployment relative to the effect (θ_1) of the level, the nearer is the short-run NAIRU to last year's unemployment.

In terms of policy, hysteresis means that, once unemployment has risen, it cannot be brought back at once to the long-run NAIRU without a permanent increase in inflation. But it can be reduced gradually without inflation rising.

Hysteresis clearly helps us to understand why inflation did not fall in Europe over the later 1980s. But there is also another important element: the fact that extra unemployment has a smaller effect on wages when unemployment is already high than it does in a tighter labour market. One can think of many reasons why wage-setters would respond in this nonlinear way. For example, if an employer found he had 2 applicants per job rather than 1, he would relax his wage by more than if he had 12 applicants rather than 11.

Thus, the large extra unemployment of the 1980s had quite a small deflationary effect. By contrast, the small excess demand of the early 1970s produced quite large increases in inflation.

5. How do real wages relate to unemployment?

The next question is, Where do real wages fit into the picture? It is often claimed that unemployment occurs because real wages are too high. Is this true? We can discuss the issue first in the long term and then in the short term. Both analyses draw on Fig. 6(*a*).

In the *long term* the issue is whether the mark-up of price over wage-cost rises with the level of economic activity; i.e., does the 'price-setting' real wage in Fig. 6(*a*) slope down to the right? This is a matter of controversy.

We can begin with the extreme case of 'normal-cost pricing', where (for a given capital stock) the price mark-up is constant. In this case, if there were a spontaneous increase in wage pressure, it would not actually have any effect on real wages. But it would raise unemployment, as illustrated in Fig. 8. Thus the problem is not that real wages are too high, but that too high real wages are desired at given unemployment. This is always the root of the problem. There can be extreme problems of wage pressure without any evidence of an actual 'wage gap', and indeed the whole concept of the wage gap tends to confuse rather than clarify.

Of course, if economic activity does raise the price mark-up, as in Fig. 6(*a*), then extra wage pressure will indeed raise real wages as well as unemployment. But the ultimate cause of both unemployment and higher real wages is the wage pressure. Unemployment and real wages are jointly determined.

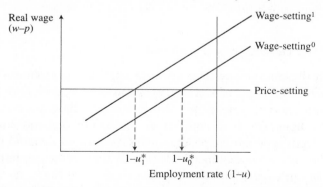

Fig. 8. *With normal-cost pricing, real wage pressure raises unemployment but not real wages.*

Turning to the *short term*, what happens to the real wage if a demand shock reduces unemployment? This depends on the structure of wage- and price-setting. To understand what is going on, it is helpful to rewrite the price equation as

$$p - w = \beta_0 - \beta_1 u - (w - w^e) \tag{1'}$$

and the wage equation as

$$w - p = \gamma_0 - \gamma_1 u - (p - p^e). \tag{2'}$$

It can be seen that, when inflation is increasing ($p - p^e > 0$, $w - w^e > 0$), the real wage is below what wage-setters intended, and above what price-setters intended. Thus, inflation is the mechanism that reconciles the struggle for shares of the national cake, by cheating both price-setters (capitalists) and wage-setters of what they intended. Hence the observed point is in the darkly shaded area in Fig. 6(*a*).[7]

But has the real wage moved up or down, compared with its equilibrium value? It depends. With equal inertia in both price- and wage-setting (i.e. $p - p^e = w - w^e$), the real wage rises so long as the wage-setting line is steeper than the price-setting line.[8] However, in practice there may be different degrees of wage and price inertia, and in most countries there is more inertia in the formation of prices than wages. Thus, in terms of our equations p^e adjusts more rapidly to p than w^e adjusts to w, making it likely that observations will be close to the 'wage-setting' line.

In fact, in our estimates real wages generally rise in a (demand-led) boom. The same is true of most of the standard macroeconomic models used in public debate. This reflects the fact that our model and theirs are very similar. So is the model of the man-in-the-street, who also believes that real wages rise in a boom. However, this is not what many economic textbooks say.

Relation to new classical macroeconomics

We should at this point make clear how our approach compares with the 'new classical macroeconomics' of Lucas (1972) and others. Both approaches have an equilibrium unemployment rate. But in the new classical model, what we call the 'price equation' is thought of as the labour demand curve of firms selling in perfectly competitive product markets. Labour demand is unaffected by money illusion or nominal inertia. It follows that real wages fall in demand-led booms. In our own approach we prefer to think of the 'price equation' as representing a locus of price–employment combinations consistent with profit-maximizing behaviour by monopolistically competitive firms. There is substantial nominal inertia in pricing largely because of staggered price-setting and the costs of frequent price adjustment.

Turning to the 'wage equation', the new classical model would call this a labour supply equation, which is held to be relevant since the labour market is continuously in balance, with workers on their supply curves. In booms, workers underestimate prices and think real wages have risen when they have not. This elicits an increased labour supply. There is however no satisfactory evidence to support the view that cyclical changes in employment correspond to changes in the amount of labour people wish to supply. As Annex 1.1 shows,* the 'intertemporal substitution' theory of fluctuations has little factual basis.

By contrast, we think of the relationship not as a supply equation but as a wage-setting equation, with wages tending to exceed the supply price of labour. If wages are set unilaterally by firms, it may still be in their interest to set them above the market-clearing level ('efficiency wages'). Or firms may be forced to do this by union bargaining.

So labour-market-clearing is not a necessary condition for equilibrium. Market-clearing is even less likely during fluctuations. Disequilibrium wage-setting does not necessarily require misperception by workers, since nominal inertia can be readily explained by overlapping wage contracts.

Although our interpretation of the structural model differs so sharply from the new classical model, it remains true that the reduced forms are indistinguishable. Equation (3′) is the so-called 'Lucas supply curve'. In Lucas's interpretation, the price surprise causes the difference in output; in ours (as in the original Phillips curve) the difference in output causes the price disturbance. But the relationship is the same.

Since the policy implications of the two approaches are so different, it is very desirable to find independent evidence (from structural relationships, surveys, and the like) that will enable us to distinguish between the two descriptions of the world. We shall be doing this repeatedly.

Another rival analysis of fluctuations is the theory of equilibrium real business cycles. This is based on the idea that fluctuations originate mainly not from demand shocks but from supply shocks to the level of productivity. This approach does have the merit of predicting that real wages rise when output rises. But there is no real reason to think that most cyclical productivity fluctuations are exogenous rather than due to differential labour hoarding or work effort over the cycle. And, worst of all, the theory implies that inflation falls when output rises, despite the clear evidence of episodes when demand pressure increased both output and inflation.

* Annexes appear at the end of the book.

6. If labour markets don't clear, why don't wages fall?

Our approach, therefore, is one in which some labour markets generally fail to clear, and jobs are rationed. The main evidence for this are the queues of applicants for many jobs. Though queues exist for jobs at all levels, skilled workers can generally get jobs in less skilled work. Thus, less skilled workers account for most of the unemployment problem. So why is there this persistent rationing of jobs?

It is not, as in some 'disequilibrium' models, because firms cannot sell all they wish on the product market. It is quite true that they cannot, but this would be so even if there were full employment. For most firms have some monopoly power and therefore set prices above marginal cost in order to maximize profit. This means that they would be happy to sell more at the price they have set, if anyone would buy it. But, unlike the unfortunate workers, who did not set the price of their labour, the suppliers of goods did set the price. The firms are therefore rationed in a quite different sense. We thus reject the goods-market rationing models of Barro and Grossman (1971) and Malinvaud (1977), who assume an arbitrarily rigid price which prevents perfect competitors from selling all they want to: we know of no mechanism that could sustain such a price.

The key problem is in the labour market and revolves around the issue of what stops wages falling when there is an excess supply of labour. There can be two classes of explanation. Either firms are not free to choose the wage, and wage bargaining forces them to pay more than they wish; or, if firms are free to choose and still pay more than the supply price of labour, it must be in their interest to do so.

Efficiency wages

We begin with the case where firms freely choose to pay a high wage in order to maintain high morale and encourage effort. It is easy to see how behaviour of this kind could lead to a pattern of wage-setting where wages are higher than the minimum at which people are willing to work—hence the queue for jobs.

Suppose that in firm i effort per worker is given by

$$E_i = e \left(\frac{W_i}{W^e}, u \right) \qquad (e_1, e_2, > 0; e_{11}, e_{12} < 0),$$
$$+ \quad +$$

where W_i is the wage in the firm and W^e the expected prevailing wage outside. High relative wages elicit effort. So does high unemployment (though high

22

unemployment diminishes the marginal effect of financial reward). Unemployment has this effect both because it affects the ease of finding another job if you lose this one, and because it affects the ease of shifting from one job to another without positive support from the current employer.

The representative firm now chooses W_i and P_i to maximize profit, which is

$$\Pi_i = R(E_iN_i) - W_iN_i = R(E_iN_i) - \frac{W_i}{E_i}\, E_iN_i,$$

where $R(\cdot)$ is revenue and N_i is employment. The firm will choose W_i to minimize cost per unit of effort (W_i/E_i), and then will choose N_i to maximize profit. The firm will always find it worthwhile to raise the wage so long as a 1 per cent rise in wages brings forth a more than 1 per cent rise in effort. But, once this ceases to be the case, the firm will stop raising wages. Thus, the optimum wage is where the elasticity of effort with respect to the wage is unity.

This can be seen clearly from the condition for choosing W_i to maximize E_i/W_i, which requires

$$W_i\frac{\partial E_i}{\partial W_i} - E_i = 0.$$

Hence

$$e_1\left(\frac{W_i}{W^e},\, u\right)\frac{W_i}{W^e} = e\left(\frac{W_i}{W^e},\, u\right),$$

where e_1 is the derivative with respect to the expected relative wage.

We now come to the crucial point about general equilibrium. If inflation is stable, the representative firm must willingly set its wage equal to the expected prevailing wage. There must be no leapfrogging and no wage–wage spiral. Thus, $W_i = W^e$ is *the* condition for equilibrium. And it is unemployment that brings this about. So equilibrium unemployment (u^*) is given by

$$e_1(1,\, u^*) = e(1,\, u^*).$$

It is helpful now to relate this to the system of price and wage equations shown in Fig. 6(a). For an individual firm facing a given demand curve, the choice of price is equivalent to the choice of employment. Thus, maximizing profit with respect to employment gives the price equation. This requires

$$\frac{\partial\Pi_i}{\partial N_i} = R'_iE_i - W_i = 0.$$

Suppose for simplicity that output equals E_iN_i. Then $R'_i = P_i(1 - 1/\eta)$, where η is the elasticity of demand facing the individual firm. It is convenient to write

23

$(1 - 1/\eta)$ as κ, which is a measure of product market competitiveness, whose maximum value is unity. Hence the real product wage determined by price-setting is

$$\frac{W_i}{P_i} = \kappa e \left(\frac{W_i}{W^e}, u \right).$$
$$\qquad\qquad + \quad +$$

But in aggregate the price in the representative firm will equal the price in all other firms $(P_i = P)$, and similarly with the wage $(W_i = W)$. So the price equation is

$$\frac{W}{P} = \kappa e \left(\frac{W}{W^e}, u \right).$$
$$\qquad\qquad + \quad +$$

As employment rises, real wages fall (as in Fig. 6(a)), but they are increased by rising inflation. Similarly, maximizing profit with respect to the wage leads to a general equilibrium wage equation

$$\frac{W}{P} = \kappa \frac{W}{W^e} e_1 \left(\frac{W}{W^e}, u \right).$$
$$\qquad\qquad\qquad - \quad -$$

As employment rises, real wages rise (again as in Fig. 6(a)).

We have so far posed the firm's problem in terms of morale and effort. But there are of course many other reasons why a firm can gain by raising its relative wages. In particular, higher wages help it to retain and recruit workers. At the same time, higher unemployment raises profits by reducing quits and vacancies. So the efficiency-wage model reflects the whole range of well established personnel-management practices. And these practices lead firms to offer wages above the market-clearing level.

What evidence is there that this sort of thing is in fact happening, i.e. that workers are receiving rents, even in the absence of unions? One piece of evidence is the queues of applicants. Other, more direct, evidence comes from the fact that wages of otherwise identical workers differ widely between firms and industries, and when individual workers move to 'high-wage' industries most of them get wage increases. The high-wage industries are mostly those where the morale of the workers matters more: they use valuable equipment, or their performance is more difficult to monitor. In this case we have an effort function which includes a firm-specific variable λ_i,

$$e \left(\frac{W_i}{W^e}, u, \lambda_i \right),$$

and the optimum wage for a firm is given by

$$e_1\left(\frac{W_i}{W^e}, u, \lambda_i\right)\frac{W_i}{W^e} = e\left(\frac{W_i}{W^e}, u, \lambda_i\right).$$

Thus, wages will be different in each firm. The law of one wage for each type of labour has been repealed. But we still have to prevent leapfrogging, and in equilibrium unemployment must be high enough to ensure that the average of the W_i does not exceed the prevailing expected wage level (W^e).

Unions and wage bargaining

In the USA, 'efficiency' considerations may well be the main source of non-market-clearing wages; after all, only around one-fifth of all workers are unionized, and fewer in the private sector. But in European countries there is no question that unions are important: in all European countries, over three-quarters of the workforce have wages that are covered by collective bargaining.

Unions have every incentive to set wages above market-clearing levels. And once again, unemployment has got to be high enough to stop leapfrogging between unions. We shall concentrate on the case where bargaining occurs in a decentralized way between each firm and its own union members, though essentially the same analysis would apply in the case of a bargain for a single industry.

In bargaining, the union's main concern is to push for higher wages. However, we cannot assume that this is their only concern, since in some cases a higher wage would lead to job losses for existing union employees.

Of course, not all job losses lead to layoffs, since they can sometimes be accommodated through the natural wastage which occurs when people quit. Thus, though in 1980 nearly half of all British workplaces cut the number of jobs, only 11 per cent of them had any compulsory redundancies (layoffs) and only 9 per cent any voluntary redundancies (with some overlap between the two).[9] The proportion of actual individuals who were made redundant was of course even lower than this—less than 5 per cent a year.

However, even if few lose their jobs, union wage policy will be restrained by fear of job loss if enough individuals *fear* that they will be unlucky. The more random the incidence of job loss, the more will wage-push be restrained by employment considerations. For simplicity, we shall assume that the workers to be laid off are selected randomly.

Apart from their anxieties about jobs, unions want higher wages. Firms, by contrast, push for lower wages. What determines the outcome? As we show in Chapter 2, a reasonable model of the bargained wage is that wage which maximizes $\beta \log(W_i - A)S_i + \log\Pi_i$. Here $(W_i - A)S_i$ represents the worker's rent: W_i is the wage paid by the firm, A is the worker's expected income outside the firm, and S_i is the probability that the worker will remain employed in this firm (which is clearly an increasing function of the level of employment which can be expected, N_i^e). β reflects the degree of union power. We discover the bargained wage by differentiating with respect to W_i. Hence

$$\frac{\beta}{W_i - A} + \frac{\beta}{S_i}\frac{\partial S_i}{\partial W_i} - \frac{N_i}{\Pi_i} = 0,$$

since $\partial\Pi_i/\partial W_i = -N_i$ by the envelope theorem. Thus, the mark-up of the wage over outside opportunities is

$$\frac{W_i - A}{W_i} = \left(\frac{W_i}{S_i}\frac{\partial S_i}{\partial W_i} + \frac{W_i N_i}{\beta\Pi_i}\right)^{-1}$$

$$= \left(\frac{N_i^e}{S_i}\frac{\partial S_i}{\partial N_i^e}\frac{\partial N_i^e}{\partial W_i}\frac{W_i}{N_i^e} + \frac{W_i N_i}{\beta\Pi_i}\right)^{-1}$$

$$= \frac{1}{\varepsilon_{SN}\varepsilon_{NW} + W_i N_i/\beta\Pi_i},$$

where ε_{SN} is the elasticity of survival with respect to expected employment, and ε_{NW} is the absolute elasticity of expected employment with respect to the wage. Clearly, a 1 per cent rise in N_i^e can at most increase S_i by 1 per cent, and in fact the effect must be less since extra workers may be hired. Thus, the elasticity ε_{SN} must be less than unity.

The other terms on the right-hand side depend on the firms' product market power and the labour intensity of production. Suppose the firm faces a product demand curve $Y_i = P_i^{-\eta} Y_{di}$, where Y_{di} is a demand index. And suppose it has a production function $Y_i = N_i^\alpha K_i^{1-\alpha}$, where K_i is the firm's capital. Then, as we show in Chapter 2,

$$\varepsilon_{NW} = \frac{1}{1 - \alpha\kappa}$$

and

$$\frac{W_i N_i}{\Pi_i} = \frac{\alpha\kappa}{1 - \alpha\kappa},$$

where $\kappa = 1 - 1/\eta$ is our measure of product market competitiveness. Hence the mark-up of the wage over outside opportunities is

$$\frac{W_i - A}{W_i} = \frac{1 - \alpha\kappa}{\varepsilon_{SN} + \alpha\kappa/\beta} \tag{6}$$

This is extremely informative. It shows that the mark-up of the wage over the outside alternative (A) is higher the higher is union power (β), the lower is product market competitiveness (κ), and the lower is labour intensity (α). Thus, the mark-up depends on the rents coming from product market power and the quasi-rents coming from fixed capital—together with the power of the union to appropriate these rents.

Thus, when we look at wages in individual industries, we are not surprised that these are higher (for given types of worker) the more concentrated and the more capital-intensive the industry. The mark-up is also higher if the average worker is unlikely to lose his job if employment falls—for example because of high natural wastage.

So much for the mark-up. The actual wage depends also on the outside opportunities for disemployed workers (A). Such workers have a chance of getting another job paying the expected prevailing wage (W^e); if not, they will get benefit (B). Their chance of getting a job is higher the less unemployment there is, and we shall assume the chance is $(1 - \varphi u)$. Thus, the expected outside income is

$$A = (1 - \varphi u)W^e + \varphi u B \qquad (W^e > B).$$

Hence, since wages in a given firm are higher when outside opportunities improve, wages will be higher the lower is unemployment and the higher are benefits.

We can now look at the aggregate economy. If we have an equilibrium with no leapfrogging, $W_i = W^e$. Unemployment adjusts to bring this about. In addition, the wage in the representative firm is, by definition, equal to the aggregate wage: $W_i = W$. Thus, from the definition of A,

$$\frac{W_i - A}{W_i} = \varphi u \left(1 - \frac{B}{W} \right),$$

and hence, using (6),

$$u^* = \frac{1 - \alpha\kappa}{(\varepsilon_{SN} + \alpha\kappa/\beta)(1 - B/W)\varphi}. \qquad (6')$$

If we take the real *level* of benefits as exogenous, this is a real wage equation, and equilibrium unemployment is found by combining it with a standard price equation. If (more realistically) we take the replacement *ratio* (B/W) as exogenous, (6') gives the direct expression for unemployment. It shows that unemployment is higher the greater the power of unions, the greater the rents from product market monopoly and fixed capital, and the higher the replacement ratio.

In this situation unemployment is involuntary. Wages have been set by a process which involves only the firm and its existing workers (the insiders). Provided the unions are strong enough, the resulting real wage exceeds the supply price of the unemployed outsiders.

Of course, if the firm could sack all its workers, this power would vanish. But the specific training embodied in the workforce makes this unprofitable, except in extreme circumstances. And two-tier wage structures, in which outsiders are hired at their supply price, are ruled out because insiders rightly fear that the extra low-wage workers would eventually dominate the union. So union bargaining leads to non-market-clearing wages and unemployment.

Clearly, if there were no rents, there would be no scope for union wage gains. It is therefore obvious that product markets in which there is easy entry for new firms are conducive to low unemployment.

Any union model of unemployment is (and always has been) a model of insider power. But a key issue that arises in the light of recent experience is, Does insider power lead to hysteresis?

Insider power as a source of hysteresis

The answer to the above question is by no means obvious. For example, suppose that the jobs of the workers who control the unions are in effect safe, regardless of feasible variations in the wage. This could easily be the case if layoffs were in order of seniority. And, if so, employment considerations would have no effect on how hard the union pushed for wages. In this case the NAIRU would be given by (6) with ε_{SN} set equal to zero—since wages would have no effect on the survival probability (of the workers who matter). The number of historically determined insiders would have no effect on this period's NAIRU.

However, suppose layoffs are by random assignment. In those firms in which there is a risk of layoffs, wages then have a material effect on the relevant chances of survival ($\varepsilon_{SN} > 0$). And if last year's workforce was large relative to this year's expected employment, a higher wage this year will certainly put existing workers' jobs at risk. Thus, ε_{SN} will be large, wage pressure lower, and unemployment lower. By contrast, if last year's workforce was small relative to this year's expected employment, then a higher wage this year will involve little extra risk, since most existing workers are already safe. Thus, ε_{SN} will be small, wage pressure higher, and unemployment higher. If last year's unemployment was high, therefore, this year's NAIRU will be higher than it would be otherwise.

But how far does such insider power actually explain hysteresis? It is not the main explanation. To investigate this question we have to use micro-data and see how far wages at the micro-level depend on lagged employment at the micro-level—as opposed to lagged employment in the outside labour market. Most studies that have examined this issue have found that the time-series movements of wages depend much more on the outside labour market than on firm-specific, or even industry-specific, factors. It is lagged unemployment in the outside labour market that matters much more than lagged employment in the firm or industry. Theory also suggests that the impact on wage-bargaining of changes in the number of insiders must be quite small. So in order to find a proper explanation of why lagged unemployment matters, we shall have to look at the behaviour of the unemployed outsiders. We come to this in Section 8.

Corporatism

Whether insider power generates hysteresis or not, it certainly increases the average level of unemployment. We would therefore expect that countries with less insider power would have lower unemployment (and perhaps lower hysteresis). Which countries are those?

Insider power requires unions. But it also requires a particular form of union organization—where unions bargain with their employers on a firm-by-firm (or possibly industry-by-industry) basis. In such a context the unions know that, if their workers become disemployed or go on strike, they have a good chance of a job in the rest of the economy. But suppose a single union bargained with a single employer's federation on behalf of the whole workforce: there is then no 'rest of the economy' on which the workers can fall back. (Alternative expected income, A, is zero, assuming that benefits are financed by taxes on employed workers.) The unions are now much weaker in the bargain. In fact, there is a good chance that under this centralized system the bargained outcome will be consistent with full employment. In addition, if the employers bargain as a whole, they will have no efficiency-wage incentive to bid up wages against each other.

We can illustrate the different union objectives in Fig. 9 and show how, if wages were set by unions (with no employer resistance), a national union would be much more likely to choose full employment. The line PP indicates the 'feasible' real wage function of the economy as set by price-setting. This has a corner at full employment. Subject to this constraint, the national union federation would like to maximize the expected income of each member of the labour force, i.e. the expected value of $(N/L)(W/P)$. So, unless the (absolute)

29

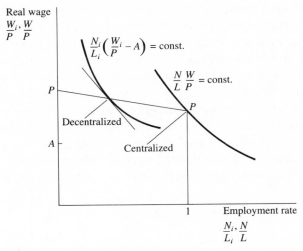

Fig. 9. *Centralized versus decentralized bargaining.*

elasticity of the real wage with respect to employment exceeds unity, which is most unlikely, the national union would choose the corner solution.

By comparison, a decentralized union can for simplicity be thought of as wishing to maximize the expected value of

$$\frac{N_i}{L_i}\left(\frac{W_i}{P} - A\right),$$

where L_i is the firm's 'share' of the labour force. This differs from the objective of the national union because there is a 'rest of the economy' to which disemployed workers can resort, which offers an expected income A. Thus, a decentralized union would never want a wage below A, and the isoquants for its objective function are thus asymptotic to A. (By contrast, the isoquants for the centralized union are much steeper and asymptotic to zero on the vertical axis.) The decentralized union is thus much less likely to want a wage consistent with full employment.

And there is a further point. A union in a single firm can make its workers better off by raising their wage relative to other wages (and thus to the general price level). A national union cannot do this. It can only move back up the line PP in Fig. 9. The single representative firm too has to end up on the line PP, but it perceives its trade-off differently, with imperfect competition providing it with scope for additional real wage increases through increasing the relative price of its product. This is shown by the steeper line in Fig. 9—leading to a second source of extra unemployment when there is decentralized bargaining.

It is thus not surprising that the ordering of countries by unemployment is roughly as follows:

Unemployment	Countries	Unions
High	EC	Pervasive and decentralized
Medium	USA	Limited
Low	Scandinavia, Austria	Pervasive and centralized

Clearly, unemployment is also affected by factors other than the system of wage determination. The other key factor that affects unemployment is the behaviour of the unemployed themselves. We come to this in Sections 8 and 9.

But first we need to ask how import prices, taxes, and productivity affect unemployment, using the framework we have just developed.

7. How do import prices, taxes, and productivity affect unemployment?

The answer is that, in the long run, they do not. If productivity, or living standards generally, had a long-run effect on unemployment, unemployment could not be untrended. And the theories we have been developing are consistent with this. Changes in taxes and import prices are in the long run borne by labour, with no change in unemployment. Similarly (at least with Cobb–Douglas production functions), productivity gains affect price- and wage-setting equally, with no change in equilibrium unemployment.

But in the short run things are very different. This is because the psychology of workers is more complicated than we have so far allowed for. Workers value not only the level of their real consumption wage, but also how it compares with what they expected it to be (or what they think is fair). For simplicity, we can think of people's expected living standards as a multiple of what they had last year. When external shocks like import price shocks, tax increases, or falls in productivity growth reduce the feasible growth of real consumption wages, this generates more wage pressure, which (in equilibrium) requires more unemployment to offset it.

We can illustrate this, first assuming efficiency wages and then wage bargaining. For simplicity, we now assume that effort is given by

$$e\left(\frac{R_i}{R_{i,-1}}, u\right) \qquad (e_1, e_2 > 0; e_{11}, e_{12} < 0),$$

where R_i is the real consumption wage and $R_{i,-1}$ is its lagged value. The real consumption wage is given by[10]

31

$\log R = \log(\text{net wage}) - \log(\text{consumer price})$

$= \log W - t_1 - t_2 - (\log P + t_3 + s_m \log P_m/P) + \text{const.}$

$= \log W/P - (t_1 + t_2 + t_3 + s_m \log P_m/P) + \text{const.}$

Here W is labour cost, t_1 is the rate of labour taxes paid by the employer, t_2 is the tax rate paid by the worker, and t_3 is the indirect tax rate. P_m/P is the price of imports relative to final output and s_m the share of imports in final output.

When import prices rise, this raises consumer prices relative to the GDP deflator (P). Thus there is a wedge ($t_1 + t_2 + t_3 + s_m \log P_m/P$) between the real product wage (W/P) and the real consumption wage (R). This wedge can be increased either by a tax increase or by a terms-of-trade shock, like an oil price rise. When this happens wage pressure increases, and in equilibrium unemployment must rise to contain it.

To check on this, we turn to the condition for the efficient wage (see Section 6). In aggregate (with $R_i = R$), this condition implies

$$e_1 \left(\frac{R}{R_{-1}}, u \right) \frac{R}{R_{-1}} = e \left(\frac{R}{R_{-1}}, u \right).$$
$$\underset{-}{} \quad \underset{-}{} \qquad\qquad \underset{+}{} \quad \underset{+}{}$$

Given the signs of the functions as indicated, a fall in R/R_{-1} must lead to a rise in u. Thus an increase in the wedge raises unemployment. Equally, if productivity growth falls, reducing R/R_{-1}, unemployment will also rise.

A similar story applies in the case of wage-bargaining. The union maximand now depends on $R_{i,-1}$ as well as $R_i - A$. As a consequence, a rise in the wedge will increase the bargained wage mark-up, and hence equilibrium unemployment.

To capture these effects, we need to modify our basic aggregate supply curve (3''') to

$$\Delta^2 p = -\theta_1(u - u^*) - \theta_{11}(u - u_{-1}) + \mu\Delta\text{wedge}, \qquad (3'''')$$

where $\Delta^2 p = \Delta p - \Delta p_{-1}$. This is quite a major modification. It means for example that a country can for a time improve its inflation–unemployment trade-off by appreciating its real exchange rate, i.e. by reducing P_m/P and hence reducing the wedge. Thus, as P_m/P falls, employment can rise with no inflationary take-off (as it did for example in the USA in 1983–5). In Fig. 10 we chart as SS the relation between non-inflationary employment and P/P_m—choosing to measure the relative price this way round in order to make clear that this relation is the non-inflationary supply curve of the economy. In other words, our supply of output (and jobs) increases as our relative price rises. By

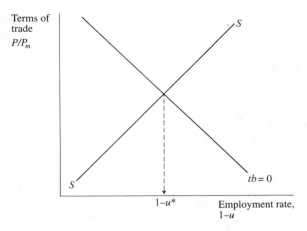

Fig. 10. *The terms of trade and the NAIRU.*

the same token, a real depreciation reduces non-inflationary employment—as the Germans regularly pointed out to the Americans in 1983–5.

Some have argued that this makes the NAIRU a useless concept, since in the short run employment can be increased without inflation rising, provided the value of the currency rises (e.g. through a fiscal expansion with a floating exchange rate). But this criticism misses the mark, for two reasons.

First, the implied loss of competitiveness will worsen the trade balance, and a trade deficit cannot be sustained indefinitely. For the trade balance relative to national income, tb, is given by

$$tb = a_0 - a_1(P/P_m) + a_2u,$$

and this shows that, if trade is to balance ($tb = 0$), a real appreciation in P/P_m will require a rise in unemployment—to restrain imports. This line for balanced trade is drawn in Fig. 10. Where the line crosses the SS line we have the long-run sustainable level of unemployment.

But there is a further point. The effect of the wedge on wage pressure probably does not last for ever. In the end, all changes in potential living standards are accepted by workers with no change in the NAIRU: it is only Δwedge that creates temporary changes in the NAIRU, and the wedge itself has no permanent effect. To this extent we never reach the long-run NAIRU shown in Fig. 10 because SS itself becomes vertical.

This framework of analysis is extremely helpful in looking at the impact of the supply shocks of the 1970s. First we had the 1973–4 commodity price shock which worsened the terms of trade for most OECD countries. This was a much more serious blow (as measured by $s_m\Delta\log P_m/P$) for most European countries

33

than it was for commodity-rich North America. And it was followed by a blow of similar magnitude in 1979–80. For some European countries the combination of the two shocks reduced living standards by around 7 per cent (see Chapter 9, Table 3).

At the same time, productivity growth slowed down throughout the world, and in many countries tax rates increased. It has been more difficult to trace the wage pressure effects of these changes in the wedge. But we shall show later how well the change in unemployment in different countries after each commodity price shock is explained by the size of that shock and by the institutional arrangements in the country.

As we have shown, real commodity prices eventually fell back in the mid-1980s to the same level as in the 1960s—since commodity prices tend to fall in world recessions (see Annex 1.2).[11] This in turn generated a world boom. But European unemployment was still high in the boom, since it had hardly recovered from the earlier recession. Why was this? As we have said, the hysteresis cannot be much explained by changes in the number of insiders. The clue lies in the behaviour of the outsiders.

8. How does job-search behaviour affect unemployment?

This is the element that has so far been lacking from our analysis. The unemployed have not appeared at all as people, whose behaviour matters— merely as pawns, whose number reconciles the claims to the national output. This is not the case, and it is time to expand the model to show how job search affects the equilibrium number of jobs.

The mechanism is this. Wage pressure builds up unless there is a sufficient excess supply of labour. (Firms bid up wages against each other and unions feel strong enough to press their claims.) But if the unemployed seek harder for jobs, this raises the effective excess supply of labour. (Firms can get workers more easily and disemployed people face fiercer competition for jobs.) Thus, if unemployed workers seek harder, there need be fewer of them in order to restrain wage pressure.

This leads us to modify our earlier wage equation to make wages depend on cu rather than u, where c measures the 'effectiveness' of the average unemployed job-seeker. To see exactly how this enters in, we shall start from a rather more structural wage function than we had originally. We shall now assume that, from the point of view of a worker facing possible unemployment, what matters is the chance of getting a job if he searches with a given effectiveness (say with $c = 1$). This chance is H/cU, where H is the number of unemployed people hired per period, U is the number of unemployed, and cU is the number of effective unemployed. But in equilibrium, the numbers hired equal the numbers becoming unemployed. If the fraction of employed workers (N) who become unemployed is s, this means that in equilibrium $sN = H$, so that

$$\frac{H}{cU} = \frac{s}{cU/N} \simeq \frac{s}{cu}.$$

This becomes the relevant variable to explain the wage pressure coming from the workers in wage bargaining.

There is also the wage pressure coming from the firms. This depends on the chances of their filling each vacancy, which (as we show in Chapter 5) is uniquely related to H/cU. So our new wage equation is

$$w - p = \gamma_0 - \gamma_1(cu/s). \tag{2$'$}$$

In equilibrium, the more effective are the unemployed (i.e. the higher is c), the lower is unemployment.

But how are we to measure c over time? One approach might be to replace it by what determines it, including the replacement ratio B/W. But there are many other factors which also affect search effectiveness, including social attitudes to work, the stigma attaching to unemployment, employers' attitudes, and so on. These are very difficult to measure; but fortunately, there is some direct evidence on c from the behaviour of unemployment in relation to vacancies.

The unemployment–vacancy relationship

Given the small amount of information economists have about how their economies work, we need to exploit to the utmost the information that vacancy data provide. In particular, we can obtain direct evidence on the effectiveness of job search (c) by examining the movement of unemployment relative to the level of vacancies.

This is because there is a 'hiring' (or 'matching') function which explains the flow of unemployed people into work. This flow (H) depends positively on the number of vacancies (V) and also on the number of effective job-seekers (cU):

$$H = h(V, cU). \tag{7}$$

Provided the market is large enough, an equiproportional increase in vacancies and in effective job-seekers will induce an equiproportional increase in hirings. Hence the chances of finding a job are given by

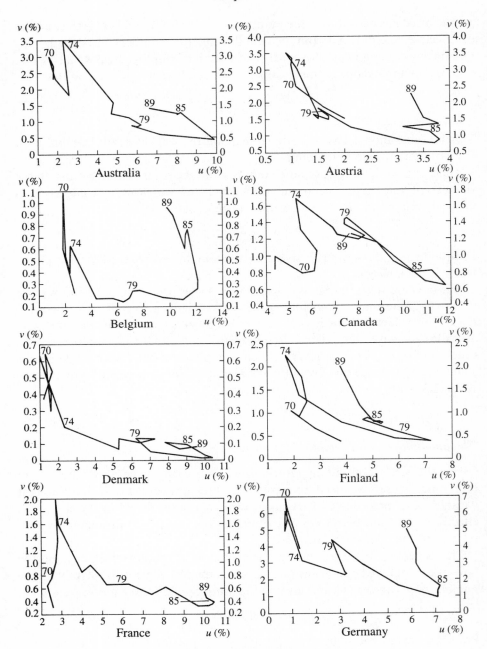

Fig. 11. *Vacancy rates* (v) *and unemployment rates* (u).

Source: Jackman *et al.* (1990).

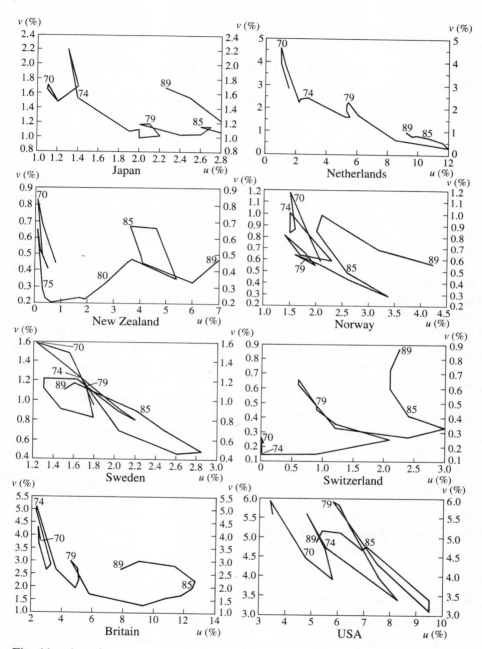

Fig. 11. (*cont.*)

$$\frac{H}{U} = c\,h\left(\frac{V}{cU}, 1\right).$$ (8)

Both (7) and (8) imply that, from knowledge of H, V, and U, we can infer changes in c.

Alternatively, we can use the fact that in equilibrium $H = sN$ to obtain the relationship

$$s = h\left(\frac{V}{N}, \frac{cU}{N}\right).$$ (8')

This is the famous Beveridge curve (or U/V curve). For given s, shifts in this curve reflect shifts in c. As Fig. 11 shows, there has been a considerable increase in many European countries in the level of unemployment at given vacancies. (In the USA it shifted out but has now shifted back.) What could account for the outward shift of the European Beveridge curve?

From what we have said so far, the explanation would have to be a fall in search effectiveness (c) among the unemployed. However, there is another possible explanation to be considered. There could have been an increase in 'mismatch' between the pattern of unemployment and vacancies across sectors (i.e. regions, industries, or skill-groups). An increase in mismatch would shift out the U/V curve; for, provided the relation (8') between U/N and V/N in each sector is the same and convex to the origin, the aggregate curve will be 'further out' if U/V differs between sectors. However, if the relevant mismatch indices are computed, it turns out that they have not risen at all since the early 1970s in Britain or in most other European countries (see Chapter 6).

So we come back to search effectiveness. Either workers have become more choosey in taking jobs, or firms have become more choosey in filling vacancies (owing for example to discrimination against the long-term unemployed or to employment protection legislation). Both are possible, and we need to be very clear about this when we use our concept of effective job-seekers (cU). Effectiveness (c) reflects not only how hard the workers look for work, but also how willing the employers are to consider them.

Factors affecting job-finding

We can now identify two measurable factors that affect c and thus job-finding—see equation (8). The first is the *benefit–income (replacement) ratio*, whose effects have been much studied in Britain and the USA, using both cross-section and time-series data. The results typically suggest that the elasticity of exit rates from unemployment with respect to the replacement ratio are of the order of 0.2–0·9.

In most European countries, though not in the USA, replacement ratios rose significantly in the 1960s or 1970s or both (Emerson 1988*b*). In Britain they rose by a half from the mid-1950s to the mid-1960s but not thereafter. This increase may have had some lagged effect on unemployment but can explain only a fraction of the increase in unemployment in the 1970s, and none of that thereafter. It is of course possible that the absolute real value of benefits also has an effect (e.g. that the relevant replacement ratio relates to incomes above some subsistence level). But this is pure speculation.

The second factor is *how long people have been unemployed.* The apparent effect of this can be seen in striking form by comparing the exit rates from unemployment of people with different durations. Fig. 12 shows this for both Britain and the USA. In the USA there are very few long-term unemployed. But in Britain, where there are many, the exit rates are much lower for the long-term unemployed. One reason for this must be that the more energetic job-seekers find jobs first, so that the long-term unemployed include a higher proportion of less energetic people. But time-series evidence makes it clear that another reason is the direct effect of unemployment duration upon a given individual. Long-term unemployment both demoralizes the individual and is also used by employers as a (biased) screening device. Thus, if the average duration of unemployment rises, we can expect the average level of c to fall. Hence unemployment will rise relative to vacancies.

The exact degree to which duration affects exit rates cannot easily be resolved from studies of individual data, owing to the problem of unobserved differences between individuals. But aggregate time-series equations indicate a considerable effect of duration structure upon average exit rates.

Moreover, in regressions of the unemployment rate on the vacancy rate and the proportion of long-term unemployed, the latter term has a significant positive effect. The same is true when the proportion of the long-term unemployed is included in a real wage equation: it increases wage pressure. In other words, the long-term unemployed are much less effective inflation-fighters, since they are not part of the effective labour supply.

Between 1979 and 1986, the proportion of unemployed who had been out of work for over a year rose from around 20 to around 40 per cent in Britain. Using the regression estimates, this in itself would explain one-third of the outward shift of the U/V curve. Similar findings apply in other major European countries.

It is noticeable in Fig. 13 that all the countries where long-term unemployment has escalated except Italy have unemployment benefits of some kind that are available for a very long period, rather than running out after 6 months (as in the USA) or 14 months (as in Sweden). In countries in which benefits are indefinitely available, employment is much less likely to rebound after a major downwards shock.

If employment does not rebound quickly, further changes may occur affecting job search. An unemployment culture may develop, through the external effect of one man's unemployment on another man's job search. If no one in your street is out of work, the social pressure to find work is much

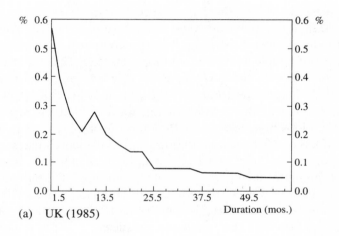

(a)   UK (1985)

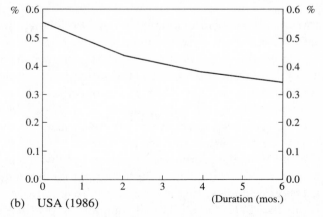

(b)   USA (1986)

Fig. 12.   *Proportion of unemployed people leaving unemployment within the next 3 months, by existing duration of unemployment.*

Sources: (*a*): see Ch. 5, Fig. 4(*c*); (*b*): see Ch. 5, Table 4.

greater than if (as sometimes happens in Britain) half the street has been out of work for some years. Mechanisms of this kind could help to explain the persistence of unemployment. Thus, if the recent history of unemployment affects the current (short-run) NAIRU, this is mainly because it affects the search effectiveness of the unemployed 'outsiders', rather than because it reduces the number of 'insiders' in work.

9. Is unemployment voluntary or involuntary?

In the last section we showed how the search behaviour of individuals affects equilibrium unemployment. At any moment there are outstanding vacancies as well as job-seekers, but it takes time to match them to each other. In consequence, unemployment and vacancies coexist. The harder people look for work, the lower unemployment will be, because wage pressure will be reduced (at any given level of unemployment).

This raises the question of whether unemployment is voluntary or involuntary. The question is fruitless. There are two aspects to reality:

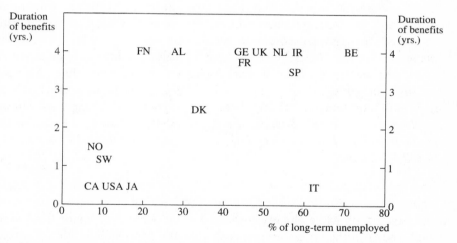

Fig. 13. *Maximum duration of benefit, 1985, and percentage of unemployed out of work for a year, 1983–1988.*

Countries with indefinite benefits are graphed as having a 4-year duration.
AL: Australia; BE: Belgium; CA: Canada; DK: Denmark; FN: Finland; FR: France; GE: Germany; IR: Ireland; IT: Italy; JA: Japan; NL: Netherlands; NO: Norway; SP: Spain; SW: Sweden; UK: United Kingdom; USA: United States.

Sources: proportion of long-term unemployed in total unemployed: OECD, *Employment Outlook*, July 1989 and July 1990, Table M; benefits: Table 5 below.

1. There *is* job rationing, because individuals cannot just pick up a job.
2. The total number of jobs *does* respond to how hard people search.

To get a proper perspective on unemployment, it is essential to hold both points in view.

However, there are two further qualifications to be made to this picture:

3. For the semi- and un-skilled, there are often in fact very few well paid vacancies. Those that appear are snapped up overnight, and there are often hundreds of applicants who are, for all practical purposes, indistinguishable. Employers report no shortage of labour to do these jobs. In Britain the proportion of employers in manufacturing who expect their output to be limited by shortages of non-skilled labour has averaged only 5 per cent over the last quarter-century (compared with 19 per cent for skilled workers). Thus, there are not many well paid vacancies for less skilled labour in what we may call the 'primary sector'. Once people get these jobs, they tend not to quit.
4. However, though well paid jobs are scarce, it is generally possible to find a badly paid one. For most of the unemployed (other than the handicapped) there is some vacancy they can pick up—in catering, cleaning, some retail stores, and small-scale repairs and maintenance. For those with sufficient enterprise, there is also self-employment. This whole sector we may call the 'secondary sector' (though in fact there is clearly a continuous spectrum of jobs). The secondary sector is market-clearing, in the sense that wages are not high enough to attract a queue of job-seekers, nor do vacancies last long since skill requirements are low. *In the secondary sector, if wages were lower employment would fall, because of reduced supply of labour; whereas in the primary sector, if wages were lower employment would grow, because of increased demand.*

Why are there people who would be willing to work in the primary sector but not in the secondary sector? It may be because it is harder to find a primary-sector job while already employed in the secondary sector than while unemployed. Another possible reason is that for some people life on unemployment income is preferable to life in the secondary sector. People vary in these respects, and for each person i there is some critical secondary-sector wage (W_i^*) at which they are just willing to work. The array of reservation wages (W_i^*) taken in ascending order provides the rising supply curve of labour to the secondary sector. Once the secondary-sector wage is determined, we know how many of those not employed in the primary sector will be employed in the secondary sector, and how many will be unemployed.

The primary and secondary sectors

We can illustrate the position in Fig. 14. The total labour force (employed plus unemployed) is L. We take this as exogenous, mainly on the grounds that the total labour force (male and female taken together) is not very responsive to changes in wages. All workers are willing to work in the primary sector. D_1 gives the demand relationship between primary employment and the primary-sector real wage (in units of general purchasing power). This wage is determined at the level shown, by the mechanism of efficiency wages or union bargaining already discussed. Thus, primary-sector employment is N_1. This leaves $L - N_1$ workers available for the secondary sector. We suppose that the distribution of reservation wages in this group is independent of its size, with a minimum equal to the minimum height of S_2 and a maximum equal to its maximum height. D_2 gives the demand relationship between secondary employment and the secondary-sector real wage. In this sector the wage and employment are determined so that the market clears, with N_2 people being employed. This leaves $L - N_1 - N_2$ ($= U$) people unemployed.

These people are both involuntarily and voluntarily unemployed. They are willing to work in the primary sector at the going wage there, but have not so far found work; they are *not* willing to work in the secondary sector at the going wage there.

This account seems to capture the way most participants (firms and workers) perceive the equilibrium of the labour market. As time proceeds, some primary-sector firms expand, others contract. Thus, some people lose jobs

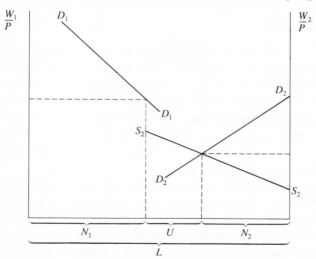

Fig. 14. *Unemployment in a two-sector model.*

43

in the primary sector and join those $L - N_1$ people outside who would like jobs in the primary sector. Some of these become unemployed, while others take secondary-sector jobs while continuing to look for better work.[12]

How long those who become unemployed remain so depends on the general equilibrium of the system. The key element is the number of primary-sector jobs, which in turn depends on the primary-sector wage. It is however extremely difficult to distinguish between the primary and secondary sector in the official statistics. The secondary sector is also a fairly small part of the manual labour market. We have discussed it because it is important to recognize the reality that for most people *some* job is available (especially of course for those with personal characteristics liked by employers).

But in order to understand how the economy changes over time, it may be good enough to proceed as though there were only one sector, whose wages and employment are determined by the kinds of mechanism discussed in Section 6.[13]

10. Why are some groups more unemployed than others?

We have proceeded so far as though all workers were the same, except that some of them have jobs and others haven't. But in fact, unemployment rates differ sharply between groups. Why is this, and how do these disparities affect the overall unemployment rate?

Causes of mismatch

As we have stressed before, unemployment mainly affects manual workers. Over three-quarters of unemployed men are manual workers. As Table 3 shows, this is mainly because they are more likely to *become* unemployed, not because they remain unemployed longer once unemployed.

Similarly, young people are more likely to be unemployed than older people, and this is again due to the fact that they are more likely to become unemployed. In fact, they remain unemployed for a rather shorter time on average than older people.

So here we have big differences in unemployment between occupations and age-groups which are persistent over time and across countries. They are not mainly related to general shifts in demand or supply, or to any resulting market disequilibrium. They are essentially equilibrium phenomena.

But they do result from *firm-level* disturbances, in which some firms are expanding and others are contracting. As firms are forced to contract, they lay

Table 3   *Unemployment by skill: flow and duration, Britain and USA*

	Britain (1984)			USA (1987)		
	Inflow rate (% per mo.)	Average duration (mos.)	Unemployment rate (%)	Inflow rate (% per mo.)	Average duration (mos.)	Unemployment rate (%)
Professional and managerial	0.50	11.2	5.3	0.74	3.0	2.3
Clerical	0.88	10.1	8.0 ⎫	1.58	2.6	4.3
Other non-manual	1.14	11.8	12.2 ⎭			
Skilled manual	1.02	14.2	12.6	1.97	2.9	6.1
Personal services ⎫	1.32	14.1	15.5	2.96	2.4	7.7
Other manual ⎭				2.84	3.0	9.4
All	0.94	12.8	10.8	2.23	2.6	6.2

Notes:

Inflow rate   = inflow/numbers employed
Outflow rate   = outflow/numbers unemployed
Unemployment rate = numbers unemployed/numbers employed-or-unemployed

Monthly inflow and outflow are measured by numbers unemployed less than 1 month. In Britain the numbers in this category on the *Labour Force Survey* (*LFS*) definition of unemployment are only 70% of those in their first month of benefit receipt. The *General Household Survey* is broadly consistent with the *LFS*.

Source: Britain: *Labour Force Survey* tapes. This only records previous occupation and industry for those unemployed for under 3 years. The unemployment rate in each occupation is computed by taking the numbers unemployed for less than 3 years who were previously employed in the stated occupation and raising it by the ratio of total unemployed to numbers of unemployed reporting their previous occupation. A similar procedure is done for those unemployed for under one month. *USA*: *Employment and Earnings*, Jan. 1988, p. 175.

off not their experienced non-manual staff, in which they have sunk much firm-specific human capital, but their direct labour and to some extent those workers most recently hired (last-in, first-out). In addition, younger workers are more prone to quit. So what we are seeing is a stochastic equilibrium, involving a persistent mismatch between the pattern of the labour force (L) and the pattern of employment (N). How such a mismatch affects the overall unemployment rate we shall consider in a moment.

But first we turn to regional unemployment differences. Here we come nearer to something with a disequilibrium (i.e. transitional) element in it. Certainly these differences are related to shifts in labour demand, and to a failure of migration to keep pace. For example, we can see how the decline of textiles caused unemployment in New England in the 1960s and 1970s, while at the same time Texas boomed; and in the 1980s there was a complete reversal, as high tech boomed and oil faltered. Similarly, in Germany the North boomed in the 1960s and unemployment was relatively high in Bavaria; by the 1980s the decline of heavy industry had completely reversed the situation.

But in other countries regional unemployment differentials are much more persistent, with unemployment always higher in the North of England and the South of Italy. The differences here are sustained by steady one-way shifts in the pattern of demand, with migration never catching up. It is a steady-state disequilibrium.

The main reason why labour demand shifts from one region to another is that labour demand shifts between industries, and different regions are intensive in different industries. Thus, the degree of regional imbalance is related to the rate of change in industrial structure. In Britain regional unemployment differences were much greater in the inter-war period than since the war—and so were the changes in industrial structure. If we compute the proportion of jobs in each industry in adjacent years and then take the changes in each proportion, we can sum the positive changes to get a measure of the proportion of employment 'changing industries'. This measure averaged 2.7 in 1924–39 and less than half as much (1.1) since 1950. The pattern for the USA is very similar (1.7 and 0.9). (The USA data relate to 1-digit and the British to 2-digit industries.)

But has turbulence increased since the 1960s in a way that could help to explain increased unemployment? The answer is a clear no. And for this reason, we are not surprised that the inflow into unemployment has not increased in most countries. The secular rise in unemployment is associated with increased duration and not with an increase in the rate of job loss.

Relation of mismatch to the NAIRU

The next issue is, How exactly do differences in unemployment rates affect average unemployment? In addressing this question, it is essential to banish the idea that the only interesting unemployment differences are those relating to disequilibrium problems of transitional adjustment. Even if age differences in unemployment reflect an equilibrium, it is still true that, by shifting labour demand from middle-aged to younger people, we could reduce the NAIRU. So we need a general framework for analysing the implications of unemployment disparities, from whatever source they may arise.

The basic idea is that, if there are unemployment disparities, this makes it more difficult to secure a low average level of unemployment. For the low-

46

unemployment labour markets overheat while there is still high unemployment elsewhere. If, instead, we could increase unemployment by x per cent where it is low, and reduce it by x per cent where it is high, this would reduce wage pressure. For wages are more sensitive to unemployment when unemployment is low than when it is high.

The problem can be analysed quite simply within our standard framework, and ignoring nominal inertia. Assuming for simplicity normal-cost pricing ($\beta_1 = 0$), the price equation can be approximated by

$$p = \beta_0 + \sum_{i=1}^{I} \alpha_i w_i \qquad (\textstyle\sum \alpha_i = 1),$$

where there are I types of labour having (log) wages, w_i. There are separate wage equations for each type of labour, which evidence suggests have the concave form

$$w_i - p = \gamma_{0i} - \gamma_1 \log u_i \qquad (i = 1, \ldots, I).$$

Substituting the wage equations into the price equation, and adding and subtracting $\gamma_1 \log u^*$, gives

$$\gamma_1 [\textstyle\sum \alpha_i (\log u_i - \log u^*) + \log u^*] = \text{const.}$$

or[14]

$$\log u^* = - \textstyle\sum \alpha_i \log(u_i / u^*) + \text{const.}$$

$$\simeq \tfrac{1}{2} \, \text{var} \, \frac{u_i}{u} + \text{const.}$$

Thus, the NAIRU depends on the variance of the relative unemployment rates. Hence equiproportional rises in unemployment rates do not increase the NAIRU. This is due to the curvature of the wage function, which empirically appears to be best represented by the double-log form.

We can now examine whether mismatch, measured in this way, has increased over time. Table 4 gives data for Britain on the variance of relative unemployment rates by occupation, age, region, and industry. There is no pattern of general increase since the mid-1970s. Similar results apply to regional and industrial patterns of unemployment in most of the main OECD countries. Though unemployment has risen, it has risen by much the same proportion in all groups—or, at least, its relative dispersion has not increased.

Turning to the shift in the U/V curve, this could be due to increased mismatch only if there were increased imbalance between the pattern of vacancies and unemployment. Imbalance of course exists, with vacancy rates low where unemployment rates are high. But there is no evidence in any major country that the misalignment has increased since the early 1970s.

This does not mean that mismatch is unimportant. If we add up the different mismatch indices in Table 4 for 1985 (treating them as independent), they have raised unemployment by some 40 per cent (half of the sum of the bottom row) above what it would otherwise be. Thus, when we come to policy, mismatch is a major issue. It is just that this is nothing new.

11. Why has unemployment differed between countries?

We are now ready to explain the differences in unemployment experience between countries. Table 1 shows the amazing spread of unemployment rates in 1990, and Table 5 gives similar data for 1983–8. Average unemployment is in 1990 roughly 9 per cent in the EC, $5\frac{1}{2}$ per cent in the USA, 2 per cent in Japan, and 3 per cent in the EFTA countries. By contrast, in the 1960s the unemployment differences were small (in absolute terms): Britain, France, Germany, Belgium, the Netherlands, the EFTA countries, and Japan all had average unemployment below $2\frac{1}{2}$ per cent; the USA had 4 per cent. Thus the challenge is to explain why the unemployment rates are now so different.

Static analysis

We shall begin with an extremely static approach to the issue, and then look more carefully at the different shocks that have affected different countries and how they have responded to them.

Table 4 *Variance of relative unemployment rates, Britain, 1974–1985 (%)*

	By occupation (5 groups)	By age (10 groups)	By travel-to-work area (322 areas)	By industry (10 groups)
1974	23	16	18	11
1975	14	19	22	13
1984	21	14	20	12
1985	22	23	24	14

Source: General Household Survey. Travel-to-work area data are available only for 1985 but have been inferred for other years, using regional data.

We began this chapter with the simplest possible Phillips curve (3″):

$$\Delta^2 p = -\theta_1(u - u^*).$$

If we let u^* depend on a vector of institutional variables z, we can rewrite this as

$$u = a_0 + a_1 z - \frac{1}{\theta_1}\Delta^2 p$$

or, for the ith country,

$$u_i = a_0 + a_1 z_i - a_2 \Delta^2 p_i. \tag{9}$$

We can then attempt to explain the average unemployment rate (1983–8) in each country by its current institutional structures (z), and the degree of disinflation ($-\Delta^2 p$).

On the basis of our analysis so far, we would expect the NAIRU to be affected by the following variables in the manner shown:

	Effect
Duration of unemployment benefits	+
Replacement ratio	+
Expenditure on national manpower policies	−
Union coverage	+
Co-ordinated bargaining by unions	−
Co-ordinated bargaining by employers	−

So the first task is to look at the basic institutional differences between countries, building up in Tables 5 and 6 a profile of national institutions which we then use to explain unemployment.

Unemployment benefits

Most EC countries except Italy have benefit systems that are more or less open-ended in duration—unemployed people can draw benefits for at least three years and often indefinitely. By contrast, in the USA and Japan the maximum is half a year and in Norway, Sweden, and Switzerland it is roughly a year. We give summary statistics for 1985 in column (3) of Table 5. In fact, all benefit systems are very complicated (Atkinson and Micklewright 1991). In Annex 1.3, Table A1, we show exactly which benefits we are counting (i.e. all those paying over $120 a month in 1985).

There is also the question of the replacement ratio. In column (4) we give the replacement ratio over the initial period of unemployment for a single man under 50. This shows gross benefits as a percentage of the most relevant gross wage. As the table shows, replacement ratios are very high in EFTA countries and Denmark and Spain, but the duration is generally limited. In most other countries they are around 50–60 per cent, except for the UK, Australia, and New Zealand, where they are rather lower.

There are two other key dimensions of benefit systems, which are not shown in the table. The first is their coverage—most usefully thought of as the proportion of the unemployed receiving benefit. Table A2 of Annex 1.3 gives some partial information on this, together with the actual outlays on benefit. Coverage is between a half and three-quarters in most European countries. In the USA it is only a third and in Japan 40 per cent.

The other key issue is the conditions for getting benefit. Such matters are extremely subtle but very important. For example, in Britain virtually no test of work availability was applied in the late 1970s and early 1980s. But from 1986 onwards people receiving unemployment benefit have been interviewed every six months under the Restart Programme and urged to find work. Fewer and fewer reasons are accepted for not taking up available jobs. A strict test of availability for work is also applied to newly unemployed people claiming benefit.

The dramatic fall in British unemployment after 1986 was partially due to these measures, which increased the effective labour supply so that, when demand surged ahead, there was only a limited increase in wage inflation. Corroborating evidence for this interpretation includes the facts that (1) vacancies did not rise despite the fall in unemployment (see Fig. 11); (2) productivity per worker grew at only 1 per cent a year at the peak of the boom; (3) semi- and un-skilled employment grew strongly; and (4) lower decile earnings fell sharply relative to the mean.

Unfortunately, there are no internationally comparable measures of administrative procedures between countries. But there is a widespread impression in Europe that the 'work test' was applied with progressively less rigour up to the early 1980s, and with rather more rigour since then. And some countries have always been tougher than others. For example, ever since the late 1930s Sweden has consciously adopted what it calls the 'employment principle' as opposed to the 'benefit principle'. This means that unemployed people are expected to look hard for work and, if necessary, to move to get it. In return, they are given major help with job search and in other ways.

Active labour market policy

In fact, countries differ sharply in the amount of 'active' help they give to the unemployed, and not only in the 'passive' help they give through unemployment benefits. Countries vary enormously in what they spend on (*a*) placement and counselling services (plus administration), (*b*) training of adult unemployed, and (*c*) direct job creation and recruitment subsidies. Since the programmes vary with the unemployment situation, the best way to measure a country's commitment to this activity is to measure expenditure per unemployed person (relative to output per worker). As Table 5, column (5) shows, the degree of commitment varies amazingly, with the Swedes doing much more

Table 5 *Unemployment experience of different countries, and treatment of the unemployed*

	(1) Unemployment rate % 1983–8	(2) % of long-term unemployed 1988	(3) Duration of unemployment benefit (yrs.) 1985	(4) Replacement ratio (%) 1985	(5) Expenditure on 'active' labour market programmes per unemployed person (as % of output per person) 1987
Belgium	11.3	78	Indef.	60	7.4
Denmark	9.0	29	2.5	90	7.9
France	9.9	45	3.75	57	3.9
Germany	6.7	47	Indef.	63	10.4
Ireland	16.4	66	Indef.	50	5.0
Italy	7.0	69	0.5	2	0.8
Netherlands	10.6	50	Indef.	70	2.7
Portugal	7.7	51	0.5	60	7.4
Spain	19.8	62	3.5	80	2.1
UK	10.7	45	Indef.	36	4.6
Australia	8.4	28	Indef.	39	2.8
New Zealand	4.6	—	Indef.	38	13.1
Canada	9.9	7	0.5	60	4.3
USA	7.1	7	0.5	50	2.4
Japan	2.7	21	0.5	60	5.6
Austria	3.6	13	Indef.	60	11.3
Finland	5.1	19	Indef.	75	12.9
Norway	2.7	6	1.5	65	9.8
Sweden	2.2	8	1.2	80	34.6
Switzerland	2.4	—	1.0	70	3.7

Sources: col. (1): see p. 526, UK is UK(1); col. (2): OECD, *Employment Outlook*, July 1990, Tables M and P; cols. (3) and (4): mainly US Department of Health and Social Services, *Social Security Programs Throughout the World 1985 (Reserve Report No. 60)*; see also OECD, *Employment Outlook*, Sept. 1988, Tables 4.3 and 4.4. Further details in Annex 1.3; col. (5): OECD, *Employment Outlook*, Sept. 1988, Table 3.1.

than any other country and Germany doing more than any other EC country. In fact, Sweden goes to the length of guaranteeing every unemployed person a temporary job if he or she has still not found a job when benefits run out (after 14 months).

Unions and wage bargaining

As we know, unemployment depends not only on the treatment of the unemployed outsiders, but also on the institutions through which wages are determined, and on how far these are dominated by insider power. In Europe unions are pervasive in wage-setting, and the percentage of workers unionized

Table 6 *Collective bargaining in different countries*

	(1) % of workers covered (3 = over 75% 2 = 25–75% 1 = under 25%)	(2) Union coordination (3 = high 2 = middle 1 = low)	(3) Employer coordination (3 = high 2 = middle 1 = low)
Belgium	3	2	2
Denmark	3	3	3
France	3	2	2
Germany	3	2	3
Ireland	3	1	1
Italy	3	2	1
Netherlands	3	2	2
Portugal	3	2	2
Spain	3	2	1
UK	3	1	1
Australia	3	2	1
New Zealand	2	2	1
Canada	2	1	1
USA	1	1	1
Japan	2	2	2
Austria	3	3	3
Finland	3	3	3
Norway	3	3	3
Sweden	3	3	3
Switzerland	2	1	3

Source: cols. (1)–(3): see Annex 1.4; cols. (4)–(5): see Ch. 2, Table 6 for sources plus data on earlier periods; col. (6): see Ch. 9, Table 11; col. (7): OECD, GDP deflator. See Annex 1.6.

rose in most countries up to 1980, since when it has fallen in a few, especially Britain. Union membership is higher in EFTA than in the EC, but in every European country except Switzerland over three-quarters of workers have wages that are covered by a collective agreement. This is shown in column (1) of Table 6.

But what matters about unions is not only whether they exist, but how centralized they are and thus who is represented in the typical union bargain. In the Nordic countries and Austria the unions operate in a highly centralized way with multi-industry national agreements. In the EC the basic system is for single-industry agreements, which are generally binding on all firms, whether they are unionized or not; however, employers may pay wages above what the industry agreement requires. So it is important whether firm-level strikes over

(4) Workers involved in strikes p.a. (per 100 workers) (1980s)	(5) Working days lost p.a. (per 100 workers) (1980s)	(6) Wage contract flexibility (index)	(7) Change in inflation 1983–88 (% points)
—	—	4	− 3.6
4.8	21.9	6	− 3.0
0.8	6.3	3	− 6.5
0.7	3.5	4	− 1.7
4.5	43.5	2	− 7.6
36.3	72.0	4	− 8.9
0.5	1.4	5	− 0.1
			− 12.7
15.0	60.5	1	− 5.8
4.6	37.8	2	1.4
11.5	37.5	6	1.1
11.6	47.1	6	1.4
3.3	56.7	2	− 1.8
0.5	12.5	1	− 0.5
0.4	0.5	4	− 0.3
0.3	—	4	− 1.9
15.2	50.0	3	− 1.6
0.7	10.8	4	− 3.5
2.9	18.5	4	− 3.8
0.02	—	0	− 0.3

wages are allowed. In Scandinavia, Germany, the Netherlands, and Portugal, they are not.

Within the EC there are big differences between countries in the degree of inter-industry co-ordination that occurs before the industry bargains begin. In Germany, for example, there is a major debate over what 'going rate' makes sense, which runs both in public and in private between the employers' and trade union federations. This leads to a pattern settlement in one industry (in one region) which is then broadly followed elsewhere. Britain is one of the least co-ordinated countries in the EC, with industry-level bargains being of minor importance and little discussion about the going rate. The system in Switzerland is also decentralized but with some employer co-ordination, and with industry-wide peace agreements outlawing firm-level strikes.

Australia and New Zealand have generally had centralized quasi-judicial setting of basic wages, modified by firm-level bargaining about 'over-award' payments. In Japan, wages in large firms are set by synchronized firm-level bargains (preceded by much general discussion), but there is also a large small-firm sector where wages are set by the employer. Finally, in Canada and the USA bargains are at firm level, but the majority of wages in the economy are set at the employer's discretion.

The systems are described in more detail in Annex 1.4. We need to classify them in a simple way that is yet the most relevant to explaining wage pressure. As we have seen, where union coverage is high, the key issue is whether unions bargain at the national level (thus taking into account the common interests of the workforce in full employment) rather than bargaining as atomistic groups of insiders (thus ignoring the effects of their actions on the general job situation or on the general price level). Of course, even where bargaining is not centralized, if the separate unions agreed on a common wage claim, this would have a similar effect.

But equally, or more, important is the employers' response. If they adopt a common position, then they will certainly not wish to concede real wages high enough to imperil full employment and thus profits. On the other hand, if they bargain one by one they will be more inclined to leapfrog each other, thinking they can achieve some efficiency wage advantage while passing on the cost in an increase of their relative prices. Thus, employer co-ordination could be even more important than union co-ordination.

We therefore construct in Table 6 crude indices of the levels at which unions co-ordinate their wage claims and employers co-ordinate their wage offers: 3 means essentially at national level, 2 at intermediate level and 1 at firm level (i.e. unco-ordinated).

Next, the table records, for interest, two measures of strike activity in the

1980s. Most of the differences are long-standing, reaching back to the Second World War, except for France, where the relative strike record has improved. Strikes are not of course a structural variable, and we shall not use them for explanatory purposes. But it gives some idea of the remarkable differences in industrial relations between countries.

Finally, there is the question of contract structure, which affects the degree of nominal inertia in an economy. If wage contracts are long, then, when nominal demand changes, current wages respond little, and unemployment changes a lot. This effect is reduced if wages are indexed, and it is also reduced if contracts are synchronized rather than overlapping. So we need an index of the extent to which contracts are flexible in the sense of being (*a*) short, (*b*) indexed, and (*c*) synchronized. If we award marks of between 0 and 2 on each of these points and then add, we have an index of contract flexibility, as shown in column (6).

Explaining cross-section differences

We can now estimate equation (9) as a cross-sectional equation for the percentage unemployment rate 1983–8 in each of 20 countries. The results are as follows (with *t*-statistics in brackets):

Unemployment rate (%) = 0.24(0.1)
$$+ 0.92(2.9) \text{ benefit duration (years)}$$
$$+ 0.17(7.1) \text{ replacement ratio (\%)}$$
$$- 0.13(2.3) \text{ active labour market spending (\%)}$$
$$+ 2.45(2.4) \text{ coverage of collective bargaining (1–3)}$$
$$- 1.42(2.0) \text{ union co-ordination (1–3)}$$
$$- 4.28(2.9) \text{ employer co-ordination (1–3)}$$
$$- 0.35(2.8) \text{ change in inflation (\% points)}$$
$$\bar{R}^2 = 0.91; \quad \text{s.e.} = 1.41; \quad N = 20$$

Thus, with six institutional variables plus the change in inflation, we can explain over 90 per cent of the differences in unemployment between countries.

As one would expect, the duration of benefit is important (we treated 'indefinite' as four years), and so is the replacement ratio. But it also helps if countries train their unemployed and take active steps to induce or provide work for them. On the bargaining side, high coverage of collective bargaining is bad for employment unless it is accompanied by co-ordinated bargaining. Co-ordination among employers is particularly important. If there is the maximum co-ordination, as in Scandinavia, a fully covered country can have lower unemployment than a country with very low coverage, where efficiency wage considerations may induce employers to leapfrog.

As it happens, the standardized regression coefficients are all about one-tenth of the *t*-statistics quoted above. So the *t*-statistics indicate well the partial contribution of the different variables to explaining the unemployment differences. These differences are thus explained in roughly equal measure by the treatment of the unemployed, and by the bargaining structures.

Dynamic analysis

But this analysis does not explain why unemployment has changed over time, or why its movement has differed between countries. There are two key points here.

1. Unemployment has moved over time because of supply shocks (changes in z, including now changes in real import prices) and demand shocks (changes in $\Delta^2 m$, the rate of nominal income growth). The extent of these shocks differs between countries.
2. The effect of any given shock depends on the country-specific parameters of the wage and price equations, which in turn depend on the institutional structure of the country.

Real and nominal wage rigidity

We begin with the second of these points. For this purpose we need to modify slightly our initial wage and price equations to allow for the fact that nominal inertia differs between countries. For example, where there are long-term, staggered wage contracts with no indexation, changes in inflation will have a much bigger effect on the mark-up of wages over prices. Thus the wage equation becomes

$$w - p = \gamma_0 - \gamma_1 u - \gamma_2 \Delta^2 p,$$

with a high γ_2 indicating a high level of nominal inertia or nominal rigidity. Similarly, the price equation will be

$$p - w = \beta_0 - \beta_1 u - \beta_2 \Delta^2 p.$$

This gives a Phillips curve

$$\Delta^2 p = -\frac{\beta_1 + \gamma_1}{\beta_2 + \gamma_2} \left(u - \frac{\beta_0 + \gamma_0}{\beta_1 + \gamma_1} \right). \tag{10}$$

Thus, as before, the NAIRU is

$$u^* = \frac{\beta_0 + \gamma_0}{\beta_1 + \gamma_1}.$$

The term $\beta_1 + \gamma_1$ reflects the degree of real wage flexibility in the economy, i.e. the degree to which extra unemployment reduces the gap between the target and feasible real wage. By the same token, the inverse, $1/(\beta_1 + \gamma_1)$, reflects the degree of real wage rigidity (RWR):

$$RWR = \frac{1}{\beta_1 + \gamma_1}.$$

This parameter is very important for two reasons. First, it tells us how the NAIRU responds to a given supply shock, i.e. a given increase in real wage push. For

$$u^* = RWR(\beta_0 + \gamma_0),$$

so that unemployment rises more the greater the degree of real wage rigidity.

Second, real wage rigidity helps to explain how strongly nominal inflation responds to unemployment. For

$$\Delta^2 p = -\frac{1}{RWR(\beta_2 + \gamma_2)}(u - u^*),$$

so that the response of inflation is inversely proportional to RWR times the level of nominal inertia ($NI = \beta_2 + \gamma_2$). It is natural to call this latter term ($RWR \cdot NI$) the degree of *nominal* wage rigidity (NWR):

$$NWR = RWR \cdot NI,$$

with

$$\Delta^2 p = -\frac{1}{NWR}(u - u^*).$$

Thus, if a country wants to reduce inflation by 1 percentage point per year, it must experience NWR extra percentage points of unemployment that year. Thus, NWR is often referred to as the 'sacrifice ratio':

$$-\frac{du}{d\Delta^2 p} = NWR = \text{sacrifice ratio.}$$

Countries differ widely in both their real and their nominal wage rigidities. From our estimates of the wage and price equations, we arrive at the estimates shown in Table 7. Real wage rigidity is much higher in most EC countries than in Japan and EFTA, with the USA lying in an intermediate position. However, when it comes to nominal wage rigidity, the USA and Canada rank high, partly because of the prevalence of long-term contracts.

The impact of the oil shocks

The importance of real wage rigidity can be seen at once, if we wish to explain inter-country differences in the impact of the oil shocks. From equation (10) we can see that, for a given wage shock $\Delta\gamma_0$, the change in unemployment over time (Δu) is given by

$$\Delta u = -\frac{\beta_2 + \gamma_2}{\beta_1 + \gamma_1}\Delta(\Delta^2 p) + \frac{1}{\beta_1 + \gamma_1}\Delta\gamma_0.$$

So for the ith country with its own parameter values,

$$\Delta u_i + NWR_i\Delta(\Delta^2 p)_i = RWR_i\Delta\gamma_{0i}. \tag{11}$$

Table 7 *Real and nominal wage rigidity*

	Real wage rigidity (RWR)	Nominal wage rigidity (NWR)
Belgium	0.25	0.04
Denmark	0.58	0.08
France	0.23	0.20
Germany	0.63	0.49
Ireland	0.27	0.31
Italy	0.06	0.14
Netherlands	0.25	0.24
Spain	0.52	0.56
UK	0.77	0.70
Australia	1.10	0.10
New Zealand	0.23	0.22
Canada	0.32	1.37
USA	0.25	0.80
Japan	0.06	0.05
Austria	0.11	0.46
Finland	0.29	1.01
Norway	0.08	0.37
Sweden	0.08	0.39
Switzerland	0.13	0.41

Source: Ch. 9, Table 2.

We can use this framework to explain inter-country differences for 19 OECD countries in the change in unemployment between the period 1969–73 and the period 1980–85. For this purpose we focus simply on the effect of the change in relative import prices between 1972 and 1981, so that

$$\Delta\gamma_{0i} = s_{mi}\Delta\log(P_m/P)_i.$$

Using the values of RWR_i and NWR_i from Table 7, the correlation of the left-hand side of equation (11) with the right-hand side of equation (11) is no less than 0.84 (with one dummy variable for Spain).

This analysis gets us only part of the way, however. It falls short in two respects. First, it focuses on only a limited period. We really need a model that explains the year-to-year dynamics of unemployment over, say, 30 years, allowing for all kinds of supply and demand shocks. Second, we need to explain the parameter values in terms of the institutional features of each country.

A general dynamic equation

With this in mind, we first obtain the reduced-form equation for unemployment by combining the short-run supply curve (Phillips curve) with the demand curve. The short-run supply curve is (10), expanded to include a term in lagged unemployment, u_{-1}, to allow for an effect of the change in economic activity upon wage and price behaviour. The demand curve is equation (4):

$$\Delta p = \Delta m + \lambda(u - u_{-1}). \tag{4}$$

After one minor modification,[15] this yields an equation of the form

$$u = bu_{-1} + (1 - b)RWR(a_0 + a_1 z' - NI\Delta^2 m). \tag{12}$$

Here b is the hysteresis coefficient, which itself increases with real wage rigidity—if unemployment does not reduce wage push, it will not reduce inflation and will therefore persist.

Thus, equation (12) ought to explain the unemployment history of every country, provided we let the coefficients vary according to the factors that should affect them. After suitable experimentation, we conclude that

		Effect
b depends on	benefit duration	+
	co-ordination	−
	labour turnover	−
RWR depends on	benefit duration	+
	co-ordination	−
NI depends on	wage flexibility	−

a_0 varies between countries but a_1 does not. The wage-push variables (z) vary over time and include the replacement ratio, a wage-militancy dummy from 1970 onwards, and $s_m\Delta\log(P_m/P)$—this latter variable taking a coefficient unity.

Thus, using pooled time-series cross-section data for 19 OECD countries (excluding Portugal) for 1956–88, we estimate the following equation (i country, t time):

$$u_{it} = b_i u_{i,t-1} + (1 - b_i)RWR_i(a_{0i} + a_1 z'_{it} - NI_i\Delta^2 m_{it})$$

where b_i, RWR_i, and NI_i are themselves functions of the variables mentioned above. The equation works well (see Chapter 9, Table 12), and its results are highly consistent with the crude cross-sectional results presented earlier in this section. It is remarkable that (ignoring the country dummies) an equation with only 12 parameters common to all countries should enable us to trace the evolution of unemployment in 19 different countries better than a set of country autoregressions with country-specific parameters and trends.

The coefficients b_i, a_{0i}, and NI_i are of course amalgams of coefficients from the wage and price equations. We leave to Chapter 9 the analysis of these structural coefficients and our attempt to explain them by institutional features of each country. But the reduced form we have just provided is fully consistent with the results.

Explaining unemployment history

The reduced-form equation above provides us with a splendid basis for discussing in greater detail the events of the 1970s and 1980s. The explanation goes as follows.

(a) Import price shocks. Most countries have been subjected to two major upward shocks to import prices—the first and second oil and commodity price shocks. The size of these shocks was much greater in Europe than in the USA, since the USA produces so much of its own raw materials. However, the more centralized countries suffered less than others because wage-bargainers were more willing to allow the shock to cut living standards.

(b) Demand shocks. By 1980 world inflation had reached a level where electorates in all countries signalled that a change was needed. Most countries restricted the rate of money growth, and most EC countries had severe budget cuts. Thus the growth rate of nominal income fell. Because of inflation inertia, this led not only to a fall in inflation but also to a fall in output and to rising

unemployment. The real impact of a given cut in the growth of nominal income was less, the more flexible was the structure of wage contracts, so that for a time unemployment rose as much in the USA as in the EC.

(c) Persistence. But in the EC unemployment persisted, while in the USA it fell rapidly after 1982. This was because persistence is much higher where benefits are open-ended in duration. The EFTA countries escaped persistent unemployment partly because unemployment rose little in the first place and partly because persistence there is low, for three main reasons: a limited duration of benefits (in most of the countries), a corporatist approach to wage-setting, and (especially in Sweden) intensive labour market policies for the unemployed.

(d) Other factors. There are also other factors at work which account for some of the deterioration in the unemployment–inflation trade-off. Of these we have been able to identify only the greater militancy of workers after the Paris events of 1968 and rising benefit replacement ratios in many countries at various times up to around 1980.

The main interest is in the policy implications. The clear message is that benefits, labour market policy, and bargaining structure play an important role in affecting the course of unemployment.

12. How can unemployment be reduced?

By bringing together all we have learned, we can now draw significant policy conclusions. Unemployment is not determined by an optimal process of allocation. Though it does perform a vital role in the redirection of labour, its level is subject to a host of distorting influences, tending to make it higher than is economically efficient. The most obvious of these distortions are

1. the benefit system, which is subject to massive problems of moral hazard (unless administered well), and
2. the system of wage determination, where decentralized unions and employers both have incentives to set wages in a way that generates involuntary unemployment, and where bargained wages create a mismatch between the pattern of labour demand and supply.

Both these systems generate negative externalities. While there may be some positive search externalities from unemployment, it is hard to suppose that these are of the same order.

61

However, the negative distortions do not mean that unemployment is too high in every country. This depends on how much else the country has done to offset them.

Policy-makers have to apply a cost–benefit approach to each possible policy option open to them in their existing circumstances. They inevitably operate in the world of the second-best and most of the forms of intervention that are proposed introduce other distortions. Even so, they may improve the welfare of millions and make an economy thrive rather than limp.

We shall begin by looking at policies towards the unemployed, including policies on benefits, since the lessons here are clearest. We shall then look at the issue of bargaining and incomes policy. Then we shall discuss the role of employment subsidies.

All these kinds of policies can help a lot. We end by discussing ones that are unlikely to help—profit-sharing, work-sharing, early retirement, and reduced employment protection.

Policies for the unemployed (benefits and active manpower policy)

(i) Benefits

The unconditional payment of benefits for an indefinite period is clearly a major cause of high European unemployment. This possible effect of the welfare system was never intended by its founders. For example, the architect of the British welfare state, Lord Beveridge, proposed in his Report (1942) that 'unemployment benefit will continue at the same rate without means test so long as unemployment lasts, but will normally be subject to a condition of attendance at a work or training centre after a certain period . . . The normal period of unconditional unemployment benefit will be six months.' He believed that, after that, 'complete idleness even on an income demoralises'.

Yet somehow this simple truth got overlooked. The unconditional welfare system worked so well in the booming 1950s and 1960s that people failed to realize that it gravely weakened the economy's self-correcting mechanism in the face of adverse shocks.

The obvious lesson is that unconditional benefits must be of limited duration. But then, what after they run out? One approach is nothing, as in the USA. This is a harsh route, in which some people end up on the scrap-heap. It also ignores the fact that benefits of even limited duration are subject to 'moral hazard' and liable to encourage an inefficient degree of unemployment. The other approach is active manpower policy.

(ii) Active manpower policy: the Swedish example

The classic example of an active manpower policy is the Swedish system. In the 1960s most foreign economists (including some of us) thought the Swedes had gone over the top. But the wisdom of their approach was proved by the fact that, even after two oil shocks, the Swedish unemployment rate never lingered over 3 per cent; long-term unemployment was never allowed to emerge, and unemployment quite soon came down to under 2 per cent. So it is worth describing the essential features of their system of manpower policy.

Benefits for the unemployed run out after 14 months, but linked to this are labour market policies to make sure that people find productive work. These have four main ingredients.

(a) The placement services (employment exchanges). These go into intensive operation from the moment a person becomes unemployed. Case loads are low—only 35 unemployed people per member of staff, compared with at least five times more in Britain. And the exchanges have excellent information on the labour market both locally and elsewhere, based on the compulsory notification of vacancies.

(b) Retraining. Hard-to-place workers are sent on high-quality training courses—in some cases, as soon as they become unemployed. Thus, economic change is welcomed as an opportunity to provide experienced workers for the industries of the future. Generally about 1 per cent of the workforce are on courses of this kind.

(c) Recruitment subsidies. If workers have not been placed within six months, employers recruiting them can be offered a 50 per cent wage subsidy lasting six months. The numbers taken up under this scheme peaked at 0.3 per cent of workers in 1984.

(d) Temporary public employment and the right to work. If all these measures fail, the public sector (mainly local authorities) acts as the employer of last resort. It provides work for up to six months, mostly in construction or the caring services. Provision is highly counter-cyclical, covering some 2 per cent of the workforce at the peak and under 0.5 per cent by 1988. Anyone whose benefit entitlement has run out is entitled to such work by law.

Such policies are expensive, and the Swedes spend nearly 1 per cent of national income on them. But, by keeping down unemployment, the programmes reduce unemployment benefits, which in the EC cost 1.5 per cent of

GNP compared with 0.7 per cent in Sweden. In the long term the Swedish programmes may be largely self-financing to the Exchequer. In terms of social cost–benefit analysis, they almost certainly pass the test.[16]

By any criteria, the Swedish labour market has performed extremely well (during the 1980s). The employment–population ratio, already the highest in the world, has gone on rising, while it has fallen in all the main EC countries. Thus, any country wishing to sustain low unemployment would do well to study the example of the Swedish manpower policies.

(iii) Policy to the long-term unemployed

The lessons here are particularly obvious for the countries of Eastern Europe which have started from a position of zero unemployment. But, for a country with high unemployment, there is also the question of how to get from here to there. In high-unemployment countries around a half the unemployed have been out of work for over a year. For such workers the chances of finding a job are very much less than for the short-term unemployed. And, for the same reason, long-term unemployment is doing much less to restrain inflation than short-term unemployment.

For these reasons, active help to the unemployed should be concentrated on the prevention of long-term unemployment. If we remove from unemployment a newly unemployed person, we are removing someone who on average would have left unemployment fairly soon anyway. If we remove a person at risk of long-term unemployment, we are removing someone who might otherwise continue much longer in unemployment. So the external benefit to the taxpayer from removing the second type of person is much greater than that from removing the first. Unless the costs are disproportionately greater, therefore, help should be concentrated on those at risk of long-term unemployment.

(iv) Displacement, substitution, and deadweight

But manpower policies are often criticized on two grounds. First, though they provide jobs for those helped, they may reduce employment for others (by 'displacing' labour in other firms, or 'substituting' for other workers in the same firm). This argument is often based on the notion that there is a limited demand for labour (arising from limited aggregate demand for products). If so, the argument is almost totally misconceived. For the aim of manpower policy is to improve the supply side of the economy, on the assumption that this is the main limiting factor, not aggregate demand.

But there will almost certainly be some substitution and displacement for supply-side reasons. For example, if long-term unemployment is greatly reduced, there may need to be some small increase in short-term unemployment in order to restrain wage pressure. In principle, the magnitude of the total effect of a policy can be determined by finding out how it affects not only the outflow rate from unemployment but also the inflow rate (the unemployment rate being determined by the ratio of the inflow rate to the outflow rate; see Chapter 5).

The second charge against manpower policy is that it often pays money for things that would otherwise have happened ('deadweight'); for example, an employer is paid for hiring someone he would have hired anyway. Transfer expenditures of this kind are undesirable if they then have to be paid for by distorting taxes. But such elements are probably a smallish issue in the overall social cost–benefit calculus of most active labour market policies.

(v) Pin-point targeting

The policies we have discussed have the major merit of being targeted directly at the problem in hand. For example, general regional aid is often advocated because there are more unemployed in one region than another. But much of it fails to relieve unemployment. In contrast, the policies we have been discussing aim directly at unemployment. They are thus highly regional, but they are regional *as a consequence* of dealing with unemployment, rather than in order imperfectly to do so. Likewise, these policies deal directly with skills mismatch where it is identified, rather than by some more general intervention.

Policies on mismatch (employment subsidies and training)

This does however raise the issue of whether there is a case for more general action to combat the mismatch across regions and across skills. Suppose there are two markets (say North and South), with higher unemployment in the North. One could approach this problem by increasing labour demand in the North or by reducing labour supply there (by out-migration). But it does not make sense to attempt both; for subsidies to employment in the North will be paid for by higher taxes in the South. This policy is bound to discourage migration.

So which policy should be attempted? If better returns to migration do little to encourage migration, then (ignoring externalities) the correct policy is to subsidize employment in the high-unemployment area. But suppose migration is very responsive, with all workers indifferent between regions at the prevailing rates of wages and employment. Then, even though there is job rationing, the classic principles of public finance apply: in the absence of externalities, there should be uniform taxation.

However, there are externalities. Migration into low-unemployment areas creates a demand for extra infrastructure, publicly financed. It may also damage the losing region. This argument, together with unresponsive migration behaviour, provides the foundation of the case for regional policy. But one must stress that other distortions that reduce migration, such as housing policy, do need urgent reform.

With skill formation, the case is somewhat different. Training suffers from the standard externality problem—that trainers are not able to trap the full social return, either because of 'poaching' or because of the tax wedge. Even though the supply response is again quite weak, this constitutes a case for favourable fiscal treatment for education and training.

As we have already said, direct policies affecting the unemployed should be judged by different criteria from those affecting the overall balance of supply and demand. This is because of the pin-point targeting which gives them their extra leverage.

The reform of wage bargaining, and incomes policy

(i) Bargaining systems

We turn now to the other key issue: the reform of wage bargaining. Here we have discovered two main points. First, other things equal, unemployment is lower the lower is union coverage and the lower is union power in each bargain. This suggests the merits of limiting the power of individual unions. But, second, for a given union coverage and union power, unemployment is lower when employers co-ordinate their wage offers at an industry or national level, and likewise when unions co-ordinate their wage claims.

So there seem to be two forms of organization that work well. One (as in the USA) has low union coverage—and preferably low union power. The other (as in Scandinavia and Austria, and to a lesser extent Germany) has high union coverage—with low union power again at the decentralized level, but with strong national unions dealing on equal terms with employers. The choice between these systems is clearly political and depends also on the size of country. But economic arguments are also relevant.

The issue is whether institutions can be created which overcome the externalities involved in decentralized wage-setting (whether by firms and/or unions). The ideal is that a consensus develops about an appropriate 'going rate' for nominal wages, which is then implemented without requiring unemployment to eliminate the wage–price and wage-wage spirals. In this context there is a role for

1. an informed national debate about what rate makes sense;
2. reports by respected bodies such as councils of economic advisers and research institutes;
3. national talks between employers and unions.

If the climate of opinion is responsible, a kind of implicit contract may emerge, as often happens in Germany and Japan, in which other bargainers follow a pattern settlement unless they face exceptional circumstances. Everyone recognizes the need for increasing flexibility in remuneration packages. But equally, it is important that most agreements stick within an accepted range of total remuneration and do not initiate a game of competitive leapfrogging.

However, this does presuppose a fairly high degree of social discipline. If this is not forthcoming, governments naturally consider direct intervention.

(ii) Conventional incomes policies

We then need to consider the case for some form of government wage controls, such as a maximum permitted percentage rate of growth of earnings. Incomes policies of this kind have been tried at many times and places.

To control inflation, the Roman Emperor Diocletian issued a wage decree in AD 301 and those who breached it were sentenced to death. The policy was abandoned as a failure after 13 years.

In AD 1971 the US President Nixon introduced a three-month wage–price freeze, followed by two years of less rigid controls. The policy clearly restrained inflationary pressure while it lasted, but proved unsustainable under the pressure of shortages of labour and goods (Blinder 1979).

In Britain there was a statutory incomes policy in 1972–4 and a voluntary one (initially agreed with the Trades Union Congress) in 1975–9. Both of these were abandoned, mainly because of union opposition. However, the second of the policies was at first remarkably successful, and helped to reduce inflation from 27 to 12 per cent in two years with no increase in unemployment. After the policy was abandoned inflation rose again. Some people said this was due to a 'catching-up effect'. But the best econometric evidence does not support the view that in Britain reductions of inflation achieved during incomes policies are automatically undone once the policies end (Wadhwani 1985).

In France an incomes policy was introduced in 1982 and inflation fell over four years from 12 to 3 per cent. The wage norms had statutory force in the public sector, and the employers' federation broadly followed the same norms.

Similarly, Belgium and Italy have, since 1982, had laws prescribing the maximum degree of wage indexation in between major renegotiations, which again implies a form of wage norm. Inflation has fallen.

Australia has a long-standing system of quasi-judicial determination of basic wage rates, above which 'overaward' payments can be negotiated. However, since 1983 the national government, in 'accord' with the union movement, has set the basic norm within which the system operates.

There are two main problems with fully centralized governmental incomes policies. First, they infringe the principle of free bargaining between workers and employers. Thus, many individual groups have a strong incentive to breach the norm. This is also the case, of course, where a norm has been bargained centrally between confederations of employers and unions. But individual groups are more inclined to accept a deal to which they are at least an indirect party. For this reason, governmental incomes policies that have the support of the confederations of employers and unions are themselves more likely to last than those that are imposed. But history suggests that nearly all such policies are eventually breached. A permanent centralized incomes policy is probably infeasible.

The second problem is that a centralized incomes policy is inherently inflexible. It is bound to impose rigidity on the structure of relative wages. But the reallocation of labour may be much easier if relative wages rise where labour is scarce and vice versa. Without this, structural unemployment is likely to become worse, unless major efforts are made, as in Sweden, to promote movement of labour between industries and regions. Incomes policies sometimes try to incorporate committee mechanisms for adjusting relativities, but these cannot work as effectively as the market.

The result is that incomes policies of this kind have always been short-lived. This does not mean they have always been useless. Indeed, a temporary incomes policy is a much better way to disinflate than having a period of high unemployment. And if unemployment is above the long-run NAIRU and there is hysteresis, a temporary incomes policy is an excellent way of helping unemployment to return to the NAIRU more quickly.

(iii) Tax-based incomes policies

One would, however, like to achieve a permanent reduction in the NAIRU itself. If this is to be through incomes policy, it must be through some mechanism other than direct controls. This leads to the proposal for tax-based incomes policy. Under this there is a norm for the growth of nominal wages, but employers are free to pay more than the norm at the cost of a substantial financial penalty. Thus, if employers need to break the norm in order to recruit labour or avoid a strike, they will do so. But all bargainers will be subject to strong disincentives to excessive settlements. Let us see more clearly how this would work.

If the free market generates excessive wage pressure, the obvious solution is to tax excessive wages. This is generally the most efficient way to deal with market failure, unless direct controls have some particular advantage. One approach is through a tax on excessive wage growth; another is through a progressive tax on wage levels. For the sake of clarity, we shall discuss them in reverse order, starting with a tax on the *level* of wages.

Suppose that the tax is paid by firms. If a firm pays its workers a gross real wage W_i, it also has to pay the Exchequer a net tax per worker of $tW_i - S$, where t is the tax rate and S a positive per worker subsidy. Hence the firm faces an *ex ante* schedule of labour cost per worker (C_i) equal to

$$C_i = W_i(1 + t) - S.$$

We assume that the scheme is self-financing, so that *ex post* in the representative firm $C_i = W_i$.

How does this reduce wage pressure and thus unemployment? The basic mechanism is that, when workers gain an extra $1 of wages, it costs the firm an extra $(1 + t)$. Thus, the firm is more willing to resist any claim, while the workers may be more anxious about making the claim because of its greater employment effect. As on p. 26, the bargained wage W_i is that which maximizes $\beta \log(W_i - A)S_i + \log\Pi_i$. Differentiating this expression with respect to W_i, the firm chooses the wage so that

$$\frac{\beta}{W_i - A} + \frac{\beta}{S_i}\frac{\partial S_i}{\partial C_i}\frac{\partial C_i}{\partial W_i} - \frac{N_i}{\Pi_i}\frac{\partial C_i}{\partial W_i} = 0,$$

where by the envelope theorem a unit rise in labour cost (C_i) reduces profit by N_i so that $\partial\Pi_i/\partial C_i = -N_i$.

Since the tax sets $\partial C_i/\partial W_i = 1 + t$, and *ex post* it is self-financing with $C_i = W_i$, the mark-up of the wage over outside opportunities is given by

$$\frac{W_i - A}{W_i} = \frac{1 - \alpha\kappa}{(1 + t)(\varepsilon_{SN} + \alpha\kappa/\beta)}.$$

The higher the tax rate, the less will wages tend to leapfrog each other. Thus unemployment will be lower. To be precise, since $W_i = W = W^e$,

$$u^* = \frac{1 - \alpha\kappa}{(1 + t)(\varepsilon_{SN} + \alpha\kappa/\beta)\varphi(1 - B/W)},$$

so that unemployment falls as the tax rate rises. A similar result holds in the case of efficiency wages.

Needless to say, it makes no difference whether the tax is levied on firms or workers.[17] But it must be progressive so that, when wages rise, labour cost rises faster than wages do; i.e., a part of wage cost must be tax-exempt, through a positive S. A proportional tax at rate t whose proceeds were given to the Martians would have no effect.

Of course, any tax introduces some distortions, even while it offsets others. A tax on weekly earnings could have severe effects on work incentives, so the tax should be levied on hourly earnings to make it as near an ideal tax as possible.

An alternative, and more understandable, policy is to tax the *growth* in hourly earnings. The upshot again is lower wage pressure and lower unemployment. But the tax bites less hard, because raising wages this year rather than next costs you taxes this year but saves you taxes next year. Thus, to achieve a given reduction in wage pressure, the tax rate has to be $1/(r - n)$ times what is needed with a wage level tax, where r is the real discount rate and n the permitted (tax-free) growth rate of real wages.

According to many people, a tax-based incomes policy is very difficult to administer. This is not true. Provided it is part of the law of the land and the definition of earnings is as for the income tax (or the social security tax), it can be readily collected from firms at the same time as they pay the withholding income tax (or the social security tax). There are, as with any tax, some obvious ways of trying to dodge the tax. Most of these can be dealt with. Even so, any tax has some distorting effects and so does TIP. But on balance we believe that, if the political will were there to implement it, in most countries it would not only decrease unemployment but would raise social welfare.

We should stress that the aim of all incomes policies is not to reduce real take-home pay but only to reduce wage pressure and thus the NAIRU. If there is diminishing marginal productivity of labour, real product wages may have to fall if there is to be more employment. But since higher output yields higher tax returns, it will normally be possible to cut tax rates when employment increases, so that real take-home pay is sustained.

Marginal employment subsidies

Incomes policy works by reducing the target real wage at given unemployment. An alternative way to reduce unemployment is to raise the feasible real wage in a way that does not lead to equal changes in the target real wage. A good way to do this is by a marginal employment subsidy.

Suppose that we subsidize at a rate s all employment above some fixed proportion of last period's employment. If the scheme is self-financing, it can be paid for by a tax on the rest of last year's employment. If the firm is monopolistically competitive, it sets prices as a mark-up on marginal cost. Thus the price equation becomes

$$p - (w^e - s) = \beta_0 - \beta_1 u.$$

The feasible real wage is increased and unemployment falls. This is an attractive way of reducing inflationary pressure.

Clearly, we do not want this process to reduce post-tax profits, but post-tax profits can be restored by reductions in the profit tax financed by proportional taxes on workers. The latter, as we have seen, would not affect unemployment.

Another way to reduce the profit mark-up is by increased product-market competition (e.g. via the 1992 programme in Europe). Under wage-bargaining (though not efficiency wages), this will reduce unemployment.

We turn now to policies that are much less likely to have this effect.

Profit-sharing

There has been much recent excitement over profit-sharing, generated by the work of Martin Weitzman. Social reformers have, of course, advocated profit-sharing for many years as a way of improving productivity—and there is good evidence to support their case. But the extra productivity would not of itself increase employment. That would require some additional mechanism.

In his original book, Weitzman (1984) proposed such a mechanism in the context of a labour market which in equilibrium is market-clearing. He argued that under the wage system firms equate the real wage to the marginal revenue product of labour. In the short period the real wage is fixed, so that any fall in marginal revenue product will reduce employment. Under profit-sharing, by contrast, competition for labour ensures that in general equilibrium the marginal revenue product equals the total remuneration of labour (i.e. the base wage plus the profit share). Hence the marginal revenue product exceeds the base wage. But, once the base wage has been set, *ex post* firms seek to employ labour up to where the marginal revenue product *equals* the base wage. So there is permanent excess demand for labour. A fall in labour demand (marginal revenue product) will not cause a fall in employment—merely in profits. Weitzman claimed that this explained the Japanese miracle.

But there are problems with the theory and with the Japanese evidence. The theory assumed that, after the package of base wage and profit share had been determined, workers would stand idly by while the firm tried to employ people,

71

thus eroding the profit share of the existing workers. It seems unlikely that workers would react in this way, rather than trying to bargain also about employment. Second, the theory assumed long-run market-clearing in the labour market. In many countries this may not be the right model, and it is easy to show that in both an efficiency wage model and our bargaining model profit-sharing would have no effect on the NAIRU.

So what about Japan? Why exactly is unemployment in Japan so low and so stable? It is not because of any of the mechanisms Weitzman describes, as the following facts make clear.

1. Output is not stable. It fluctuates (about its trend) more than in most countries. It responds to monetary shocks exactly as elsewhere.
2. Nominal prices are affected by cost factors and not simply by demand.
3. Excess demand for labour, as reported by firms, is rather lower than in other countries.
4. It does not appear that employment is determined in the short run by base wages.

Having said all this, the basic fact remains that employment in Japan *is* stable compared with elsewhere. What happens is roughly as follows. Only 40 per cent of Japanese workers are in the organized sector (where bonuses are paid); another 30 per cent are employees in the small-firm sector, and 30 per cent are family workers. When output fluctuates, employment in the formal sector fluctuates quite a lot. But employment in small firms varies much less. This is quite simply because the flexibility of pay per worker is so high in the market-clearing small-firm sector, while it is much less high in large bonus-paying firms. Thus, Japan's stable employment record is due mainly to the wage flexibility in the small-firm sector.

This flexibility has the result that in Japan the total labour input (hours $\times$ employment, HN) fluctuates less than other countries. On top of this, the Japanese value their human capital highly, so they use hours per worker (H) as a shock-absorber more than most other countries, further dampening fluctuations in employment (N). In addition, the labour force (L) shrinks in recession, as 'secondary' female workers shrink back home. This makes unemployment ($L - N$) even more stable than employment (compared with other countries).

So what does the Japanese evidence tell us about profit-sharing? Since the intermediate predictions of Weitzman's theory are not borne out, one can say either that his theory is wrong or that Japan is not a case of profit-sharing. There is a lot to the latter view. While some 25 per cent of remuneration is in bonuses, much of this is indeed a fixed element. Thus, we must probably conclude that Japan provides little evidence either for or against profit-sharing.

Even so, we would support profit-sharing as a device to improve productivity and industrial relations. As a device to reduce unemployment, it is no straightforward panacea.

Early retirement and work-sharing

Two policies that are very popular would be clearly counter-productive. The first is the policy of reducing the labour force by early retirement. As we have shown, it is the unemployment rate that equilibrates the labour market. If the size of the labour force is reduced, the equilibrium unemployment rate is unaffected. Employment has to fall to eliminate the wage pressure that would otherwise emerge, as the supply of labour becomes more scarce relative to the demand. Thus, early retirement does not make jobs available for people who would otherwise be unemployed: it just reduces employment.

This is what reasonable theory says, and it is confirmed by the evidence. In time-series regressions wage behaviour is affected not only (positively) by employment but also (negatively) by the size of the labour force—and the absolute elasticities are of roughly equal size. Moreover, if one compares countries, it is striking that early retirement has expanded most in countries with the greatest increase in unemployment. In Japan, where retirement behaviour is unchanged, unemployment has not risen at all. This suggests that early retirement is not an effective means of reducing unemployment. It is an excellent way of making a country poorer.

The other policy with the same effect is work-sharing. The idea here is to redistribute the available work to more people. But once again, the available work is not a given—that is the 'lump-of-output fallacy'. The equilibrium unemployment rate is independent of hours of work. Thus, if hours are reduced and employment rises for a while, wage pressure will soon increase and the amount of work available will have to be reduced. Employment will revert to its former level.

We can understand why this happens by taking our wage-setting models, inserting hours, and making W_i represent the hourly wage. The conclusion from theory is confirmed by time-series regressions, which show that hours do not affect the relation between wage pressure and the unemployment rate. Again, the countries that have reduced hours most have been those where unemployment has grown most. In Japan and the USA, with fairly steady unemployment, hours have fallen little. Thus, cuts in hours provide a poor antidote to unemployment. But they certainly provide a lower standard of living.

Employment protection legislation

Another policy of importance relates to the laws of employment protection. In most European countries the law requires that, when a worker is laid off, he be given advance notice, severance pay (redundancy payments), and a satisfactory reason (as opposed to 'unfair dismissal').

Laws of this kind must reduce the rate of flow into unemployment (S/N), and this effect tends to reduce unemployment. But such laws also discourage hiring, since firms are less willing to hire workers whom they cannot later dismiss without incurring costs. Thus, the outflow rate from unemployment (H/U) is also reduced. In equilibrium the outflow from unemployment has to equal the inflow ($H = S$). Thus

$$\frac{U}{N} = \frac{S/N}{H/U}.$$

Unemployment is reduced by employment protection only if the inflow rate (S/N) falls more than the outflow rate (H/U). Studies on this matter yield ambiguous results.

On balance, employment protection laws are probably bad for employment, since they strengthen insider power and encourage the payment of efficiency wages to motivate workers who cannot be threatened with dismissal. But there are equity arguments in their favour, and the evidence on adverse employment effects is not strong enough to warrant a total abandonment of the practice.

Demand management

On the supply side, we have seen that there exist policies which would really help (policies towards the unemployed, towards wage determination, and marginal employment subsidies)—and some others which would probably not. What about the demand side?

This is not mainly a book about the demand side of the economy, or about 'stabilization policy'. We would make only two comments.

First, when hysteresis is strong, it is very important to avoid big rises in unemployment. If inflation is too high, it is better to eliminate it by small amounts of extra unemployment over a longish time period than by anything approaching 'cold turkey' (see Annex 1.5). Had this been understood in 1980, much of the disaster of European unemployment could have been avoided.

Second, once inflation is at an acceptable level, it is normally desirable to avoid disturbances to nominal demand, by holding the growth of nominal demand stable. But should inflationary supply shocks happen, the case for some accommodation through faster nominal demand growth is stronger the higher the degree of hysteresis. Stabilization policy should be highly sensitive to the supply mechanisms of the economy.

13. Summary

We began with a set of ten questions, which we have taken some time to answer. If we had been quicker, we might simply have said:

1. Unemployment is in equilibrium when it is high enough to eliminate the leapfrogging of wages over each other and to make the planned mark-up of wages over prices (the target real wage) consistent with the planned mark-up of prices over wages (the feasible real wage).

2. There is, however, 'nominal inertia' in price- and wage-setting so that the system can easily depart from equilibrium as a result of shocks. Moreover, once unemployment is away from the long-run NAIRU, it takes some time to return. If recent unemployment is high, inflation falls only if unemployment is above the *short-run* NAIRU.

3. In the steady state, lower unemployment requires lower real labour costs but not necessarily lower real take-home pay.

4. Equilibrium unemployment is not market-clearing. Firms may find it profitable to pay wages above market-clearing levels in order to motivate workers. Unions may also keep wages up, even when there is excess supply of labour.

5. Unemployment is raised by adverse demand shocks and adverse supply shocks (such as rises in relative import prices). But in the very long term unemployment is independent of import prices, taxes, and productivity.

6. But unemployment is also affected by the search behaviour of the unemployed, and is higher when the unemployed search less (whether because of unemployment benefits or because of the demoralization arising from long-term unemployment).

7. For most people there is also a secondary sector of the labour market, where wages clear the market and jobs are available. If workers are not taking these jobs, it is because the jobs are too unpleasant or ill-paid relative to the quality of life while unemployed.

8. Unemployment rates are much above average for less skilled workers,

young people, and people in disadvantaged regions. These disparities tend to raise the overall unemployment rate.

9. The different experience of different countries depends on the way they treat unemployed people (benefits and active manpower policy) and their wage-bargaining systems—together with the shocks they have been subjected to.

10. There is plenty we can do to reduce unemployment. It is far from natural, and not beyond our power to control.

Notes

1. This is related to the finding that, when unemployment is regressed on lagged unemployment, the coefficient on the latter is close to unity. For Britain, annual data for 1900–89 give

$$u_t = 0.0041 + 0.934\, u_{t-1}$$
$$(0.039)$$

and for the USA they give

$$u_t = 0.0080 + 0.877\, u_{t-1}$$
$$(0.051)$$

(s.e. in brackets). However, this kind of exercise assumes an unvarying stochastic 'unemployment process', which we do not.
2. The equation corresponding to Fig. 5(c) is

$$\Delta^2 p = 7.34 - 0.95u + 0.17t$$
$$(3.2) \quad (3.5) \quad (2.3)$$

where $\Delta^2 p$ is the annual change in inflation (% points), u is the unemployment rate (%) and $t = $ date $- 1990$. The time trend (0.17) is used to calculate detrended unemployment. Clearly, a time trend is a very inadequate way to model supply shocks, and most of this book is concerned with seeking better ways to do so—see in particular Ch. 9.
3. The long-run equilibrium rate of unemployment is also often called the 'natural' rate (Friedman 1968). We avoid this usage which smacks of inevitability.
4. Broadly speaking, the relevant chapters are as follows:

Question	Section of Ch. 1	Chapter of the book
1	3	8
2	4	8, 2 (Sect. 7), 3 (Sect. 4), 7, 9
3	5	8, 9
4	6	2, 3, 4
5	7	2, 3, 4
6	8	5
7	9	5
8	10	6
9	11	9
10	12	10

5. A more accurate term would be non-increasing inflation rate of unemployment, but the common usage is NAIRU.
6. If u_{-2} also affects Δp, the short-run NAIRU may lie above u_{-1} if unemployment has risen rapidly.
7. During disinflation the observations are in the corresponding area to the left.
8. Solving (1′) and (2′) for $w - p$ shows that

$$w - p - (w^* - p^*) = \frac{\gamma_1(w - w^e) - \beta_1(p - p^e)}{\beta_1 + \gamma_1}.$$

Suppose that in the first period after a shock $w^e = w^*$ and $p^e = p^*$; then

$$\frac{w - w^*}{p - p^*} = \frac{\gamma_1}{\beta_1}$$

so that

$$\Delta \log w > \Delta \log p \text{ if } \gamma_1 > \beta_1.$$

9. Millward and Stevens (1986), Table 8.8. The redundancy figures are based on Chapter 2, Table 5.
10. The consumer price is

$$P_c = P^{1-sm} P_m^{sm} = P(P_m/P)^{sm}$$

11. Annex 1.2 gives a model of the world economy, endogenizing commodity prices.
12. There is also a flow into unemployment from the secondary sector, arising from the temporary nature of much secondary-sector employment. However, those who make this transition are likely to return quite quickly to other secondary-sector jobs.
13. It is also probably the case that changes in primary employment cause almost equal changes in unemployment (though not of course quite one for one).

$$-\frac{dU}{dN_1} = 1 - \frac{N_2}{N_2 + U} \frac{1}{1 + \eta^S/\eta^D}$$

where η^S is the elasticity of S_2 and η^D is the elasticity of D_2, both evaluated at the point of intersection. If η^S is high, this is close to one.
14. Set $u_i/u = x$. Expanding x around $\bar{x}$ gives

$$\log x \simeq \log \bar{x} + \frac{1}{\bar{x}}(x - \bar{x}) - \frac{1}{2}\frac{1}{\bar{x}^2}(x - \bar{x})^2.$$

Since $\bar{x} = 1$ and $\sum \alpha_i = 1$,

$$\sum \alpha_i \log x_i \simeq 0 + 0 - \frac{1}{2}\sum \alpha_i (x_i - \bar{x})^2.$$

Thus, provided $(\alpha_i - L_i/L)$ is independent of u_i/u,

$$\sum \alpha_i \log u_i/u \simeq -\frac{1}{2}\sum \frac{L_i}{L}\left(\frac{u_i}{u} - 1\right)^2.$$

15. We replace Δp_{-1} by Δm_{-1}. This is based on rational expectations (see Ch. 8), with $\Delta^2 m$ white noise. In the absence of rational expectations, we could still include $\Delta^2 m$ but with extra lags on u.
16. Control group studies of the effect of the programmes on individuals do not show a totally clear pattern of results (Björklund 1990). But two caveats are important. First, there have been no experiments using random assignment. But, second, the programmes may help to create a pro-work ethic and may have important externalities that can only be judged by looking at the overall performance of the system compared with

other countries, and not by comparing the experience of one Swede with another. For a full description of the Swedish system see Layard *et al.* (1991).

17. To analyse a tax on workers, make take-home pay (W_i) equal to $C_i(1 - t) + S$ and differentiate the objective function with respect to W_i.

Microfoundations

2

Wage Bargaining and Unions

UNIONS are often blamed for unemployment. Is this fair? Do unions always raise unemployment? Or does it depend on how they operate?

A few casual facts suggest that unions might cause unemployment. In particular, there is the contrast between Europe and the USA. First there are the long-term trends. Since the 1950s unemployment has risen fairly steadily in Europe, but not in the USA. At the same time, unionization has been falling steadily in the USA, while it has been stable or rising in most European countries for most of the period.

Then there is the medium-term issue of persistance. Both Europe and the USA had sharp rises in unemployment in the early 1980s. But in Europe the unemployment stayed high, while in the USA it has fallen sharply. Could this be an effect of high unionization in Europe—giving greater power to the employed 'insiders' and inhibiting re-employment of the unemployed 'outsiders'?

These pieces of evidence seem pretty unfavourable to unions. But against this simple conclusion must be set two further facts. First, in the 1980s European unions have lost significant legal rights in some countries, especially Britain. But unemployment has not fallen below where it was in 1979. Is this because the scope of union bargaining has changed? In the 1970s there was more bargaining over manning than there is now. Can it be that bargaining over manning helps to maintain the number of 'good jobs', and that the end of 'overmanning' thus leads to unemployment?

A second key piece of evidence comes from the experience of Sweden, Norway, and Austria—countries with the highest unionization in the Western world and some of the lowest unemployment. Is this explained by the fact that, in those countries, bargaining is at the whole-economy level—a kind of corporatist national compact? By contrast, bargaining elsewhere is mainly at firm or industry level. Does whole-economy bargaining ensure that the interests of the outsiders are properly represented? Is employment safe where there are centralized unions?

From all these questions, it is obvious that the effects of unions on unemployment must depend upon how they operate. In this chapter we shall try to analyse the effects of five main dimensions in which the role of unions may vary. We shall see how unemployment is affected by

  (i) union power within the bargaining unit;
 (ii) whether bargaining covers manning ratios ('featherbedding');
(iii) the fraction of workers covered by collective bargaining;
(iv) the degree of centralization of bargaining;
 (v) the number of insiders.

The first four questions relate to the long-run equilibrium of the system. The last relates to short-run dynamics and the speed with which a system returns to equilibrium.

It may help if at this stage we state our broad conclusions somewhat baldly.

(i)   Union power

In Europe union power rose up to the late 1970s and has since fallen. The rise was due to increased legal protection (e.g. against dismissal for union activities), and perhaps also to greater affluence and the occurrence of more two-earner families—enabling workers better to withstand the privations of a strike. Since around 1980 union power has fallen in some European countries, especially Britain, owing to the removal of various union rights (e.g. in relation to strikes and the closed shop). In the USA, by contrast, union power has diminished steadily throughout the period, as employers have devoted more resources to opposing union organization (Freeman and Medoff 1984).

Our theoretical investigations suggest that these changes do matter, and that where unions are decentralized increased union power always increases unemployment (see Sections 2 and 5).

(ii)   Featherbedding

The next issue is the effect of featherbedding. If workers negotiate an easy life for themselves, with favourable manning ratios and crew sizes, does this increase total employment by increasing the number of workers producing a given output? In Britain such negotiations have become less common in the 1980s. Partly in consequence of this, productivity growth has been restored. Many people believe that the 'demanning' that has occurred, as management regained unilateral control over the work environment, has been a major cause of increased unemployment.

This could happen if those who lose their union jobs are unwilling to take less well-paid jobs in the market-clearing secondary sector. But it could go the other way. For, when union workers' effort is increased, this can raise the real wage in all sectors of the economy. Hence workers without union jobs will be more willing to take jobs in the competitive sector. Hence total employment can rise, even though union employment falls. On balance it seems likely that, even though demanning could raise unemployment in the short run, in the long run a shift to managerial discretion is likely to lower unemployment (Sections 4 and 5).

(iii)   Union coverage

What of the effect of union coverage (i.e. the proportion of workers whose wages are fixed by collective agreements)? In the USA only a quarter of workers are covered, compared with over three-quarters in most European countries. Can an increase in the number of 'good jobs' lead to an increase in total employment? Once again, this is unlikely (with decentralized bargaining) if in the process wages are reduced in the 'bad-job' sector, so that workers outside the union sector have less incentive to take jobs (Section 5).

(iv)   Centralization

Why is unemployment so low in Scandinavian countries? The answer is in part that in those countries wage bargaining is highly centralized. Under decentralized bargaining the bargainers take the national level of job opportunities as given and ignore the effect of their own decisions upon the job opportunities open to other workers. But under centralized bargaining, where one union organization bargains on behalf of the whole workforce, this externality is internalized. In addition, the fruitless process whereby one group tries to raise its wages relative to other workers' wages (and thus relative to prices) is short-circuited. Thus, with centralized bargaining the union is unlikely to push for wages that will create unemployment (Section 6).

(v)   Unions and persistence of unemployment

Reverting to decentralized unions, not only do they raise the average level of unemployment but they also make unemployment persist longer after shocks. This is because, when workers bargain, they push harder if there is only a small number of insiders (in which case there is less risk of further job loss from a given wage settlement) (Section 2). In addition unions may increase the degree of nominal inertia, and thus increase the response of unemployment to changes in nominal demand (Section 7).

Structure of the chapter

To derive our conclusions, we begin with a whole range of facts (Section 1). We then proceed to build a set of models whose relevance is supported by the evidence of Chapters 4 and 9.

Most of our analysis is concerned with decentralized union bargaining. In Section 2 we develop our basic model. Bargaining is over wages, and employers then determine employment. In Section 3 we discuss why employment is not generally bargained over. Section 4 shows what difference it makes if manning patterns are bargained over. In Section 5 we introduce a non-union sector, with unions still operating in a decentralized manner. In Section 6 we move to the case of centralized bargaining and analyse its effects. Finally, in Section 7 we look at how union bargaining can affect the degree of nominal inertia in wages, and thus the impact of demand shocks on the level of unemployment.

1. Basic facts and bargaining theory

To develop sensible models about the effects of unions, we must first discover some basic facts about how unions operate. That is the purpose of this section, but as a guide to what follows we shall begin by stating our stylized conclusions.

1. The fraction of workers covered by union-negotiated rates is over three-quarters in most of Europe, but under a quarter in the USA. In Scandinavia and Austria bargaining is highly centralized, but it is less so elsewhere.
2. Union democracy means that unions maximize the welfare of the median member. Only employed workers have votes.
3. Recruits are paid the same as existing workers, for reasons we discuss.
4. Unions do not bargain over employment as such, for reasons we discuss. These include the fact that most firms are hiring workers to replace quits rather than laying workers off.
5. However, workers are concerned about the *ex ante* risk of layoff, which is perceived as the same for all workers in an enterprise (random assignment).

6. Firms pay no unemployment insurance to laid-off workers, for reasons we discuss.
7. Unions do bargain over conditions of work, including in many cases crew size, manning ratios, and other variables that may affect employment.
8. The union never gets everything it wants. Thus, we rejct the 'monopoly union' model and use instead the 'right to manage' model where wages are bargained over and the firm selects employment *ex post*.
9. When workers strike for a wage above the supply price of labour, firms do not sack them. This is mainly because of the human capital embodied in the workforce, which is the main source of insider power.
10. Most bargains are in fact made without a strike, since a strike would dissipate the joint surplus of firm and workers.

These will be the operating assumptions on which we build our models. Impatient readers can accept them and move to p. 99; others may prefer to examine our evidence.

Union density and coverage

To form a view of the role of unions, we begin with the crude data on union membership. As Table 1 shows, union membership is much higher in Europe than in the USA. In 1986 it was 17 per cent in the USA compared with 40–50 per cent in Germany, Italy, and the UK and over 80 per cent in Denmark, Finland, and Sweden. In addition, the trends are quite different. In the USA union density has been falling ever since the mid-1950s, mainly because of the determined efforts of employers to prevent union organization (Freeman and Medoff 1984).[1] In Europe union density rose strongly in the 1970s and has continued to rise in Sweden and Denmark. Only in Britain, Italy, and the Netherlands have there been significant falls in the 1980s.

Moreover, the unionization figures greatly understate the difference in the proportion of workers covered by collective agreements. In the USA 'coverage' exceeds membership by only about 10 per cent (Freeman and Medoff 1984). But in Europe the great majority of workers are covered by collective agreements even if they are not union members. In Britain, for example, two-thirds of workers are formally covered by collective agreements (Table 2). But others are covered by statutory Wages Councils consisting of equal numbers of workers' and employers' representatives plus an independent chairman: for most practical purposes, this is a form of collective bargaining. And between 1975 and 1982 the Fair Wages Resolution applied to all workers, giving them a legal claim to the generally prevailing wage for their occupation and area.

Table 1 *Percentage of workers unionized*

	1970	1979	1986/7	Change 1970–9	1979–86
Belgium	66	77	—	+ 11	—
Denmark	66	86	95	+ 20	+ 9
France	22	28	—	+ 6	—
Germany	37	42	43	+ 5	+ 1
Ireland	44	49	51	+ 5	+ 2
Italy	39	51	45	+ 12	− 6
Netherlands	39	43	35	+ 4	− 8
UK	51	58	50	+ 7	− 8
Australia	52	58	56	+ 6	− 2
New Zealand	43	46	—	+ 3	—
Canada	44	49	51	+ 5	+ 2
USA	31	25	17	− 6	− 8
Japan	35	32	28	− 3	− 4
Austria	64	59	61	− 5	+ 2
Finland	56	84	85	+ 28	+ 1
Norway	59	60	61	+ 1	+ 1
Sweden	79	89	96	+ 10	+ 7
Switzerland	31	34	33	+ 3	− 1

Note: Non-agricultural employees only.

Source: Blanchflower and Freeman (1990).

Similarly in Germany, the government of the region (*Land*) has the power to extend collective agreements to non-union workers and this is often exercised. In France, Italy, Spain, and Portugal bargained rates have an application far beyond the unionized workforce.

The systems of wage determination in the 20 main OECD countries are described in some detail in Annex 1.4. It is difficult for Americans to grasp the difference between the European and US labour markets, but a clear illustration of the difference is the response of women's pay to equal pay legislation. In the relatively flexible US labour market, the response was certainly not striking (O'Neill 1985); by contrast, in Britain women's relative pay rose by 15 per cent in the last three years of the phasing-in of the Equal Pay Act, and has stayed there ever since. This is because individual pay is largely determined by collectively bargained rates of pay. The negotiated hourly pay scales used to differ for men and women by on average 15 per cent (Zabalza and Tzannatos 1985); they then became the same. Similar changes in the relative pay of men

Table 2 *Percentage of workers covered by collective agreements in Britain, 1984*

	Private		Public
	Manufacturing	*Services*	
Manual	79	53	100
Non-manual	79	40	100

Note: According to the Workplace Industrial Relations Survey (WIRS), there was no systematic change between 1980 and 1984 in these percentages. Somewhat in contrast, the *New Earnings Survey* shows the following percentages covered by collective agreements:

		1973	1978	1985
Men:	Manual	83	78	71
	Non-manual	60	59	56
Women:	Manual	72	71	62
	Non-manual	65	67	65

Source: Millward and Stevens (1986: Tables 9.3, 9.4, 9.9, 9.10). Based on the WIRS.

and women have occurred in Australia and other countries, by precisely the same mechanism (Layard and Mincer 1985).

To picture the process of collective bargaining, it is important to have an idea of the level at which it occurs (Table 3). In the USA, nearly half the workers involved have their pay set by a multi-employer deal. (In this case any simultaneous bargain, explicit or implicit, over the numbers employed is

Table 3 *Workers covered by collective bargaining analysed by level of bargain*

	USA	*Britain (private sector)*			
		Manufacturing		*Services*	
		Manual	*Non-manual*	*Manual*	*Non-manual*
Multi-employer	43	30	13	50	40
Single employer					
Multi-plant	40	24	33	33	45
Single plant	17	46	53	17	15
	100	100	100	100	100

Sources: *USA*: Freeman and Medoff (1984: Table 2.5). Data relate to major collective agreements, 1980 (covering over 1000 workers). *Britain*: Millward and Stevens (1986: Tables 9.7, 9.13). Data relate to 'most important level of bargaining', 1984.

clearly impossible.) Most of the other US bargains are company-wide agreements. A similar pattern of settlements holds in Britain, except that almost all public-sector pay deals are national in coverage.

Union decision-making

The next question is, 'On whose behalf do the unions bargain?' They bargain essentially on behalf of their members, nearly all of whom are existing workers. Former workers, even if they go on paying their dues, generally lose voting rights or cease to attend meetings.

Doubtless union officials have their own objectives, which may include empire-building. But union democracy generally imposes quite severe limits on the bargaining position of union officials (Farber 1986). In general union members elect their executive committees for fairly short tenures (with the possibility of electing their full-time officials for much longer tenures). Union members often vote directly on whether or not to accept wage offers and on whether to go on strike. Thus, whatever the shortcomings of the theory, we shall assume that union decisions are made at the behest of the median voter.

What is bargained over?

So what do unions bargain over?

(i)   Wages

All bargains certainly cover wages. In Europe wages are generally negotiated each year, while in the USA and Canada the bargain typically covers three years. With such long contract periods, it is not surprising that some contingent elements are included in the contract. However, these are generally confined to cost-of-living clauses. It is certainly unusual for any contract to link future wages to future employment. (The latter is sometimes now assumed in the implicit contracts literature, which we find unhelpful for reasons given in Annex 2.1.)

Unions almost always insist that firms pay the same wage to new workers as to the existing workers with the same qualifications. They successfully resist most proposals for two-tier wage structures, for two reasons. Two-tier wages provide an incentive for the firm gradually to replace existing workers by others. And even if this did not happen, low-wage workers would eventually become a majority—and high-wage workers would have lost majority support for a strike threat to protect their own wages.[2]

Apart from wages, what else is bargained over?

(ii) Employment

Employment is almost never bargained over as such. Indeed, US contracts typically include a 'management rights' clause, asserting for example that the company 'will determine the extent of any required force adjustments'. As we shall see, British contracts are not usually as extreme as this. But the total size of the workforce is rarely a subject of routine negotiation.

To find the facts on this, Oswald (1987) wrote to the largest 60 US and 60 British unions. His questionnaire began, 'Does your union normally negotiate over the number of jobs as well as over wages and conditions?' Only 2 US respondents said Yes (out of 19) and only 3 British respondents said Yes (out of 18). In Britain the main exceptions were the miners' and printers' unions, which are notorious but untypical. In addition, it is unusual for the number of redundancies to be settled by bargaining (even though there may be negotiations over terms of severance).

It has bothered many economists (starting with Leontief 1946) that a bargain should be struck which did not cover a subject like employment, which both sides might be thought to care about. Hence some authors have assumed that there *must* at least be an implicit bargain about employment (McDonald and Solow 1981, 1985). But such assumptions are not supported by the evidence.[3]

So why is employment not bargained over? The reason is that existing workers do not care about the level of employment in the firm as such: they care about whether their own job is safe. In most firms in most years there are no layoffs (see below), so that employment is well above the level needed for job security. Some workers leave each year and others are hired. Existing workers can expect to keep their jobs unless things turn out particularly badly.

However, if things do turn out badly, some workers will be fired. This is what concerns existing workers. One might suppose that it would be efficient to have *ex post* bargains about the scale of layoffs. However, there are asymmetries of information. It is impossible for workers to be sure how much trouble the firm is in. There may or may not be a risk of shut-down if too few redundancies are accepted. Grossman and Hart (1981) have suggested that these problems might be overcome by agreements on a wage–employment locus along which firms would operate, but this has never been heard of and is evidently too difficult to negotiate.

In any case, the efficiency costs of not bargaining over layoffs are much less than one would suppose from the standard (Leontief/McDonald–Solow) analysis of the efficiency costs of not bargaining over employment (see Section 3). So in general, workers leave the employment decision to the managers without restrictions. Though the scale of layoffs is sometimes bargained over, this is rare.

In the USA there is an additional reason why bargaining over layoffs is uncommon. This is that a strike in pursuit of an employment objective is illegal[4] (Staiger 1990). So employers can simply refuse to negotiate, and it is in their interest to do so.

Oswald (1987) has suggested a further reason why bargaining over employment is relatively rare. This is that, when layoffs do occur, they quite often occur in a pre-assigned order. In such a case the median voter feels a lot safer than he would if layoffs were allocated among existing workers by purely random assignment. Given the evidence quoted below, we do not think this point should be given excessive weight.

So just how common are layoffs? In Britain the great majority of firms have no layoffs. Even in 1980 (one of the worst post-war years) only 11 per cent of establishments that remained in business dismissed any workers (Millward and Stephens 1986: Table 8.8). One reason for the low rate of layoffs is the relative stability of employment at the level of the establishment in Britain. In a normal year total annual establishment-level falls in employment amount to only 4 per cent of total employment (see Table 4). As in most countries, British workers who become unemployed lose all contact with their previous employer, and, indeed, in 1978 only 33 per cent returned eventually to the same industry (*Employment Gazette*, January 1981).

The situation in the USA is somewhat different (see Table 4). We do not know how many establishments lay off workers in a year. But there is much more variability of employment at the level of the establishment than in Britain. In a year of steady unemployment, total establishment-level falls in employment amount to 10 per cent of total employment. This induces a high flow of dismissed workers into unemployment. Some of these are 'temporary layoffs'; i.e., they remain associated with a firm awaiting recall while receiving publicly provided unemployment insurance. However, as Lilien and Hall (1986) point out, temporary layoffs accounted for only about 17 per cent of the unemployed in 1976–82. And only about three-quarters of these are eventually rehired. Thus, temporary layoffs are not a central part of US unemployment, and in most other countries the system does not exist. So we need to give it no special attention.

The implications of all this depend a lot on whether the firm-level employment changes are forecastable. What is striking is that, except for adjacent years, the changes are uncorrelated over time, and the correlation over adjacent years is only 0.24 and negative (Leonard 1987). Thus, employment change appears difficult to forecast.

Table 4 *Layoffs and employment adjustment (years of roughly stable employment)*

	USA 1980	UK 1978
	(as % of employment)	
(1) Gross job losses p.a. (12-month comparison)	10	4
(2) Job-losers entering unemployment p.a.	18	4
(3) All entrants to unemployment p.a.	35	12
(4) Individuals employed at beginning of year and no longer employed by same firm at end of year	28	15
(5) Total job separations p.a. (manufacturing)	48	24
(6) Total layoffs p.a.(manufacturing)	20	
(7) Gross job losses p.a. (manufacturing)	9	

Notes: Gross job losses measure the falls in employment at the level of the establishment between one week and the same week 12 months later. In addition, there are substantial gross job losses which occur because of fluctuations in employment which get reversed during the year. These fluctuations include the creation and destruction of temporary jobs (e.g. because of seasonal employment). The end of temporary jobs is an important source of job loss among entrants to unemployment. Thus, one cannot compare rows (1) and (2) and infer that natural wastage is not an important method of employment adjustment. (But note also the size of row (6).)

Sources: *USA*, row (1): Leonard (1978: Table 6.6). This relates to Wisconsin only. The figures show that the position in manufacturing is very broadly similar to non-manufacturing. It is therefore also relevant to examine the data in Davis and Haltiwanger (1990)—see row (7). (2): See Johnson and Layard (1986: Table 16.9) and Table 2 in Ch. 5 below. (3): Ch. 5 below, Table 2; (4): Hall (1982: 717); (5): Employment and Training Report of the President 1982, Table C.13; (6): Ibid.; (7): Davis and Haltiwanger (1990).

UK, row (1): see Layard and Nickell (1980: 71). (2): see Johnson and Layard (1986: Table 16.10) and Table 3 in Ch. 5 below; (3). Ch. 5, Table 3. (4): Johnson and Layard (1986: Table 16.7). (5): DE, *Employment Gazette*, Feb. 1980, p. 130.

Since the danger of job loss is a real *ex ante* risk facing many workers, we need to know how it will affect bargaining behaviour. This clearly depends on the method of deciding who gets laid off and on the terms for laid-off workers.[5] These matters are almost invariably covered in the terms of bargains in the USA and in 90 per cent of bargains in Britain (see Table 5).

(iii)   Layoff criteria

In deciding who is laid off in a contraction, seniority is almost always a major criterion, 'other things equal'. In other words, last-in, first-out (LIFO) is an important principle (Oswald 1987; Oswald and Turnbull 1985).[6] However, in written contracts this principle is always subject to the qualification that the

Table 5 *Percentage of union establishments for which each item is generally bargained over: Britain, manual unions,[a] 1980 and 1984*

	1980	1984
Physical working conditions	92	78
Redeployment within establishment	80	62
Manning levels[b]	76	55
Size of redundancy payments	—	46
Major changes in production methods	65	—
Recruitment	69	38
Holiday entitlement	96	—
Length of working week	95	—
Capital investment	39	—
Pensions	76	—

[a] Non-manual union bargaining is very similar.

[b] Manning levels refers to manning ratios.

Sources: Daniel and Millward (1983: 197, 182); Millward and Stevens (1986: 248).

efficiency of the plant be maintained. Thus it is not the case that, if a plant contracts, the only workers who leave are those most recently recruited. For a contraction generally involves running down one part of the operation more than another. So LIFO is a principle that applies within each workshop and even within each craft, rather than across the board. And even at that level, it is not uniquely decisive. For example, a recent British survey of 350 establishments in various parts of the country asked the following question: 'If you have used enforced redundancy in the last three years, which criteria did you use?' The percentages of estalishments reporting each of the following criteria were (Oswald and Turnbull, 1985):

LIFO	64
Least competent or skilled	47
Poor work/attendance record	26
Others	40
	177

Thus it is not true that, if a wage bargain leads to redundancies in an establishment, everybody can tell in advance who will go. If workers fear a 10 per cent fall in employment, it is not true that 10 per cent of workers expect to go and 90 per cent feel safe; nor is it true that all workers face a 10 per cent chance of going. But, since it is probably nearer the truth, we shall proceed as though within a firm any layoffs are by random assignment.

(iv)   Unemployment insurance

The next issue is the financial and other rights of those laid off. The main support in all countries comes from the state.[7] This consists of weekly unemployment benefit. In addition, in most European countries employers are legally obliged to make a one-off payment (Emerson 1988*a*). In Britain this amounts very roughly to one week's pay per year of service.

But in addition to these legal obligations, employers often negotiate further payments. The main form of this is higher severance pay, and private unemployment insurance is fairly rare (contrary to the assumptions of much implicit contracts literature). In Britain about one-third of all redundant workers get extra severance pay, either as an *ex gratia* payment or resulting from a bargain with the union (IMS 1981). Some of these extra payments are to encourage voluntary redundancy, though some also go to compulsory layoffs. The total amount of money paid above the statutory requirement is about the same as the total paid on a statutory basis (Metcalf 1984*a*). It is however almost unknown for firms to pay workers who are made redundant any *regular* payment.[8]

The situation in the USA is somewhat different. There is no statutory severance pay, but in manufacturing one-half of union agreements specify one-off severance pay, and a similar number specify continuing supplementary unemployment benefit. Such schemes are rare in the service sector.[9] The elementary theory of bargains can probably afford to overlook these schemes. It should certainly assume that workers do not want to be made redundant.

There are probably many reasons why the unions do not bargain for full insurance. First, there is the problem of moral hazard—firms and unions fear that some workers might opt for paid leisure. Second, LIFO-type layoffs mean that only a limited proportion of union members would gain from a policy for which all paid. We shall assume that the only unemployment insurance comes from public authorities.

(v)   Manning ratios

Although unions do not generally bargain over employment, they do bargain over conditions of work, including how hard workers have to work. A key determinant of the latter is the level at which machines, shops, or offices are manned, or the size of crew (for example in trains or ships). Unions also care about this because of its effect upon employment.

As Table 5 shows, three-quarters of bargains in the UK used to cover manning ratios, though by 1984 the proportion had fallen to just over a half. Bargaining over crew size is also common in the USA (Johnson 1990). Some writers have concluded that unions are thus in effect bargaining over employment (e.g. McDonald and Solow 1981). This is not correct. At most, they are bargaining over the ratio of capital to labour employed per shift. This does not determine employment, since

1. the quantity of capital can be changed, and is not normally bargained over, and
2. the number of shifts per machine can be varied from zero upwards.

It seems far better to think of bargaining over manning ratios as a form of bargaining over effort. This is the approach we adopt later in the chapter.

Union power

The union never gets everything it wants. It bargains. Thus we reject an excessively simple model in common usage—the model of the 'monopoly union'. Under this model the union chooses wages on its own, with no bargaining. Apart from being patently false, this model may give rise to the 'paradox of the shrinking union': as union members leave, existing members jack up wages progressively so that no hiring occurs. The paradox is, however, no paradox, since the premiss is false.

But what does determine the outcome of the power struggle between a union and its employer? The key element in the situation is the ability of both sides to halt production. The firm's power depends on the right to lock-out or fire. The union's power depends on the right to organize and strike. The union may indeed have some power through threats of overtime bans, work-to-rule, and go-slow, even when it has no right to strike (as in much of the US public sector). But in general, the right to strike is crucial. This power is upheld by law, and we must therefore look briefly at the legal framework of union power.

In the USA most strikes come about after the expiry of legally binding contracts. A union can negotiate with employers only if it wins a ballot of workers in which the majority say they wish to be represented by the union. If this occurs, all workers may or may not have to join the union (i.e. work in a 'union' shop), depending on whether the employer agrees. However, in some states having 'right-to-work laws' the union shop is illegal. Most unions have votes on strikes.

The unionization rate has fallen sharply in the USA. As old firms decline and new ones grow, the unions continually need to extend their organization in order to stand still. They have been increasingly unsuccessful at this, largely because of more effective management opposition, including the illegal firing of union organizers. According to Freeman and Medoff (1984), 'from 1960 to 1980 the number of charges involving a firing for union activity rose threefold, and the number of workers awarded back pay or reinstated to their jobs rose fivefold . . . In 1980 one in twenty workers who voted for a union got fired.' Given the small penalties involved, such increased sophistication on the part of employers represents an effective loss of union power.

In Britain the legal position is different. Subject to certain legal limits, any union can call its members on strike at any time in support of their own interests (though most strikes over wages occur during the annual negotiation of wages). From 1906 until the 1970s, the basic bargaining rights of unions were unchanged but were exercised with increasing effectiveness during the later 1960s and 1970s. In 1975 trade union immunities from civil action were extended. In addition, the introduction of unfair dismissal laws in 1971 made it much more difficult and costly for firms to sack workers for any reason, including unreasonable union activities. Thus, in Britain, as elsewhere in Europe, employment laws helped to strengthen insider power (Emerson 1988*a*; Lindbeck and Snower 1989).

Since 1980, Britain has had a series of laws reducing union power in many different directions (Metcalf 1990; Brown and Wadhwani 1990; Freeman and Pelletier 1990; Towers 1989). Over the same period, in Britain as in many other countries, there has been much less strike activity. But it is difficult to know how far this is due to higher unemployment and how far to different laws.

In some countries strikes are a much less important method for dispute resolution than in Britain, the USA, France, or Italy. In Norway and Sweden, 'peace agreements' between national unions and employers rule out the use of strikes in supplementary firm-level bargains. In Germany, strikes over wage disputes at the level of the firm are illegal. Peace agreements are also common in Switzerland. These arrangements may help to explain the good unemployment record in those countries.

Arbitration arrangements are also very important. For example, until 1984 New Zealand (another low-unemployment country till then) had a system of compulsory arbitration at the request of either side. This helped to restrain wage pressure.

An obvious question is, Why do firms ever agree to pay workers more than the supply price of labour—as they clearly do when there are involuntary unemployment and job queues? To put the matter more brutally, why do firms not sack all workers the moment they strike for more than the supply price of labour? The answer is that, though firms may have the legal right to do so, it is against their interest—owing to the firm-specific human capital embodied in the workforce. Only when the union's wage demand is so high that the firm finds it cheaper to hire a new workforce do we get exceptional incidents like the sacking of Murdoch's print-workers in London in 1985–6 or of the US air-traffic controllers in 1981.

However, the crucial fact about strikes is that they are comparatively rare. Few workers are involved each year in most countries (see Table 6). Strikes occur in only about 15 per cent of contract negotiations in the USA and

Table 6 *Percentage of workers involved in strikes per year, 1950s–1980s*[a]

	1950s	*1960s*	*1970s*	*1980s*[b]	*(Working days lost per year per 100 workers, 1980s)*
Belgium	4.7	0.7	2.2	—	(—)
Denmark	0.6	1.4	4.1	4.8	(21.9)
France	7.6	10.9	8.7	0.8	(6.3)
Germany	0.6	0.2	0.8	0.7	(3.5)
Ireland	1.0	0.3	3.4	4.5	(43.5)
Italy	10.8	17.5	46.8	36.3	(72.0)
Netherlands	0.4	0.4	0.5	0.5	(1.4)
Spain	—	—	13.9	15.0	(60.5)
UK	2.9	5.5	10.6	4.6	(37.8)
Australia	1.0	12.1	23.7	11.5	(37.5)
New Zealand	3.4	2.9	10.2	11.6	(47.1)
Canada	1.8	2.6	5.8	3.3	(56.7)
USA	3.5	2.6	2.5	0.5	(12.5)
Japan	3.0	2.6	3.2	·0.4	(0.5)
Austria	1.0	2.1	0.4	0.3	(—)
Finland	3.8	2.0	17.1	15.2	(50.0)
Norway	0.7	0.3	0.4	0.7	(10.8)
Sweden	0.2	0.1	0.5	2.9	(18.5)
Switzerland	0.04	0.01	0.03	0.02	(—)

[a] Data exclude France 1968; Spain 1986–7; Austria 1950–2; Switzerland 1961, 1973, 1987; and New Zealand 1986–7.

[b] 1980s means 1980–7.

Sources: *Workers involved in strikes*: ILO *Yearbook of Labor Statistics*, various years; *Total employment*: OECD, *Main Economic Indicators* (*Historical statistics*), various years, and OECD, *Economic Outlook*, no. 45 (June 1989), except Spain and New Zealand, for which various editions of the *Yearbook of Labor Statistics* were used.

Canada (see Kennan and Wilson 1989) and this is high by international standards: for example, in Britain between 1979 and 1986 the proportion was only $2\frac{1}{2}$ per cent (CBI data).

The reason why strikes are rare is that in most firms the marriage between the firm and its workers generates an economic surplus. This surplus would be lost during a strike (i.e. during a temporary separation).

Bargaining theory

So what does determine the outcome of a bargain, even when there is no strike? The answer is precisely that, if there *were* a strike or lock-out, both sides would lose owing to the loss of firm revenue from which to pay wages and obtain profit. Both sides, therefore, have an incentive to settle.

The problem is analogous to that of dividing a continuous supply of cake between two parties. What makes the parties agree at the outset is that, if they do not agree, they will get no cake at all until they do. It can be shown that, on two assumptions, this would drive the bargainers to split the cake equally (Binmore *et al.* 1986). These assumptions are that

1. both sides have the same discount rate, and
2. neither side gets any extra income from other sources while the disagreement is going on.

This is the starting point in the analysis. If we now relax the two assumptions, we find the following.

1. If the discount rates differ, the party with the higher discount rate will be less willing to go without cake, and will therefore accept a reduced share of cake in order to prevent this happening.
2. If one side gets some extra income from elsewhere as a result of a disagreement, that party will be more willing to tolerate a disagreement and thus will be able to insist on a higher share of cake. This party is said to have a higher 'fallback'.

Thus, one can show that if Y_i is the cake which one party receives per period, r_i its discount rate, and $\bar{Y}_i$ its fallback income per period, the supply of cake $\bar{Y}$ will be divided between the two parties to maximize

$$(Y_1 - \bar{Y}_1)^{r_2/r_1}(Y_2 - \bar{Y}_2) \qquad \text{s.t.} Y_1 + Y_2 = \bar{Y}.$$

This is shown in Annex 2.2. If we apply it to the problem of bargaining between a union and a firm, the problem is to maximize

$$(V - \bar{V})^{\beta}(\Pi - \bar{\Pi}) \qquad \text{s.t. the relevant constraints,}$$

99

where V is the union objective function, Π the firm's profit per period, and $\bar{V}$ and $\bar{\Pi}$ the relevant 'fall-backs'.

In this context β is lower the higher the relative discount rate of the union: a higher union discount rate reduces union bargaining power and helps to account for the oft-alleged imbalance of bargaining power between workers and firms. Most institutional changes of the kind we have discussed earlier impact on $\bar{V}$ and $\bar{\Pi}$, and impact on them differentially. However, to model this differential impact by changes in $\bar{V}$ and $\bar{\Pi}$ is clumsy and involves a multiplication of symbols. For all practical purposes, an institutional change favouring unions can be adequately represented by an increase in β and vice versa. This is how we shall represent it.

Following hallowed usage, we shall refer to the term $(V - \bar{V})^{\beta}(\Pi - \bar{\Pi})$ as the *Nash maximand*, since Nash (1950, 1953) first proposed a formulation of this kind. One remaining point is important. The 'outside option' available to each partner if the marriage is dissolved has no effect on the bargain, provided the bargain gives both parties more than they could get elsewhere. If, however, the bargaining solution given above would give one partner less than that, the 'outside option' becomes a binding constraint, and the bargain that is struck gives that partner an amount just equal to his 'outside option'.

2. How unions affect unemployment

Union objectives

We can now use this framework to examine the outcome of a firm-level bargain in an economy of many identical firms (indexed i), all unionized. We start at the firm level and then move to the general equilibrium. We shall assume that the union is concerned only with existing workers and wishes to maximize the expected utility of its median voter.

In this section we shall ignore effort and assume that bargaining is over wages only. With no risk aversion, the union wishes to maximize the expected income of the median voter. Since we assume that layoffs are by random assignment, this is the same as the expected income of every worker. (No substantive results would alter if we assumed that individual utility was isoelastic in income.) Thus, the objective of the union associated with the ith firm is given by

$$V_i = S_i W_i + (1 - S_i) A,$$

where W_i is the real wage in firm i measured in units of GDP (throughout this chapter), S_i is the probability of being employed in the same firm next period (the 'survival' probability), which is clearly dependent on the wage bargain, and A is the expected real income of a worker who loses his job in the firm.[10] The wage is bargained at the beginning of the period and there is an element of uncertainty about some aspect of the firm's performance during the period. The expected 'alternative' income (A) is given by

$$A = (1 - \varphi u)W^e + \varphi uB,$$

where W^e is the expected outside real wage, B is the real unemployment benefit, and φ is a constant which depends positively on the discount rate and negatively on the turnover rate.[11] We assume, for simplicity, that the outside wage is the only aggregate variable that is not known at the time wages are bargained. Thus there is perfect foresight about u, B, and the aggregate price level.

We now have to consider the question of strike income ($\bar{V}_i$). Some unions have strike pay, but this should be included only if it is paid from a fund including mainly workers from outside the bargaining unit. Thus, the main relevant incomes are earnings from other temporary jobs which strikers pick up during the strike, plus unemployment benefits in so far as these are payable.[12] Thus we can approximate $\bar{V}_i$ by

$$\bar{V}_i = (1 - \theta u)W^e + \theta uB.$$

If we assume for simplicity that $\theta = \varphi$, then $\bar{V}_i = A$ and

$$V_i - \bar{V}_i = (W_i - A)S_i.$$

Turning to the firm, its income is its profit. Since fixed charges are incurred whether or not there is a strike, the excess income when there is no strike consists of operating profit. So as not to multiply symbols, we shall henceforth use the symbol Π to mean operating profit, with $\bar{\Pi} = 0$. Thus, using the Nash-bargaining maximand, the bargain is that which maximizes

$$\Omega = (W_i - A)^\beta S(W_i)^\beta \Pi_i^e(W_i),$$

where β measures union power.

The bargaining outcome

We can now trace out the implication of the bargain for

(i) the firm-level wage,
(ii) the aggregate wage, and
(iii) equilibrium unemployment.

(i)   The firm-level wage

The bargained wage must satisfy

$$\frac{\partial \log \Omega}{\partial W_i} = \frac{\beta}{W_i - A} + \frac{\beta}{S}\frac{\partial S}{\partial W_i} - \frac{N_i^e}{\Pi_i^e} = 0, \tag{1}$$

since $\partial \Pi_i^e / \partial W_i = - N_i^e$ by the envelope theorem, N_i^e being expected employ-ment. Clearly, $\partial S / \partial W_i$ is negative. Multiplying by W_i and inverting gives the wage mark-up over alternative income as

$$\frac{W_i - A}{W_i} = \frac{1}{-\dfrac{W_i}{S}\dfrac{\partial S}{\partial W_i} + \dfrac{W_i N_i^e}{\beta \Pi_i^e}} = \frac{1}{\varepsilon_{SW}(W_i) + (\beta \gamma(W_i))^{-1}}, \tag{2}$$

where ε_{SW} is the *absolute* elasticity of the survival probability with respect to the wage and $\gamma = \Pi_i^e / W_i N_i^e$.

In order to analyse this equation, we need to look at the functions $\varepsilon_{SW}(W_i)$, $\gamma(W_i)$ in more detail. Life is much simpler, and little of substance is lost, if we assume at the outset that production is Cobb–Douglas and product-demand is constant elasticity. Comments on the non-Cobb–Douglas case will be made in the text. Thus we have, for firm i,

$$\text{Production: } Y_i = N_i^\alpha K_i^{1-\alpha} \tag{3}$$

$$\text{Demand: } \quad Y_i = (P_i)^{-\eta}\tilde{\theta}_i Y_{di} \tag{4}$$

where Y_i is value added output, K_i is the pre-determined capital stock, P_i is the real price of the firm's value added, Y_{di} is a demand index, and $\tilde{\theta}_i$ is a random variable whose value is revealed only after wage bargaining. Price, output, and employment are set by the firm *ex post*.

As a consequence of profit maximization, we have the marginal revenue product condition,

$$N_i/K_i = (W_i/P_i\alpha\kappa)^{-1/(1-\alpha)}, \tag{5a}$$

where $\kappa = 1 - 1/\eta$. κ is an indicator of product market competitiveness. In much of what follows, we shall refer to κ simply as competitiveness unless we have to distinguish it from international competitiveness, as in Chapter 8.

Using (3), (4), and (5), we are able to solve out for employment as

$$N_i/K_i = \tilde{\varphi}(W_i K_i^{1/\eta}/\alpha\kappa Y_{di}^{1/\eta})^{-1/(1-\alpha\kappa)}, \tag{5b}$$

here $\tilde{\varphi} = \tilde{\vartheta}^{1/\eta(1-\alpha\kappa)}$. This random variable we suppose, without loss of generality, to have a unit mean. Consequently expected employment, N_i^e, satisfies

$$N_i = N_i^e \tilde{\varphi}. \tag{6}$$

It is then easy to show that *ex post* maximum profit (Π) satisfies

$$\Pi_i = \frac{1 - \alpha\kappa}{\alpha\kappa} W_i N_i,$$

and hence the relative share of profit (γ) is a constant given by

$$\gamma = \frac{1 - \alpha\kappa}{\alpha\kappa}. \tag{7}$$

So with the Cobb–Douglas assumption, the profit share is independent of W_i and is decreasing in both labour intensity, α, and competitiveness, κ.

Now consider the survival function S. We suppose that on the union side, the group of individuals who are party to the wage bargain consists of the employees who remain with the firm from the previous period after voluntary quitters have left. This group are N_{Ii} in number and may be termed the 'insiders'. So if δ is the exogenous voluntary quit rate, we have

$$N_{Ii} = (1 - \delta)N_{i-1}, \tag{8}$$

where N_{i-1} is employment in the previous period.

After employment is determined by the firm, the insiders have first call on the available jobs. An individual's probability of survival is, therefore,

$$1 \text{ if } N_i > N_{Ii}; \qquad \frac{E(N_i \mid N_i \leqslant N_{Ii})}{N_{Ii}} \text{ if } N_i \leqslant N_{Ii}.$$

The survival function $S_i(W_i)$ is thus given by

$$S_i = \text{prob}(N_i > N_{Ii}) + \frac{E(N_i \mid N_i \leqslant N_{Ii})}{N_{Ii}} \text{prob}(N_i \leqslant N_{Ii})$$

$$= P\left(\tilde{\varphi} > \frac{N_{Ii}}{N_i^e}\right) + \frac{N_i^e}{N_{Ii}} E\left(\tilde{\varphi} \mid \tilde{\varphi} \leqslant \frac{N_{Ii}}{N_i^e}\right) P\left(\tilde{\varphi} \leqslant \frac{N_{Ii}}{N_i^e}\right)$$

$$= S(N_{Ii}/N_i^e(W_i)). \tag{9}$$

Survival depends simply on the number of insiders relative to expected employment. Furthermore, it is obvious that survival is more likely if employment is expected to grow rather than to contract (i.e. $S' < 0$).

In the light of equation (9), it is convenient to write the *absolute* elasticity of survival with respect to the wage, $\varepsilon_{SW}(W_i)$, as

$$\varepsilon_{SW}(W_i) = \varepsilon_{SN}\left(\frac{N_{Ii}}{N_i^e(W_i)}\right)\varepsilon_{NW}, \tag{10}$$

where

$$\varepsilon_{SN} = \frac{\partial S}{\partial N_i^e}\frac{N_i^e}{S} > 0,$$

and

$$\varepsilon_{NW} = \left|\frac{\partial N_i^e}{\partial W_i}\frac{W_i}{N_i^e}\right|.$$

The latter is simply the wage elasticity of employment, which (5*b*) immediately indicates is

$$\varepsilon_{NW} = (1 - \alpha\kappa)^{-1}. \tag{11}$$

We can now return to our *partial equilibrium wage function* (2), and using (10) and (11) as well as our expression for γ in equation (7), we can rewrite it as

$$\frac{W_i - A}{W_i} = \frac{1 - \alpha\kappa}{\varepsilon_{SN}(W_i) + \alpha\kappa/\beta}. \tag{12}$$

Note that $\varepsilon_{SN} = \varepsilon_{SN}(N_{Ii}/N_i^e(W_i))$ with N_i^e given by equation (5*b*). The properties of the survival function and its elasticity are set out in Annex 2.3, the most important being that $\varepsilon'_{SN} > 0$. This tells us that, if employment is expected to rise rapidly ($N_I \ll N^e$), an additional insider has little impact on survival since everyone is likely to survive anyway, whereas if it is contracting ($N_I > N^e$), an additional insider has a significant impact on the average survival rate.

Working through the comparative statics of (12) enables us to see that the mark-up of wages over the outside option (A) is higher,

1. the greater is union power (β);
2. the lower is product market competitiveness (κ);
3. the lower is the labour intensity of the firm (α);
4. the smaller is the number of insiders (N_{Ii}) relative to the firm's capital (note equation (5*b*));
5. the greater is the firm's demand (Y_{di}) relative to its capital (note equation (5*b*)).

So wages are higher not only when unions are more effective, but also when there are more rents of various kinds to be raided, including both product market rents (item 2 above) and quasi-rents on fixed capital (item 3).

Thinking about the forces affecting wage mark-ups given in (12), the order of magnitude of the wage mark-up in reality is in the range 0.05–0.15, and the numerator of the right-hand side is around 0.3. (Note $\alpha\kappa$ is the share of labour.) Consequently the denominator of the right-hand side must be in the range 2–6. Since ε_{SN} is typically less than $\frac{1}{2}$ (see Annex 2.3), $\alpha\kappa/\beta$ must be in the range 1.5–5.5. So the chief force restraining wage pressure is likely to be employer resistance ($\alpha\kappa/\beta$) rather than workers' fear of job loss (ε_{SN}).

(ii) The aggregate wage

Because firms are identical, $W_i = W$, $P_i = 1$, $N_{Ii}/N_i^e = N_I/N^e$. Since $A = (1 - \varphi u)W^e + \varphi u B$, the aggregate mark-up $(W - A)/W$ is

$$\frac{W - A}{W} = (1 - \varphi u)\left(\frac{W - W^e}{W}\right) + \varphi u \left(1 - \frac{B}{W}\right).$$

Hence using (12) and the following text, the aggregate wage equation can be written as

$$\left(1 - \frac{B}{W}\right) = \frac{1 - \alpha\kappa}{[\varepsilon_{SN}(N_I/K, W) + \alpha\kappa/\beta]\varphi u} - \left(\frac{1}{\varphi u} - 1\right)\left(\frac{W - W^e}{W}\right), \quad (13)$$

where the ε_{SN} function is increasing in W and in the number of insiders relative to capital, N_I/K. (Note that $\varepsilon_{SN} = \varepsilon_{SN}(N_I/N^e) = \varepsilon_{SN}[(N_I/K)(W/\alpha\kappa)^{1/(1-\alpha)}]$ using the aggregate version of (5a).) Thus the aggregate wage (W) is affected in the same way as the firm-level wage by union power (β), product market competitiveness (κ), labour intensity (α), and the ratio of the number of insiders to capital (N_I/K). In addition, the level of real benefits (B) has a positive effect on real wages, and unemployment (u) and wage surprises ($(W - W^e)/W$) have a negative effect. The latter is essentially a nominal inertia effect arising from the fact that (outside) wage *expectations* influence the wage bargain.

Because we are focusing in this chapter on wage-setting behaviour and its implications for equilibrium unemployment, we are ignoring any nominal inertia on the price side. Thus our price equation/employment function is given by the aggregate version of (5a); that is,

$$\frac{N}{K} = \left(\frac{W}{\alpha\kappa}\right)^{-1/(1-\alpha)} \quad (14)$$

Since $N = (1 - u)L$, this equation together with the wage equation determines unemployment (u) and the real wages (W) as a function of the wage surprise.[13]

We shall have more to say about this wage equation (13) when we discuss hysteresis (and in Chapter 4), but, for the moment, we consider the equilibrium level of unemployment.

(iii)   General equilibrium unemployment

Here we need to eliminate the surprise, so that $W = W^e$. If wage expectations are formed on the basis that inflation follows a random walk (i.e. if $\Delta \log W = \Delta \log W_{-1} + v$, where v is white noise and Δ is the difference operator), then

$$\frac{W - W^e}{W} = \log W - \log W^e = \log W - \log W_{-1} - \Delta \log W_{-1} = \Delta^2 \log W. \quad (15)$$

So when expectations are fulfilled, $\Delta^2 \log W = 0$ and inflation is constant. In this case equilibrium unemployment corresponds to stable inflation and can be referred to as the NAIRU.

In equilibrium, unemployment is stationary and, assuming a constant labour force, so is employment. So using our definition of insiders in equation (8),

$$N_I = (1 - \delta)N_{-1} = (1 - \delta)N,$$

and since $N^e = N$, the elasticity ε_{SN} can be written

$$\varepsilon_{SN} = \varepsilon_{SN}(N_I/N^e) = \varepsilon_{SN}(1 - \delta). \quad (16)$$

Thus in stationary equilibrium, ε_{SN} is a constant which depends only on the rate of voluntary quitting, δ. (Note that if the labour force is growing, then ε_{SN} will also depend on the rate of growth of the labour force, g_L, since $N_I = (1 - \delta)N_{-1} = (1 - \delta)(1 - g_L)N$.)

So from the aggregate wage equation (13), we see that in equilibrium ($W = W^e$) we have

$$1 - B/W = \frac{1 - \alpha\kappa}{(\varepsilon_{SN} + \alpha\kappa/\beta)\varphi u}. \quad (17)$$

Furthermore, from the price–employment equation (14), we have

$$W = \alpha\kappa(K/N)^{1-\alpha} = \alpha\kappa(K/L)^{1-\alpha}/(1 - u)^{1-\alpha}, \quad (18)$$

where L is the labour force. This can be thought of as the aggregate price-setting equation which, when combined with the wage equation by eliminating the real wage, W, reveals that equilibrium unemployment, u^*, satisfies

$$u^*[1 - (1 - u^*)^{1-\alpha}B/\alpha\kappa(K/L)^{1-\alpha}] = \frac{1 - \alpha\kappa}{(\varepsilon_{SN} + \alpha\kappa/\beta)\varphi}. \quad (19)$$

So equilibrium unemployment is an increasing function of normalized benefits $(B/(K/L)^{1-\alpha})$, union power (β) and the exogenous quit rate (δ), and a decreasing function of competitiveness (κ). However this applies only if real benefits (B) are exogenous. If, as seems more likely, the replacement ratio $(B/W = b)$ is set exogenously by government social policy, then equilibrium unemployment follows directly from (17) as

$$u^* = \frac{1 - \alpha\kappa}{(\varepsilon_{SN} + \alpha\kappa/\beta)(1 - b)\varphi}. \tag{20}$$

In this case we have the interesting result that equilibrium unemployment is independent of the productivity measure K/L.[14]

This is a key finding which helps us to understand why, in the union context, unemployment is untrended in the very long run. If the production function is Cobb–Douglas (not a bad assumption) and benefit replacement rates are kept stable, then unemployment in the long run is independent of capital accumulation and technical progress. Indeed, the same is true without Cobb–Douglas if K/L rises at the same rate as labour-augmenting technical progress so that the real rate of profit and relative factor shares remain stable. If, however, the elasticity of substitution is less than one, capital accumulation (with no technical progress) raises the share of labour and reduces unemployment.

In the discussion so far we have taken capital as exogenous, as we generally do in this book. However, one might wish to suppose that in the very long run there is a required rate of return on capital (r). In this case real product wages are determined by r and by the degree of product market competitiveness, κ. Suppose the aggregate production function is $Y = Kf(N/K)$, where K is 'variable' capital and firms are identical as before. Then factor proportions N/K will satisfy

$$r = [f(N/K) - (N/K)f'(N/K)]\kappa.$$

Thus r determines factor proportions, which in turn determine the real product wage according to

$$W = f'(N/K)\kappa. \tag{21}$$

In this model, for given r, the ratio of distributive shares (γ) in our model (see equation (2)) is again independent of wages, but this is now the case *regardless* of the production function.[15]

Taxes, terms of trade, and real wage resistance

We can now ask, Do increases in taxes affect unemployment? A proportional tax on labour has no effect provided the net replacement ratio is unaffected. For suppose that labour income and benefits are taxed at rate t. Then the Nash maximand becomes

$$\Omega' = [W_i(1 - t) - A(1 - t)]^\beta S_i^\beta \Pi_i^e = (W_i - A)^\beta S_i^\beta \Pi_i^e(1 - t)^\beta, \qquad (22)$$

where W_i continues to mean real labour cost and A retains its original definition. Since the effect of the taxes on the maximand is multiplicative, equilibrium unemployment is unaffected. And since pricing behaviour is unchanged, so is real labour cost—meaning that labour bears the full cost of the tax. Likewise, a profits tax would fall on profits.

What if we now move to an open economy and examine the effect of rises in relative import prices? The conclusion is again the same. Events which alter the price of consumption relative to value added have no effect on the level of equilibrium unemployment. They simply change the numeraire of the Nash maximand. The result is that unemployment is unaffected, and wage-earners and firms bear the cost in proportion to their incomes.

These results are very important, because they deny the existence of 'real wage resistance'. Such resistance occurs if, when taxes on labour rise or the terms of trade shift adversely, workers attempt to protect their living standards by maintaining their net incomes, hence exerting upward pressure on real labour costs. But the fact that the Nash maximand is multiplicative in tax rates, and thus bargained labour costs are unaffected, seems to indicate that we should not expect real wage resistance, even in the short run.

There are, however, two possible routes through which real wage resistance might occur. First, and less important, is the possibility that union members might have utility functions that are not isoelastic. In the tax-adjusted Nash maximand (22), tax rates will continue to appear multiplicatively if union members are risk-averse rather than risk-neutral, so long as their utility functions are isoelastic. This no longer applies with non-isoelastic utility and hence real wage resistance then becomes a possibility. However, this is hardly a solid foundation for what appears to be a pervasive phenomenon (see Chapter 4 (Section 7) or Chapter 9). In fact, of course, the essence of real wage resistance derives from the fact that individual utility depends not only on the absolute level of current real income but also on that level relative to what has been achieved in the recent past. Thus, two individuals may have the same current real income, but if in one case it has recently risen and in the other case it has recently fallen, the latter will feel worse off than the former. The evidence for this is not simply commonplace observation but derives from extensive work by psychologists based on so-called adaptation theory (see e.g. Brickman and Campbell 1971, or Argyle 1987).

In the light of this, we might suppose that individual employed union members have a utility function of the form

$$\text{Utility} = W_i(1 - t) - a\bar{W}_i(1 - \bar{t}),$$

where $\bar{W}_i$, $\bar{t}$ are moving averages of past labour costs and tax rates, respectively. In this case, it is easy to show that wages and unemployment are increasing in $t - \bar{t}$ and decreasing in $W_i - \bar{W}_i$, and hence that we have short-run real wage resistance. Of course, if taxes and wage growth are stationary, there is no effect, but an increase in taxes or a fall in wage growth will have an impact that will continue for as long as people have not yet fully adapted to the change. The same is true of changes in the terms of trade.

Hysteresis

We have yet to examine how unions affect the persistence of unemployment disturbances after a shock. As we have seen in our discussion of aggregate wages (equation (13) and the following text), wage pressure is decreasing in the number of insiders, and since these reflect last period's employment, we have the potential here for unemployment dynamics. More formally, following our definition of the number of insiders in equation (8), we have in aggregate

$$N_I = (1 - \delta)N_{-1} = (1 - \delta)(1 - u_{-1})L. \tag{23}$$

Combining this with (13) and (14) enables us to write our aggregate wage equation as

$$1 - B/W = -\left(\frac{1}{\varphi u} - 1\right)\left(\frac{W - W^e}{W}\right)$$

$$+ \frac{1 - \alpha\kappa}{\left(\varepsilon_{SN}\left[\frac{L}{K}\left(\frac{W}{\alpha\kappa}\right)^{1/(1-\alpha)}(1 - \delta)(1 - u_{-1})\right] + \alpha\kappa/\beta\right)\varphi u}. \tag{24}$$

Wages are, therefore, decreasing in current unemployment (u) and increasing in lagged unemployment (u_{-1}). Thus wage pressure at given unemployment is higher if unemployment is falling than if it is rising. The reason is quite simply that insiders are less worried. This is the foundation for insider hysteresis or so-called membership dynamics (see Blanchard and Summers 1986).

Before going on to consider unemployment dynamics, it is worth looking briefly at the amount of hysteresis we can expect to be generated by these insider effects. If we suppose that the benefit replacement ratio ($B/W = b$) is exogenous, and omitting nominal inertia, our wage equation can be rewritten as

$$\varepsilon_{SN}\left[\frac{L}{K}\left(\frac{W}{\alpha\kappa}\right)^{1/(1-\alpha)}(1-\delta)(1-u_{-1})\right] = -\alpha\kappa/\beta + \frac{1-\alpha\kappa}{\varphi u(1-b)}. \quad (25)$$

Taking differentials, we find that the ratio of the u_{-1} effect to the u effect (evaluated at $u = u_{-1}$) is given by[16]

$$\frac{u_{-1}\ \text{coefficient}}{u\ \text{coefficient}} = \frac{(1-\delta)(1-b)\varphi u^2\varepsilon'_{SN}}{(1-\alpha\kappa)(1-u)}. \quad (26)$$

We show in Annex 2.3 that ε'_{SN} is unlikely to exceed 7, and, setting $\varphi = 2$ (see n. 11), $1 - \alpha\kappa =$ share of profit $= 0.3$, $1 - \delta < 0.9$, $b = 0.5$, $u = 0.05$, the expression takes the maximum value 0.07. So, for reasonable values, the hysteresis effect arising from insiders is small, a point worth bearing in mind when we look at the empirical evidence in Chapters 4 and 9.

In the light of this, we can now consider unemployment dynamics. For simplicity, we assume that the benefit replacement ratio, $B/W = b$, is exogenous. In this case, making use of the price/employment equation (18), we can rewrite our aggregate wage equation (24) as

$$u = \frac{1-\alpha\kappa}{\left[\varepsilon_{SN}\left(\frac{(1-\delta)(1-u_{-1})}{1-u}\right) + \alpha\kappa/\beta\right]\varphi(1-b)} - \frac{1-\varphi u}{\varphi(1-b)}\frac{W-W^e}{W}. \quad (27)$$

This is the dynamic unemployment equation, with nominal shocks operating via the wage surprise term. If we linearize about $u = u_{-1} = \bar{u}$ and $W = W^e$, we can write (27) as

$$(u - u^*) = \alpha_1(u_{-1} - u^*) - \alpha_2\frac{W-W^e}{W}, \quad (28)$$

where

$$\alpha_1 = \omega/(1+\omega) < 1, \qquad \omega = \frac{(1-\alpha\kappa)(1-\delta)\varepsilon'_{SN}}{(\varepsilon_{SN} + \alpha\kappa/\beta)^2\varphi(1-b)}, \qquad \alpha_2 = \frac{1-\varphi\bar{u}}{\varphi(1-b)},$$

noting that ε_{SN}, ε'_{SN} are both functions only of $(1-\delta)$ and u^* is given by equation (20). So the hysteresis coefficient (α_1) is increasing in union power (β) and the benefit replacement ratio (b) and decreasing in the degree of product market competition (κ). Note that the parameter ω can be written as

$$\frac{(1-\delta)(1-b)\varphi u^{*2}\varepsilon'_{SN}}{1-\alpha\kappa},$$

using the expression for u^* in equation (20), and comparison with (26) immediately reveals that we can expect this also to be small. So the degree of unemployment persistence arising from insider power is probably not going to be very significant in practice.

It is convenient at this stage to define the short-run equilibrium level of unemployment, u_s^*, which is also a short-run NAIRU if $(W - W^e)/W = \Delta^2 \log W$. This is the level of unemployment consistent with no surprises (constant inflation), for a *given level of* u_{-1}. So from (27),

$$u_s^* = \frac{1 - \alpha \kappa}{\left[\varepsilon_{SN} \left(\dfrac{(1 - \delta)(1 - u_{-1})}{1 - u_s^*} \right) + \alpha \kappa / \beta \right] \varphi(1 - b)},$$

or, using the linear version (28),

$$u_s^* = (1 - \alpha_1) u^* + \alpha_1 u_{-1}. \tag{29}$$

The short-run equilibrium level of unemployment is a weighted average of the long-run equilibrium and last period's unemployment.[17] If last period's unemployment is high, unemployment can be reduced only part of the way towards the long-run equilibrium unless there is to be inflationary pressure.

There is, as we have said, much dispute as to how far unions care about employment, which we have been assuming they do. The question is not really well posed. In situations where employment is likely to rise they are not likely to be much concerned, since all existing members' jobs are safe. In cases where it is likely to fall, they are highly concerned.

Clearly, turnover provides an important protection for existing workers: if employment changes are not too large, these can be accommodated by natural wastage, without layoffs. In fact, for the representative firm—for which expected employment is, in equilibrium, constant—it is clear that without uncertainty there would be no layoffs. Thus, without uncertainty, the union could have no local concern about employment. In such a case ε_{SW} is zero and there is no hysteresis.

This is the logical implication of any steady-state certainty model of the representative firm—and such models are still in common use. But in a more reasonable view of the world, (a) there is uncertainty at the firm level and (b) firms differ in whether employment is expected to rise or fall. Thus it is right to include the term ε_{SW} in a model of unemployment and to think of it as a weighted average of its value in different firms. Given this, bargaining behaviour provides a clear, albeit small, source of hysteresis in aggregate unemployment.

3. Bargaining over employment? A digression

We have so far assumed that, though unions may care about employment, they
do not bargain over it. As a broad generalization, this is true. The occasional
exception is in contracting firms, and they bargain not about employment but
about layoffs. As we have said, this is what efficient bargaining is about.

By contrast, most of the efficient bargaining literature asserts that there
ought to be bargaining over employment, even when conditions are unchanging. Since the literature generally assumes that demand is known with
certainty, let us assume this. We can then show that, since firms experience
turnover, the majority of firms will be hiring workers, so that unions are locally
indifferent to employment. Hence employment will not figure in any efficient
bargain. Even firms that are contracting will generally make efficient bargains
of the type that involve no layoffs, rather than ones involving the standard
McDonald–Solow efficiency conditions. Indeed, in general the McDonald–
Solow conditions would be grossly inefficient, and both parties could do better
by ignoring them—which is why they do so.

We shall begin with the case where the conditions do apply, i.e. a situation
where demand is very low relative to the number of insiders. We shall then
demonstrate how, with turnover, the situation eventually converges to one
where the union is no longer concerned about employment. The analysis will
be first diagrammatic and then algebraic.

We begin with the standard situation analysed by McDonald and Solow
where the number of inside 'members' (N_I) is so high that not all of them will
be employed, even if bargaining is over employment as well as wages. For
simplicity, we assume constant marginal utility of income. The position is then
as illustrated in Fig. 1(a). The union objective function is

$$V_i = (W_i - A)\min\left(\frac{N_i}{N_{Ii}}, 1\right).$$

The union indifference curves are, therefore, kinked. For $N_i < N_{Ii}$ they are
rectangular hyperbolas asymptotic to $W_i = A$ and $N_i = 0$; while for $N_i > N_{Ii}$
they are horizontal, since the union places no value on further employment.
Given constant marginal utility of income, the contract curve is vertical. Thus
the bargained level of employment, N_i^*, is 'strongly efficient', since it maximizes
the joint surplus of firms and workers. The bargained wage is, say, W_i^* (point
P). Since N_i^* is less than the number of insiders (N_{Ii}), some workers will have to
be out of work.

We now move on to period 2 (see Figure 1(b)). Of the N_i^* workers employed
last year, δN_i^* have left through natural wastage. The zone of horizontal

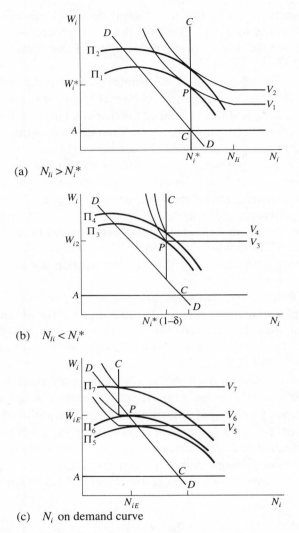

(a) $N_{Ii} > N_i^*$

(b) $N_{Ii} < N_i^*$

(c) N_i on demand curve

Fig. 1.   *Bargaining over wages and employment.*

CPC indicates the contract curve.

indifference curves is therefore extended leftwards, since for any level of employment greater than $(1 - \delta)N_i^*$ the union places no value on extra employment—once all jobs are guaranteed, all the union wants is extra pay. Given this set of indifference curves, the contract curve becomes vertical at $N_{Ii} = N_i^*(1 - \delta)$.

113

The optimal wage is now W_{i2}. But the efficient bargain leads not to N_i^*, as in McDonald–Solow, but to $N_i^*(1 - \delta)$. Thus the efficient bargain, though not the same as in McDonald–Solow, is still to the right of the demand curve (at point P).

Now move on. The efficient level of employment shrinks still further. Eventually we reach a point where the efficient bargain gives a wage and employment combination just to the right of the demand curve. What happens next? Owing to turnover, the number of insiders falls below the number of workers demanded at last period's wage. So in that neighbourhood the union indifference curve is now flat where it crosses the demand curve. Since the isoprofit curves are also flat along the demand curve, the contract curve lies (locally) along the demand curve. This is illustrated in Fig. 1(c), which shows the steady-state equilibrium of the firm.

We have reached the normal situation that exists in most firms; i.e., hiring occurs (unlike in the McDonald–Solow model). The firm hires enough workers to make up for those who leave, and the efficient bargain is on the demand curve.

The conclusion differs from that of McDonald and Solow only because we assume that disemployed workers lose their voting rights in the union and their connection with the firm. By contrast, McDonald and Solow assume permanent attachment and no hiring. The thinking behind their assumption is based on temporary layoffs. But in fact, as we have said, temporary layoffs comprise only 17 per cent of the unemployed in the USA, and only three-quarters of these actually return to the same firm. In other countries the system of temporary layoffs barely exists and almost none of the unemployed return to the same firm. (In Britain only 33 per cent return to the same industry!) Thus we miss a key element of reality by assuming a fixed membership.

Reverting to our own assumptions, we can use algebra to fill out our conclusions. The objective is always to choose W_i and N_i to maximize

$$\Omega = (W_i - A)^\beta \left[\min \left(\frac{N_i}{N_{Ii}}, 1 \right) \right]^\beta (R(N_i) - W_i N_i),$$

where R is the firm's revenue function. Because there is bargaining over wages, the wage always satisfies

$$\frac{\partial \log \Omega}{\partial W_i} = \frac{\beta}{W_i - A} - \frac{N_i}{R(N_i) - W_i N_i} = 0 \tag{30}$$

or

$$W_i = \frac{\beta}{1 + \beta} \frac{R(N_i)}{N_i} + \frac{1}{1 + \beta} A. \tag{30'}$$

Thus wages are a weighted average of average revenue and the outside option.

But what about employment? We can begin with the McDonald–Solow situation where $N_i < N_{Ii}$ and we have an interior solution. Hence N_i is determined by

$$\frac{\partial \log \Omega}{\partial N_i} = \frac{\beta}{N_i} + \frac{R'(N_i) - W_i}{R(N_i) - W_i N_i} = 0. \tag{31}$$

Comparison of (30) and (31) reveals at once that

$$W_i - A = -(R'(N_i) - W_i)$$

or

$$R'(N_i) = A.$$

This defines N_i^* and is the 'strong efficiency' result depicted in Fig. 1(*a*).

However, once turnover has reduced N_{Ii} below N_i^*, the union is uninterested in having employment as high as N_i^*. The contract curve is now vertical at $N_i = N_{Ii}$. As turnover proceeds, N_{Ii} falls and so does employment. From (30′) the wage rises since average revenue rises. At each point the union indifference curve is kinked at $N_i = N_{Ii}$. As N_{Ii} falls over time, we eventually reach a point where the contract point lies on the demand curve. In such a situation the union is happy to allow employment to be determined by the firm, given the wage. It behaves as if it only cares about wages. Bargaining about employment ceases.

What the above analysis makes clear is that bargaining over wages (only) does not in normal circumstances involve anything like the level of efficiency loss that is implied by the McDonald–Solow-style model in which $N_{Ii} > N_i^*$. Typically N_I is less than N_i^* and hiring occurs.

Before going on, it is interesting to compute some numbers for the path of wages in the previous analysis, assuming that production is given by $Y_i = N_i^\alpha$. Ignoring, for simplicity, imperfections in the product market (which do not affect the argument), real revenue $R(N_i) = N_i^\alpha$. Hence

$$R'(N_i) = \alpha \frac{R(N_i)}{N_i}.$$

Since wages are always given by

$$W_i = \frac{\beta}{1 + \beta} \frac{R(N_i)}{N_i} + \frac{1}{1 + \beta} A,$$

it follows that at N_i^* (where $R' = A$) the wage mark-up is given by[18]

$$\frac{W_i - A}{W_i} = \frac{1 - \alpha}{1 + \alpha/\beta}. \tag{32}$$

This is the wage level in Fig. 1(*a*). By contrast, when employment is on the demand curve (where $R' = W$) the wage mark-up is

$$\frac{W_i - A}{W_i} = \frac{1 - \alpha}{\alpha/\beta}. \tag{33}$$

This is the wage in Fig. 1(*c*). It is appreciably higher than that in panel (*a*): the smaller number of insiders has, in effect, increased union power. The wage in panel (*b*) is intermediate.

We can now ask what would happen if, starting from equilibrium (i.e. on the demand curve), the level of demand were to fall substantially. Unless the demand shifts were very large, employment would fall to N_{Ii} but no lower. Thus we would move to a situation such as that in Fig. 1(*b*) and wages would fall as well as employment. This is 'concession-bargaining', and it certainly occurs on some occasions. With a very large fall in demand we could move to a situation like Fig. 1(*a*), with greater falls in wages and also employment.

And what if demand rises? On the Cobb–Douglas assumption there is no reason for wages to change since we remain on the demand curve and equation (33) continues to apply. But employment will rise. All this seems eminently reasonable. Firms do raise employment when demand rises, contrary to some of the more prevalent insider theories.[19]

If this section presents an interesting overall framework for thinking about bargaining, why do we not use it more generally in this book? There are two reasons. First, most firms are hiring labour. Yet in Fig. 1(*a*) and (*b*) this is not the case. Second, the analysis overlooks the uncertainty issue, which for the typical firm is quite well handled by the method of Section 2.

General equilibrium

Before we leave the issue of bargaining over employment, we shall ask one further question—about its general equilibrium effects. Would unemployment in the steady state be reduced if firms and unions always bargained over employment, rather than over wages only? In the case where demand is known with certainty, the answer is no.

This holds both in the steady state and (given a Cobb–Douglas production function) in the 'McDonald–Solow' case where employment is less than the number of insiders. The steady-state result is clear since there is no difference between bargaining over employment and wages on the one hand and bargaining over wages only.

But it is less obvious in the case where employment is less than the number of insiders. The reason for the result is this. Bargaining over employment effectively raises the power of the union since a push for wages would now involve less risk of job loss. Thus, as we shall show, wages are higher both in the representative firm and in all other firms.

The position is illustrated in Fig. 2. With bargaining over employment, the contract point is at P_N—to the right of the demand curve. But if the production function is Cobb–Douglas, this point lies directly above the contract point on the demand curve corresponding to bargaining over wages only (point P_W). Thus employment is unchanged.

To prove this result we begin with the basic point that unemployment is given as an identity by

$$\varphi u \left(1 - \frac{B}{W} \right) \equiv \frac{W - A}{W},$$

using the definition of A. Thus, assuming an exogenous replacement ratio ($B/W = b$), the wage mark-up is the key to understanding unemployment. Under bargaining over wages and employment, as we have seen, the wage mark-up with a Cobb–Douglas production function is given by equation (32):

$$\frac{W - A}{W} = \frac{1 - \alpha}{1 + \alpha/\beta}.$$

Under bargaining over wages only (with employment depending on wages), the wage is given by maximizing

$$\Omega = (W_i - A)^\beta N(W_i)^\beta \Pi,$$

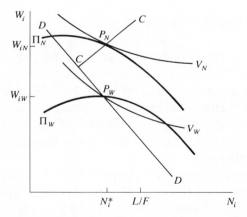

Fig. 2. *Bargaining over wages and employment (at P_N) and over wages only (at P_W): the general equilibrium comparison under Cobb–Douglas.*

117

and so, in aggregate, the first-order condition becomes

$$\frac{\beta}{W-A} + \frac{\beta}{N}\frac{dN}{dW} - \frac{N}{R(N)-WN} = 0$$

or

$$\frac{W-A}{A} = \frac{1}{\varepsilon_{NW} + WN/\beta\Pi}.$$

One might suppose that including the direct job consequences of wage-push (represented by ε_{NW}) would reduce the mark-up, until one reflects that the lesser power of labour will lower the relative share of wages WN/Π. Thus in the Cobb–Douglas case the mark-up in the 'right to manage' case becomes

$$\frac{W-A}{W} = \frac{1}{\dfrac{1}{1-\alpha} + \dfrac{\alpha}{\beta(1-\alpha)}} = \frac{1-\alpha}{1+\dfrac{\alpha}{\beta}},$$

which is exactly the same as when bargaining over both wages and employment (equation 32).

Of course there is nothing sacrosanct about Cobb–Douglas. In Layard and Nickell (1990) we show that, with an elasticity of substitution greater than unity, efficient bargaining will actually reduce aggregate employment. But what we have said should be sufficient to dispel any simple-minded impression based on partial equilibrium analysis that the whole economy would be more efficient if only unions could bargain over employment.

4. Does featherbedding create jobs?

Though workers rarely bargain over employment, they do bargain over conditions of work. These conditions include such questions as the number of workers per machine/train/aircraft, etc. Such bargaining over manning levels leads employers to use more workers per machine than they otherwise would— in other words, to 'overmanning' or 'featherbedding'. But does more workers per machine mean more workers in total? Does overmanning reduce unemployment, or the reverse?

This is relevant not only to policy choice. It also affects our interpretation of history. For example, one theory of the rise in British unemployment in the 1980s states: 'In the 1970s overmanning reduced productivity but also reduced unemployment; in the 1980s per contra overmanning was cut, causing higher productivity and also higher unemployment.'

To investigate whether these suggestions are plausible, we have to model the manning level in the most fruitful way. We believe it is most helpful to think of the manning level in terms of the effort (E) required of the worker. The firm likes effort and has a production function where effort is multiplicative with employment. The worker dislikes effort and has, for illustration, a utility function of $Wg(E)$ where W is weekly real earnings, and $g' < 0$. We shall also suppose that the absolute elasticity $(-Eg'/g)$ is increasing in effort, which is tantamount to assuming that g is not too convex and is always true if it is concave.[20]

As before, we have a large number of identical firms, labelled i. Thus, following the model of Section 2, the elementary union objective function is now

$$V_i = S_i W_i g(E_i) + (1 - S_i)A,$$

where

$$A = (1 - \varphi u)Wg(E) + \varphi uB$$

and W is the outside wage, E is outside effort, and B is utility of benefits. In this case we assume perfect foresight concerning aggregate variables, so we ignore nominal inertia. If, for simplicity, $\bar{V}_i = A$, the Nash maximand is

$$\Omega = (W_i g(E_i) - A)^\beta S(W_i, E_i)^\beta \Pi^e(W_i, E_i),$$

where note that both the survival probability and the firm's profit are functions of wages and effort. We can examine the outcome first when wages and effort are both bargained over, and then when the employer sets effort and only wages are bargained over.

Bargaining over wages and effort

Let us first examine the outcome of a bargain over both wages (W_i) and effort (E_i). The first-order condition for wages is

$$\frac{\partial \log \Omega}{\partial W_i} = \frac{\beta g(E_i)}{W_i g(E_i) - A} + \frac{\beta}{S} \frac{\partial S}{\partial W_i} - \frac{N_i^e}{\Pi_i^e} = 0 \tag{34}$$

or, in terms of the mark-up,

$$\frac{W_i g(E_i) - A}{W_i g(E_i)} = \frac{1}{\varepsilon_{SW}(W_i, E_i) + 1/\beta\gamma(W_i, E_i)}, \tag{35}$$

where both ε_{SW} and the relative share of profit γ are generally functions of wages and effort.

119

Similarly, we can determine the bargained level of effort by noting that[21]

$$\frac{\partial \log \Omega}{\partial E_i} = \frac{\beta W_i g'(E_i)}{W_i g(E_i) - A} + \frac{\beta \partial S}{S \partial E_i} + \frac{W_i N_i^e}{\Pi_i^e E_i} = 0,$$

which rearranges to yield

$$\frac{W_i g(E_i) - A}{- W_i g'(E_i) E_i} = \frac{1}{\varepsilon_{SE}(W_i, E_i) + 1/\beta\gamma(W_i, E_i)}, \tag{36}$$

where $\varepsilon_{SE} = \partial \log S/\partial \log E_i$.

As in Section 2, we must now look more closely at the functions S and γ, and again we assume a constant elasticity of product demand and a Cobb–Douglas technology. Demand is given by equation (4), whereas production is now given by

$$Y_i = (E_i N_i)^\alpha K_i^{(1-\alpha)}. \tag{3'}$$

The marginal revenue product condition corresponding to (5a) in Section 2 is

$$N_i/K_i = (W_i/P_i \alpha \kappa)^{-1/(1-\alpha)} E_i^{\alpha/(1-\alpha)} \tag{5a'}$$

and employment is given by

$$N_i/K_i = \tilde{\varphi}(W_i K_i^{1/\eta}/\alpha \kappa \, Y_{di}^{1/\eta})^{-1/(1-\alpha\kappa)} E_i^{\alpha\kappa/(1-\alpha\kappa)}, \tag{5b'}$$

where all symbols are as in Section 2. As before, the relative share of profit (γ) is given by $(1 - \alpha\kappa)/\alpha\kappa$ (see equation (7)) and the survival function depends only on N_{Ii}/N_i^e (see equation (9)), N_{Ii} being the number of employees concerned with the bargain. The elasticities $\varepsilon_{SW}, \varepsilon_{SE}$ can be written

$$\varepsilon_{SW} = \varepsilon_{SN} \varepsilon_{NW} = \frac{\varepsilon_{SN}}{1 - \alpha\kappa}, \qquad \varepsilon_{SE} = \varepsilon_{SN} \varepsilon_{NE} = \frac{\alpha\kappa\varepsilon_{SN}}{1 - \alpha\kappa},$$

using (5b'), and hence wages and effort in firm i satisfy

$$\frac{W_i g(E_i) - A}{W_i g(E_i)} = \frac{1 - \alpha\kappa}{\varepsilon_{SN} + \alpha\kappa/\beta} \tag{37}$$

$$\frac{W_i g(E_i) - A}{- W_i g'(E_i) E_i} = \frac{1 - \alpha\kappa}{\alpha\kappa(\varepsilon_{SN} + 1/\beta)}, \tag{38}$$

with

$$\varepsilon_{SN} = \varepsilon_{SN}(N_{Ii}/N_i^e)$$

and

$$N_i^e = K_i (W_i K_i^{1/\eta}/\alpha\kappa \, Y_{di}^{1/\eta})^{-1/(1-\alpha\kappa)} E_i^{\alpha\kappa/(1-\alpha\kappa)}.$$

Comparative statics leads to a number of interesting effects on effort. In particular, it can be shown that an increase in union power (β) or outside opportunities (A) will reduce effort but an increase in product market competitiveness (κ) will tend to raise it. On the other hand, the comparative-static effects on wages are hard to sign although it is probable that they will be the same as under the model of Section 2 which ignored effort. Thus, an increase in union power or outside opportunities will probably raise wages.

Turning to long-run equilibrium, by setting $W_i = W$, $E_i = E$, and noting that ε_{SN} is a function only of $(1 - \delta)$ in a stationary state, we find from (37) and the expression for A that u^* is given by

$$u^* = \frac{1 - \alpha\kappa}{(\varepsilon_{SN} + \alpha\kappa/\beta)(1 - b)\varphi}, \tag{39}$$

where the exogenous replacement ratio b is now given by $B/Wg(E)$, and is thus defined as a ratio of utilities. (Recall that B is the utility of being on benefit, including the utility value of leisure.) This expression for u^* is thus identical to that found in equation (20) above.

Turning now to the desirability of effort bargaining, so long as the production function is unaffected by the rights of management, it will always be efficient (i.e. maximize Ω) if workers and managers bargain over effort as well as wages. But the evidence (for Britain at least) is that when managers become stronger (β low), there is less bargaining over manning practices (see Table 5). Why would this happen?

If both parties care about effort, their joint surplus can be increased by bargaining over it (unless the very act of such bargaining involves excessive real costs). It follows that at least one party will gain from the extra scope for bargaining, and that party will be able to insist that bargaining is extended to cover the extra dimension of effort. In fact, of course, it is workers who will gain.[22] The gain to workers from effort-bargaining will be greater in absolute terms the greater is union power β. So workers will insist on bargaining over effort.

Now suppose that effort-bargaining has a cost. For example, the production set may be reduced when managers lose their discretionary control at the workplace. If β is high, effort-bargaining may still improve the workers' lot (at the partial equilibrium level). But if β is low, they may do better if decisions are left to managers than if they are bargained over, with the resultant cost.

Thus, it is interesting to examine the case where managers determine effort and only wages are bargained over. Does a shift to this arrangement increase unemployment, via demanning, as many people have argued happened in the UK in the 1980s?

Bargaining over wages only (with effort set by management)

In a wholly unionized economy (with Cobb–Douglas production functions and utility equal to $Wg(E)$), the answer to the above question is no. The unemployment rate is exactly the same whether the unions bargain over effort or not; for the unemployment rate is in both cases given by equation (39).[23] Thus the attempt to create employment by overmanning in fact creates no extra jobs at all in aggregate.

But it does reduce effort. The employer, if free to set effort, chooses it taking into account the effect of effort on the wage he will have to pay in the wage bargain. This knowledge is contained in equation (37), which shows the wage that would be selected for a given level of effort. This equation implies that in the individual bargain, with A exogenous, the elasticity of wages with respect to effort is given by

$$\frac{E_i}{W_i}\frac{\partial W_i}{\partial E_i} = \frac{\left|\dfrac{E_i g'}{g}\right| + \dfrac{(1-\alpha\kappa)gW_i\varepsilon_{SN}}{(\varepsilon_{SN}+\alpha\kappa/\beta)^2 A}\left|\dfrac{E_i\partial\varepsilon_{SN}}{\varepsilon_{SN}\partial E_i}\right|}{1 + \dfrac{(1-\alpha\kappa)gW_i\varepsilon_{SN}}{(\varepsilon_{SN}+\alpha\kappa/\beta)^2 A}\dfrac{W_i\partial\varepsilon_{SN}}{\varepsilon_{SN}\partial W_i}}. \tag{40}$$

Knowing this relationship, the employer will choose effort to minimize cost per unit of effort (W_i/E_i). This requires the standard 'Solow' condition

$$\frac{E_i}{W_i}\frac{\partial W_i}{\partial E_i} = 1$$

and is illustrated in Fig. 3. From (40), this implies that the effort elasticity satisfies

$$\left|\frac{E_i g'}{g}\right| = 1 + \frac{(1-\alpha\kappa)}{(\varepsilon_{SN}+\alpha\kappa/\beta)^2}\frac{gW_i\varepsilon_{SN}}{A}\left(\frac{W_i\partial\varepsilon_{SN}}{\varepsilon_{SN}\partial W_i} - \left|\frac{E_i\partial\varepsilon_{SN}}{\varepsilon_{SN}\partial E_i}\right|\right). \tag{41}$$

To sign the last term on the right-hand side, we note that ε_{SN} is a function of N_{Ii}/N_i^e, so that

$$\frac{W_i\partial\varepsilon_{SN}}{\varepsilon_{SN}\partial W_i} - \left|\frac{E_i\partial\varepsilon_{SN}}{\varepsilon_{SN}\partial E_i}\right| = \frac{\varepsilon'_{SN}}{\varepsilon_{SN}}\frac{N_{Ii}}{N_i^e}(|\varepsilon_{NW}| - \varepsilon_{NE})$$

$$= \frac{\varepsilon'_{SN}}{\varepsilon_{SN}}\frac{N_{Ii}}{N_i^e}\left(\frac{1}{1-\alpha\kappa} - \frac{\alpha\kappa}{1-\alpha\kappa}\right) > 0.$$

Hence, from (41),

$$\left|\frac{E_i g'}{g}\right| > 1. \tag{42}$$

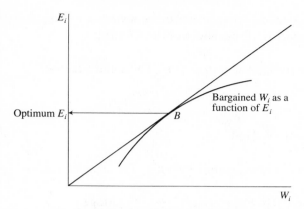

Fig. 3. *The firm's choice of effort.*

Comparison of the two cases

To compare how effort varies when it is set unilaterally rather than by bargaining, we compare the level of effort in equations (41), (42) (unilateral setting of effort) with that in equations (37), (38) (effort set by bargaining).

Manipulating (37), (38) yields

$$\left|\frac{E_i g'}{g}\right| = \frac{\alpha\kappa(\varepsilon_{SN} + 1/\beta)}{\varepsilon_{SN} + \alpha\kappa/\beta} < 1 \qquad \text{since } \alpha\kappa < 1, \qquad (43)$$

and comparison with (42) immediately reveals that effort is lower under bargaining since $|E_i g'/g|$ is increasing in effort.

But how will total welfare vary when there is bargaining over effort? At the partial equilibrium level, when one firm moves to bargaining over effort (A unchanged), the combined welfare of both parties to the bargain must improve unless the production function changes. But in long-run general equilibrium, when all firms shift to effort bargaining, things are different. We know that when the economy shifts to bargaining over effort, employment is unchanged but effort falls. So what happens to the profit of each firm and the utility of each worker? In general equilibrium, the demand-side equation (5a') reveals that

$$N/K = (W/\alpha\kappa)^{-1/(1-\alpha)}E^{\alpha/(1-\alpha)},$$

and hence, given that employment is fixed, if effort falls wages must also fall. Indeed, we can be more precise and note that

$$\Delta\log W = \alpha\Delta\log E, \qquad (44)$$

123

where Δ refers to the change when we switch to effort-bargaining. Let us consider the effect on firms and workers in turn.

(*a*) *Profits in the representative firm.* These fall because

$$\Pi_i = \frac{1 - \alpha\kappa}{\alpha\kappa} W_i N_i$$

and W_i falls with N_i fixed.

(*b*) *Welfare of the representative worker.* The change here is

$$\Delta\log(W_i g(E_i)) = \Delta\log W_i - \left| \frac{E_i g'}{g} \right| \Delta\log E_i$$

$$= \Delta\log E_i \left(\alpha - \left| \frac{E_i g'}{g} \right| \right). \tag{45}$$

In signing this we know that when firms set effort unilaterally, $|E_i g'/g| > 1$ and when there is effort bargaining, $|E_i g'/g| > \alpha\kappa$ (see equation (43)). So we cannot be certain that the relevant value of $|E_i g'/g|$ is greater than α. However, if κ is close to unity (perfect competition), the expression is highly likely to be positive (recall $\Delta\log E_i < 0$), and hence the fall in effort probably more than compensates workers for the real wage fall induced by the introduction of effort-bargaining.

To summarize, effort-bargaining will fail to increase employment,[24] and it will reduce output, profits, and real wages. However, the fall in real wages will probably be more than compensated for by the reduction in effort, making workers better off.

Effort in a two-sector model

So much for the case of a wholly unionized economy. If there is also a secondary sector with a competitive labour market, things are more complicated. Before setting up the two-sector model, therefore, we need to look at how productivity is determined in that context. First we need to examine how firms in the secondary sector set effort. In a competitive labour market each firm has to offer the going level of utility ($\bar{U}_c$). Hence in the competitive sector $Wg(E) = \bar{U}_c$. The firm wants to minimize W/E subject to that constraint, and therefore chooses E to maximize $Eg(E)$. So in the competitive firm effort satisfies $|E_i g'/g| = 1$, whereas recall that in the union sector effort satisfies $|E g'/g| < 1$ with effort-bargaining (featherbedding) and $|E_i g'/g| > 1$ with the firm setting effort (no featherbedding). So the effort ranking is: effort (no featherbedding) > effort (competitive) > effort (featherbedding). We are now ready to examine the two-sector case from a whole variety of angles.

5. A world with good and bad jobs

We have so far considered a world where all firms are unionized and have found that unemployment is (on reasonable assumptions)

1. increased by higher union power and higher product market power, and
2. unaffected by featherbedding.

But in many countries there is also a competitive, market-clearing sector of the manual labour market. We need to check whether these conclusions still hold in that context. And we also want to know what happens if there are changes in the fraction of firms that are unionized.

For this purpose we shall assume that union jobs are good jobs, which anyone would be willing to take, but which are in limited supply. By contrast, anybody who wants it can get a competitive-sector job, but only a fraction (v) of people who do not get union jobs are willing to take one of these. We shall initially assume this fraction to be constant.[25] It follows that, if union employment rises by 1 per cent of the labour force, competitive employment falls by v per cent of the labour force and the overall employment rate rises by $(1 - v)$ per cent. Thus, when union employment rises, total employment rises. So we can now examine how union employment (and thus total employment) changes, where there are changes in (*a*) union power, (*b*) the scope of bargaining (featherbedding), and (*c*) the coverage of collective bargaining.

For this purpose we need to develop the relevant demand curve and wage equation. In analysing demand, we shall stick with the model used in the previous section. Firms in both sectors have the same capital stock and face the same demand curves. So, from equation (5*b'*), each firm in the union sector employs N_{ui} workers, where

$$N_{ui} = \bar{B} W_u^{-\pi} E_u^{\pi - 1}, \qquad \pi = (1 - \alpha\kappa)^{-1}, \qquad (46)$$

where $\bar{B}$ is a constant which is the same for all firms and W_u, E_u are real labour costs and effort in union firms. Given that employment in firms in the competitive sector is given by a similar equation, the relative demand for labour in the two sectors is

$$N_u/N_c = \lambda(W_u/W_c)^{-\pi}(E_u/E_c)^{\pi-1}, \tag{47}$$

where λ is the ratio of union to non-union firms in the economy, or an index of union coverage. Note that N_c must also equal the supply of labour to the competitive sector. Since we shall (in this section) measure employment always as a fraction of the labour force, we have

$$N_c = v(1 - N_u). \tag{48}$$

So the relative demand function is

$$\frac{N_u}{1 - N_u} = \lambda v(W_u/W_c)^{-\pi}(E_u/E_c)^{\pi-1}. \tag{49}$$

This is graphed, with effort constant, as *DD* in Fig. 4.

The wage equation comes from the standard union mark-up equation (37); that is,

$$\frac{W_u g(E_u) - A}{W_u g(E_u)} = \frac{1 - \alpha\kappa}{\varepsilon_{SN} + \alpha\kappa/\beta} = \mu(\beta), \text{ say.} \tag{50}$$

Since we are only concerned with comparing long-run equilibria, we can treat ε_{SN} as a constant since in equilibrium it depends only on $(1 - \delta)$ (see equation (16)). Ignoring benefits, outside income (A) is given by

$$A = N_u W_u g(E_u) + N_c W_c g(E_c)$$
$$= N_u W_u g(E_u) + v(1 - N_u) W_c g(E_c), \qquad \text{from (48).}$$

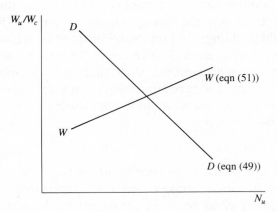

Fig. 4. *A world with good and bad jobs.*

126

Substituting into (50) and rearranging gives us the relative wage equation,

$$W_u/W_c = \frac{v(1 - N_u)}{1 - \mu - N_u} \left(\frac{g(E_u)}{g(E_c)}\right)^{-1}. \tag{51}$$

The relative union wage is increasing in N_u and is graphed, with effort constant, as WW in Fig. 4. We are now in a position to analyse our original questions.

(i) Change in union power

If we initially ignore the consequences for effort in the union sector (recall that effort in the competitive sector satisfies $|E_c g'(E_c)/g(E_c)| = 1$ and remains fixed throughout—see previous section), then a rise in union power (β) shifts up the relative wage function (WW), since μ rises; and hence the union relative wage will rise and union employment will fall. Total employment will also fall. But when union power rises, effort falls in the union sector, and this will tend to raise the demand for union workers. To see this, note that eliminating the relative wage between the demand function (49) and the wage function (51) yields

$$\frac{N_u(1 - N_u)^{\pi - 1}}{(1 - \mu(\beta) - N_u)^\pi} = \lambda v^{-(\pi - 1)}(g(E_u)/g(E_c))^\pi (E_u/E_c)^{\pi - 1}. \tag{52}$$

The left-hand side is increasing in N_u and β, and the right-hand side is decreasing in E_u.[26]

So the fall in effort generates an offsetting effect on union employment. However, unless the impact of union power on effort is very large, this effect will not typically dominate and we would expect union employment to fall in response to a rise in union power.[27] In consequence total employment will fall, since only a fraction of those disemployed in the union sector will be willing to work in the competitive sector.

By the same token, a fall in union power, such as occurred in Britain in the 1980s, would cause a rise in employment. Many observers, however, have argued that the unemployment of the 1980s has been exacerbated by demanning because of falls in union power. As we shall now show, such a thing is possible, if the fall in union power leads to a discrete abandonment of bargaining over effort.

(ii) Shift from featherbedding

If we shift away from featherbedding, then union effort will rise (see previous section). With union power initially held constant, the wage function (WW) will shift to the left in Fig. 4 and the demand function (*DD*) will move to the right. This certainly raises relative union wages, but what of its impact on employment? The fact that the right-hand side of (52) is decreasing in effort immediately reveals that union employment, and hence total employment, will fall.

This effect is however probably offset by two forces. First, there is the simultaneous effect of the fall in union power (β), which tends to shift down the wage function. Second, there is the likelihood that the fraction of non-union workers willing to work in the competitive sector may rise. This is because the fall in union employment will reduce the bargaining power of union workers and, with a given feasible average real wage, thus raise utility in the competitive sector. For utility in the union sector, $W_u g(E_u)$ will fall relative to that in the competitive sector, $W_c g(E_c)$—see equation (51). Because of the higher competitive-sector utility, workers without union jobs have a greater incentive to take jobs in the competitive sector.[28] The key issue then is how far the labour supply to the competitive sector responds to any rise in real wages in that sector. If, as Minford (1983) assumes, the supply to the competitive sector is very elastic, then an end to restrictive practices is always good for employment.

One important empirical conclusion from the above analysis is that, even when unions become weaker, their relative wage may rise if bargaining over effort is abandoned (Nickell *et al.* 1989; Machin and Wadhwani 1991*a*). This may help to explain the substantial rises in real wages in Britain in the 1980s. (For a further discussion, see Chapter 4, Section 4.) But one cannot infer that the loss of union power also caused a fall in overall employment.

(iii) Changes in union coverage

A quite different kind of change is a shift in the number of firms whose wages are determined by collective bargaining (rather than competitively).[29] An increase in union coverage (rise in λ) shifts the relative demand curve for unionized labour (49) to the right. It thus increases union employment. Hence total employment rises, provided the fraction of non-union workers who accept competitive jobs is constant. But once again, if the supply to the competitive sector is elastic enough, a rise in union coverage, by depressing competitive-sector wages, will lead to a contraction of employment (see, again, Minford 1983).[30] This result is increasingly likely the nearer one is to complete unionization. For, when an additional firm becomes covered, there is a consequential rise in real effort-adjusted wages for the firm's workers—which implies a given cost to be spread over all competitive-sector workers. The fewer competitive-sector workers there are, the greater the fall in living standards per competitive-sector worker. Eventually the fall will become so great that the negative effect on v will outweigh the benefit through the increase in the number of good jobs. On balance, our view is that over most relevant ranges an increase in coverage reduces total employment, unless offset by a change in national bargaining arrangements—the next key issue.

6. Corporatism: centralized versus decentralized bargaining

So far unions have not come well out of our analysis. But we have been concerned only with decentralized unions. What if there is a single centralized union bargain? How does the degree of centralization in bargaining affect the equilibrium level of unemployment?

This issue is important, because countries differ so much in their degree of centralization. At one end of the spectrum, bargaining goes on at the level of the firm or plant, as we have so far assumed. This is the most common situation in Britain and the USA. At the opposite extreme, the unions bargain as a united whole with a single all-industry national employers' federation. Scandinavia and Austria approximate to this corporatist model. In between are countries where most bargaining is nationally organized, but on an industry-by-industry basis (see Annex 1.4).

Crouch (1985) and Bruno and Sachs (1985) have suggested that all this makes a substantial difference. And our theories and evidence confirm this.

A national bargain between unions and employers

Let us first consider fully centralized bargaining. This changes the whole situation—in five specific ways.

1. Most important, the union objective function changes, since there is no longer a world of employment outside the bargaining unit to which disemployed union members can resort. Thus, whereas in decentralized bargaining the alternative expected income (A) is

$$A = (1 - \varphi u)W + \varphi uB,$$

in centralized bargaining the only alternative to employment in the bargaining unit is life on benefit. Yet, going further, benefits are paid for by taxes on all workers and all workers are now in the bargain. So workers in the bargain can no longer impose the cost of benefits on other workers. Thus in effect we have

$$A = 0.$$

129

There is no place to go. This makes the union objective function not

$$V_i = S_i W_i + (1 - S_i)A,$$

as in the decentralized union, but

$$V = SW.$$

In this formulation, unions continue to be concerned only with the welfare of existing workers. However, it seems likely that, if they are involved in a whole-economy bargain, the unions may in addition take a strong interest in the unemployed. In this case we might argue that their objective takes the form

$$V = \frac{N}{L}W \qquad (N \leqslant L),$$

where, up to full employment, gains in employment (N) are valued as highly as reductions avoided.

Because there is no place to go ($A = 0$), we escape the externality problems inherent in firm-level bargaining. For in firm-level bargaining the bargainers take the general level of unemployment as given—ignoring the fact that their own actions will affect the jobs open to other workers. They also ignore the fact that, if union workers end up on benefit, these benefits have to be paid for by workers in other firms.

Thus a centralized union, even if it did not have to bargain with employers, would be likely to choose a real wage consistent with full employment. To see this, consider the problem of a centralized union maximizing NW subject to $N \leqslant L$ and $W = W(N)$, the latter showing the feasible real wage (based on pricing behaviour) as a function of the level of employment. ($W(N)$ corresponds to the aggregate employment equation (18).) This maximization requires

$$\frac{\partial \log NW}{\partial \log W} = \frac{\partial \log N}{\partial \log W} + 1 \leqslant 0.$$

The value should be negative if the constraint $N \leqslant L$ is binding and zero otherwise; for, if at full employment a rise in the wage would give no increase in NW, then full employment should be chosen. Thus full employment will be chosen so long as

$$\left| \frac{\partial \log W}{\partial \log N} \right| < 1.$$

In other words, if we plot the feasible real wage, given by pricing behaviour, against the level of employment, the absolute slope must be less than unity.

The picture is drawn in Fig. 5. The iso-welfare line ($WN/L = $ const.) is a rectangular hyperbola, asymptotic to both axes. Provided the feasible wage locus (PP) has an absolute elasticity of less than unity, the result is a corner solution.

This condition is highly likely to be satisfied. For example, with a Cobb–Douglas production function ($Y_i = N_i^\alpha$) and monopolistic competition ($Y_i = P_i^{-\eta} \bar{Y}$),

$$P_i(1 - 1/\eta) = W_i/\alpha N_i^{\alpha-1},\tag{53}$$

so that in aggregate, with $P_i = P = 1$ and $W_i = W$,

$$\left| \frac{\partial \log W}{\partial \log N} \right| = (1 - \alpha).$$

In the extreme case, $\alpha = 1$ and the feasible wage is flat. Other versions of simple mark-up pricing also have that implication.

Thus, full employment (allowing for frictions) would be the natural outcome of centralized bargaining. To understand why this outcome differs from decentralized bargaining, we can compare it with the situation where a decentralized monopoly union has an objective function written for simplicity as

$$V_i = \frac{N_i}{L_i} W_i + \left(1 - \frac{N_i}{L_i} \right) A = \frac{N_i}{L_i}(W_i - A) + \text{const.},$$

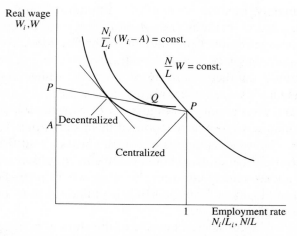

Fig. 5. *Centralized versus decentralized bargaining.*

where L_i is the firm's share of the total labour force. It maximizes this, subject to the inverse demand curve $W_i = W_i(N_i)$.

The main difference is the change in the objective function. To illustrate this, we draw iso-welfare curves ($V_i = $ const.) on the same diagram as before (Fig. 5). The iso-welfare curves for V_i are not asymptotic to the horizontal axis; instead, as N_i goes to infinity, W_i goes to A. One such curve is drawn through point Q. As can be seen, the fact that there is somewhere else to go ($A > 0$) makes full employment much less likely.

2. We can now add in a second consideration. The trade-off between real wages and employment will in fact be flatter at the whole-economy level than at the level of the single monopolistically competitive enterprise. This can be seen by going back to equation (53), which, after substituting for product demand and the production function, gives

$$W_i = \alpha\kappa N_i^{-(1-\alpha\kappa)} \bar{Y}^{1/\eta}.$$

Hence

$$\left|\frac{\partial \log W_i}{\partial \log N_i}\right| = 1 - \alpha\kappa.$$

Since product-market competitiveness (κ) is less than unity, unions now feel more able to raise real wages, because they can exploit not only the quasi-rent of capital but also the product-market rents coming from imperfect substitution between products.

Thus the actual level of employment under decentralized bargaining is at a point such as that indicated by the arrow in the diagram. It differs from full employment mainly because there is no alternative employment to that provided through the bargain (i.e. $A = 0$), but also because of a more favourable real wage employment trade-off at the firm level. To put that latter point in colloquial language, under decentralized bargaining one man's wage increase is mainly another man's price increase, while under centralized bargaining one man's wage increase is the same man's price increase.[31]

There appears, even among colleagues, to be considerable confusion over these issues, which is why we have laboured them somewhat. The key to clear thought is this. The wage bargain is of course always about the money wage. But when centralized bargainers choose a wage in conditions of given money demand, they always understand how this wage will in turn affect the overall price level and employment. Thus, it is fully legitimate to think of bargainers as in effect choosing the real wage.

We have not so far considered the role of the employers' association. If the supply of labour is completely inelastic, it is clearly in the interest of employers to pay as little as possible. In a centralized bargain any incentive employers might have to raise absolute wages in order to raise relative wages (as in efficiency wage models) is eliminated. They will therefore always want the full-employment wage, which would give them maximum profit. The stronger they are, the more likely is full employment.

3. One reason for greater employer resistance at the whole-economy level is the greater cost of concessions by employers. This follows directly from the flatness of the real wage employment trade-off. A decentralized employer can pass on real wage increases into increases in the relative prices of their products: centralized employers cannot do this. The loss of profit from a unit wage increase, which is N for a decentralized employer, is more than that for a national employers' association.[32] This factor will stiffen employer resistance.

4. Another important factor working in the same direction is the fallback income of workers during the strike $(\bar{V})$. If there were a general strike, there would be little chance of workers taking casual work while on strike, and the national strike fund would be owned by parties to the bargain so there would be no 'external' strike pay. For all intents and purposes, we should have $\bar{V} = 0$. The two preceding factors make full employment very likely, even if the union federation did not want it.

5. A fifth favourable factor is that in centralized bargains the union can take into account fiscal economies of scale.[33] Suppose for example that all government expenditure is on public employment and is financed by a proportional tax (t) on workers.[34] Thus, if all workers are paid the same, the government budget constraint (with no borrowing) is

$$T + N_G = tN = t(N_G + N_P),$$

where T are transfers (in wage units), N_G are government workers, and N_P are private-sector workers. If total employment expands, and with it the tax base, either the public can gain from better public services or the tax rate can be cut. Let us assume the latter. Then

$$\frac{\partial t}{\partial N_P} = -\frac{t}{N}.$$

Thus when employment increases and real product wages fall, the real consumption wage $W(1 - t)$ may rise; for

$$\frac{\partial \log W(1 - t)}{\partial \log W} = 1 - \frac{1}{1 - t}\frac{\partial t}{\partial N_P}\frac{\partial N_P}{\partial \log W}\frac{N_P}{N_P}.$$

Provided employment increases sufficiently when wages fall, this expression can be negative. The required condition (for the real wage employment trade-off) is

$$\left| \frac{\partial \log W}{\partial \log N_P} \right| < \frac{t}{1-t} \frac{N_P}{N}.$$

But even if cuts in gross pay do not increase real after-tax wages, they may still increase the union's objective function $W(1-t)N$. This increases as wages fall, provided that

$$\frac{\partial \log W(1-t)N}{\partial \log W} = 1 + \frac{N_P}{N} \frac{\partial \log N_P}{\partial \log W} \left(\frac{t}{1-t} + 1 \right) < 0$$

or

$$\left| \frac{\partial \log W}{\partial \log N_P} \right| < \frac{1}{1-t} \frac{N_P}{N},$$

an easier condition to satisfy. Provided unions take increasing fiscal returns into account, they will choose full employment if this condition is satisfied. If they do not take increasing fiscal returns into account in a mixed economy, they will choose full employment if

$$\left| \frac{\partial \log W}{\partial \log N_P} \right| < \frac{N_P}{N}.$$

This shows how full employment is more likely if centralized bargains take into account fiscal economies of scale.

Implications of the open economy

So far we have considered the matter in relation to a closed economy. We now need to consider the elasticity of labour demand at the firm and economy level in an open economy.

This will show that the contrast between decentralized and centralized bargaining is less stark in an open economy. For at the whole economy level the real wage–employment trade-off becomes steeper owing to the fact that, if employment is to grow, real wages have to fall not only to reduce the marginal product of labour, but also to improve competitiveness in order to maintain the balance of trade.

The consumer price index (P_c) is now not equal to the GDP deflator (P), but is given by[35]

$$\log P_c = (1 - s_M)\log P + s_M \log P_M + \text{const.},$$

where s_M is the share of imports in consumption and P_M the price of foreign goods. If we measure all other prices relative to the GDP deflator (as we do throughout this chapter), we set $P = 1$ and thus $\log P = 0$. Hence

$$\log P_c = s_M \log P_M + \text{const.}$$

Thus, ignoring fiscal issues, the real consumption wage varies with employment according to

$$\frac{\partial \log(W/P_c)}{\partial \log N} = \frac{\partial \log W}{\partial \log N} - \frac{\partial \log P_c}{\partial \log N} = \frac{\partial \log W}{\partial \log N} - s_M \frac{\partial \log P_M}{\partial \log N}.$$

As employment expands, a real depreciation is needed to balance trade. So $\partial \log P_M / \partial \log N$ is positive. This implies that the trade-off between real wages and employment is now given by[36]

$$\frac{\partial \log W/P_c}{\partial \log N} = \frac{\partial \log W}{\partial \log N} - \frac{s_M s_N}{\varepsilon_X + \varepsilon_M - 1},$$

where s_N is the share of labour and ε_X, ε_M the price elasticity of exports and imports. Real wages fall more when employment rises.

Hence centralized bargaining is slightly less likely to produce full employment if an economy becomes open. By contrast, decentralized bargaining is slightly more likely to produce full employment when a given economy becomes open. For η will always become higher if a given economy becomes open and more firms are competing together (as in Europe after 1992). And this in turn will reduce the share of profit and hence will cut wage pressure and unemployment.

A national bargain between unions and government

We have not so far allowed any role for government in a central wage bargain. But in some countries where there is a single bargain the government does become involved (e.g. Austria), and the bargain is essentially between the union and the government.[37] Even so, this leads to very similar conclusions about the employment outcome. For employment (N) has got to be the main objective of the government. This gives $\Omega = (WN)^\beta N$, with full employment, if, at $N = L$, we have

$$\frac{\partial \log \Omega}{\partial \log W} = \beta \left(1 + \frac{\partial \log N}{\partial \log W} \right) + \frac{\partial \log N}{\partial \log W} < 0.$$

This guarantees full employment if

$$\left|\frac{\partial \log W}{\partial \log N}\right| < \frac{1-\beta}{\beta}.$$

Full employment is of course more likely the weaker are the unions.

Industry-level bargaining

Our conclusion so far is that centralized wage bargaining is good for employment. Does this mean that, starting from any decentralized position, a partial move towards centralization is always good? The answer is no. It may be that employment is

> highest in fully centralized bargaining;
> next highest in fully decentralized bargaining;
> worst in national single-industry bargaining.

Among academics, this has been argued forcibly by Calmfors and Driffill (1988), and at the policy level decentralized bargaining has been praised by the present British government (Department of Employment 1988) and the Donovan Committee (1968).

Decentralized bargaining would be better than national single-industry bargaining if the elasticity of demand for labour facing the industry were markedly lower than that facing the individual firm. This could not happen if the products of all firms were equally good (or bad) substitutes for the products of all other firms, as we have so far assumed.[38] But in reality, there are clearly groupings of firms whose products are closer substitutes for each other than for other goods (e.g., Ford and BMW are closer substitutes for each other than they are for cornflakes). If the unions at Ford and BMW bargain as one, they collectively face a less elastic demand for their labour than either group would face, bargaining on its own with its own firm.[39]

Thus, if we compare firm- with industry-bargaining, the relevant elasticity of labour demand $\varepsilon_{SW} = \varepsilon_{SN}\varepsilon_{NW}$ would be lower at the industry level. But by how much?

Let us first examine the elasticity of demand facing a single firm. Suppose the demand for the output of the ith firm in the jth industry is given by

$$Y_{ij} = \left(\frac{P_{ij}}{P_j}\right)^{-\eta} Y_j,$$

where Y_j is an index of industry output, P_j is the average price in the jth industry, and all prices are in real terms. To analyse the determination of labour demand, we shall for simplicity assume a production function $Y_{ij} = N_{ij}$. It follows that

$$\frac{\partial \log Y_{ij}}{\partial \log P_{ij}} = -\eta + \frac{\partial \log P_j}{\partial \log P_{ij}}\left(\eta + \frac{\partial \log Y_j}{\partial \log P_j}\right) = -\eta + v(\eta - \sigma),$$

where η is the elasticity of substitution between firms *within* the industry, σ is the elasticity of substitution *between* industries, and v is the share of the firm in the total output of the industry.[40] Hence

$$\left|\frac{\partial \log Y_{ij}}{\partial \log P_{ij}}\right| = (1 - v)\eta + v\sigma > \sigma \qquad \text{(since } \eta > \sigma\text{).}$$

Clearly, $\sigma < \eta$, since the products of different industries are less close substitutes than the products of different firms within an industry. Thus, if firms bargain one by one their demand elasticity is greater than σ, but if the bargaining is industry-wide the demand elasticity is σ. However, in an open economy a country's share of any industrial market may be quite small, so there remain many substitutes within the same industry. Industry bargaining does little to eliminate competition and reduce the elasticity of demand for labour. Thus in a very open economy, industry-wide bargaining may be only slightly more harmful to employment than fully decentralized bargaining.

The preceding analysis related to the case where industry-wide bargaining involves horizontal collaboration between firms producing the same product. However, industry-wide bargaining also involves vertical collaboration between firms at different stages in the production process. Collaboration of this kind raises the effective share of labour in total cost, and this increases the elasticity of demand for labour. This works in the opposite direction.

Thus, all things considered, partial centralization is unlikely to be significantly worse than total decentralization. But full centralization is better for unemployment than either.

A much more important issue is the effect of variable levels of union coverage (discussed in the previous section). In our judgement, allowing for reasonable supply responses in the competitive sector, unemployment levels rise monotonically with union coverage—provided bargaining is non-centralized. But once coverage becomes high enough, centralization becomes possible, and in that case unemployment is again low (see Table 7). This is what gives the misleading impression that intermediate levels of centralization are bad. But for given levels of coverage, there is no reason to suppose this is so. This interpretation is consistent with the empirical analysis of Chapter 1.

Table 7 *Schematic analysis of unemployment*

Union coverage	Centralization of bargaining	
	Decentralized	*Centralized*
High	High	Low
Middle	Medium	n.a.
None	Low	n.a.

7. Trade unions and nominal inertia

An important achievement of trade unions, which we have up to now taken for granted, is that they have formalized the contract of employment between a firm and its workers. While the main purpose has been to improve the working conditions and job security of union members, a significant, though perhaps unintended, consequence has been to impart a substantial degree of inflexibility into wage adjustment. In a casual labour market, employers can alter their wage offers rapidly in response to changes in market conditions. But with formal contracts, firms are obliged to adhere to the terms of the contract, and this prevents them adjusting wages until the contract expires or can be renegotiated.

For a long time it has been known that union wages are less flexible than non-union wages. The union wage mark-up, for example, generally moves counter-cyclically (Lewis 1963). At the aggregate level, in international comparisons wage inflexibility has often been correlated with union density (or with associated measures of the extent of formalization of the labour market such as the proportion of workers employed in large firms: see Chapter 9).

Employment contracts typically (though not invariably) specify a given money wage to be paid over the length of the contract, and the inflexibility created is thus an inflexibility of money wages. Money wage inflexibility, or nominal inertia, will give rise to unemployment of a standard Keynesian type. A fall in nominal aggregate demand will cause unemployment because money wages will not fall in response. Twenty-five or thirty years ago this way of thinking would have been at the centre of any explanation of unemployment. Our position in this book is that, while such considerations matter in explaining short-run changes in unemployment, they have very little to contribute to an understanding of the big variations in unemployment in the medium term with which we are mainly concerned.

The key point is that, while contracts stipulate a money wage, economic logic, common sense, and empirical evidence all suggest that workers and firms

138

are interested not in nominal magnitudes as such, but rather in the real values to which they correspond. If the inflation rate goes up, workers will demand, and firms will be willing to concede, higher money wage increases than otherwise. Thus, when bargaining, firms and unions are concerned to set a money wage, given their expectations about prices.

Early attempts to model the formation of price expectations were based on adaptive expectations—the idea that expectations of the future would depend on the experience of the past. In such models, fluctuations in employment would arise only to the extent that expectations were slow to adjust. Some early attempts to model the formation of price expectations (Solow 1969) did suggest that there were quite long lags in the adjustment of expectations of inflation to the actual inflation rate. But, as inflation rates increased in the later 1960s and early 1970s, the estimated lag became shorter, and with it the duration of the impact of changes in aggregate demand on employment.

With the advent of rational expectations in the early 1970s, the role of contracts in creating nominal inertia was further attenuated. Under rational expectations, the expected price underlying any wage bargain would be an optimal forecast and the outcome would thus deviate from equilibrium only because of 'shocks' (events that had not been predicted at the time the contract was drawn up). Clearly, shocks could create unemployment in a world of wage contracts, because the parties are temporarily locked into the agreement and cannot renegotiate; but equally, such effects cannot last for longer than the duration of the contract itself other than via endogenous sources of persistence (e.g. hysteresis). Once the contract has ended, new negotiations can take full account of the new information.

In Britain and in most European countries, wage contracts typically last for a year. In the USA, in the unionized sectors of the economy three-year contracts are quite common (Taylor 1983). It is sometimes suggested that this may account for the greater degree of nominal inertia which appears to characterize the American economy (Grubb *et al.* 1983, and see Chapter 9 below). But the low degree of unionization in the USA casts some doubt on this explanation. It is difficult to explain the persistence of high unemployment in Europe, which in many countries has lasted for the best part of ten years, by the constraints of contracts which themselves typically last only for one year.

There is, however, one approach which suggests that contracts may create persistence in unemployment lasting longer than the length of the contracts themselves, even when price expectations are formed rationally so that errors in price expectations do not persist. This can occur when contracts are 'staggered', that is, when different groups of workers negotiate at different times in the year. In these circumstances, if any one group agrees a cut in its money wage it will suffer a reduction, at least temporarily, in its real wage and in its wage relative to other groups of workers. This approach usefully formalizes Keynes's intuition that in a decentralized economy it would be difficult to change the general level of money wages (which, as such, would be of no great concern to workers) without disrupting the pattern of relative wages (about which workers are deeply concerned).

The significance of staggered contracts is that the disruption of relative wages during the adjustment to a nominal shock can be reduced if the adjustment itself proceeds at a slower pace. This point was first demonstrated by Phelps (1978), but more fully developed by Taylor (1979; 1980). A version of the model taking as its basis the behaviour of rational trade unions was developed by Jackman (1984; 1985).

The basic idea can be seen most easily in a model where there are annual wage contracts and just two unions, bargaining at different times in the year, say half a year apart. The economy is subject to a deflationary shock, which for example requires a cut in money wages (relative to previous trend) of 10 per cent. If the unions were each to adjust their money wage in full at the first opportunity, members of the first union would suffer a 10 per cent fall in their relative wage for half a year, and no subsequent compensation. By contrast, if each union were to embark on a policy of setting its wage 1 per cent below the other's at each negotiation until the new equilibrium was reached, the adjustment process would take five years instead of six months, but the maximum disruption of relativities would be 1 per cent; and because of the alternating pattern of relative wage differentials, neither union would have gained or lost overall in terms of real income during the adjustment process.

This example describes the principle behind the mechanisms at work. Rational behaviour with perfect foresight leads to a partial adjustment mechanism converging to the new equilibrium (Taylor 1979; Blanchard and Fischer 1989: 395–8). The choice of speed of adjustment involves exactly the trade-off described above. This trade-off depends on the importance trade unions attach to wages as against employment (Jackman 1985).

Staggered contracts then provide an institutional mechanism which can in principle lock an economy on to an inappropriate level (or growth path) of money wages and hence cause persistent unemployment in response to nominal shocks, even when price expectations are formed rationally.

The main weakness of staggered contracts as an explanation of persistent unemployment is that the theory does not seem able to explain why on some occasions the rate of change of money wages appears very stable, while on others it seems able to adjust very rapidly. In Britain, for example, money wages increased by 14.3 per cent in the year to September 1979, by 26.1 per cent in the year to September 1980, but by only 9.3 per cent in the year to September 1981. Wage increases thereafter stabilized, in the range of 7–8 per cent per year, until 1987. It is difficult to explain the stability of money wage growth in the face of mass unemployment in the mid-1980s by a model of nominal inertia when wage inflation fell so rapidly in response to the economic downturn in 1981.

While in other countries movements in money wages in the early 1980s were less dramatic, after the first oil price shock the average rate of wage inflation in the seven largest OECD countries rose to nearly 18 per cent by the end of 1974, but had fallen back to little over 10 per cent by the end of 1975. The average remained close to 10 per cent for the rest of the 1970s despite higher average rates of unemployment. Again, it seems hard to believe that the forces of nominal inertia are enormously powerful when wage inflation can vary so much from one year to the next.

There is thus *a priori* evidence that nominal inertia induced by staggered contracts is not the main cause of the large-scale medium-term movements in unemployment with which we are mainly concerned. None the less, we do believe that nominal inertia has an important role to play in explaining the causes and propagation of economic shocks (see Chapter 9) and that contracts are a more important source of such inertia than the curious idea that workers are unaware of the current price level when determining their labour supply.

In the theoretical literature, there are three types of objections to models based on staggered contracts. They are:

1. that staggering wage settlement dates, rather than synchronizing them, is not privately efficient for firms;
2. that the models provide no theoretical rationale for fixed-length rather than state-dependent contracts; and
3. that the inefficiencies in the system could easily be removed by the simple expedient of indexing the contract wage to the price level.

It is not our intention to mount a theoretical review of this area, for which see Blanchard and Fischer (1989: ch. 8). But it is worth briefly summarizing why we find these objections unconvincing.

1. Given that firms differ so much in the scope and complexity of their wage-bargaining negotiations, and that the time taken to reach a settlement is itself never known in advance, it is clear that wage bargaining can be synchronized effectively only if it is centralized. In a decentralized system, the advantages to an individual firm of 'bunching' (timing its wage settlements to be at the same time as many other firms) seem small relative to firm-specific factors

affecting the timing of negotiation, not to mention the benefits, particularly to smaller firms, of letting others establish a 'going rate' prior to their own negotiations (Ball and Cecchetti 1988).

2. It is a well established result that, if there are fixed costs of changing prices, the optimal strategy is a rule that prices should be changed whenever their deviation from equilibrium reaches a certain level (this is termed an Ss rule: see Chapter 7, or Blanchard and Fischer 1989: ch. 8). If firms adopt such a price-setting rule, individual prices will be inflexible over a certain range, but the aggregate price level will not necessarily be subject to inertia because those prices that do change will change by larger amounts (Caplin and Spulber 1987).

But this optimal rule is based on the assumption that the equilibrium is known and the costs are solely those of implementing the change in prices (often termed 'menu costs'—i.e. the costs of reprinting menus or price lists to carry the new prices). Wage bargaining is concerned with determining the new level of wages, and hence the timing of negotiations cannot be determined by a rule that depends on the outcome being already known.

3. Indexation of wage contracts will help under the assumptions of perfect competition. If employment depends only on the real wage, and a deflation of demand causes unemployment by causing a fall in prices relative to a given level of money wages, then clearly, indexation of wages to prices will resolve the problem. But under imperfect competition, prices may not be very sensitive to demand in the short term (see Chapter 7) and employment will change when demand changes, with a given level of real wages. In these circumstances indexation will not help. With one-year contracts, the main shocks to the price level often come from supply-side factors, such as oil prices or tax changes, rather than from demand. From the employment standpoint, to raise money wages in response to an increase in oil prices or taxes would be counter-productive, and inappropriate indexation could do more harm than good.

Our conclusion is that trade unions provide an institutional environment within which nominal inertia can arise. The mechanism is staggered wage contracts, which prevent a uniform adjustment of money wages. Nominal inertia could in principle provide an explanation for medium-term persistence of unemployment arising from demand shocks. Our argument at this point is that nominal inertia is a very partial explanation of the persistence of unemployment. We will go on to show that it does account for some of the variation across countries in the response to demand shocks in the short run. However, the main sources of medium-term variation in unemployment must be sought elsewhere. We return to an empirical investigation of all these issues in Chapter 9.

8. Summary

We can now baldly summarize the argument of this chapter.

1. Unions generally bargain over wages and manning ratios. They do not bargain over total employment because in the most typical cases (where new workers are being hired) the level of employment is of no interest to existing workers. However, where jobs are being lost, there is sometimes (especially outside the USA) bargaining over layoffs. But layoffs are generally left to management discretion—and the wage bargain takes the risk of layoff into account.

2. At the firm level the bargained wage is higher the more powerful the union and the less elastic the demand for labour (with rents and quasi-rents up for grabs). The wage is also higher the lower is unemployment.

3. In aggregate, the bargained wage has to be in line with prevailing wage levels outside, and in equilibrium expectations must be fulfilled. This determines the requisite level of unemployment, which depends on the same variables as the bargained wage (given outside wages).

4. Since wages affect job security less when underlying unemployment is falling, wage pressure is higher when unemployment is falling. Thus, high unemployment last period raises wage pressure and leads to a high level of non-inflationary unemployment. This is the basic insider mechanism of hysteresis.

5. When management becomes sufficiently strong to take unilateral decisions over manning ratios, this increases productivity in the union sector and decreases employment there. It decreases total employment unless the general increase in real wages encourages enough of the non-union workers to take jobs in the competitive sector.

6. A fall in union coverage also reduces the number of 'good jobs'. However, it is unlikely to reduce total employment so long as the induced rise in the competitive wage encourages enough of the non-union workers to take jobs in the competitive sector.

7. Centralized bargaining is conducive to full employment. This is because the bargainers internalize all the employment effects of the wage bargain.

8. Trade unions can create nominal inertia (inflexible money wages) because wage bargaining and collective agreements reduce the frequency of wage adjustment. If wage contracts are staggered over the year, such nominal inertia could in principle persist over long periods of time. In practice, the rate of wage inflation does vary quite significantly in the short run, suggesting that nominal inertia is a very partial explanation of the persistence of unemployment. A systematic empirical investigation of nominal inertia is given in Chapter 9.

Notes

1. Another reason is the overpricing of union labour—with a union mark-up much greater in the USA then elsewhere (Blanchflower and Freeman 1990).
2. In some insider–outsider models (Lindbeck and Snower 1989) it is assumed that incumbent workers protect themselves against this by allowing new hires to move up on to the 'insider' pay scale after a period. But in this case the authors have no explanation of involuntary unemployment, since the wage for new hires could be low enough to make the present value of employment equal to that of unemployment. The authors might reply that capital market imperfections prevent the entry wage falling below subsistence, but in practice it is generally well above this.
3. Econometric attempts to ascertain whether there is efficient bargaining have been based on the McDonald–Solow model in which there are always unemployed insiders. (Examples are Brown and Ashenfelter 1986, and MaCurdy and Pencavel 1986.) But, as we show in Sect. 3, this model is in most cases inappropriate, and tests based on it tell us little. (See also Ch. 4, Sect. 4.) Moreover, the tests were in the newspaper printing industry which is highly untypical.

   We should also record that, in a later survey of British unions (Clark and Oswald 1989) covering 91% of TUC membership, the following answers were obtained (replies weighted by union size): 'Is the level of employment usually decided by the employer?' Yes 96%; No 4%. 'Does your union usually negotiate over the total number employed at an establishment as well as over their wages and conditions?' Yes 29%; No 71%. The authors do not fully explain the relation between these two sets of answers.
4. That is, the union loses legal protection under the National Labour Relations Act. In consequence, the firm always has the power to enforce a wage-only system of bargaining. This will generally lead to higher profit than bargaining over both wages and employment (see Sect. 3 below).

   While there does exist a range of the contract curve which improves profit as well as union utility (when compared with wage-only bargaining), the firm is likely to end up at a point on the contract curve where it is worse off (e.g., it would do so with a Cobb–Douglas production function).
5. From the workers' point of view, it is also important that they know as far ahead as possible if they are going to lose their jobs. Thus in Britain the law has two requirements. First, the firm must tell the union of any planned redundancies well in advance. There is also a period of notice that must be given to each individual worker: this is roughly one week per year of service. On top of this, unions often bargain for longer periods. In the USA practice has varied (Ehrenberg and Jakubson 1988), but since 1988 the law has required that individuals be given advance notice, except in small firms.
6. Other evidence in support of LIFO in Britain is the small number of workers each year who get statutory redundancy payments (for which two years' service is required). In the year 1978 these amounted to about $1\frac{1}{2}$ per cent of the workforce, compared with a flow of job-losers into unemployment equal to about 4 per cent of the labour force.
7. In most countries, support for the unemployed is financed by general taxes or contributions, unrelated to the previous layoff rate of the firm. However, in the USA the

144

employer's rate of contribution to unemployment insurance funds is heavily experience-rated. This does not affect the union's approach to bargaining, but it does affect employer behaviour. As Feldstein (1975, 1976) and Topel (1983) show, employers are less likely to lay off workers where they are more heavily experience-rated.

8. There may be temporary payments to workers who are on temporary short-time or layoff (of which, short-time, such as 4 days a week, is the most common). Some workers also have guaranteed week agreements under which they get paid for (say) 40 hrs. a week, whether they actually work or not—so long as they are not made redundant.

9. In 1980 the proportion of workers in union establishments with over 1000 employees who were covered by these schemes were as follows (Oswald 1986):

	Mfg (%)	Non-mfg (%)
Severance pay	54	27
Supplemental unemployment benefit	51	4
Wage employment guarantee (WEG)	13	20

The WEGs guarantee a certain annual income regardless of weeks worked. Supplemental unemployment benefit is quite rare in non-union firms.

10. This is a crude one-period approach. In principle, union members would bargain over next period's wage, knowing that this in turn determines the probability distribution of the number of insiders next period, which in turn affects the outcome of next period's wage negotiation. A higher wage this period increases the survival probability next period associated with a given wage next period. This encourages more union wage-push this period but also (by the same token) more employer resistance this period.

The analytics of this problem are immensely complicated and, if soluble, are unlikely to yield much more insight than the present simplified approach. (See Roberts 1989 for a dynamic treatment.)

11. In a stationary environment, the present value of an unemployed person is V_u where

$$V_u = \frac{1}{1+r}[B + hV_n + (1-h)V_u],$$

where present values are calculated at the beginning of each period and payments are made at the end. At the end of the period the individual is paid B and has an exit probability h into a job, where the present value is V_n. If not, he remains unemployed with the same present value. The expected present value of being employed is, by symmetry,

$$V_n = \frac{1}{1+r}[W^e + sV_u + (1-s)V_n],$$

where s is the exit rate from employment to unemployment. Solving, the flow equivalent of V_u is

$$rV_u = (1-\psi)W^e + \psi B$$

where $\psi = (r+s)/(r+s+h)$. But if unemployment is constant, exits = entries, so that $hu = s(1-u)$. Hence $\psi \simeq (r+s)u/(ru+s) \simeq (1+r/s)u = \varphi u$ where the relevant r and s may each be of the order of 20%.

12. On the income of British workers on strike, see Gennard (1981; 1982).

13. Note that in principle (13) and (14) determine N, W as a function of W^e. N then determines Y, and real aggregate demand (Y_d) is endogenous (since $Y = Y_d$ from the

aggregate version of equation (4)). Thus with exogenous nominal demand, Y_d then determines the aggregate price level. The logic of this is easier to see in Ch. 1, where nominal prices are shown explicitly.

14. Note that, if we define full utilization output in the economy ($\bar{Y}$) by $\bar{Y} = L^{\alpha}K^{1-\alpha}$, then potential productivity $\bar{Y}/L = (K/L)^{1-\alpha}$.

15. Note that, if there is free entry, the elasticity of product demand (η) is endogenous and depends on the number of firms. This in turn depends on the zero profit condition and the level of fixed capital costs.

16. Taking differentials of equation (25) gives

$$\frac{\varepsilon'_{SN}(1-\delta)}{(1-\alpha)}\mathrm{dlog}W - \varepsilon'_{SN}\frac{(1-\delta)}{(1-u)}\mathrm{d}u_{-1} - \varepsilon'_{SN}(1-\delta)\mathrm{dlog}K/L = \frac{\alpha\kappa}{\beta^2}\mathrm{d}\beta - \frac{(1-\alpha\kappa)}{\varphi(1-b)u^2}\mathrm{d}u,$$

where we have used the price–employment equation (18) and set $u = u_{-1}$.

17. If the unemployment equation is second-order (as empirically found in Layard and Nickell 1987) with, for example,

$$(u - u^*) = \alpha_{11}(u_{-1} - u^*) - \alpha_{12}(u_{-2} - u^*),$$

then the short-run NAIRU can exceed u_{-1} if u_{-2} is large enough, even if u^* is less than u_{-1}.

18. As a matter of curiosity, this is the same wage level as would result from the right-to-manage model with $N_i < N_{Ii}$, see below.

19. Lindbeck and Snower's views on this point vary (see Lindbeck and Snower 1989). But the basic logic of their model implies a similar conclusion to ours, although for a different reason. They believe the insiders have the power to force wages up to the level at which they will all be sacked. Initially they do not push wages that far because the firms would not wish to employ all the insiders. But, as turnover proceeds, wages must eventually reach this ceiling. At this point a rise in demand would raise N_i but not W_i, while a fall in demand would cut W_i and not N_i.

20. This assumption is also necessary to ensure a solution to the firm's choice of effort in a competitive economy. Under competition, the firm chooses effort to minimize the wage per unit of effort subject to a given level of utility $Wg(E)$ which is competitively determined. This is tantamount to maximizing $Eg(E)$, a problem whose second-order condition implies that $-Eg'(E)/g(E)$ is increasing in effort.

21. Omitting i subscripts, assuming that $Y = f(EN)$ implies

$$\Pi = R(f(EN)) - WN$$

$$\frac{\partial\Pi}{\partial N} = R'f'E - W = 0$$

$$\frac{\partial\Pi}{\partial E} = R'f'N = \frac{WN}{E} \text{ (from the above equation).}$$

22. The workers will not of course push their case beyond the point where firms' profits fall below their outside option.

23. When firms set effort, the wage bargain still satisfies (37), and therefore in general equilibrium (39) will still give the level of unemployment.

24. This may not be quite right if benefits are indexed to wages rather than to utility in

146

work. In the former case, the ratio of benefits to utility in work will fall under effort bargaining, and hence unemployment will fall and employment rise. This effect is likely to be minor, however.

25. e.g. because benefits are a constant fraction of competitive-sector wages.

26.

$$\frac{\partial}{\partial E_u}[(g(E_u))^\pi E_u^{\pi-1}] = \pi g^\pi E_u^{\pi-2}\left(\alpha\kappa - \left|\frac{E_u g'(E_u)}{E_u}\right|\right) < 0$$

since $|E_u g'(E_u)/E_u|$ is always greater than $\alpha\kappa$ (see (42), (43)).

27. Extensive manipulation reveals that union employment will fall if

$$\hat{\varepsilon}_g = \mathrm{dlog}\left|\frac{Eg'(E)}{g(E)}\right|/\mathrm{dlog}E > \frac{\varepsilon_{SN}(1-\mu-N_u)}{1+\beta\varepsilon_{SN}}. \tag{i}$$

Now consider the world in which all firms are unionized. Then, in equilibrium, the impact of union power on effort is given by

$$\hat{\varepsilon}_g \mathrm{dlog}E/\mathrm{dlog}\beta = \frac{-\mu\varepsilon_{SN}/\beta}{(\varepsilon_{SN}+1/\beta)} \qquad \text{(differentiate equation (43)).}$$

The impact of union power on equilibrium unemployment is given by

$$\partial\mathrm{log}u^*/\partial\mathrm{log}\beta = \frac{(\alpha\kappa/\beta)\mu}{(\varepsilon_{SN}-\alpha\kappa/\beta)(1-\alpha\kappa)} \qquad \text{(differentiate equation (39)).}$$

Thus

$$\frac{|\partial\mathrm{log}E/\partial\mathrm{log}\beta|}{\partial\mathrm{log}u^*/\partial\mathrm{log}\beta} = \frac{\varepsilon_{SN}}{(\beta\varepsilon_{SN}+1)\hat{\varepsilon}_g}\frac{(\beta\varepsilon_{SN}+\alpha\kappa)(1-\alpha\kappa)}{\alpha\kappa}.$$

Now let us investigate the consequences in this economy, if the effort utility function g has the property that $\hat{\varepsilon}_g$ does not satisfy the inequality (i). Thus, if $\hat{\varepsilon}_g$ satisfies $\hat{\varepsilon}_g < \varepsilon_{SN}(1-\mu-N_u)/1+\beta\varepsilon_{SN}$, then it follows that

$$\frac{|\partial\mathrm{log}E/\partial\mathrm{log}\beta|}{\partial\mathrm{log}u^*/\partial\mathrm{log}\beta} > \frac{(\beta\varepsilon_{SN}+\alpha\kappa)(1-\alpha\kappa)}{\alpha\kappa(1-\mu-N_u)} > \frac{1-\alpha\kappa}{1-N_u}. \tag{ii}$$

So if, in our two-sector economy, the union sector is around 50% and the share of profit is around 30%, then $(1-\alpha\kappa)/(1-N_u)\simeq0.6$. Then inequality (ii) implies that, in our fully unionized economy, were union power to rise enough to raise equilibrium unemployment from 4% to 6% (i.e. a rise of 50%), effort would simultaneously fall by at least 30%! (0.6 × 50.) So if the effort utility function did not satisfy inequality (i), then it would imply that, in a fully unionized economy, a rise in union power which was enough to raise unemployment by a mere 2 percentage points would also be enough to reduce effective employment (*EN*) by more than 30%. In the light of this somewhat startling consequence, it seems likely that the g function will typically satisfy inequality (i). Otherwise effort is simply too responsive to exogenous changes.

28. For a full analysis of the comparative statics of the case being discussed, see an earlier draft of this book (available on request).

29. This is not the same as a change in the proportion of the workforce unionized, which if it occurs *within* a firm leads to an increase in union power but not in coverage.

30. This is true of a country in which the trade balance is unchanged. It is not true of a region within a country where increased unionization can raise non-union wages via the

so-called threat effect (Freeman and Medoff 1984: 158–9). The result must then be a loss of competitiveness for the whole region concerned. However, Freeman and Medoff do observe that increased unionization does reduce the wages and employment of non-union *secondary*-sector workers, while raising the wages of non-union primary-sector workers (in 'good' jobs). One other point. Freeman and Medoff (1984) claim that unions raise productivity (*ceteris paribus*). If so, a rise in union coverage would shift out the real wage frontier of the economy. This could obviate the need for a fall in competitive-sector real wages. (Freeman and Medoff's view is that unions raise productivity but raise wages more, thus reducing profits.)

31. It is natural to ask what is the position for partial centralization. For example, what is the elasticity of demand if one-half of all firms agree to bargain together? The answer is that, since each firm faces a demand curve $Y_i = P_i^{-\eta} \bar{Y}$, where P_i is the real price (relative to the general price level), the elasticity of demand with respect to the real wage remains $1/(1 - \alpha\kappa)$ for the aggregate of firms in a bargain when they all change their real wage. But there is an important force towards wage moderation coming from a quite different quarter; for, if employment changes in half the economy, this alters the opportunities open to workers disemployed in this half of the economy—by changing the overall unemployment rate. Bargainers will take this into account. Thus, as bargains cover an increasing share of the labour force, they will become more moderate (Jackman 1990). The only force operating in the other direction is that discussed on pp. 136–38, which we do not consider important in most open economies.

32. Under decentralized bargaining, if W_i is real wages and Π_i real profit, then

$$\Pi_i = R_i(N_i) - W_i N_i$$

and

$$\frac{\partial \Pi_i}{\partial W_i} = -N_i + (R_i' - W_i)\frac{\partial N_i}{\partial W_i} = -N_i.$$

Under centralized bargaining, $\Pi = f(N) - WN$ and

$$\frac{\partial \Pi}{\partial W} = -N + (f' - W)\frac{\partial N}{\partial W}$$

$$= -N + \left(\frac{W}{1 - 1/\eta} - W\right)\frac{\partial N}{\partial W}$$

$$= -N\left(1 + \frac{1}{(\eta - 1)(1 - \alpha)}\right).$$

33. This derives from the notion that economic expansion spreads the cost of given public services over a larger tax base, reducing the average tax cost per unit of GNP (Blanchard and Summers 1987).

34. This formulation avoids ambiguities to do with Okun's law.

35. We are assuming that the price of consumption is equal to the price of all final expenditure.

36. When employment increases, the income effect on imports has to be offset by an equal absolute effect of real depreciation on exports minus import costs. Hence, assuming unit income elasticity of imports,

$$\mathrm{dlog}\,Y = (\varepsilon_X + \varepsilon_M - 1)\mathrm{dlog}\,P_M.$$

The changes in employment and output are related by

$$\mathrm{dlog}\,Y = s_N\mathrm{dlog}N.$$

Thus

$$\left|\frac{\mathrm{dlog}P_M}{\mathrm{dlog}N}\right| = \frac{s_N}{\varepsilon_X + \varepsilon_M - 1}.$$

37. Even in countries where the government stands aloof from the process of wage-bargaining, its actions may yet affect the outcome. For a country like Sweden, Calmfors and Horn (1985) have suggested the following model. The union determines wages, and the government then responds by setting public employment in a way that makes up a part of the resulting employment gap. They have argued that in certain circumstances this type of government response could actually increase unemployment (see Annex 2.4). The reasoning is not however persuasive, and it is not in any case clear why the government would persist in an ineffective policy.

38. The demand function we have been using is based on the CES utility function

$$U = \sum_i Y_i^{(1-1/\eta)},$$

where Y_i is the output of the ith firm.

39. We are comparing a situation where either (a) the workers of Ford and BMW negotiate a single deal with Ford and BMW combined, or (b) the Ford workers bargain with Ford, and the BMW workers with BMW. We do not consider the more complicated case where a single union represents the workers in both firms but negotiates separately with each.

40. This result can be rigorously derived assuming a two-level CES utility function,

$$U = \sum_j \left(\sum_i Y_{ij}^{1-1/\eta}\right)^{1-1/\sigma}.$$

3

Efficiency Wages

In the last chapter we discussed how union power might generate wage pressure that required unemployment to damp it down. However, unions are a newer phenomenon in human history than unemployment. Moreover, widespread unemployment seems to exist in some countries where union power is very weak. So what could be producing the excess wage pressure in those contexts?

The most obvious explanation is that firms tend to bid up wages against each other. Unemployment is needed not to stop unions from leapfrogging but to stop firms doing so.

Why would a firm want to pay more than its rivals? It is a commonplace in industrial relations that a wise firm uses wages as an instrument to 'recruit, retain, and motivate' its workers. It does not passively pay some going wage, but actively adopts that wage which maximizes its profits. It is easy to see how behaviour of this kind could lead to unemployment.

For most of this chapter we shall deal in a 'one-sector' world where all firms pay efficiency wages, though we shall argue that adding a market-clearing sector has very similar effects to those shown in the last chapter. The model is of monopolistic competition in the product market with identical firms, as before.

We begin in the first section with the simplest explanation of the theories, and a refutation of the 'bonding critique'. In Section 2 we look more deeply at the motivational processes lying behind the simple theories. We then discuss evidence (Section 3), before considering the dynamic effect of efficiency wage considerations in generating persistent unemployment after a shock such as the oil price rise.

1. 'Recruit, retain, and motivate': basic theory

Let us take 'recruit, retain, and motivate' in reverse order.

Motivation

Suppose that each worker produces E units of output where effort (E_i) in the ith firm depends on the firm's relative wage and also on unemployment:

$$E_i = e\left(\frac{W_i}{W^e}, u\right) \qquad (e_1, e_2 > 0;\ e_{11}, e_{12} < 0). \qquad (1)$$

Here W_i is the real wage in the firm (in units of GNP) and W^e the wage which the worker could expect to receive elsewhere. Workers work harder if they feel they are being treated relatively well, and also if the world outside is bleak (making it more important to please the boss). High unemployment not only raises effort, but also reduces the effect of wages upon effort.

If output in the firm depends on total effort, E_iN_i, the firm chooses wages and employment to maximize profits, Π_i, given by

$$\Pi_i = R(E_iN_i) - W_iN_i = R(E_iN_i) - \left(\frac{W_i}{E_i}\right)E_iN_i,$$

subject to the way in which wages affect effort (equation (1)), R being the real revenue function. This problem can be solved in two stages. First the firm chooses wages to minimize the cost per unit of effort (W_i/E_i). Then it chooses employment to maximize profit, given wages and effort (already determined by the chosen wage).

To minimize W_i/E_i wages must be raised so long as effort rises faster than wages. At the optimum, both rise at the same rate and we have

$$\frac{\partial E_i}{\partial W_i}\frac{W_i}{E_i} = 1.$$

This 'Solow condition' is illustrated in Fig. 1.[1] It implies that

$$e_1\left(\frac{W_i}{W^e}, u\right)\frac{W_i}{W^e} = e\left(\frac{W_i}{W^e}, u\right). \qquad (2)$$

This is the *partial equilibrium or firm-level wage equation*, giving the firm's wage as a function of the expected outside wage and the level of unemployment.

In general equilibrium, unemployment has to be high enough to stop the firm setting its wage higher than the expected prevailing level, which will also

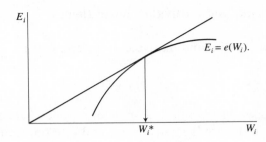

Fig. 1. *The efficient wage.*

$e(W_i)$ is the effort function; W_i^* is the 'efficiency' wage.

equal the actual level; otherwise there would be further leapfrogging. Hence $W_i = W = W^e$, and *equilibrium unemployment* (u^*) is given by

$$e_1(1, u^*) = e(1, u^*). \tag{3}$$

Note that, as with our union model, productivity changes have no impact on u^*.

To relate this analysis to the framework of aggregate wage and price equations, we can proceed more cumbrously to differentiate profits with respect to, first, wages and then employment. This gives

$$\frac{\partial \Pi_i}{\partial W_i} = R' \frac{e_1}{W^e} N_i - N_i = 0 \tag{4a}$$

and

$$\frac{\partial \Pi_i}{\partial N_i} = R'e - W_i = 0. \tag{4b}$$

Suppose, for illustration, we use our standard constant elasticity demand and Cobb–Douglas production functions from Chapter 2 (equations (4) and (3′)); that is,

$$Y_i = (P_i)^{-\eta} Y_{di}; \qquad Y_i = (E_i N_i)^\alpha K_i^{1-\alpha}, \tag{5}$$

where Y_i is value added output, P_i is the real price, and K_i is the predetermined capital stock. Then we have aggregate wage and price equations (setting $W_i = W$, $P_i = 1$, $N = (1 - u)L$) corresponding to (4a) and (4b):

$$W = \alpha \kappa \frac{W}{W^e} e_1 \left(\frac{W}{W^e}, u \right) \left[e \left(\frac{W}{W^e}, u \right) (1 - u) \frac{L}{K} \right]^{-(1-\alpha)}, \tag{6}$$

$$W = \alpha \kappa e \left(\frac{W}{W^e}, u \right) \left[e \left(\frac{W}{W^e}, u \right) (1 - u) \frac{L}{K} \right]^{-(1-\alpha)}, \tag{7}$$

where recall that L is the labour force and $\kappa = 1 - 1/\eta$, the index of product market competitiveness. These equations have the standard slopes shown in Chapter 1 (so long as α is not too small).[2]

One other point. We should not abandon our belief in efficiency wage theory if we do not find the wage elasticity of effort to be exactly unity. One possibility is that the production function is more complex. Another is that bargaining may be in progress, together with efficiency wage considerations affecting employers. In this case, even with $Y_i = E_i N_i$, the wage elasticity of effort will, in equilibrium, be less than one (see Annex 3.1).

We can now quickly check that the structure of the firm's problem is identical to what we have just analysed if it is concerned not with motivation but with retention or recruitment.

Retention

Firms often (and universities, sometimes) use wages to stop their workers leaving. This is because most firms have monopsony power (at least, in terms of their ability to affect the rate at which workers flow out). Thus the quit rate is

$$q = q\left(\frac{W_i}{W^e}, u\right) \qquad (q_1, q_2 < 0; q_{11}, q_{12} > 0)$$

Quitting matters because firms have to incur real hiring and training costs, θ, whenever a quitter is replaced. Thus the firm's steady-state profits are[3]

$$\Pi_i = R(N_i) - \left[W_i + \theta q\left(\frac{W_i}{W^e}, u\right)\right] N_i.$$

Clearly, this expression is basically similar in form to the one used earlier. It can be solved by first minimizing the cost per worker (i.e. the term in brackets) and then choosing employment. The wage and price equations have the appropriate signs (under the same conditions as the effort model). Equilibrium unemployment (u^*) is determined by an equation analogous to (3) but not involving unit elasticity of the quit function. u^* increases as relative training costs (θ/W) increase, or as exogenous turnover propensities rise.

Recruitment

Finally, we can turn to the issue of recruitment. Most firms believe that they can fill their vacancies quicker if they raise their relative wages. Hence hires (H_i) are given by

$$H_i = h\left(\frac{W_i}{W^e}, u\right) V_i \qquad (h_1, h_2 > 0;\ h_{11}, h_{12} < 0),$$

where V_i is the firm's vacancies (see Chapter 5). The firm has sN_i leavers per period and wishes to replace them. The firm can secure the necessary flow of recruits either by raising wages or by creating vacancies. But both involve costs: higher wages raise the wage bill, and higher vacancies involve a net cost per empty workplace of, let us say, φ.

The firm's profits are

$$\Pi_i = R(N_i) - \left(W_i + \varphi\frac{V_i}{N_i}\right) N_i.$$

Since $V_i = H_i/h(\ )$ and in a steady state the firm sets $H_i = sN_i$,

$$\Pi_i = R(N_i) - \left(W_i + \frac{\varphi s}{h\left(\dfrac{W_i}{W^e}, u\right)}\right) N_i.$$

This is a very similar expression to those given earlier. The wage is chosen to minimize the net cost of labour, including hiring costs. As before, the aggregate wage and price equations have the proper slopes. An increase in the turnover rate (s) or in the cost of vacancies (φ) raises equilibrium unemployment. (A fuller version of this model appears in Chapter 5, Section 7.)

Source of the problem and the bonding critique

Why exactly do efficiency wages lead to non-clearing labour markets? The problem is that the firm is using the wage for two purposes:

1. to motivate, recruit, and retain workers, but also
2. to determine employment.

If, instead, the first purpose could be secured by some other instrument, then the wage could perform the second function only, falling until it cleared the market.

For example, suppose that workers who quit paid for the cost of hiring and training their successors. Then profits would be

$$\Pi_i = R(N_i) - (W_i + \theta q - \theta q)N_i = R(N_i) - W_i N_i.$$

The employer would wish to pay the lowest possible wage, and thus wages would fall until the market cleared.

For this reason, critics of efficiency wage theory have asked why workers would not be forced to post a bond when they joined the firm, which they would then forfeit when they quit or were found shirking. Alternatively, they would pay a once-for-all entry fee when they arrived, and have it repaid towards the end of their working lives.

Partly for legal reasons (see below), we do not observe bonds. But we do indeed observe elements of entry fees. New entrants often start on lower wages and progress upwards (Lazear 1986).

But there is a limit to this arrangement, because of moral hazard. If employers exploit workers early in their careers and, in return, have to overpay them later, there is a major danger that they will try unfairly to rid themselves of the overpaid workers. Reputational sanctions might not be enough to prevent this, and firms are not, therefore, able to use this incentive device to any great extent.

A second problem arises from capital market imperfections, which make it difficult for workers to survive on very low starting wages (Akerlof and Katz 1989). However, some have argued that, even if starting wages cannot be too low, beginners can be expected to work very hard, thus reducing their wage per unit of effort. But once again, there are limits to the extent of extra effort that can be extracted from some, but not all, workers on the same shop-floor. There is also the danger of loss of worker good-will (see 'Gift exchange', in Section 2 below).

So there may be practical reasons why employers are forced to use the general level of wages as an instrument of personnel policy. And this in turn leads to non-market-clearing—as evidenced by the length of job queues. There are queues for non-union jobs paying above minimum wages, and there are noticeable queues for minimum wage jobs—showing that employers have not removed all attraction from such jobs by making the workers work unusually hard (Holzer *et al.* 1988).

We do know that bad behaviour by workers is a real problem in many firms—for example, workers pilfer about 1 per cent of the GNP from their employers (Dickens *et al.* 1989). If bonding were possible, the correct strategy for the firm would be to require bonds far in excess of any potential damage, spend little on monitoring, and impose penalties on those caught far in excess of the damages they have wrought. However, as the Merchant of Venice was lucky enough to discover, super-compensatory damages are not allowed in law. There are also the other problems with bonding or its equivalent which we have discussed. In consequence, firms spend a lot on detecting employee crime. They also use wages as an instrument to secure good behaviour from their workers. For, as two experts on employee theft conclude, 'the most important control against employee theft is a good salary or wage' (Lipman and McGraw 1988).

Crucial issue of the size of wage effects

Whether efficiency wages matter depends entirely on how strongly wages affect worker behaviour. If the effect is very great, the incentive to leapfrog is very great and equilibrium unemployment will be high.

To see this, let us take a special case of the first model (Summers 1988). We set[4]

$$E_i = (W_i - A)^\lambda \qquad (\lambda < 1),$$

where $A = W^e(1 - u)$. The firm sets $\partial \log E_i / \partial \log W_i = 1$, which requires

$$\frac{\lambda W_i}{W_i - A} = 1.$$

Thus the partial equilibrium wage mark-up equation is

$$\frac{W_i - A}{W_i} = \lambda, \qquad (8)$$

with the firm's wage mark-up being higher the more effort responds to wages.

In equilibrium, with $W_i = W = W_i^e$, the wage mark-up equation implies that

$$u = \lambda.$$

Thus, unemployment is higher the greater is the incentive to leapfrogging.[5]

Many firms: the law of one price is repealed

We can now allow for the obvious fact that the return to high morale may be greater in some firms than in others. It is more important that train-drivers are alert than that postmen are, even though similar attributes may be required for each job. This in turn produces higher wages for train-drivers than postmen, and longer job queues.

To illustrate this, suppose that the real revenue function has the form

$$R_i = R_i(E_i^{\alpha_i} N_i),$$

where α_i varies across jobs. If marginal variations in effort are important, α_i is high, as with the train-driver. In this case, it is easy to show that the wage satisfies the generalized 'Solow condition',

$$\frac{\partial \log E_i}{\partial \log W_i} = \frac{1}{\alpha_i}.$$

If we now use the functional form specified in the previous section ($E_i = (W_i - A)^{\lambda}$), then the wage in each job is determined by

$$\frac{W_i - A}{W_i} = \alpha_i \lambda \qquad (i = 1, \ldots, n).$$

Thus, for identical types of labour, with identical average opportunities, wages differ according to how much efficiency responds to wages. The law of one price has once again been repealed—this time by the unilateral actions of employers.

To find the overall employment rate, we note that, with $A = W^e(1 - u)$,

$$W_i = W^e(1 - u)\frac{1}{1 - \alpha_i \lambda},$$

so that in equilibrium, with $EW_i = W = W^e$,

$$1 - u^* = \frac{1}{E\left(\dfrac{1}{1 - \alpha_i \lambda}\right)},$$

where E is the expectation. The right-hand side is the harmonic mean of $(1 - \alpha_i \lambda)$, confirming the positive relation between u and average $\alpha_i \lambda$.

When we come to investigate the evidence for efficiency wages, we have to rely heavily on inter-firm wage differences in order to see whether these do indeed conform to the mechanisms which might lead to efficiency wages. But first we need to look more closely at the mechanisms themselves.

2. Underlying mechanisms

We shall again begin with the issue of motivation, and then turn to recruitment and retention. There are various ways in which higher wages could induce workers to perform better.

1. Higher wages might increase workers' identification with the firm and their general willingness to co-operate. This is sometimes called the 'gift exchange'—'I treat you well and you treat me well' (Akerlof 1982; Kaufman 1984). Higher wages might be especially necessary if there were high profits and workers felt it unfair if they got no share in these.

2. Higher wages might discourage individual 'shirking', by giving the worker more to lose if he were caught and fired (Shapiro and Stiglitz 1984).
3. Higher wages might discourage collective disruption, including the danger of union organization (the 'threat effect').

Let us look at these in turn.

Gift exchange

In most situations workers cannot be monitored in full, nor can their job be exactly specified. Some initiative is required, and the success of the operation depends on the employer being able to trust the workers to try hard. To induce workers to do more than the minimum that they could get away with, the firm in return has to give something. *It* therefore pays more than the minimum *it* could get away with (Akerlof 1982). Thus it is in the firm's interest to pay more than the supply price of labour.

In choosing its optimum wage, the firm knows that workers have some idea of a 'fair wage'. The worker's effort depends on the relation between the fair wage (W_f) and the wage actually paid by the firm. The fair wage is higher the higher are expected wages in other firms (W^e), but it is lower if unemployment is higher. Thus effort is given by

$$E_i = e(\underset{+}{W_i}, \underset{-}{W_f}) \qquad \text{where } W_f = h(\underset{+}{W^e}, \underset{-}{u}).$$

A natural specialization of this is

$$E_i = e\left(\underset{+}{\frac{W}{W^e}}, \underset{+}{u}\right),$$

as we have used it before.

The fundamental concept here is reference group theory, which most of us know to be true by introspection. This says that our morale and willingness to perform depends importantly on what we get relative to what we see our likes getting. A striking confirmation came from the studies of the American soldier in the Second World War: combat soldiers were little more dissatisfied than those at home, since the former compared themselves with soldiers at home and the latter compared themselves with civilians (Stouffer *et al.* 1949*a* and *b*).

(i)   Individual effort unobservable

It is important to stress that, like all models of efficiency wages, this one has to be concerned with those dimensions of effort which cannot easily be observed and measured.[6] If effort can be measured and paid for (with no transaction costs), then there is no reason for wage-setting behaviour to cause unemployment.

To see this, we start from the truism that there will always, in the equilibrium of any economy, be some minimum level of utility that a firm must offer its workers. Call this $\bar{U}$. Utility depends on total remuneration (W_i) and effort (E_i). So, if the firm can observe both wages and effort, it will choose to pay no W_i, E_i combination that provides utility higher than $\bar{U}$:

$$U(W_i, E_i, W^e, u) = \bar{U} \qquad (U_W, U_{EE} > 0, U_{EW}, U_{WW} < 0; U_E \gtrless 0).$$

Thus there will be full employment.

The analysis is as follows. The firm chooses W_i and E_i to minimize W_i/E_i subject to the $\bar{U}$ constraint. This is illustrated in Fig. 2. The optimum E_i, W_i are at point P. The employer can either lay down E_i and W_i himself, or (more conveniently) offer a price per unit of effort and let the individual choose his own level of effort. (The appropriate price equals the slope of the line OP.) In either case, the worker performs at P and

$$W_i = f(\bar{U}, W^e, u) \tag{9}$$

and

$$E_i = g(\bar{U}, W^e, u). \tag{10}$$

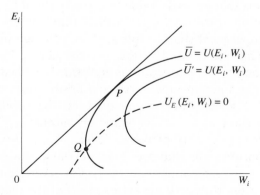

Fig. 2.   *Determination of effort when it is observable.*
$U_E(E_i, W_i) = 0$ is the effort function (the dashed curve).

The demand for labour is, say,

$$E_i R'(E_i N_i) = W_i, \tag{11}$$

and the model is closed by the full-employment condition

$$N_i = L/F. \tag{12}$$

Since in general equilibrium $W_i = W^e$ and $u = L/F - N_i$, the model determines N_i, W_i, E_i, and $\bar{U}$.

By contrast, if effort is unobservable, the employer has to rely on his lump-sum payment (W_i) to provide the motivation. The employer knows that, given W_i, the worker will choose E_i to maximize $U(W_i, E_i, \ldots)$. Hence

$$U_E(W_i, E_i, \ldots) = 0.$$

This is the *effort function*, which we have hitherto written in explicit form as[7]

$$E_i = e(W_i) \qquad (e' > 0). \tag{13}$$

This curve is a locus of points such as Q. No employer would *choose* to operate on this curve since, if $U = \bar{U}$, point P gives him the higher profit. But, if effort is unobservable, he is forced to do so.

Given the effort function, he selects a wage such that

$$\frac{\partial \log E_i}{\partial \log W_i} = 1. \tag{14}$$

This wage will in general not clear the market.[8]

One final point. In the bargaining models of the previous chapter, effort had to be clearly observable. Thus, in any complete view of the world there are dimensions of effort that are observable (e.g. the speed of the production line, number of operations performed), and others that are less so (e.g. whether tasks are done properly, whether people are using enough initiative). Observable effort, as we have said, can be either prescribed (e.g. by the speed of the production line, the number of operations performed) or elicited by piece-work payments. But, as co-operative teamwork and flexible responses have become more important at work, both piece-work and the production line have become less important as modes of work organization. The unobservable elements of effort (e.g. quality of work, degree of initiative) have probably become more important. The employer must of course be able to observe their consequences in aggregate, otherwise he could never figure out his $e(W_i)$ function. But he cannot observe the actual effort at the individual level. It is this kind of unobservable effort with which we are exclusively concerned in this chapter.

(ii) Rent-sharing

We have so far assumed that workers' goodwill depends only on relative wages and is unaffected by the firm's ability to pay. This leads to an optimum wage that bears no explicit relation to the profitability of the firm. In real life, however, wages of similar workers do vary positively with the profitability of the enterprise. In the absence of collective bargaining, the obvious explanation for this is that workers expect to be paid more if the firm is profitable and to slack off if they are not paid more—they feel hard done by (Kahneman *et al.* 1986; Frank 1985). Thus, in the effort function the elasticity λ depends positively on, say, last period's profits per worker. Hence, and following equation (8), the mark-up is

$$\frac{W_i - A}{W_i} = \lambda[(\Pi_i/N_i)_{-1}] \qquad (\lambda' > 0).$$

Wages will be higher when lagged profits per worker are high.

An alternative explanation of rent-sharing (i.e. the correlation of wages and profitability) is the theory of 'expense-preference'. According to this, managers like not only profits but a peaceful life. Peace can be bought with high wages. Hence, when managers have high profits, they spend part of them in wages.

Formally, we may suppose that managerial utility in the ith firm is given by $U(\Pi_i, W_i)$ and that both profits and wages are in the managers' eyes normal goods. But profits depend negatively on wages and positively on other variables X_i:

$$\Pi_i = \Pi(W_i, X_i).$$
$$- \quad +$$
(15)

The manager maximizes $U(\Pi_i, W_i)$ subject to (15). If exogenous forces (X_i) make his firm more profitable, he will 'spend' some of this advantage on profits and some on wages—at least so long as (15) is additively separable or devoid of perverse interactions.

Thus, expense preference has the same rent-sharing prediction as the gift-exchange efficiency wage. But it relies on the managerial theory of the firm (and thus on the weakness of the shareholders). Efficiency wage theory is perhaps preferable.

Shirking

We turn now to a quite different model of motivation. In this the worker dislikes work. He is however willing to do it in order to get a wage income rather than risk becoming unemployed. *If he works*, his net income is

$$W_i - e_i,$$

where e_i is the disutility of work (in money units). If he slacks, his net income is W_i, but he runs a risk p of being caught and sacked. And, if sacked, his expected net income is (for simplicity) $(W - e)(1 - u)$, where W is the outside wage and e the disutility of effort expected in other jobs. Thus, *if he slacks*, his expected net income is

$$(1 - p)W_i + p(W - e)(1 - u).$$

He will not slack so long as

$$W_i - e_i > (1 - p)W_i + p(W - e)(1 - u)$$

or

$$W_i > \frac{e_i}{p} + (W - e)(1 - u).$$

The firm will therefore pay a wage of $e_i/p + (W - e)(1 - u)$. Since all other firms do the same, the *aggregate wage equation* is

$$W = e\left(\frac{1 - p}{pu} + 1\right).$$

Wages are higher, the lower is the unemployment rate and the chance of being caught—and the higher the required effort. Given the price equation, this determines the aggregate unemployment rate. The labour market does not clear.

This model is a simplified version of Shapiro and Stiglitz (1984). The basic mechanism is this. The firm cannot force a worker to work. It must make work so attractive that the worker does not choose to shirk (and thus risk losing his job). The firm therefore has an incentive to pay more than other employers. If there is no unemployment, so that the worker can always pick up another job, the firm will have to pay more than other employers, in order to make its own workers work. This will unleash a wage–price spiral. But, if there is enough unemployment, then an equilibrium is possible in which one firm can make its workers only as well off as in other firms and yet elicit work effort. *This is because workers cannot be sure of getting another job.* Thus, unemployment acts as a 'worker-disciplining device'. There must be just enough of it to eliminate the incentive for firms to pay wages that leapfrog the wages paid by other employers.

Critics of this theory ask why workers are not forced to put up bonds of good behaviour. We have already discussed this issue and have provided two answers. The first is moral hazard: if slacking is not exactly definable, the firm has an incentive to sack marginal workers and collect the bond. Only really good information in the labour market would restrain it. The other answer is imperfect capital markets, already discussed.

Threat effect

We have so far shown how firms can use wages to prevent disruptive action by individuals acting one by one. The firm also wishes to prevent collective disruption. In general, collective disruption requires a union to organize it. So, to prevent collective disruption, firms try to keep out unions. A key way to do this is to pay the union wage, or something near to it. In general, if c is the cost of organization (per worker), the firm can keep out the union if it pays

$$W_i > W_u - rc,$$

where W_u is the union wage, and r the discount rate. We should not be surprised to find that non-union employers willingly pay more in industries that are heavily unionized and where the union wage is high. Models of this kind can clearly generate a non-clearing labour market, resembling closely that obtained when all wages are set by bargaining.

Recruitment and retention

If firms have monopsony power, they also have an incentive to pay higher wages in order to recruit and retain workers. We have already discussed this mechanism in the context of homogeneous labour.

With heterogeneous labour the incentive is even greater. Suppose that, when a firm advertises some semi-skilled jobs, it is unable to evaluate the talents of the applicants and selects at random. If it offers a low wage, it will fail to attract good applicants, because they will already be receiving a higher wage elsewhere. But if it raises the wage, the average quality of applicants will improve. It will continue raising the wage so long as the proportional change in average quality exceeds the proportional change in wages. It will stop raising the wage when this elasticity becomes unity.

To make this model plausible, we have to assume that, the longer workers stay with an employer, the more their talents are recognized. As a result of this there is, in the world from which applicants are drawn, a correlation between wages and productivity. But firms hiring workers either do not know precisely the applicants' existing wages or do not totally believe what they are told. Firms may also wish to avoid low pay for fear of losing their best workers,[9] who could most easily find other jobs.

3. Evidence

What evidence is there to support efficiency wage theories—and which of the various mechanisms does the evidence best support? There are two main types of evidence. First, there is direct evidence of the effects of wages on motivation, retention, and recruitment. Second, there are features of the wage structure that can only be explained by efficiency wage considerations. Though the firm's wage policy has always been a central topic in the theory of personnel management, it is a new one for empirical research and the evidence as yet is fairly sketchy, especially on the first of the two issues listed above.

Benefits of paying more

The clearest evidence of the benefits of higher wages concerns their effects on the quitting behaviour of otherwise identical workers. Pencavel (1972) found an elasticity of around 8, which might be sufficient to justify the higher wage, but Krueger and Summers (1988) and Dickens and Katz (1987) get much smaller figures. As regards recruitment, Holzer *et al.* (1988) show that higher wages lead to more applicants per vacancy, though the effect is not strong. Krueger and Summers (1986) show that higher wages reduce absenteeism. Employers certainly believe that wages affect all these things (Kaufman 1984).

Perhaps the most general test of the theory is to estimate directly a value added production function which includes W_i/W and u. This should capture whatever increases in value added come from the effects of relative wages on recruitment and retention as well as motivation. Wadhwani and Wall (1990*a*) estimate such a function on a panel of firms and conclude that relative wages raised output with an elasticity of up to unity. Levine (1988), using US establishments, finds an elasticity of 0.41. Such a number can be quite consistent with the efficiency wage model if production is a function not simply of EN or if efficiency wages coexist with wage-bargaining (for which see Annex 3.1).

Regarding the effect of unemployment on production, Wadhwani and Wall found that unemployment raised productivity with an elasticity of about 0.05; high unemployment also reduced the positive effect of relative wages on output (i.e. $e_{12} < 0$).

Evidence from the wage structure

We turn now to the evidence from the wage structure. We shall consider this in much more detail in the next chapter, but a brief overview is in place here.

It has long been a commonplace that apparently identical workers employed by different firms in the same street may earn wages differing by 40 per cent or more (Slichter 1950; MacKay *et al.* 1971). Competitive theory would offer two explanations of this:

1. the workers are not really identical, and the better paid are more able; or
2. the jobs are different, and the higher paid jobs are less pleasant.

However, these factors cannot explain anything like all the observed differentials. For, if this were where the differentials came from, they would not lead to differences in quitting or in job queues.[10]

Moreover, inter-industry wage differences remain large, even after controlling for measured working conditions and for measurable ability variables (which also, of course, pick up the effects of that part of unmeasured ability that is correlated with measured ability). More strikingly, panel data on individuals suggest that, when the same individual moves from a high-wage to a low-wage industry (or vice versa), he experiences a wage change of the same order as the average wage difference (*ceteris paribus*) between the two industries (Krueger and Summers 1988). This suggests that unmeasured ability differences cannot adequately account for the inter-industry wage differences.

So what does explain the inter-industry wage differences? First we need to record some of the basic facts about the pattern of these differences, speculating rather loosely on their implications. Then we need to look at regressions which explain the differentials by the characteristics of the industry, and see whether efficiency wage theory tells us that these are the relevant differences.

The main stylized facts about the industry wage structure are shown in Table 1, together with our conclusions about which efficiency wage story, if any, they support (Krueger and Summers 1987, 1988). The first striking fact is the similarity of relative wages in different countries and over time. Beginning with cross-country comparisons, the correlation of relative wages across countries is very high, even when communist countries are compared with capitalist. Figure 3, for example, shows the correlation between the USA and Japan. This suggests a major importance for technological factors (determining the different responsibilities of workers in different industries), as compared with differential product-market power or union activity. Similarly, the correlation over time (Fig. 4) again suggests that technological factors may be more important than unions. It is also true that relative wages are very similar for union and non-union workers, which could reflect the common influence of technological factors or a threat effect.

Finally, however, there is the extremely striking fact that inter-industry wage

Table 1 *The stylized facts: which efficiency wage theories do they support?*

	Gift exchange (with differential payoff to goodwill)	Shirking (with differential costs of shirking and monitoring)	Threat (with differential rates of unionization)	Quit (with differential costs of training)	Hiring (with differential costs of vacancies)
Industry wage differential similar:					
In all countries	√	√		√	√
Over time	√	√		√	√
For union and non-union workers	√	√	√	√	√
In all occupations	√				
Industry wages vary positively with:					
K/L	√	√	√	√	√
Profits	√		√		
Union coverage	√		√		

Source of stylized facts: Krueger and Summers (1987, 1988), Katz (1986*b*), Dickens and Katz (1987).

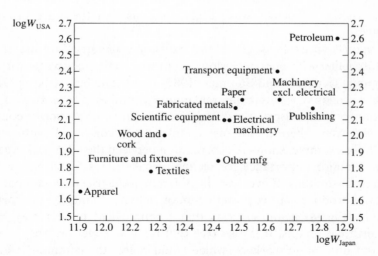

Fig. 3. *Industrial wages in the USA and Japan, 1982.*

Source: Krueger and Summers (1987), based on ILO, *Yearbook of Labour Statistics*.

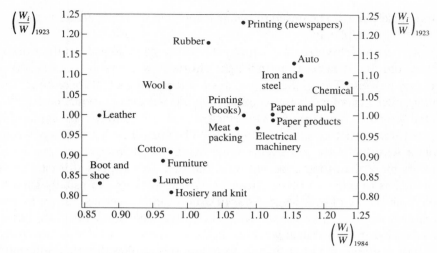

Fig. 4. *Wage differentials over time, USA, 1923 and 1984.*

Industry wage as proportion of average wage.
Source: Krueger and Summers (1987).

relativities are very similar in different occupations (Katz 1986*b*). This is not at all consistent with a technological approach. Why should the responsibilities of office workers, janitors, technicians, and operatives in different industries all vary in proportion? It seems most unlikely. This fact is much more supportive of the gift exchange model, with inter-industry wage differentials coming from common rent elements. Alternatively (for consistency with our earlier results), they could come from a technological difference affecting some occupations plus a good-will requirement that the wages of all occupations are affected.

We ought not, however, to be trying to select one theory against another but rather to be seeing just how important different elements are in explaining complex reality. This is done, as always, by regression analysis. We can take the industry wage (standardized for measured ability plus any correlates of unmeasured ability) and regress this on the characteristics of the industry (see Dickens and Katz 1987). The most powerful explanatory variables are the capital–labour ratio, profitability (profits/sales), and union coverage. The first is consistent with a technological approach, the second specifically with gift exchange (or union bargaining), and the third with union bargaining and a threat effect.

Striking evidence of the importance of capital intensity comes from the wage policy of Henry Ford (Raff and Summers 1987; Raff 1988). In 1914 he introduced mass-production assembly lines, which increased the returns to

167

worker discipline. So he raised the wage from \$2 to \$5 a day, attracting a queue of 10,000 job applicants.

Since small firms are less capital-intensive, have lower product-market power, and find it easier to monitor the efforts of workers, it is not surprising that they pay less. Thus, efficiency wages will tend to be a feature of large firms, with smaller firms forming a secondary, market-clearing labour market.

One obvious question is, Do efficiency wages help us to explain the occupational structure of unemployment? The answer is this. Efficiency wages explain why there are job queues: employers find it in their interest to pay workers more than their expected wage outside. This applies at least as much to skilled as to other workers. However, skilled workers can usually get a less skilled job but at a lower wage. Thus in equilibrium we see less unemployment for skilled workers: they simply experience job queues for skilled jobs but not for unskilled. For unskilled workers, however, there may be 'nowhere to go'. When their employers offer them a premium, this implies that their alternative involves either a chance of unemployment or, *if* there is a secondary sector, a job there at a lower wage which they may not be willing to accept.

4. Efficiency wages and the persistence of unemployment

So far we have used efficiency wage theory to explain the stationary equilibrium level of unemployment. We could readily extend it to allow for a secondary market-clearing sector as in Chapter 2: we need simply replace the union wage equation with an efficiency wage mark-up equation like (8). There is no need to repeat the analysis.

The issue we now need to consider is how far efficiency wage theory enables us to explain the dynamic path of non-inflationary unemployment after a shock. The most obvious mechanism is through the effect of unemployment duration on the effectiveness of the unemployed. When a worker's efficiency is affected by labour market tightness, his real concern is with the chance of getting a job. This depends not simply on aggregate unemployment, but also on the effectiveness of the unemployed (c). As we explain in Chapter 5, the dynamics of c will explain persistence.

However, there may be another important mechanism through which efficiency wages can generate persistence after a supply shock. Suppose that efficiency is determined by wages relative to what people 'expect' for themselves, rather than what they forecast others to receive. This 'expected' wage involves a mixture of what people actually forecast for themselves and what they feel entitled to (Layard 1980). Suppose that what people expect for themselves ($\hat{W}_i$) adapts slowly to the experience of actual wages. Then, if productivity falls—or, indeed, if there is any exogenous reduction in available consumption wages, as after an adverse shift in the terms of trade, for example—this can require an awful lot of unemployment to bring expectations ($\hat{W}_i$) into line with what is feasible.[11]

To formalize this in a simple fashion, suppose that output is given by

$$Y_i = \gamma E_i N_i, \tag{16}$$

where γ reflects productivity, although it can also be thought of as capturing terms-of-trade effects. In the light of our previous discussion,

$$E_i = e(W_i/\hat{W}_i, u),$$

where $\hat{W}$ is the 'expected' real wage which adjusts to the prevailing wages via

$$\Delta \log \hat{W}_i = \lambda(\log W_i - \log \hat{W}_i). \tag{17}$$

This firm chooses W_i, N_i to maximize profit, and this yields

$$\kappa e_1(W_i/\hat{W}_i, u) = \hat{W}_i/\gamma, \qquad \kappa e(W_i/\hat{W}_i, u) = (\hat{W}_i/\gamma)(W_i/\hat{W}_i).$$

These follow from (6), (7), setting $\alpha = 1$. Since firms are identical, in aggregate we have

$$\Delta \log \hat{W} = \lambda(\log W - \log \hat{W}), \tag{18}$$

$$\kappa e_1(W/\hat{W}, u) = \hat{W}/\gamma; \qquad \kappa e(W/\hat{W}, u) = (\hat{W}/\gamma)(W/\hat{W}). \tag{19}$$

In the long run, $W/\hat{W}$ will be unity (by (18)). Then (19), with $W = \hat{W}$, determines long-run equilibrium unemployment, u^*, and W/γ. But in the short-run, with $\hat{W}$ predetermined, u and $W/\hat{W}$ are functions of the 'expected' wage relative to productivity ($\hat{W}/\gamma$).

Suppose that, starting from long-run equilibrium, there is an adverse terms-of-trade shock and γ falls. $\hat{W}$ will not at once adjust, so $\hat{W}/\gamma$ rises. It is easy to check that this raises unemployment (see Johnson and Layard 1986). It also reduces $W/\hat{W}$, so $\hat{W}$ starts falling. Eventually, both W and $\hat{W}$ converge on each other at a new reduced level and u returns to its long-run level, u^*. The process is illustrated in Fig. 5.

It is clear that this is a real wage resistance story and illustrates how real wage resistance can arise without unions. What evidence is there for this story? At the micro level Wadhwani and Wall (1990*a*) provide some evidence that, other things being equal, past real wages do have a negative effect on effort. And at the macro level there is the frequent evidence that past wages do have a positive effect on current wages (e.g. Grubb *et al.* 1982, or Chapter 9).

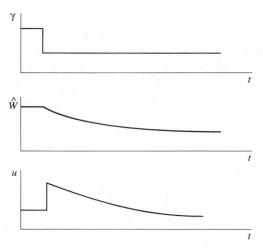

Fig. 5. *Effect of a fall in productivity upon unemployment.*

More generally, the model does seem to give considerable insight into the problems of the 1970s and early 1980s. For in oil-importing countries, the oil shock reduced the level of the feasible real wage, and there was also a fall in the trend growth of total factor productivity. Wage behaviour did not at once adjust fully to this, with the rise in $\hat{W}/\gamma$ causing a rise in the labour share in value added in most countries. This model seems to offer a powerful explanation of the early phases of high and persistent unemployment, and it is firmly based in the notion of the efficiency wage.

5. Summary

We can, as before, state some bald conclusions from this chapter.

1. Personnel management has always involved the use of wages to 'recruit, retain, and motivate' workers. Wages designed for this purpose do not clear the market: they produce job queues.

2. There are many reasons why a firm may gain by paying wages above the market-clearing level: through increased good-will, less malpractice by individual workers, a reduced threat of unionization, lower hiring and training costs, and lower vacancies. When worker effort is difficult to observe, better motivation could not equally well be achieved by the posting of bonds or by steeply sloping earnings profiles. The main reason for this is moral hazard— the risk that the firm will cheat.

3. Much evidence supports the efficiency wage theory. Wages differ between

identical workers in different firms, and these wage differences produce differences in quit rates and application rates and in total factor productivity. The wage differences between industries are rather stable over both time and space, and are positively related to capital intensity, profitability, and unionization. This is because effort is more crucial in capital-intensive industries, and workers expect to be paid more for their efforts when profits are high. Firms that pay high in one occupation pay high in others—since workers' perceptions of the fair wage are influenced by the wages of their colleagues.

4. Efficiency wage theory also helps to explain the persistence of unemployment after a supply shock. Workers base their notion of the 'fair wage' upon what wages have been in the past. If an adverse supply shock reduces productivity, as after the oil price shocks, the 'fair wage' will not fall initially. In consequence, the profit-maximizing wage will rise relative to productivity—thus raising unemployment.

Notes

1. This depends of course on the labour input being characterized by the multiplicative form E_iN_i. The Solow formulation is in Solow (1979), for which Leibenstein (1963) was a precursor.
2. In the wage equation (6), $\partial \log W/\partial u = e_{12}/e_1 - (1-\alpha)e_2/e + (1-\alpha)/(1-u) < 0$ if α is not too small, and in the price equation (7), $\partial \log W/\partial u = \alpha e_2/e + (1-\alpha)/(1-u) > 0$. In any event, note that the price equation slopes upwards more steeply than the wage equation, whatever the value of α.
3. In a more rigorous analysis, we should maximize the discounted value of profits in a dynamic context and then take the steady state. If this is done and the discount rate is low, the steady-state first-order conditions are the same as those for a profit function with the steady state imposed.
4. Strictly, to fit the earlier model, we could write

$$E_i = \left(\frac{W_i}{A} - 1\right)^{\lambda} = (W_i - A)^{\lambda}A^{-\lambda}.$$

   This has the same first-order conditions as the maximand in the text.
5. Also, if $Y_i = E_iN_i$, then in general equilibrium $W = \kappa e = \kappa(\lambda W)^{\lambda}$, so that

$$W = \kappa^{\frac{1}{1-\lambda}}\lambda^{\frac{1}{1-\lambda}}$$

   which increases in λ. This model is taken from Summers (1988).
6. Akerlof's examples raise problems here. They generally relate to measured output being higher than some required level (see Akerlof 1982, 1984). But our interpretation in the text corresponds to what most readers know to be the case either as employees, employers, or both.
7. $e' > 0$ since $E_{EW}dW_i + U_{EE}dE_i = 0$ and $U_{EW} < 0$, $U_{EE} > 0$.
8. For convenience of illustration, we have here used the simplest efficiency wage model in which $E_i = e(W_i)$ rather than $e(W_i/W^e, u)$, since it suffices to make the point. The equilibrium of the system with no relative wage terms would be given by (13) and (14) determining E_i and W_i, and (11) then determining N_i.
9. The standard assumption here is that pay in the firm is less closely related to productivity than it would be outside. This is difficult to rationalize in the context of a representative firm, but could perhaps be handled in a more complex model. Weiss (1980) uses self-employment as the alternative sector, where everyone gets paid his product; but this is totally unrealistic.
10. It is of course possible that higher wages can induce people to do nasty jobs for a limited time, but not for as long as they would do other jobs. In this case higher wages in some jobs could be explained by non-pecuniary factors—with the wage differences insufficient to lead to equal quit rates. This approach requires the relative disamenity of different jobs to vary according to how long the person has been doing them.
11. What follows is based on Johnson and Layard (1986). See also Grubb et al. (1982; sect. 5) for an attempt at empirical implementation. In this account the main event of the 1970s was a fall in the trend *growth* of productivity. The theory offered in the present text can be readily adjusted to handle changes in trend, rather than changes in levels.

172

4

Wage Behaviour: The Evidence

IT is time to review systematically the evidence on wage determination, to see how far it confirms the models we have been developing. The key feature of these models is that wages are *not* set to clear the market. So they all imply that identical individuals can be paid differently for reasons going far beyond mere compensation for differential job amenities. This contrasts starkly with wage determination in a competitive labour market. In this case the wage paid to a given type of worker doing given work would be the same, whatever the employer. In addition, this wage would change in the same way in all firms, reflecting only overall external market conditions. And, excepting compensating differentials, wage changes in a firm would be independent of the internal features of the firm.

Is this what we observe? Are wages for the same type of work equalized in all firms? And, if not, how far does the internal situation in the firm affect them? In this chapter we survey the evidence on what does determine wage levels and wage changes.

We begin in Section 1 with the evidence on individual pay, and highlight in particular the differences between pay in different industries. Then in Section 2 we bring evidence to bear from panel data on the economic position of firms and industries. In the context of a general model of wage formation, we investigate the extent to which wages are determined by 'outside' forces (e.g. unemployment, the outside wage) relative to 'inside' forces (e.g. productivity, union power, the number of insiders). This provides the natural framework for most of what follows.

In Section 3 we look at the characteristics of the firm, since in both union and efficiency-wage stories rent-sharing occurs. We therefore examine the effect on wages of both firm size and product market power. We show how in small firms, with little market power, wages may often be determined entirely by external factors.

We then turn to the effects of unions on wages (Section 4). We examine the evidence on whether unions bargain over employment and then look at the union mark-up and its change over time, taking 1980s Britain as a case-study. In Section 5 we consider the important issue of the impact of unemployment on wages. We look first at what determines the size of the unemployment effect and then we analyse the evidence on dynamics or hysteresis. This leads on to the question of whether the long-term unemployed are less effective, in terms of their impact on wage-bargaining, than the short-term unemployed.

The next issue (Section 6) is the effect of productivity and productivity growth. Do wages grow faster (as newspapers urge they should) in firms or industries where productivity growth is faster? Or is there sufficient pressure from the external market to ensure that wage growth is independent of productivity growth? In Section 7 we investigate the evidence in favour of real wage resistance and ask whether such resistance is permanent or temporary. We also consider the direct impact of benefits on wages.

Finally, the effect of aggregate demand on output depends importantly on the degree of nominal inertia in wages. Some of the evidence is surveyed in Section 8.

1. Is the labour market competitive? Inter-industry evidence

The traditional view of the wage structure derives from Adam Smith's theory of compensating wage differentials:

The whole of the advantages and disadvantages of the different employments of labour and stock must, in the same neighbourhood, be either perfectly equal or continually tending to equality. If in the same neighbourhood, there was any employment evidently either more or less advantageous than the rest, so many people would crowd into it in the one case, and so many would desert it in the other, that its advantages would soon return to the level of the other employments. (Smith 1976)

This basic notion of compensating differentials has nowadays been formalized in theoretical models which allow for heterogeneous jobs as well as heterogeneous labour, so that (provided we assume perfect information and no mobility costs) all workers with the same worker and job characteristics obtain the same wage (S. Rosen 1986).

But this view has, of course, been questioned for many years. Slichter (1950) and Lester (1952) found large pay disparities across apparently similar people and establishments, and these findings were echoed in a later British study (MacKay *et al.* 1971), which used information on 75,000 workers in 66 engineering plants and found wage differentials that were not readily explicable by non-pecuniary factors.

Inter-industry wage differentials

These unexplained differentials have received much attention recently— especially those between industries. Krueger and Summers (1988) estimate standard wage equations using cross-section data on individuals. They use data from the US Current Population Surveys for 1974, 1979, and 1984. Their equations include human capital and demographic controls like education, age, sex, race, union status, marital status, and veteran status. But on top of these, the authors include industry and occupation dummy variables, and find evidence for substantial industry wage differentials (ranging from + 38 per cent in the petroleum industry to − 37 per cent in private household services).

The employment-weighted standard deviation of the industry dummy coefficient was found to be about 15 per cent. The industry variables were found to be relatively important explanatory variables for variations in earnings. For example, adding the industry controls (when all the other variables are already included) led to a fall of 4 percentage points in the standard error of the regression for log wages. This is of the same order as the effect of adding all human capital variables (education, age, tenure) when all other variables are already included.

Of course, even in a competitive labour market such industry wage differentials could, in principle, result from shifts in labour demand associated with less than perfect short-run labour mobility between sectors. However, the differentials appear to be extremely stable over time. Krueger and Summers find that the correlation of the estimated industry wage premia for 1974 and 1984 was 0.97. (It is also interesting that the correlation between crude industry wage differentials for 1984 and the unskilled wages by industry in 1923 is 0.56 (see Chapter 3, Fig. 4).) This makes any explanation based on the short-run immobility of labour exceedingly implausible.

Unobserved labour quality

So the competitive model would have to explain the industry differentials by either unmeasured ability or unmeasured differences in job amenity. We begin with the first of these. Krueger and Summers address the problem of unmeasured labour quality by using longitudinal data, and therefore compare the wages of the same person as he or she switches industry. Provided that unmeasured labour quality is valued equally in different industries, this provides an unbiased estimate of the pure 'industry' effect. For suppose an individual i has constant unmeasured ability A_i and a vector of other characteristics X_i, some of which may vary over time. If he works in industry j in year t he will be paid a log wage (w_{it}) given by

$$w_{it} = \alpha A_i + X_{it}\beta + \sum_j \theta_j D_{ijt} + u_{it}, \tag{1}$$

where D_{ij} is an industry dummy variable which is equal to 1 only if the individual is in that industry (otherwise 0), and θ_j represents the effect on wages of being in industry j. Clearly, a single-period regression, omitting A_i, would lead to biased estimates of the effects of being in a particular industry if industries differ in the unmeasured ability of their workers. However, this problem is eliminated if we can observe the same person in two different periods. Then, assuming that the individual's ability A_i is unchanged, we have

$$\Delta w_{it} = \Delta X_{it}\beta + \sum_j \theta_j \Delta D_{ijt} + \Delta u_{it}. \tag{2}$$

Thus, a regression using changes over time leads to an unbiased estimate of the industry effects.

For this purpose, Krueger and Summers use the matched sample from the Current Population Survey (CPS) which gives data on wages, industry, and other variables for the same workers in two successive Mays. Because there is evidence that many of the reported industry-switchers did not truly switch industry, they report 'measurement-error-corrected estimates'. They then find that the wage-change regression gives essentially similar estimated inter-industry wage differentials to the regression based on wage levels in a single period. In other words, workers moving from high- to low-wage industries were found to experience a wage decrease, while those moving from low- to high-wage industries got a wage increase. Further, these wage changes were similar to the wage differentials estimated using data on wage levels.

However, Murphy and Topel (1987) also use data on wage changes, and find that these indicate much smaller industry wage effects than those obtained using data on wage levels. To be specific, they first estimate $\hat{\theta}_j$ from a wage-level equation (1). They then include in their wage-change equation the difference ($\Delta\hat{\theta}$) between the $\hat{\theta}$ relevant to the individual's final and initial industry. Their wage-change regression is

$$\Delta w_{it} = \Delta X_{it}\beta + \delta\Delta\hat{\theta}_{it} + \Delta u_{it}. \tag{3}$$

If the estimated cross-sectional industry differentials were true industry effects, we should expect $\delta = 1$, whereas the 'ability differences' view implies $\delta = 0$.

Murphy and Topel estimate δ as 0.29 (the OLS estimate is lower at 0.15), and they can reject both the above extreme hypotheses.

Three factors explain why the results are so different from Krueger and Summers. First, the measurement error problem is dealt with by instrumental variables—instrumenting $\Delta\hat{\theta}$ with a variable known to be accurate in their sample (the industry–occupation classification of the individual in the final year). Second, they classify jobs throughout by industry-cum-occupation. Clearly, occupational wage differentials are much more likely to reflect unmeasured ability than industry wage differentials, but that is not the point at issue. Third, they use the March CPS, which records only the annual earnings in the two years being compared, and the individual's current industry and primary industry in the previous year. Thus, the wages are not precisely recorded for the industries to which they purport to relate.

The discussion so far is based on the idea that ability commands the same premium in all industries. But suppose some industries can use ability better than others. These industries will on average attract more able workers and will pay more. Assuming some uncertainty about any individual worker's ability, it is possible that workers who move into high-wage industries are those who are revealed to have high ability. Gibbons and Katz (1989) construct a formal model where inter-industry wage differentials can be entirely explained by unobservable utility differences, and where workers moving from a high-wage industry to a low-wage industry do experience a wage decrease (because they are revealed to have low ability) and vice versa. This illustrates that there are at least two endogeneity problems inherent in first-differenced regressions using longitudinal data—whether a worker changes jobs may be endogenous, as may be the industry of the new job the worker finds.

We may deal with the first of these problems by focusing on people who move for exogenous reasons. For this purpose both Krueger and Summers and Gibbons and Katz (1989) used the 1984 CPS Displaced Workers Survey, which relates to workers who lost a job during 1979–84 as a result of plant closings— so that their job loss was exogenous. Moreover, in these data the ratio of false industry transitions to reported industry transitions is much smaller than in the matched CPS samples. For each worker the survey provides information on current wage and industry as well as pre-displacement wage and industry. Using these longitudinal data on wage changes, Krueger and Summers find similar industry effects to those obtained from the cross section analysis of wage levels. Gibbons and Katz use equation (3) to estimate δ and find it to be between 0.63 and 0.88.

So industry-switchers were found to experience wage changes of nearly the same size as the industry wage differences estimated from cross-section data. However, these longitudinal estimates still fail to deal with the endogeneity bias caused by the choice of the new industry of the displaced worker.[1] This can be investigated by examining whether the change in wage when an individual moves from industry i to industry j is the same size (in absolute terms) as when an individual moves from j to i. Krueger and Summers investigated this issue and found no significant differences, which suggests that the endogeneity issue need not worry us greatly.

Compensating differentials

A second possible explanation for the industry differentials is that they may exist as a way of compensating employees for non-wage aspects of the industry. Krueger and Summers add various controls for working conditions to their cross-section equation. These include hours, health hazards on the job (two dummies), shift work (two dummies), commuting time, two variables indicating the extent of choice of overtime, and two variables indicating whether the physical work conditions are pleasant. On including these, Krueger and Summers find that their new estimates of inter-industry wage structure are highly correlated with their previous estimates, and that, if anything, the standard deviation of wage differentials *rises* after the addition of controls for working conditions, suggesting that industry net wages may be less equal than gross wages.[2] Of course, attempting to estimate the effects of working conditions on wages without appropriate controls for ability is an extremely dangerous exercise, for more capable workers are more likely to take jobs with better working conditions. (Income effects imply that workers with greater earning capacity will 'spend' some of it on better working conditions.) Consequently, the coefficient on 'bad' working conditions in a cross-section wage equation will be biased downwards, and this may explain why studies based on cross-section data have been unable to document compensating differentials for many obvious job attributes.

Ideally, therefore, one should estimate the equation for wage changes, having also included information on the change in working conditions. Brown (1980) represents an early attempt to use longitudinal data in this area. However, he too finds that some of the coefficients on job characteristics that might be expected to generate equalizing differences in wage rates are wrong-signed or insignificant. Following this, Duncan and Holmlund (1983) argue that measures of working conditions can be rather inaccurate, for they often assign the *average* occupational or industrial characteristic to individual respondents. Instead, Duncan and Holmlund use self-reported changes in working conditions. They do find that an index of dangerous working conditions is associated with a compensating differential in the change formulation, but not in the level formulation. Unfortunately, however, they did not test for the existence of pure industry wage effects.

The evidence so far suggests that there exist wage differences that cannot be explained by an appeal to compensating differentials.

Indirect evidence on compensating differentials

This view is supported by the relationship between wages on the one hand, and quit rates and job queues on the other. If industry wage premia do reflect equalizing differences, they should not be associated with lower quits, which is what Pencavel (1972) and Krueger and Summers find. Thus, quitting behaviour is consistent with the view that industry wage premia reflect rents to 'good' jobs.[3]

Alternatively, one might use job applications data to test for the existence of rents in the labour market. Holzer *et al.* (1988) detect a weak, positive relationship between job application rates and industry wage premia. This may be consistent with either the existence of rents or the possibility that unqualified applicants apply for high-wage jobs (which also require greater skills) because, given that employers cannot observe skills accurately, there must be a non-zero probability of obtaining the job.

The occupational structure of industry wage premia

Further evidence on the existence of rents comes from the remarkable fact that industries paying well in one occupation also pay well in others. In a competitive market it would be easy to see why workers on oil platforms get rewarded for the fact that their work is dangerous; however, there is no reason for clerical workers in a petroleum company to be paid more than the prevailing average wage for clerical workers. Yet Dickens and Katz (1987) found that, if one occupational group in an industry was highly paid, then all categories of workers in that industry tended to be highly paid. It is extremely difficult to explain this finding in terms of arguments relating to unobserved ability or compensating differentials, for relative skill requirements and working conditions are likely to vary significantly between different occupations in any given industry.

International evidence on inter-industry wage differentials

Several studies have found a high rank correlation in industry wages among developed capitalist economies. Table 1 documents correlations between industry wages in a variety of countries. In the main, the correlations are quite high (largely in the 0.7–0.9 range), and it is primarily the closed, command economies (e.g. USSR, Poland) and the developing countries (Bolivia, Mexico) whose wage structures differ somewhat from those prevailing in the developed, capitalist economies. Since these data do not control for other personal

Table 1 *Correlations of log manufacturing wages among countries, 1982*

	Canada	France	Japan	USA	Germany	USSR	UK	Bolivia
Canada	1.00	0.85	0.82	0.92	0.83	0.41	0.88	0.43
France		1.00	0.95	0.90	0.87	0.71	0.93	0.45
Japan			1.00	0.89	0.86	0.84	0.93	0.59
USA				1.00	0.85	0.33	0.95	0.51
Germany					1.00	0.78	0.90	0.49
USSR						1.00	0.81	0.34
UK							1.00	0.56
Bolivia								1.00
Yugoslavia								
Norway								
Mexico								
Sweden								
Korea								
Poland								

	Yugo-slavia	Norway	Mexico	Sweden	Korea	Poland
Canada	0.61	0.67	0.55	0.79	0.75	0.45
France	0.84	0.80	0.52	0.84	0.81	0.47
Japan	0.88	0.80	0.58	0.81	0.82	0.65
USA	0.79	0.67	0.81	0.82	0.86	0.70
Germany	0.77	0.74	0.51	0.84	0.87	0.50
USSR	0.63	0.47	0.57	0.54	0.41	0.64
UK	0.75	0.70	0.74	0.83	0.84	0.63
Bolivia	0.43	0.41	0.54	0.45	0.40	0.46
Yugoslavia	1.00	0.65	0.44	0.78	0.75	0.50
Norway		1.00	0.33	0.74	0.65	0.38
Mexico			1.00	0.46	0.43	0.23
Sweden				1.00	0.82	0.47
Korea					1.00	0.43
Poland						1.00

Source: Krueger and Summers (1987).

characteristics, they have no clear implications for the validity of the competitive model, but they confirm that institutional differences are not the main cause of inter-industry wage differences.

To sum up, while it is difficult ever to refute a hypothesis, it is hard to explain many aspects of the inter-industry wage structure in terms of a competitive model of the labour market. We need, therefore, to determine why firm-specific factors are at work in generating non-compensating wage differentials.

2. The effect of outside and inside factors

We begin with a quite general approach in which we examine how far firm-specific factors do influence the wages that firms pay. The view that wages reflect both inside and outside forces receives considerable support from survey evidence. For example, the Confederation of British Industry's Databank Survey annually asks its 1200 respondents about the factors that may have affected the most recent settlement. Some responses are in Table 2. Several external forces, including comparisons with other employees in the same company/industry/locality and comparisons with pay increases nationally, are seen to be important. In addition, internal considerations like profitability and the risk of redundancy also appear to be extremely influential in determining pay settlements. We have already discussed theoretical models which are consistent with these findings: here we just reiterate them in a form that is amenable to econometric analysis.

A union model with insiders

The model here is the same as that in Chapter 2 (Section 2). We show there (equation (12)) that the bargain over wages yields the following outcome for the ith firm:

$$\frac{W_i - A}{W_i} = \frac{1 - \alpha\kappa}{\varepsilon_{SN}(W_i) + \alpha\kappa/\beta}, \qquad (4)$$

where W_i is the wage, A is the expected income of a worker who loses his job in the firm, ε_{SN} is the elasticity of job security (or the survival probability) with respect to expected employment, β is a measure of union power, α is the labour exponent in the production function, and κ is a measure of product-market competitiveness ($\kappa = 1 - 1/\eta$, where η is the product demand elasticity). Furthermore, ε_{SN} can be written as

$$\varepsilon_{SN} = \varepsilon_{SN}(N_{Ii}/N_i^e(W_i)), \qquad N_i^e(W_i) = K_i(W_i/\alpha\kappa P_i^e)^{-1/(1-\alpha)} \qquad (5)$$

181

Table 2 *Factors influencing pay settlements: percentage of respondents citing the factor as 'very important*[a]*', Britain*

	1979/80	1980/1	1981/2	1982/3	1983/4
Factors exerting an upward pressure on level of pay settlements					
Level of establishment/company profits	11	11	16	19	21
Management able to pass on substantial part of pay increase in prices	6	4	3	4	4
A need to improve ability to recruit/retain labour	22	7	6	5	9
Cost-of-living increases	60	47	45	36	40
Industrial action threatened	2	2	2	1	3
Industrial action taken	3	2	1	2	2
Factors exerting downward pressure on level of pay settlements					
Level of establishment/company profits	45	62	60	53	45
Management unable to pass on a substantial part of any pay increase in prices	38	56	52	52	51
Risk of redundancy if large pay increase awarded	20	43	35	27	21
Other[b]	2	6	3	4	3
Other factors influencing level of settlement					
Comparisons with other employees in same company	24	23	23	24	21
Comparisons with other employees in same industry	21	12	13	15	17
Comparisons with other employees in locality	27	17	15	14	18
Comparisons with general level of pay and/or pay increases nationally	26	16	16	18	19
Repercussions of national/district agreement negotiated by an employer organization to which you are a party	16	10	10	10	9
Repercussions of national/district agreement negotiated by an employer organization to which you are not a party but nevertheless follow	6	4	4	2	3

[a] Numbers are based on firms that belong to the CBI Databank.

[b] Question labelled 'Other' has changed over the period. In 1979/80 it dealt with the impact of direct tax cuts; in 1980/1 with that of government exhortation, and in 1981/2, 1982/3, and 1983/4 with that of employee involvement policies.

Source: Gregory *et al.* (1985).

(these equations being based on Chapter 2, equations (5a) and (10)), where N_{Ii} is the size of the group of workers engaged in the wage-bargain (insiders), N_i^e is expected employment, and P_i^e is the expected price of output.

In this context, we shall define A in a slightly more general way than in Chapter 2; that is,

$$A = W^e[1 - \varphi(u, z_s)] + B\varphi(u, z_s), \tag{6}$$

where φ reflects the probability of a displaced worker not gaining employment elsewhere, W^e is the expected outside wage, and B is the benefit level. φ is increasing in aggregate unemployment (u). The variable z_s reflects all factors that raise the chances of a displaced worker obtaining alternative employment *at given levels of u*. These include anything that generates less competition for jobs from the existing unemployed. For our purposes in this chapter, the key variable is the proportion of long-term unemployed in the unemployment pool. If the long-term unemployed are less active in searching for work or are less attractive to employers, then an increase in the long-term proportion will obviously reduce the competition for jobs and raise the probability of a displaced worker gaining alternative employment. (See Chapter 5 for extensive analysis and evidence on this issue.) This discussion indicates that

$$\varphi_1 = \partial\varphi/\partial u > 0, \qquad \varphi_2 = \partial\varphi/\partial z_s < 0. \tag{7}$$

On the basis of (4), (5), and (6), we can look explicitly at the impact of all the relevant variables on firm-level wages, by computing log differentials. Taking the lower-case letters, w, p, k, n, as logs, we have

$$\mathrm{d}w_i = \lambda_i[\mathrm{d}p_i^e + (1 - \alpha)(\mathrm{d}k_i - \mathrm{d}n_{Ii})]$$

$$+ (1 - \lambda_i)\left(\mathrm{d}w^e - \frac{\varphi_1(1 - b)}{1 - \varphi(1 - b)}\mathrm{d}u - \frac{\varphi_2(1 - b)}{1 - \varphi(1 - b)}\mathrm{d}z_s\right.$$

$$\left. + \frac{\varphi}{1 - \varphi(1 - b)}\mathrm{d}b\right) + \frac{\alpha\kappa(1 - \alpha\kappa)}{\lambda_d(\beta\varepsilon_{SN} + \alpha\kappa)^2}\mathrm{d}\beta, \tag{8}$$

where b is the benefit replacement ratio B/W^e, λ_i is given by

$$\lambda_i = \frac{(1 - \alpha\kappa)N_I\varepsilon_{SN}'}{(\varepsilon_{SN} + \alpha\kappa/\beta)^2(1 - \alpha)N^e}\left(\frac{W^e}{W}[1 - \varphi(1 - b)] + \frac{(1 - \alpha\kappa)N_I\varepsilon_{SN}'}{(\varepsilon_{SN} + \alpha\kappa/\beta)^2(1 - \alpha)N^e}\right)^{-1}, \tag{9}$$

and λ_d is the denominator of λ_i, which is positive. Note also that $0 \leqslant \lambda_i < 1$.

This equation is the foundation for our analysis of the empirical evidence. Wages are a weighted sum of the firm-specific or 'inside' factors (notably price, p_i^e, and a measure of productivity, $k_i - n_{Ii}$) and the outside factors (w^e, u, z, b), with union power β generating an additional term. The parameter λ_i may thus be termed the 'insider weight'. This equation is, however, based on a particular union bargaining model, and we must also consider what happens with non-union wage determination.

Non-union wage models

It is widely believed in the literature that internal factors may affect wages in non-union settings as well (see e.g. Blanchard and Summers 1986). Before explaining why, we must note that the internal factors that we are concentrating on (productivity, price) do not lead to a rise in a firm's wages in the standard efficiency wage model. In this case wages are determined by the 'Solow condition' that the effort–wage elasticity is unity, and only variables that influence a worker's effort affect wages. So, if a firm's revenue function is of the form $\Phi_i R(E_i N_i, K_i)$ where e is effort, N is employment, Φ_i reflects factors that shift the revenue function like technical progress or demand, and z are a set of market factors that influence effort (e.g. unemployment), then wages are only a function of W^e and z, and Φ_i, K_i have no role to play. Of course, if the revenue function takes the more general form $\Phi_i R(N_i, E_i, K_i)$, then wages will depend on Φ_i, but in general the sign is ambiguous.

However, suppose we have an efficiency-wage model of the turnover type (see Chapter 3, Section 1) but explicitly taking account of vacancies. Wages are then set to influence accessions in order to ensure that the firm operates as near to full capacity as possible. In this case we have a wage model which has a structure almost identical to equation (8).[4] To be more explicit, suppose we have fixed coefficients, *ex post*. So if the firm has capital stock, K_i, then the number of available job slots, N_i^*, is given by

$$N_i^* = K_i v, \tag{10}$$

where v is constant for purposes of wage determination but varies through time. Assume next that we have a production function of the form

$$Y_i = N_i (K_i / N_i^*)^{1-\alpha} \qquad (N_i \leqslant N_i^*). \tag{11}$$

We can thus define the number of vacancies as $(N_i^* - N_i)$, each vacancy reflecting an unfilled job slot. (For a full discussion of vacancies, see Chapter 5.) If we now have an accessions function $a(W_i/A)$, $a' > 0$, which captures the flow of accessions per vacancy, then employment must satisfy

$$N_{it} - N_{it-1} = a(W_{it}/A_t)(N_i^* - N_{it}) - sN_{it}, \tag{12}$$

where s is the fixed separation rate. Note that A is again given by (6).

Within this framework, we show in Annex 4.1 that, if the firm sets wages and employment, then wages will satisfy

$$dw_i = \lambda_i[dp_i^e + (1 - \alpha)(dk_i - dn_i^*)] + (1 - \lambda_i)$$

$$\times \left(dw^e - \frac{\varphi_1(1 - b)}{1 - \varphi(1 - b)}du - \frac{\varphi_2(1 - b)}{1 - \varphi(1 - b)}dz_s + \frac{\varphi}{1 - \varphi(1 - b)}db \right), (13)$$

where in this case the weight (λ_i) is given by

$$\lambda_i = \left(1 + \frac{a\eta_a}{s(1 + \eta_a) + r + a} \right)^{-1}, \qquad (0 < \lambda_i < 1), \qquad (14)$$

r being the discount rate and $\eta_a = a'W_i/aA$, the accessions elasticity.

The form of equation (13) is almost identical to that generated by the union model in equation (8). There are only two notable differences. In the union model, we have the capital stock normalized on the number of 'insiders', N_{Ii}, whereas in the non-union model it is normalized on N_i^*, the exogenous number of available job slots. Second, there is, of course, no union power term in the non-union model.

The insider weight (λ) and the form of the wage equation

Returning to the union model, on the basis of (8) we can write a firm-specific log-linear wage equation of the form

$$w_i = c_0 + \lambda_i[p_i^e + (1 - \alpha)(k_i - n_{Ii})] + (1 - \lambda_i)(w^e - c_1u + c_2z_s + c_3b) + c_4\beta, \quad (15)$$

where

$c_1 = \varphi_1(1 - b)/[1 - \varphi(1 - b)] > 0,$

$c_2 = -\varphi_2(1 - b)/[1 - \varphi(1 - b)] > 0,$

$c_3 = \varphi/[1 - \varphi(1 - b)] > 0,$

$c_4 = \alpha\kappa(1 - \alpha\kappa)/\lambda_d(\beta\varepsilon_{SN} + \alpha\kappa)^2 > 0.$

The non-union model based on (13) is identical except that n_{Ii} is replaced by n_i^* and the union power term (β) is missing. It is also worth noting the form of the aggregate wage equation, which, assuming identical firms, may be written as

$$w - p = \frac{c_0}{\lambda} - \frac{1 - \lambda}{\lambda}c_1u - (p - p^e) - \frac{1 - \lambda}{\lambda}(w - w^e) + (1 - \alpha)(k - n_I)$$

$$+ \frac{1 - \lambda}{\lambda}c_2z_s + \frac{1 - \lambda}{\lambda}c_3b + \frac{c_4}{\lambda}\beta. \qquad (16)$$

Equations (15) and (16) provide us with a general framework for analysing wages at the micro and macro levels. We can thus expect aggregate (real) wages to be influenced by unemployment (u, negative), price and wage surprises, which are essentially nominal inertia effects ($p - p^e$, $w - w^e$, negative), some measure of trend productivity (positive),[5] the number of insiders (n_I, negative), factors that raise the chances of an unemployed entrant being offered a job (z_s, positive), the benefit replacement ratio (b, positive), and union power (β, positive). The only obvious missing effects are those arising from real wage resistance. In Chapter 2 (Section 2) we saw that real wage resistance effects do not arise in the union bargaining model, where individual utility depends only on the level of real wages, and this is the foundation of equations (15) and (16). However, once we allow individual utility to depend on *changes* in real wages as well, then real wage resistance becomes an important feature of wage determination which must be considered in any empirical analysis. (See Chapter 2 (Section 2) and also Chapter 3 (Section 4) for a model of real wage resistance in the efficiency wage context.)

It is clear from both (15) and (16) that the weight attached to 'inside' or firm-specific factors (λ_i) plays a key role in the structure of wage equations. At the micro level, λ_i reflects the extent to which wages at the firm level adjust to actual or prospective company performance. Furthermore, the adjustment tends to be in the direction of employment stabilization. Thus, when output prices or the capital stock shift, wages shift in the same direction. This tends to counter the natural movement of employment. This type of wage 'flexibility' in response to firm-specific factors is often thought of as being a desirable property of wage formation. It is, however, non-competitive in the long run; for, of course, in a competitive labour market firm-specific factors have no role to play. Finally, at the aggregate level, it is worth noting that the coefficient on unemployment is decreasing in λ.

Given the importance of the λ parameter, it is worth seeing what we can say about its determinants. If we look at the definition given in equation (9), we find two very interesting results: namely that λ is increasing in union power (β), and that it is decreasing in the degree of product-market competition (κ). We now turn to the evidence on the form of the micro-wage equation and the size of λ.

Evidence on the insider weight (λ) and inside factors

The fact that a firm's wages are influenced by firm-specific factors such as output prices and productivity comes as no surprise to managers. As we have seen in Table 2, when they are asked, they always note productivity/profitability as a key factor in wage-setting. This is true for manual and non-manual, union and non-union workers alike, as Blanchflower and Oswald (1988*a*) demonstrate (see Table 3).

These results are confirmed in a number of econometric studies at both firm and industry level. Thus, Nickell and Wadhwani (1990*b*) estimate a firm-level equation based on (15), using data on a panel of 219 UK quoted companies, and find a significant role not only for own price and productivity but also for measures of the financial health of the company. Similar results are obtained by Brunello and Wadhwani (1989) and Brunello (1990) for a sample of large Japanese manufacturing companies. Related results along the same lines are reported in M. Gregory *et al.* (1987), using the Confederation of British Industries (CBI) Pay Data Bank, and in Blanchflower *et al.* (1990) on a large cross-section of British establishments.

Table 3 *Factors influencing the level of pay in the most recent settlement,*[a] *Britain (%)*

	Manual workers		Non-manual workers	
	Union sector[b]	Non-union sector	Union sector[b]	Non-union sector
All establishment could afford	11	5	9	7
Increasing cost of living	34	29	37	32
Going rate in industry	15	23	13	19
Merit/individual performance	4	20	5	33
Published norms	3	2	3	4
Internal pay structure	2	3	6	15
External pay structure	15	15	9	11
Government regulation	6	3	10	2
Strikes	1	0	0	0
Profitability/productivity	34	35	37	38
Economic climate	9	2	13	3
Other	13	7	15	6
Not answered	8	3	11	1
No. of establishments (= 100%)	488	613	356	904

[a] Question asked was, 'What factors influenced the level of pay decided upon in the most recent settlement?'

[b] Union status of establishment based on whether or not unions were recognized at the workplace for purposes of bargaining.

Source: 1984 Workplace Industrial Relations Survey, from Blanchflower and Oswald (1988*a*).

At the industry level, Nickell and Kong (1988) present evidence for a number of British manufacturing industries, and Holmlund and Zetterberg (1989) do the same for a panel of industries from Sweden, Norway, Finland, West Germany, and the USA. These studies are again based on equation (15) and illustrate the importance of industry-specific factors for the non-Scandinavian countries. In a related study, Freeman and Katz (1987) use a panel of US industries and report that wage changes are linked to changes in sales.

Overall, therefore, we have a number of studies that indicate that wages at the firm level can usefully be thought of as being influenced by firm-specific or 'inside' factors as well as by outside or market-based variables which are familiar from competitive explanations of wage determination. The next step is to see what can be said about the weight attached to these firm-specific factors (λ_i). In Table 4 we list the point estimates obtained in various countries, usually from the manufacturing sector. The pattern of results here is quite striking. In Scandinavia the insider weight is zero, a result that is surely related to the centralization of wage-bargaining in those countries.[6] In the UK and Germany λ is small but significant, whereas in both the USA and in large Japanese firms it is substantial. This evidence of wage 'flexibility' at the firm level is to be expected in Japan, which has very stable employment in large firms, but in the USA, where employment is rather flexible, it is perhaps more surprising. However, it is consistent with the results reported in Bell and Freeman (1985) and Freeman and Katz (1987). Finally, the very large value of λ evident in China reflects the impact of the reforms in the early 1980s (which encouraged enterprises to pay wages related to performance), allied to the almost complete absence of a labour 'market' of the type found in the OECD countries.

What evidence do we have on the determinants of λ? In our theoretical

Table 4 *Estimates of λ, the weight attached to firm-specific factors in wage determination*

	λ	Source
Germany	0.10	Holmlund and Zetterberg (1989)
UK	0.08–0.15	Nickell and Wadhwani (1990*b*)
USA	0.30	Holmlund and Zetterberg (1989)
Japan (large firms)	0.33	Brunello and Wadhwani (1989)
Finland	0	Holmlund and Zetterberg (1989)
Norway	0.03	Holmlund and Zetterberg (1989)
Sweden	0.04	Holmlund and Zetterberg (1989)
China	0.60–0.75	Hay and Liu (1990)

discussion we note that λ should be increasing in union power, and decreasing in the degree of product-market competition. The evidence on union power is mixed. Nickell and Wadhwani (1990*b*) find no effect of union coverage on λ. On the other hand, Nickell and Kong (1988) find that industries with more powerful unions have higher levels of λ. This latter result is not, however, reflected in the numbers reported in Table 3, where the impact of productivity or profitability on wages is the same in both union and non-union establishments. Furthermore, the Scandinavian countries all have powerful unions and no detectable insider effects. This latter result, along with the inconclusive evidence previously noted, suggests that perhaps the distinction is not between union and non-union firms, but between decentralized union–firm bargains and the rest. It may be in the presence of these decentralized bargains that high levels of λ are observed. This fits in with both the Scandinavian and US evidence.[7]

Turning to the evidence on the relationship between product-market structure and λ, we do not have much to go on. Nickell and Kong (1988) find that industries with higher levels of concentration tend to have higher values of λ (controlling for union power). Brunello and Wadhwani (1989) look at the distinction between small and large firms, and find that the insider weight is consistently greater in large firms, both in the UK and in Japan. Finally, there is some evidence to suggest that firms with greater product-market power are more likely to have decentralized (as opposed to industry-wide) wage-bargaining.

To summarize, there is a considerable body of evidence that firm-specific or inside factors are important in wage determination, and that the degree to which they are important varies systematically across countries. There is weaker evidence that inside factors are less important when bargaining is centralized or when product markets are more competitive. In the next section we shall consider more generally the relationship between product-market characteristics and wages. In subsequent sections we look at various specific key issues in the light of the general framework encapsulated by equation (15).

3. The effect of the characteristics of the firm

It is much easier for workers to obtain higher wages if there are rents or quasi-rents which they can lay their hands on. This means there must be product-market power and/or sufficient installed capital. In this section we focus on characteristics of the firm, including size and product-market power.

Chapter 4

Firm size and wages

We begin with the simple evidence that larger firms pay higher wages, and then ask why this should be. There is evidence dating back to at least Lester (1967) that 'large' employers pay more than 'small' employers, even after including all the standard controls. Brown and Medoff (1989) argue that, even after they include most observable controls for differences in labour quality, an employee working at an establishment with employment one standard deviation above average earns 6–15 per cent more than a similar employee at a location one standard deviation below average. There is also some evidence of a company-size effect that is additional to the establishment-size effect. Further, the size effect is present in the wages of most kinds of workers.

Much of the discussion on whether or not this employer-size effect on wages is consistent with a competitive labour market parallels that regarding inter-industry wage differences (see Section 2). Thus, one obvious possibility is that larger firms employ workers of better (unobserved) quality. Brown and Medoff (1989) report some results based on longitudinal data. They find that the wage differential by size, when estimated using longitudinal data, ranges from 55 to 95 per cent of that estimated using cross-section data. So, as in the case of inter-industry wage differences, provided that unobserved ability is valued equally in large and small firms, the size wage-differential cannot be explained mainly by an appeal to unobserved ability. Moreover, the observation that workers of all kinds benefit from the differential does undermine the explanation based on unobserved ability differences, since it is unlikely that all the occupations at a large firm will require the greater ability.

A second obvious possible explanation for the size wage-differential is differences in working conditions. Brown and Medoff (1989) included detailed industry and occupation controls (which should capture at least some of the variation in working conditions), but find the differential to be largely unaffected. They also experiment with including various direct controls for working conditions, but they find that, if anything, the estimated differential rises. If differences in working conditions are to explain the wage differential, we would require working conditions to be worse in large firms. Unsurprisingly, Brown and Medoff (1989) discover that there is a significant negative relationship between good job characteristics and establishment size in only 4 of the 42 job characteristics variables that they experiment with. Further, they find that employees in large firms are less likely to quit, which is consistent with the view that employer-size wage premia reflect rents to good jobs (though also with other explanations).

It is sometimes argued (e.g. Freeman and Medoff 1984) that one reason for the size wage-differential is that large firms are more likely to follow union-avoidance policies (which, among other things, involves paying higher wages). But Brown and Medoff (1989) show that there are size wage-effects for workers that are already unionized, so union-avoidance efforts cannot be the only reason for size wage-differentials.

Another commonly offered explanation for size wage-differentials is that large firms might find it more difficult to monitor their workers. In the setting of the efficiency-wage model, this would lead to larger firms paying higher wages. However, Brown and Medoff (1989) report that the size wage-premium is, if anything, higher for piece-rate workers than for standard-rate workers. Since monitoring difficulties should be largely absent among piece-rate workers, this does make an explanation of the size wage-premium based on monitoring costs less plausible.

This does not, though, rule out all efficiency-wage-based explanations. There is considerable evidence that firms with a large share of the product market tend to be more profitable. Other things being equal, larger firms are more likely to have a higher market share, and hence to be more profitable. If 'fair' wages have important motivating effects, profitable firms may find that it pays them to offer higher wages. The above provides some evidence for the most obvious explanation of why large firms pay more: they have greater product-market power, which means that there are higher rents for unions (workers) to get their hands on.

Product-market power and wages

In terms of the evidence, both Pugel (1980) for the USA and Carruth and Oswald (1989) for the UK show the link between wages and profits. But other authors have tried to model product-market power directly. While some early studies detect such a link between wages and the industry concentration ratio, the relationship does not seem particularly robust to the inclusion of detailed labour quality controls (Dickens and Katz 1987). However, it is not obvious that the concentration ratio for the *industry* in which a firm operates is an appropriate measure of the *firm*'s market power. Instead, it is the individual firm's market share that has a positive impact on its profitability, and not the extent of concentration in the industry in which it operates (e.g. Ravenscraft 1983, or Schmalensee 1989: stylized fact 4.11). To reflect whether the firm was one of the large or small firms in its market, Stewart (1990) uses data from the UK Workplace Industrial Relations Survey which includes the response of management to a question about the number of competitors faced by the firm. The author divides the sample into two categories: the 'competitive' sector (if the manager said that his firm had many competitors), and the sector with market power (if the market was dominated by the organization, or if there were fewer than five competitors). He then finds that, among establishments in the competitive sector, there is no significant union–non-union wage differential unless there is both high union coverage in the industry and a closed shop. In his sample, only 4 per cent of establishments facing competitive conditions satisfied these requirements. By contrast, there are significant union–non-union differentials in firms with market power.[8]

An alternative way to study the effects of product-market power on wages is to examine the effects of changes in government regulation. Rose (1987) examines the effects of the trucking regulatory reforms of the late 1970s and early 1980s in the USA. The US trucking industry had been regulated since 1935. These regulations included stringent entry controls and collective rate-making. There was evidence documenting the existence of monopoly profits in the industry. Deregulation led to entry of new firms, expansion of existing firms, and greater price competition. Rose finds that between 1979 and 1985 there was a decline of approximately 40 per cent in the size of the union wage differential in trucking. This is consistent with considerable rent-sharing by the union workers.

However, deregulation does not always appear to be accompanied by significant wage reductions. Card (1989) finds that there was no significant decline in the relative earnings of airline employees after deregulation. This finding could have several possible explanations. First, it may be that non-price competition had already dissipated potential regulatory rents and thus, because firms did not earn substantial rents under regulation, there would be no reason to expect a relative decline in airline industry wages. Second, it could be argued that the deregulation did not, in the end, reduce the market power of airline firms. So the evidence from airline deregulation is of a rather inconclusive character. However, overall, we conclude that product-market power does affect the level of wages.

Capital intensity

Finally, we should note the clear evidence that wages are higher in firms that are more capital-intensive (e.g. Krueger and Summers 1988). This must reflect at least two forces at work. First, there are more quasi-rents to be exploited. But, second, the importance of having the work well done may be greater, so that firms paying efficiency wages have an incentive to pay more. This is related to the issue of wage changes and productivity growth which we discuss in Section 6.

4.   The effect of unions

This section is mainly devoted to the impact of unions on wages, but before getting down to this question we first discuss some of the empirical work on the issue of bargaining over employment.

Bargaining over employment?

In Chapter 2, we noted a number of reasons why we consider bargaining over employment in general, and 'efficient' bargaining in particular, to be unimportant, both in theory (Section 3) and in practice (Section 1). There have, however, been numerous econometric studies which investigate this issue (Brown and Ashenfelter 1986, MaCurdy and Pencavel 1986, and Card 1986, 1988, on US data; and Carruth *et al.* 1986, Alogoskoufis and Manning 1991, Bean and Turnbull 1988, Andrews and Harrison 1989, and Nickell and Wadhwani 1990*a* on UK data). These have typically been based on the fixed-membership (greater-than-employment) union objective, which we feel to be inappropriate for the reasons discussed in Chapter 2 (Section 3). However, it is worth briefly discussing the results of these studies taken at face value, for they raise a number of interesting issues.

Many of the earlier studies are based on an investigation of the appearance of outside labour market variables in the labour demand curve. The idea here is that if we have Nash bargaining, and if the union and firm contributions to the Nash objective are of the form

$$V_i - \bar{V} = (W_i - A)N_i^{\gamma}, \qquad \Pi_i - \bar{\Pi} = R(N_i) - W_iN_i,$$

then the contract curve has the form

$$R'(N_i) = (1 - \gamma)W_i + \gamma A.$$

(The notation here is the same as that used in Chapter 2, so R is real revenue and A is the expected outside wage.) Comparing the contract curve with the labour demand curve,

$$R'(N_i) = W_i,$$

we see that the appearance of A in the former is the distinguishing feature.

Three points may be noted about this method of attacking the problem. If the labour demand curve is treated as a special case of the contract curve, the hypothesis to investigate is $\gamma = 0$. But this is simply the hypothesis that unions do not care about employment—not quite what we are interested in, as Andrews and Harrison (1989) point out. The problem here is that the contract curve should not be taken as the maintained hypothesis. In fact, as we shall see later, efficient bargaining and 'right-to-manage' bargaining, where the employer sets employment, are non-nested hypotheses and neither is a special case of the other. The hypothesis $\gamma = 0$ is merely the condition that makes the contract curve coincident with the labour demand curve, which is not the hypothesis of interest.

A second point worth noting is that, if the union contribution to the Nash bargain takes the form $N_i^{\gamma_1}(W_i/A)^{\gamma_2}$, then the contract curve is

$$R'(N_i) = (1 - \gamma_1/\gamma_2)W_i.$$

So here we have an example where A does not enter the contract curve. The third point is that, if there are efficiency wages, so that revenue has the form $R[e(W_i/A)N]$, where e is the effort function, the labour demand curve does include outside labour market variables. Thus, as Bean and Turnbull (1988) note, we can have efficient bargaining with outside wages absent from the contract curve and right-to-manage bargaining with outside wages appearing in the labour demand curve. So, while most of the above studies find some role for outside wages in determining employment, it is not clear what this fact signifies.

If we wish to proceed with this type of investigation, it is clear, as both Andrews and Harrison (1989) and Alogoskoufis and Manning (1991) recognize, that the two hypotheses of interest must be nested within a more general model. The obvious such model is that suggested in Manning (1987), where we allow two stages of bargaining of the form:

2nd stage: $\max_{N_i}[N_i^{\gamma}(W_i - A)]^{\beta_n}[R(eN_i) - W_iN_i]$ given W_i,

            solution: $N(W_i, A, \beta_n)$

1st stage: $\max_{W_i}\{[N(W_i, A, \beta_n)]^{\gamma}(W_i - A)\}^{\beta_w}\{R[eN(W_i, A, \beta_n)] - W_iN(W_i, A, \beta_n)\}$.

In this model, β_w reflects the power of the union in the wage bargain, β_n the power of the union in the employment bargain. Efficient bargaining then corresponds to the restriction $\beta_w = \beta_n$, and right-to-manage bargaining corresponds to the restriction $\beta_n = 0$. The two restrictions are clearly not nested. In Annex 2 we demonstrate the following facts. (*a*) The absence of efficiency-wage considerations ($e = 1$) imposes no obvious restrictions on the wage and employment equations generated by this model. (*b*) In the presence of efficiency wages, one cannot discriminate, in general, between efficient and right-to-manage bargaining. (*c*) If one asserts, *a priori*, that efficiency wages are absent, then one can discriminate between efficient and right-to-manage bargaining.

In the light of these facts, it is clear that any attempt to investigate bargaining structures by studying wage and employment patterns is fraught with difficulty. One approach, which seems promising, is to argue that, because union wages are set at discrete intervals whereas employment is adjusted continuously, we might assert that wages are predetermined in the solution to the second-stage bargain given above ($N_i = N(W_i, A, \beta_n)$). Card (1988) and Nickell and Wadhwani (1990a) pursue this approach, with the results of the latter coming down slightly in favour of efficiency wages.

The union–non-union mark-up

We turn now to the effect of unions on wages. In the standard bargaining model, unions raise wages and the union–non-union mark-up affects how much unemployment results from unions' actions.

There is an enormous number of estimates of union relative wage effects (see Lewis 1986, and the references therein). Conceptually, we wish to estimate

$$\text{mark-up} = \frac{W_i^U - W_i^N}{W_i^N}, \tag{17}$$

where W_i^U = earnings of a union member, W_i^N = potential earnings of the *same* individual if he did not belong to a union. Typically, investigators estimate earnings functions of the form

$$\ln W_i^U = X_i \beta^U + u_{1i}, \tag{18a}$$

$$\ln W_i^N = X_i \beta^N + u_{2i}, \tag{18b}$$

with the average differential then being given by $\bar{X}(\hat{\beta}^U - \hat{\beta}^N)$, where $\bar{X}$ is the average value of the relevant characteristics.

The standard procedure consists of estimating (18) on individual cross-section data by OLS. For the USA, Lewis (1986) concludes, on the basis of 143 estimates over the period 1967–79, that the average mark-up is 0.15 (the estimates range between 0.07 and 0.22). In the UK there has been much less work in this area, but data on individuals yield estimates in the range of 8–10 per cent (Stewart 1983), while work on establishment data yields estimates in the range of 0–14 per cent (see Blanchflower and Oswald 1988a).

We need to enter an important caveat regarding these OLS estimates, because they fail to take into account the possibility that union status is endogenous. A standard argument (Freeman and Medoff 1984, or Lewis 1986) is that these OLS estimates may be biased *upward* because the employer responds to a higher imposed wage by employing workers of higher unobservable (to the econometrician) quality, since he now has a longer queue of applicants. However, C. Robinson (1989) argues that the OLS coefficient may easily be biased *downward*. For example, suppose that the non-union sector is characterized by production processes where there is scope for individual 'initiative', and individual outputs are readily observed. By contrast, assume that the union sector is characterized by production processes where a team structure means that all operatives on the production line are equally productive. Now, if workers who can excel in the non-union sector do not apply for jobs in the union sector, it is possible that the concentration of ability outside the union sector leads to an underestimate of the trade union wage differential.

The empirical evidence on the direction of the above biases is somewhat mixed. One may attempt to deal with the problem of union endogeneity in a variety of ways. The methods used include instrumental variable (IV) methods, or inverse Mills (IM) ratio methods (Heckman 1979) applied to cross-section data. Alternatively, one may attempt to deal with the problem of unobserved labour quality by using longitudinal data on those who switch jobs and union status. Most estimates using either IV or IM methods suggest that there is a rise in the union differential relative to OLS estimates. However, most estimates based on longitudinal data suggest that the differential is smaller than that suggested by cross-section OLS estimates. However, Chowdhury and Nickell (1985) and C. Robinson (1989) argue that longitudinal estimates using OLS are biased downward because of the problem of measurement error. Using IV estimates to deal with this, they generate measures of the differential which tend to be slightly higher than the cross-section OLS estimates.

Thus, we can safely conclude that union coverage raises an individual's wage somewhat—and probably more in the USA (where coverage is fairly low) than in Britain (where it is high). One should, though, beware of using the mark-up measures as a summary statistic for the effect of unions on wages. First, these mark-up estimates do not measure the effect of unions on wages in the sense of telling us how the average wage would differ if there were no unions. This is because the effect of unions on the non-union sector is likely to be complicated—the increase in labour supply will lower wages, but the 'threat' of possible unionization will lead non-union firms to raise wages in order to avoid unionization.

Second, the extent of union organization in an industry may also matter. If industry unionization increases, this will reduce the ability of buyers to substitute non-union for union products, and thereby will lower the elasticity of demand for those workers who are organized—thus leading to higher wages. Overall, the evidence supports the notion that industry union density is positively related to the earnings of both union and non-union workers

(Podgursky 1986). This also accords with the results of Nickell and Wadhwani (1990*b*), where it is found that increases in industry union density lead to higher average wages in a firm.

It is also important to stress that unions are not the only source of non-market-clearing wages. This is especially the case in the USA, where union membership is low.

Variation over time in the mark-up

Despite these caveats, it is interesting to learn what we can from the time-series behaviour of the estimated union mark-ups. This is particularly interesting in the European context, where wage pressure at given unemployment rose noticeably (in aggregate wage equations) from 1969 onwards. It was widely felt at the time that this was due to a new form of more militant, less deferential behaviour by workers following on the Paris events of 1968.

Unfortunately, there are no year-by-year cross-sectional data on individuals in any European country that cover the relevant period. But Layard *et al.* (1978*a*) use data on 3-digit industries in Britain to estimate for each year the effect of union coverage on the industry wage, controlling for a number of variables. Their estimates do not claim to measure accurately the *level* of the union mark-up, but they do reflect how wages have changed from year to year in more (relative to less) highly unionized industries. The coefficient on union coverage updated to 1987 moves as follows (averages of annual data):[9]

1956–9	*1960–4*	*1965–9*	*1970–4*	*1975–9*	*1980–4*	*1985–7*
0.15	0.17	0.19	0.27	0.27	0.32	0.22

The estimates appear to show a strong rise in the mark-up at the end of the 1960s with a fairly stable mark-up thereafter until the mid-1980s.[10]

It may be surprising that the union mark-up did not fall more sharply from 1980 onwards—between 1975–9 and 1980–4—given the successive reductions that occurred in the legal powers of unions. The most significant change was the restriction of the post-1906 'immunities', under which unions in a trade dispute were protected from suit for breach of contract. Under the 1980 and 1982 Employment Acts, there is now generally no immunity when action is taken against employers who are secondary to the dispute, or when a worker pickets away from his own place of work. The definition of a 'trade dispute' was also significantly narrowed to exclude, for example, political disputes. Further, the Trade Union Act (1984) restricted immunities to the case where particular balloting requirements were complied with. The effect of the narrowing of immunities is that substantial damages can now be awarded against unions in a variety of tort actions, and failure to pay may result in a sequestration of assets.

One reason why the mark-up did not fall more sharply may have been the recession. According to Gregg Lewis, this tends to hold up union relative to non-union wages because of the temporary stickiness of the former. However, an alternative possibility is related to our discussion of effort bargaining in Chapter 2 (Section 4), which also indicates why real wage growth in Britain has been so strong in the 1980s despite the dramatic rise in unemployment from 1979 to 1983. The basic results from that section are as follows. If unions and firms bargain over both wages and effort, we would expect the weakening of unions to lead to a rise in effort but probably a fall in wages. However, if there are fixed costs associated with bargaining over effort, it is possible, once unions are weak enough, that they might cede to managers the control over working practices (e.g. manning levels). At this point we have the situation where managers set effort, and the results of Chapter 2 (Section 4) now tell us that effort will rise, *as also will wages*. If this was happening in union firms, this would explain both the stability of the union mark-up in the early 1980s and the buoyancy of real wage growth.

So what is the evidence? First, as already noted in Chapter 2, there was a significant fall in bargaining over manning levels in particular, and work practices in general, between 1980 and 1984 (see Chapter 2, Table 5). Second, we know that significant changes in working practices occurred over the 1980–4 period. During that time the CBI Pay Databank suggests that 60 per cent of bargaining groups agreed on at least one concession with regard to productivity (Cahill and Ingram 1987). And the UK Workplace Industrial Relations Survey suggests that organizational change (defined as 'substantial changes in work organisation or work practices') occurred in 27 per cent of establishments. Further, this was around twice as likely to occur in unionized establishments (Machin and Wadhwani 1991a). The latter finding is consistent with the fact that unionized firms experienced faster productivity growth than their non-union counterparts over the 1980–4 period although not subsequently (Nickell *et al.* 1989).

Third, there is independent evidence suggesting that the removal of restrictive practices *was* sometimes associated with a pay rise as a *quid pro quo*. For example, in the UK Workplace Industrial Relations Survey, managers said that organizational change in itself increased the earnings of those manual workers directly affected in about 28 per cent of the cases, although it was also associated with a decrease in earnings in 16 per cent of establishments (as one would expect, if there was no change in bargaining arrangements). Among those establishments that did increase earnings, 30 per cent agreed that the 'higher rates [were] agreed as part of the agreement to accept the change' (Machin and Wadhwani 1991*b*). There is also some evidence from the CBI Databank that groups who made productivity concessions appeared to receive higher pay settlements.

During the 1980–4 period unionized firms were more likely to invest in new plant and machinery (UK Workplace Industrial Relations Survey data, reported in Machin and Wadhwani 1991*a*). When firms making major investments were asked how pay responded to this investment, we find that pay fell in only about 1 per cent of the cases, and rose in 28 per cent. Going further, the higher investment in union firms may have been caused in part by the removal of restrictive practices. So, overall, there is substantial evidence that one reason for the resilience of the union–non-union mark-up is the differential investment and productivity growth between union and non-union firms.

Turning to overall real wages, these rose by 1.7 per cent a year between 1981 and 1988 despite high unemployment. An obvious explanation is the high rate of productivity growth (2.2 per cent a year), stimulated in the main by better working practices and (latterly) some recovery of investment.

5. The effect of unemployment

It is widely believed, and has been at least since the publication of Phillips (1958), that a high level of unemployment serves to depress wages. Literally innumerable aggregate and sectoral time-series wage equations exhibit significant negative coefficients on unemployment, and we need not summarize them here. Two points are worth noting, however. First, there are rather few studies of wages at the firm level that focus on time-series effects. Examples include Nickell and Wadhwani (1990*b*), Brunello and Wadhwani (1989), and Christofides and Oswald (1989), which reveal negative unemployment effects for Britain, Japan, and Canada, respectively, although it should be noted that these tend to be more important for smaller firms. Second, there are a number of cross-section studies, for example those by Blanchflower and Oswald (1990) or Blackaby *et al.* (1990), where individual wages are related to local unemployment rates. These cross-section studies will capture a mix of the wage equation and the long-run equilibrium migration condition which slopes the other way (that is, in migration equilibrium high wages go with high unemployment, low wages with low unemployment, *ceteris paribus*: see Chapter 6, Section 2). Consequently, they do not identify what is required.

Taking the evidence that unemployment influences wage-bargaining as read, the first topic of interest is what we can say about the factors that affect the size of this unemployment effect. Turning back to our fundamental relationships given by (15), (16), we see that the (absolute) unemployment coefficient is given by

$$
\text{Absolute unemployment coefficient}
\begin{cases}
\text{eq. (15)} = \dfrac{(1 - \lambda)\varphi_1(1 - b)}{1 - \varphi(1 - b)}, & (19a) \\[3mm]
\text{eq. (16)} = \dfrac{(1 - \lambda)\varphi_1(1 - b)}{\lambda[1 - \varphi(1 - b)]}, & (19b)
\end{cases}
$$

where b is the benefit replacement ratio and the function $\varphi = \varphi(u, z_s)$ captures the probability that an individual losing his job is unable to find work in a given period. The z_s variables tend to reduce this probability, making it easier to find work at given levels of unemployment. As we have already noted, the important z_s variable for our purposes is the proportion of long-term unemployed.

From the expressions for the unemployment coefficient given in (19), we have the following results. The unemployment effect is decreasing in the insider weight (λ), and hence increasing in product-market competitiveness (κ) and decreasing in union power (β), following the discussion in Section 2. Furthermore, it must be decreasing in the benefit replacement ratio b. Indeed, arguing by analogy, the unemployment effect will be decreasing in anything that raises the generosity of the benefit system, notably the length of time for which benefits are payable (the duration of benefits).[11] The coefficients in (19) have nothing more to tell us, but there is another important factor arising from our discussion of centralized bargaining in Chapter 2 (Section 6). Here, we argue that wages are likely to be more responsive to unemployment under centralized bargaining.

So what is the evidence on all these issues? From firm and industry studies, we have the following. In Nickell and Kong (1988: Table 4), we find that the aggregate unemployment effect on wages in an industry is decreasing in both union power in that industry and product-market concentration; Brunello and Wadhwani (1989) discover that wages are much more responsive to unemployment in small firms than in large ones, both in Britain and in Japan; and, using British cross-section data, Blanchflower (1989) finds that regional unemployment has twice the effect on wages in small firms as in large firms. All these results are consistent with our hypotheses.

Using macro evidence across countries, there has been some work on the centralization issue, and the evidence in Bean *et al.* (1986), Newell and Symons (1985, 1987a), and Alogoskoufis and Manning (1988) suggests some positive relationship between the unemployment effect and the degree of centralization.

This is confirmed in Chapter 9 (Table 7), where we also find evidence relating the unemployment effect positively to the proportion of small firms in the economy and negatively to benefit levels and, more significantly, to benefit durations. Overall, therefore, although relevant evidence is somewhat thin, it does appear to point in the expected direction.

Before turning to unemployment dynamics, one final point worth considering is the linearity of the unemployment effect. Looking at (19), the fundamental derivative here is clearly φ_{11}. If φ_{11} is negative, the *absolute* unemployment effect on wages is likely to be concave. Now φ_{11} reveals how the impact of an extra point of unemployment on the probability of being unable to find work changes as unemployment increases. Intuitively, one would expect the direction of this effect to be negative because, as unemployment increases, the extra unemployed would make less and less difference in the competition for available jobs. Thus, if there is one job available and the number of unemployed rises from 1 to 2, the chances of one of them getting it falls from 1 to 1/2, whereas if the number of unemployed rises from 10 to 11, the chances fall only slightly from 1/10 to 1/11.

Consider a more formal argument based on a model due to Hall (1977). Suppose U unemployed are searching randomly over V vacancies. If each jobseeker makes one application per period, the probability that no seeker applies for a given vacancy is

$$\left(1 - \frac{1}{V}\right)^U \simeq e^{-U/V}.$$

So the number of hires (H) is the number of vacancies times the probability that a vacancy is applied for, namely,

$$H = V(1 - e^{-U/V}).$$

Thus, the probability of an unemployed individual failing to obtain a job (φ) is

$$\varphi = 1 - \frac{H}{U} = 1 - \frac{V}{U}(1 - e^{-U/V}).$$

It is then simple to show that this is concave in U/V.[12] We shall not go into the evidence on the issue of the linearity of the unemployment effect here in great detail, since it is considered in Chapter 6. However, it is a commonplace that in many countries wage equations appear to perform better when u is replaced by $\log u$ or u^{-1} (see e.g. Grubb 1986).

Unemployment dynamics

In Chapter 2 (Section 2) we introduced the notion of hysteresis arising from membership dynamics in the union bargaining model. The idea was that, when employment falls as the consequence of an adverse shock, in the subsequent period the number of participants in the wage bargain is reduced. This then generates upward pressure on wages because the smaller number of 'insiders' have a higher probability of survival at any given wage. And this in turn serves to prolong the impact of the shock. In terms of the aggregate wage equation, we saw this effect translated into a positive coefficient on lagged unemployment (see Chapter 2, equation (24)), which, when combined with the standard contemporaneous negative effect, generates a change effect of unemployment. It is this that we term the 'hysteresis effect' in wage-setting.

Returning to our fundamental firm-specific wage equation (15), insider hysteresis appears once we specify the number of insiders (n_{Ii}). This we suppose to be the number of employees remaining at the end of the previous period once the voluntary quitters have left (see Chapter 2, equation (8)). Thus we have

$$n_{Ii} = \log(1 - \delta) + n_{i,-1}, \tag{20}$$

δ being the quit rate. Equation (15) therefore becomes

$$w_i = c_0 + \lambda_i[p_i^e + (1 - \alpha)(k_i - n_{i,-1}) + (1 - \alpha)\log(1 - \delta)]$$
$$+ (1 - \lambda_i)(w^e - c_1 u + c_2 z_s + c_3 b) + c_4\beta. \tag{21}$$

Recall that, in a non-union setting, this effect does not typically occur, although Lindbeck and Snower (1988) construct a non-union model that has similar consequences. In any event, evidence for such membership dynamics must be based on the presence of negative lagged employment effects in firm or sectoral wage equations.

In fact, the existing evidence is weak. Nickell and Wadhwani (1990b) find such an effect for one sample of UK companies, but it is not robust across other samples. However, they do find the effect to be more important in decentralized union bargains. Furthermore, neither Holmlund and Zetterberg (1989) nor Brunello and Wadhwani (1989) found any consistent evidence of such an effect for other countries. In the light of our finding in Chapter 2 (Section 2), that for reasonable parameter values we would expect membership hysteresis effects to be small, perhaps all this is hardly surprising.

It is, however, worth noting briefly an extreme version of this model proposed by Blanchard and Summers (1986), which supposes that unions choose wages in order that, on average, existing employees retain their jobs. From equation (5), and ignoring voluntary quits, this reveals that wages satisfy

$$w_i = 1n\alpha\kappa + p_i^e + (1 - \alpha)(k_i - n_{i,-1}). \tag{22}$$

This is, of course, a special case of our model with $\lambda_i = 1$, which is far higher than any estimates yet obtained (see Section 2). So this model is perhaps best thought of as illustrative rather than realistic.

Insider hysteresis is not the only foundation for unemployment dynamics. Recall that wages are increasing in z_s, those factors that make it easier for a displaced employee to find an alternative job. As we have already noted, the proportion of long-term unemployed in the unemployment pool is a key variable of this type, so long as the long-term unemployed are ineffective competitors for jobs. So if we denote the long-term proportion by LTU (i.e. the proportion unemployed for more than 52 weeks) and assume a constant labour force l, we may write the aggregate version of (21) as

$$w - p = \frac{c_0}{\lambda} - \frac{(1-\lambda)}{\lambda}c_1 u + c_{11}(1-\alpha)u_{-1} + \frac{(1-\lambda)}{\lambda}c_2 LTU - (p - p^e)$$

$$- \frac{(1-\lambda)}{\lambda}(w - w^e) + (1-\alpha)(k - l) + \frac{(1-\lambda)}{\lambda}c_3 b + \frac{c_4}{\lambda}\beta, \tag{23}$$

where we replace z_s by LTU and incorporate $(1 - \delta)$ into the constant. We have introduced a parameter $c_{11} < 1$ on the u_{-1} term to capture the fact that insider hysteresis occurs only in certain types of wage bargain.

How then does the long-term proportion, LTU, generate unemployment dynamics? Here we must rely on some facts. When unemployment rises, the inflow of new entrants naturally tends to reduce the long-term proportion. However, in the long run higher unemployment tends to be associated with a high long-term proportion. Thus we have a typical relationship of the form

$$LTU = \alpha_0 + \alpha_1 u - \alpha_2 \Delta u, \tag{24}$$

an example of which may be found in Chapter 9 (Table 15). The α coefficients in this equation will, of course, tend to be high in those economies with a high long-term proportion at given levels of unemployment. Substituting into (23) and rearranging yields

$$w - p = \frac{c_0}{\lambda} - \left(\frac{(1-\lambda)}{\lambda}(c_1 - c_2\alpha_1) - c_{11}(1-\alpha) \right) u$$

$$- \left(\frac{(1-\lambda)}{\lambda}c_2\alpha_2 + c_{11}(1-\alpha) \right) \Delta u - (p - p^e) - \frac{(1-\lambda)}{\lambda}(w - w^e)$$

$$+ (1-\alpha)(k - l) + \frac{(1-\lambda)}{\lambda}c_3 b + \frac{c_4}{\lambda}\beta. \tag{25}$$

So the hysteresis term in Δu depends, for its impact, on insider dynamics and long-term unemployment effects. The former are likely to be more important in the union sector, particularly if bargaining is decentralized, whereas the latter will clearly be more significant in those economies with a high proportion of long-term unemployed. In Chapter 5 we shall pursue these duration effects in more detail, but the evidence from both firm-level and aggregate wage equations suggests that they may be important. Nickell and Wadhwani (1990*b*) and Nickell (1987) find a strong positive impact of the long-term proportion in the British economy, and Franz (1987) finds similar effects for Germany. Also, duration effects now feature in the wage equations of many of the main UK macroeconometric models (London Business School, National Institute, and Bank of England, for example). Thus, in Chapter 9 we demonstrate that the long-term proportion is a key determinant of the hysteresis coefficient in the wage equation, across the OECD countries.

Finally, it is worth remarking that, while there is not a great deal of evidence on the causes of unemployment dynamics, their existence can hardly be doubted. For example, the wage equations of both Coe and Gagliardi (1985) and Alogoskoufis and Manning (1988) are replete with hysteresis terms for many of the OECD countries.

6.   The effect of productivity

Some theoretical considerations

Different sectors of the economy normally experience different rates of productivity growth. The implications of this for sectoral patterns of wages and employment, and for unemployment overall, depends importantly on the wage-setting mechanism.

We shall analyse a variety of possibilities in the context of a simple formulation of sectoral price, wage, and employment determination. These are based on the standard constant elasticity structure of production and demand used in Chapter 2, although now we add a technical progress term. Thus, we have[13]

$$\text{Production: } Y_i = \Phi_i N_i^\alpha K_i^{1-\alpha}; \qquad \text{Demand: } Y_i = (P_i/P)^{-\eta} Y_{di}. \qquad (26)$$

where Φ_i reflects technical progress, and P_i, P are nominal prices, as usual in this chapter.

Following the standard analysis, our sector may be described by the following three equations:

Demand = production: $\eta(p_i - p) = -\alpha(n_i - k_i) + (y_{di} - k_i) - \varphi_i,$ (27)

Pricing/employment: $(1 - \alpha)(n_i - k_i) = -(w_i - p_i) + \alpha\varphi_i,$ (28)

Wage-setting: $w_i = \lambda_i[p_i^e + (1 - \alpha)(k_i - n_{i,-1}) + \alpha\varphi_i] + (1 - \lambda_i)w^e.$ (29)

Note that all constants and variables with which we are not currently concerned are omitted to reduce clutter (e.g., u is missing from the wage equation). So these equations can thus be viewed as being in 'differential' form. Equation (28) is the marginal revenue product condition (i.e. equation (5)), and (29) is the standard wage equation (15), setting the number of insiders, n_I, equal to last period's employment, n_{-1}.

Consider the short- and long-run determination of wages and employment. Solving out yields

Short-run wages:
$$w_i = \frac{-\lambda_i}{1 - \lambda_i}(p_i - p_i^e) + \frac{(1 - \alpha)\lambda_i}{1 - \lambda_i}\Delta n_i + w^e.$$ (30)

Long-run wages:
$$w_i = w.$$ (31)

Short-run employment:
$$\left[1 + \frac{(1 - \alpha)\eta\lambda_i}{[\alpha + (1 - \alpha)\eta](1 - \lambda_i)}\right](n_i - k_i)$$

$$= \frac{(1 - \alpha)\eta\lambda_i}{[\alpha + (1 - \alpha)\eta](1 - \lambda_i)}(n_{i,-1} - k_i)$$

$$- \frac{\eta}{[\alpha + (1 - \alpha)\eta]}(w^e - p) + \frac{1}{[\alpha + (1 - \alpha)\eta]}(y_{di} - k_i)$$

$$+ \frac{\alpha\eta - 1}{[\alpha + (1 - \alpha)\eta]}\varphi_i$$

$$+ \frac{\eta\lambda_i}{[\alpha + (1 - \alpha)\eta](1 - \lambda_i)}(p_i - p_i^e)$$ (32)

Long-run employment:

$$(n_i - k_i) = -\frac{\eta}{[\alpha + (1 - \alpha)\eta]}(w - p)$$

$$+ \frac{1}{[\alpha + (1 - \alpha)\eta]}(y_{di} - k_i) + \frac{\alpha\eta - 1}{[\alpha + (1 - \alpha)\eta]}\varphi_i.$$ (33)

On the basis of these, we may now examine a number of special cases.

205

(i) 'Competitive' labour market ($\lambda_i = 0$)

Here wages in each sector are unaffected by sector-specific factors in either the short or the long run. Employment adjusts to productivity shifts immediately, there being no dynamics in the employment relationship. (We have, of course, omitted employment adjustment costs from this analysis.) If we have turbulence across sectors generated by sector-specific demand or productivity shocks, employment will adjust rapidly in both expanding and contracting sectors, although there may be some unemployment as workers move from the latter to the former.

(ii) Pure insider model ($\lambda_i = 1$)

In this case $w_i = p_i^e + (1 - \alpha)(k_i - n_{i-1}) + \alpha\varphi_i$ from (29), and (30) reveals that employment follows a random walk, namely

$$\Delta n_i = \frac{1}{1 - \alpha}(p_i - p_i^e).$$

This is the Blanchard–Summers (1986) model again, with wages adjusting to set expected employment equal to the current number of insiders. All shocks have permanent effects and relative sectoral wages reflect sectoral productivity movements. However, as there is no evidence that λ_i is ever close to unity, this case need not be taken seriously.

(iii) Insider–outsider model ($0 < \lambda_i < 1$)

This is the standard model. Following an anticipated increase in productivity (φ_i), sectoral employment changes (equation (32)), and because of this sectoral wages tend to move in the same direction (see (30)). But this is only a short-run effect. In the long run, the insider–outsider model generates exactly the same wage/employment effect as the 'competitive' model, since the long-run equations are independent of λ_i. This is a very important result—which, incidentally, does not depend on our special Cobb–Douglas assumptions.

It tells us that, despite the fact that insiders can capture productivity improvements in the form of higher wages in the short run, in the long run competitive forces assert themselves. So even in this case, sectoral variations in productivity do not lead to *permanent* sectoral differences in wages. Essentially this is because the growth in employment is accompanied by falls in the industry price, which then exerts downward pressure on the industry wage. This, of course, is consistent with the oft-cited finding of Salter (1966), that in a cross-section of industries long-period changes in industrial wages are uncorrelated with long-period changes in total factor productivity.

Hence, provided that $\lambda < 1$, the size of λ does not affect the implication of the above model that, in the long run, the relative wage structure is independent of relative productivity differences. Essentially, while the direct effect of an increase in φ_i may be to raise w_i, its indirect effect is to reduce w_i by reducing p_i. In the long run, these two effects exactly offset each other.

The other important feature of this case is the fact that, following a shift in productivity or demand, employment will change only sluggishly because of the role of insiders in wage-setting. The consequence of insider activity is thus very similar to that of employment adjustment costs in this context. As with the competitive case, when we have industrial 'turbulence', there will be some frictional unemployment as workers move from contracting to expanding firms. The fact that contractions and expansions take place only gradually is probably likely to reduce such unemployment, if anything.

Asymmetries in wage adjustment

Over the years, there has been much interest in the possible downward rigidity of wages, and there have been many attempts to provide micro-foundations for such rigidity (e.g. implicit contract models). However, we have seen that wages do respond to a significant extent to firm-specific factors, and hence the view that wages are rigid is too simple. But it remains possible that there are asymmetries.

We see from equation (30) that firms with expanding employment will exhibit a wage premium, whereas those with contracting employment show a wage discount. As we have already noted, there will be some frictional unemployment associated with industrial turbulence arising from random demand or productivity shocks across sectors. Now suppose that λ is asymmetric, being higher in good times. This is the situation where workers are happy to take a wage hike when demand or productivity is high, but less happy to do the reverse when demand is low. Then we have a case where expanding firms have a high wage premium and slow adjustment, and contracting firms have only a small discount and rapid adjustment. This will clearly exacerbate frictional unemployment because workers are thrown out of work rapidly but hired in their new sectors only slowly. The opposite asymmetry will, of course, have the opposite effect.

The empirical evidence

We have already noted the evidence for a positive value of λ (at least for large firms) when we use industry/firm data. The finding of Salter (1966), that, in a cross-section, long-period changes in relative industrial wages are uncorrelated with long-period changes in total factor productivity, does not, of course, imply that $\lambda = 0$. As we have seen, our basic model (equations (27), (28), (29)) implies that the relative product price falls as total factor productivity rises. This ensures that in the long run sectoral wages are unaffected by sectoral productivity shifts even when the insider weight (λ) is positive, so long as it is less than unity. The relevant cross-section restrictions across equations (28) and (29) that are required to ensure this outcome are tested, using industry-level data, by Nickell and Kong (1988). They are unable to reject the relevant restrictions.

There remains the issue of possible asymmetries in adjustment.

Testing for asymmetric insider effects

One way of attempting to test for asymmetries is to divide the sample into two groups: those firms with above-average productivity growth, and the rest. One may then allow the coefficients in the wage equation to differ systematically between the two groups. This is the approach followed in Bell and Freeman (1985). Define the dummy variable associated with this as *DBF* (i.e., *DBF* = 1 if relative productivity growth is positive).

There are, though, several possible objections to the above procedure. One drawback is that it fails to allow for the possibility that the fortunes of firms may change over time. A second problem is that, in our model, insiders are really concerned about the level of output next period, relative to the number of insiders today. To accommodate both these objections, we may define a dummy variable

$$DIN = \begin{array}{l} 1 \text{ if } (y - n_{-1}) - (y_{-1} - n_{-2}) > 0, \\ 0 \text{ otherwise,} \end{array}$$

where y refers to the *real* values of sales.

However, a difficulty associated with using both the above measures is that output is not exogenous, but is, of course, influenced by the wage outcome. Therefore, Nickell and Wadhwani (1990*b*) fit an equation explaining sales as a function only of lagged variables, and use this to generate expected sales shifts. They then use a dummy taking the value 1 when real sales are expected to rise. An alternative method is to pick years when the economy as a whole could be said to be experiencing a recession, then define a dummy which takes the value 0 during an economy-wide recession.

In all, Brunello and Wadhwani (1989) use four different types of dummy variables, which are interacted with the insider effects, in order to assess the extent to which these responses are asymmetric. They conduct this exercise for both Japanese and British firms. Their results depend on the particular dummy variable used. For Japan, in two cases there is support for the view that wages are more responsive to insider effects when times are good, while in the other two cases the opposite is true. For the UK, three of the four experiments support the view that wages are more responsive to insider effects in 'bad' times.

As for other evidence, Freeman and Katz (1987) use *DBF* and find that, for the USA, wages were more responsive to insider effects in 'bad' times. However, Holzer and Montgomery (1990) discover exactly the opposite for a sample of US companies. Using cross-section data, Blanchflower (1989) finds that, in the UK, workplaces where employment is expected to rise pay significant wage premia; those facing a decline in employment do not set lower pay.

All in all, the evidence on asymmetries appears to be rather inconclusive, and this area, especially, deserves further research.

7. Real wage resistance and benefit effects

The notion of real wage resistance

Real wage resistance occurs when firms' labour costs rise in response to exogenous changes which tend to reduce workers' living standards. Thus, if income taxes increase and unionized workers put in for, and obtain, higher wages in order to compensate, we have real wage resistance in action. We have seen in Chapter 2 (Section 2) and Chapter 3 (Section 4) how real wage resistance can arise in both union bargaining and efficiency-wage models. We now look at the evidence.

The key variable here is the so-called 'wedge'. This is the gap between the real labour costs of the firm, on the one hand, and the real, post-tax consumption wage of the worker, on the other. Thus, if the log of real labour cost is $w + t_1 - p$, where t_1 is the tax rate on labour paid by employers and p is the value added price, and the log of the real post-tax consumption wage is $w - t_2 - p_c$, where t_2 is the tax rate on employee earnings (including social security taxes) and p_c is the consumer price index, then the wedge is given by

$$\text{wedge} = (w + t_1 - p) - (w - t_2 - p_c),$$

or

$$\text{wedge} = t_1 + t_2 + (p_c - p).$$

(34)

The wedge thus consists of the tax rates applying to both employers and employees and the price of consumer goods relative to value added. The key elements of $(p_c - p)$ are t_3, the tax rate on goods, and $s_m(p_m - p)$, which is the real price of imports $(p_m - p)$ times the share of imports (s_m). Any rise in the wedge generates the potential for real wage resistance by reducing living standards at fixed levels of real labour cost. Real wage resistance actually occurs if real labour costs respond positively to elements of the wedge. If there is such a positive response, then the wedge will influence equilibrium unemployment.

The models that illustrate the possibility of real wage resistance indicate that such effects are likely to be temporary rather than permanent. So we are interested in the evidence for both the existence and the duration of wedge effects on wages.

Real wage resistance: the evidence

Evidence that elements of the wedge have permanent effects on (product) wages appear in a variety of papers. Knoester and van der Windt (1987) find that employee taxes have a permanent impact on wages in 10 OECD countries, although Calmfors (1990) reports no effect for three out of four Nordic countries (Denmark, Finland, and Norway), finding a positive effect only for Sweden. Payroll taxes, however, appear to affect labour costs in the long run in all the Nordic countries except Finland (see Calmfors 1990: Table 3). Both Modigliani *et al.* (1986) and Padoa-Schioppa (1990) find significant, permanent tax effects for Italy. There is also evidence of permanent import price effects for Finland, Norway, and Sweden (Calmfors 1990), and for the UK (Chapter 9 below: Table 15). Overall wedge effects are found to be significant in 5 out of 15 OECD countries (Belgium, France, Ireland, Sweden, USA) in Bean *et al.* (1986).

However, it is hard to imagine that real wage resistance really is permanent; and the cross-section evidence reported in OECD (1990*a*: annex 6A) indicates that, in the long run, rises in the wedge are borne entirely by labour. But this same source, which draws on work by James Symons and Donald Robertson, shows that short-run wedge effects are both very important and very long-lasting. Thus, on average, for 16 OECD countries, a 1 per cent rise in the wedge induces an immediate rise in labour costs of $\frac{1}{2}$ per cent, and nearly half of this effect remains after five years. Given the further lags in the system, operating via hysteresis, this implies that a change in the wedge can have a significant impact on unemployment for at least a decade. In the light of this fact, it is hardly surprising that empirical researchers find it very hard to discriminate between permanent and temporary effects. To summarize, therefore, we have plenty of evidence that taxes and import prices have very long-lasting effects on product wages, and hence on the equilibrium of the economy, operating via real wage resistance.

Benefit effects

From our basic wage models (15), (16), it is clear that we should expect to see significant benefit effects on wages. However, the evidence here is very thin, not least because in many countries important changes in the benefit system are very infrequent. There is some evidence of relatively small effects for the UK, where benefit changes are more frequent than most (see Beenstock *et al.* 1985; Layard and Nickell 1986*b*; and Chapter 9 below: Table 15), although Minford (1983) reports very large effects, probably because of omitted variables (see Nickell 1984). For other countries, few have found important effects (see Newell and Symons 1985; Calmfors 1990), although in our pooled regression across 19 OECD countries in Chapter 9 (Table 12) we can see a significant impact of the replacement ratio on unemployment. Overall, therefore, there is little evidence of effects of benefit levels on wages. This is not to say, however, that the benefit system is not important. As we see in Chapters 1 and 9, it is a crucial factor in explaining differences in the unemployment experiences of various countries. The important mechanism is not, however, via the direct effect of benefit levels on wages, but more via the impact of the benefit system as a whole on the effectiveness of the unemployed in reducing wages, and on the duration structure of unemployment.

8. Nominal inertia

The widespread utilization of fixed-term nominal wage contracts indicates that nominal inertia in wage-setting must exist, although it may, of course, be attenuated by the inclusion of cost-of-living adjustments (COLA) in the terms of the contract. Furthermore, as we have seen in Chapter 2 (Section 7), if wage contracts are 'staggered', this will tend to increase the degree of inertia in the aggregate. In the light of this, it is clear that the extent of nominal inertia in wage-setting should depend positively on the duration of wage contracts or agreements, and negatively on the extent of synchronization and indexation.

In order to measure the extent of nominal inertia, the standard method is to investigate the degree to which *ex post* real wages are negatively affected by unanticipated increases in inflation. For, the stickier are nominal wages, the more will workers lose out in the short run because of unexpected increases in prices. In the context of aggregate wage equations, the following results seem fairly robust (see Alogoskoufis and Manning 1988; Bruno and Sachs 1985; and Chapter 9 below). Nominal inertia in wage-setting tends to be high in North America and in the European economies with centralized bargaining institutions, and low in Japan.

The standard arguments used to explain these results are as follows. First, wage contract durations in North America tend to be long. Second, under centralized bargaining, the bargainers recognize the direct impact of nominal wage increases on future aggregate price increases and hence moderate their response of nominal wages to current price increases in order to avoid a wage–price spiral. Third, in Japan wage negotiations are co-ordinated in the 'Spring Offensive' (or Shunto) and hence are highly synchronized. As we have already noted in Chapter 2 (Section 7), the first argument, at least when applied to the USA, does not carry a great deal of conviction, because, while wage contracts are indeed lengthy in the union sector (three years is standard), the union sector itself covers less than 20 per cent of the workforce. However, as we shall see in Chapter 9, there does appear to be some relationship between the structure of union wage contracts and the extent of nominal wage inertia.

9. Summary

We can baldly summarize our main conclusions.

1. Wages differ between industries and firms in ways that go beyond the effect of differences in ability or working conditions.

2. These extra differences arise because wages reflect not only outside forces (such as unemployment and wages in the external market) but also inside forces (such as value added per worker and the number of 'insiders' whose jobs are at stake). There is some evidence that inside factors are more important when wage-bargaining is decentralized and when product markets are less competitive.

3. Wages are higher in larger firms. This is mainly because large firms have higher product-market power and, in some cases, more powerful unions.

4. Union power increases wages. However, in the UK context there is no evidence of any significant change in the union–non-union mark-up during 1975–84. The fact that it did not appear to fall after 1979, despite the anti-union legislation of the early 1980s, may well be because restrictive practices (featherbedding) have been reduced, raising both productivity and real wages in the union sector.

5. The level of outside unemployment does have a clear effect on wages, confirming the existence of a long-run NAIRU. Furthermore, unemployment has a bigger impact on the wages of small firms operating in competitive product markets. At the economy-wide level, unemployment has a greater effect on wages when bargaining is centralized, and when unemployment benefits are low and available for only a limited period.

There are also hysteresis effects, coming from two sources. One is a membership effect, whereby wage pressure is higher if the number of 'insiders' whose jobs are at stake is low. The evidence for this effect is somewhat uncertain. The other is the fact that, if the unemployed 'outsiders' include a high proportion of long-term unemployed, this also raises wage pressure because the long-term unemployed are ineffective fillers of vacancies.

6. Although relative wages do respond to differences in relative value added per head, it is probably true that in the long run sectoral differences in the rate of technical progress leave the relative wage structure unchanged. This is because higher technical progress lowers the product price.

7. Real wage resistance is a significant feature of many economies. The evidence suggests that a 1 per cent rise in the wedge between real labour costs and net consumption wages induces an immediate rise in the former of $\frac{1}{2}$ per cent. While this effect is not permanent, it probably has a significant impact on unemployment for a decade or more.

8. There is some evidence to suggest that nominal inertia in wage-setting is systematically related to the key features of wage contracts, namely duration, synchronization, and indexation, with the first of these tending to raise nominal inertia, the latter two tending to reduce it.

Notes

1. For a full discussion see Gibbons and Katz (1989).
2. For a general survey of the evidence on compensating differentials, see Rosen (1986).
3. However, Katz (1986b) points out that it may also be consistent with pure compensating differentials if different workers have different tastes. For example, suppose there is a disamenity that only some workers care about, but there are enough of them to warrant a compensating differential for the marginal worker. Therefore, the infra-marginal worker earns rents and will be less likely to quit. By contrast, firms without the disamenity have low wages and no workers earning rents. Hence we will observe low quits where there are high wages. It is, however, also easy to construct examples going in the opposite direction.
4. This model is analogous to the dynamic monopsony model of Mortensen (1970).
5. The measure we have in mind is one of the form $k - n^*$, where n^* reflects the number of job slots associated with k as in the second of our two wage models. More generally, one should think of $k - n^*$ as the trend level of capital intensity, which is, of course, directly related to trend productivity. Thus, in (16) as it is written, we would have two terms, $(1 - \alpha)(k - n^*) - (1 - \alpha)(n_t - n^*)$. That is, the absolute number of insiders would typically be normalized on some non-cyclical level of employment in order to neutralize the impact of variations in the overall scale of the economy.
6. When discussing the behaviour of wages in the Nordic countries, it is important to be aware of the issue of wage drift, i.e. wage increases in excess of those centrally negotiated. It is possible that the central negotiations are merely a veil, with variations in drift offsetting the centrally negotiated wages. Calmfors (1990) has surveyed the evidence on this issue and concludes that the central negotiations are important because their effect on wage drift is relatively minor (see his p. 57, item (x)).
7. Again, however, not all the evidence points the same way. Pissarides and Moghadam (1990) find that sector-specific factors are no more important in their impact on relative wages in the USA and the UK than they are in Sweden and Finland.
8. Note, though, that Stewart is unable to find any role for the product-demand elasticity perceived (by managers) to be faced by the organization. So, although product-market conditions are seen to matter, they need to be modelled in a more complex fashion than using estimates of the product-demand elasticity.
9. Annual data in Layard and Nickell (1989: Annex Table 29b).
10. Shah (1984) and Stewart (1983), using individual data, report mark-ups for 1968 and 1975 that differ little from each other (around 8%), but Shah fails to control for firm size, which is highly correlated with unionism. Symons and Walker (1988) and Stewart (1987) find fairly stable mark-ups for the period 1980–4.
11. The duration of benefits may also influence the unemployment coefficient in another way. From (19), the coefficient is increasing in φ_1, which measures the impact of a one-point increase in the unemployment rate on the probability that a displaced worker will fail to find a job. This is likely to be influenced by the proportion of long-term unemployed in the unemployment pool, in the sense that the higher this proportion is, the smaller will be the impact of more unemployment on the probability of finding a job. Since benefit duration is almost certain to be positively related to the long-term

214

proportion (see Chapter 9, Table 9, for evidence), then again, longer benefit durations will tend to reduce the unemployment coefficient.

12. Let $U/V = x$. Then

$$\varphi = 1 - x^{-1}(1 - e^{-x}),$$

$$\varphi'' = -\frac{2}{x^3}[1 - e^{-x}(1 + x + \tfrac{1}{2}x^2)] < 0,$$

since $1 + x + \tfrac{1}{2}x^2 < e^x$.

13. We have assumed that technology is Cobb–Douglas. However, the basic character of all our results is preserved under more general technological assumptions.

5

Job Search: The Duration of Unemployment

THE story so far has focused on firms and workers and left little role for the individual unemployed person. But is the behaviour of unemployed people themselves important in determining how many people are unemployed or which people they are? How important are the attitudes and the motivation of unemployed people, and how are these affected by financial incentives, labour market institutions, and government policies? Do the recruitment strategies of employers matter, and how important is the role of (public and private) employment agencies and other labour market intermediaries in bringing together information on job vacancies and unemployed workers?

In this chapter we shall argue that such factors make an important contribution to understanding both the level of unemployment and the causes of its persistence in the aftermath of shocks. Our basic claim is that the NAIRU or equilibrium rate of unemployment depends not only on the wage-pressure factors discussed in previous chapters, such as unions, real wage resistance, and the generosity of the benefit system, but also on what we term the 'search effectiveness' of the unemployed. In this we include everything (other than the overall pressure of demand in the labour market) that affects the speed with which the unemployed find jobs—that is, the efficiency with which information about vacancies is transmitted, the time and effort the unemployed devote to job search, their 'choosiness' with regard to vacancies and job offers, and the recruitment practices of employers.

Search effectiveness can be influenced, for example, by a change in the unemployment benefit regime which affects the incentives for unemployed people to look for work or to accept job offers. It can be affected by employment protection legislation which makes employers cautious about taking on unemployed people. It can be affected by the duration structure of unemployment, because for many reasons the search effectiveness of long-term unemployed people is less than that of the short-term unemployed. (We have already discussed this point in the previous chapter (Section 5), but we now consider it in more detail.) It can also depend on how well the attributes of the unemployed match those of the available vacancies, but we defer consideration of this major and very important question to the next chapter.

The most striking evidence as to the role of search effectiveness in explaining changes in unemployment in recent years comes from looking at job vacancies. Changes in aggregate demand, or in wage pressure, increase unemployment by reducing the number of jobs available. With more unemployed chasing fewer jobs, the number of job vacancies would be expected to fall. But in fact, in many countries, while the unemployment rate has risen substantially over the last twenty years, the vacancy rate is relatively unchanged (see Fig. 11 in Chapter 1). Increased unemployment at a given vacancy rate suggests a decline in the search effectiveness of the unemployed.

This chapter then is concerned with the behaviour of the unemployed as job-seekers—the process by which they search for work and the impact of labour market institutions—and with how such factors affect the unemployment rate.

The hiring function

There is only one basic idea: the hiring function. This says that the number of hirings (which we will initially identify with the number of people who leave unemployment)[1] per period (H) depends on the number of vacancies (V) and the number of effective job-seekers (cU), where U is the number of unemployed people and c is their average effectiveness. It also depends on the degree of mismatch between unemployment and vacancies, but we will defer the problem of mismatch to the next chapter. Thus, ignoring mismatch,

$$H = h(V, cU).$$

Each hiring involves a marriage between a vacancy and an unemployed person. In a marriage market of reasonable size the number of marriages will double as the numbers of men and women double, even if the numbers of each sex are unequal. The same is true in the labour market.[2] Thus $h(\cdot)$ is linearly homogeneous in V and cU—an assumption not refuted by the evidence (see below). Dividing both sides by cU then implies that the outflow rate from unemployment depends only on the ratio of vacancies to unemployment and on the 'effectiveness' of the unemployed:

$$\frac{H}{U} = ch\left(\frac{V}{cU}, 1\right). \tag{1}$$

This is the aggregate relation determining outflow rates. We will also argue (p. 234 below) that an individual i, with effectiveness c_i, will have a probability of leaving unemployment given by his individual effectiveness c_i and the same aggregate variables as above; i.e.,

$$h_i = c_i h\left(\frac{V}{cU}, 1\right). \tag{2}$$

Equations (1) and (2) provide the framework for this chapter. In our discussion we start with the *individual* probability of finding a job. We examine factors that affect individual effectiveness, looking in particular at the effect of unemployment benefit and the length of unemployment which the person has already experienced. This analysis is mainly cross-sectional.

We then move on to the *aggregate* outflow rate and attempt to explain its behaviour over time. The latter is particularly important for the light it sheds on the increase in the aggregate unemployment rate. In a steady state it is convenient to think of the unemployment rate (U/N) as

$$\frac{U}{N} \equiv \frac{S}{N}\frac{U}{S},$$

where S is the inflow into unemployment. Here

1. S/N is the rate at which people leave employment for unemployment—in other words, the 'inflow rate'—and
2. U/S is, in a steady state, the average time for which those who enter unemployment remain there—in other words, the 'average duration'.

Hence, in a steady state

> Unemployment rate = Inflow rate × Ave. duration.

In addition, since in a steady state the inflow (S) equals the outflow (H), we can always think of the average duration (U/S) as the inverse of the outflow rate (H/U):

$$\frac{U}{S} = \frac{1}{H/U} \qquad \text{(if } H = S\text{)},$$

or

$$\text{Ave. duration} = \frac{1}{\text{Outflow rate}}.$$

Thus

$$\text{Unemployment rate} = \frac{\text{Inflow rate}}{\text{Outflow rate}}.$$

218

The secular increase in unemployment in most countries between the 1960s and the 1980s is arithmetically 'due to' an increase in average duration (a fall in the outflow rate), rather than a rise in the inflow rate. However, this does not provide a self-contained explanation of the rise in unemployment, since the fall in the outflow rate depends on the V/U ratio which also has to be explained.

So how does the flows approach in this chapter actually help us to explain the changes in unemployment? To answer this, we need to embed it in our original model.

Relation to overall model

As explained in Chapter 1, it is most reasonable to suppose that wage behaviour depends on the average duration of unemployment for an unemployed person of given effectiveness,[3] cU/H. Since in a steady state $H = S = sN$, this implies that

$$w - p = \gamma_0 - \gamma_1 \frac{cU}{sN} + z, \tag{3}$$

where z reflects standard wage pressure variables (e.g. unions or the 'wedge'). At the same time, pricing behaviour determines the equilibrium real wage from the side of prices:

$$p - w = \beta_0 - \beta_1 \frac{U}{N}. \tag{4}$$

Equations (3) and (4) provide a model of the equilibrium unemployment rate, and show that, in addition to the wage-pressure variables included in equation (3), it depends (inversely) on c and (positively) on s.

However, there is little direct evidence on c. The best evidence in fact comes from shifts in the hiring function. For, if

$$H = h(V, cU),$$

we can identify c from shifts of the hiring function. (Again, we set aside the problem of mismatch: see Chapter 6, Section 6.) Alternatively, we can look at shifts in the steady-state U/V curve. In a steady state $H = sN$, so that (given constant returns to scale in hiring)

$$s = h\left(\frac{V}{N}, c\frac{U}{N}\right). \tag{5}$$

In the simple case of normal cost pricing ($\beta_1 = 0$), the unemployment rate (U/N) is, other things equal, inversely proportional to c (equations (3) and

(4)). By the same token, the vacancy rate is independent of c (equation (5)). Thus, a fall in search effectiveness might help to explain why vacancies have altered so little despite the huge change in unemployment.

This brings us back to where we started. In a world where economists have little certain knowledge, the shift of the U/V curve provides us with vital clues to the sources of the rise in unemployment. Large shifts indicate that a major part of the rise is due to changed behaviour of workers and employers in the filling of vacancies. And, as we shall show in the case of the UK, a part of this altered behaviour can be attributed to the demoralizing and stigmatizing effects of long-term unemployment.

Layout of chapter

Our procedure in the chapter is as follows. First, we set out some of the basic aggregate data on the duration of unemployment and on the negative relation between individual exit rates and the length of time a person has been unemployed (Section 1). Next, we develop the theory of an individual's chances of finding work, showing the role of the reservation wage (Section 2). In Section 3 we turn to evidence on individual job-search behaviour and conclude that for many people, much of the time, unemployment is not a particularly productive activity. We then consider the evidence, based on individual cross-section data, concerning the impact upon a person's search effectiveness of factors such as the replacement ratio and unemployment duration (Section 4).

After this we look at the aggregate time series and estimate the hiring function from time-series data (Section 5). This is the heart of the chapter. To complete the model, in Section 6 we consider the inflow into unemployment as an endogenous variable, and attempt to explain its movement over the cycle and thus to derive the U/V curve. Finally, in Section 7 we turn to the determination of vacancies, and develop a model where this is grounded explicitly in the optimizing behaviour of firms.

1. Unemployment duration: the facts

Unemployment can be viewed as a pool with an inflow and an outflow (see Fig. 1). The change in unemployment is the excess of inflow (S) over outflow (H):

$$\Delta U = S - H.$$

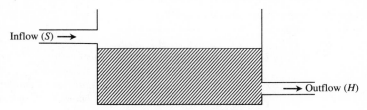

Fig. 1.   *The pool of unemployment.*

This is illustrated for Britain in Fig. 2. When $S = H$, unemployment is constant and we have a 'steady state'. Since in most years unemployment changes relatively little, it is extremely helpful to see what is happening in that situation. As already noted,

$$\frac{U}{N} \equiv \frac{S}{N}\frac{U}{S},\tag{6a}$$

or, in a steady state,

$$\text{Unemployment rate} = \text{Inflow rate} \times \text{Ave. duration.}\tag{6b}$$

Table 1 shows this decomposition for a number of countries. Since inflow data are shaky or absent in most countries, we proxy the monthly inflow by the number of people who, at a point of time, have been unemployed for one month or less. (This equals the monthly inflow minus about one-half of those

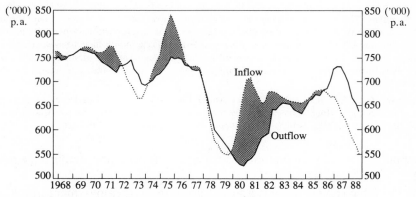

Fig. 2.   *Unemployment inflow and outflow: Britain, males, 1968–1988.*

Shaded area indicates increase in unemployment.

Source: unpublished Department of Employment Consistent ('X-11') Series.

221

Table 1 *Unemployment rates and flows, 1988*

	(1) Unemployment rate (%)	(2) Inflow rate (% per month)	(3) Steady-state average duration (mos.)	(4) Turnover rate (% of employees hired in last year)
	U/N	S/N	U/S	
Low flow, high duration				
Belgium	8.3	0.2	50	
Denmark	9.4	0.8	11	
France	11.1	0.6	21	12
Germany	6.6	0.4	16	
Ireland	20.0	0.7	30	
Italy	8.6	0.2	36	
Netherlands	10.1	0.4	25	
Spain	23.6	0.2	105	
UK	9.1	0.9	10	18
High flow, low duration				
Australia	7.8	1.4	6	25
Canada	8.3	2.6	3	27
USA	5.8	2.2	3	29
Low flow, low duration				
Finland	5.3	1.1	5	19
Japan	2.6	0.5	5	12
Norway	3.3	1.1	3	
Sweden	1.6	0.5	3	

Note: The number of unemployed who have durations of less than one month have been taken as the monthly inflow. This excludes roughly one half of those whose completed unemployment duration is less than one month. Average duration is exaggerated in the same proportion as inflow is understated. For Finland and USA, the numbers with durations less than one month have been calculated on the basis of a uniform distribution of durations of, respectively, less than two months and less than five weeks. This further exaggerates average duration, particularly for Finland. The figures for Finland relate to 1987.

Sources: col. (1): CEP–OECD Data Set (see Annex 1.6, Table A3), recalculated as % of employed labour force; col. (2): OECD data (used in *Employment Outlook*, July 1990, Chart 1.2); col. (3): col. (1) ÷ col. (2); col. (4): OECD, *Employment Outlook*, July 1989, Table 5.14, 1987 data.

who find jobs within the first month.[4]) Durations are computed using equation (6*b*).

As the table shows, there is a huge variation in unemployment inflow rates and durations across countries. Unemployment durations are very low in North America, and inflow rates rather high. By contrast, in the EC inflow rates are quite low but durations are huge. And the 'virtuous' countries

Table 2 *Unemployment duration and flows: USA*

	(1) Unemployment rate (%) (U/N)	(2) Inflow per month[a] (%) (S/N)	(3) Steady-state average completed duration of all spells (mos.) (U/S)	(4) Average uncompleted duration of current spells (mos.)
1962	5.9	2.2	2.7	3.4
1963	6.0	2.2	2.6	3.2
1964	5.5	2.2	2.5	3.1
1965	4.7	1.8	2.4	2.7
1966	3.9	1.9	2.1	2.4
1967	4.0	1.9	2.1	2.0
1968	3.7	1.8	2.0	1.9
1969	3.6	1.8	2.0	1.8
1970	5.2	2.4	2.2	2.0
1971	6.3	2.4	2.6	2.6
1972	5.9	2.4	2.5	2.8
1973	5.1	2.3	2.3	2.3
1974	5.9	2.6	2.3	2.3
1975	9.2	2.9	3.1	3.3
1976	8.3	2.8	3.0	3.6
1977	7.6	2.8	2.8	3.3
1978	6.5	2.6	2.5	2.7
1979	6.2	2.6	2.4	2.5
1980	7.7	2.9	2.7	2.7
1981	8.2	3.0	2.8	3.2
1982	10.7	3.4	3.2	3.6
1983	10.6	3.1	3.5	4.6
1984	8.1	2.8	2.9	4.2
1985	7.8	2.8	2.7	3.6
1986	7.5	2.7	2.8	3.5
1987	6.6	2.5	2.6	3.3
1988	5.8	2.3	2.5	3.1
1989	5.6	2.3	2.4	2.7

[a] Estimated by assuming a uniform distribution of durations of less than 5 weeks.

Sources: 1962–87: *Economic Report of the President*, 1989, Tables B.34, B.41; 1988–9: *Monthly Labor Review*, July 1990, Tables 5 and 10.

(Norway, Sweden, Finland, and Japan) have both low inflow and low duration. As column (4) shows, there is some relation between inflow rates and the general turnover rate in a country.

We can now ask how unemployment changes over time. How much is due to changes in flow and how much to duration? In the USA the answer is about half and half, while in the UK it is mainly duration. This is shown in Tables 2 and 3 and Fig. 3. Similar figures are given for other countries in Annex 5.1. In some of these countries inflows to unemployment have increased considerably

Table 3   *Unemployment duration and flows: Britain, males (exluding school-leavers)*

	(1) *Unemployment* *rate (%)* *(U/N)*	*(2)* *Inflow per month* *(%)* *(S/N)*	*(3)* *Average completed* *duration of all* *spells (mos.)* *(U/S)*	*(4)* *Average* *uncompleted* *duration of current* *spells (mos.)*
1967	2.4	1.6	1.5	6.3
1968	2.7	1.6	1.7	6.5
1969	2.7	1.6	1.7	6.9
1970	3.0	1.6	1.8	7.0
1971	3.6	1.7	2.1	7.0
1972	4.2	1.5	2.7	8.2
1973	2.9	1.4	2.0	8.8
1974	2.9	1.6	1.8	8.3
1975	4.3	1.9	2.3	7.2
1976	5.9	1.7	3.5	8.1
1977	6.2	1.7	3.7	9.0
1978	6.1	1.3	4.5	9.3
1979	5.4	1.3	4.3	10.0
1980	6.5	1.6	4.1	10.4
1981	11.4	1.6	7.0	10.0
1982	13.8	1.7	8.1	14.2
1983	14.8	1.7	9.0	18.0
1984	14.7	1.6	9.3	20.8
1985	14.9	1.6	9.2	22.2
1986	15.2	1.7	8.9	24.5
1987	14.4	1.7	8.7	24.5
1988	11.3	1.4	8.0	24.0
1989	8.6	1.2	7.0	20.6

Sources: Cols. (1) and (2): Jackman *et al* (1989: Table 1), updated from *Employment Gazette*. Col. (3): Col. (1) ÷ Col. (2). Col. (4): 1967–78, Main 1981; 1979–89, *Employment Gazette*, Table 2.6.

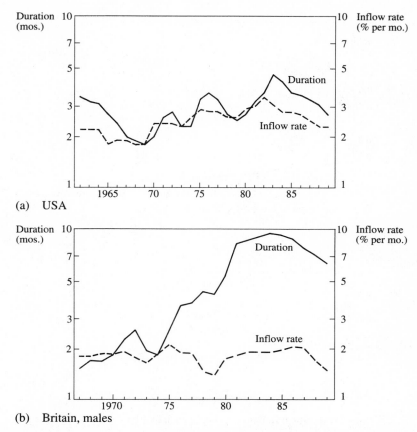

Fig. 3. *Inflow rates and duration of unemployment, USA and Britain, 1962–1989.*
Sources: USA: Table 2; *Britain*: Jackman *et al.* (1989), updated from *Employment Gazette*.

in the last fifteen years. But in the majority of countries, it is the variation of average duration that is the key issue.

Distribution of spell lengths

The average duration of unemployment gives only a limited picture of what is actually happening. For there is a huge variation in the length of spells of unemployment. Figure 4 shows the distribution of male unemployment experience in Britain in 1985. Panel (*a*) shows what proportion of a cohort of entrants remains unemployed as time passes—it is, if you like, a survival curve where 'survival' means remaining unemployed. In a steady state this survival

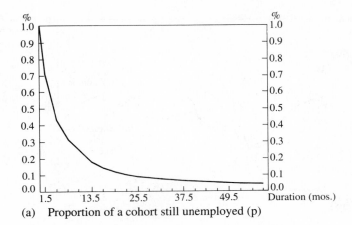

(a)   Proportion of a cohort still unemployed (p)

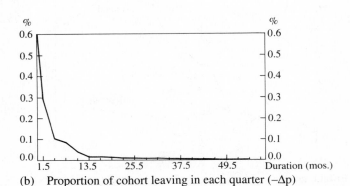

(b)   Proportion of cohort leaving in each quarter ($-\Delta p$)

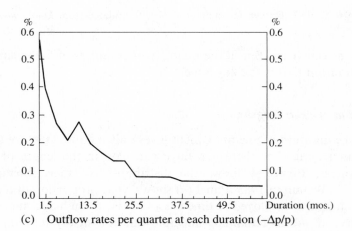

(c)   Outflow rates per quarter at each duration ($-\Delta p/p$)

curve shows, at a point of time, the relative numbers of unemployed people who have been unemployed for each duration.

This is not the same as the distribution of completed spell lengths (for any cohort, and thus for all cohorts). To find this we need to take the slope of the survival curve, which shows the numbers of people *leaving* unemployment between adjacent durations. This is shown in panel (*b*).

Finally, we can examine what proportion of survivors to each duration leave unemployment in the subsequent three-month period. This 'hazard rate' is calculated by expressing panel (*b*) as a proportion of panel (*a*), which is done in panel (*c*). This panel shows how the outflow rate in Britain is much lower at the longer durations. The chances of getting a job after five years' unemployment is one-tenth the chances for a newly unemployed person.

Differences of this sort are found in other countries, though they are somewhat less extreme. Table 4 gives data on Australia and the USA. (However, in the USA, as Katz (1986*a*) points out, if workers on recall are excluded, the decline is almost entirely eliminated.)

A key issue running through this chapter is whether these differences are *due to duration* or merely reflect heterogeneity among entrants, those with low job-finding probability remaining unemployed longer. If the differences are due to duration, it then becomes important to understand also how the stock of unemployment at each duration comes about, and what determines the average uncompleted duration among the unemployed. Typically, the average duration of uncompleted spells among the current stock of unemployed ($\bar{d}$) is

---

Fig. 4. *The experience of unemployment: Britain, males, 1985.*

The data relate to registered unemployment, and come from the *Employment Gazette*.

Source: *Panel* (*c*): The basic data are those in panel (*c*). These show the outflow rates between April and July 1985 for those with the indicated durations in April. All but one of these rates come from taking the stock of unemployed for duration *d* in April and comparing it with those unemployed for duration $d + 1$ in July (or, where the stock data cover two quarters, $d + 2$ in October or, for four-quarter categories, $d + 4$ in the following April). The very first outflow rate, for those who just became unemployed, is computed as

$$2 \left(1 - \frac{\text{stock of the unemployed under 3 mos. in Apr.}}{\text{inflow, Jan.–Apr.}} \right).$$

This is based on the assumption that the outflow rate over the first three months is constant, so that by the end of a quarter the remaining stock excludes one-half of those who leave within the first three months of their unemployment.

Panel (*a*): This follows from panel (*c*) by recursion.

Panel (*b*): This is the differences in panel (*a*).

Table 4 *Exit rates per month from unemployment, by duration, USA and Australia (%)*

	USA (1986)	Australia (1987)
Under 5 weeks	55	58
5–11 weeks	44	39
11–26 weeks	38	34
Over 26 weeks	34	23
All	46	33

Note: The data show the proportion of people with the given initial duration who were no longer unemployed one month later. In Australia the ranges of initial duration were 4, 13, and 25 weeks (not 5, 11, and 26).

Source: OECD, *Employment Outlook*, Sept. 1988, Table 2.12.

higher than the average duration of completed spells among all those who ever enter unemployment $(\bar{t})$. For example, in 1989 the figures were as follows:

	Ave. uncompleted length of spell among unemployed stock $(\bar{d})$	Ave. completed length of spell for entrants to unemployment $(\bar{t})$
Britain (males)	21 mos.	7 mos.
USA	3 mos.	2 mos.

How can this paradox be explained? The first point to note is the relation between completed and uncompleted spell lengths. History contains many spells. If we regard the moment of observation as randomly selected, then any spell which is observed at all will on average be observed halfway through. Hence in a steady state,

Ave. uncompleted length of spell among unemployed stock $(\bar{d})$ = $^1/_2$ ave. completed length of spell among unemployed stock.

So how long is the latter? What is the relation between the size of (i) the average completed spell for a cohort of entrants $(\bar{t})$, and (ii) the average completed spell among the stock of the currently unemployed $(2\bar{d})$? The latter must be longer, and can easily be very much longer.

This is illustrated in the following example. Suppose that in each week 51 spells begin, of which 50 last for 1 week and 1 lasts for 50 weeks:

228

Completed duration	No. of spells beginning p.w.
1 week	50
50 weeks	1
All spells	51

The average spell lasts roughly 2 weeks.

But, if we look at the unemployed at any point in time, we shall find 50 unemployed people in the course of a 1-week spell and an equal number in the course of a 50-week spell (1 person from each of the last 50 cohorts):

Completed duration	No. of unemployed people
1 week	50
50 weeks	50
All unemployed people	100

Thus, spells lasting 50 weeks account for as much unemployment as spells lasting 1 week. And the average unemployed person is in a spell whose completed length is $25\frac{1}{2}$ weeks.

The reason is of course that, in computing the average length of all spells, each spell gets counted once; but, in computing the average length of all spells current at a particular moment, long spells are more heavily represented. In fact, the probability that a spell appears is proportional to its length.

So, suppose the probability distribution of spells (among entrants) is $g(t)$. Clearly, in a steady state $U = S\Sigma tg(t) = S\bar{t}$, and the average length of spell for entrants is $\bar{t}$. This is the first statistic we were interested in.

To find our second statistic, we note that the number of weeks of unemployment represented by current spells is $S\Sigma t^2 g(t)$, and we divide this by U. Thus,

$$\text{Ave. completed duration of current spells} = \frac{\Sigma t^2 g(t)}{\Sigma tg(t)}$$

$$= \bar{t}\left(\frac{\Sigma t^2 g(t) - \bar{t}^2}{\bar{t}^2} + 1\right)$$

$$= \bar{t}\left(1 + \frac{\text{var}(t)}{\bar{t}^2}\right).$$

This measure can be many multiples of $\bar{t}$. So long as it is more than twice $\bar{t}$, the average uncompleted duration ($\bar{d}$) will exceed $\bar{t}$. Whether it does depends on the form of $g(t)$.

229

To get a feel for this, it is convenient to start from the benchmark case where all individuals have a constant exit probability (h), independent of duration. In this case we can see that both measures must be the same ($\bar{d} = \bar{t}$). For if h is independent of duration, the remaining expected duration for unemployed people will be the same as it was when they first became unemployed. So, *if h is constant,*

$$\frac{\text{Ave. completed duration}}{\text{of entrants } (\bar{t})} = \frac{\text{Ave. remaining duration}}{\text{of the stock.}}$$

But we have also shown that it always holds (owing to random choice of moment) that

$$\frac{\text{Ave. remaining duration}}{\text{of the stock}} = \frac{\text{Ave. uncompleted duration}}{\text{of the stock } (\bar{d}).}$$

Hence, *if h is constant,*

$$\frac{\text{Ave. completed duration}}{\text{among entrants } (\bar{t})} = \frac{\text{Ave. uncompleted duration}}{\text{among the stock } (\bar{d}).}$$

In fact, we generally observe that $\bar{d} > \bar{t}$. This is the corollary of the fact that the exit rates are lower at the longer durations. So what does determine exit rates and the way they vary with duration?

2. Job search: theory

To answer this question, we need to develop a general theory of job-finding. When a typical unemployed person looks for work, there are three stages involved:

1. He collects information about job vacancies.
2. He decides to apply for some of the vacancies that he learns of.
3. He (generally) accepts the offer of any job for which he has applied.

We shall first focus on stage 2, bearing in mind that an individual will in general only apply for those vacancies which he expects he will accept. Which vacancies will he apply for?

Vacancies come with different pre-assigned wages and conditions. This wage dispersion can exist because the 'efficiency wage' differs between firms, or because some firms face more powerful unions than others, or because of differences in an individual's productivity in different jobs. If W_i denotes the wage (adjusted for non-pecuniary attributes of the job), vacancies have a density $f(W)$ with cumulative distribution $F(W)$. For convenience we shall assume that the individual learns of one job vacancy per 'period'. In deciding whether to apply for it, he compares the expected present value of getting the job with the expected present value of not getting it.

What will be the lowest-wage job for which he applies? To answer this question we have to know how easy it is, having taken a job, to look for and obtain a better one.

Costless search on the job

If a person can take a job and go on looking for a better one (with equal chances of success), he will obviously take any job paying more than the net income he gets while unemployed (B). For he can then carry on searching on a higher income than when he was unemployed. So the reservation wage is

$$W_c = B,$$

and he applies for every job paying more than B.[5]

The chance that he will make an application depends on the distribution of vacancies by wage (W). We shall call this chance $p(W_c)$, where

$$p(W_c) = \text{Prob}(W > W_c) = 1 - F(W_c).$$

The chance of getting a job if he applies is λ (taken as a constant). So, if the individual learns of one job per 'period', his chance of getting a job each period is $p(W_c)\lambda$. With costless search on the job, this is $p(B)\lambda$.

Search on the job impossible

Suppose, by contrast, that on-the-job search was impossible or that employers were unwilling to steal each other's labour (perhaps thinking mobile labour to be excessively mobile). The unemployed person now has a higher reservation wage, below which he will not apply; for, by accepting a job, he now rules out the possibility of continuing to search thereafter and thus creeping up the wage distribution. Whatever job he takes he has to live with, and he is therefore willing to reject some jobs paying more than B in order to keep open the chance of getting a still better job.

If the wage distribution of vacancies is taken as constant, his correct strategy, on these assumptions, is again to select a constant reservation wage (W_c), and keep on applying to all jobs paying more than that. If he applies for no job this period, his position next period will be exactly the same as now, and he should therefore use exactly the same decision rule next period as now. Thus, he has the same simple decision rule in each period:

Apply if $W > W_c$.

How will W_c be selected? A very low W_c would be a mistake because the chances of a much better wage coming along are quite high (high expected returns) and it would be worth incurring the lowish cost of another period of search (since W_c is a low income to forgo). Equally, a very high W_c would be a mistake because the chances of a much better wage coming along are quite low (low expected returns), and the cost of continuing to search are high (since W_c is now a high income to forgo). The optimum W_c is where the cost of another period of unemployment just equals the expected return.

To calculate the cost, we proceed as follows. If the individual accepts a job at the reservation wage, his income next period would be W_c; so the cost of searching another period is $W_c - B$. And what is the expected return from one more period of search? This equals the chance that next period a job will be secured paying more than W_c *times* the present value of the extra wage that could then be expected over and above the reservation wage. If any job taken would last for ever, the expected return is

$$\text{Expected return} = \lambda \text{Prob}(W > W_c)\frac{E(W \mid W > W_c) - W_c}{r}$$

$$= \frac{\lambda}{r} p(W_c)[\bar{W}(W_c) - W_c],$$

where $\bar{W}(W_c) = E(W \mid W > W_c)$.

The reservation wage (W_c) is selected so that the cost of remaining unemployed when W_c is rejected ($W_c - B$) equals the expected return. Hence W_c is determined by

$$W_c = B + \frac{\lambda}{r} p(W_c)(\bar{W}(W_c) - W_c).$$

If this were the end of the matter, he might choose a reservation wage substantially higher than B. However, we now need to allow for the fact that the job an unemployed person takes is not likely to last for ever. If it ends and the individual becomes unemployed again, the return has come to an end. Suppose s is the probability per period that the stream comes to an end. Then the expected present value of the return is

$$\text{Expected return} = \frac{\lambda}{r + s} p(W_c)(\bar{W}(W_c) - W_c),$$

which may be small if s is large. We then have

$$W_c = B + \frac{\lambda}{r + s} p(W_c)(\bar{W}(W_c) - W_c). \tag{7}$$

The reservation wage is lower (closer to B) the higher are r and s. Thus, key issues in thinking about the reservation wage include the duration of post-unemployment jobs ($1/s$) and the discount rate (r).

An alternative (and more general) approach to deriving this formula is based on dynamic programming. This is shown in Annex 5.2.

Search on the job possible but costly

An intermediate case is where on-the-job search is possible, though at some cost. Because on-the-job search is costly, the reservation wage will be higher than B; but it will not be as high as implied by equation (7), since it is still possible to search having taken a job.

Implications for theory of job-finding

We can now complete our review of how a person finds work. We have so far considered only stage 2 of the process of job-finding. As we have seen, the proportion of vacancies that an individual will apply for depends on his reservation wage (W_c), which in turn depends (in the three possible cases we have considered) on B. Hence the fraction of vacancies for which he will apply depends on B relative to the mean of the wage distribution (μ_w). Thus B/μ_w is one determinant of the individual's 'effectiveness' as a job-seeker.

Next we consider stage 3—the question of whether the individual's application is successful. This clearly depends on his personal characteristics (q_i) as perceived by employers. These may be characteristics he had when he became unemployed, or ones acquired later through the (demoralizing or stigmatizing) experience of unemployment. Obviously, the probability of success depends also on the general economic climate, since this affects the degree of competition for jobs.

Finally, we consider stage 1—the question of how many vacancies the individual hears of per period. This will depend on the returns to information acquisition and on the costs.[6] The returns will depend on all the factors we have already considered—the likelihood of applying, the likelihood of success, and also the gain if successful. Turning to the costs of information acquisition, these are mainly psychic (though there is some cash cost). People differ a lot in their experience of the costs of looking for work. So these costs again depend

233

on personal characteristics (q_i), either original or acquired through unemployment.

Thus, there are two sets of factors that affect whether an individual finds a job:

1. individual factors ($B_i/\mu_w, q_i$);
2. the degree of competition for vacancies from other job-seekers (V/cU).

Note that we now index (by i) factors specific to individuals, with no index implying aggregate variables common to all individuals. Recalling our framework at the beginning of the chapter (equation (2)), we write the probability that an individual finds a job as

$$h_i = c_i h \left(\frac{V}{cU}, 1 \right),$$ (2)

where, given our discussion above, we now have

$$c_i = c \left(\frac{B_i}{\mu_w}, q_i \right).$$

So

$$h_i = c \left(\frac{B_i}{\mu_w}, q_i \right) h \left(\frac{V}{cU}, 1 \right).$$ (2′)

We shall consider estimates of (2′) on individual data in Section 4.

Equations (2) and (2′) introduce a specific, multiplicative functional form. This carries with it the implication that a change in economic conditions affects the outflow probabilities of all individuals in equal proportion. A 10 per cent increase in the number of vacancies, other things equal, will increase everyone's chance of getting a job in the same proportion.

The multiplicative function stems directly from the normal assumption made about matching (Hall 1977—see our note 2). This is that, if two or more unemployed people arrive at the same vacancy, the job goes to the person who got there first. While this appears to us the most reasonable base-case assumption in the market for manual labour, a case can be made for an alternative view, based on the idea that hiring decisions are made by ranking job applicants, and taking the best qualified person (Butters 1977; Blanchard and Diamond 1990). On this view of things, well-qualified people always find it reasonably easy to find jobs; their outflow rates are relatively invariant to economic conditions. In recessions, the available jobs go to those best qualified and the burden of unemployment falls disproportionately on the least skilled.

Blanchard and Diamond examine a specific version of the ranking hypothesis according to which firms rank workers according to the length of time for which they have been unemployed. They choose the job applicant with the shortest unemployment duration. We investigate their idea empirically in Section 5 below, which examines outflow rates at different durations.

3. Job search: the facts

The issues

But first we need to examine the basic facts about job search in order to see whether there is any evidence that job search is more difficult when conducted on the job. If it were, this could have two important implications.

First, it would imply that most unemployment was a productive phenomenon, as argued by Alchian (1969). (This argument was rejected by Tobin 1972—who argued that employed workers get better information about jobs than those who are unemployed[7] and thus have lower job-search costs.)

Second, if the cost of on-the-job search could be reduced easily, major efforts should be made to do so—for example, by opening labour exchanges during weekends and evenings and even subsidizing employers to fill vacancies with employed rather than unemployed workers.

To throw light on the cost of on-the-job search, we need to find out:

- how much searching unemployed people do which could not be done by the employed (*answer*: not much);
- how much re-employed people seek to move from job to job (*answer*: a significant minority of those re-employed continue to search for a better job);
- how successful employed job-seekers are, compared with unemployed (*answer*: probably at least as successful);
- how quickly the re-employed become unemployed again (s) (*answer*: for a significant proportion, rather quickly); and
- what discount rates the unemployed use (r) (*answer*: high).

In this section we review the relevant available evidence for Britain and the USA. Our conclusion (with one qualification) is going to be that off-the-job search is not typically more productive than on-the-job search, and that unemployment does not exist because of high costs of on-the-job search. The qualification is that search for a high-quality job may be more successful when unemployed than if employed in a low-quality job.

We begin by reviewing evidence on the three stages of the job-search process.

Chapter 5

(i) Time spent searching for information

For Britain we begin by looking at the time that unemployed people spend searching, using the DHSS cohort study of unemployed men who became unemployed in autumn 1978, i.e. just before the second oil shock and the big rise in unemployment. This evidence is directly comparable with the evidence of a number of surveys in the USA, carried out at much the same time. (More recent evidence for the UK is discussed in a later section.)

In the 1978 survey, unemployed men were asked how much time and money

Table 5 *Search intensity, by duration of unemployment: Britain, males, 1978/9*

	6 weeks			16 weeks	12 months
	All (1)	*'Short-spell'* (2)	*'Long-spell'* (3)	*All* (4)	*'Long-spell'* (5)
Time spent searching (hours per week)					
Up to 5	46	58	54	50	64
6–9	18	14	16	20	17
10 or more	36	27	30	30	20
	100	100	100	100	100
Median	6	5	5	5	4
Money spent searching (£ per week)					
Nothing	22	29	26	24	42
Under £1	29	26	35	35	34
£1–£3	28	27	26	26	18
£3 or more	21	19	13	15	6
	100	100	100	100	100
Median	1	0.75	0.75	0.75	0.25

Notes: 'Short-spell' people are those who found jobs within 3 mos.; 'long-spell' remained unemployed for over a year.

The median times are calculated on the basis that responses were given to the nearest hour. Median money spent is rounded to the nearest £0.25.

The average weekly earnings of male manual workers in Oct. 1979 were £96.94 (*Employment Gazette*, Feb. 1980: 136). Price inflation between 1979 and 1990 was about 100 per cent.

Sources: cols. (1)–(3): Moylan *et al.* (1982: Tables 5, 13); col. (4): Social and Community Planning Research (SCPR), Cohort Study of Men Registering as Unemployed, Preliminary Report, 2nd Stage (mimeo), Tables 59, 63; col. (5): SCPR Preliminary Report, 3rd Stage, Tables 55, 56.

they had spent on job search during the previous week. The results are summarized in Table 5. Those concerned were interviewed three times, about 6 weeks, 16 weeks, and 12 months after they became unemployed. In analysing the results, we shall distinguish between the 'short-spell' unemployed, who found jobs within three months and remained continuously employed throughout the rest of the year, and the 'long-spell' unemployed, who were continuously unemployed throughout the year.

The frequency distribution of search intensity is skewed, with the bulk of people not spending very much time or money on search, while a minority searched very actively.[8] For this reason, the median is a more representative statistic than the mean.[9] Table 5 shows a median search time of little more than 5 hours per week. Interestingly, the time spent on job search does not seem to differ greatly between those who find jobs quickly and those who remain unemployed (compare columns (2) and (3)): there is no immediate evidence of 'heterogeneity' among the unemployed in respect of search intensity. Nor does the time spent on search diminish very much with the duration of unemployment (compare columns (3) and (5)); there is little immediate evidence of 'duration-dependent' behaviour, either.

However, if time spent on job search does not decline, the effectiveness of the time spent on job search does appear to decline with duration. The annual Labour Force Surveys for Britain include questions on methods of job search.

Table 6   *Search intensity in the USA, 1976*

	Unemployed for at least 4 weeks		
	Men	*Women*	*All*
Time spent searching (hours per week)			
Up to 5	52	69	59
5–10	20	25	29
More than 10	27	7	12
	100	100	100
Median	5	3	4

Note: The time spent searching per week is one-quarter of the reported figures on time spent in the previous four weeks.

Source: Rosenfeld (1977: Table 3).

It is instructive to group these methods into those involving direct contact with employers as against more passive methods, such as looking at job advertisements and visiting job centres. In 1986, 61 per cent of benefit claimants with less than 6 months of unemployment had engaged in 'employer contact' search in the 4 weeks before their interview; by contrast, only 42 per cent of those unemployed for over 6 months had searched in this way (McCormick 1991).

Table 5 also gives the reported financial costs of search. These are very small. Again, there is little difference between short-spell and long-spell unemployed, but among the long-spell unemployed the money spent on searching does appear to decline quite substantially with the duration of unemployment. This is presumably because they become increasingly hard up.

In the USA, the available information on hours spent on job search is much less detailed than in Britain, but the results of a survey carried out in May 1976 are presented, in comparable form to Table 5, in Table 6. The US survey was of a sample of people unemployed in May 1976, who had already been unemployed for at least 4 weeks. (The average uncompleted duration of unemployment of the group is about 20 weeks[10]). Hence, in terms of sample

Table 7   *Methods of job search by unemployed men in Britain, 1978/9*

| | Percentages of workers | | | | |
| | *Unemployed at 1st month* | | | *Unemployed at both 1st and 4th month* | |
	All (1)	*'Short-spell'* (2)	*'Long-spell'* (3)	*At 1st month* (4)	*At 4th month* (5)
Newspapers	83	78	80	85	85
Job Centres					
Self-service	77	79	84	81	82
Talking to staff	60	54	63	73	56
Asked people					
Former workmates	29	23	22	28	27
Workers in					
other firms	42	38	33	42	37
Friends	50	54	40	32	28
Relatives	31	33	23	48	45
Approached possible					
employers direct	28	48	28	37	41

Note: Table indicates the percentage using each method. Many people used more than one method.

Sources: cols. (1)–(3): *Employment Gazette*, Aug. 1982, pp. 336, 339; cols. (4)–(5): SCPR Preliminary Report 2nd Stage, Table 56.

characteristics, the US survey is probably closest to the second interview in the British cohort study, when the median time since becoming unemployed was 16 weeks.[11] The main finding is the remarkable similarity between the results of the American and the British surveys, with the same median figure for unemployed men of 5 hours per week spent on search.

If job search is a productive activity, it is difficult to explain why people spend only 5 hours a week searching when the normal work-week is, say, 40 hours. More immediately, it suggests that workers might be expected to take a job during the time they are not searching rather than remaining in enforced idleness. Why might they not do so?

One possibility is that, though search time may not take up many hours, effective search requires the worker to be available, to make job applications or attend interviews at any time, rather than having to fit these activities around the requirements of an existing job. Our next three tables give information about how workers spend their search time (Tables 7 and 8), and about which source of information actually led them to the job they finally got (Table 9). In Britain, job search takes place primarily through 'intermediaries'—newspapers, employment exchanges, or word of mouth—rather than by means of direct approaches to possible employers (see Table 7). These methods of job search do not on the face of it appear incompatible with having a job at the same time. In the USA, by contrast, over 70 per cent of the unemployed search for jobs by means of direct approaches to employers (see Table 8).

Evidence on how people find their jobs in the USA is provided in a survey of successful job-seekers (both employed and unemployed) carried out in January 1973 (see Table 9). This confirms the greater importance of direct employer

Table 8 *Methods of job search in the USA, June 1990*

| | Percentages of workers | | |
	Men	Women	Total
Employment agency			
Public	24	20	22
Private	8	9	9
Friends/relatives	23	16	20
Answered advertisements (or			
placed them)	37	40	38
Direct approach to employers	73	72	72

Source: Employment and Earnings Report, July 1990, Table A-19.

239

Table 9 *How jobs were found: Britain and USA*

| | (1)
Britain | (2)
USA | | |
| | *Unemployed men
finding work by 4th
month, 1978/9* | *January 1973 survey of
successful job-seekers* | | |
		Men	*Women*	*All*
Newspapers	15	12	16	14
Public employment agencies	22	5	5	5
Asked people	31	31	24	28
Direct approach to employer	20	35	35	35
Other/not stated	12	17	20	18
	100	100	100	100

Sources: col. (1): Moylan *et al.* (1984: Table 4.4); col. (2): Rosenfeld (1975: Table 1).

contacts in the USA and the relative unimportance of public employment agencies.

About half of this US sample of successful job-seekers were unemployed at the time they were looking for work, and the rest were employed. Interestingly, the median search time of the sample of employed and unemployed job-seekers in 1973 was about the same as that of the 1976 sample of unemployed workers only—that is, 5 hours (Bureau of Labor Statistics *Bulletin* no. 1886, 1975: 14). In the British cohort study of the unemployed, by contrast, those who had found work but were still seeking for better jobs appeared to spend much less time on job search than did unemployed job-seekers, with a median search time of 3 hours per week as against 5 hours for unemployed job-seekers (SCPR Preliminary Report, 2nd Stage: Table 59).

(ii) Number of job applications

Given information on job vacancies, workers decide which jobs to apply for. But how many applications do they make? In the British cohort study people were asked how many jobs they had applied for, and in Table 10 the responses are summarized for those who had been continuously unemployed up to the fourth month. The median number of job applications was under one a month. In a 1980 study, Daniel (1990: 185) found an average of two job applications per month during the first six weeks of unemployment, falling to an average of

Table 10   *Number of job applications, males: Britain and USA*

| No. of applications in first 4 mos. | Britain, 1978/9 All unemployed at 16 wks. | | USA, 1976 All unemployed for at least 4 wks. | |
	Incl. all applications (%) (1)	Incl. only applications for known vacancies (%) (2)	No. of applications over past 4 wks.	(%) (3)
0	18	32	0	0
1, 2	19	32	1, 2	14
3, 4	17	14	3–5	22
5–9	15	7	6–10	27
10–19	10	6		
20–29	7	3	More than 10	37
30 or more	12	4		
	100	100		100
Median	4	2		8
Median applications per month	1	0.5		8

Sources: cols. (1) and (2): SCPR Preliminary Report, 2nd Stage, Table 66; col. (3): Rosenfeld (1977: 40).

one per month by the tenth month of unemployment, and thereafter remaining constant. A more recent British study in Leeds and Sheffield in 1982 (a time of deep recession) found a mean job application rate below 0.7 per month; the application rate was only slightly lower for longer-term unemployed people.

The results from the British cohort study can be compared with those of the US May 1976 survey. There is a very substantial difference between the two countries in the median number of job applications (eight per month in the USA as against only 1 per month in Britain).[12] The greater use of direct approaches to employers as a method of search in the USA may lead more immediately to job applications than methods of job search using intermediaries. Even so, the median number of applications reported by British unemployed men seems remarkably low. Again, it would not seem to be too difficult for someone in employment to manage this number of applications (of which, anyway, only a proportion would lead to interviews). As we show later, the behaviour of the unemployed in Britain had changed somewhat by 1987.

(iii)   Acceptance of job offers

The next issue is whether job applicants refuse offers of work. The answer is that most take their first job offer. In the US 1976 survey of the unemployed, only 8.5 per cent of job-seekers had rejected a job offer (Akerlof *et al.* 1988*b*: 539).

Further evidence from the USA can be derived from the 1980 Employment Opportunity Pilot Projects (EOPP) survey (Barron *et al.* 1985). Employers were asked, for the last job they had filled, how many people had turned a job offer down. The answer was about 20 per cent. These job offers would have been made to employed as well as unemployed job applicants. Another study, using the EOPP household survey, reports that 33 per cent of job offers to unemployed people were rejected (Blau and Robins 1990).

Turning to Britain, a Manpower Services Commission (MSC) study of the flow into unemployment in May 1980 established that, within the first six weeks of unemployment, 13 per cent of job-seekers had turned down job offers (Daniel 1981). Of job-seekers who had found work by the end of the six weeks, 15 per cent had turned down at least one offer, though in some of these cases this may simply reflect the consequences of having a number of applications under consideration at the same time. Of those unemployed at the end of the six weeks, 12 per cent had turned down job offers. Daniel also reports that job rejection is, as might be expected, more common among non-manual than among manual workers. Another British study established that job rejection is more common among the short-term than among the long-term unemployed. The study showed that in June 1980 12 per cent of men who had then been unemployed for at least 16 months had rejected a job offer, while only 4 per cent of this sample rejected a job offer during the subsequent 15-month period from June 1980 to September 1981 (White 1983).[13]

The fact that job refusal among the long-term unemployed is less common than among unemployed people as a whole, combined with the evidence cited above that the long-term unemployed search for work much like others, implies that long-term unemployed people are less likely to leave long-term unemployment, simply because they receive few or no job offers. Of course, this could be the result of an elaborate deception whereby they apply for jobs which they know they have no hope of getting; but it seems more plausible to think that the long-term unemployed face greater obstacles to finding work as a result of their personal characteristics, employer discrimination, or the consequences of lengthy unemployment itself.

(iv)   More recent evidence for Britain

We have so far confined our comparison of US and British job search behaviour mainly to the 1970s, when evidence is available for both countries and unemployment rates were similar. There is however further evidence for Britain in spring 1987, when unemployment was very much higher and efforts had begun to tighten the administration of unemployment benefit. The relevant tables, referred to below, are in the Appendix at the end of this chapter.

By 1987 the application rate for newly unemployed people had increased to around 3 per month (see Table A1). This compares with around 1 per month in 1978 and 2 per month in 1980. (Application rates were similar after seven weeks and nine months.) However, the time spent on job search had changed little[14], and there had been some rise in real expenditure on job search (from about £2 to £3.50 a week in 1987 prices)—see Table A2. For the 1987 cohort (unlike the 1978 cohort), success in finding a job was somewhat associated with search intensity (see Table A3).

Information on job acceptances and refusals by the 1987 cohort is shown in Table A4. Compared with the MSC 1980 study, there appears to have been some fall in the proportion of job offers refused. Within seven weeks of becoming unemployed, 29 per cent of men had obtained jobs and 7 per cent had refused jobs. Both these figures were down on 1980, but the second more so.

At the first interview, 14 per cent of the men in the 1987 cohort who were not in work said that they were not seeking work. (The corresponding figure for 1978 was 16 per cent.) At the second interview, nine months after the start of unemployment, 22 per cent of those still unemployed reported that they were not seeking work. (The nearest equivalent figures from 1978 were 23 per cent after four months and 33 per cent after a year: Wood 1982: Table 114; Erens and Hedges 1990: Table 801.) So, by spring 1987 there had been no marked change in these respects.

A surprising feature of the 1987 cohort is that those who had not looked for work at all were as likely to be back in work at the time of the first interview as those who had looked for work. This might be because workers who expected to be recalled to work by their former employers saw no need to search. As Table A5 shows, 17 per cent of those who returned to work within 26 weeks of becoming unemployed did so as a result of an approach by an employer or by returning to a former employer. (In the 1978 study, 9 per cent of those not in work and not seeking work four months after becoming unemployed were not searching because they expected to return to a former job.) In 1987 nearly one-half of the men not in work and not seeking work gave 'waiting to start a job', 'education', 'training', or a 'government scheme' as their reason for not searching; health and retirement were also important reasons for not searching. Clearly, those not in work and not seeking work are very heterogeneous.

There is also information on failure to search among the stock of unemployed. The 1986 Labour Force Survey showed that 26 per cent of those who were claiming benefit because of unemployment had not sought work in the four weeks before being interviewed. This proportion fell somewhat in the following years and was 19 per cent in 1989.

Surveys of those unemployed for over six months and claiming benefit, carried out for the Department of Employment, suggest that in London and the West Midlands failure to search is less common than indicated by the Labour Force Survey. The London survey, carried out in July 1988, found that 12 per cent of claimants had not sought work in the previous four weeks (Meadows *et al.* 1988). The West Midlands survey of April 1989 showed the same proportion of claimants not seeking work as the London survey (Cooper 1989). An October 1979 survey of those unemployed for over three months in Bristol also found that 14 per cent of those unemployed for over six months had not looked for work in the previous four weeks, and that 8 per cent of those unemployed for between three and six months had not looked for work in the previous four weeks (Griffin 1990).

The location of the interviews for the Department of Employment surveys may have caused selection bias. The interviews were conducted in unemployment benefit offices immediately after claimants had signed to say they were available for work. While the interviews were carried out in reasonable privacy by an independent research centre, those who were not seeking work may have been less willing to volunteer for interview. So the Labour Force Survey results are probably more reliable. This makes the finding, common to both the London and West Midlands surveys, that nearly 5 per cent of claimants reported that they had never looked for work even more disturbing.

(v)   *Job-to-job movement*

We can now ask what happens when people eventually find work. Do they keep looking, or do they stay in the same job for a long time? The majority of people taking jobs stop searching, but a significant proportion take a job while intending to go on looking for another one: one-fifth of those in the 1978 cohort study who found jobs within four months were continuing to look for other jobs (SCPR Preliminary Report, 2nd Stage: Table 42). In the survey, one-third said they continued their search after finding their initial jobs, and of those three-quarters did subsequently (i.e. within 20 months) change (or lose) the first job (Daniel 1983: 255). Indeed, according to Daniel, people often take jobs to provide 'a more secure base than unemployment for an extended job search' (1983: 253). The Labour Force Survey provides supporting evidence: while only about 5 per cent of employed workers engage in job search, the proportion of those people now in work but recently unemployed who are looking for another job is around three times higher (see Table 11).

(vi)   Re-entry to unemployment

Many of those who find work quickly become unemployed again because they lose their jobs. Of the British 1978 cohort, 40 per cent of those who found a job within the first 12 months became unemployed again within that period. Of these, 36 per cent had only one job in the year, 46 per cent had two jobs, and the rest had three or more jobs (all within a year), as well as at least two spells of unemployment (Moylan *et al.* 1982: 337). The rate at which the 1987 cohort lost the first job they found was also very high: 41 per cent of men finding a job within nine months left at least one job within that period; of those who had at least one job, 22 per cent had two jobs and 8 per cent had three or more jobs (Ehrens and Hedges 1990: 131 and Table 502).

In the USA, unemployment is concentrated among teenagers to a much greater extent than in Britain. Clark and Summers (1979: 54) estimate an average duration for post-unemployment jobs held by teenagers of less than three months, and argue that with such short job durations the payoff from acquiring better job information would be minimal.

Table 11   *Percentage of employees currently engaged in on-the-job search, by status 12 months earlier: Britain, 1984*

Current occupation	Employed 12 mos. earlier	Unemployed 12 mos. earlier
Managerial and professional	4.8	17.4
Clerical and related	5.3	13.6
Other non-manual	4.5	8.0
Skilled manual	3.9	10.6
General labourers	4.0	27.3
Other manual	4.8	16.6
All	4.7	15.0

Source: 1984 Labour Force Survey.

(vii) Effectiveness of on-the-job search

Turning briefly to wider evidence on the effectiveness of on-the-job search, there is clearly a large amount of job-to-job movement, as the British data in Annex 5.3 show. These data also show, interestingly, that employed job-seekers get a job more quickly than unemployed job-seekers. As the unemployed accept most job offers, this means that employed job search is more productive than unemployed job search in generating job offers.

Employed people's greater success is partly because of their advantage over the unemployed in access to information. Hence, even if their reservation wage is higher than that of the unemployed, they are more likely to find a job worth taking. Employers also seem to like them more. A survey carried out in 1986 showed that one-half of employers regarded unemployment as an undesirable attribute in a job applicant (Meager and Metcalf 1987). Case-studies indicated that long-term unemployment prevented applicants being selected for interview, irrespective of their other characteristics. Long-term unemployment was less damaging to the employment prospects of manual workers: employers' recruitment procedures for manual workers tended to include little if any pre-selection for interview, the most obvious stage at which long-term unemployment might debar an applicant. There was evidence of less discrimination against the long-term unemployed in areas of high long-term unemployment, and in occupations where there were labour shortages.

(viii) Discount rates

There remains the question of the discount rates which unemployed people use. These can be estimated econometrically. They can also be guessed by looking at the capital market position of the unemployed. Do unemployed people run down financial assets or borrow to maintain their consumption, or do they simply consume less? If the latter, their discount rates could be very high.

In the 1978 British cohort study, men were asked how much savings they had both at six weeks and at 12 months. The main findings (Table 12) were that a majority (about two-thirds) of the men had virtually no savings at either six weeks or 12 months, but that a small minority had substantial savings. (These men were mainly retired people with occupational pensions, who had not yet reached the age of 65.) There was no evidence of savings being run down.

Later British studies broadly confirm the 1978 results. Those aged under 35 in a sample of the 1983 inflow into unemployment did not, on average, reduce their savings or increase their borrowings to limit the fall in their consumption

Table 12   *Savings of the unemployed: Britain, 1978/9*

Savings	All		Continuously registered unemployed	
	1st month	*12th month*	*1st month*	*12th month*
None	53	51	58	65
Up to £250	24	22	7	7
£250–£500	5	8	2	1
£500–£1250	4	5	4	4
£1250+	9	10	21	21
Not stated	4	4	7	3
	100	100	100	100

Source: SCPR, 3rd Stage, Table 80.

during 15 months of unemployment, but those aged 35 and over increased their net debt by about £400 on average (Heady and Smyth 1989). The 1987 cohort study shows that those unemployed for no more than nine months reported an increase in net debt from an average of £435 before becoming unemployed to £525 when they returned to work (Garman and Redmond 1990; see also Table A6). Like the 1978 cohort, just over one-half of the 1987 cohort had no savings when their unemployment started.

(ix)   Choosiness

Finally, it is important to know how far the unemployed are putting obstacles in their own way by being unwilling to consider a whole range of available jobs. This is a difficult question. It is certainly not true that the unemployed are unwilling to consider jobs in different industries or occupations. The two British cohort studies and the American 1976 survey found that the majority of the unemployed take jobs in different industries and/or occupations from their previous job (Tables 13 and A7). In the Policy Studies Institute (PSI) survey, only one-half of those questioned claimed to be looking for particular types of jobs; the other half were looking for, 'within broadly defined limits, any kind of job' (Daniel 1983: 252).

As far as earnings are concerned, in both British cohort studies those who returned to work were earning on average about the same in real terms as in their previous jobs. However, about one-third had taken a cut in real earnings, and in the 1978 study about half of these took a substantial cut—of £10 or

Table 13 *Jobs taken by the unemployed (%)*

	Britain, 1978/9	USA, 1976	
	Men	All (incl. women)	Men aged 25–59
In same industry	33	36	55
In same occupation	40	33	47
In same industry and occupation	25	24	38

Note: Employment was classified under 14 broad industries and 17 occupations in Britain.

Source: col. (1): Moylan and Davies (1981: 30); cols. (2) and (3): Clark and Summers (1979: 48, Table 9).

more in gross weekly earnings in 1978 prices (Moylan and Davies 1981: 30–1; Erens and Hedges 1990: 140–7). An analysis of American data from the Michigan Panel on Income Dynamics in the period 1972–6 found that earnings immediately after a period of unemployment were significantly less than earnings before the spell (Chowdhury and Nickell 1985).

The Department of Employment survey of those unemployed for over six months in London found that 45 per cent of job-seekers were not restricting their search to any particular kind of work, and that a large majority of those who limited their search were seeking jobs in occupations that were well represented among the vacancies found in a parallel survey of employers (Meadows *et al.* 1988). The main exception was the 12 per cent who were looking for work only in the arts, fashion, design, or media—areas of limited job opportunity, even in London. So there is evidence that a small minority of the unemployed are reducing their chances of employment by restricting their area of job search. The Bristol survey of people unemployed for over three months found that just over half were not specific about the type of work they were seeking (Griffin 1990).

The Department of Employment surveys do indicate, however, that travel-to-work times have a major effect on job applications by the unemployed. More strikingly, Daniel (1990: 142–3) found that in the May 1980 survey, access to motorized transport was the single most important factor associated with unemployment duration. In similar vein, in the recent West Midlands study, Cooper (1989) has suggested that, given the locations of the unemployed and vacancies (particularly for less skilled jobs), a change in expectations about travelling times by employers as well as by the unemployed is needed if the West Midlands labour market is to work effectively.

A study of unemployed people of all durations in Leeds and Sheffield in 1982 found that the median of the maximum acceptable one-way journey-to-work times in both cities was one hour, twice the median of maximum acceptable times reported by those unemployed for over six months in the 1988 West Midlands and 1989 Bristol surveys. Yet, job applications by the unemployed in Leeds and Sheffield were spatially limited, with strong preferences for job locations in the city centres and close to the main radial roads served by the principal bus routes. There were far fewer applications per job vacant in areas that were less easily accessible.

The 1987 cohort study collected information on travel-to-work times in the last job (if any) in the year before becoming unemployed and in jobs obtained in the nine subsequent months. For both men and women, the distribution of travel-to-work times is remarkably similar before and after unemployment (Erens and Hedges 1990: Tables 309 and 711).

(x)   Conclusion

From all this evidence, we conclude that there is little reason for an unemployed individual to reject a job paying more than benefits in order to search more effectively. But there is one important qualification. Employers offering good jobs may well use a person's current position as a screening device. While unemployment is a bad signal, being in a low-quality job may well be a worse one (McCormick 1990). Moreover, a person who has just taken one job and now seeks another may look like a high-turnover risk. These factors may indeed deter people taking low-quality jobs, by reducing their chances of successfully applying for a better one. Little is known about these mechanisms.

To formalize this line of thought, we can use our two-sector model of earlier chapters. According to this, jobs of some kind are freely available in the secondary sector at a wage that clears the market. From such jobs it is possible to look for primary-sector work, but the chances of success are somewhat reduced. Thus, an individual will take a secondary-sector job if it pays a wage above benefit *B* plus an appropriate risk premium. He will then continue to search for a better job. Other unemployed people will not take a secondary-sector job; but once they get a primary-sector job, they will stop looking. We believe this account squares well with the facts laid bare in this section.

We are not saying that job search is unimportant; the proper matching of individual workers to individual vacancies is important for productivity and for job satisfaction. But unemployment exists mainly because wages in the primary sector lead to job-rationing. Wages in that sector may be affected by the supply price of labour, but do not clear the market. Workers are not deterred from taking jobs by the thought that employment and job search are incompatible activities. However, because of job rationing in the primary sector, benefits (B), and the possible bad signal from taking a job in the secondary sector, their best strategy may be to remain unemployed until a suitable vacancy turns up.

4. Determinants of duration: cross-section evidence

The basic model

The next task is to explain the outflow of individuals from unemployment. There have been a large number of studies of this, nearly all of which are more or less loosely based on the simple search model described in Section 2.

In its standard form, we may write the conditional probability that an unemployed individual leaves unemployment, or his 'exit rate' (h_i), as

$$h_i = \lambda_i p(W_{ci}), \tag{8}$$

where $p(W_{ci})$ is the probability (per period) that the individual makes a job application and λ_i is the probability that he is selected for the job, having applied. In this standard model, the reservation wage, W_{ci}, is given by

$$W_{ci} = B_i + \frac{\lambda_i}{\psi_i} p(W_{ci})(\bar{W}(W_{ci}) - W_{ci}), \tag{9}$$

where $\bar{W}(W_{ci}) = E(W \mid W > W_{ci})$, the conditional expectation of the wage in the prospective job, and ψ_i depends on the discount rate and the probability (per period) of leaving this prospective job (see equation (7)). This is a very simple variant of the standard model which may easily be extended to incorporate the utility of leisure, search intensity, and so on (see e.g. Narendranathan and Nickell 1985). Furthermore, it can also be extended rather crudely to take account of on-the-job search. If it is just as easy to search on the job as it is to search while unemployed, then, as we have noted, the individual simply takes the first job that pays more than the benefit level (i.e., $W_{ci} = B_i$). In the more complex case where on-the-job search is more costly than unemployed search, some weight is attached to the second term in (9), namely, the expected pay in the prospective job. We could incorporate this case into (9) by allowing ψ_i to be a decreasing function of relative on-the-job search costs. As these fall, ψ_i rises and the reservation wage falls towards the benefit level. While (9) is not formally the correct equation in this case, it still captures the main forces at work.

The main drawback of this simple model is that it is based on a stationary environment. Major sources of non-stationarity arise because of time variation in benefits (B) and the probability that the applicant will be selected (λ). In some countries, benefits change with the duration of unemployment spells and may even disappear completely after some point. The chances of selection for a job applicant may change either because external labour market conditions change (e.g., a rise in U/V will raise the degree of competition for vacancies) or because employers systematically base their hiring decisions on the elapsed duration of unemployment spells, discriminating against those with longer durations.

Job search in a non-stationary environment has been studied extensively, with the most complete analyses appearing in Mortensen (1987) and van den Berg (1990a). (Earlier studies include Mortensen 1977; Burdett 1979.) Thus, for example, suppose that either B or λ is expected to drop suddenly after duration T, otherwise remaining constant. Then van den Berg (1990a) demonstrates that the reservation wage follows the path set out in Fig. 5. In particular, as Mortensen (1987) indicates, there is a very sharp fall in the reservation wage during the two or three weeks preceding duration T. Corresponding to this will be a significant rise in the exit rate during the same period.

Empirical implementation

In order to implement this kind of framework to analyse duration data, the standard approach is to work with the conditional probability of leaving

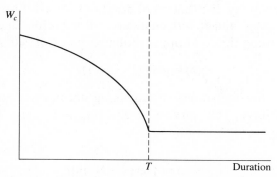

Fig. 5.   *The reservation wage when B or λ fall discretely at duration T.*

251

unemployment, or the exit rate (h_i), which is also known as the hazard. This is the fundamental behavioural concept in studying the duration of unemployment. The simplest method of proceeding is to note the determinants of the reservation wage from (9) and then insert these into (8), writing the hazard in a general form as

$$h(t) = h(B_{it}/\mu_{wi}, q_i, V/U, t), \tag{10}$$

where μ_{wi} is the mean of the wage distribution associated with available vacancies, q_i is a set of personal characteristics which determine λ and ψ, and V/U is the vacancy–unemployment ratio which varies over time and also influences λ and ψ (see equation (2')). In practice, the ratio V/U may also be person-specific, in the sense that it may refer to the region and occupation of the individual concerned. Note that benefits are normalized by the mean of the wage distribution since, as Mortensen (1986) demonstrates, expected-wealth-maximizing search models generally imply homogeneity of degree zero in benefits and a scale parameter of the wage distribution.

A more sophisticated procedure is to make use of the exact form of (9) in the process of estimation, thereby identifying separately the functions λ and ψ, and the parameters of the wage distribution. This relies heavily on assumptions made about the various functional forms, but does provide estimates of the impact of exogenous variables on the reservation wage as well as expected duration. Examples of this latter approach include Yoon (1981), Lancaster and Chesher (1983), Lynch (1983), Narendranathan and Nickell (1985), Wolpin (1987), and van den Berg (1990*a*). Here, however, we shall concentrate on the former approach in order to keep the exposition straightforward.

When we come to empirical work, we have data on how long people remain unemployed (t_i) rather than on their probabilities of leaving. Hence to estimate the parameters of the hazard function, we need to see how the hazard rate relates to the probability distribution of durations (or exit times). If $g(t)$ is the density function of exit times, with cumulative distribution function $G(t)$, then the hazard $h(t)$, being the conditional probability of exit, satisfies

$$h(t) = g(t)/(1 - G(t)), \tag{11}$$

where $1 - G(t)$ is the probability of remaining unemployed to time t (or the 'survival' probability). This survival probability is in turn, by integration, equal to

$$1 - G(t) = \int_0^t \exp(-h(\tau)) d\tau. \tag{12}$$

The standard form used for the hazard is the so-called mixed proportional hazards model, where $h(t)$ is written as

$$h_i(t) = v\exp(x'_{it}\beta)f(t). \tag{13}$$

The vector x'_{it} represents the observed variables in (10), whereas v is a random variable, which captures unobserved variables, and is usually taken to be orthogonal to x. $f(t)$ is the 'baseline hazard' which captures the variation of the hazard with duration. In order to make this model operational, we must specify a distribution for v, namely $H(v)$. Then the observed survivor function in the sample $(1 - \bar{G}(t))$ is given by

$$1 - \bar{G}_i(t) = \int_0^\infty \int_0^t \exp[-v\exp(x'_{it}\beta)f(\tau)]d\tau dH(v), \tag{14}$$

where $\bar{G}_i(t)$ now reflects the distribution of v. This is then used to form the likelihood function appropriate to the sample. Thus, if we have a random sample of entrants into unemployment who are followed for T_0 periods, the likelihood function has the form

$$L = \prod_{i\in I}\bar{g}_i(t_i)\prod_{j\in J}[1 - \bar{G}_j(T_0)],$$

where I is the set of individuals who left unemployment prior to T_0, at duration t_i, and J is the group who remained unemployed until T_0.

The fundamental problem facing the researcher is how to model the baseline hazard $f(t)$ and the 'error' distribution $H(v)$. In a formal sense, non-parametric identification of both f and H is possible so long as we assert that $H(v)$ has a finite mean. (See Ridder 1990 for a complete analysis.) In practice, however, things are rather tricky. If we misspecify $H(v)$, this will certainly corrupt our estimates of the baseline hazard $f(t)$, and maybe even our estimates of the impact of the regressors β. The corruption of the baseline hazard arises from the omitted heterogeneity problem. Thus, the average hazard of a heterogeneous group will decline solely because the 'best' individuals exit most rapidly, leaving a group of lower and lower average 'quality' as duration increases. (See Lancaster and Nickell 1980, or Heckman and Singer 1984, for a formal treatment.) All is not lost, however. If the choice of a function to capture the baseline hazard is flexible enough, then estimates of the elasticity of expected duration with respect to the x-variables are generally satisfactory whatever the choice of $H(v)$. (See Ridder 1987 for a complete treatment.) The instability of the impact of the regressors in response to changes in $H(v)$, found by Heckman and Singer (1984), is probably due to their choice of the highly inflexible Weibull baseline hazard $(f(t) = \alpha t^{\alpha-1})$. On the other hand, to get the baseline hazard right, a flexible choice of $H(v)$ is an absolute requirement.

In practice, the simplest choices are Weibull for $f(t)$ and gamma for $H(v)$; that is,

$$f(t) = \alpha t^{\alpha-1}, \qquad H(v) = (\gamma^{\gamma}/\Gamma(\gamma))v^{\gamma-1}\exp(-v\gamma), \qquad (15)$$

which was first used by Lancaster (1979). Note that the Weibull forces the baseline hazard to be monotone, which in most cases is probably not flexible enough, at least for obtaining accurate estimates of the impact of time-varying regressors. (See Meyer 1990 for some relevant experiments.) Thus, for example, Nickell (1979b) used a quadratic for the baseline hazard and found it to be non-monotonic.

To make things more flexible, the obvious procedure is to use non-parametric methods for either $f(t)$ or $H(v)$, or both. Methods for allowing full flexibility for the baseline hazard are detailed in Cox (1972) and Prentice and Gloeckler (1978) and were used successfully in this context by Meyer (1990) in conjunction with the gamma form of $H(v)$. To allow full flexibility for $H(v)$, Heckman and Singer (1984) suggest mass point methods, whereby $H(v)$ is modelled using a discrete set of values $v_1, v_2, \ldots, v_m$ with probabilities Π_1, $\Pi_2, \ldots, \Pi_m$, allowing m to be chosen by the data. Five mass points ($m = 5$) is typically adequate. Meyer (1990) reports an attempt to use both these non-parametric methods simultaneously, but found it difficult to compute the discrete distribution for v. So, despite the theoretical identifiability of such a completely flexible model, it seems hard to make it work in practice. This is rather unfortunate, because estimates of the true baseline hazard would be most informative on the issue of duration dependence. Thus, if we can control for time variation in the benefit system and the tightness of the labour market, we may be able to identify effects arising from loss of motivation by the unemployed or duration-based discrimination by employers. However, if we cannot obtain reliable estimates of the baseline hazard, then we are unable to obtain evidence of these kinds of effects from cross-section duration data.

Evidence on benefit and other effects

The most interesting results arising from the analysis of duration data are those concerned with the impact of unemployment benefits. However, before looking at the actual numbers, one or two points are worth making about their interpretation. Suppose we find that a 1 per cent rise in unemployment benefit tends to raise average unemployment duration by x per cent. Does this mean that unemployment will rise by x per cent? The answer is No. First, it tells us nothing about benefit effects on the inflow into unemployment. Second, the duration effect of benefits is *ceteris paribus* on wages. It is a *labour supply* effect. After a rise in benefits, wages will rise and this will attenuate the general equilibrium effect on durations and hence on unemployment. What it does tell us is the extent to which benefits influence the effectiveness of the unemployed in searching for work. This, of itself, is a very important issue.

The basic result is that the elasticity of expected duration with respect to benefits is generally in the range 0.2–0.9 depending on the state of the labour market and the country concerned, although estimates as low as 0 (Atkinson *et al.* 1984) and as high as 3.3 (Ridder and Gorter 1986) may be found. Standard estimates for the UK range from the early findings of Nickell (1979*a*) and Lancaster (1979) of around 0.8 to the more recent estimates of 0.3 reported by Narendranathan *et al.* (1985). There is some suggestion here that benefit elasticities tend to be lower during periods of high unemployment. (For further discussion of this view, see van den Berg 1990*a*.) However, it is also true that only in the later (1985) study were data on actual benefits available, with the earlier studies using imputation. In the USA, the most recent estimate by Meyer (1990) is 0.88, although this is high relative to previous estimates, as discussed in Meyer's paper. In a highly informative structural study, van den Berg (1990*a*) discusses the implications of the Dutch benefit system. Here there is a sharp decline in benefits for some workers after two years' duration, as the system switches from insurance-based to welfare-based support. His results indicate that the duration elasticity of insurance benefits is around 0.15, whereas for the welfare benefits it is 0.5. Unlike the USA, the Netherlands has a high proportion of long-term unemployed, and the relatively high elasticity with respect to the benefits of the two-year-plus group indicates how much of an impact reducing this long 'tail' has on average durations.

This last is one of only a very few studies which consider the implications of significant changes (usually reductions) in benefits as the unemployment spell gets longer. In many countries there are no significant changes, but in some, such as the USA, benefits effectively cease after some point. Two notable studies in this area, using US data, are those by Katz and Meyer (1988) and Meyer (1990). Both studies report that the exit rate rises very sharply just before the time when benefits are due to lapse, exactly as might be expected if the reservation wage follows the path shown in Fig. 5. However, care must be taken with the interpretation here, because some of this rise is due to the fact that many workers are recalled by their previous employers shortly before their benefits run out. This suggests that firms' recall policies are not unrelated to the structure of the benefit system. In any event, Katz and Meyer (1988) find a strong impact of benefit duration on unemployment duration. A one-week increase in potential benefit duration leads to an increase in the average duration of unemployment spells of 0.16–0.20 week. Comparable results for Canada are reported in Ham and Rea (1987).

One or two other aspects of benefit effects are worth noting. For example, Narendranathan *et al.* (1985) find that young workers are significantly more responsive to benefit changes than older workers, and van den Berg (1990*a*) finds that those with lower levels of human capital are more responsive than the rest. Finally, it is generally the case that the effects of benefits and potential earnings are consistent with zero degree homogeneity.

What evidence is there of duration dependence? The fact that benefits typically decline somewhat over spells would lead naturally to exit rates increasing, and it is generally the case that, once heterogeneity is controlled for, exit rates are estimated to be relatively flat or rising. However, what is of real interest is the path of exit rates once the effect of declining benefits has been removed, for only then can we observe the possibility of declining exit rates arising from a falling off of motivation or employer discrimination. The evidence on this is very thin, although Meyer (1990) discovers no hint of a declining hazard, controlling for the benefit path, except perhaps in the first two or three weeks. However, as we have already noted, accurately estimating the baseline hazard is a very tricky business.

Finally, we should mention some other standard results. The exit rate usually decreases with age, is higher for married as opposed to single men, and is typically lower for individuals in regions or occupations with high unemployment rates (or U/V ratios).

5. Determinants of duration: time-series evidence

We now turn to time-series evidence on what determines the outflow from unemployment. As we saw in Table 3 and Annex 5.1, average durations have risen and outflow rates fallen hugely in many countries. This is partly due to the fall in the ratio of vacancies to unemployment. But that is by no means sufficient to explain it all. This is clear from Fig. 6, which plots for Britain on a log scale the outflow (H), unemployment (U), and vacancies (V). Suppose the hiring function were logarithmic with

$$\ln H = \alpha \ln V + (1 - \alpha)\ln U + \text{const.}$$

Then we should see in our graph that $\ln H$ was a weighted average of $\ln V$ and

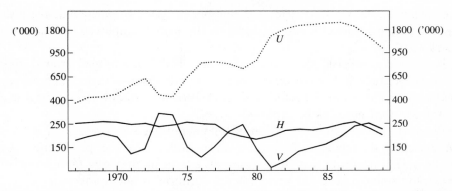

Fig. 6. *Male unemployment (U), male monthly outflows (H), and vacancies (V), Britain, 1967–1989.*

Sources: Jackman *et al.* (1989), plus update from *Employment Gazette*.

ln$U$ plus a constant. Yet in fact, ln$H$ falls sharply relative to any possible weighted average.

What could explain this shift? As we have argued, the outflow rate should also depend on the effectiveness of job-seekers (c) and on U/V mismatch. We discuss U/V mismatch in the next chapter and show that it is a relatively stable factor. This focuses our attention on the effectiveness of the unemployed, which can be undermined by:

1. increased choosiness of employers in general (e.g. arising from employment protection laws discouraging hiring);
2. increased ineffectiveness of the unemployed themselves, because of demoralization from long-term unemployment or an increased relative utility of unemployment;
3. increased choosiness of employers arising from the unemployed being less attractive (e.g. there being more long-term unemployed).

Employment protection laws are quite strict in most European countries (though not in the USA). In many countries they became stiffer during the 1960s and 1970s, with some relaxation in the 1980s (Emerson 1988*a*). In Britain, for example, there were three main stiffenings of the regulations. The Redundancy Payments Act 1965 introduced statutory payments when a worker is made redundant, the costs of which fell, initially in part but since 1986 in full, on the employer. The Industrial Relations Act 1971 established legal rights against unfair dismissal. The Employment Protection Act 1975 extended the periods of notice required before a termination. During the 1980s the laws have become less strict in a number of ways. In particular, the laws against unfair dismissal no longer apply to any worker employed less than two years.

It is widely believed that employers have been discouraged from hiring workers because it has become more costly to dismiss them. The survey evidence on this is not particularly clear (Daniel and Stilgoe 1978), but it is a hypothesis that needs to be explored.

We next consider the motivation of the unemployed as job-seekers. This is influenced by the replacement ratio, by the conditions for receipt of benefit, by neighbourhood effects (e.g. the hysteresis effects of previous high levels of unemployment), and by the uncompleted duration of unemployment.

In Britain neither the replacement ratio nor the duration of benefits has altered much since the mid-1960s, and the effect of these variables cannot therefore be traced in the recent time series. (We have already noted the significance of these factors in accounting for differences in unemployment rates across nations.) But equally important are the job-search conditions required of benefit recipients. There is evidence of increasing lenience of administration in Britain from the mid-1960s through the 1970s (Layard 1986). Since 1986 conditions have been substantially tightened, with marked apparent effects on outflow rates (see Chapter 10).

Finally, there is the effect of uncompleted duration of unemployment on the motivation and morale of workers, and on the extent to which they are stigmatized by employers. There are three main elements to the idea that the duration of unemployment can effect a worker's chance of finding a job:

1. effects on job search;
2. effects on the worker's skills, motivation, and morale;
3. job screening and employer perceptions.

With regard to the first of these, most of the evidence suggests that search activity declines but only to a rather small extent with duration of unemployment. Most of the British surveys already cited (though not all) suggest that job search and job applications do not fall off greatly with duration. It is nevertheless the case that when long-term unemployed people make job applications they are less likely to be called to interview, and if called to interview are less likely to be offered a job.[15]

Why do employers discriminate against the long-term unemployed, and are they rational to do so? Many employers believe that the long-term unemployed are unmotivated and lacking in relevant skills and work habits. As noted above, some automatically reject applications from long-term unemployed people purely on the basis of unemployment duration. When long-term unemployed people are called to interview, employers report that they often perform very badly, appearing anxious and depressed (P. Robinson 1988).

The key issue is whether the long-term unemployment *causes* demotivation and demoralization, or whether it is simply that the least enthusiastic and energetic people have most difficulty in finding jobs, and therefore the long-term unemployed consist largely of people with such characteristics. Studies both in Britain and the USA find evidence of the adverse effect of prolonged spells of unemployment on motivation and morale. A study of school-leavers in Leeds in the UK found evidence of a direct impact of unemployment on motivation (Banks and Jackson 1982). For school-leavers with similar scores on the General Health Questionnaire while still at school, those who became unemployed tended to develop symptoms of psychological ill-health, while the psychological health of those who found jobs tended to improve. Similar findings have been reported from the Michigan Panel Study on Income Dynamics in the USA.

A review of the literature concluded that the psychological impact of job losses was typically rapid, with significant impairment at an early stage of unemployment (Warr 1987). Further deterioration was likely if unemployment continued, until a plateau of poor mental health was reached after between three and six months. (However, the motivation and morale of the long-term unemployed did not decline further as their period of unemployment lengthened.)

These conclusions are supported by recent studies. A UK survey of the 1983 inflow into unemployment assessed psychological health after three months' unemployment and a year later (Heady and Smyth 1989). A comparison between those who were continuously unemployed for 15 months and those who were in full-time work at the time of the second assessment indicates that both groups had very much the same level of psychological well-being after three months' unemployment; but those in work a year later showed a marked improvement in psychological well-being when compared with those who had remained unemployed. A similar result was obtained from a longitudinal analysis of a stock of unemployed people using 1986 data from local labour markets in Britain (Burchell 1990).

This direct evidence of the effect of duration on motivation does not establish an effect on outflow rates. For this purpose it is better to look directly at the effect of duration on outflow rates.[16] We have already seen the sharp differences in British exit rates at different durations (Fig. 4(*c*)). We can also see from Figs. 7 and 8 (which use a log scale) that the ratios between these exit rates are rather stable over time. As we shall explain shortly, this is inconsistent with the view that the differences in exit rates reflect pure heterogeneity, and

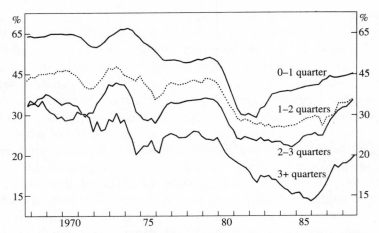

Fig. 7. *Percentage of unemployed people with given duration leaving unemployment within the next quarter: Britain, males, 1968–1988.*

Four-quarter centred moving average; log scale.

Source: Jackman and Layard (1991) plus update.

also inconsistent with a pure ranking model (*à la* Blanchard and Diamond). It is consistent with the view that the differences in outflow rates reflect duration-dependence, with the exit rate at duration d given by

$$h_d = c_d h \left(\frac{V}{cU}, 1 \right).$$

We will test this assumption more rigorously later. For the present we shall proceed with it and see how well it helps us to explain the fall in exit rates.

We therefore construct an index of the effectiveness of the unemployed in year t by taking the exit rates (h) at each uncompleted duration (d) in any arbitrarily selected year o (h_{do}) and weighting them by the proportion of the unemployed at that duration in year $t(f_{dt})$. Thus the index is

$$\hat{c}_t = \sum_d h_{do} f_{dt}.$$

Figure 9 graphs the log of this index. The analysis here, and in what follows, is confined to male outflow and unemployment, because female outflow and unemployment are so much affected by varying benefit regulations.

To see whether the index provides a valid (partial) explanation for the fall in exit rates, we embed it in our standard hiring function. In log-linear form this is

$$\log\frac{H}{U} = \log\hat{c} + b_1\log\frac{V}{\hat{c}U} + b_2X$$

$$= (1 - b_1)\log\hat{c} + b_1\log(V/U) + b_2X$$

where X includes U/V mismatch, employment protection, lagged unemployment (to reflect hysteresis), seasonals, and time. We ran this regression on quarterly data for Britain from 1968(IV) to 1988(IV), measuring U and V by their values at the beginning of each quarter and including some dynamics. Apart from seasonals and time, none of the X-variables is significant and they are therefore excluded. The estimated equation is (t-statistics in brackets)

$$\log\frac{H}{U} = 0.33\log\hat{c} + 0.19\log\frac{V}{U} + 0.33\log\left(\frac{H}{U}\right)_{-1} - 0.65\frac{t}{100} + \text{seasonals} \qquad (16)$$
$$\quad\;\; (1.8) \qquad\quad (6.6) \qquad\qquad (2.7) \qquad\qquad\quad (3.7)$$

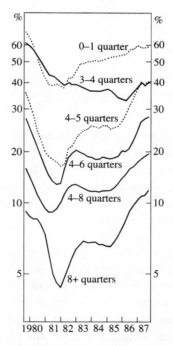

Fig. 8. *Percentage of unemployed people with given duration leaving unemployment within the next quarter: Britain, males, 1979–1987.*

Four-quarter centred moving average; log scale.

Source: Jackman and Layard (1991) plus update.

261

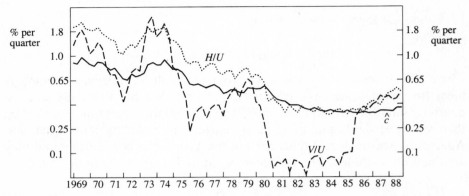

Fig. 9. *Quarterly outflow rate (H/U), effectiveness index (ĉ), and V/U ratio: Britain, males, 1969–1988.*

Male unemployment and outflows; all vacancies.

Source: sources to Jackman and Layard (1991).

This gives a long-run relationship,

$$\log\frac{H}{U} = 0.49\log\hat{c} + 0.28\log\frac{V}{U} - 0.97\frac{t}{100} + \text{seasonals}.\qquad(17)$$

We tested for constant returns to scale by including $\log U$ separately and it was not significant. As regards $\hat{c}$, the Wald test that $(0.49 + 0.28)$ is not different from unity gives 1.37 $(\chi^2_{0.05}(1) = 3.84)$, consistent with the assumption of constant returns to scale. The long-run elasticity with respect to the V/U ratio is of the same order as that of 0.3 estimated by Pissarides (1986). But we now have an important additional explanation of the fall in H/U coming from the growth of long-term unemployment.

There are two obvious possible sources for the negative time trend. The first is employment protection. One should bear in mind the general downward trend in job mobility in most European countries over the last 25 years. Even though it is difficult to isolate the relationship econometrically, it does seem reasonable to assume that employment protection played a role in producing this trend. The second force is the reduced pressure from the authorities to seek work (up to 1986), together with any general changes in the work ethic. However, the most important conclusion we draw from the preceding analysis is that a part of the fall in outflow rates can be explained by the rise in long-term unemployment.

262

Heterogeneity versus state-dependence

This conclusion is derived from an index based on the assumption that the pattern of duration-specific exit rates reflects duration-dependence rather than heterogeneity. But some would argue that the pattern of exit rates simply reflects heterogeneity among those entering unemployment. This latter view is not consistent with any reasonable interpretation of the British time series, as the following argument shows.

Suppose that there were pure heterogeneity, and that for a given unemployed individual the exit probability from unemployment is independent of duration and given by

$$h_i = c_i \bar{h},$$

where c_i reflects only antecedent individual characteristics, and

$$\bar{h} = h\left(\frac{V}{cU}, 1\right),$$

reflecting the state of the job market. Suppose too that the proportion of new entrants with each level of c is, like the inflow to unemployment, fairly stable.

Now let us compare two steady states in the labour market, one where conditions are good ($\bar{h} = \bar{h}_1$) and the other where times are bad ($\bar{h} = \bar{h}_2$). Our argument is that, in the absence of state-dependence, although there will be many more long-term unemployed people in steady state 2 (where things are bad), the average quality of the unemployed is in fact the same in the two states.

The exit probabilities of type i people in the two states are $c_i \bar{h}_1$ and $c_i \bar{h}_2$. So the corresponding average durations are $1/c_i \bar{h}_1$ and $1/c_i \bar{h}_2$. Thus, the stock of each type of unemployed person, which is equal to the inflow multiplied by the duration, changes in the same proportion for each type. Thus, provided the structure of the inflow is constant, the proportion of each type of unemployed person in the unemployed total is the same. So the average quality of the employed is unchanged. All that happens is that the overall exit rate (h) falls by the multiple $\bar{h}_2/\bar{h}_1$. The same happens to the exit rate of new entrants (h_N). Hence

$$\frac{h}{h_N} = \text{const.}$$

What are the facts? The British data are shown in Table 14. Between 1969 and 1985 the overall exit rate fell by five-sixths, while the exit rate of new entrants fell by only just over one-half. Thus the ratio h/h_N fell by 60 per cent.

Table 14 *Overall exit rate and exit rate of new entrants: Britain, males. Quarterly rates: 1984 = 100*[a]

	Overall exit rate, h (1)	Exit rate of new entrants h_N (2)	h/h_N (3)	$\hat{c}/c_N$ (4)
1969	597	255	234	282
1970	544	245	222	266
1971	428	216	198	237
1972	375	222	169	201
1973	505	249	203	241
1974	532	242	220	266
1975	381	199	191	226
1976	269	184	146	173
1977	259	183	141	166
1978	222	157	141	151
1979	231	167	138	154
1980	186	129	145	159
1981	118	94	126	127
1982	109	104	105	112
1983	106	102	104	104
1984	100	100	100	100
1985	103	107	96	98
1986	108	112	96	97
1987	125	125	100	99
1988	139	128	109	104

[a] Annual averages of quarterly rates.

Source: Jackman and Layard (1991).

This is very close to the fall of 65 per cent in our index $\hat{c}$. It lends powerful support to the view that the average effectiveness of the unemployed has been reduced by long-term unemployment, relative to the effectiveness of the newly unemployed.

The data are *not* consistent with the view that the correlation of measured $\hat{c}$ and H/U (which are both functions of duration structure) is simply due to some unmeasured common cause affecting both, rather than to duration-dependence. For suppose that $\bar{h}$ fell because of some unmeasured cause. Then, it is true, measured $\hat{c}$ would fall and so would H/U. But, under pure heterogeneity, h/h_N would have remained constant.

To put the same point another way, under pure heterogeneity exit rates would have fallen less at the longer durations. This is because the average quality of unemployed people will rise, and it will rise more the longer the duration. For the probability p of remaining unemployed to duration d is

$$p = (1 - c_i \bar{h})^d,$$

and

$$\Delta \log p = - \left(\frac{c_i d}{1 - c_i \bar{h}} \right) \Delta \bar{h}.$$

The term in parentheses increases with c_i and with d. Thus we ought to observe a much less steep fall in exit rates at the longer durations. But we do not, as Figs. 7 and 8 show. So the pure heterogeneity story does not hold up if exit rates are given by $h_i = c_i \bar{h}$.

But what if there were pure heterogeneity but the exit probability function were not multiplicative, but more interactive instead? As already shown, theory suggests the multiplicative form (see equation (1)). But even so, we have tested for the implications of more complex interactions and found no supporting evidence (Jackman and Layard 1991).

These considerations also lead us to reject the functional forms implied by the pure ranking model. As Blanchard and Diamond (1990) show, it is an implication of their theory that long-duration unemployment outflow rates are more sensitive to aggregate economic changes than are short-duration ones. But duration-specific outflow rate equations for Britain show an unsystematic pattern in terms of the effect of the V/U ratio on the outflow rate (see, again, Jackman and Layard 1991).

However, though we have on reasonable assumptions rejected pure heterogeneity, and also the pure ranking model, we have certainly not established pure state-dependence. In fact, there must be some heterogeneity, and indeed, the fact that our index $\hat{c}$ falls by more than h/h_N itself might be taken as evidence for some degree of heterogeneity. But we believe that the resemblance between columns (3) and (4) in Table 14 is of great significance and has important policy implications.

One final point. Throughout this analysis we have assumed that all vacancies are filled by unemployed people. This is not in fact the case. In Annex 5.3 we show how the analysis can be modified to take into account employed job-seekers. But we also show that, in Britain at least, allowing for this does not improve the fit of our estimates. This is presumably because of deficiencies of the data.

US evidence

For the USA, Blanchard and Diamond (1989*a*) have estimated a hiring function with rather different coefficient estimates from ours. This may be because they use a different dependent variable. Theirs is the total of hirings ($\bar{H}$), including not only unemployed people but also employed people and people from outside the labour force. They explain this by the levels of vacancies and unemployment. Using monthly data for 1968(2) to 1981(12), they find (*t*-statistics in brackets)

$$\log\bar{H} = 0.54\ln V_{-1} + 0.35\ln U_{-1} - 0.15(t/100) + \text{const.}$$
$$\quad\quad (6.9) \quad\quad\quad (3.9) \quad\quad\quad (2.4)$$

Blanchard and Diamond test for constant returns to scale and it is not rejected. They also test for departures from log-linearity (using a CES function) and find no reason to reject log-linearity.

Their regression gives a higher weight to vacancies than ours. However, this may reflect the fact that, in our regression, vacancies are underweighted relative to unemployment because the dependent variable excludes employed people who fill vacancies. By contrast, in their regression the unemployed are underweighted relative to vacancies because they do not include the employed job-seekers included in the dependent variable. Blanchard and Diamond assume that the unemployed are a good proxy for all job-seekers. But for Britain at least this has not been the case, with employed job-seekers sometimes falling as unemployment rises.[17]

The Blanchard–Diamond result can be easily grasped by looking at Fig. 10. This shows that the outflow is a weighted average of unemployment and vacancies, plus a relatively small downward drift. In Britain the downward drift is much bigger.

6. Unemployment inflow and the U/V curve

So far we have concentrated on the outflow from unemployment. But to understand the general equilibrium of the system, we need also to look at the inflow to unemployment.

Time-series analysis

The data on inflows into unemployment in Britain over time have been presented in Fig. 2. There is a marked cyclical pattern, with the inflow higher during periods of economic downturn such as 1975 and 1980–1.

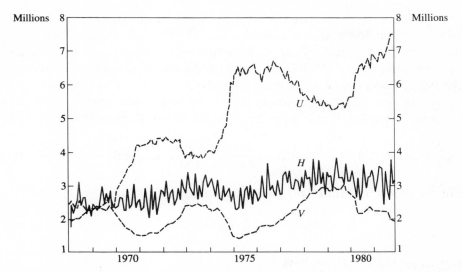

Fig. 10. *Unemployment (U), monthly hires (H), and vacancies (U), USA, 1968–1981.*

Source: Blanchard and Diamond (1989a: fig. 5); adjusted unemployment.

The inflow into unemployment comprises people who lose their jobs (by reason of redundancy, dismissal, or because the job was temporary), those who voluntarily quit their job, and new entrants to the labour force. Of the inflow, job-losers are the largest category (see pp. 269–72 below), and the cyclical pattern of inflows also appears to be dominated by the tendency for job losses to increase in the downturn. (One might expect voluntary quits and, to a lesser extent, new entrants to the labour force to fall when labour market conditions are bad.)

To analyse the time-series behaviour of the inflow rate more formally, we ran a regression analysis on quarterly data on inflows for 1969(IV) to 1989(I) for Britain.[18] The results were:

$$\log\frac{S}{N} = -0.42 - 0.0014\log\frac{V}{U} - 0.071\Delta\log\frac{V}{U} + 0.869\log\left(\frac{S}{N}\right)_{-1}$$
$$\quad (2.4)\quad (0.2)\qquad\qquad (2.5)\qquad\qquad (14.7)$$

$$-\ 0.0105\frac{t}{100} + \text{seasonals}$$
$$\quad (0.3)$$
\hfill (18)

267

This equation suggests that the level of economic activity has no long-run effect on the inflow rate, and provides only very weak evidence of a negative time trend. The main influence on inflow is the change in the vacancy–unemployment ratio, which can be taken as a measure of economic shocks. In the steady state, it seems legitimate to take the inflow rate as constant.

We can now construct a steady-state relationship between U and V. The long-run hiring function is given by equation (17) in Section 5:

$$\log\frac{H}{U} = \text{const.} + 0.49\log\hat{c} + 0.28\log\frac{V}{U} - 0.97\frac{t}{100} + \text{seasonals.} \qquad (17)$$

For the inflow, equation (18) gives, in the long run,

$$\log\frac{S}{N} = \text{const.}$$

Hence, setting $S = H$, we have

$$\text{const.} = 0.72\log\frac{U}{N} + 0.28\log\frac{V}{N} + 0.49\log\hat{c} - 0.97\frac{t}{100}. \qquad (19)$$

This inverse relationship between the unemployment and vacancy rates constitutes the U/V curve, or Beveridge curve. The negative time trend shows that the curve in Britain has been shifting out as time proceeds. This time trend is sometimes ascribed to employment protection legislation: however, our analysis suggests that the time trend can be ascribed to a reduction in the outflow rate (hiring rate) rather than a fall in the inflow rate. This could be because employment protection has done more to reduce hiring than to affect firing. (But for a contrary view see Bentolila and Bertola 1990.) We have, however, pointed to a number of other possible explanations of the time trend in the outflow rate in Section 5. In the British context, a major factor shifting the U/V curve outwards has been the rise in long-term unemployment, which reduces search effectiveness and hence $\hat{c}$ in the outflow rate equation.

Outside the steady state, we observe significant dynamic effects in both the outflow rate equation (16) and the inflow rate equation (18). For example, a sharp fall in vacancies will lead to a big rise in the inflow rate and a fall in the hiring rate, causing unemployment to rise. Thereafter, the inflow rate falls back (as the rate of decline of V/U slows down) and the number of hirings increases (because U is higher). So the rate of increase of unemployment slows down. The system ultimately reaches a new equilibrium with a higher rate of unemployment. However, during the adjustment, the inflow is not equal to the outflow, so the economy is not on the U/V curve as described by equation (19).

Characteristics of the inflow

The people at most risk of becoming unemployed are the young and those employed in unskilled manual or personal service jobs. In Britain, the monthly inflow rate into unemployment for men aged under 20 is two-and-a-half times the average for the labour force as a whole, while for men in unskilled manual or personal service jobs unemployment inflow rates are more than four and more than eight times the national average, respectively (Stern 1983). Highly correlated with these features, however, is the duration of the job: a man who has been in a job for less than a year is six times as likely to become unemployed as the average employee. Stern argues that job tenure is in fact the key influence, and that once the duration of job tenure is controlled for the effect of age disappears.

The spring 1987 cohort study shows that monthly inflow rates for both men and women aged under 20 were just over twice the labour force average (Erens and Hedges 1990: Table 102). The difference from Stern's analysis of the autumn 1978 cohort may reflect seasonal factors. There are fewer school-leavers in the spring than in the autumn. We discuss the impact of different inflow rates across occupations in explaining differences in occupational unemployment rates in the next chapter.

Reasons for becoming unemployed

Before leaving the subject of inflow, we need to ask, How exactly do people come to be unemployed?[19] Table 15 shows the stock of unemployed in the USA and Table 16 the composition of the stock and the inflow. As can be seen, the distribution of reasons for becoming unemployed is generally similar for the inflow and for the stock. Not many of the unemployed are there because they quit their previous employment—job-leavers account for only about 0.8 percentage points of unemployment. By contrast, people who lost their jobs account for a much larger portion, which fluctuates according to the state of the business cycle: it is never less than three times the number of job-leavers, and sometimes as high as eight times that number. Job-losers include people whose jobs have disappeared or who have been dismissed for personal reasons, but the latter are a minority. (The job may have disappeared either because it was temporary or because of a cut-back in regular work.)

The rest of the unemployed are people who were not previously in the labour force, either because they had never worked before (around 0.8 points of unemployment) or because they had worked before but had dropped out of the labour force in the meantime. This category of re-entrants made up 28 per cent

Table 15   *The unemployed stock, by reasons for unemployment: USA*

	% of labour force (excl. armed forces)				
	Lost last job	*Left last job*	*Re-entered labour force*	*Seeking first job*	*Total unemployed*
1974	2.4	0.8	1.6	0.7	5.6
1975	4.7	0.9	2.0	0.9	8.5
1976	3.8	0.9	2.0	0.9	7.7
1977	3.2	0.9	2.0	1.0	7.1
1978	2.5	0.8	1.8	0.9	6.1
1979	2.5	0.8	1.7	0.8	5.8
1980	3.7	0.8	1.8	0.8	7.1
1981	3.9	0.8	1.9	0.9	7.6
1982	5.7	0.8	2.2	1.1	9.7
1983	5.6	0.7	2.2	1.1	9.6
1984	3.9	0.7	1.9	1.0	7.5
1985	3.6	0.8	2.0	0.9	7.2
1986	3.4	0.9	1.8	0.9	7.0
1987	3.0	0.8	1.6	0.8	6.2
1988	2.5	0.8	1.5	0.7	5.5
1989	2.4	0.8	1.5	0.5	5.3

Source: *Employment and Training Report of the President*, 1989, Tables B32, B41; *Monthly Labor Review*, May 1990, Tables 9, 48.

of the unemployed in 1989. It was rather less for adult men, but was 29 per cent for youths and 39 per cent for women (see Table 16).

This raises important difficulties in thinking about the duration of unemployment. For a high proportion of re-entrants to unemployment are in fact people who were unemployed before they left the labour force and thus have a sequence: unemployment–out of labour force–unemployment. We do not really know why they stopped looking for work for a time and were therefore classified as being out of the labour force. Some writers, such as Clark and Summers (1979), have stressed that a substantial number of them say that they 'want a regular job now', even though they are not looking for one; others have stressed the weak labour force attachment of the out-of-labour-force group (Feldstein and Ellwood 1982; Flinn and Heckman 1983). But one should, at any rate, be aware of the fact that roughly half of all unemployment spells in the USA end in withdrawal from the labour force rather than in a job. These spells are roughly the same length as the spells that end in jobs, but the average duration of the two types of spells obviously makes it appear easier to get a job than it really is.

Table 16 *The unemployed stock and inflow, by reasons for unemployment: USA 1989*

	Temporary layoff	Lost last job	Left last job	Re-entered labour force	Seeking first job	All unemployed
Stock						
Men (20 and over)	19	45	14	19	3	100
Women (20 and over)	11	27	17	39	6	100
Young people (under 20)	4	13	17	29	38	100
All stock	13	33	16	28	10	100
Inflow						
Men (20 and over)	24	36	16	22	3	100
Women (20 and over)	12	19	19	43	6	100
Young people (under 20)	5	11	18	29	37	100
All inflow	15	23	18	32	12	100

Note: Inflow figures exclude about half of those who leave unemployment within 5 weeks of entry as they have been calculated from the numbers unemployed for less than 5 weeks.
Source: *Employment and Earnings*, Jan. 1990, Tables 12, 13.

Table 17 *The unemployed, by main reason for unemployment: Britain, spring 1989*

	Last job ended within 3 years		Last job ended over 3 years ago	Seeking first job	All reasons
	Lost job	Left job			
Men	33	24	35	8	100
Non-married women	21	28	36	16	100
Married women	19	44	34	3	100
All unemployed	27	29	35	8	100

Source: *Employment Gazette*, May 1990, Table 1, p. 266.

In Britain the data from the Labour Force Survey and the 1987 cohort study are somewhat differently presented and do not distinguish re-entrants to the labour force. The Labour Force Survey gives no information on those who have not worked in the last three years, but we can be sure that over half the men who did so lost their job (see Table 17). Thus, in Britain, as in the USA, over half of unemployed men lost their last job.

The cohort study also gives information on employment status in the year before becoming unemployed and on time spent in that status. On average, men in the inflow to unemployment in spring 1987 spent three weeks of the previous year out of the labour force and women 14 weeks. Time 'out of labour force' includes time out of work but not signing on for benefit, but excludes periods of sickness while unemployed and time on government training schemes.[20] So re-entrants to the labour force are clearly a smaller component of the inflow to unemployment than in the USA.

Of the inflow, 73 per cent had had a full-time job in the previous year. Of these, 66 per cent had clearly lost their last job, while only 22 per cent said they had decided to leave (Erens and Hedges 1990: Table 218).

7. Determinants of vacancies

Thus far we have used vacancies to explain the unemployment outflow (and inflow). This leaves us with the final question: How are vacancies determined? If we begin with the facts, we are bound to notice that, despite huge changes in unemployment, vacancy rates have a strong tendency to return to their original level.

The most obvious explanation of this, as we argued in the introduction to this chapter, is that changes in search effectiveness are a major issue, and that such changes affect unemployment but not vacancies. To pursue this idea, we now ask in more detail what vacancies actually are, how they arise, and what determines the equilibrium vacancy rate in the economy.

The concept of a vacancy

A common-sense definition of a vacancy is that used by the UK's National Survey of Engagements and Vacancies, i.e. a job that is 'currently vacant, available immediately and for which the firm has taken some specific recruiting action during the past four weeks'. Even if there is unemployment, a firm paying the prevailing wage cannot hire as many workers as it wants instantaneously. Instead, firms indicate that they need labour by announcing vacancies. They can of course attract more labour by offering higher wages, but there is a limit to the extent to which they will want to do this. They can also attract more labour by announcing more vacancies, but again, there is a limit to the extent that they will do this. The reason is that a vacancy must be genuine. If a firm advertises y vacancies, it must be ready to employ y (properly qualified) people if they turn up. If it refused to do this, its future advertisements would carry little conviction. This means that vacancies are related to the genuine hiring needs of the firm.

It would be convenient to think of the sum of employment and vacancies as being equal to the number of 'productive jobs' that firms can provide. But in principle, firms might find it worth their while to declare more vacancies than they have productive jobs, if they expect that on average they will not be able to fill all their vacancies. Against this is the risk that they may then have to hire more people than they want, if people turn up. Under what circumstances will they take this risk?

Clearly, a small firm will often be in a position where it has lost no workers of a given kind in the recent past. It will not therefore have any incentive to declare 'pre-emptive vacancies' in excess of its current requirements. By contrast, a large firm may know that it loses on average x workers per period and that, to recruit on average x workers, it needs y vacancies ($y > x$). It may therefore declare pre-emptive vacancies, so that the sum of vacancies and employed exceeds the number of 'productive jobs', defined as the number of jobs for which there is a corresponding capital stock.[21]

We therefore pose the following question. Suppose a firm has made a long-run choice of the wage it pays to its workers, its capital stock, and its capital intensity of production. This gives it M 'genuine jobs', where M is the capital stock divided by the embodied capital–labour ratio. The probability that each worker leaves is s and the probability of filling a vacancy is p. Will the expected profit of the firm be greater if it has M established posts or $M + 1$ established posts? (If it has M posts it will advertise $M - N$ jobs when it has N workers; if it has $M + 1$ posts it will advertise $M + 1 - N$.)

The first issue is what proportion of posts will on average be occupied. To answer this, note that in a steady state the following unconditional probabilities must be equal:

(*a*) the probability that a given post becomes empty;
(*b*) the probability that it becomes occupied.

If n is the probability that the post is occupied, (a) = (b) implies that $sn = p(1 - n)$ where p is the probability of filling a vacancy. Hence $n = p/(p + s)$. This is the proportion of posts that are occupied on average.

We can now compare the firm's expected profits when it has M and $M + 1$ posts. In the first case expected profits Π are

$$\Pi_M = (y - w)M\frac{p}{p + s},$$

where y is net output per worker and w the wage. In the second case expected profits are

$$\Pi_{M+1} = y(M + 1)\frac{p}{p + s} - y\left(\frac{p}{p + s}\right)^{M+1} - w(M + 1)\frac{p}{p + s}.$$

The first two terms represent expected output. The first term is expected output as it would be if there were $(M + 1)$ genuine jobs. But, since there are only M such jobs, expected output is less than this by y times the probability of there being $M + 1$ workers, since in that case one worker would produce nothing. This is the second term. The third term is the cost of labour.

Hence it will be unprofitable to have an extra post if

$$(y - w)\frac{p}{p + s} < y\left(\frac{p}{p + s}\right)^{M+1}$$

or

$$M < \frac{\ln\left(1 - \frac{w}{y}\right)}{\ln\left(\frac{p}{p + s}\right)}.$$

Realistic values suggest that this requires M to be less than 70.[22] Thus, unless an establishment employs more than 70 workers of any particular type, it will not have pre-emptive vacancies. Presumably, this is unlikely to occur in any establishment employing less than about 500 workers in total, of all types. In Britain, three-quarters of workers work in establishments employing less than 500 workers.[23] So it seems reasonable to focus on the case where firms have no pre-emptive vacancies. We shall therefore assume that firms declare vacancies only when they have unused capital.

The determinants of vacancies

We now consider a model in which wages are set by firms.[24] Most firms believe that they can fill their vacancies more quickly if they raise their relative wages. Hence a firm's hires (H_i) are given by

$$H_i = h\left(\frac{W_i}{W}, \frac{cU}{V}\right) V_i \qquad (h_1, h_2 > 0; h_{11}, h_{12} < 0),$$

where V_i is its vacancies. The firm has sN_i leavers per period and wishes to replace them. The firm can secure the necessary flow of recruits either by raising wages or by creating vacancies. But both involve costs: higher wages raise the wage bill, and higher vacancies involve a net cost per empty workplace of, let us say, φ.

The firm's profits are

$$\Pi_i = R(N_i) - \left(W_i + \varphi\frac{V_i}{N_i}\right) N_i.$$

Since $V_i = H_i / h(\ )$, and in a steady state[25] the firm sets $H_i = sN_i$,

$$\Pi_i = R(N_i) - \left[W_i + \frac{\varphi s}{h\left(\frac{W_i}{W^e}, \frac{cU}{V}\right)}\right] N_i.$$

The firm then chooses W_i to maximize Π_i. This gives

$$1 = \frac{\varphi s}{\left[h\left(\frac{W_i}{W^e}, \frac{cU}{V}\right)\right]^2} \frac{h_1\left(\frac{W_i}{W^e}, \frac{cU}{V}\right)}{W^e}.$$

At the aggregate level, in general equilibrium $W_i = W^e = W$. And we may suppose the cost of a workplace to be proportional to the general wage level with, say, $\varphi / W^e = \varphi'$. Thus, equilibrium of the wage determination process implies that

$$\left[h\left(1, \frac{cu}{v}\right)\right]^2 = \varphi' s\, h_1\left(1, \frac{cu}{v}\right),$$

where v is the vacancy rate. There is also the flow equilibrium relationship (U/V curve),

$$s = h(v, cu). \tag{5}$$

These two relationships determine u and v. If search effectiveness falls, unemployment rises but the vacancy rate is unchanged. This seems a reasonable first approximation to what has happened in a number of countries. The same result would hold if wages are determined by union bargaining.

8. Summary

In this chapter we have examined the behaviour of unemployed people and the operation of labour market institutions, and have focused on the questions of how such factors affect the equilibrium rate of unemployment and its persistence over time. Our findings are as follows.

1. In a steady state, the unemployment rate is the product of the inflow rate and the average duration of unemployment spells. In Britain, and in many European countries, the rise in unemployment has taken the form of an increase in duration rather than an increase in the inflow rate.

2. In Britain newly unemployed people in 1987 made only 3 applications per month: in 1978 the comparable figure was 1–2 per month—compared with 8 per month in the USA.

3. We find clear evidence that the experience of unemployment has an adverse effect on search effectiveness, and that the long-term unemployed experience considerable difficulty in getting back into work. An implication of this is that unemployment may persist in the aftermath of a severe recession, because of the adverse effects of the long-term unemployment caused by the downturn on the subsequent effectiveness of the labour market in matching unemployed workers to jobs.

4. There is good evidence that benefit levels influence the average duration of unemployment spells, with the elasticity typically being in the range 0.2–0.9. Cross-section data on the USA suggest that the duration of benefit availability is important, a 1-week rise tending to raise average durations by around 0.2 week.

5. Voluntary quits form only a small proportion of the inflow into unemployment. Most people entering unemployment do so because their jobs come to an end, or they are dismissed from them. Inflows rise in a downturn and fall in a recovery.

6. If free to do so, firms choose wages and vacancies simultaneously to maximize profits. This process, together with the flow equilibrium condition (or u/v curve), determines the equilibrium levels of unemployment and vacancies.

Appendix: Job search of unemployed people in Britain, 1987

Table A1 *Number of job applications, Britain, 1987*

	Men %	Women %	All[a] %
No. of applications (excl. any which were successful) in first 7 weeks since becoming unemployed			
None	21	27	24
1–4	29	35	32
5–9	20	18	19
10–19	14	9	12
20–29	5	4	5
30 or more	10	5	8
Not stated	1	1	–
	100	100	100
Median	5	3	4

[a] The percentages in the third column are expressed as a proportion of those giving a response.

Source: Erens and Hedges (1990: Table 828).

Chapter 5

Table A2 *Search intensity in Britain, by week of interview, 1987/8*

	Men		Women	
	7 wks. (1)	9 mos. (2)	7 wks. (3)	9 mos. (4)
Time spent searching (hours per week)				
Less than $5\frac{1}{2}$	44	46	67	71
$5\frac{1}{2}$ to $9\frac{1}{2}$	17	17	15	12
$9\frac{1}{2}$ or more	39	37	18	17
	100	100	100	100
Median (hours)	7	7	4	3
Money spent searching (per week)				
Nothing	10	10	12	15
Under £2	25	31	39	44
£2–£6	41	39	39	37
£6 or more	24	20	10	4
	100	100	100	100
Median (£)	3.50	2.75	2	1.75

Note: Percentages are expressed as a proportion of those giving a response. The medians are calculated assuming uniform distributions within each of the bands.

Sources: Erens and Hedges (1990: Tables 823, 825).

278

Table A3 *Search intensity in Britain, by week of interview: men and women, 1987/8*

	Interview						9 months
	7 weeks						
	Period after first interview in which work found				*Did not find work*	*All*	*Unemployed at both interviews*
	Within 4 weeks	*5–13 weeks*	*14–16 weeks*	*27–32 weeks*			
	(1)	*(2)*	*(3)*	*(4)*	*(5)*	*(6)*	*(7)*
Time spent searching (hours per week)							
Up to $5\frac{1}{2}$	40	43	42	59	64	53	56
$5\frac{1}{2}$ tp $9\frac{1}{2}$	16	18	21	16	14	16	15
$9\frac{1}{2}$ or more	44	39	37	25	22	31	29
	100	100	100	100	100	100	100
Median (hours)	8	7	7	5	4	5	5
Money spent searching (per week)							
Nothing	6	8	7	10	17	11	12
Under £2	21	27	29	36	37	30	36
£2–£6	46	40	43	41	36	40	38
£6 or more	27	25	21	13	10	19	14
	100	100	100	100	100	100	100
Median (£)	4.25	3.50	3.25	2.25	1.75	3.00	2.25

Note: See notes to Table A1.

Sources: cols. (1)–(5): Erens and Hedges (1990: Tables 824, 827); cols. (6) and (7): Erens and Hedges (1990: Tables 823, 825).

Table A4 *Job acceptances and refusal by the unemployed: Britain, 1987/8 (%)*

	First interview, 7 wks. after becoming unemployed			Second interview, 9 mos. after becoming unemployed		
	Men	*Women*	*All*	*Men*	*Women*	*All*
Obtaining a job						
by first interview	29	32	30			
between interviews				35	25	31
Refusing a job						
by first interview	7	7	7			
between interviews				11	16	13

Source: Erens and Hedges (1990: Tables 501, 829 and p. 185).

Table A5 *How the unemployed found jobs: Britain, 1987/8 (%)*

	Those finding work within 9 mos. of becoming unemployed			Period of unemployment before finding work (Men and Women)			
	Men	*Women*	*All*	*Up to 4 weeks*	*5–13 weeks*	*14–26 weeks*	*27–34 weeks*
Newspapers	15	18	16	11	21	17	14
Public employment agencies	25	16	22	20	22	23	28
Asked people	25	21	24	24	20	23	32
Direct approach to new employer	11	8	10	11	10	10	8
Returned to former employer	6	10	7	7	10	4	4
Approach by employer	9	10	9	10	7	13	8
Private employment agency	5	12	7	11	6	5	4
Other/ not stated	4	6	5	5	5	6	4
	100	100	100	100	100	100	100

Source: Erens and Hedges (1990: Table 610).

Table A6 *Savings and debts of the unemployed who returned to work within nine months of start of unemployment: Britain, 1987/8 (%)*

	Last job	Entering unemployment	Return to work
Savings[a]			
None	53	55	56
Up to £500	16	18	18
£500–£1000	7	5	4
£1000–£3000	8	7	6
£3000+	7	8	6
Not stated	8	8	11
	100	100	100
Debts			
None	69	61	63
Up to £500	11	17	17
£500–£1000	5	6	6
£1000–£3000	7	7	8
£3000+	4	4	3
Not stated	3	3	4
	100	100	100

[a] Savings were higher when entering unemployment than in the last job because of redundancy payments.

Source: Erens and Hedges (1990: Tables 1214, 1217).

Table A7 *Jobs taken by the unemployed: Britain, 1987/8 (%)*[a]

	Men	Women	Men and women
In same industry	44	53	47
In same occupation	44	59	50

[a] Employment was classified under 10 broad industries and 16 occupations.

Source: Erens and Hedges (1990: 118).

Notes

1. This ignores two problems. First, many hirings are not from unemployment but of people who already have jobs. A few are from out of the labour force. In the UK, about half of vacancies are filled by employed people (Smith 1988). The problem of employed job-seekers is discussed in Annex 5.2. Second, many of those who leave unemployment drop out of the labour force. This is not a major issue for adult males, but it is more significant for women and (in the USA) youths. In Britain the 1987 cohort study showed that 90% of men and 76% of women who had left the register in the first 9 months after becoming unemployed had returned to work for at least part of the period. In recent years there has also been a tendency, partially induced by changes in regulations, for unemployed people to leave unemployment to register as ill. This is particularly the case with elderly long-term unemployed people, the number of whom has increased substantially in the 1980s.

2. An example of such a function is given by Hall (1977) and Pissarides (1979). Suppose U unemployed job-seekers are searching randomly over V vacancies. If each seeker makes one application per period, the probability that seeker i applies for vacancy j is $1/V$. The probability that no seeker applies for vacancy j is

$$\left(1 - \frac{1}{V}\right)^U \simeq e^{-U/V}$$

Thus, if firms are prepared to hire any applicant,

$$\frac{H}{V} = 1 - e^{-U/V} \qquad \text{or} \qquad H = V(1 - e^{-U/V}),$$

and the function $H = h(V,U)$ exhibits constant returns to scale.

3. In the union model, cU/H reflects the chances that a worker made unemployed or a striker will find alternative work. In the efficiency-wage model, it again measures the cost to the worker of becoming unemployed. As Annex 5.2 shows, this variable is also uniquely related to the employer's ease of job-filling.

4. It is thus less than the estimate of unemployment inflow for the USA based on the Current Population Survey. However, it is known that this is an overestimate, arising from the over-reporting of changes of state. For rival estimates of inflows and duration in the USA, see Poterba and Summers (1986) and Abowd and Zellner (1985). Both give longer durations than crude CPS data; this is especially true of Poterba and Summers.

5. In practice, the individual will not apply for very high-wage jobs. If his chances of being offered a high-wage job paying more than, say, w_{max} are very low, it will not be worth bearing the cost of applying and the likely pain of rejection. This feature can be modelled by introducing a cost of application and/or a pain of rejection and making the probability of success vary inversely with the wage. With appropriate assumptions, this will give a maximum wage above which a job-seeker will not apply. However, it remains the case that on reasonable assumptions the fraction of vacancies for which a person applies falls as B rises.

6. For a full optimizing approach to the intensity of search, see Pissarides (1990).

7. Tobin was mainly discussing a worker's decision whether or not to quit his existing job

in order to look for another. But the point is also relevant (though less striking) in relation to an unemployed worker's decision whether to take a job or to remain unemployed while searching.

8. The published figures group together all those spending more than 10 hours per week on search. However, in the interviews responses were classified in intervals up to 40 hours. About 5% report spending more than 30 hours per week on search, including 2% spending more than 40 hours per week (Social and Community Planning Research (SCPR), Cohort Study of Men Registering as Unemployed, Preliminary Report, 2nd Stage (mimeo): Table 62).

9. The fact that there is no detail as to the distribution of hours spent on search within the 0–5 hours group, where most of the observations occur, makes it impossible to calculate the mean at all accurately.

10. About three-quarters of all the unemployed were unemployed for over 4 weeks (Rosenfeld 1977: 40). From national data, the average duration of uncompleted spells in 1976 for the stock of unemployed was 15.8 weeks. Since one-quarter have a duration of less than 4 weeks, the average duration of the remaining three-quarters must be of the order of 20 weeks.

11. In the British sample, of those unemployed at the time of the second interview, about 10% had experienced one or more spells of full-time work between the onset of unemployment and the time of the second interview (Moylan and Davies 1981: 29, supplemented from unpublished data.)

12. This may be partly definitional: American men who make no job applications are not classified as unemployed.

13. A third British study found that 15% of those currently unemployed in September 1982 had rejected any job offer (Jones 1989).

14. The median times are not strictly comparable, as the time categories in the 1978 study were not clearly defined. The assumption made to calculate the median search times in Table 5 may underestimate the time medians by half an hour (private information from the DSS). This problem does not affect the 1987 study.

15. There is evidence both in Britain and in Austria (Winter–Ebmer 1989) that employment exchanges are much less likely to send long-term unemployed people to job interviews.

16. For earlier work on this effect see Budd *et al.* (1988) and Franz (1987).

17. If employed job-seekers are J, then

	J/N	U/N	$(J + U)/U$	$\hat{E}/H$
1977	0.050	0.053	1.94	1.77
1981	0.032	0.102	1.32	1.66
1983	0.045	0.133	1.34	1.62
1984	0.060	0.137	1.44	1.69

Source: Labour Force Survey. $\hat{E}$ estimated total engagements; H outflow from unemployment.

18. The regression is based on the consistent data on inflows supplied by the Department of Employment which is plotted in Fig. 2. The variable $\hat{c}$ was not significant and has therefore been omitted.

19. Data on the stock of the unemployed, both for the USA and for Britain, show no evidence of massive differences in the durations of unemployment for people who

283

become unemployed for different reasons (Marston 1976: 191; Layard *et al.* 1978*b*: 80). Analysis of data from the DHSS Cohort Study on the inflow into unemployment in Britain unexpectedly suggests that leaving a job voluntarily increases duration (Narendranathan *et al.* 1985).

20. On average, men spent 2 weeks out of work but not signing and women 3 weeks (Erens and Hedges 1990: Table 203).
21. See e.g. Holt and David (1966): 'a company with just the right number of tool makers will *always* have vacancies for tool makers to replace those who quit to work for other companies. Because it takes time for the search process required to fill a vacancy, a company will not wait to *start* its search until the worker is needed. Instead, it will create a vacancy in anticipation of the need.'
22. The share of wages in value added in manufacturing is about 75%. According to the National Survey of Engagements and Vacancies, the engagement rate in Britain in April–July 1977 was 0.7% per week. Since the vacancy rate in May 1977 was 2.1%, the proportion of vacancies filled per week was 33%. Hence $p/(p + s) = 33/33.7$, and the critical value of M is 66.6.
23. In 1986, 71% of employment was in firms employing under 500 people (Bannock and Daly 1990). In addition, a number of those employed in larger firms work in establishments employing less than 500 people.
24. This model has in fact already been discussed in Chs. 3 and 4 as an example of 'efficiency wages'.
25. A full dynamic solution to the firm's problem yields the same solution as the static approach presented here, provided the discount rate r is sufficiently small.

6

Mismatch: The Structure of Unemployment

As everybody knows, unemployment rates differ widely between occupations and between regions, as well as across age, race, and (sometimes) sex groups. The striking thing is how stable these differences are. In all countries, unskilled people have much higher unemployment rates than those with skills. Similarly, youths have higher rates than adults. In addition, in most countries (though not in the USA) regional differences are highly persistent—with unemployment always above average for example in the North of England and the South of Italy.

The first task is to document these differences (Section 1) and then to explain them (Section 2). An obvious question is why occupational and geographical mobility does not eliminate the differences between unemployment rates in different occupations and different regions. We attempt to answer this question. Thus, our main focus is on the *persistent* imbalance between the supply and demand for labour across skill groups, regions, and age groups. But there are additional imbalances which are *temporary*. Suppose for example there are two occupations that have the same average unemployment rate over time, but in one year demand shifts from one occupation to the other. This will produce a temporary imbalance until corrected.[1] Such one-off structural shocks have aroused great interest in relation to the issue of real business cycles (see Lilien 1982). They are also clearly of interest to the unemployed themselves. But they account for a fairly small fraction of the inequality among unemployment rates observed in the average year. In any event, our framework encompasses both kinds of phenomena (since both reflect imbalances between the demand and supply of labour), and we shall refer to both by the generic title 'mismatch'.

The next question is how the structure of the unemployment rates is related to the average level of unemployment. Many people in Europe attribute the

285

rise in unemployment to increased imbalances between the pattern of labour demand and supply—in other words, to greater mismatch. The question is, Have exogenous forces raised average unemployment by changing the structure of the unemployment rates? To answer this we need to develop a relevant measure of mismatch, consistent with our overall framework of explanation. We develop the theory in Section 3 while in Section 4 we offer empirical evidence in support of our framework. The general conclusion is that, while mismatch is a serious problem, in most countries it has not increased over time.

Since the structure of unemployment affects the average level of unemployment, what (if anything) should be done to alter the structure? The standard recipes are to shift demand towards the sectors with high unemployment rates, and to shift supply away from them. As we show in Section 5, this must be right when supply is effectively exogenous. However, the more elastic supply becomes, the less strong is the case for intervention—except where standard resource misallocation arguments (externalities or taxation wedges) apply. These arguments may indeed be important, so that jobs should be shifted towards less congested regions and people should be shifted into highly skilled occupations.

Thus far the discussion of mismatch is entirely in terms of differences in employment rates, i.e. in the ratio between total labour demand and total labour supply. But it is also instructive to look at inter-group differences in the ratio of vacancies to unemployment, i.e. in the ratio of excess labour demand to excess labour supply. We explore this in Section 6 and ask how mismatch of this kind affects the location of the aggregate U/V curve.

We ought at this point to issue a health warning. Despite its obvious importance, the topic of mismatch has so far been subject to remarkably little rigorous analysis.[2] The propositions of this chapter are therefore particularly exploratory.

1. The structure of unemployment: some facts

Occupational differences

The most striking difference in unemployment rates is between skill groups. In Britain and USA the unemployment rate of semi- and un-skilled workers is over four times that of professional and managerial workers (see Table 1(*a*)). A simple measure of the dispersion of the unemployment rates is the coefficient of variation (using relative labour forces as weights). For reasons given in Section 3, we use as our fundamental measure of mismatch the square of this—in other words, the *variance of relative unemployment rates* (var(u_i/u)). In Britain the

Table 1(a)   *Unemployment by occupation: Britain and the USA (%)*

	Rates (%)			% of unemployed		
	Men	*Women*	*All*	*Men*	*Women*	*All*
Britain, 1985						
Professional and managerial	2.9	4.8	3.3	7	6	7
Other non-manual	5.9	6.8	6.7	10	48	23
Skilled manual	11.3	8.0	10.9	41	8	29
Semi-skilled manual (incl. personal services)	19.1	11.5	15.0	28	36	31
Unskilled manual	28.5	3.2	17.0	14	2	10
All	11.2	8.8	10.2	100	100	100
var(u_i/u)	44%	10%	22%			
USA, 1987						
Professional and managerial	2.2	2.4	2.3	10	11	10
Other non-manual	3.7	4.7	4.3	13	40	25
Skilled manual	6.0	6.4	6.1	22	3	14
Personal services	7.5	7.8	7.7	13	28	19
Semi- and un-skilled manual	9.3	9.9	9.4	43	19	32
All	6.2	6.2	6.2	100	100	100
var(u_i/u)	24%	19%	21%			

Notes: Unemployment is classified by occupation in last job. The unemployment rate in an occupation is the number unemployed who were previously in an occupation relative to the numbers employed plus unemployed. Since many of the unemployed have never worked or do not record previous occupation, the national unemployment rate ('All') exceeds the mean of the occupational unemployment rates. In calculating var(u_i/u), u is the mean of the occupation-specific unemployment rates.

Source: *General Household Survey*; *Employment and Earnings*.

variance across occupations was 22 per cent in 1985, much the same as in the USA.

In Table 1(*b*) we provide data for other countries (but with no skill breakdown of manual workers). Focusing on the ratio between manual and non-manual unemployment rates, the striking thing is how low this is in Germany (a result of their training system?).

Table 1(b) *Unemployment rate by occupation: various countries, 1987 (%)*

	USA	Australia[a]	Austria	Canada	Finland
Professional and technical	2.2	2.0	2.7	4.7	1.8
Administrative and managerial	2.6	2.1	0.9	4.5	—
Clerical and related	4.2	3.3	3.8	7.4	2.5
Sales	4.9	5.0	4.5	6.7	4.0
Service	7.7	6.1	8.4	11.6	4.1
Agriculture	7.1	3.8	1.7	10.0	2.7
Other manual	8.0	6.2	6.2	10.9	7.1
Average of above	5.4	4.5	4.8	8.2	4.0
All	6.2	8.0	4.7	8.9	5.0
Ratio of manual to non-manual unemployment rate	2.27	1.94	1.82	1.88	2.29
var(u_i/u) (%)	18.5	15.0	19.9	11.2	28.1

[a] Australia 1986, [b] Germany 1985.

Notes: See notes to Table 1(a). Occupational Classifications according to International Standard Occupational Classification. The first 4 categories are treated as non-manual.

Source: ILO *Year Book*, 1988.

Over time, the pattern of occupational unemployment rates is remarkably stable, as revealed by the correlation between the rates in the mid-1970s and mid-1980s (see Table 2). But has the spread altered? The answer is that in no country except Sweden is there any evidence of increased mismatch since the late 1970s, though in the USA there is some evidence of increased occupational imbalance since the early 1970s.

The next question is, Where do the occupational differences in unemployment rates come from? Are they due to differences in duration or in inflow rates? As a broad generalization, mismatch stems more from differences in inflow rates than in duration. This is certainly true of occupational differences (see Table 3). Unemployment is highest in those occupations that have high general turnover.

Closely related to differences in occupational unemployment rates are differences in educational unemployment rates. Since education (unlike occupation) is a relatively stable personal characteristic, these rates are in many ways more meaningful. However, except in the USA and Britain, it is difficult to find time-series data on these rates, so we confine ourselves here to the

Germany[b]	Ireland	New Zealand	Norway	Spain	Sweden
6.5	3.2	1.7	0.7	6.1	1.2
4.3	3.7	1.0	0.2	2.9	—
—	6.0	2.8	1.2	8.2	1.0
8.6	8.6	3.6	1.3	7.5	1.8
6.6	9.7	3.9	1.6	13.0	3.2
3.2	2.5	5.0	0.7	13.2	2.8
10.2	18.2	5.3	2.3	13.7	2.1
7.4	9.3	3.7	1.4	11.4	1.7
7.5	17.7	4.1	1.5	20.5	1.9
1.49	2.26	2.01	2.19	1.88	2.03
11.4	45.1	14.9	25.3	7.2	16.7

snapshot in Table 4. It confirms the much greater problems experienced in most countries by people without good academic or vocational qualifications.

Region

Unemployment rates also differ greatly between and within regions. But the regional differences are much less than the occupational differences (see Table 5). For example, in Britain the variance of relative unemployment rates across ten regions is only about 6 per cent, compared with a variance of 21 per cent across five occupations. Only when one gets down to travel-to-work areas do major geographical differences emerge. Across Britain's 322 travel-to-work areas, the variance of relative unemployment rates is 24 per cent; but in the USA, even when we go to the variance across states, it is still only about 8 per cent.

Turning to the variance in other countries, we provide comparable data in Table 6. These show the high persistence of regional differences in some countries (Italy, UK, Japan, Germany) and the total absence of persistence in

Chapter 6

Table 2 *Dispersion of occupational unemployment rates*

(a) var(u_i/u) (%)

	UK (5)	USA (7)	Australia (7)	Canada (7)	Germany (6)	Spain (7)	Sweden (8)
1973		13.1					9.0
1974	23.3	15.1					9.6
1975	14.0	20.2		12.3			7.6
1976	20.5	14.0		9.2	8.8	15.2	12.1
1977	21.0	12.3	13.8	10.7		15.7	12.5
1978	16.2	12.4	18.4	9.5	9.1	16.4	12.4
1979	24.4	15.2	14.3	10.9		19.7	12.8
1980	20.4	22.7	15.1	12.4	9.1	20.6	12.4
1981	21.2	21.1	17.2	13.3		20.0	15.9
1982	21.4	25.1	17.4	15.1	16.9	21.4	17.3
1983	22.8	21.5	25.7	13.6		21.1	15.9
1984	20.5	19.9	22.2	11.2	14.1	16.7	12.1
1985	22.3	20.6	19.7	11.3	11.4	12.9	13.3
1986		20.6	15.0	10.8		11.1	16.6
1987		18.5		11.2		7.2	16.7
Correlation between first and last years	0.87	—	0.92	0.95	0.86	1.00	0.83

(b) Ratio of manual to non-manual unemployment rates

	UK (5)	USA (7)	Australia (7)	Canada (7)	Germany (6)	Spain (7)	Sweden (8)
1973		1.80					1.74
1974	1.76	1.93					1.78
1975	1.74	2.18		1.89			1.65
1976	2.13	1.94		1.71	1.04	2.08	1.91
1977	2.12	1.85	1.68	1.78		2.14	1.93
1978	1.78	1.85	2.16	1.70	1.18	1.95	2.04
1979	2.27	2.04	1.97	1.80		1.99	2.02
1980	2.34	2.46	1.97	1.92	1.27	2.04	1.96
1981	2.41	2.39	1.86	1.97		1.98	2.25
1982	2.53	2.58	2.14	2.04	1.69	1.86	2.34
1983	2.57	2.46	2.36	1.97		1.75	2.22
1984	2.20	2.38	2.46	1.86	1.60	1.99	1.95
1985	2.45	2.42	2.14	1.87	1.49	1.91	1.85
1986		2.41	1.93	1.86		2.00	1.98
1987		2.27		1.88		1.88	2.02

Notes: See Table 1(a). Numbers in brackets are numbers of categories. Bars indicate break in series.

Sources: UK: *General Household Survey* (breakdown as in Table 1(a)); *Others*: ILO *Yearbook* (breakdown as in Table 1(b), which amalgamates skilled and non-skilled manual workers). For the USA, Employment and Earnings uses different classifications before and after 1983, but the trend in each sub-period is as shown above.

Table 3 *Unemployment by occupation: inflow and duration, Britain and USA*

	Britain (1984)			USA (1987)		
	Inflow rate (% per month) (S/N)	Ave. duration (mos.) (U/S)	Unemployment rate (%) (U/L)	Inflow rate (% per month) (S/N)	Ave. duration (mos.) (U/S)	Unemployment rate (%) (U/L)
Professional and managerial	0.50	11.2	5.3	0.74	3.0	2.3
Clerical	0.88	10.1	8.0	1.58	2.6	4.3
Other non-manual	1.14	11.8	12.2			
Skilled manual	1.02	14.2	12.6	1.97	2.9	6.1
Personal services	1.32	14.1	15.5	2.96	2.4	7.7
Other manual				2.84	3.0	9.4
All	0.94	12.8	10.8	2.23	2.6	6.2

Note: The sources listed below provide data on *L*, *N*, *U*, and *S* (inflow). These are then used to produce 'steady-state' estimates of duration. However, the estimate of monthly inflow is an underestimate, comprising all those unemployed at a point in time who became unemployed in the previous month. (It thus excludes those who enter and leave within a month.) In Britain the numbers in this category on the *Labour Force Survey* definition of unemployment are only 70% of those in their first month of benefit receipt. The *General Household Survey* is broadly consistent with the *LFS*.

Source: Britain: *Labour Force Survey* tapes. This only records previous occupation and industry for those unemployed for under 3 years. The unemployment rate in each occupation is computed by taking the numbers unemployed for less than 3 years who were previously employed in the stated occupation and raising it by the ratio of total unemployed to numbers of unemployed reporting their previous occupation. A similar procedure is carried out for those unemployed for under one month. *USA*: *Employment and Earnings*, Jan. 1988, p. 175.

the USA and Australia. Thus, while the correlation coefficient of mid-1970s and mid-1980s unemployment rates across British regions is 0.92, across the US states it is − 0.33.

How has dispersion altered? In no country is there any important increase since the mid-1970s, and in Britain it is now markedly lower than in the early 1970s. As regards the cyclical pattern of mismatch, we have investigated this only for Britain. The figures are plotted in Fig. 1(*a*) and show a clear tendency for regional mismatch to fall in downturns and rise in upturns. In other words, in a downturn unemployment rises proportionately more in the low-unemployment regions. Even so, employment falls more slowly in the low-unemployment regions, bringing about substantial changes in the pattern of employment. To look at the degree of 'turbulence' in the pattern of regional

Table 4 *Unemployment rate, by highest education level, 1988 (%)*

		Degree	Sub-degree	Vocational	Upper secondary	Other	All
Australia	M	2.6	4.2	4.7	6.4	9.5	6.3
	F	5.5	6.8	—	7.7	7.8	7.3
Austria	M	0.8	—	3.1	3.4	5.5	3.5
	F	2.4	—	3.1	2.9	4.9	3.7
Belgium	M	3.2	—	—	4.6	9.0	6.9
	F	7.7	—	—	15.9	22.4	17.4
Canada	M	3.4	6.3	—	8.5	11.2	7.9
	F	5.5	7.2	—	9.8	12.7	9.0
Finland	M	1.2	—	—	4.0	9.2	7.4
	F	0.7	—	—	3.2	5.6	4.6
Germany	M	3.0	3.0	5.9	5.5	14.4	6.9
	F	6.9	8.8	8.2	8.1	12.9	9.4
Greece	M	4.2	8.1	—	7.3	3.9	4.8
	F	12.7	14.1	—	18.7	6.2	9.9
Italy	M	3.3	—	—	9.2	6.2	6.7
	F	9.3	—	—	20.0	15.3	16.3
Netherlands	M	4.4	4.3	—	4.8	10.9	7.5
	F	11.4	10.7	—	10.3	16.5	13.2
Norway	M	0.4	—	—	1.1	2.2	1.5
	F	1.1	—	—	2.4	2.2	2.1
Spain	M	9.9	11.3	—	18.8	14.7	15.5
	F	27.4	21.8	—	33.7	17.9	24.4
Sweden	M	0.8	1.4	2.2	1.4	2.1	1.8
	F	0.8	0.8	2.1	1.5	2.2	1.8
UK	M	3.7	—	8.1	7.7	14.8	10.4
	F	4.7	—	10.1	7.0	11.3	9.7
USA	M	1.8	4.3	—	6.7	10.7	5.6
	F	2.1	3.6	—	5.4	9.6	4.8

Note: 'Sub-degree' is some post-secondary education but not a degree (only identified in some countries). 'Vocational' includes any vocational qualification below a degree (only identified in some countries).

Source: OECD, *Employment Outlook*, July 1989, pp. 85–6.

Table 5   *Unemployment by region, 1988*

	Inflow rate (% per month) (Inflow/N)	Average duration (mos.) (U/Outflow)	Unemployment rate (%) (U/L)
Britain			
South East	0.80	5.7	5.3
East Anglia	0.83	4.7	4.9
South West	1.03	5.0	6.2
West Midlands	0.97	7.6	9.0
East Midlands	0.97	6.4	7.5
Yorks. and Humbs.	1.20	6.8	9.7
North West	1.30	7.2	10.9
North	1.47	7.0	12.2
Wales	1.40	6.2	10.6
Scotland	1.50	6.9	11.7
Total	1.07	6.4	8.0
var(X_i/X)	5.7%	2.0%	10.6%
USA			
New England (1)			3.1
New York and New Jersey (2)			4.1
Middle Atlantic (3)			4.9
South East (4)			5.6
Central: North East (5)			6.0
Central: South West (6)			7.8
Central: North West (7)			4.9
Mountain (8)			5.8
Pacific (9)			5.3
North West (10)			6.2
Total			5.4
var (u_i/u)			4.1%

Note: Numbers in brackets are standard numbers for each region in the USA.

Source: Britain: *Employment Gazette*, Oct. 1988, Table 2.23. The data do not relate to a steady-state. The data relate to benefit recipients in Summer 1988. *USA*: *Employment and Earnings*, May 1989, Table 3.

employment, we can compute $\frac{1}{2}\Sigma\left|\Delta(N_i/N)\right|$ indicating what fraction of all jobs in the economy have 'changed region'. This is plotted in Fig. 1(*c*) and shows a marked redistribution of employment during the 1979–81 downturn.

One naturally asks whether the problems of the 1980s can be attributed in general to a greater pace of change in the pattern of employment between regions. To answer this we compute the regional turbulence index

Table 6   *Dispersion of regional unemployment rates*
var (u_i/u)

	Australia (8 reg.)	Canada (10 reg.)	France (22 reg.)	Germany (11 reg.)
1974	3.5	—	7.1	—
1975	3.1	7.1	3.9	—
1976	2.1	7.9	3.8	—
1977	1.5	8.5	3.5	3.6
1978	1.4	8.3	3.9	5.0
1979	2.0	9.3	4.0	6.6
1980	1.4	8.7	3.7	6.3
1981	2.9	10.4	3.2	4.9
1982	1.6	4.9	3.0	4.3
1983	0.8	3.2	3.1	4.2
1984	2.0	5.1	3.2	5.9
1985	2.6	7.1	2.8	7.3
1986	1.8	8.2	2.8	8.3
1987	2.8	9.5	2.8	—
Correlation between first and last years	−0.11	0.67	0.50	0.83

Note: Numbers of regions are given in brackets.

Source: OECD, Regional Database on unemployment and labour force except for UK, which is based on Savouri (1989). British data for 1967–73 are 12.8, 13.3, 14.9, 13.7, 14.3, 15.2, 17.5.

$(\frac{1}{2}\Sigma |\Delta(N_i/N)|)$ for a number of countries. Table 7 gives averages of this for different decades. Only in Britain and the USA is the degree of turbulence any higher in the recent past than in the 1960s, and in Britain this turbulence was concentrated in the early 1980s.

Industrial differences

We can turn now to differences in industrial unemployment rates. These are a less clear concept than any other. For when industrial rates are computed, unemployed people are attributed to the industry in which they were last employed, and many eventually find employment elsewhere. As Table 8 shows, unemployment is well above average in construction. And in bad times manufacturing too gets hit. But durations are remarkably similar in all industries, with unemployment differences being due to different turnover rates.

Finland (12 reg.)	Italy (20 reg.)	Japan (20 reg.)	Sweden (24 reg.)	Britain (10 reg.)	USA (51 reg.)
39.0	—	7.6	—	14.3	—
26.4	—	4.1	—	7.2	—
15.8	—	4.3	17.1	4.5	5.3
16.6	14.3	7.2	14.6	4.9	4.4
13.8	12.4	7.4	15.5	6.7	3.7
13.1	12.5	7.1	11.7	8.8	3.9
19.2	18.1	6.9	15.6	9.2	5.0
22.4	13.1	5.9	16.4	6.6	5.6
20.0	11.5	5.0	13.7	5.6	5.5
16.9	9.3	5.9	10.4	5.4	5.2
22.1	7.9	6.4	11.0	5.1	6.0
23.5	9.7	6.6	11.6	5.0	5.1
20.5	13.6	5.8	14.8	5.1	6.6
18.8	19.6	5.4	14.5	6.3	7.8
0.91	0.84	0.91	0.69	0.92	−0.33

The pattern of industrial unemployment rates is remarkably constant, as is shown in the correlations in Table 9. And there is no sign except perhaps in Australia that the dispersions have increased over time. This does not mean that the process of industrial restructuring is not an important source of unemployment. As Table 10 shows, about 1 per cent of jobs 'change industry' each year. But, contrary to popular belief, there is no evidence that this process has been accelerating. People seem constantly to forget the massive restructurings of the past, such as the huge exodus from European agriculture in the 1950s and 1960s which was accompanied by so little unemployment.

In fact, in most countries except the USA the rate of structural shift has been slowing down. And in Britain there is no difference between the level now and the level in the mid-1960s, as Fig. 1 shows. Both turbulence and industrial mismatch increase in downturns,[3] but in the late 1980s they were at normal levels. Where there is a remarkable difference in both Britain and the USA is between the 1930s and the post-war period. As Fig. 2 shows, there is every

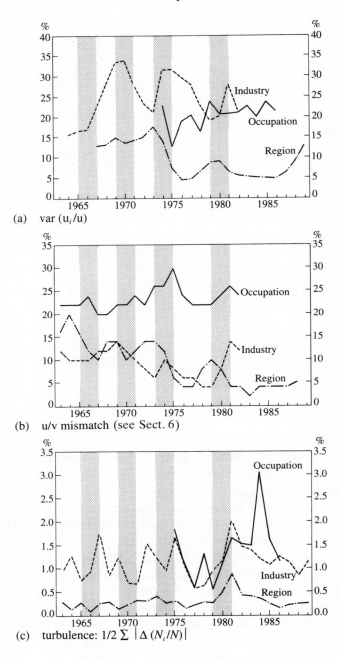

(a)   var (u_i/u)

(b)   u/v mismatch (see Sect. 6)

(c)   turbulence: $1/2 \sum |\Delta (N_i/N)|$

Table 7 *Regional turbulence indices (averages of annual values) per cent* $\frac{1}{2}\sum |\Delta(N_i/N)|$

	1960s	1970s	1980s
France (22 reg.)	—	0.93	0.99
Germany (11 reg.)	0.52	0.45	0.38
Italy (20 reg.)	0.73	0.46	0.71
UK (10 reg.)	0.23	0.28	0.37
Australia (8 reg.)	0.49	0.48	0.51
Canada (10 reg.)	0.51	0.46	0.53
USA (10 reg.)	0.40	0.61	0.54
Finland (12 reg.)	—	0.66	0.51
Sweden (24 reg.)	—	0.35	0.50

Note: Numbers of regions are given in brackets.

Sources: OECD, Regional Database on Labour Force and Unemployment except for the USA and UK. *For the USA*: 1952–75: *Employment and Training Report to the President*, 1982, Table D-1; 1975–88: US Bureau of Labor Statistics, *Employment and Earnings*, various issues. *For the UK*: 1951–68: Dept. of Employment and Productivity, *British Labour Statistics, Historical Abstract, 1886–1968*, 1971, Table 131; 1969–70: CSO *Regional Statistics,* no. 12, 1976, Table 8.1; 1971–89: *Employment Gazette, Historical Supplement* no. 2, Nov. 1989, Table 1.5. Annual data available on request.

reason to think of 1930s unemployment as being due significantly to the 'problems of the declining industries'.

Age, race, and sex

Unemployment is, of course, almost everywhere more common among young people than among adults (see Table 8). Very often, the difference results from higher inflow rates—and certainly not from unusual duration. The youth unemployment problem was accentuated in the 1980s by a big rise in the relative number of youths, reflecting the baby boom of the late 1950s and 1960s. In consequence, much more attention has been devoted to youth unemployment than to any other aspect of unemployment. (See for example

Fig. 1. *Fluctuations in mismatch and turbulence, Britain, 1963–1990.*

Shaded areas = downturns.

Sources: (*a*) Industry: ILO, *Yearbook of Labour Statistics*, various issues; regional: CSO, *Regional Trends* and *Regional Statistics*, various issues; occupation: see Schmitt (1990*a*). (*b*) Jackman and Roper (1987: Table 2), updated using *Employment Gazette*. (*c*) Industry: see Fig. 2; regional: see Table 7; occupation: see Schmitt (1990*b*).

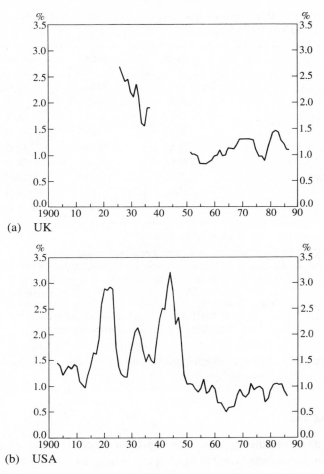

(a) UK

(b) USA

Fig. 2. *Industrial turbulence index (five-year moving average).*

$$\tfrac{1}{2}\sum |\,\Delta(N_i/N)\,|\,.$$

Sources: *UK industrial employment statistics*: 1924–39: Department of Employment and Productivity, *British Labour Statistics, Historical Abstract, 1886–1968*, London: HMSO, 1971; Table 114. 1948–68: ibid., Table 132; 1969–70: Department of Employment and Productivity, *British Labour Statistics Yearbook, 1972*, Table 63. 1971–89: *Employment Gazette, Historical Supplement no. 2*, Nov. 1989, Table 1.2. *Note*: For the years 1948–70, the data represent 24 industry orders, the 1948–59 data for 1948 SIC, and the 1959–70 data for 1958 SIC. The data for 1971–89 are for 25 industry orders from 1980 SIC. For the lists of the respective industries, see the above sources.

US industrial employment statistics: 1901–55: *Historical Statistics of the United States: Colonial Times to 1970, pt. I*: D127–41. 1955–88: US Department of Labor, Bureau of Labor Statistics, 'Employment and Earnings', May 1989: Table B1; *Note*: Index is for 8 divisions.

Table 8   *Unemployment by industry, age, race, and sex: Britain and USA*

	Britain (1984)			USA (1987)		
	Inflow rate (% per month) (S/N)	Average duration (mos.) (U/S)	Unemploy-ment rate (%) (U/L)	Inflow rate (% per month) (S/N)	Average duration (mos.) (U/S)	Unemploy-ment rate (%) (U/L)
Industry						
Agriculture	0.82	10.6	8.0	4.88	2.4	10.5
Manufacturing	0.88	16.6	12.7	2.06	3.1	6.0
Construction	1.57	12.7	16.6	4.52	2.9	11.6
Energy	0.76	10.1	7.1			
Services	0.90	11.6	9.4			
Transportion and public utilities				1.57	3.0	4.5
Distribution				2.96	2.5	6.9
Finance and service industries				2.08	2.5	4.9
Age						
16–19	3.33	8.5	22.1	10.15	2.0	16.9
20–24	1.33	15.3	16.9	4.46	2.4	9.7
25–54	0.74	13.1	8.8	1.76	3.0	5.0
55–64	0.47	19.2	8.3	0.97	3.7	3.5
Race						
White	0.92	12.6	10.4	2.15	2.6	5.3
Other	1.43	17.6	20.1	5.14	2.9	13.0
Sex						
Male	0.78	16.1	11.2	2.28	2.9	6.2
Female	1.17	9.7	10.2	2.87	2.3	6.2
All	0.94	12.8	10.8	2.54	2.6	6.2

Note: see Table 3.

Source: *Britain*: *Labour Force Survey* tapes (see Table 3); *USA*: *Employment and Earnings*, Jan. 1988, pp. 160, 166, 169, 170, 174, 175.

Table 9 *Dispersion of industrial unemployment rates, 1973–1987*
var(u_i/u) (%)

	UK (9)	USA (9)	Australia (7)	Canada (9)	Germany (9)	Spain (9)	Sweden (7)
1973	21.2	7.3					
1974	31.8	9.3	4.1				8.7
1975	31.8	15.3	5.7		17.6		5.1
1976	29.9	8.1	8.1	7.6	13.0	59.0	7.6
1977	28.3	6.1	8.9	9.8	12.0	60.3	2.7
1978	22.9	5.8	11.9	10.6	11.1	54.4	7.5
1979	19.1	5.8	8.3	8.9	11.3	57.2	3.7
1980	20.1	10.6	8.6	10.6	10.0	53.6	3.2
1981	28.2	9.4	9.6	8.3	9.5	48.6	6.2
1982	21.8	13.9	11.1	12.5	11.7	41.2	5.7
1983		11.0	24.3	12.7	10.4	37.2	4.7
1984		8.7	10.4	10.9	11.1	34.7	3.8
1985		8.8	5.9	9.2	12.3	26.5	3.6
1986		9.9	9.1	8.3	11.7	19.9	5.2
1987		9.0	9.9	7.1	10.0	11.9	4.0
Correlation between first and last years	0.86	0.89	—	0.95	0.80	0.96	0.81

Notes: Numbers of industrial sectors are given in brackets. Bars indicate breaks in series. Correlations are not calculated across breaks.

Source: ILO *Yearbook*.

successive issues of the OECD *Employment Outlook*.) For this reason we shall concentrate mainly on other dimensions of mismatch. We shall also say little about race differences, which are acute and reflect mainly differences in inflow rates into unemployment, or about sex differences, which in most but not all countries are fairly small.

2. How the structure of unemployment is determined

Why do unemployment rates differ across groups? In thinking about this, it is essential to distinguish between situations according to whether the labour force structure is exogenous or endogenous. In the short run the labour force is already allocated between groups. But in the long run migration is possible between skill-groups and regions, though not normally between sexes and

Table 10 *Industrial turbulence indices (averages of annual rates) (%)*
$\frac{1}{2}\sum|\varDelta(N_i/N)|$

	1950s	1960s	1970s	1980s
Belgium (8)	0.94	0.94	0.96	0.89
France (8)	1.04	0.96	0.68	0.65
Germany (8)	1.35	1.15	0.92	0.64
Italy (8)	2.18	1.43	1.11	1.29
Netherlands (8)	0.74	0.89	0.96	1.14
Spain (8)	1.55	1.19	1.53	1.36
UK (24/25)	0.91	1.12	1.17	1.27
Australia (8)	—	1.76	1.21	1.40
Canada (8)	—	—	0.83	0.90
USA (8)	0.93	0.67	0.89	0.96
Austria (8)	—	—	1.10	1.08
Sweden (8)	—	1.45	1.52	0.67
Switzerland (8)	—	0.90	0.99	0.50

Note: Numbers of industrial sectors are given in brackets.

Source: OECD, *Labour Force Statistics*, various years, except for the USA and UK; see also sources to Fig. 2.

races. There *is* migration between age-groups, but it is unfortunately exogenous. We shall begin with the case where the labour force is taken as given, and then turn to the case where migration occurs and a long-run equilibrium has been established.

Labour force exogenous

In the short run, the disposition of the labour force across sectors is given. Employment is determined by the pattern of labour demand and the process of wage formation. For simplicity we can suppose that output (Y) is produced by a CES production function that is homogeneous of degree one in the different types of labour (N_i):

$$Y^\rho = \varphi\sum \alpha_i N_i^\rho \qquad (\rho \leqslant 1, \ \Sigma\alpha_i = 1),$$

where $\rho - 1 = -1/\sigma$, σ being the elasticity of substitution.[4] Ignoring imperfect competition, the *labour demand* for the ith type of labour is then given by

$$W_i = \alpha_i\varphi\left(\frac{N_i}{Y}\right)^{-1/\sigma} = \alpha_i\left(\frac{N_i}{L_i}\frac{L_i}{L}\right)^{-1/\sigma} X \qquad (i = 1, \ldots, n), \qquad (1)$$

where W_i is the real wage, L_i the labour force in the ith sector, and X the productivity factor $\varphi(Y/L)^{1/\sigma}$. The coefficient α_i is an indicator of the productivity of labour of type i.

Wages in each sector are determined by the *wage function*, which we shall write as

$$W_i = \gamma_i f\left(\frac{N_i}{L_i}\right) X \qquad (f' > 0) \qquad (i = 1, \ldots, n), \qquad (2)$$

where the coefficient γ_i is an indicator of 'wage push'. The evidence for this formulation will be discussed later. Its theoretical basis, as described in earlier chapters, is a mixture of bargaining outcomes, efficiency wages, and pure labour supply.[5]

The demand function and the wage function are drawn in Fig. 3. Taken together, they determine the unemployment rate of each group as an increasing function of its wage-push relative to productivity (γ_i/α_i) and also of its relative size (L_i/L):[6]

$$u_i = g^1\left(\frac{\gamma_i}{\alpha_i}, \frac{L_i}{L}\right)$$
$$\quad + \quad +$$

$$W_i = g^2\left(\alpha_i, \gamma_i, \frac{L_i}{L}, X\right)$$
$$\quad + \quad + \quad - \quad +$$

Thus, if an age-group increases in relative size, its unemployment rate will go up and its wage rate down. (The demand curve as drawn shifts left, since a given N_i corresponds to a lower N_i/L_i.) This is exactly what happened to youths in the USA as a result of the baby boom (see Freeman and Bloom 1986).

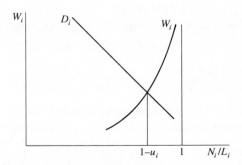

Fig. 3. *Employment and wages in a single sector: labour force given.*

Equally, the unemployment rate of a group will be affected by its turnover rate. For wage push develops if it is easy for unemployed people to find work. At a given unemployment rate, the chances of finding work are proportional to the rate at which jobs are being left. Thus the wage-push variable (y_i) is higher, the higher is turnover. This helps to explain why unemployment is higher for young people.

Labour force endogenous

The preceding analysis applies to differences in unemployment across regions, occupational levels, or educational levels only in the short run. In the longer run the number of people in each occupation or region itself depends on wages and job opportunities. Migration can change the share of the total labour force in each sector. Migration into a sector (M_i) depends on the extent to which expected income in the sector exceeds that elsewhere. It also depends on the costs of belonging to the sector (e.g. on the associated training costs or the climatic discomfort).[7] Thus, the net in-migration rate (M_i/L_i) is given by

$$\frac{M_i}{L_i} = h \left(W_i \frac{N_i}{L_i} \bigg/ (1 + c_i) X \right) \qquad (i = 1, \ldots, n), \qquad (3)$$

where c_i reflects the differential costs of belonging to the sector.

Suppose initially that we define the long-run equilibrium as a condition of zero net migration. Then in equilibrium the *zero-migration condition* gives

$$W_i \frac{N_i}{L_i} = (1 + c_i)\zeta X \qquad (i = 1, \ldots, n), \qquad (3')$$

where $\zeta = h^{-1}(0)$. This is the long-run supply condition for the choice of sectors. The equalization of net advantages requires that, if a sector has higher employment, it will have to have lower wages. This relationship reflects long-run migration behaviour, and could therefore be expected to show up in cross-sectional evidence. On the other hand, once workers are in a sector, they will press for the setting of higher wages if employment is higher. This relationship repeated year after year could be expected to show up in time-series evidence.

To understand why unemployment rates differ between sectors, we combine (3') and (2) to obtain

$$u_i = j^1 \left(\underset{+}{\frac{\gamma_i}{1 + c_i}} \right),$$

$$W_i = j^2 \underset{+ \ + \ +}{(\gamma_i, \ c_i, \ X)}.$$

We note that relative unemployment rates and wage rates in the long run are determined by supply-side factors alone: demand conditions determine only the absolute magnitude of employment and of the labour force in each sector.

To see more clearly what is happening, we can note that there are $(n - 1)$ independent zero-migration conditions (3'), n wage equations (2), n demand equations (1), and the identity $\Sigma L_i \equiv L$, which together determine W_i, N_i, and L_i. But the unemployment rates themselves are determined by supply factors, and demand 'then' allocates the labour force between sectors.

The partial equilibrium for a sector is illustrated in Fig. 4. As before, the wage-setting relation shows that wages rise as higher employment creates wage push. This reflects the way in which workers behave once they are in a sector. On the other hand, their migration decisions imply that higher wages must be associated with lower employment to equalize the net advantages of the different sectors.

So long as the differential wage push in a sector is in proportion to its cost differential, the sector will have the same unemployment as elsewhere. But if the wage push is excessive, higher unemployment must result—otherwise the sector would continue to attract labour.

Thus consider, for example, the standard human capital model, where occupation 1 requires one more year of schooling than occupation 2. Making use of (3'), we have that under full employment

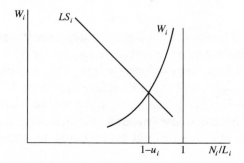

Fig. 4. *Employment and wages in a single sector: labour force endogenous, zero migration equilibrium.*

$$\frac{W_1}{W_2} = 1 + r = \frac{1 + c_1}{1 + c_2},$$

where r is the discount rate, while, allowing for unemployment,

$$\frac{W_1(N_1/L_1)}{W_2(N_2/L_2)} = \frac{1 + c_1}{1 + c_2}.$$

So long as $W_1/W_2 = 1 + r$, the unemployment rates will be equal. But suppose the differential is squeezed (because $\gamma_1/\gamma_2 < 1 + r$). Then the uptake of schooling will fall until the unskilled unemployment rate has risen sufficiently relative to the skilled.

A similar model was used by Harris and Todaro (1970) to explain urban unemployment in poor countries. If the urban wage gap (W_1/W_2) is excessive relative to any cost differences, people will pile into the towns until there is sufficient urban unemployment ($N_1/L_1 < 1$). Thinking along similar lines, Hall (1970) showed that unemployment differences between US cities were positively correlated with their wage rates. A similar model was earlier used to explain the unemployment of educated people in India by excessive wages for the educated (Blaug *et al.* 1969).

So let us ask, How well does the notion that unemployment depends on $\gamma_i/(1 + c_i)$ explain the pattern of unemployment rates? There is strong evidence in Tables 3 and 8 that those occupations and industries with high turnover rates (and thus high γ_i) have high unemployment rates. Wage pressure will also be higher the greater the union strength. Thus, other things being equal, union power in an occupation or industry will increase its unemployment rate, as will factors increasing the firms' incentive to pay efficiency wages.

With regard to training costs (c_i), occupations where these are high do tend to have low unemployment rates. This is partly because, for reasons of compensating differentials, their wages have to be high, with the result that they are kept well above the level of unemployment benefits.

Across regions, as we have seen, unemployment is also higher in those regions that have high turnover. But typically, unemployment differences are greater than can be adequately explained on this basis. And in many countries, like Britain and Italy (but not the USA), the pattern of regional unemployment differences is highly persistent. The out-migration of labour from the high-unemployment areas is only just sufficient to keep pace with the transfer of jobs. Thus there is a steady-state migration of both jobs and workers, with relative unemployment rates and relative wages very stable. Regions like the North of England or the South of Italy provide a steadily decreasing share of total employment, and this downward drift in employment share is matched by a downward drift in the share of the labour force. Matters are often made worse by the fact that the 'natural' growth rate of population (arising from the difference between new entrants and retirements) is higher in the regions that are losing jobs. We also need to allow for this.

Labour force endogenous with steady-state migration

We can easily handle these long-run steady-state patterns with two small modifications of our earlier framework. First, employment is changing at a steady-state rate $\hat{N}_i$ (which differs across sectors). This arises because of exogenous shifts in demand (e.g. changes in its industrial mix), with relative wages unchanged. Since the employment rate (N_i/L_i) is constant, in this dynamic steady state it follows that

$$\hat{L}_i = \hat{N}_i = \text{const.}$$

In addition, there is (as between regions) a differential 'natural' growth of working population (corresponding to the difference between new entries and exits from the population of working age).[8] A region has problems if its natural population growth Π_i exceeds its employment growth rate.

To see this, we have to extend our equation (3) to show how the labour force changes not only because of net migration, $h(\cdot)$, but also because of natural population growth (Π_i). This gives

$$\hat{L}_i = h\left(W_i \frac{N_i}{L_i} \middle/ (1 + c_i) X \right) + \Pi_i.$$

Since the unemployment rates are constant in the steady state, with $\hat{L}_i = \hat{N}_i$, it follows that

$$h\left(W_i \frac{N_i}{L_i} \middle/ (1 + c_i) X \right) = \hat{N}_i - \Pi_i.$$

Thus, at given W_i a region will have a higher employment rate (N_i/L_i) if its rate of job creation exceeds its rate of population growth.

On the other hand, a sector where the natural growth rate of population is high will have a high unemployment rate. Turning back to Fig. 4, in such a region the long-run labour supply relation (LS_i) is shifted down—raising unemployment and lowering wages. This helps to explain persistent high unemployment, as in southern Italy and Ireland. People have constantly wondered why one-off injections of jobs into such areas have had no enduring effect on their unemployment rates. Our story shows why. It also helps to explain low unemployment in skilled occupations. If skilled jobs are always increasing faster than unskilled jobs, this will tend to lower steady-state unemployment in the skilled occupations.

The analysis in this section is out of line with traditional analyses of structural unemployment, which emphasize the role of one-off demand shifts. However, as we showed in Section 1, there are such striking persistent differences in unemployment rates that we feel these deserve the primary attention.

3. How mismatch is related to the NAIRU

The preceding analysis provides a complete account of the unemployment rate for each separate group and thus also of the aggregate unemployment rate. Thus, in principle, our theory could stop at this point. However, many people are interested in explaining aggregate unemployment without going through the daunting task of explaining each of the individual rates. In particular, people ask, Does increased structural imbalance help explain the recent high unemployment in Europe?

So is there some simple index by which one could assess how the structure of unemployment is related to its average level (both of course being endogenous)? The answer is Yes. The basic idea goes back to Lipsey (1960). It is worth beginning with an analogous framework to his, before modifying it in the direction of greater rigour. Figure 5 sets out the wage function, assumed to be the same for each of two equal-sized groups. $\overline{W}$ is the feasible average real wage, based on pricing behaviour. If both unemployment rates are equal, aggregate unemployment is at A. If the two unemployment rates differ but the

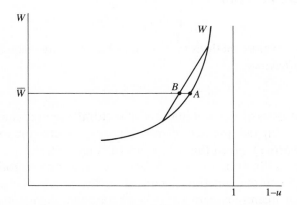

Fig. 5. *Introductory presentation of mismatch and the NAIRU.*

average wage remains at $\bar{W}$, the average unemployment will have to be at B. Thus, overall unemployment is higher. The further apart the unemployment rates, the higher the average unemployment.

This result depends entirely on the convexity of the wage function, for which there is some evidence (see below). But the formulation above is unrigorous, and insufficiently general. For example, it assumes identical wage functions for each group, which, on reasonable assumptions, turns out to be unnecessary.

To see this, and to derive the relevant mismatch index, we begin with the feasible set of real wages, given by the price function. For simplicity, we shall assume constant returns to scale in the different types of labour. If we also initially assume a Cobb–Douglas production function,

$$Y = \varphi \prod_i N_i^{\alpha_i} \qquad (\Sigma \alpha_i = 1),$$

the nominal price level (P) is given by

$$P = \prod_i W_i^{\alpha_i} / \kappa \varphi,$$

where κ is the index of product-market competitiveness.

Setting the price level at unity and taking logs, the price function gives a *feasible real wage frontier*,

$$A = \Sigma \alpha_i \log W_i, \tag{4}$$

where $A = \log(\kappa\varphi)$. In addition, we shall assume double logarithmic wage functions. (Evidence for the UK follows; for other countries see e.g. Grubb 1986.) Thus, the *wage functions* are

$$\log W_i = \gamma_{0i} - \gamma_1 \log u_i. \tag{5}$$

Substituting the wage functions into the feasible real wage frontier (4) gives an *unemployment frontier*,

$$A = \Sigma \alpha_i \gamma_{0i} - \gamma_1 \Sigma \alpha_i \log u_i. \tag{6}$$

This shows the locus of all combinations of sectoral unemployment rates which are consistent with the absence of inflationary pressure (or, more generally, wage/price surprises), given the behaviour of wage-setters.

This frontier is illustrated in Fig. 6 for the case of two sectors of equal size ($\alpha_1 = \alpha_2 = \frac{1}{2}$). Since the function is convex to the origin, the lowest possible *average* level of unemployment ($u_{\min}$) is where unemployment is the same in both sectors.[9] This occurs at point P in the diagram. If, instead, the unemploy-

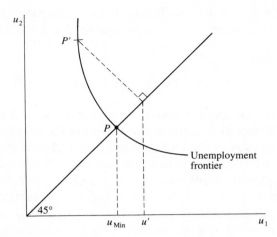

Fig. 6. *The unemployment frontier.*

Wages responding to own-sector unemployment.

ment rates differ, as at P', average unemployment is higher—in this case it is u'. The further apart the different unemployment rates, the higher their average level.

We can readily derive an expression that shows how average unemployment is related to the dispersion of the unemployment rates across sectors. We start from (6) and add $\gamma_1 \log u$ to both sides and divide both sides by γ_1. This gives

$$\log u = \text{const.} - \Sigma \alpha_i \log \frac{u_i}{u},$$

since $\Sigma \alpha_i = 1$. Expanding $\log u_i/u$ around 1 gives[10]

$$\log u \simeq \text{const.} - \Sigma \alpha_i \left(-\frac{1}{2} \right) \left(\frac{u_i}{u} - 1 \right)^2$$

$$= \text{const.} + \frac{1}{2} \text{var} \frac{u_i}{u}. \tag{7}$$

The minimum level of log unemployment is now given by the constant, $((\Sigma \alpha_i \gamma_{0i} - A)/\gamma_1)$ and occurs when unemployment rates have been equalized. But if unemployment rates are unequal, unemployment rises in proportion to $\frac{1}{2}\text{var}(u_i/u)$.

Given equation (7), the natural index of the structure of unemployment is $\frac{1}{2}\text{var}(u_i/u)$. It measures the proportional excess of unemployment over its minimum. Since it is zero if in each sector labour demand (N_i) bears the same proportion to labour supply (L_i), it is natural to give it the name 'mismatch' (MM).[11] Thus

$$MM = \frac{1}{2} \text{var} \frac{u_i}{u} = \log u - \log u_{min}.$$

As the data in Section 1 showed, mismatch on this definition has not increased. In other words, we cannot use changes in the structure of unemployment as an explanation of the higher average level of unemployment rates.

At this point we need to deal with a misconception. We do not mean that the *number* of unemployed people who are 'mismatched' has failed to rise; for if unemployment rises for some other reason and the proportional mismatch is constant, the absolute numbers mismatched will rise. This corresponds well with the feeling of many Europeans that there are now more people who are structurally unemployed than used to be the case. The point is that it is possible for this to be true without structural factors being the main reason.

Clearly, this need not mean that mismatch is unimportant. In fact, the figures we gave earlier for Britain show precisely how important it is. In 1985 the variances of relative unemployment rates were

Across 7 occupations	0.22
Across 322 travel-to-work areas	0.24
Across 10 industries	0.14
Across 10 age groups	0.22
Across 2 race groups	0.03
Across 2 sex groups	0.01
	0.86

Assuming these imbalances to be orthogonal, we can add them together and conclude that the degree of mismatch equals, at most, half their sum, 0.43. In fact, there is likely to be some degree of correlation, but even then mismatch could easily account for one-third of total unemployment—a serious matter.

Qualifications

Clearly, the measure of mismatch that we have developed is very model-specific. It depends on our assumptions about

1. the curvature of the price function;
2. the curvature of the wage function;
3. the assumption that wages depend on unemployment in the sector in question and not in some leading sector.

310

How much do things change if we vary these assumptions?

The first assumption is not that important. Suppose for example that the production function is CES with an elasticity of substitution σ between each type of labour. Then we show in Annex 6.1 that the appropriate measure of mismatch is

$$MM = \frac{1}{2}[1 - \gamma_1(\sigma - 1)]\text{var}\frac{u_i}{u}.$$

In general, the elasticity of substitution between skill-groups, age-groups, sex-groups, and regional products exceeds unity (e.g. Hamermesh 1986; Layard 1982). But γ_1 is quite small—of the order of 0.1 (see below). Thus $\gamma_1(\sigma - 1)$ will not be large. However, it is true, as one would expect, that for a given dispersion of u_i/u mismatch declines as types of labour become more substitutable. It is also true (given $\sigma > 1$) that mismatch declines as wage flexibility (γ_1) increases. Since $\sigma > 1$, mismatch may equal somewhat less than half of $\text{var}(u_i/u)$.

But many people object to the notion that mismatch should be measured by relative unemployment differentials. They feel that absolute differences are what matter—so that for constant $\text{var}(u_i/u)$ mismatch will have risen if average unemployment is higher.

In fact, however, our result follows even if, more generally,

$$\log W_i = \gamma_{0i} - \gamma_1 \frac{u_i^\lambda - 1}{\lambda} \qquad (-\infty < \lambda \leqslant 1; \lambda \neq 0),$$

where the parameter λ determines the curvature of the wage function. With $\lambda = 1$ the function is linear, and as λ falls the curvature increases (with wages tending to $\gamma_{0i} - \gamma_1 \log u$ as λ tends to zero). The level of unemployment is now determined by[12]

$$\frac{u^\lambda - 1}{\lambda} = \frac{\Sigma \alpha_i \gamma_{0i} - A}{\gamma_1} + \frac{(1 - \lambda)u^\lambda}{2}\text{var}\left(\frac{u_i}{u}\right).$$

As $\lambda \to 0$, this tends to

$$\log u = \frac{\Sigma \alpha_i \gamma_{0i} - A}{\gamma_1} + \frac{1}{2}\text{var}\left(\frac{u_i}{u}\right),$$

but whatever λ, u is increasing in $\text{var}(u_i/u)$. Only relative unemployment matters, whatever the curvature of the wage function. Needless to say, if there is no curvature ($\lambda = 1$) there is no problem of mismatch, whatever the variance.

However, the evidence supports the notion of positive curvature and we shall in the next section provide some evidence in support of the log formulation.

Leading sector issue

However, all the analysis so far is postulated on the basis that wages in a sector depend only on the unemployment rate in the same sector. This is not how many analysts of mismatch think. Suppose, instead, that wages depend only on unemployment in some leading sector (like the South of England or electrical engineering) whose unemployment rate is denoted u_L. Then

$$\log W_i = \gamma_{0i} - \gamma_2 \log u_L,$$

and the unemployment function is

$$A = \Sigma \alpha_i \gamma_{0i} - \gamma_2 \log u_L.$$

This tells us the minimum unemployment we can have in the leading sector before general overheating emerges in the economy. There is no point in having unemployment higher than u_L anywhere else since it would have no effect on wage pressure. On the other hand, presumably unemployment elsewhere cannot be lower than in the leading sector (since the leading sector is likely to be the tightest market). Thus[13]

$$MM = \log u - \log u_L.$$

This is typically much greater than mismatch as measured on the assumption that wages respond to unemployment in each sector (rather than in the leading sector only). For, with a given set of unemployment rates, the minimum level of unemployment is much higher in the 'own-sector' case than the unemployment rate in the 'leading-sector' case. In the own-sector case, equation (6) shows that the same wage pressure is generated by $\Sigma \alpha_i \log u_i$ as by $\Sigma \alpha_i \log u_{\min}$ (with all rates equal). Thus, since $\Sigma \alpha_i = 1$,

$$\log u_{\min} = \Sigma \alpha_i \log u_i.$$

In words, the minimum level of unemployment ($u_{\min}$) is then the *geometric mean* of all the actual unemployment rates. But in the leading-sector case it is given by u_L, which is the lowest of all the rates. Thus, the gap between u and $u_{\min}$ is greater in the leading-sector wage model than it is when wages respond to own-sector unemployment.

For those who like diagrams, the point is illustrated in Fig. 7. Assuming that the leading sector is the one with the lowest unemployment rate, the unemployment frontier becomes a right angle. As we have drawn the actual pattern of

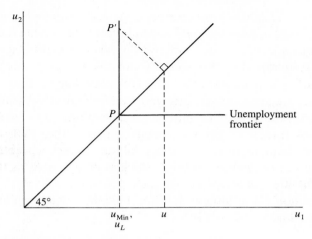

Fig. 7. *The unemployment frontier.*

Wages responding to leading-sector unemployment.

unemployment at P', sector 1 is the leading sector and actual unemployment greatly exceeds $u_{\min}$.

So have we grossly underestimated mismatch by ignoring the leading-sector issue? This depends on whether the leading-sector theory of wages is right. Before addressing this question, we should consider one further possibility: that wages in one group depend simply on the aggregate unemployment rate:

$$\log W_i = \gamma_{0i} - \gamma_1 \log u.$$

In this case there is no mismatch, as we have defined it, since the NAIRU is independent of the distribution of unemployment and depends only on its average.

4.   Evidence on sectoral wage behaviour and on mobility

Regional wage behaviour (Britain)

To check on our model, the first issue to study is the wage determination equation (2). We do this first in relation to regional wage behaviour, beginning with Britain. The key question is whether or not regional unemployment is an important factor in the determination of regional wages, as asserted in (2). We investigate the following general time-series wage equation:

$$w_{it} = a_{0i} + a_{0t} - a_1 \log u_{it} + a_2 w_{it-1},$$

313

where w_i is log real hourly wages for male manual workers in manufacturing (in GDP units) and u_i is the regional unemployment rate. Note that we include a region effect (a_{0i}) and a time dummy (a_{0t}), where i is the region subscript, t is the time subscript. The time-dummy effect is of vital importance since it will capture *all* aggregate variables that influence wages. These will include (i) productivity trends, (ii) aggregate and leading-region unemployment, and (iii) all wage-pressure factors common to all regions (e.g. benefits, unions, taxes, terms of trade). If regional unemployment rather than aggregate or leading-sector unemployment is the key labour market variable, we should obtain a long-run coefficient on $\log u_i$ which is comparable to the aggregate unemployment effect in a typical UK wage equation.

Fitting equation (8) to annual data for 1975–89 for ten regions, using the New Earnings Survey, we obtain

$$w_{it} = a_{0i} + a_{0t} - 0.068\log u_{it} + 0.40w_{it-1} \qquad \text{(s.e.} = 0.0106).$$
$$\quad\quad\quad\quad\quad (4.7) \quad\quad\quad\quad (6.3)$$

Thus we find that regional wages respond to local unemployment with a long-run elasticity of 0.11 which is slightly larger than the typical aggregate elasticity of around 0.10 (Layard and Nickell 1986*b* or Chapter 9 below, Table 15).

These results provide powerful evidence in favour of our assertion that regional wages are strongly influenced by the regional labour market. If we drop the time effects and include either leading-sector or aggregate unemployment, these come in with a significant positive coefficient, with the regional unemployment coefficient remaining significantly negative (Jackman *et al.* 1991). These positive coefficients on the aggregate unemployment variables are simply capturing the impact of omitted wage-pressure effects which come into play when we drop the time dummies.

Turning to the curvature of the wage–unemployment relationship, the log of unemployment dominates the effect of the absolute level of unemployment. If both terms are included, we obtain

$$w_{it} = a_{0i} + a_{0t} - 0.0521\log u_{it} - 0.23u_{it} + 0.373w_{it-1} \qquad \text{(s.e.} = 0.0105).$$
$$\quad\quad\quad\quad\quad (2.8) \quad\quad\quad\quad (2.1) \quad\quad (5.9)$$

This implies that the effect of unemployment on log wages is given by

$$\frac{\partial w_{it}}{\partial u_{it}} = -\frac{0.0521}{u} - 0.23,$$

where the first effect is much the larger influence at standard levels of unemployment. (If only the linear term is included, the standard error rises to 0.0110.)

The linear term reduces the magnitude of mismatch but not its qualitative nature. To be precise, the effect of mismatch on the NAIRU is now
not $\frac{1}{2}\text{var}(u_i/u)$ but

$$\frac{1}{2}\left(1 + \frac{0.23u}{0.05}\right)^{-1}\text{var}(u_i/u).$$

We should briefly contrast these estimates with the 'wage curves' estimated
from cross-section data by Blanchflower and Oswald (1990). When estimated
across British regions, these show $\partial w/\partial u$ becoming positive at high levels of
unemployment. This is probably because the cross-sectional data capture a
mixture of the wage equation and the long-run supply equation—the latter
having the opposite slope to the former (see Fig. 4).

Regional wage behaviour (USA)

Similar analyses have been made for wage determination at the level of US
states, using annual data for 1975–88. Given the lack of stability in unemployment rankings across US states, there is no plausible leading sector. But it is
interesting to look at the effects of state-level unemployment. Again, the
powerful influence of local unemployment is apparent, as we see from the
following regression:

$$w_{it} = a_{0i} + a_{0t} - 0.028\log u_{it-1} + 0.68w_{it-1} \qquad \text{(s.e.} = 0.026).$$
$$\phantom{w_{it} = a_{0i} + a_{0t} - }(5.1)\phantom{\log u_{it-1} + }(23.0)$$

This gives an unemployment elasticity for wages of 0.09.

Regional labour mobility

As regards the regional model, the next relationship to be investigated is the in-
migration function (3). The equation is

$$\frac{M_i}{L_i} = b_1\log\left(\frac{N_i/L_i}{N/L}\right) + b_2\log\left(\frac{W_i}{W}\right) + b_3\log\left(\frac{P}{P_i}\right) + b_{4i},$$

or, for estimation purposes,

$$\frac{M_i}{L_i} = b_1(u - u_i) + b_2(w_i - w) + b_3(p - p_i) + b_{4i}.$$

Here P refers to house prices.

The equation was fitted to annual data for the UK for 1968–86 (see Savouri
1989) and the results were

315

$$\frac{M_i}{L_i} = 0.081(u - u_i) + 0.058(w_i - w) + 0.010(p - p_i) + b_{4i} \qquad \text{(s.e.} = 0.0031).$$

$$\quad (2.7) \qquad\qquad (3.9) \qquad\qquad (1.6)$$

Interestingly, the equation is consistent with the idea that the real wages and the employment rates have the same proportional effect on migration. Pissarides and Wadsworth (1989) have argued that the absolute rate of migration falls when the general level of unemployment is high, but we were unable to find such an effect.

For the USA we estimated the following equation for 1975–88:

$$\frac{\Delta L_i}{L_i} - \frac{\Delta L}{L} = 0.546(u - u_i) + 0.013(w_i - w) + b_i.$$

$$\qquad (7.8) \qquad\qquad (0.5)$$

For the USA we do not have data on local price levels. This may be one reason why we find no significant effect of local wages, though this problem is common in US studies (Greenwood 1985). But local unemployment has a much more powerful effect than in Britain.

Occupational wages and mobility

Turning to occupational wages, in Britain these appear to respond negatively to unemployment in the occupation with an elasticity well above 0.1. In consequence, the relative wages of manual workers have fallen sharply in the 1980s.

We have not been able to undertake any similar analysis for other European countries, owing to lack of data on unemployment by occupation. But we are struck by the fact that in no other European country except Denmark have wage differentials increased during the 1980s as they have in Britain (see Table 11); and in France and Belgium they have narrowed. This may be a partial clue to high European unemployment.

Turning to skill formation, there is a strong effect of wages on the choice of skill. Thus, if we interpret M_i as the excess of entrants to departures in a skill group, the number of entrants is highly sensitive to expected earnings. In the USA the earnings elasticity of entrants has been variously estimated in the range 1–4 (Freeman 1986), while in the UK Pissarides (1981b, 1982) gives figures of $\frac{1}{2}$–$1\frac{1}{2}$. Relative unemployment effects on educational choice are less well determined.

Thus, taking a unit elasticity and a working life of 50 years, we can infer that, if wages in a skill group are higher by 1 per cent, numbers in the skill group will

Table 11 *Non-manual wages relative to manual wages, 1970–1986*
Index 1980 = 100

	Belgium	Denmark	France	Germany	Holland	Italy	UK
1970	—	—	—	—	—	—	—
1971	—	—	—	—	—	—	—
1972	—	—	1.19	0.96	—	1.27	—
1973	—	—	1.15	0.97	—	1.23	0.95
1974	—	—	1.11	0.97	—	1.17	0.97
1975	1.03	1.10	1.09	0.97	0.99	1.12	0.96
1976	1.01	1.09	1.04	0.98	1.01	1.05	0.95
1977	1.01	1.08	1.02	0.99	0.99	1.01	0.96
1978	1.01	1.03	1.02	0.99	1.00	1.02	0.97
1979	1.01	1.02	1.01	1.00	1.00	1.04	0.98
1980	1.00	1.00	1.00	1.00	1.00	1.00	1.00
1981	0.99	1.00	0.98	1.00	1.01	0.98	1.01
1982	0.98	1.01	0.95	1.00	1.01	0.95	1.00
1983	0.97	1.03	0.93	1.01	1.02	0.95	1.06
1984	0.97	1.04	0.94	1.02	1.00	0.98	—
1985	0.97	1.06	0.94	1.02	0.98	1.01	1.04
1986	0.97	1.08	—	1.02	—	—	1.07

Source: *Eurostat Review*, 1970–80, 1977–86. Manual: gross hourly earnings, all industries (Table 3.6.1); Non-manual: gross monthly earnings, all industries (Table 3.6.12).

rise by some 0.02 per cent per annum above what they would be otherwise. This is of the same order as the effect on a region's labour force if wages in the region are higher by 1 per cent (see above).

5. Policy implications

Are there any policies that can improve things when there is mismatch? Policies commonly advocated include

1. Shifting the jobs towards the workers (e.g. by cutting employers' taxes in those sectors where unemployment is high);
2. Shifting the workers towards the jobs (e.g. by subsidies to migration or training).

Frequently both are advocated (e.g. by Johnson and Layard 1986). But is the analysis correct?

An illustrative case (W₂ totally rigid)

We shall begin with the highly simplified case of two skill-groups, with the skilled wage (W_1) perfectly flexible and the unskilled wage (W_2) perfectly rigid. There is then full employment in the skilled labour market, and unemployment in the unskilled. If unemployed leisure is of zero value (as we shall assume throughout), this outcome is clearly inefficient.

What is the appropriate policy response? We shall begin with the case where the labour forces (L_1 and L_2) are given. This is illustrated in Fig. 8. In this situation two things are clear.

1. An employment subsidy to employers hiring unskilled workers would increase unskilled employment. This would have to be financed. Since it is unrealistic to posit lump-sum taxation, we shall assume that any employment subsidies have to be financed by other employment taxes. In the present case this implies a tax on skilled labour. Since wages of skilled labour are perfectly flexible and labour supply is inelastic, this tax involves no efficiency costs. Skilled workers remain fully employed, and the increased employment of unskilled workers raises employment and thus output.

2. Equally, if we could turn unskilled workers into skilled workers, this would increase (gross) output. For suppose we transfer one individual from group 2 to group 1. Employment in the skilled sector will rise, since W_1 is flexible; and (to the first approximation) employment in the unskilled sector will be unaffected, since W_2 is fixed. To find the output effects we shall assume that $Y = F(e_1 L_1, e_2 L_2)$ where e_i is the employment rate. If we have one more

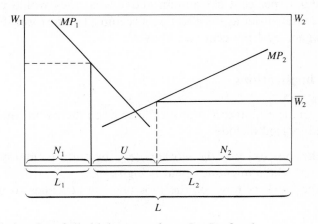

Fig. 8. *Skilled and unskilled labour markets:* L_1, L_2 *fixed.*
W_1 *flexible,* $\bar{W}_2$ *rigid.*

skilled worker, output rises by approximately F_1. This is the net social return to training. By contrast, the net expected private return is $(F_1 - e_2 F_2)$ which is much lower. This appears to suggest a case for subsidies to training and migration.

Thus, on the line of reasoning so far, we should be willing to subsidize both employment in group 2 and migration into group 1. These are the arguments commonly heard. But they will not really stand up. For subsidies to migration can be evaluated only within a general theory of migration behaviour. Once we do this, we realize that the employment tax on skilled workers (proposal 1) will reduce skilled wages and thus discourage migration. The migration subsidy (proposal 2), when amortized, would be equivalent to an employment *subsidy* to skilled workers, partially or wholly offsetting the initial tax. Is there any sense in such a combined operation? The answer is that employment taxes and migration subsidies cannot be thought of as distinct entities. The only question is what should be the net taxes paid by each group of workers.

Let us pursue this issue in the context of our simple example, and ask: 'Suppose there were initially no taxes on either group and W_2 is rigid. Is there any subsidy to one group, paid for by a tax on the other, that would increase output?'

Net output is

$$Y = F(e_1 L_1, e_2 L_2) - c_1 L_1,$$

where c_1 is the amortized cost of training. We want to maximize this, subject to the constraints, including those coming from migration behaviour. In the steady state this implies the *zero-migration condition*, which for simplicity can be written in the additive form

$$W_1 e_1 = W_2 e_2 + c_1.$$

In other words, net expected income in sector 1 ($W_1 e_1 - c_1$) equals expected income in sector 2, the private and social costs of training (c_1) being for the present assumed the same.

If all wages were fully flexible, we should have full employment in both sectors ($e_1 = e_2 = 1$). This would maximize net output, as is illustrated in Fig. 9. If, however, W_2 is rigid, output is reduced. The migration condition becomes (with $e_1 = 1$)

$$W_1 = \bar{W}_2 e_2 + c_1.$$

The question is, If we start from zero taxes, is there any self-financing scheme of employer taxes and subsidies that would increase net output?

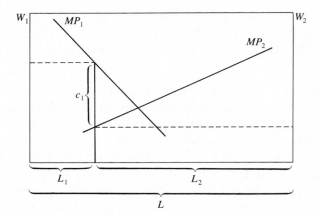

Fig. 9. *Skilled and unskilled labour markets*: L_1, L_2 *variable.*
W_1, W_2 *flexible.*

The answer is No. For, given that $L_2 = L - L_1$, the change in net welfare when policy changes is

$$(F_1 - e_2 F_2 - c_1)\mathrm{d}L_1 + F_1 L_2 \mathrm{d}e_2.$$

But private choice has already set the first term to zero. So policy action can improve welfare only if it can alter the employment rate of the unskilled.

But this it cannot do (even though it can change L_1 and L_2). For, if $\bar{W}_2$ is fixed, so is W_1. Hence, by the zero-migration condition, e_2 is fixed.

To see why W_1 cannot change, note that (under perfect competition in product markets)

$$\mathrm{d}W_1 = \mathrm{d}F_1 - \mathrm{d}t_1.$$

where t_i is the net employer tax per worker of type i, and W_i is take-home pay. The real wage frontier implies

$$\mathrm{d}F_1 = -\frac{N_2}{N_1}\mathrm{d}F_2,$$

while the government budget constraint implies

$$-\,\mathrm{d}t_1 = \frac{N_2}{N_1}\mathrm{d}t_2.$$

But since W_2 is fixed, $\mathrm{d}F_2 - \mathrm{d}t_2$ is zero and hence $\mathrm{d}F_1 - \mathrm{d}t_1$ is also zero. There is no scope for improving things. The best taxes and subsidies are no taxes and subsidies. Though unemployment involves an externality, it is not an externality that can be offset by these kinds of taxes and subsidies.

There are two basic qualifications to this. First, if there is an external social cost or benefit, this must be corrected by taxation or subsidy. And second, if individuals differ in their costs, there may well be a case for taxing the costly sector. But to investigate these issues, let us proceed to the more general situation where all wages are partially flexible and taxes are non-zero.

We begin with the case where the labour forces are exogenous and observe the potent role of policy. Then we proceed to the case where the labour forces are endogenous and policy analysis is more complex.

Labour force given

To find the ideal tax structure, we maximize net output subject to a revenue requirement and to the wage functions and labour demand functions. The problem is

$$\max_{t_i, W_i, e_i} \quad Y = F(e_1 L_1, e_2 L_2)$$

$$+ \varphi(t_1 e_1 L_1 + t_2 e_2 L_2 - R)$$
$$+ \psi_1(W_1 - f^1(e_1)) + \psi_2(W_2 - f^2(e_2))$$
$$+ \theta_1(W_1 + t_1 - F_1) + \theta_2(W_2 + t_2 - F_2),$$

where R is a revenue requirement, W_i is take-home pay, $f^i(e_i)$ are the wage functions, and t_i is a per-worker tax levied on employers. This requires

$$\frac{\partial Y}{\partial t_i} = \varphi e_i L_i + \theta_i = 0,$$

$$\frac{\partial Y}{\partial W_i} = \psi_i + \theta_i = 0,$$

which imply $\psi_i = \varphi e_i L_i = -\theta_i$; and in addition,

$$\frac{\partial Y}{\partial e_i} = F_i L_i + \varphi t_i L_i - \psi_i \frac{\partial W_i}{\partial e_i} - \theta_i F_{ii} L_i$$

$$= L_i \left(W_i + t_i + \varphi t_i - \varphi e_i \frac{\partial W_i}{\partial e_i} + \varphi e_i L_i F_{ii} \right) = 0.$$

Hence we have the standard Ramsey-like condition that[14]

$$\frac{t_i}{W_i} = \frac{\varphi}{1 + \varphi} \left(\frac{1}{\eta_S} + \frac{1}{\eta_D} \right) - \frac{1}{1 + \varphi}, \tag{9}$$

321

where η_S is the wage elasticity of employment in the wage function and η_D is the wage elasticity of employment in demand. The tax rate should be higher the more flexible are wages and the less elastic demand. In general, unskilled labour markets are likely to have relatively inflexible wages and relatively elastic demand.

Concentrating on wage flexibility, if the wage function is double-log, then $\partial\log W_i/\partial\log u_i$ will be similar (e.g. $-\alpha$) in all groups and

$$\frac{\partial\log W_i}{\partial\log e_i} = -\frac{\partial\log W_i}{\partial\log u_i}\frac{e_i}{u_i} = \alpha\frac{1-u_i}{u_i}.$$

Hence wage flexibility will be inversely proportional to unemployment. Thus, taxing flexible markets means taxing those with low unemployment. So long as t_1/W_1 is too low, output could be increased by raising t_1 and lowering t_2, thus stimulating employment where wages are inflexible and reducing it where they are flexible.

This argument has been used to justify subsidies to less skilled labour financed by taxes on skilled labour. It is a standard conclusion in much of the theory of manpower policy.

Labour force endogenous

But the above argument is valid only if the labour force is exogenous (e.g. by age, race, or sex). If the labour force is endogenous, everything changes. We shall show that, if there are no externalities, efficiency requires that the absolute level of the net tax (after netting out any subsidy) should be roughly equal for all groups. More precisely, the 'expected' net tax burden should be equal: that is, groups with lower employment rates should pay proportionately higher taxes.

The problem now is to maximize net output, $F(e_1L_1,e_2L_2) - c_1L_1$, subject to the budget constraint, the two wage functions, the two demand functions, *and the zero-migration condition*. The policy instruments are t_1 and t_2, but to examine the properties of the optimum we again choose the full set of variables $(L_1, t_1, t_2, W_1, W_2, e_1,$ and $e_2)$ to maximize net output. Thus, we have

$$\max_{t_i,W_i,e_i,L_1} \quad Y^* = F(e_1L_1,e_2L_2) - c_1L_1$$

$$+ \varphi(t_1e_1L_1 + t_2e_2L_2 - R)$$
$$+ \psi_1(W_1 - f^1(e_1)) + \psi_2(W_2 - f^2(e_2))$$
$$+ \theta_1(W_1 + t_1 - F_1) + \theta_2(W_2 + t_2 - F_2)$$
$$+ \lambda(W_1e_1 - W_2e_2 - c_1),$$

where the last (and additional) constraint is the zero-migration constraint, enabling us to determine L_1.

Adding this zero-migration constraint changes everything. The focus of the analysis shifts to the first-order condition for L_1. This is[15]

$$\frac{\partial Y^*}{\partial L_1} = F_1 e_1 - F_2 e_2 - c_1 + \varphi(t_1 e_1 - t_2 e_2)$$

$$= W_1 e_1 - W_2 e_2 - c_1 + t_1 e_1 - t_2 e_2 + \varphi(t_1 e_1 - t_2 e_2) = 0. \qquad (10)$$

The zero-migration condition ensures that the first three terms sum to zero, so that optimality requires that

$$t_1 e_1 = t_2 e_2. \qquad (11)$$

Expected taxes should be equal in each sector.[16] The Ramsey-type equation (9) is no longer valid since it fails to take into account the migration condition. *Thus, even in the presence of wage rigidity and differential unemployment, the classic principles of public finance apply and there is no case for differential taxation unless there are externalities (other than simply unemployment itself).*

However, there may well be externalities. The most obvious are the congestion externalities from regional migration. Suppose that net output is not $Y - c_1 L_1$ but $Y - c_1 L_1 - c_s L_1$, where the costs c_1 are privately borne but the remaining social costs c_s are not. Then the optimality condition becomes

$$t_1 e_1 = t_2 e_2 + \frac{c_s}{1 + \varphi}.$$

The congested sector should pay higher taxes in the standard Pigovian manner in order to equate the private and social returns to migration. This argues for increased taxes in regions that are congested (typically low unemployment regions)[17] and subsidies to skill formation, where there is an external benefit that is not privately appropriated.

There is however a more subtle form of externality. We have so far allowed only for one type of 'original' labour, which can then be allocated between two sectors. However, in fact there may be different types of original labour, say of different ability or taste, for whom there are different costs (c_i) of entry to sector 1. Thus the average cost (c_1) per sector 1 worker is an increasing function of L_1. Thus if $C(L_1)$ is the total cost of L_1, the migration condition is

$$W_1 e_1 - W_2 e_2 - C' = 0 \qquad (C', C'' > 0).$$

Optimality now requires

$$\frac{\partial Y^*}{\partial L_1} = (W_1 + t_1)e_1 - (W_2 + t_2)e_2 - C' + \varphi(t_1e_1 - t_2e_2) - \lambda C'' = 0,$$

where λ is the multiplier on the supply condition $e_1 W_1 - e_2 W_2 - C' = 0$. Hence

$$t_1 e_1 = t_2 e_2 + \frac{\lambda C''}{1 + \varphi}. \tag{12}$$

The extent of the expected tax differential $(t_1 e_1 - t_2 e_2)$ is higher the less responsive migration is to changes in financial incentives; for λ and φ are positive,[18] and C'' is the inverse of the supply response $\mathrm{d}L_1/\mathrm{d}W_1$, suitably discounted.

As we have seen, both regional and occupational labour forces respond very slowly to wage differentials, which could make the last term in (12) quite important (even after multiplication by the discount rate). Thus (even without standard externality arguments) there is certainly some efficiency case for lower absolute tax rates on occupations and regions with low employment rates. But the standard externality arguments differ sharply between occupations and regions, favouring tax concessions for high-skill groups and tax penalties for congested regions.

Of course, the whole discussion has as a premise the assumption that unemployment of a group affects only the wages of that group. If there is a leading sector whose employment rate pushes up wages elsewhere, that sector generates external disbenefits which make it a candidate for extra taxation. The reader will find it easy to modify our framework to deal with that case.

What we have said in this section is not the last word on tax progressivity. There are well-known equity arguments in its favour which we have not considered. There is also the case for progressive taxes to discourage wage pressure (see Chapter 10). In that context we recommend a linear tax structure $(tW - S)$ with quite high t and a high flat rate subsidy S. But the implication of the present chapter is that, if it is possible to have different subsidies (S_i) for different groups, the optimal tax structure (in the absence of externalities) involves $(tW_i - S_i)e_i$ being equated between groups.

6. Mismatch and the unemployment–vacancy relationship

We have not so far referred to vacancies in discussing mismatch. This is because we believe that the main issue is the mismatch between the total labour force of each type (L_i) and employment (N_i): hence our index MM. However, it is helpful to use the shift of the aggregate U/V curve to isolate changes over time in the effectiveness of the unemployed. We cannot do this without first isolating the effect of mismatch on the location of the U/V curve. Hence we need an index of mismatch between U and V, which we shall call MM'.

Theory

We need to see how differences in the ratio U_i/V_i across different groups affect the location of the aggregate U/V curve. Suppose, first, that each group had the same U/V curve based on the hiring function

$$H_i = A V_i^\alpha U_i^{1-\alpha}.$$

If the entry to unemployment in each sector is $S_i = sN_i$, where s is the entry rate (assumed common to all groups), then in the steady state (with $H_i = sN_i$) the U/V curve is

$$s = A \left(\frac{V_i}{N_i}\right)^\alpha \left(\frac{U_i}{N_i}\right)^{1-\alpha} \tag{13}$$

This is shown in Fig. 10.

If U/N and V/N were always the same for each group, then the national aggregate U/V curve would be identical to that shown in the figure. But if group 1 was at P_1 and group 2 at P_2 (and the two groups were of equal size) the aggregate national observation would be at P. This follows from the convexity of the relationship, and implies that inequalities in U_i/V_i always increase U/N at given V/N.

The same is true even if the hiring functions differ, as they do (see below). To

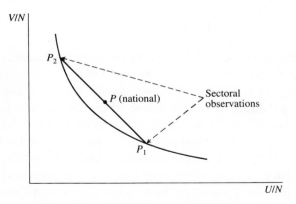

Fig. 10. *The U/V curve of a group.*

see the quantitative effect of variations in the U_i/V_i ratios, we can begin by modifying the hiring function (13) for each group to obtain

$$\frac{S_i}{A_i} = v_i^{\alpha} u_i^{1-\alpha},$$

where $u_i = U_i/N_i$ and $v_i = V_i/N_i$. We then multiply and divide the right-hand side by $v^{\alpha} u^{1-\alpha}$ and take a weighted average of all the equations. This gives

$$\Sigma f_i \frac{S_i}{A_i} = \left[\Sigma f_i \left(\frac{v_i}{v} \right)^{\alpha} \left(\frac{u_i}{u} \right)^{1-\alpha} \right] v^{\alpha} u^{1-\alpha},$$

where $f_i = N_i/N$. The term in brackets is a matching index, which has a maximum value of unity when the U_i/V_i ratio is the same in all groups.[19] At this point the aggregate unemployment rate is as low as it can be, for a given level of vacancies. But, as the U_i/V_i ratios diverge, the aggregate U/V curve shifts out.

It is natural to measure mismatch by the proportion to which unemployment is higher than it could be at given vacancies. Thus, U/V mismatch is measured by

$$MM' = \log u - \log u_{\min} = -\frac{1}{1-\alpha} \log \left[\Sigma f_i \left(\frac{v_i}{v} \right)^{\alpha} \left(\frac{u_i}{u} \right)^{1-\alpha} \right].$$

This is approximately[20]

$$MM' \simeq \frac{1}{2} \alpha (\sigma_{v_i/v}^2 + \sigma_{u_i/u}^2 - 2\rho_{u_i v_i} \sigma_{u_i/u} \sigma_{v_i/v}),$$

where σ is the standard deviation and ρ the correlation coefficient (positive or negative).

Evidence

Let us examine the size of this mismatch index and its movements over time. Table 12 shows relative vacancy rates and relative unemployment rates by occupation, region, and industry in Britain in 1982. To obtain the mismatch index we need a value for α, which can be taken as approximately $\frac{1}{2}$ (Pissarides 1986; Jackman *et al.* 1987; Blanchard and Diamond 1989*a*).[21] Using this value for α, Table 13 shows the movement of the mismatch index over time. The striking thing is the very small magnitude of the index, and the fact that it has not risen over time. In other words, any shift that has occurred in the aggregate u/v curve has also been a shift in the average u/v curve for each sector.

Jackman and Roper (1987) present similar evidence for France, Germany,

Table 12   *Unemployment rates and registered vacancy rates, by occupation, region, and industry: Britain, 1982*

	u_i/u	v_i/v
Occupation		
Managerial and professional	0.32	0.49
Clerical and related	0.80	1.05
Other non-manual	0.84	1.93
Skilled manual	0.87	0.84
Other manual	1.87	1.31
Region		
South East	0.73	1.10
South West	0.89	1.30
East Midlands	0.92	0.92
West Midlands	1.24	0.67
Yorks and Humberside	1.11	0.74
North West	1.24	0.77
North	1.39	0.85
Wales	1.30	1.22
Scotland	1.17	1.24
Industry		
Agriculture	0.94	0.31
Mining and quarrying	0.88	0.12
Manufacturing	1.03	0.66
Construction	2.13	1.03
Gas, electricity, and water	0.33	0.31
Transport	0.68	0.48
Distribution	0.86	1.31
Services	0.53	1.36
Public administration	0.68	1.31

Notes: Unemployment data relate to previous occupation and industry of unemployed registered at Job Centres. *Vacancy rates* relate to vacancies registered at Job Centres.

Sources: Occupation: Employment Gazette, June 1982, Tables 2.11, 3.4 (employment figures from *Labour Force Survey*); *Region: Vacancies: Employment Gazette*, Dec. 1985, Table 3.3; *Employment: Regional Trends*, 1985, Table 7.1; *Unemployment: Employment Gazette*, June 1982, Table 2.3 (made consistent with unpublished Department of Employment continuous series); *Industry: Employment Gazette*, June 1982, Table 3.3, and July 1982, Table 2.9.

Table 13 *U/V mismatch: time-series: Britain, 1963–1988*

| | Mismatch index (%) | | |
| | $$2\left[1 - \sum_{\alpha} \frac{N_i}{N}\left(\frac{u_i}{u}\,\frac{v_i}{v}\right)^{\frac{1}{2}}\right]$$ | | |
	Regional *(9 groups)* (1)	*Industrial* *(24 groups)* (2)	*Occupational* *(24/18 groups)* (3)
1963	16	12	22
1964	20	10	22
1965	16	10	22
1966	12	10	24
1867	10	12	20
1968	14	12	20
1969	14	14	22
1970	10	12	22
1971	12	10	24
1972	14	8	22
1973	14	6	26
1974	12	10	26
1975	6	8	30
1976	4	6	24
1977	4	6	22
1978	8	4	22
1979	10	4	22
1980	8	8	24
1981	4	14	26
1982	4	12	24
1983	2	—	—
1984	4	—	—
1985	4	—	—
1986	4	—	—
1987	4	—	—
1988	5	—	—

Source: Authors' calculations, based on data published in successive issues of the *Employment Gazette*.

Note: The index is $MM' = -\frac{1}{1-\alpha}\log\Sigma \simeq -\frac{1}{1-\alpha}(\Sigma - 1) = \frac{1}{1-\alpha}(1 - \Sigma)$ since Σ is close to unity. We set $\alpha = 1/2$.

Netherlands, Austria, Finland, Norway, and Sweden. Except in Sweden, there is no evidence of increased mismatch.

As regards the cyclical behaviour of mismatch, this was illustrated in Fig. 1 using the index MM'. It shows a tendency for regional mismatch to fall in downturns and for industrial mismatch to rise.

Much has been made of the latter phenomenon by Lilien (1982). He has argued that fluctuations in unemployment are often *caused* by exogenous shifts in labour demand between industries, producing mismatch and hence changes in unemployment. But can we reasonably think of these cyclical shifts in mismatch as exogenous? If they were, we should expect the resulting mismatch to increase not only unemployment but also vacancies. As Abraham and Katz (1986) and Blanchard and Diamond (1989a) show, this is not what happens when we see a short-run rise in the turbulence index. Instead, unemployment rises and vacancies fall. Thus the notion that business downturns are typically initiated by structural demand shifts is implausible.

However, over the longer term the degree of turbulence in industrial structure *is* clearly an important factor affecting unemployment. But for this purpose we need to take a moving average of the index. If we do this, we find that industrial turbulence in the 1930s was double its post-war average in both Britain and the USA, and the same was true of Britain in the 1920s. Thus it is quite appropriate to blame a part of inter-war unemployment on the 'problems of the declining industries'.

Further evidence on occupations

Finally, we present some evidence on the duration of occupational vacancies in Britain. This is given in Table 14. The first point concerns the vacancy rates. These are based on a national survey which included all vacancies rather than adjusted data based on vacancies registered at Job Centres. It shows no clear tendency for higher vacancy rates in more skilled occupations; but the turnover rate is very much lower in these occupations. From this it follows that the duration of vacancies is very much longer in the skilled occupations. (The situation was very similar in 1977, the year of the only other national survey of vacancies; see Jackman *et al.* 1984: 45.)

All of this raises obvious questions about which occupations are facing labour shortages. When employers in manufacturing were asked, 'Do you expect your output to be limited by shortages of (*a*) skilled labour and (*b*) other labour?' only 4 per cent replied Yes for 'other labour' compared with 20 per cent for 'skilled labour'. These replies coincide with the view that, from the employers' side, the proper pressure of demand variable is the duration of

Table 14 *Differences between occupations in vacancy flows and stocks: Britain*

	Unemployment (1984)		
	Inflow rate (% per month) (1)	Average duration (mos.) (2)	Unemployment rate (%) (3)
Managerial and professional	0.50	11.2	5.3
Clerical	0.88	10.1	8.0
Other non-manual	1.14	11.8	12.2
Skilled manual	1.02	14.2	12.6
Semi- and unskilled manual	1.32	14.1	15.5
All	0.94	12.8	10.8

	Vacancies (1988)			% of firms reporting shortage of labour (Jan. 1988) (7)
	Engagement rate (% per month) (4)	Duration of vacancies (mos.) (5)	Vacancy rate (Jan.) (%) (6)	
Managerial and professional	1.0	2.2	2.2	
Clerical	2.3	1.5	3.4	Skilled 20
Skilled and semi-skilled manual	2.8	1.2	3.4	
Retail and catering, personal services	5.8	0.9	5.1	Other 4
Unskilled manual	3.8	0.6	2.1	
All	2.8	1.0	2.9	

Source: *Unemployment*: see Table 3; *Vacancies*: IFF Research Limited, *Vacancies and Recruitment Study*, May 1988: col. (4) = Engagements ÷ employed (Table 4.3); col. (5) = col. (6) ÷ col. (4); col. (6) = Vacancies ÷ employed (Appendix 9); *Labour shortages*: CBI, *Industrial Trends Survey*.

vacancies, rather than the vacancy rate. We must however note that from the point of view of workers the comparable duration (of unemployment) is similar in all groups, and it is the unemployment *rates* that differ. We have not yet found a satisfactory way of interpreting these fascinating data.

7. Summary

It may be helpful to bring together baldly some of the main arguments of the chapter.

1. There are huge differences in unemployment rates between occupations, regions, age-groups, and races. These differences are for the most part very persistent and do not reflect the legacy of structural shocks. They are however quite closely related to differences in turnover rates (i.e. in the rate of entry to unemployment), with differences in unemployment durations playing a minor role.

2. Unemployment rate differences between age-groups are affected by demographic factors. But unemployment differences between occupations and regions can only be explained jointly with mobility between groups. In each case, high unemployment is associated with low costs of entry and high levels of wage push. Where (as in Britain but not the USA) regional unemployment differences are highly persistent, these importantly reflect steady-state differences in job growth relative to the natural growth of population.

3. One naturally asks whether the rise in European unemployment can be explained by increased mismatch. To investigate this we assume (and later check) that wage behaviour in a sector is caused primarily by unemployment in *that* sector, rather than by unemployment in some leading sector. Given this assumption, the relevant index of mismatch is half the variance of the relative unemployment rates. On this basis, mismatch has increased in no country we studied except Sweden. But the *level* of mismatch still in Britain explains at least one-third of all unemployment.

4. As regards policy, if the members in each group are exogenous (e.g. as in each age-group), then it pays to subsidize employment where it is low and to tax employment where it is high. But where workers choose their sectors (as with occupations and regions) the matter is more complex. If there are no standard 'externalities' (other than unemployment), no leading sector in wage determination, and all workers are identical, there is no efficiency case for any tax/subsidy scheme to improve the structure of unemployment rates. Contrary to the standard notions of 'manpower policy', expected taxes should be equal for all groups.

But tax/subsidy arrangements should be used to discourage bad externalities (e.g. congestion in low unemployment regions), to promote good externalities (e.g. skill training), and to discourage overheating in any leading sectors. In addition, where workers vary (upward-sloping supply curves) it may be right to subsidize employment in high-unemployment groups.

5. Finally, we examine the mismatch between unemployment and vacancies. We show that this mismatch has not worsened either, and cannot be used to explain the outward shift of the U/V curve that has occurred in many countries.

Notes

1. Note that a temporary shock in favour of a high unemployment group will actually reduce the total imbalance.
2. Honourable exceptions are Lipsey (1960), Archibald (1969), Baily and Tobin (1977), Johnson and Blakemore (1979).
3. This is not because turbulence creates mismatch which creates aggregate unemployment, as Lilien (1982) argues. (For a clear rebuttal of Lilien's position see Abraham and Katz 1986.) Rather, it is because aggregate shocks are highly sectorally unbalanced — and thus create both aggregate unemployment and more turbulence and more mismatch. They particularly affect high unemployment sectors (e.g. construction). See also Section 6 of this chapter.
4. Where the sectors considered are regions, we could introduce an equivalent CES utility function where σ reflected substitution elasticities between the products of different regions.
5. Neither bargaining theory nor efficiency wage theory has so far made much progress in explaining the wages of one group out of many groups employed. This is a key area for research. Honourable exceptions to this remark include Lazear (1989), who showed how envy could lead employers to prefer more egalitarian wage structures than otherwise. A related argument is developed in Akerlof and Yellen (1990).
6. X is not of course exogenous but can be solved for by substituting $N_i(= (1 - u_i)L_i)$ into the production function.
7. It is best to think of W_i as measuring the wage in terms of its power to purchase market bundles of goods.
8. This arises from differential age structures and differential changes in participation rates.
9. This assumes $\alpha_i \simeq L_i/L$, for the minimization of u requires

$$\min_{u_i} \Sigma \frac{L_i}{L} u_i - \lambda(\Sigma \alpha_i \log u_i - \text{const.});$$

that is,

$$\frac{L_i}{L} - \lambda \frac{\alpha_i}{u_i} = 0.$$

If $\alpha_i = L_i/L$, this requires $u_i = \lambda$ (all i).
10. This assumes either that the weights α_i (which are shares of wage bill) are equal to L_i/L (which are shares of labour force), or that $(\alpha_i - L_i/L)$ is independent of u_i/u.
11. Note that mismatch is the proportional excess of actual unemployment over the unemployment needed to yield the same wage pressure if all unemployment rates were equal. Readers familiar with the Atkinson (1970) index of inequality will note the close correspondence between his measure and our mismatch measure. Atkinson measured inequality as the proportion by which actual output exceeded the output needed to yield the same social welfare if individual incomes were equal.

12. Let

$$\gamma_1 \frac{u_i^\lambda - 1}{\lambda} = f(u_i)$$

$$f(u_i) \simeq f(u) + f'(u)(u_i - u) + \tfrac{1}{2}f''(u)(u_i - u)^2.$$

So

$$A = \Sigma\alpha_i\gamma_{0i} - \Sigma\alpha_i f(u_i)$$

$$= \Sigma\alpha_i\gamma_{0i} - \gamma_1\left(\frac{u^\lambda}{1-\lambda} + 0 + \tfrac{1}{2}(1-\lambda)u^{\lambda-2}\Sigma\alpha_i(u_i - u)^2\right).$$

This gives

$$u^\lambda = \left(\frac{1 + \lambda\,(\Sigma\alpha_i\gamma_{0i} - A)/\gamma_1}{1 - \frac{\lambda(1-\lambda)}{2}\operatorname{var}\frac{u_i}{u}}\right).$$

Since $0 < u < 1$, $\Sigma\alpha_i\gamma_{0i} - A < 0$ and u is increasing in $\operatorname{var}(u_i/u)$ for all values of λ.

13. Of course, wages could depend both on own-sector unemployment (u_i) and on leading-sector unemployment (u_L):

$$\log W_i = \gamma_{0i} - \gamma_1\log u_i - \gamma_2\log u_L.$$

Thus

$$\log u = \frac{\Sigma\alpha_i\gamma_{0i} - A}{\gamma_1 + \gamma_2} + \frac{\gamma_1}{\gamma_1 + \gamma_2}\frac{1}{2}\operatorname{var}\left(\frac{u_i}{u}\right) + \frac{\gamma_2}{\gamma_1 + \gamma_2}\log\left(\frac{u}{u_L}\right).$$

14.

$$\frac{1}{\eta_S} = \frac{e_i}{W_i}\frac{\partial W_i}{\partial e_i} \qquad \text{and} \qquad \frac{1}{\eta_D} = \frac{e_i L_i}{W_i}\frac{\partial F_i}{\partial(e_i L_i)}.$$

Strictly, the latter is $1/\eta_D$ only if t_i is small.

15. There are two further terms which sum to zero. These are

$$-\theta_1(F_{11}e_1 - F_{12}e_2) - \theta_2(F_{21}e_1 - F_{22}e_2) = \varphi e_1(e_1 L_1 F_{11} + e_2 L_2 F_{21})$$
$$- \varphi e_2(e_1 L_1 F_{12} + e_2 L_2 F_{22})$$
$$= \varphi e_1(0) - \varphi e_2(0) \text{ (by Euler's Theorem)}.$$

16. In the case of a migration subsidy of s paid to workers who get trained and employed in sector 1, we arrive at exactly the same conclusion. The tax condition is

$$(t_1 - s)e_1 L_1 + t_2 e_2(L - L_1) - R = 0.$$

The migration condition is

$$e_1(W_1 + s) - e_2 W_2 - c_1 = 0.$$

Hence $\partial Y^*/\partial L_1 = 0$ implies $(t_1 - s)e_1 - t_2 e_2 = 0$. The conclusion would be unaffected if costs were a proportion of $W_2 e_2$.

17. One should note that there is also a benefit externality, whereby unemployment benefit reduces the incentive to leave high-unemployment regions.

18. φ is positive, because a reduction in R raises Y. As regards λ, if the zero-migration constraint did not hold and people could be physically allocated to sectors, the optimum allocation would be given by (10), with c_1 replaced by C'. We can assume that in this situation $t_1e_1 - t_2e_2 > 0$: in other words, we should want to have a smallish number of unskilled people and then subsidize their employment to keep them in work. But we cannot achieve this since by equation (10) this would reduce incentives to migrate below the acceptable level. It follows that, if there is a supply equilibrium constraint, an additional incentive to move would raise welfare. Hence $\partial Y^*/\partial$ (net return) $= \lambda > 0$.

19. We seek to

$$\max_{U_i, V_i} \Sigma \left(\frac{V_i}{V}\right)^\alpha \left(\frac{U_i}{U}\right)^{1-\alpha} + \lambda(\Sigma V_i - V) + \varphi(\Sigma U_i - U)$$

This requires $\alpha(V_i/U_i)^{\alpha-1}(1/V)^\alpha(1/U)^{1-\alpha} + \lambda = 0$ (all i). If $V_i = \theta U_i$ (all i),

$$\Sigma \left(\frac{V_i}{V}\right)^\alpha \left(\frac{U_i}{U}\right)^{1-\alpha} = \Sigma \left(\frac{\theta U_i}{\theta U}\right)^\alpha \left(\frac{U_i}{U}\right)^{1-\alpha} = \frac{\Sigma U_i}{U} = 1$$

20. Expanding $(v_i/v)^\alpha(u_i/u)^{1-\alpha}$ around $v_i/v = u_i/u = 1$, we have

$$\left(\frac{v_i}{v}\right)^\alpha \left(\frac{u_i}{u}\right)^{1-\alpha} \simeq 1 + \alpha\left(\frac{v_i}{v}-1\right) + (1-\alpha)\left(\frac{u_i}{u}-1\right)$$
$$+ \tfrac{1}{2}\alpha(\alpha-1)\left(\frac{v_i}{v}-1\right)^2 + \tfrac{1}{2}(1-\alpha)(-\alpha)\left(\frac{u_i}{u}-1\right)^2$$
$$+ (1-\alpha)\alpha\left(\frac{v_i}{v}-1\right)\left(\frac{u_i}{u}-1\right).$$

Hence

$$\Sigma\frac{N_i}{N}\left(\frac{v_i}{v}\right)^\alpha\left(\frac{u_i}{u}\right)^{1-\alpha} \simeq 1 - \tfrac{1}{2}\alpha(1-\alpha)\left(\sigma^2_{v_i/v} + \sigma^2_{u_i/u} - 2\text{cov}_{v_i/v, u_i/u}\right).$$

Note also that this equals

$$1 - \tfrac{1}{2}\alpha(1-\alpha)\Sigma\frac{N_i}{N}\left[\left(\frac{v_i}{v}-1\right) - \left(\frac{u_i}{u}-1\right)\right]^2 = 1 - \tfrac{1}{2}\alpha(1-\alpha)\Sigma\frac{N_i}{N}\left(\frac{v_i}{v}-\frac{u_i}{u}\right)^2.$$

Thus it is closely related to the index

$$MM'' = \Sigma\frac{N_i}{N}\left|\frac{v_i}{v}-\frac{u_i}{u}\right| = \Sigma\left|\frac{V_i}{V}-\frac{U_i}{U}\right|,$$

used in Jackman and Roper (1987), and in Fig. 1(b).

21. See Ch. 5, equations (17) and (17'), and the discussion following (17'). See also Annex 5.2.

7

The Pricing and Employment Behaviour of Firms

In previous chapters, we have discussed wage-setting behaviour at great length because this is crucial for understanding unemployment. However, unemployment is a general equilibrium phenomenon; and so, in order to analyse the macroeconomics of unemployment, we must devote attention also to the product-market behaviour of firms. Indeed, in the macroeconomic model in the next chapter, firms' price-setting behaviour is one of the key elements in determining the response of unemployment to exogenous shocks.

The vital features of price determination in this regard are, first, the degree to which demand influences prices; second, the extent to which prices are more influenced by demand in the short run than in the long run; and third, the degree of nominal inertia or price stickiness. The second of these is a hysteresis effect and ties up with our more usual notion of hysteresis in the following way. Suppose the level of economic activity (or demand) influences prices and wages in the short run but not in the long run. (That is, there are effects from the rate of change of economic activity but not from its level.) Then any exogenous shock to economic activity will tend to have a permanent impact because, once the shock is no longer in force, the changed level of economic activity will have no impact on wages and prices. There is, therefore, no tendency for the economy to move back to its original state. This may be thought of as *pure* hysteresis. Any tendency in this direction, where there are short-run change effects but long-run level effects are also present, may thus be thought of as partial hysteresis.

In order to see this kind of effect in action from the price side, consider the following simple log-linear model based on the framework set out in Chapter 1.

Price-setting: $\qquad\qquad p - w = \beta_0 + b_1 y_d + b_{11} \Delta y_d + \varepsilon_p$

Wage-setting: $\qquad\qquad w - p = \gamma_0 - \gamma_1 u + \varepsilon_w$

Production (Okun's law): $\quad y_d = -\alpha u$

Prices are influenced by demand (y_d), with the short-run effect ($b_1 + b_{11}$) being greater than the long-run effect (b_1). To complete the model, we have a standard wage equation with a negative level effect from unemployment but no change term, and a simple Okun's law relationship between demand and unemployment. ε_p, ε_w represent price and wage shocks. Using Okun's law to eliminate demand from the price equation, we have

$$p - w = \beta_0 - \beta_1 u - \beta_{11} \Delta u + \varepsilon_p \qquad (\beta_1 = b_1\alpha, \beta_{11} = b_{11}\alpha).$$

Then, using the wage equation to eliminate $(p - w)$ gives us the dynamic unemployment model,

$$u = \frac{\beta_{11}}{\gamma_1 + \beta_1 + \beta_{11}} u_{-1} + \frac{(\gamma_1 + \beta_1)}{\gamma_1 + \beta_1 + \beta_{11}} u^* + \frac{(\varepsilon_p + \varepsilon_w)}{\gamma_1 + \beta_1 + \beta_{11}}.$$

Here u^* is the equilibrium level of unemployment ($= (\beta_0 + \gamma_0)/(\beta_1 + \gamma_1)$: see Chapter 1, equation (3)). So unemployment is influenced by wage and price shocks, and the persistence of these shocks is governed by the parameter β_{11} which depends directly on the impact of the change term in the price equation. Thus, we see clearly that hysteresis is not exclusively a wage-setting phenomenon.

In this chapter we study all three features of price-setting noted above using a variety of models, and we also consider the interaction between price-setting and employment determination. In Section 1 we consider a simple static model and focus on the impact of demand on price-setting. In the next section we introduce an adjustment cost model where there are convex costs associated with changing both prices and employment. We conclude here that it is price adjustment costs which generate nominal inertia, whereas employment adjustment costs produce hysteresis in price-setting.

The problem with assuming convex adjustment costs in price-setting is that such costs seem so unrealistic. So in the two remaining sections we consider other possible sources of nominal inertia. First, we look at the possibility of price changes occurring at discrete intervals, with prices in different sectors changing at different times. This is generally referred to as 'staggering'. Second, we consider optimal price-setting in response to fixed costs of changing prices. This seems more realistic than convex adjustment costs, although harder to analyse. Under general conditions, however, they appear to have similar effects.

Chapter 7

1. A static model of price and employment behaviour

In this section, we consider a static model of the firm and analyse the ways in which demand can influence prices. We also look at the evidence on this matter. In order to keep things simple, we shall ignore capital and technical progress. So we suppose our economy consists of F identical firms, labelled i, with a technology of the form

$$Y_i = N_i^\alpha \qquad (\alpha > 0), \tag{1}$$

where Y_i is value added output and N_i is employment. Each firm faces a demand function of the form

$$Y_i = (P_i/P)^{-\eta} \exp y_{di} \qquad (\eta > 1), \tag{2}$$

where P_i is the value added price for the firm, P is the aggregate price level, and y_{di} is an index of demand. To maximize profit, the firm sets marginal revenue equal to marginal cost; that is,

$$\kappa P_i = \frac{1}{\alpha} W_i Y_i^{(1-\alpha)/\alpha}, \tag{3}$$

where recall that $\kappa = 1 - 1/\eta$, our index of product-market competitiveness.

The three equations (1), (2), (3) determine prices, output, and employment in terms of aggregate prices (P), wages (W_i), and demand (y_{di}). The mark-up of prices on marginal cost is $1/\kappa$ which is decreasing in the demand elasticity. Marginal costs may slope up or down depending on whether α is less or greater than unity, being flat when $\alpha = 1$. This parameter thus effectively captures short-run returns to scale.

Using (2) and (3), we may solve out for prices in terms of exogenous factors, and if we write this in log-linear form, we have

$$p_i = -\mu_1 \log \alpha \kappa + \mu_1 w_i + (1 - \mu_1)p + \frac{(1-\alpha)}{\alpha}\mu_1 y_{di}, \tag{4}$$

where $\mu_1 = \alpha(1 - \kappa)/(1 - \alpha\kappa)$ and the lower-case letters refer to logarithms. Prices are a weighted sum of the firm's own wage costs (w_i) and competitors' prices (p), with the second-order conditions ensuring that $\mu_1 > 0$ (equivalent to $\alpha\kappa < 1$). Interestingly, if marginal costs are decreasing ($\alpha > 1$), then competitors' prices have an inverse effect ($\mu_1 > 1$). The firm's output then becomes very elastic with regard to outside prices.

Focusing on the aggregate equation, this may be obtained by setting $p_i = p$, $w_i = w$, $y_{di} = y_d$, firms being identical. Thus (4) becomes

$$p - w = - \log\alpha\kappa + \frac{(1 - \alpha)}{\alpha} y_d. \tag{5}$$

The price mark-up on wages thus depends on two terms, the first reflecting the price mark-up on marginal cost (note $\log(1/\kappa) = -\log\kappa$) and the second reflecting marginal cost itself. Demand effects on prices can operate via either of these two terms since it is quite feasible for the demand elasticity (η) to vary systematically with the level of demand.

Demand effects on prices

Much of the evidence suggests that prices tend to be rather unresponsive to demand fluctuations. (See, for example, Coutts *et al.* 1978, Encaoua and Geroski 1986, and Brack 1987 for evidence from a number of countries.) There is also fairly general agreement that demand effects on prices tend to be weaker if firms operate in a less competitive environment. (See, again, Encaoua and Geroski 1986 and Brack 1987, who also discuss the theoretical background to this result.) However, at this point the consensus stops. In equation (5) we see that demand can influence prices via the mark-up on marginal cost and via marginal cost itself.

Marginal cost may increase with demand for a variety of reasons. As the firm operates closer to full capacity, it will have more workers on overtime or evening and night shifts, when hourly pay is higher. It will bring into operation less efficient machines and plant, which have higher associated production costs. The question then is, Are these effects big enough to generate significantly rising short-run marginal costs? The evidence on this is sketchy, particularly because the issue becomes complex in the presence of employment adjustment costs and associated labour hoarding.

In certain industries, we *know* that marginal costs are rising. For example, in electricity supply, plants and generators are formally ranked in terms of efficiency, with the least efficient being brought into operation only at times of peak load. We also know that delivery lags in manufacturing rise strongly in booms (see Carlton 1989). If marginal costs are constant or even falling, why do firms keep customers waiting rather than make more profit by producing the goods and supplying them immediately? Of course, it could be argued that the goods cannot be produced any faster because the firms are operating at 'full capacity'. But this is tantamount to arguing that marginal costs become very large at full capacity and must, therefore, be increasing in its vicinity.

On the other hand, in studies of inventory behaviour it has been noted that the variance of production is often larger than the variance of sales (see e.g.

West 1988). This is indicative of a weak role for production smoothing relative to stock-out costs (the costs associated with running out of stocks of finished goods and turning customers away), and hence of a relatively flat marginal cost schedule. Econometric evidence also tends to be conflicting. Bils (1987), using data from a large number of US manufacturing industries, concludes that short-run marginal costs are, indeed, increasing.[1] Ramey (1988), however, comes to the opposite conclusion when she estimates a structural model of production and inventory behaviour, again using data on US manufacturing industries. Flaig and Steiner (1990) also find falling marginal costs in the majority of German manufacturing industries. This latter result is perhaps more persuasive, since it avoids the strong restrictions imposed on the technology in Bils, for example. There is also some evidence from automobile manufacturers. Berndt *et al.* (1990) find that all three of the major US car companies (General Motors, Ford, and Chrysler) have declining marginal costs. On the other hand, Aizcorbe (1990), using plant-level data on inputs and production-line speeds, comes up with a textbook U-shaped marginal cost schedule.

Overall, therefore, the evidence is not overwhelming in either direction. Indeed, it is perfectly possible for marginal costs to go both ways in the sense that they could easily be flat or even falling with demand up to some point, beyond which they start rising as full capacity is approached. This seems a very plausible scenario.

Turning to the other element of the price mark-up on wages, namely the mark-up on marginal costs, it is clear that this will shift with demand if the elasticity of demand (η) does so and in the opposite direction. (Note that $d/d\eta$ $(1/\kappa) < 0$.) So if a firm or an industry faces a demand curve whose elasticity rises in booms, this will tend to generate a negative demand effect on prices. A variety of arguments support this notion. Bils (1989) suggests that, in a world where customers become attached to firms, it is during booms that firms have a greater incentive to attract customers, thereby reducing their prices when demand is higher. (Related arguments may be found in Stiglitz 1984 and Ball and Romer 1990.) Rotemberg and Saloner (1986) argue that it is more difficult to enforce collusion between oligopolistic firms during booms because the incentives for undercutting are greater at this time. This again leads to increased downward pressure on the mark-up when demand is high. (See Rotemberg and Woodford 1989 for further results on this model.)

The evidence on these issues is thin. Not surprisingly, in view of his finding that marginal cost rises with demand, Bils (1987) discovers a counter-cyclical mark-up of prices on marginal cost. Equally unsurprisingly, Flaig and Steiner (1990) find the mark-up on marginal cost to be pro-cyclical. On the other hand,

Berndt *et al.* (1990) find a pro-cyclical mark-up at General Motors and Ford, and a counter-cyclical mark-up at Chrysler! Other investigations in this area, for example Domowitz *et al.* (1986a, 1986b), make no real attempt to measure marginal cost, contenting themselves with average variable cost. Consequently they tend to confound the separate questions of the shape of the marginal cost curve and the mark-up of prices on marginal cost.

In conclusion, prices tend to be relatively unresponsive to demand, but whether this is because marginal costs are increasing with demand and the price mark-up on marginal cost is falling, or because marginal costs are falling with the mark-up rising, or because they are both flat, is not something we are, as yet, able to answer. However, it does seem probable that marginal costs are rising once the firm gets close to full capacity.

Prices and employment

Corresponding to the profit-maximizing condition (3) is an alternative form, namely, the marginal revenue product condition. This is obtained by substituting employment for output in (3) using the production function to obtain

$$\alpha \kappa P_i N_i^{-(1-\alpha)} = W_i, \tag{6}$$

the left-hand side being the marginal revenue product of labour. So long as $\alpha \neq 1$, we may solve (6) to obtain

$$N_i = \left(\frac{W_i}{\alpha \kappa P_i} \right)^{-1/(1-\alpha)} \tag{7}$$

If the product market is competitive ($\kappa = 1(\eta = \infty)$), P_i is exogenous to the firm and α must be less than unity. Equation (7) then becomes the marginal productivity condition and is a standard labour demand function (just as equation (3) is then a standard output supply function). However, if the firm is a price-setter, equation (7) simply reveals a relationship between employment and product wages which must hold if the firm is maximizing profit. It is not a labour demand function because prices are chosen jointly with employment. However, it does reveal that, if the price mark-up on marginal cost $(1/\kappa)$ shifts systematically with demand, then so does the standard marginal productivity relation between real wages and employment. This breaks the negative link between employment and real wages which is a typical feature of the response of an economy to aggregate demand shocks when the product market is competitive. (Note: this link is also broken if $\alpha > 1$.)

It is clear from (6) and (7) that, if $\alpha = 1$, the marginal product of labour is constant and (7) no longer exists. However, even if the technology has this form, it is still possible to generate a relationship between employment and wages if the average (hourly) pay per employee increases with the number of employees. Given that capital and technology are implicitly fixed, this implies a rise in average pay per employee as capital is used with greater intensity. This could easily happen because, as employment per unit of capital increases, a higher proportion of employees work overtime or on weekends or on evening or night shifts, all of which tend to carry a wage premium. Suppose therefore that wages have the form

$$W_i \left(N_i/N^* \right)^v \qquad (v > 0),$$

where N^* is a baseline level of employment and v captures the extent to which wages rise as employment moves above the baseline. Then the marginal revenue product condition may be solved out as

$$N_i = \left(\frac{N^{*-v}}{\alpha \kappa} \frac{W_i}{P_i} \right)^{-1/(1+v-\alpha)}, \tag{7'}$$

which remains intact even if the marginal product of labour is constant ($\alpha = 1$).

Finally, it is worth noting that the aggregate version of the marginal revenue product condition (7) may be written, in log-linear form, as

$$n = f + \frac{1}{(1-\alpha)} \log \alpha \kappa - \frac{1}{(1-\alpha)} (w - p), \tag{7''}$$

where $f = \log F$, F being the number of firms in the economy. This reveals that, if the price mark-up on marginal cost ($1/\kappa$) falls as demand increases, the standard marginal productivity schedule will shift to the right with an increase in demand. This yields the potential for a simultaneous increase in employment and real wages in response to a demand shock.

2. Dynamic models of prices and employment with convex adjustment costs

Adjustment costs

Having looked at the nature of demand effects on price-setting, we now turn our attention to hysteresis and nominal inertia. To do so, it is essential to operate in a dynamic framework. So we suppose that there are costs of changing both prices and employment. The costs of changing employment are well documented, arising as they do from costs associated with both hiring and firing. The evidence here is summarized in Nickell (1986)[2] and indicates that, in the USA, the sum of hiring-and-firing costs for white-collar workers totals between two weeks' and two months' pay, whereas for blue-collar workers they are around one-fifth as great. In European countries the legislative framework is rather stricter so the equivalent costs would be considerably higher (see e.g. Burda 1988 and Bentolila and Bertola 1990).

In contrast, the costs of changing prices are not well documented. That some costs must be incurred goes without saying. Prices must be relabelled, catalogues and menus reprinted. Such costs, often termed 'menu' costs, are, presumably, quite small. An additional cost, emphasized by Okun (1981), for example, is that associated with customer dissatisfaction if prices change too frequently or erratically. However, as Carlton (1986) notes, many changes in price are very small (e.g. less than $\frac{1}{2}$ per cent). However, in another paper (Carlton 1985), evidence is presented on the degree to which firms allow fluctuations in demand to be absorbed by changes in delivery delays rather than price changes, which is surely indicative that some significant costs of such changes must be perceived.

In this section, we shall follow Rotemberg (1982) and suppose that adjustment costs are quadratic. The arguments against such an assumption are well known. There are clearly fixed elements in both price and employment adjustment costs, and the very fact that price changes are discrete and often at large intervals indicates that price adjustment costs cannot be strictly convex. However, the analytical convenience of this assumption is considerable and many of the conclusions that may be drawn from models of this type are robust to changes in the assumption.

We intend to model price adjustment costs in two different ways. Thus, we suppose that they have the possible forms

$$\tfrac{1}{2}b_p(p_{it} - p_{it-1})^2, \tag{8a}$$

$$\tfrac{1}{2}b_p[p_{it} - p_{it-1} - (p_t^e - p_{t-1})]^2. \tag{8b}$$

The first of these simply asserts that price adjustment costs depend solely on the absolute change in price; the second emphasizes the customer dissatisfaction argument and supposes that adjustment costs are incurred only if the firm deviates from expected aggregate inflation. These latter seem more realistic, for, as Sims remarks,

if there were such a thing as an economy with a rock-solid inflation rate of 40 percent, plus or minus 2 percent, per year, institutions would surely adapt, so that prices would be announced in catalogs and wage contracts with smooth growth paths paralleling the smooth aggregate price path. Nominal rigidity would set in about this price path in much the same form as we see around the zero inflation rate in low-inflation economies. (Sims 1988: 77)

The aim of the model

The aim of this model is to demonstrate how the adjustment costs cause the firm to smooth both prices and employment. This will yield a pricing equation that has prices adjusting towards the static equilibrium (equation (5)) in a way that exhibits both nominal inertia and hysteresis. Nominal inertia arises from the costs of adjusting prices, whereas the hysteresis effect is generated by the employment adjustment costs. This latter comes about because, when there are costs associated with changing employment, short-run marginal costs increase more rapidly than long-run marginal costs because of the incomplete adjustment of employment in the short run. This generates a degree of upward pressure on prices, in response to increases in demand, which is greater in the short run than in the long run. Hence we have a positive effect arising from *changes* in demand, as well as the level effect.

The strategy we pursue in working out the model is first to derive the static equilibrium that would occur in the absence of adjustment costs, and then to analyse the dynamic adjustment to this equilibrium using the standard methods of dynamic optimization.

The static equilibrium

The general structure of the model is based on the previous section, although we shall now suppose that prices are set prior to employment and wages. So we are introducing two potential elements of inertia into price-setting, one arising from the costs of adjustment and the other arising from the fact that prices must be set before wages are revealed. Later we shall be able to identify the different terms in the price equation which are generated by these two sources of stickiness.

In order to analyse the adjustment cost model, we start by considering the static equilibrium levels of prices and employment in the new context where prices are set 'at the beginning of the period'. Following the argument up to equation (4), it is easy to see that in this case the static equilibrium price p_i^* (that is, the price which would rule in the absence of adjustment costs) is given by

$$p_i^* = -\mu_1 \log \alpha \kappa + \mu_1 w_i^e + (1 - \mu_1)p^e + \frac{(1 - \alpha)}{\alpha}\mu_1 y_{di}^e,$$

where recall that $\mu_1 = \alpha(1 - \kappa)/(1 - \alpha\kappa)$. It is convenient to write this more succinctly as

$$p_i^* = \mu_0 + \mu_1 w_i^e + (1 - \mu_1)p^e + \mu_2 y_{di}^e. \tag{9}$$

Notice that the expectations appear because none of the right-hand variables is known when prices are set.

Supposing that employment is set after these variables are revealed, then the level of employment is chosen by the firm in order to produce that quantity of output which it is able to sell at the predetermined price. So the static equilibrium level of employment corresponding to p_i^* comes from the demand for output (2) and the production function (1), and is thus given by

$$\alpha n_i^* = -\eta(p_i^* - p) + y_{di}. \tag{10}$$

There is however a hidden assumption here, namely, that the firm always supplies whatever is demanded at the predetermined price. This remains so even if, for example, the marginal cost of doing so exceeds the price. This assumption may not be too bad, however, given that in normal times price tends to exceed marginal cost by a substantial margin (see e.g. Hall 1988*b* or Flaig and Steiner 1990).

Corresponding to the price equation is the marginal revenue product condition. From the fact that marginal revenue is equated to expected marginal cost, we have from (6)

$$p_i^* + \log\alpha\kappa = w_{\ i}^{\ e} + (1 - \alpha)n_i^{*e}. \tag{11}$$

Taking expectations of (10) and subtracting this from (10) itself gives

$$n_i^* = n_i^{*e} + \frac{\eta}{\alpha}\left(p - p^e\right) + \frac{1}{\alpha}\left(y_{di} - y_{di}^e\right).$$

Hence, using (11), actual employment is given by

$$n_i^* = \frac{1}{(1 - \alpha)}\log\alpha\kappa - \frac{1}{(1 - \alpha)}\left(w_i - p_i^*\right) + \frac{1}{(1 - \alpha)}\left(w_i - w_i^e\right)$$

$$+ \frac{\eta}{\alpha}\left(p - p^e\right) + \frac{1}{\alpha}\left(y_{di} - y_{di}^e\right). \tag{12}$$

This corresponds to equation (7) in the previous section, the only change being the presence of a series of surprises or innovations generated by the predetermined nature of price-setting.

The dynamic price equation

The next step is to solve the dynamic optimization problem. In order to do this, we first approximate the profit objective of the firm by a quadratic form, so that the first-order conditions are linear and may be solved analytically. So we approximate real profit, $\pi(p_i)$, by a Taylor expansion around p_i^* (see equation (9)) to obtain

$$\pi(p_i) \simeq \pi\left(p_i^*\right) - \frac{\theta}{2}\left(p_i - p_i^*\right)^2,$$

where note that $\pi'(p_i^*) = 0$ because p_i^* is the optimum price, and $\theta = -\pi''(p_i^*) > 0$. So, including quadratic employment adjustment costs of the standard type and price adjustment costs ($8a$), the firm at t will choose a price and employment path to solve

$$\min E_t \sum_{s=0}^{\infty} \varphi^s \left[\frac{\theta}{2}\left(p_{it+s} - p_{it+s}^*\right)^2 + \frac{b_p}{2}\left(p_{it+s} - p_{it+s-1}\right)^2\right.$$
$$\left. + \frac{b_n}{2}\left(n_{it+s} - n_{it+s-1}\right)^2\right],$$

subject to the constraint that demand is satisfied in each period, namely,

$$\alpha n_{it+s} = -\eta(p_{it+s} - p_{t+s}) + y_{dit+s} \qquad \text{(all } s \geqslant 0). \tag{13}$$

This constraint follows immediately from (1) and (2) in exactly the same way as (10). As already noted, the assumption that demand is satisfied in every period may not be wholly satisfactory, particularly in our dynamic context. However, for our present purpose it will not be too misleading and we shall have more to say on this general question in the next chapter.

To solve this constrained optimization problem, the first step is simply to substitute out the constraint. So using (13), we eliminate the employment terms from the firm's objective, which reduces to

$$\min E_t \sum_{s=0}^{\infty} \varphi^s \left[\frac{\theta}{2}\left(p_{it+s} - p_{it+s}^*\right)^2 + \frac{1}{2}\left(b_p + \frac{b_n\eta^2}{\alpha^2}\right)(p_{it+s} - p_{it+s-1})^2\right.$$
$$- \frac{\eta^2 b_n}{\alpha^2}(p_{it+s} - p_{it+s-1})(p_{t+s} - p_{t+s-1})$$
$$\left. - \frac{\eta b_n}{\alpha^2}(p_{it+s} - p_{it+s-1})(y_{dit+s} - y_{dit+s-1})\right].$$

The first-order conditions for this problem may be obtained by differentiating the objective with respect to p_{it+s}. So that they may be written in a simple fashion, it helps to define some new symbols as follows:

$$\tilde{p}_{it+s} = p_{it+s} - p^e_{t+s}$$

$$\alpha_1 = b_p + b_n \eta^2 / \alpha^2$$

$$\hat{p}_{it+s} = p^*_{it+s} - p^e_{t+s} + \frac{b_p}{\theta}\left(\varphi \Delta p^e_{t+s+1} - \Delta p^e_{t+s}\right)$$

$$- \frac{b_n \eta}{\theta \alpha^2}\left(\varphi \Delta y^e_{dit+s+1} - \Delta y^e_{dit+s}\right).$$

Then the first-order conditions for our problem can be written

$$\varphi \alpha_1 \tilde{p}_{it+s+1} - [\theta + \alpha_1(\varphi+1)]\tilde{p}_{it+s} + \alpha_1 \tilde{p}_{it+s-1} = -\theta \hat{p}_{it+s} \qquad (s > 0).$$

Thus we obtain a second-order difference equation (or Euler equation) which is typical for problems of this type. The solution is standard and is given by

$$\tilde{p}_{it} = \lambda \tilde{p}_{it-1} + (1-\lambda)(1-\varphi\lambda)\sum_{j=0}^{\infty}(\varphi\lambda)^j \hat{p}_{it+j},$$

where λ is the unique stable root of the quadratic equation[3]

$$\varphi\alpha_1\lambda^2 - [\theta + \alpha_1(\varphi+1)]\lambda + \alpha_1 = 0. \qquad (14)$$

In order to see how the general price level behaves, we may aggregate by noting that $p_i = p$, $y_{di} = y_d$, $w_i = w$. Furthermore, to generate a clean and simple structure, we suppose that expectations are static, namely, $y^e_{dt+s} = y^e_{dt}$, $p^e_{t+s} = p^e_t$, $w^e_{t+s} = w^e_t$. We then obtain, after some manipulation,

$$p_t = p^*_t - (1-\varphi\lambda)\frac{b_p}{\theta}\Delta p_t - \left(\frac{\lambda}{1-\lambda} - (1-\varphi\lambda)\frac{b_p}{\theta}\right)\left(p_t - p^e_t\right)$$

$$+ (1-\varphi\lambda)\frac{b_n\eta}{\alpha^2\theta}\left(y^e_{dt} - y_{dt-1}\right), \qquad (15)$$

where p^*_t is given by the aggregate version of (9), namely,

$$p^*_t = \mu_0 + \mu_1 w^e_t + (1-\mu_1)p^e_t + \mu_2 y^e_{dt}. \qquad (16)$$

Equation (15) is the key to understanding price dynamics since it reveals precisely how prices move relative to their static equilibrium level. There are two nominal inertia terms, both negative:[4] the first in Δp_t and the second in the form of a surprise, $p_t - p^e_t$.

It is worth noting, first, why we refer to terms of this type as 'nominal inertia terms'. The general form of the relevant part of the equation is

$$p_t = p_t^* - \omega_1 \Delta p_t - \omega_2 (p_t - p_t^e) \qquad (\omega_1, \omega_2 > 0).$$

This can be rewritten as

$$p_t = (\omega_1' p_t^* + \omega_2' p_{t-1} + \omega_3' p_t^e),$$

where $\omega_1', \omega_2', \omega_3' > 0$ and $\omega_1' + \omega_2' + \omega_3' = 1$.[5] Thus, p_t is a convex combination of the 'equilibrium' price (p_t^*), last period's price (p_{t-1}), and the expected price (p_t^e). Suppose the equilibrium price (p^*) shifts. Then it is clear that the response of the actual price (p) is sluggish for two reasons: first, because p_{t-1} is unaffected by the change in p^* and thus a 'proportion' ω_2' of the actual price does not move at all; second, because p_t^e will move one for one with the change in the equilibrium price (p^*) only if all the factors that cause this change are in the information set determining the price expectation. In the probable event that they are not, p_t^e will not move one for one with the change in p^*, and hence a 'proportion' ω_3' of the actual price will not respond fully. So the presence of terms of the form Δp_t or ($p_t - p_t^e$) in equation (15) captures this sluggish price response to nominal shifts and they are thus called nominal inertia terms.

The final term in equation (15) indicates that *changes* in demand will have a positive impact on prices relative to their equilibrium level. This is a hysteresis effect in the sense that a long-run upward shift in the level of demand will have no impact on price relative to equilibrium price, but in the short run will cause a positive deviation. This hysteresis effect is generated by employment adjustment costs. (Note the appearance of b_n in the coefficient.) The idea here is that, when there are employment adjustment costs, or indeed adjustment costs associated with any other factor of production, then marginal costs are steeper in the short run than in the long run, when all factors are fully adjusted. As a consequence, prices are more responsive to demand in the short run than in the long run and hence we have a hysteresis effect.

Equation (15) is generated using the simple price adjustment cost form (8a). If we assert that price adjustment costs are associated with changes in prices *relative* to the expected rate of inflation, as in (8b), then (15) takes the simpler form:

$$p_i = p_t^* - \frac{\lambda}{1-\lambda}\left(p_t - p_t^e\right) + (1 - \varphi\lambda)\frac{b_n \eta}{\alpha^2 \theta}\left(y_{dt}^e - y_{dt-1}\right). \qquad (15')$$

So the only nominal inertia term is the price surprise with the lagged dependent variable term having disappeared. This is, perhaps, more satisfactory than the previous case, because it is hard to believe that nominal price responses would have a fixed degree of sluggishness whatever the rate of inflation. Indeed, any firm following such a rule would rapidly go out of business if inflation rose to a very high level.

It is clear from (15′) that the extent of the nominal inertia that arises from price adjustment costs depends positively on the parameter λ. From (14), it is easy to show that λ is decreasing in the parameter θ/α_1 where

$$\theta/\alpha_1 = \theta \bigg/ \left(b_p + \frac{b_n \eta^2}{\alpha^2} \right).$$

From this we see that the extent of nominal inertia is increasing in both adjustment cost parameters (b_p, b_n).[6]

Finally, we may consider the full price equation obtained by using (16) to eliminate the equilibrium price (p^*) from (15′). After some manipulation, we find

$$p_t - w_t = - \log \alpha \kappa + \frac{1 - \alpha}{\alpha} y^e_{dt} - \left(w_t - w^e_t \right) - \frac{\lambda \alpha + \eta(1 - \alpha)}{\alpha(1 - \lambda)} \left(p_t - p^e_t \right)$$

$$+ \frac{(1 - \varphi \lambda) b_n \eta[\alpha + \eta(1 - \alpha)]}{\alpha^3 \theta} \left(y^e_{dt} - y_{dt-1} \right). \tag{17}$$

This is simply the dynamic version of the static equation (5), where nominal inertia terms in the form of price and wage surprises, and the hysteresis term arising from employment adjustment costs, have been added. The nominal inertia terms arise both from price adjustment costs and from our assumption that prices are set at the beginning of the period.

Adjustment costs and the extent of nominal inertia

Since price adjustment costs are likely to be small, the question arises as to whether any nominal inertia that arises from such costs is also liable to be small. In order to give some idea of the orders of magnitude involved, suppose we only have price adjustment costs, setting employment adjustment costs to zero. From (15′) or (17), we see that the key term is $\lambda/(1 - \lambda)$.[7] If this is small, then price adjustment costs contribute little to nominal inertia.

Now if we additionally assume that the discount factor (φ) is unity, then using (14), the relationship between λ and price adjustment costs (b_p/θ) is given by

$$\frac{\lambda}{1 - \lambda} = \frac{1}{2} \left[\left(\frac{z + 3}{z - 1} \right)^{1/2} - 1 \right], \tag{18}$$

where $z = 1 + \theta/b_p$. To keep things simple, if we suppose $\alpha = 1$, then $\theta (= -\partial^2\pi^*/\partial p^2)$ is given by

$$\theta = \eta(\eta - 1)\pi^*, \tag{19}$$

where η is the demand elasticity and π^* is the firm's optimal profit. Suppose $\eta = 2$ and the adjustment cost of changing prices by 1 per cent more than the expected rate of inflation is x per cent of profits. Then, using the adjustment cost formula (8b), we have

$$\frac{b_p}{2.10^4} = \frac{x\pi^*}{10^2} = \frac{0.01\theta x}{\eta(\eta - 1)},$$

from (19). So if x is 1/10 per cent, then $b_p/\theta = 10$ and $\lambda/(1 - \lambda) \simeq 2.7$, indicating a very high level of nominal inertia. Suppose x is a mere 1/100 per cent: then $b_p/\theta = 1$ and $\lambda/(1 - \lambda) \simeq 0.62$, which still represents a high level of inertia. Even if x is a negligible 1/1000 per cent, $\lambda/(1 - \lambda) \simeq 0.09$ which, while small, is not negligible. So, even if price adjustment costs are very small, they are still capable of generating a considerable degree of price stickiness. The reason for this is clear. The cost, in terms of forgone profit, of setting a non-optimal price is only a second-order magnitude in the region of the optimum because the optimum is a stationary point. Hence it pays firms to deviate from the optimum by a considerable amount to save even a small sum in terms of adjustment costs. This fact is, of course, the foundation of the 'near-rational' models of the business cycle discussed in Mankiw (1985) and Akerlof and Yellen (1985).

To summarize, therefore, both price adjustment costs and the fact that prices are set before the aggregate price level is revealed lead directly to price stickiness. Employment adjustment costs, on the other hand, lead to hysteresis in pricing behaviour.

Dynamic employment behaviour

Corresponding to the dynamics of price behaviour displayed in (17) is an employment equation which is the dynamic version of the marginal revenue product condition set out in (7''). To derive this, we first note that the aggregate version of (13) is

$$\alpha n_t = \alpha f + y_{dt}, \tag{20}$$

where recall that $f = \log F$ (the number of firms) and that, because firms are identical, prices cancel in the aggregate. This results from the fact that firms supply whatever is demanded at the predetermined price. Next we reorganize (17) as

$$p_t - w_t = -\log \alpha \kappa + \frac{1-\alpha}{\alpha} y_{dt} + \frac{\lambda_1}{\alpha}\left(y_{dt} - y_{dt-1}\right)$$

$$- \left(w_t - w_t^e\right) - \frac{\lambda \alpha + \eta(1-\alpha)}{\alpha(1-\lambda)}\left(p_t - p_t^e\right) - \frac{1-\alpha+\lambda_1}{\alpha}\left(y_{dt} - y_{dt}^e\right), \quad (17')$$

where $\lambda_1 = (1 - \varphi\lambda)b_n\eta[\alpha + \eta(1 - \alpha)]/\alpha^2\theta$. Finally, we simply substitute out y_{dt}, using (20), to obtain after some rearrangement

$$n_t = \frac{1}{1-\alpha+\lambda_1}\left[\log \alpha \kappa + (1-\alpha)f + \lambda_1 n_{t-1} - (w_t - p_t)\right.$$

$$\left. + \left(w_t - w_t^e\right) + \frac{\lambda \alpha + \eta(1-\alpha)}{\alpha(1-\lambda)}\left(p_t - p_t^e\right) + \frac{1}{\alpha}\left(1 - \alpha + \lambda_1\right)\right.$$

$$\left.\left(y_{dt} - y_{dt}^e\right)\right]. \tag{21}$$

This is the dynamic marginal revenue product condition which reduces to (7) if we set $\lambda_1 = 0$ and eliminate the surprise terms. Furthermore, if we eliminate the surprise terms only, it then has the same structure as the competitive labour demand function, although the latter is, of course, a very different animal, with prices being exogenously given at the firm level rather than being set by the firm itself. Finally, it is worth emphasizing that when firms set prices the price equation and the marginal revenue product condition are simply two sides of the same coin and are more or less interchangeable.

3. Time delays and staggered price-setting

The previous model, based on convex adjustment costs, highlights two factors generating nominal inertia, one being the setting of prices before aggregate information is revealed, and the other being the cost of adjusting prices. We now wish to get away from the somewhat artificial convex adjustment cost framework and to focus more deeply on these two factors. In this section, we concentrate on the first of these.

Prices are set before aggregate information is revealed, either because they are set in advance of the relevant period or because they are set concurrently but there is some delay in the transmission of the aggregate information. That such delays exist cannot be denied, but they tend to be short: aggregate price information is announced monthly in many economies with a delay that is often less than two months. Consequently the lags involved here are not substantial, and it is better to focus on the possibility of prices being set at discrete intervals.

It is obvious that, if prices can only be changed at discrete intervals, this is tantamount to an assertion that prices are sticky. Furthermore, the degree of stickiness depends on the length of the interval. In order to get away from this apparent triviality, we can follow two approaches. First, we can suppose there are fixed costs of changing prices and analyse the optimal frequency of price changes. This we consider in the next section. Second, we can investigate the possibility that significant aggregate price stickiness can arise even if there are only very small time delays at the micro level.

Consider the following simple example from Blanchard (1987). Suppose there are vertical interactions in which a final good (labelled n) is produced in n stages of production, each lasting one 'period'. The first good (labelled 1) uses only labour and the subsequent ones, only the good produced in the previous stage. At each step there is a delay captured by the dependence of the ith price (p_i) on a weighted average of the current value of the $(i-1)$th price and its expectation formed in the previous period. Thus, in general, we have

$$p_{it} = (1 - a)p_{(i-1)t} + aE_{t-1}p_{(i-1)t} \qquad (i = 2, \dots, n), \qquad (22)$$

and also

$$p_{1t} = E_{t-1}w_t.$$

If we suppose wages are known in advance ($E_{t-1}w_t = w_t$) but price expectations are static ($E_{t-1}p_{it} = p_{it-1}$), then we have

$$
\begin{aligned}
p_{1t} &= w_t \\
p_{2t} &= (1 - a)p_{1t} + ap_{1t-1} &&= [(1 - a) + aL]p_{1t} \\
p_{3t} &= (1 - a)p_{2t} + ap_{2t-1} &&= [(1 - a) + aL]p_{2t} \\
&\;\;\vdots &&\;\;\vdots
\end{aligned}
$$

$$p_{nt} = (1 - a)p_{(n-1)t} + ap_{(n-1)t-1} = [(1 - a) + aL]p_{(n-1)t}$$

where L is the lag operator. This implies a final aggregate price equation of the form

$$p_{nt} = [(1 - a) + aL]^{n-1}w_t,$$

which has a mean lag on w_t of $(n - 1)a$ 'periods' which is $(n - 1)$ times the mean lag embodied in each of the individual equations (a 'periods'). So even if the mean lags are small at each stage, the final mean lag could be large if there are many stages.

However, suppose price expectations are formed rationally, with wages again known in advance. The system becomes

$$p_{1t} = (1 - a)p_{(i-1)t} + aE_{t-1}p_{(i-1)t} \qquad (i = 2, \ldots, n), \qquad (23)$$
$$p_{1t} = w_t,$$

where expectations are now model-consistent. Then taking expectations of (23) yields

$$E_{t-1}p_{it} = (1 - a)E_{t-1}p_{(i-1)t} + aE_{t-1}p_{(i-1)t} = E_{t-1}p_{(i-1)t} \qquad (i = 2, \ldots, n),$$
$$E_{t-1}p_{1t} = w_t.$$

Consequently $E_{t-1}p_{it} = w_t$, all i, and substituting back into (23) yields $p_{it} = w_t$, all i. So there is no build-up of the lag once expectations are assumed to be rational. But this is not the end of the story. We know from the work of Taylor (1979) and Blanchard (1983) that if price-setting is staggered over time we again find that the aggregate lag is longer than the micro lag even under rational expectations.

In the light of this, the question naturally arises as to whether the staggering of price increases across firms is an equilibrium phenomenon. Consider an individual firm. Suppose the aggregate price level increases: will this induce a rise in the individual firm's price? If we take equation (4) as providing the optimal pricing decision at the individual firm level, we find that

$$\frac{\partial p_i}{\partial p} = \frac{1 - \alpha}{\alpha + \eta(1 - \alpha)} \left(\eta + \frac{\partial y_{di}}{\partial p} \right). \qquad (24)$$

There are two forces at work here. Suppose, first, that marginal costs are increasing ($\alpha < 1$), so the term outside the large bracket is positive. A rise in the aggregate price level induces a rise in the individual firm's price which is proportional to the elasticity of demand η. This comes about because the rise in competitors' prices allows a rise in the firm's own price without fear of loss of custom. However, there is an offsetting effect arising from the fall in overall demand induced by the rise in the aggregate price level (note $\partial y_{di}/\partial p \leqslant 0$). We know that $\eta > 1$, so what of the size of $|\partial y_{di}/\partial p|$? The term y_{di} reflects the demand facing the ith firm which we may take to be some proportion of total demand. Assuming that the share itself does not depend on the aggregate price level, we are only concerned with the impact of aggregate prices on aggregate real demand. So long as the elasticity of real demand with respect to real balances is not greater than unity, then $|\partial y_{di}/\partial p| \leqslant 1$ and a rise in the aggregate price level has an unambiguously positive effect on the ith firm's price. This we take to be the most likely case, and so, if marginal costs are increasing, p_i is likely to be increasing in the aggregate price level. On the other hand, if marginal costs are decreasing ($\alpha > 1$), then p_i is probably decreasing in the aggregate price level since the term outside the bracket in (24) is now negative.

If $\partial p_i/\partial p > 0$, this surely militates against staggering. The more other firms' prices move together, the greater is the incentive for any individual firm to raise its own price, along with the others. Such an effect will obviously lead to bunching, at least in response to common shocks. However, it is equally obvious that staggering will appear if individual firms face deterministically staggered shocks. Thus, if y_{di} moves up for half the firms in even periods and half in odd periods, then some staggering will clearly take place (see e.g. Ball and Romer 1989). This argument does, however, seem rather artificial. The overall implication seems to be that where marginal costs are increasing we can expect bunching, whereas where they are decreasing staggering may be more common.

Another possibility is analysed in Okun (1981) and more formally in Ball and Cecchetti (1988). This arises from the natural incentive for a firm to wait, before making pricing decisions, in order to see what other firms will do. The difficulty in this type of model is to specify who goes first. In a 'steady state' the answer is, presumably, that the firm which goes first is the firm which went first last time round because it will be most out of line relative to the average. This last thought leads naturally to the notion that each firm's price-setting decision clearly depends on its own history as well as on the position of others. So the general strategy should be to consider optimal price changing in response to a mixture of individual and aggregate shocks. That is, we should allow firms to change prices when it is optimal for them to do so rather than at fixed intervals as in the staggering stories. The use of fixed intervals leads to price equations with simple nominal lags. It seems most unlikely that such equations could be robust to significant changes in the economic environment, particularly with regard to the inflation rate. If inflation, and hence the rate of change of costs, were increasing, no firm would ever stick to a pricing strategy that kept its price fixed over an exogenously given period. So the models discussed in this section are best thought of as providing some suggestive examples as to how inertia might develop via aggregation.

4. Optimal pricing with fixed costs of adjustment

We have already considered optimal price adjustment under quadratic adjustment costs and the results, while useful, suffer from the drawback that such adjustment costs are somewhat unrealistic. So in this section we look at the opposite extreme, that of fixed costs of adjustment.

The simplest story is that due to Sheshinski and Weiss (1977), who envisage a monopolistic firm producing a non-storable good with fixed costs of price adjustment, facing an environment where aggregate inflation is proceeding at a constant rate. Suppose that without adjustment costs the firm's (log) price is p_i^*, which rises at the constant aggregate inflation rate. Then Sheshinski and Weiss demonstrate that the optimal strategy of the firm is to raise its price p_i to a level $S + p_i^*$ each time p_i^* reaches $p_i + s$, where S,s are constants which depend on the cost of adjustment and the aggregate inflation rate. It is worth noting that they also show that faster aggregate inflation does not necessarily lead to more frequent price adjustment. The optimal strategy is illustrated in Fig. 1 and is known as an *Ss* rule. It is clear that the time between each price adjustment is constant. Such *Ss* rules remain optimal for certain very special stochastic inflation rules (see Sheshinski and Weiss 1983) but are not, otherwise, correct. For example, once the good becomes storable, the *Ss* rule does not work because customers will simply concentrate their purchases before each jump. Not surprisingly, some randomization of price changes is then required, as Benabou (1989) demonstrates.

However, the implications of *Ss* rules are of some interest because they do not necessarily lead to aggregate price inertia of any significance. Caplin (1985) shows that, in an economy with identical firms operating *Ss* rules of the above kind and facing firm-specific shocks, the price distribution across firms tends to be uniform.[8] Furthermore, Caplin and Spulber (1987) then demonstrate that, if nominal demand in the economy rises smoothly, the aggregate price level rises in proportion, despite the fact that individual firms are only raising prices at discrete intervals. The idea here is simply that, as nominal demand rises, in

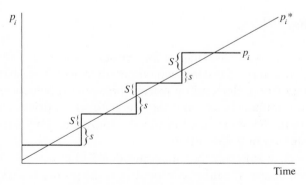

Fig. 1. *An optimal Ss pricing rule.*

each small interval of time the firms with the lowest prices jump up to the top and the average price just keeps pace with nominal demand. It is clear that under these circumstances there is no aggregate price inertia and neutrality prevails. This result breaks down, however, if nominal demand falls as well as rises or if nominal demand jumps. Possible consequences are discussed in Tsiddon (1987) and in Blanchard and Fischer (1989: ch. 8), the overall conclusion being that aggregate prices again exhibit some inertia.

A more sophisticated model, based on fixed costs of price adjustment, is that due to Ball *et al.* (1988). This is a dynamic model of staggered price-setting (as in Section 3), but the length of time between price changes is endogenous. The important results concern the equilibrium frequency of price changes. This is increasing in the aggregate rate of inflation, the variances of both aggregate and firm-specific shocks, and the second derivative of the profit function with respect to price. This last is a measure of the cost to the firm of deviating from its static profit-maximizing price. Generally speaking, this cost is increasing in the elasticity of demand,[9] which reveals that we can expect firms in more concentrated industries to have a higher degree of price rigidity, a result that is consistent with the evidence presented in Carlton (1986: 655) and Encaoua and Geroski (1986).

In general, therefore, fixed costs of adjustment will lead to nominal inertia in aggregate price-setting, but the precise analytical form of this inertia is hard to discern except under certain special cases. There are, however, some reasons for expecting that nominal inertia will be lower if general inflation is higher, if the economy is subject to more variable shocks, and if there is a higher level of product-market competition. Furthermore, the faster and more smoothly nominal demand is rising, the closer one gets to the Caplin–Spulber neutrality result.

5. Summary

The main arguments of this chapter can be summarized as follows.

1. The key features of pricing behaviour upon which we have focused are the long-run impact of demand on prices, the extent to which prices are sticky in response to nominal shocks, and the degree to which prices respond more to demand shifts in the short run than in the long run. This last is termed the extent of hysteresis in price-setting.

2. The evidence suggests that long-run demand effects are weak and that such effects are bigger, the more competitive is the product market. Prices tend to increase with demand either because marginal costs rise or because the

mark-up of price over marginal costs rises. So overall demand effects could be weak either because marginal costs rise but the mark-up falls, or because marginal costs fall but the mark-up rises, or because they are both flat. Such empirical evidence as we possess does not allow us to discriminate decisively between these hypotheses.

3. Nominal inertia arises naturally from the assumption that there are costs associated with changing prices, and we have considered a variety of models that illustrate this point. These models suggest that such nominal stickiness will be higher, the lower is the general level of inflation and the lower is the variance of both aggregate and firm-specific shocks. A lower level of product-market competition will also tend to raise nominal inertia. Finally, we find that hysteresis in price-setting is liable to arise when there are significant costs of adjusting factors of production, particularly labour.

Notes

1. Hall (1988a), however, argues that Bils does not convincingly rebut the view that the additional labour costs incurred when working at full capacity are not true costs but merely part of the overall contractual agreement with workers. For example, workers are promised a given number of overtime hours per year as part of their explicit or implicit contract.
2. See e.g. Oi (1962), Rees (1973: table 9) and Barron *et al.* (1985).
3. This solution is standard. It first appeared in the economics literature in Tinsley (1971) and is comprehensively discussed in Sargent (1978) or Nickell (1986).
4. Note, from (14), that $\dfrac{\lambda}{1 - \lambda} - (1 - \varphi\lambda)\dfrac{b_p}{\theta} = \dfrac{(1 - \lambda)(1 - \varphi\lambda)b_n\eta^2}{\alpha^2(1 - \lambda)\theta} > 0.$
5. In fact, $\omega'_1 = (1 + \omega_1 + \omega_2)^{-1}$, $\omega'_2 = \omega_1\omega'_1$, $\omega'_3 = \omega_2\omega'_1$.
6. Ball and Romer (1990) find, in the context of a different framework, that the extent of nominal inertia is inversely related to the size of the demand effect on prices. From (5) we see that the demand effect is negatively related to α. It is easy to show that θ is decreasing in α, so that if b_n is small, θ/α_1 is also decreasing and hence λ is increasing in α. So the same result applies here if employment adjustment costs are small.
7. Note that the coefficient on $(p - p^e)$ in (17) is
$$\frac{\lambda\alpha + \eta(1 - \alpha)}{\alpha(1 - \lambda)} = \frac{\lambda[\alpha + \eta(1 - \alpha)]}{(1 - \lambda)\alpha} + \frac{\eta(1 - \alpha)}{\alpha},$$
which is an increasing function of $\lambda/(1 - \lambda)$.
8. In fact, Caplin solves the problem with regard to inventories rather than prices, but the formal structure is exactly the same so the result carries over.
9. This is certainly true in the model of Section 2 (see equation (19) for a special case) and in the model of Blanchard and Fischer (1989: ch. 8, equation (8)).

The Macroeconomic Outcome

8

The Macroeconomics of Unemployment

IN this chapter we provide a macroeconomic framework for analysing unemployment. Our 'typical' economy consists of a large number of identical price-setting firms facing downward-sloping demand curves for their output. Wages are set by a variety of methods and, generally speaking, are not competitively determined. Many particular assumptions that we use have little significance in the final analysis and are made simply for expositional convenience. The implications of alternative assumptions will be discussed from time to time in order to illustrate this point.

In what follows, we do not provide any extensive analysis of the behavioural models underlying our equations, as these have been dealt with in previous chapters. We consider first a simple closed-economy model with price-setting firms and non-competitive wage determination.[1] Despite these latter features, the model has the 'natural rate' property that, in the long run, only supply-side factors influence the equilibrium level of activity. In Section 2 we look at the dynamics of the model in response to demand shocks, technology shocks, and wage shocks. Here we emphasize the key role of three sets of parameters: those that capture the extent to which the level of economic activity influences wage- and price-setting; those that represent hysteresis effects where *changes* in activity influence wages and prices; and those that reflect nominal inertia or wage/price stickiness.

Section 3 brings out the main implications of the model, and impatient readers can begin at this point. The section focuses on the unemployment–inflation trade-off and the NAIRU. Here we specialize the previous model by assuming that the expectations-generating mechanism is such as to make price surprises synonymous with changes in inflation. In Section 4 we proceed to a discussion of the open economy whose equilibrium we define to have no inflationary surprises *and* balanced trade. Finally in Section 5 we analyse the unemployment–inflation trade-off in the open-economy context.

1. A closed-economy model

Technology, demand, and pricing behaviour: the firm

Our purpose here is to describe the behaviour of firms (labelled i). These are identical and have a constant-returns technology of the form

$$y_i - k_i = \alpha(n_i - k_i) + \varepsilon_i, \tag{1}$$

where lower-case letters refer to logarithms, y = value added output, k = capital stock, n = employment, and ε = technology shock (mean zero, serially independent).[2] This technology should be thought of as a log-linear approximation to a general form rather than as Cobb–Douglas. The capital stock is fixed at the beginning of each period. Since firms are identical, we also have a corresponding aggregate technology,

$$y - k = \alpha(n - k) + \varepsilon. \tag{2}$$

Turning to the structure of demand, we first define $\bar{y}$ as the level of output in the economy corresponding to full utilization of resources. That is,

$$\bar{y} - k = \alpha(l - k), \tag{3}$$

where l = the fixed labour force[3] and the technology shock is set to its mean level. We next suppose that the real level of demand in the economy (y_d) is given by

$$y_d = \sigma_1 x + \sigma_2(m - p), \tag{4}$$

where x = a measure of fiscal stance (although it may include any other exogenous real factors influencing demand), m = money stock, and p = value added price (GDP deflator). This equation reflects the reduced form of a simple IS–LM system.[4]

Firms being identical, demand is allocated equally between them. If f is the log of the number of firms, demand for each is thus $y_d - f$. We then specify the demand curve facing the firm as

$$y_{di} = -\eta(p_i - p) + y_d - f, \tag{5}$$

where p_i is the firm's value added price, p is the aggregate value added price, and η is the elasticity of demand.[5]

Firms' decisions are taken in the following fashion. Prices are set at the beginning of the period on the basis of expectations of future demand and costs. Wages, output, and employment are set during the period. Output is determined by firms simply supplying whatever is demanded at the predetermined price. Employment is then set to produce the output.

Two points are worth noting. First, the ordering of events reflects an arbitrary assumption whose purpose is to introduce some nominal inertia into the system without making the model unduly complex. Second, the assumption that firms supply what is demanded at the predetermined price rules out any role for rationing and the like. It is clear that this may reflect irrational behaviour if the marginal cost of production rises above the price when supplying the output. Ignoring this problem, and the associated role of inventories and delivery lags, obviously reflects a gross simplification. However, we feel that in explaining unemployment it is a simplification worth making so long as we recognize the possibility that prices (or effective prices) may rise very rapidly in certain sectors when full capacity is reached. The key feature of the economy that is captured by the type of imperfect competition model we propose is that demand presents itself directly to firms rather than being mediated by an exogenously given price, as under perfect competition. This feature reflects the crucial fact that, in 'the real world', the majority of firms set prices and are willing to supply more output when more is demanded, even if the price is unchanged.

Turning now to the issue of pricing behaviour, firms plan output and set prices in order to maximize profit. Given the demand function (5), planned output (y_i^p) and the price of output (p_i) must satisfy

$$y_i^p = -\eta(p_i - p^e) + y_d^e - f, \tag{6}$$

where the superscript e refers to expectation.[6] Expected marginal cost (mc) at this planned level of output is given by

$$mc_i^e = w_i^e + b_2(y_i^p - k_i) + \text{const.}, \tag{7}$$

where w_i^e is the expectation of future labour costs per employee (including firms' labour taxes).[7] Given our constant returns assumption, the parameter b_2 must be non-negative. However, little in what follows hangs on this point, and the possibility that increasing returns leads to a negative value of b_2 need not be ruled out.

The price that maximizes short-run profit is then given by

$$p_i = \log[\eta/(\eta - 1)] + mc_i^e, \tag{8}$$

where $\eta/(\eta - 1)$ is the standard price mark-up on marginal cost. As already noted in Chapter 7 (Section 1), this mark-up may vary systematically with demand fluctuations in either a counter- or a pro-cyclical fashion. Making this dependence explicit gives

$$\log[\eta/(\eta - 1)] = \text{const.} - b_1(y_d^e - \bar{y}), \tag{9}$$

363

where we have written the mark-up as counter-cyclical.[8] Substituting (7) and (9) into (8) enables us to write the price equation as

$$p_i - w_i^e = b_0 - b_1(y_d^e - \bar{y}) + b_2(y_i^p - k_i). \tag{10}$$

The price mark-up on expected wages thus depends on demand and on the ratio of planned output to the capital stock. As already noted, we have no very strong priors as to the signs of either of these effects.

Finally, we may note that actual output is determined by *ex post* demand; that is,

$$y_i = -\eta(p_i - p) + y_d - f, \tag{11}$$

and employment is then determined by the production function (1).

Equations (1), (6), (10), (11) provide a complete description of the firm's behaviour. Given demand, wage/price expectations, and capital, these equations determine planned and actual output (y_i^p, y_i), prices (p_i), and employment (n_i). To keep things simple, we have made a number of explicit assumptions as well as a number of implicit ones. In particular, we have ignored adjustment costs and hours of work. Some of the implications of this will be discussed later.

Wage determination

As we have already seen in Chapters 2–4, wages may be determined by a variety of methods and in this chapter we do not propose to be too specific. We see wages as being influenced by firm-specific or 'insider' factors, such as productivity and the well-being of the existing workforce, and by 'outsider' factors, such as wages paid elsewhere and the general state of the labour market. In order to make these notions more precise, we begin by focusing on the insider aspect and deriving the relationship between product wages, employment, and productivity within the firm. If the firm expects to pay a wage w_i^e, then the relationship between expected product wages and planned output is given by the price equation (10). If we define planned employment (n_i^p) as that level required to produce planned output (i.e. $y_i^p - k_i = \alpha(n_i^p - k_i)$), then the relationship between the expected product wage and planned employment is given by

$$p_i - w_i^e = b_0 - b_1(y_d^e - \bar{y}) + b_2\alpha(n_i^p - k_i). \tag{12}$$

This is derived simply by substituting the production function into (10).[9]

Using (10), we now define the 'insider' wage as the level that would, at some average level of demand ($\bar{y}_d$), lead the firm just to employ these workers who are party to the wage bargain, the insiders, who are n_{Ii} in number, say. So the insider wage, w_i^I, is given by

$$w_i^I = p_i - b_{01}' - b_2\alpha(n_{Ii} - k_i), \tag{13}$$

where $b_{01}' = b_0 - b_1(\bar{y}_d - \bar{y})$. This is the wage that would tend, on average, to stabilize employment in the firm at n_{Ii}. The idea underlying this formulation is to capture the notion, discussed extensively in Chapter 2, that the insiders are simply concerned with raising wages up to the point where their own jobs are at risk. If this were the only mechanism influencing wage determination and firms had no say in the matter, the insider wage would be the actual wage outcome and we have the pure insider model of Blanchard and Summers (1986) (see Chapter 4, Sections 2 and 6).

As in Chapter 2, we suppose the insiders consist of the existing employees less the proportion δ who quit voluntarily. Thus we have

$$n_{Ii} = n_{i-1} - \delta.$$

Substituting this into (13) yields

$$w_i^I = p_i - b_{01} + b_2\alpha(k_i - n_{i-1}), \tag{14}$$

where $b_{01} = b_{01}' - b_2\alpha\delta$. So the insider wage is decreasing in last period's employment because the more employees who are party to the wage bargain, the less upward pressure they can exert on wages without fear of job loss.

As we have seen in previous chapters, however, outside factors are also important. In general, firms are constrained by the necessity to recruit, retain, and motivate their workforces. So we define the 'outsider' wage, w_i^o, to be a function of wages available elsewhere, modified by the chances of obtaining another job, the attractiveness of the unemployed state, and related factors. Thus we have

$$w_i^o = w^e + c_0 - c_1 u - c_2\Delta u + c_3\hat{z}_w, \tag{15}$$

where u is the aggregate unemployment rate, w the aggregate wage, and $\hat{z}_w$ other factors such as the generosity and coverage of unemployment benefits. We have *expected* aggregate wages because we suppose that, when wages in firm i are determined, full information about the aggregate wage is not available. Our measure of the chances of obtaining another job depends not only on the unemployment rate but also upon its change. This latter effect captures the notion that it may be harder to obtain work if unemployment has recently risen ($\Delta u > 0$), because the competition for jobs will be more intense. The reason for this is that recently unemployed persons are both more active in looking for work and more attractive to employers than the longer-term unemployed. This kind of effect is discussed fully in Chapters 4 and 5.

We now suppose that the actual wage outcome (w_i) is a weighted sum of the insider and outsider wages, and so we have

$$w_i = \lambda[p_i - b_{01} + b_2\alpha(k_i - n_{i-1})]$$
$$+ (1 - \lambda)(w^e + c_0 - c_1 u - c_2 \Delta u + c_3 \hat{z}_w) + \hat{z}_{1w}. \tag{16}$$

We have added a further variable, $\hat{z}_{1w}$, which reflects other exogenous factors that may be important in wage determination. Two such are worth mentioning explicitly. First, a firm with a more powerful union may simply have a higher wage level, *ceteris paribus* (see Chapter 2 and Chapter 4, Section 4). Second, workers may resist wage adjustments associated with changes in the wedge between product wages and consumption wages (post-tax wages deflated by retail prices). In other words, if tax changes raise the product wage relative to the consumption wage, workers may resist any reduction in their living standards, leading to upward pressure on the product wage (see Chapter 2, Section 2 and Chapter 4, Section 7). The firm-specific wage equation (16) has the standard form which is discussed at length in Chapter 4 (Section 2). In particular, it is worth recalling that the insider weight (λ) usually lies between 0 and 0.3.

This completes our model of price, wage, output, and employment determination for the ith firm, and it simply remains to aggregate.

The aggregate economy

Aggregation here is straightforward, given our assumption of identical firms and a constant labour force. We have the following:

Production: $y - k = \alpha(n - k) + \varepsilon$ (17)
(equations (2), (3))

$$\bar{y} - k = \alpha(l - k) \tag{18}$$

Output: $y = y_d$ (19)
(equations (6), (11))

$$y^p = -\eta(p - p^e) + y_d^e \tag{20}$$

Demand: $y_d = \sigma_1 x + \sigma_2(m - p)$ (21)
(equation (5))

Expected demand: $y_d^e = \sigma_1 x^e + \sigma_2(m^e - p^e)$ (22)

Pricing: $p - w^e = b_0 - b_1(y_d^e - \bar{y}) + b_2(y^p - k)$ (23)
(equation (10))

Wages:
(equation (16))

$$w = \lambda[p - b_{01} + b_2\alpha(k - n_{-1})]$$
$$+ (1 - \lambda)(w^e + c_0 - c_1 u - c_2 \Delta u + c_3 \hat{z}_w) + \hat{z}_{1w} \quad (24)$$

Unemployment: $u = l - n$ \hfill (25)
(definition)

In order to see how this model operates, we first list the exogenous and pre-determined variables, namely, k, l, m, m^e, x, x^e, $\hat{z}_w$, $\hat{z}_{1w}$, n_{-1}, ε, w^e, p^e. Given these, (22) determines expected demand, and (18), (20), (23) then determine prices, which are set at the beginning of the period. During the period, (21) yields actual demand, which then determines output via (19) and hence employment from the production function (17). Unemployment is given by (25), and finally, wages are given by (24). In general, there is no reason why expectations should be fulfilled.

Before proceeding further, it is useful to restrict ourselves to certain key variables and to reorganize the model into three equations for unemployment, prices, and wages. Equations (17), (18), (19) imply a direct relation between demand and unemployment, namely

$$y_d - \bar{y} = -\alpha u + \varepsilon. \quad (26)$$

This follows immediately from the production function and from the fact that firms supply what is demanded. Thus, for given ε, a rise in unemployment is always accompanied by a fall in demand and vice versa. So to argue, as many do, that changes in unemployment are due to changes in demand is close to a tautological statement. Of course, in some cases, an exogenous demand shock may be the initiating factor lying behind a change in unemployment. However, in many situations it is supply-side shocks of various kinds that are the driving force, with demand simply accommodating. This is particularly true in the case of longer-term shifts in unemployment.

Taking (18), (20), and (23), the price equation reduces to

$$p - w = b_0 + (b_2 - b_1)(y^e_d - \bar{y}) - (w - w^e) - b_2\eta(p - p^e) - b_2\alpha(k - l). \quad (27)$$

This is written in the form of a price mark-up on wages which depends on the level of expected demand, wage, and price surprises, which reflect nominal inertia and the capital–labour force ratio, capturing trend productivity. It is worth noting that the demand effect can go either way; for, as we have already noted, we have no strong evidence on the signs of b_2 or b_1, let alone their difference. The evidence reported in Chapter 7 does, however, suggest that demand effects on prices appear to be relatively small, whichever way they go.

Using (24) and (25), the wage equation can be rewritten as[10]

$$w - p = \gamma_0 - \gamma_1 u - \gamma_{11}\Delta u - \gamma_2(w - w^e) + b_2\alpha(k - l) + z_w. \tag{28}$$

The wage mark-up on value added prices depends, in its turn, on unemployment, the change in unemployment, wage surprises, trend productivity, and exogenous wage pressure variables such as union and benefit effects.

Several points are worth noting. First, changes in unemployment influence wages both because of insider effects and because of the duration composition effects which were discussed with reference to outsider forces (see Chapter 4, Section 5). Second, the theory of wage determination we have espoused implies that the impact of trend productivity on the price mark-up on wages is exactly the same as that on the wage mark-up on prices. This has strong implications, as we shall see. Finally, the three equations (26), (27), (28), along with the definition of demand in (21), are sufficient for a complete analysis of the economy both in long-run equilibrium and in response to shocks.

We define long-run equilibrium as a situation where exogenous factors are kept fixed and expectations are fulfilled. We also fix the predetermined capital stock. If expectations are fulfilled, $w = w^e$, $p = p^e$, $y_d = y_d^e$, and hence (27), (28) become

$$p - w = b_0 + (b_2 - b_1)(y_d - \bar{y}) - b_2\alpha(k - l), \tag{29}$$

$$w - p = \gamma_0 - \gamma_1 u + b_2\alpha(k - l) + z_w, \tag{30}$$

where note that $\Delta u = 0$ because equilibrium is a stationary state. Setting $\varepsilon = 0$ in (26), we can solve (26), (29), (30) for the equilibrium levels of unemployment, real wages, and demand. The equilibrium level of demand simply means that level of demand which is consistent with price and wage expectations being fulfilled. These levels are given by

$$u^* = \frac{b_0 + \gamma_0 + z_w}{\gamma_1 + (b_2 - b_1)\alpha}, \tag{31}$$

$$(w - p)^* = \frac{[(b_2 - b_1)\alpha\gamma_0 - b_0\gamma_2]}{\gamma_1 + (b_2 - b_1)\alpha} + \frac{(b_2 - b_1)\alpha z_w}{\gamma_1 + (b_2 - b_1)\alpha} + b_2\alpha(k - l), \tag{32}$$

$$y_d^* = -\alpha u^* + \bar{y}. \tag{33}$$

Corresponding to this equilibrium will be a level of output and employment given by (25) and (17). Furthermore, the mix of monetary and fiscal policy will determine the price level from (21).

There are some important features of this stationary state. First, the equilibrium level of unemployment depends only on the exogenous wage pressure variables (z_w) and the parameters of the wage/price equations and the production function. In particular, it is worth noting that one of these parameters is b_0, part of the mark-up of prices on marginal costs. Should this rise exogenously, because of a reduction in product-market competition, for example, this will tend to raise the equilibrium unemployment level. Second, the equilibrium level of unemployment does not depend on the capital–labour force ratio, which influences only the real wage. This arises from the equality of coefficients on this trend productivity term in the price and wage equations. Were these coefficients to differ, then unemployment would either rise or fall continuously with trend productivity growth. The absence of such a trend in unemployment over the centuries is, therefore, consistent with this framework. Nevertheless, it would be straightforward to amend our model so that the equilibrium level of unemployment depended on the predetermined capital stock. For example, we might suppose that we had a fixed-coefficients technology and that the capital stock was below the level required to sustain the equilibrium level of employment. This is, of course, a rather extreme scenario, but we present some less extreme thoughts along these lines in Annex 8.1, where such capital constraints can occur, at least in the short run.

A third key feature of the model is that it is fundamentally of the 'natural rate' type: that is, exogenous demand-side factors do not influence the equilibrium. This is so despite the fact that we have made no assumptions concerning 'market-clearing' in the traditional sense. Indeed, real wages could have been set exogenously by unions, for example, and this natural rate property would remain. However, it must be emphasized that the use of the word 'natural' here does not imply that the equilibrium is, in any sense, either desirable or unalterable. The fact that the equilibrium is conditional on the exogenous wage pressure variables (z_w) allows plenty of latitude for policy measures to influence long-run unemployment. Indeed, as we shall argue in Chapters 9 and 10, many of the factors that explain long-run differences in unemployment across countries are the consequence of explicit acts of policy. These acts of policy are not, however, of the standard monetary or fiscal kind.

Multiple equilibria

Before proceeding to the dynamics of this model, it is worth noting how multiple equilibria can exist within this framework. To see where these might arise, note that we can write our price equation (29), in equilibrium, as

$$p - w = b_0 - (b_2 - b_1)\alpha u - b_2\alpha(k - l), \qquad (29')$$

making use of (26) to replace demand deviations by unemployment. Then we can see that equilibrium unemployment (equation (31)) is that level which ensures that the real wage generated by price-setting (equation (29′)) is consistent with that determined by wage-setting (equation (30)). Of course, in this context a unique equilibrium is ensured by the linearity of the model. However, there is nothing sacrosanct about linearity, and as soon as we recognize that the impact of unemployment on the price mark-up on wages in (29′) can go either way, the prospect of multiple equilibria opens up. Recall that the parameter b_2 reflects the slope of the marginal cost function. With increasing returns, this could be negative. The parameter b_1, on the other hand, captures the extent to which demand reduces the price mark-up on marginal cost, a possibility that arises if there is more competition in booms, for example. So either this latter effect or increasing returns (or both) can easily lead to $(b_2 - b_1)$ being negative and hence to the price mark-up on wages rising with unemployment. With sufficient nonlinearity, it is then easy to see how we can have one equilibrium with high unemployment, where low real wages from the labour market are consistent with a high price mark-up on wages, and another equilibrium with low unemployment, where high real wages are consistent with a low price mark-up on wages. Examples of such multiple equilibria are discussed in Murphy *et al.* (1987) and Manning (1990), based on increasing returns, and in Chatterjee and Cooper (1989), based on greater competition in booms. It should, however, be noted that multiple equilibria of this type are rarely looked for, and never found, in any empirical investigation. (For an extensive search, see Carruth and Oswald 1988.) So we shall proceed with an investigation of the dynamics of our standard linear model and ignore the possibility of multiple equilibria from now on.

2. The dynamics of the model

The basic framework

In order to investigate how the economy responds to shocks, we simply focus on the wage and price equations along with the definition of demand, (21), and the relationship between demand and unemployment, (26). We shall also generalize the wage and price equations so that our results do not depend crucially on the timing of events given in the previous section. Our generalized price equation has the form

$$p - w = \beta_0 + \frac{\beta_1}{\alpha}(y_d - \bar{y}) + \frac{\beta_{11}}{\alpha}\Delta(y_d - \bar{y}) + \frac{\beta_1'}{\alpha}(y_d^e - \bar{y}) - \beta_{21}(p - p^e)$$
$$- \beta_{22}(w - w^e) - \beta_3(k - l) - \frac{\beta_4'}{\alpha}\varepsilon. \tag{34}$$

Thus we allow prices to depend on actual levels and changes in demand as well as expected demand (cf. equation (27)). The coefficients on these terms are divided by α to ensure that the equation takes on a simple form when demand is replaced by unemployment. It is particularly important to note the introduction of the negative term in the technology shock, ε, which appears alongside the addition of actual rather than expected demand terms. Actual demand appears in the price equation when price is set in relation to actual rather than expected marginal cost. Actual marginal cost falls with positive technology shocks; hence the negative sign.

In this more general framework we have the same demand equations as before, which we repeat for convenience:

$$y_d = \sigma_1 x + \sigma_2(m - p), \tag{35a}$$

$$y_d - \bar{y} = - \alpha u + \varepsilon. \tag{35b}$$

If we make use of the second of these to eliminate demand from the price equation (34), we obtain

$$p - w = \beta_0 - \beta_1 u - \beta_{11}\Delta u - \beta_1'u^e - \beta_{21}(p - p^e) - \beta_{22}(w - w^e)$$
$$- \beta_3(k - l) - \frac{\beta_4}{\alpha}\varepsilon, \tag{36}$$

where $\beta_4 = \beta_4' - \beta_1 - \beta_{11}$. For simplicity, we set the lagged productivity shock to zero. This version of the price equation has unemployment capturing the demand effect on prices, which is more convenient in the present context since unemployment is the variable of interest. It is important to note that the parameter associated with the productivity shock (β_4) must be positive; for, if productivity moves favourably $(\varepsilon > o)$, marginal cost and hence prices will fall *at given levels of employment (and unemployment)*.

We next generalize the wage equation by allowing expected as well as actual unemployment to play a role, and also by including price surprises (cf. equation (28)). Again, we are now allowing for a more general timing of events than was assumed in the previous section. Our new equation thus has the form

$$w - p = \gamma_0 - \gamma_1 u - \gamma_{11}\Delta u - \gamma_1'u^e - \gamma_{21}(p - p^e)$$
$$- \gamma_{22}(w - w^e) + z_w + \beta_3(k - l). \tag{37}$$

To see how this economy responds to exogenous shocks, we assume that expectations are model-consistent (i.e. 'rational'). We do this because we wish to isolate those forces keeping the economy away from equilibrium which do not depend on model-inconsistent expectations. We consider a variety of shocks, namely:

Money supply: $m = m_{-1} + \varepsilon_m.$ (38a)

Fiscal policy: $x = \bar{x} + \varepsilon_x.$ (38b)

Wage pressure: $z_w = \bar{z}_w + \varepsilon_w.$ (38c)

As with the technology shock ε, we taken ε_m, ε_x, ε_w to be serially independent with mean zero.

The key parameters and the competitive model

Before presenting the results, it is worth mentioning three features of the model which will prove to be important. The first is the long-run impact of economic activity on price- and wage-setting, as captured by the four parameters β_1, β_1', γ_1, γ_1'. All of these are probably non-negative although, as we have already noted, the β parameters could be negative as long as the remainder are large enough to ensure a sensible stable equilibrium. Note, in this case, that equilibrium unemployment is given by

$$u^* = \frac{\gamma_0 + \beta_0 + \bar{z}_w}{\beta_1 + \beta_1' + \gamma_1 + \gamma_1'}. \tag{39}$$

The second feature is the extent of hysteresis in both price- and wage-setting, captured by the parameters β_{11} and γ_{11} which should be non-negative. We have already discussed some of the reasons for hysteresis in wage-setting in this chapter (see also Chapters 2 and 4), but, as we have seen in Chapter 7, it is also likely to arise in price-setting. Thus, for example, employment adjustment costs will ensure that increases in output (falls in unemployment) will raise marginal costs, and therefore prices, by more in the short run than in the long run. Alternative mechanisms are discussed in Annex 8.1 and also in Chapter 7. Finally, the third feature is the extent of nominal inertia or wage/price stickiness. This is captured by the four parameters β_{21}, β_{22}, γ_{21}, γ_{22}. Generally speaking, we expect these to be non-negative and not to exceed unity, in order to rule out the possibility that wage/price expectations have a negative effect on actual wages or prices.

In order to clarify the role of these key parameters, it is worth noting how they emerge in a competitive market-clearing framework, which is a special case of the model discussed here. Suppose we restrict our price and wage equations (36), (37) to have the form

$$p - w = \beta_0 - \beta_1 u - \beta_{11}\Delta u - \beta_3(k - l) - \frac{\beta_4}{\alpha}\varepsilon, \tag{36'}$$

$$w - p = \gamma_0 - \gamma_1 u - \gamma_{11}\Delta u + \beta_3(k - l) + z_w. \tag{37'}$$

Then, noting that $u = l - n$, we may rearrange to obtain

$$n = - \frac{\beta_0}{\beta_1 + \beta_{11}} + \frac{\beta_{11}}{\beta_1 + \beta_{11}} n_{-1} + \frac{\beta_3}{\beta_1 + \beta_{11}} k - \frac{1}{\beta_1 + \beta_{11}} (w - p)$$

$$+ \frac{\beta_4}{\alpha(\beta_1 + \beta_{11})} \varepsilon, \tag{36''}$$

$$n - l = - \frac{\gamma_0}{\gamma_1 + \gamma_{11}} + \frac{\gamma_{11}}{\gamma_1 + \gamma_{11}} (n - l)_{-1} + \frac{1}{\gamma_1 + \gamma_{11}} (w - p)$$

$$- \frac{\beta_3}{\gamma_1 + \gamma_{11}} (k - l) - \frac{z_w}{\gamma_1 + \gamma_{11}}. \tag{37''}$$

The first of these, (36″), is a standard dynamic labour demand function. The short-run wage elasticity is $(\beta_1 + \beta_{11})^{-1}$ and the long-run elasticity is $1/\beta_1$. This immediately reveals that the parameters which reflect the impact of economic activity on prices are inversely related to the labour demand elasticity. The relationship between hysteresis in price-setting and employment adjustment costs also emerges clearly, for the key parameter (β_{11}) captures the impact of the lagged dependent variable.

The second equation, derived from the wage equation, is an intertemporal labour supply function. The lagged dependent variable here would arise from habit persistence, for example, and reflects the hysteresis effect, γ_{11}. The negative effect of the trend productivity term $(k - l)$ captures the impact of the normal or long-run real wage on labour supply which is a key feature of the intertemporal labour supply model. The short-run labour supply elasticity, $(\gamma_1 + \gamma_{11})^{-1}$, depends on the degree of intertemporal substitution, and is inversely related to the parameters that capture the impact of economic activity on wage-setting.

To summarize, in the competitive context, the hysteresis terms in price- and wage-setting derive from the degree of persistence in labour demand and supply, whereas the activity effects are inversely related to the demand and supply elasticities. So the model can be given a traditional, real business cycle interpretation. It is, of course, also possible to introduce nominal inertia into this competitive framework. A typical method is to suppose that suppliers of labour are unaware of the aggregate price level when taking their decisions, thereby introducing p^e as opposed to p in the labour supply function (see e.g. Alogoskoufis 1983).

Finally, it is worth emphasizing that our basic structure encompasses the wide variety of models discussed in previous chapters as well as the competitive framework. Thus, for example, the impact of economic activity or unemployment on wage-setting may have little to do with labour supply elasticities and much more to do with the structure of wage-bargaining in a unionized environment (see Chapter 2) or the precise way in which wages are set in an efficiency wage context (see Chapter 3). Which of these is a correct description of reality varies both across countries and across sectors within countries. The fact that our framework subsumes them all ensures that it is widely applicable.

The response to shocks

In order to work out the solution to this model under consistent expectations, we first use (35a), (35b) to replace unemployment and demand in (36) and (37) by fiscal and monetary policy terms. We then take expectations and solve for the price and wage surprises.[11] Having obtained these, we use the price and wage surprises to solve (36) and (37) for real wages and unemployment in terms of the shocks. Deviations of unemployment from equilibrium may then be shown to follow the path

$$(u - u^*) = \frac{b_{11} + \gamma_{11}}{(\beta_1 + \beta_1' + \beta_{11}) + (\gamma_1 + \gamma_1' + \gamma_{11})}(u - u^*)_{-1}$$

$$- \frac{1}{\alpha\Delta}[(1 + \beta_{21})(1 + \gamma_{22}) - (1 - \beta_{22})(1 - \gamma_{21})](\sigma_1 \varepsilon_x + \sigma_2 \varepsilon_m)$$

$$+ \frac{1}{\alpha\Delta}\left[[(1 + \beta_{21})(1 + \gamma_{22}) - (1 - \beta_{22})(1 - \gamma_{21}) - (1 + \gamma_{22})\frac{\sigma_2 \beta_4}{\alpha} \right] \varepsilon$$

$$+ \frac{1}{\alpha\Delta}[\sigma_2(1 - \beta_{22})]\varepsilon_w, \tag{40a}$$

where

$$\Delta = (1 + \beta_{21})(1 + \gamma_{22}) - (1 - \beta_{22})(1 - \gamma_{21}) + \frac{\sigma_2}{\alpha}[(1 + \gamma_{22})(\beta_1 + \beta_{11})$$
$$+ (1 - \beta_{22})(\gamma_1 + \gamma_{11})]. \tag{40b}$$

Taking each term in turn, it is clear that persistence is generated by hysteresis in both wage- and price-setting. If the change effects of economic activity on price- and wage-setting (β_{11}, γ_{11}) are large relative to the level effects ($\beta_1, \beta_1', \gamma_1, \gamma_1'$), shocks may drive the economy out of equilibrium for long periods of time. If there are no level effects ($\beta_1 = \beta_1' = \gamma_1 = \gamma_1' = 0$), then we have a pure hysteresis model with no equilibrium, and unemployment following a random walk (Blanchard and Summers 1986).

Turning to the impact effect of the shocks, we can first consider those from the demand side. Their impact on unemployment is increasing in nominal inertia, both in price- and in wage-setting ($\beta_{21}, \beta_{22}, \gamma_{21}, \gamma_{22}$), and is decreasing in the size of the activity effects on prices and wages ($\beta_1, \beta_{11}, \gamma_1, \gamma_{11}$). Only actual rather than expected changes in activity have an effect here. The fact that wage and price stickiness are important for the transmission of demand shocks is, of course, a standard result, but it is worth emphasizing the role of activity effects in stabilizing the economy. As we shall see in Chapter 9, this is a key factor in explaining unemployment patterns in different countries.

The parameter that captures the impact of real balances on demand, σ_2, also has an important part to play. If this parameter is small, fiscal policy shocks tend to have a larger impact relative to those arising from monetary policy. This, of course, corresponds to the situation where the demand for goods is interest-inelastic and the demand for money is interest-elastic.

Favourable technology shocks have two kinds of impact on unemployment. Nominal inertia tends to induce a rise in unemployment, but this is offset in part or in whole by the direct effect on price-setting (recall $\beta_4 > 0$). Furthermore, the impact on output is always positive since the overall coefficient on ε can never exceed $1/\alpha$. (Note that $y - \bar{y} = -\alpha u + \varepsilon$, and since u can never rise by more than ε/α, y must increase with ε.)

Finally, we have wage pressure shocks. Their positive impact on unemployment and negative effect on output is attenuated by nominal inertia and is eliminated entirely if β_{22} is unity (as in the simple model of Section 1). This occurs because, if prices are set before the wage shock is revealed, the wage shock has no impact on prices and hence no impact on demand, output, or employment. As with demand shocks, bigger effects of activity on wage- and price-setting reduce the real impact of wage shocks and tend to stabilize the economy. This point has profound real-world implications, as we shall again see in Chapter 9.

Turning now to the impact effect of these shocks on real wages, it is straightforward to show that positive technology shocks tend to raise real wages, and the same is true of positive wage shocks. The former occurs essentially because the demand for labour is raised; the latter is obvious. More interesting is the impact of demand shocks on the real wage. Using (40a), (34), (35), (36), it is easy to show that real wages will fall in response to a positive demand shock if and only if

$$(\gamma_1 + \gamma_{11})(\beta_{21} + \beta_{22}) < (\beta_1 + \beta_{11})(\gamma_{21} + \gamma_{22}). \tag{41}$$

So a demand increase and the corresponding rise in employment will be associated with a falling real wage if wages are stickier than prices $(\gamma_{21} + \gamma_{22} > \beta_{21} + \beta_{22})$ and activity has a bigger impact on price-setting than on wage-setting $(\beta_1 + \beta_{11} > \gamma_1 + \gamma_{11})$. These results are important because they reveal precisely what determines the cyclical behaviour of real wages. If cycles are predominantly generated by aggregate demand shocks allied to nominal inertia, real wages can be either pro-cyclical or counter-cyclical depending on the parameter configurations. Two particular cases are worth noting. If the product market is competitive and there is, consequently, no nominal inertia in price-setting $(\beta_{21} + \beta_{22} = 0)$, real wages will be counter-cyclical. On the other hand, if there is no demand effect on price-setting $(\beta_1 + \beta_{11} = 0)$, as would be the case under pure 'mark-up' pricing, real wages will be pro-cyclical. An alternative view of cycles, preferred by real business cycle theorists, is that cycles are predominantly caused by technology shocks with little or no nominal inertia. In this case real wages are positively related to output and are thus pro-cyclical.

Next, let us look at the impact of shocks on price surprises. These are given by

$$p - p^e = \frac{1}{\Delta\alpha}[(1 + \gamma_{22})(\beta_1 + \beta_{11}) + (1 - \beta_{22})(\gamma_1 + \gamma_{11})](\sigma_1\varepsilon_x + \sigma_2\varepsilon_m)$$

$$- \frac{1}{\Delta\alpha}[(1 - \beta_{22})(\gamma_1 + \gamma_{11}) + (1 + \gamma_{22})(\beta_4 + \beta_1 + \beta_{11})]\varepsilon$$

$$+ \frac{1}{\Delta}(1 - \beta_{22})\varepsilon_w.$$

As we note in the next section, over the last two decades positive (negative) price surprises have been associated with rising (falling) inflation. So this equation tells us that positive demand and wage shocks lead to positive price surprises (rising inflation), whereas favourable technology shocks generate negative price surprises (falling inflation).

To summarize, positive *demand shocks* rely on price/wage stickiness for their favourable real effects,[12] generate positive price surprises (rising inflation), and can be associated with real wage movements in either direction. Positive *technology shocks* tend to raise output and real wages, and are associated with negative price surprises (falling inflation). Employment will also tend to rise unless nominal inertia is very strong. In this case nominal inertia is not a prerequisite for real effects. Positive *wage pressure shocks* generate positive price surprises (rising inflation) and tend to raise real wages and lower employment, but their real effects are attenuated by price/wage stickiness.

Finally, the persistence of all these shocks depends critically on the extent of hysteresis in both price- and wage-setting.

It is worth noting that there has been much recent discussion as to which of these types of shock is the dominant cause of business cycles. It was generally assumed until the mid-1970s that demand shocks were the key driving force, and much attention was focused on the sources of the nominal inertia that is necessary if these shocks are to have real effects. (Lucas 1972 is the classic paper here.) However, with successive oil shocks and the productivity slow-down, attention turned to the supply side, and the view that technology shocks are highly significant finds expression in the real business cycle model (see e.g. Kydland and Prescott 1982, or Eichenbaum and Singleton 1986). As we have seen, nominal inertia is no longer necessary in such real models and fluctua-tions are generated even if both labour and product markets are perfectly competitive with complete information. However, these real models do tend to generate an association between rises in output and negative price surprises (falling inflation).

3. The unemployment–inflation trade-off and the NAIRU

Expectations formation and the NAIRU

As yet, we have made only passing references to inflation. Of course, our model determines the price level, and from the previous section it is clear that both price and wage surprises have a key role in the transmission of shocks. However, inflation, as such, does not appear to play a significant part in the story. Yet in the past three decades the control of inflation has been one of the fundamental aims of macroeconomic policy in the OECD economies. And the NAIRU has entered the language of economics.

In order to bring inflation to the centre of the stage, we shall suppose that expectations are based on the view that the rate of inflation follows a random walk.[13] If

$$\Delta p = \Delta p_{-1} + v \qquad (v \text{ white noise}), \tag{42}$$

then we may write

$$p^e = p_{-1} + \Delta p_{-1},$$

and hence

$$p - p^e = \Delta p - \Delta p_{-1} = \Delta^2 p. \tag{43}$$

So, under this assumption about expectations formation, price surprises are synonymous with changes in inflation. Since such expectations are clearly not model-consistent ('rational'), how can their use in any theoretical analysis be justified? The answer is that over the last two decades inflation processes in most OECD countries have had a root very close to unity, and consequently the expectations formation mechanism set out in (43) is a realistic and sensible one. It should, however, be emphasized that such an assumption will make the model very period- and country-specific. The discussion in this section, therefore, will be inadequate for most economies in the inter-war period or for economies experiencing hyperinflation, for example. Furthermore, our assumed expectations mechanism would surely break down if monetary policy were set to induce rising inflation for a very long period. In such cases, however, our overall framework may still be relevant, provided we replace 'inflation' by whatever derivative of price is currently untrended.

The unemployment–inflation trade-off

Bearing these caveats in mind, let us consider a simplified version of our model where the price equation (36) has the form

$$p - w = \beta_0 - \beta_1 u - \beta_{11}\Delta u - \beta_2\Delta^2 p - \beta_3(k - l) \tag{44}$$

and the wage equation (37) is

$$w - p = \gamma_0 - \gamma_1 u - \gamma_{11}\Delta u - \gamma_2\Delta^2 p + z_w + \beta_3(k - l). \tag{45}$$

So only price surprises appear in the wage and price equations. The connection between demand (y_d) and unemployment remains as before, although we shall now ignore technology shocks. Furthermore, given the stickiness of prices, we may safely suppose real demand is exogenous in the short run. Thus we have

$$y_d - \bar{y} = -\alpha u \qquad (y_d \text{ exogenous}). \tag{46}$$

So, for given levels of y_d, k, l, z_w, the three equations (44), (45), (46) provide us with the time paths of wages, prices, and unemployment. More informatively, the equations give us unemployment, the real wage, and the change in inflation ($\Delta^2 p$).

It is immediately clear that equilibrium unemployment (u^*) is the level consistent with no surprises, which in this case is synonymous with constant inflation. So u^* is also a NAIRU[14] and is given by solving (44) and (45) with $\Delta^2 p = 0$; that is,

$$u^* = \frac{(\beta_0 + \gamma_0) + z_w}{\beta_1 + \gamma_1}. \tag{47}$$

If we now eliminate the real wage from (44) and (45) and use (47), we find the relationship between $\Delta^2 p$ and $u - u^*$ given by

$$\Delta^2 p = \frac{-(\beta_1 + \gamma_1)(u - u^*) - (\beta_{11} + \gamma_{11})\Delta u}{(\beta_2 + \gamma_2)}. \tag{48}$$

This represents the unemployment–inflation trade-off and is the fundamental supply-side constraint for this closed economy. (Some authors refer to this equation as the Phillips curve.) Given that expectations are formed in the particular way described in the initial part of this section, the effects of aggregate monetary and fiscal policy, as well as other types of demand shock, are constrained by this relationship. The only way that this constraint can be relaxed is to induce a fall in u^*.

Looking at this constraint another way, we can use (47) to rewrite (48) as

$$(\beta_1 + \gamma_1 + \beta_{11} + \gamma_{11})u = (\beta_{11} + \gamma_{11})u_{-1} + (\beta_0 + \gamma_0) - (\beta_2 + \gamma_2)\Delta^2 p + z_w. \tag{49}$$

From this, and taking a year as the period under consideration, we see that a 1 per cent fall in the annual rate of inflation ($\Delta^2 p = -1$ per cent for one period) 'costs' a cumulated total of $(\beta_2 + \gamma_2)/(\beta_1 + \gamma_1)$ percentage-point years of unemployment. For, following the 1 per cent fall in inflation, unemployment is $(\beta_2 + \gamma_2)/(\beta_1 + \gamma_1 + \beta_{11} + \gamma_{11})$ per cent higher than its initial level in the first period, $(\beta_2 + \gamma_2)(\beta_{11} + \gamma_{11})/(\beta_1 + \gamma_1 + \beta_{11} + \gamma_{11})^2$ per cent higher than its initial level in the second, $(\beta_2 + \gamma_2)(\beta_{11} + \gamma_{11})^2/(\beta_1 + \gamma_1 + \beta_{11} + \gamma_{11})^3$ per cent higher than its initial level in the third, and so on. The sum total of these effects is $(\beta_2 + \gamma_2)/(\beta_1 + \gamma_1)$. Furthermore, because of the linearity of (49), this total is unaffected by the length of the period over which inflation falls. Thus, a fall in inflation of $\frac{1}{2}$ per cent per year for two years 'costs' exactly the same number of percentage-point years of unemployment. This cost, $(\beta_2 + \gamma_2)/(\beta_1 + \gamma_1)$, is often termed the 'sacrifice ratio'—that is, the total amount of extra unemployment required to reduce inflation by one point—and it depends on the extent of nominal inertia relative to the sum of the activity effects on wage- and price-setting. Another name for it is the degree of nominal wage rigidity (NWR) or simply nominal rigidity (see e.g. Grubb *et al.* 1983).

On the real side, a permanent 1 per cent rise in wage pressure (z_w up by 1 per cent permanently) leads to a long-run increase in unemployment of $(\beta_1 + \gamma_1)^{-1}$ percentage points. This is the inverse of the activity effects on prices and wages and is sometimes known as the degree of real wage rigidity (RWR) (see, again, Grubb *et al.* 1983). It simply records the long-run unemployment consequences of an autonomous rise in wage pressure which is just enough to induce an impact effect on real wages of 1 per cent at constant unemployment and inflation.

Returning to the basic trade-off equation (48), we can provide a simple diagrammatic analysis (as in Chapter 1, Fig. 6). Suppose first that the hysteresis terms are omitted ($\beta_{11} = \gamma_{11} = 0$). The resulting trade-off is illustrated in Fig. 1. The price and wage lines represent (44) and (45) in $(w - p)$, $(1 - u)$ space, with $\Delta^2 p$ set at zero. We use the employment rate $(1 - u)$ on the axis in order to emphasize the relationship between the price and wage lines and demand and supply curves, although it must again be noted that the wage equation will generally have little to do with the labour supply function as normally defined. The NAIRU is u^*, and if demand is high enough to reduce unemployment to u', the economy moves to a point B with inflation rising as given in (48). The speed at which inflation rises is proportional to the vertical distance between the two lines, DC; and the precise point at which the economy operates is determined by the slopes of the lines and the extent of nominal inertia in the two equations. The ratio $BD:BC$ is simply β_2/γ_2, so if prices are stickier than wages, $\beta_2 > \gamma_2$ and B is closer to the wage line as in the figure. In fact, the real wage is given by

$$(w - p)' - (w - p)^* = - \frac{(\beta_2 \gamma_1 - \gamma_2 \beta_1)(u' - u^*)}{\beta_2 + \gamma_2}, \tag{50}$$

so that if there is a positive demand shock, real wages will fall if and only if $\beta_2 \gamma_1 < \gamma_2 \beta_1$, a result we have already seen in a more complex form (equation (41)).

Nonlinear unemployment effects

Until now we have supposed that the impact of unemployment on (log) wages is linear. There are, however, a number of reasons for believing this relation-

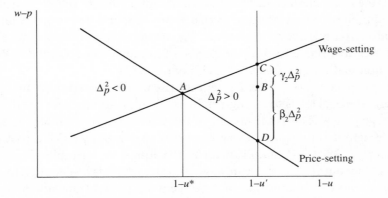

Fig. 1. *The unemployment–inflation trade-off.*

ship may be concave, as we have seen in Chapters 4 and 6. That is, as unemployment rises, the downward pressure which it exerts on (log) wages is decreasing at the margin. This notion has a long history exemplified by the fact that the relevant line is known as the Phillips *curve* rather than the Phillips *line*. Indeed, Lipsey (1960) produced a simple and elegant aggregation argument to justify the curvature. Compositional effects may also be important here. In our discussion of hysteresis in wage equations, we mentioned the possibility that recently unemployed persons are both more active in looking for work and more attractive to employers. So the higher the proportion of such individuals in the unemployment pool, the more effective are the unemployed as a whole in exerting downward pressure on wages. Since, in the long run, this proportion will tend to be lower at a higher level of unemployment, this will automatically introduce concavity in the wage–unemployment relationship.

Suppose, then, that the u term in the wage equation is replaced by $-g(u)$, $g' > 0$, $g'' < 0$. The implications are best seen diagrammatically and are illustrated in Fig. 2. When wage pressure is low ($z_w = z_{w1}$), we have equilibrium unemployment u_1^*. If unemployment is actually at $u_1 > u_1^*$, then inflation falls at a rate proportional to D_1C_1. At a higher level of wage pressure ($z_w = z_{w2}$), we have a higher equilibrium rate, u_2^*. Suppose unemployment is set at u_2 such that $u_2 - u_2^* = u_1 - u_1^*$. Then it is clear that inflation now falls at a rate proportional to D_2C_2, which is far lower than D_1C_1 despite the fact that unemployment is as far above the equilibrium rate in both cases. This is the most significant consequence of concavity. As the equilibrium rate gets higher, excess unemployment is less and less effective at reducing inflation.

Another implication of Fig. 2 is that, if the price and wage lines are rather flat in the region of equilibrium, the inflationary or deflationary consequences

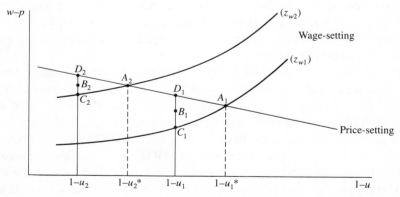

Fig. 2. *The unemployment–inflation trade-off with concave unemployment effects.*

of a move away from equilibrium may be very small indeed, and the constraints imposed by the position of the equilibrium are also small.

The role of hysteresis

Having looked at the model without the hysteresis terms, we may now reintroduce them and consider our basic model as exemplified by equations (44) and (45). From equation (48), it is clear that hysteresis effects can exert a strong influence on short-run inflationary pressure. Suppose, for example, that the hysteresis coefficients β_{11}, γ_{11} are considerably larger than the level coefficients β_1, γ_1. Then if u is above u^* and is kept fixed, $\Delta^2 p$ will be negative and inflation will be falling. But now suppose that demand is raised so that unemployment moves back towards u^*. Then the Δu term in (48) will be negative and will exert inflationary pressure which could easily dominate the deflationary pressure arising from $u > u^*$. Thus, hysteresis can give the appearance that the long-run equilibrium level of unemployment is closer to its current level than is actually the case.

In order to emphasize this point, let us define the short-run NAIRU (u_s^*) as that level of unemployment which is consistent with stable inflation *during the current period*. Thus, setting $\Delta^2 p = 0$ in (48), we have

$$- (\beta_1 + \gamma_1)(u_s^* - u^*) - (\beta_{11} + \gamma_{11})(u_s^* - u_{-1}) = 0$$

or

$$u_s^* = \frac{(\beta_1 + \gamma_1)u^* + (\beta_{11} + \gamma_{11})u_{-1}}{(\beta_1 + \gamma_1 + \beta_{11} + \gamma_{11})}. \tag{51}$$

So the short-run NAIRU is a weighted average of last period's unemployment rate and the actual NAIRU. If the hysteresis coefficients are dominant ($\beta_{11} + \gamma_{11} \gg \beta_1 + \gamma_1$), then u_s^* is much closer to u_{-1} than to u^*, and during the current period the economy behaves as if its equilibrium is close to last period's actual rate, whatever that may be.

This is illustrated graphically in Fig. 3. The lines 'Prices'', 'Wages'' represent the relationships between real wages and unemployment, given u_{-1}, and have slopes $- (\beta_1 + \beta_{11})$ and $(\gamma_1 + \gamma_{11})$ respectively; the lines 'Prices', 'Wages' are the relationships with Δu set equal to zero and have slopes $- \beta_1$ and γ_1 respectively. It is clear that 'Prices'' and 'Prices', 'Wages'' and 'Wages' will cross when $u = u_{-1}$. A' represents the short-run NAIRU and the figure reveals the inflationary consequences of moving to u. The rise in inflation in the current period is proportional to $D'C'$ despite the fact that u is well above u^*. It is clear therefore that, if policy-makers are worried about inflation, hysteresis is very

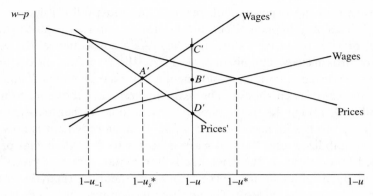

Fig. 3. *The short-run NAIRU.*

useful when it comes to the downward pressure on inflation consequent on raising unemployment, but it will cause serious problems when it comes to reducing unemployment from levels that are high relative to equilibrium. Compared with an economy without hysteresis, its presence makes it easier, in terms of inflation, to raise unemployment and harder to reduce it.

The consequences of an increase in wage pressure

Suppose there is an autonomous increase in wage pressure, z_w. The consequences, in the absence of hysteresis, are illustrated in Fig. 4, with the wage curve shifting to the left and equilibrium unemployment rising from u^* to u_1^*. If real demand, and hence unemployment, remains fixed initially, the economy moves to a point such as B with higher real wages and rising inflation. If the

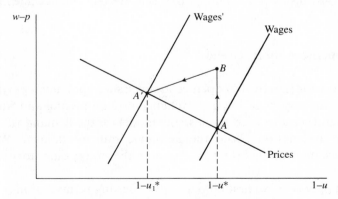

Fig. 4. *A rise in wage pressure.*

383

rise in wage pressure is permanent, real demand must fall if inflation is to be stabilized. This may happen either autonomously, via real balance effects for example, or as a result of a shift in policy. As a consequence, the economy moves towards its new equilibrium at A'. As the economy moves, inflation continues to rise along with unemployment and we have a state of 'stagflation', which is typical of such shocks. The real wage remains above its equilibrium level, and at this stage the rise in unemployment looks rather 'classical'. When the economy reaches its new equilibrium at A', unemployment is now higher, inflation is stabilized, and the real wage is higher to the extent that prices are influenced by demand. If the price line is horizontal, that is if prices are not influenced by demand as in simple 'mark-up' theories, then the real wage reverts back to its original level. The additional unemployment then appears to be entirely 'Keynesian', despite the fact that it has arisen from pressure on wages.

The lesson here is that, while autonomous wage pressure variables are the key to understanding unemployment in the long run, the view that this process operates via higher real wages is misconceived (along with the related notion of the wage gap[15]). Under mark-up pricing, for example, the equilibrium real wage is unchanged when unemployment increases as a consequence of rising wage pressure. More generally, the increase in the equilibrium real wage results from the pricing behaviour of firms only, with no influence from labour market considerations. The reason for this is that, while wage determination reveals the demands of wage bargainers at given unemployment, the price-setting behaviour of firms governs the real wage that is actually available. The sharpest expression of this point arises with mark-up pricing when the real wage that is available in the long run is independent of the level of activity. Workers may then press for higher real wages as much as they wish. Their quest is wholly unsuccessful, and all that is achieved is higher unemployment.

4. The open-economy model

We next allow for the effect of open-economy issues upon unemployment. The key point is the impact of the real exchange rate on pricing and wage-setting behaviour. But we also need to close the model on the demand side, and this requires an assumption about the exchange rate mechanism. We assume floating rates, but this makes no difference to the supply-side story with which we begin.

On the supply side, we first note that price-setting behaviour may change in the international context. It has been suggested that a rise in international competitiveness (c) makes the demand facing domestic firms less elastic[16] (see e.g. Bhaskar 1988), and, if this is the case, then the price mark-up on marginal cost will be increasing in c. If we revert to our basic model of Section 1, we may recall that the price that maximizes short-run profit for the ith firm is given by

$$p_i = \log[\eta/(\eta - 1)] + mc_i^e, \tag{8}$$

where η is the demand elasticity and mc is (log) marginal cost (equation (7)). The mark-up of price on marginal cost now depends not only on demand, as in equation (9), but on competitiveness, and so we have an extended mark-up equation,

$$\log[\eta/(\eta - 1)] = \text{const.} - b_{11}(y_d^e - \bar{y}) + b_{12}c^e, \tag{9'}$$

where c is (log) competitiveness, defined as

$$c = e + p^* - p,$$

p^* is the world price of output in foreign currency, and e the price of foreign currency (i.e., a rise in e represents a depreciation of the domestic currency). Putting together (8) and (9′) with the definition of marginal cost given in (7) gives us the open-economy version of the firm's price-setting equation (10), namely

$$p_i - w_i^e = b_0 - b_{11}(y_d^e - \bar{y}) + b_{12}c^e + b_2(y_i^p - k_i). \tag{10'}$$

Recall that marginal cost depends on the ratio of planned output to capital, $y_i^p - k_i$.

If we now insert the aggregate version of this revised equation into our aggregate model (see p. 366), we end up with a basic price equation of the form

$$p - w = b_0 + (b_2 - b_{11})(y_d^e - \bar{y}) - (w - w^e) - b_2\eta(p - p^e)$$
$$+ b_{12}c^e - b_2\alpha(k - l), \tag{27'}$$

which is the open-economy version of (27). So now the price mark-up on wages depends not only on demand, nominal inertia, and trend productivity, but also on competitiveness.

Turning to wage-bargaining, recall that among the wage pressure variables there is the real wage resistance effect generated by the wedge between product wages and consumption wages (see Chapter 4, Section 7). This wedge includes not only taxes on labour but also the discrepancy between the GDP deflator and the consumer price index (p_c). In addition to excise taxes, this depends on the real price of imports, $e + p_m^* - p$, where p_m^* is the price of imports in foreign currency. So, if there is real wage resistance, a rise in the real price of imports induces upward pressure on the product wage. If we write the real price of imports as

$$e + p_m^* - p = (p_m^* - p^*) + (e + p^* - p)$$
$$= (p_m^* - p^*) + c,$$

then we can treat $(p_m^* - p^*)$, the world relative price of imported goods, as an exogenous source of wage pressure, and competitiveness as the endogenous part. So we can add these effects into our basic equation from Section 1 (equation (28)) to obtain

$$w - p = \gamma_0 - \gamma_1 u - \gamma_{11} \Delta u - \gamma_2 (w - w^e) + b_2 \alpha (k - l) + z_w + \gamma_{12} c, \quad (28')$$

where z_w now includes $(p_m^* - p^*)$ and we have included competitiveness explicitly. Note that an improvement in competitiveness *raises* wage pressure by making consumption goods more expensive relative to domestic value added output.

Finally, there remains the question whether the impact of competitiveness on price- and wage-setting persists in the long run or is simply a short-run phenomenon. Note that, if these were permanent effects, the impact of a rise in competitiveness on price-setting would enable firms to set a higher mark-up on costs and therefore to improve permanently their domestic profit share, *ceteris paribus*. Equally, a permanent effect of competitiveness on wage-setting implies that workers are able to offer real wage resistance indefinitely. Neither is perhaps very plausible, so we may suppose that, in the end, these effects disappear. However, as we have already seen in Chapter 4 (Section 7), real wage resistance effects may influence unemployment for at least a decade, so investigating their 'equilibrium' consequences is an appropriate strategy.

Extending the demand side

In the open-economy context the demand side must be treated in greater depth, and so we set out a complete *IS–LM* system. Suppose we have

$$\text{IS curve:} \quad y_d = \sigma_1 x - \sigma_2 (i - \dot{p}^e) + \sigma_3 c \quad (52)$$

$$\text{LM curve:} \quad m - p = -l_1 i + l_2 y_d, \quad (53)$$

where x now includes not only fiscal stance but also an indicator of world economic activity and the world relative price of imports $(p_m^* - p^*)$, i is the domestic nominal interest rate, and $\dot{p}^e$ is expected inflation. Next assume we have uncovered interest parity, namely,

$$i = i^* + \dot{e}^e, \quad (54)$$

where i^* is the foreign nominal interest rate and $\dot{e}^e$ is the expected rate of exchange rate depreciation.

In order to close the model, we must also specify $\dot{e}^e$, and so we suppose that

$$\dot{e}^e = \dot{p}^e - \dot{p}^{*e} - \omega(c - c^*), \qquad (55)$$

where c^* is the long-run expected level of competitiveness[17] and $\dot{p}^{*e}$ is expected foreign inflation. So expected depreciation is simply the inflation differential modified by a tendency for the exchange rate to help competitiveness towards its long-run expected level. If we write down the reduced form of the demand side, we obtain

$$y_d = \sigma_{11}x + \sigma_{12}r^* + \sigma_{13}(m - p) + \sigma_{14}\dot{p}^e + \sigma_{15}c^*, \qquad (56)$$

$$c = -c_{11}x + c_{12}r^* + c_{13}(m - p) + c_{14}\dot{p}^e + c_{15}c^*, \qquad (57)$$

where $r^* = i^* - \dot{p}^{*e}$, the foreign real interest rate, and all the parameters are positive.[18] If $\omega = 0$, then $\sigma_{11} = \sigma_{15} = c_{15} = 0$. So if expected depreciation depends only on relative inflation rates, then (as in Mundell–Fleming) fiscal policy has no impact on demand because it is entirely offset by exchange rate shifts. Of course, if inflationary expectations ($\dot{p}^e$) are influenced by fiscal stance, this is no longer the case.

The key point, however, is that with predetermined prices both demand and competitiveness are exogenous to the model though they can be manipulated by fiscal and monetary policy (via the fiscal stance part of x, and the money supply m in (56) and (57)).[19] Of course, under model-consistent expectations, expected demand (y_d^e) and expected competitiveness (c^e) cannot be manipulated at will, and only the surprises will count. With this caveat in mind, however, we shall suppose that the model can now be analysed treating demand (y_d) and competitiveness (c) as exogenous in the short run.

In the light of this, we can now take the open-economy version of our model as consisting of the price and wage equations (27'), (28') along with the relationship between demand and unemployment (26) and the demand equations (56), (57). Given expectations, these equations determine demand, competitiveness, unemployment, wages, and prices, with output and employment being determined by the production function (17) and the definition of unemployment (25). In equilibrium, we have $p = p^e$, $w = w^e$, $y_d = y_d^e$, $c = c^e$, $\varepsilon = 0$; and this yields

$$u^* = \frac{(b_0 + \gamma_0) + z_w + (b_{12} + \gamma_{12})c}{\gamma_1 + (b_2 - b_{11})\alpha}, \qquad (58)$$

$$(w - p)^* = \frac{(b_2 - b_{11})\alpha\gamma_0 - b_0\gamma_2}{\gamma_1 + (b_2 - b_{11})\alpha} + \frac{(b_2 - b_{11})\alpha z_w}{\gamma_1 + (b_2 - b_{11})\alpha} \tag{59}$$

$$+ \frac{[\gamma_{12}\alpha(b_2 - b_{11}) - \gamma_1 b_{12}]}{\gamma_1 + (b_2 - b_{11})\alpha} c + b_2\alpha(k - l),$$

$$y_d^* = -\alpha u^* + \bar{y}. \tag{60}$$

These equations may be contrasted with their equivalents in the closed-economy model (equations (31), (32), (33) above). In this case, while there remain competitiveness effects on price- and wage-setting ($b_{12}, \gamma_{12} \neq 0$), we have a whole set of unemployment rates consistent with no surprises, depending on the level of competitiveness. The more competitive the economy, the higher is equilibrium unemployment. This is because of the wage pressure generated by the lower living standards associated with the higher level of competitiveness (more expensive imports). Thus, in order to obtain a lower level of unemployment with no surprises, fiscal and monetary policy can simply be adjusted to raise demand and lower competitiveness appropriately. Given that we have one degree of freedom here, the question is, How should we define equilibrium? The most natural method is to impose a trade balance condition, since a persistent deficit or surplus is hardly consistent with a stationary equilibrium.[20] Of course, as Carlin and Soskice (1990) emphasize, while it may be hard to run an indefinite deficit, running a permanent surplus may not be such a serious problem. However, we shall stick with our definition of equilibrium in order to keep things straightforward.

In order to complete the model, therefore, we must specify an equation for the trade balance (surplus) as a proportion of potential income, tb. This we suppose to depend positively on competitiveness and negatively on demand (in deviation form), so we have an equation of the form

$$\delta_2 tb = c - \delta_0 - \delta_1(y_d - \bar{y}) + z_c, \tag{61a}$$

where z_c reflects exogenous factors tending to improve the balance of trade. The level of competitiveness consistent with trade balance, c', is thus given by

$$c' = \delta_0 + \delta_1(y_d - \bar{y}) - z_c. \tag{61b}$$

Then our equilibrium is defined by (58), (59), (60), (61), and equilibrium unemployment ($\hat{u}$) is given by

$$\hat{u} = \frac{(b_0 + \gamma_0) + z_w + (b_{12} + \gamma_{12})(\delta_0 - z_c)}{\gamma_1 + (b_2 - b_{11})\alpha + (b_{12} + \gamma_{12})\delta_1\alpha}. \tag{62}$$

So in the no-surprise, trade balance equilibrium, the level of unemployment is influenced not only by wage pressure (z_w), but also by any exogenous factors which improve the balance of trade (z_c). This latter will, however, apply only so long as there remain competitiveness effects on wage- or price-setting. If these die away in the very long run, then the trade balance terms will disappear.

Corresponding to this equilibrium level of activity, there exist equilibrium levels of demand and competitiveness given by

$$\hat{y}_d - \bar{y} = -\alpha \hat{u}; \qquad \hat{c} = \delta_0 - \delta_1 \alpha \hat{u} - z_c. \tag{63}$$

So monetary and fiscal policy must be consistent with these levels (via (56) and (57)); otherwise the economy will move away from equilibrium. In the next section we consider how the open economy behaves in response to various kinds of shock.

5. The behaviour of the open economy

In order to keep things simple, we shall extend the NAIRU model of Section 3 to the open-economy framework. Thus, we suppose that only price surprises enter the wage and price equations and that these have the $\Delta^2 p$ form. So, following on from (27) and (28), the price and wage equations corresponding to (44) and (45) become

$$p - w = \beta_0 - \beta_1 u - \beta_2 \Delta^2 p + \beta_{12} c - \beta_3 (k - l), \tag{44'}$$

$$w - p = \gamma_0 - \gamma_1 u - \gamma_2 \Delta^2 p + \gamma_{12} c + z_w + \beta_3 (k - l), \tag{45'}$$

where we omit the hysteresis terms. (The role of hysteresis is no different here, so further exploration of this aspect of the economy is unnecessary.) As before, we ignore technology shocks and so the model is completed by the demand–unemployment relationship and the trade balance equation,

$$y_d - \bar{y} = -\alpha u, \qquad \delta_2 tb = c - \delta_0 - \delta_1 (y_d - \bar{y}) + z_c. \tag{64}$$

Competitiveness and demand are determined by (56) and (57), and, as always, output and employment are given by the production function and the relationship between output and demand (17) and (19)).

The four equations given in (44'), (45'), (64) form the supply side of the open-economy model. For given levels of real demand (y_d) and competitiveness (c), determined by (56) and (57), the supply side determines real wages ($w - p$), the change in inflation ($\Delta^2 p$), unemployment (u), and the trade balance (tb). The latter two are given directly in (64), while solving out (44'), (45') and using (64) gives the real wage and the change in inflation as

$$w - p = \frac{\beta_2\gamma_0 - \gamma_2\beta_0}{\beta_2 + \gamma_2} + \frac{\gamma_1\beta_2 - \gamma_2\beta_1}{\alpha(\beta_2 + \gamma_2)}(y_d - \bar{y})$$

$$+ \frac{\gamma_{12}\beta_2 - \gamma_2\beta_{12}}{\beta_2 + \gamma_2}c + \beta_3(k - l) + \frac{\beta_2 z_w}{\beta_2 + \gamma_2}, \tag{65}$$

$$\Delta^2 p = (\beta_2 + \gamma_2)^{-1}\left[(\beta_0 + \gamma_0) + \frac{\beta_1 + \gamma_1}{\alpha}(y_d - \bar{y}) + (\beta_{12} + \gamma_{12})c + z_w\right]. \tag{66}$$

These equations, along with (64), enable us to determine the impact of demand and competitiveness on the key supply-side variables. Thus, for example, suppose demand is fixed at a high level, generating low unemployment. Then (64) and (66) reveal how the choice can be made between an adverse trade balance and low rises in inflation or a favourable trade balance and high rises in inflation, by selecting (respectively) a low or a high level of competitiveness. If competitiveness is low, imports are cheap and wage pressure is low, and if competitiveness is high we have the opposite. This suggests that we have a trade-off between the trade balance and inflation—and indeed unemployment as well, since demand may also vary.

To exhibit this trade-off, all we need do is eliminate y^d and c from the two equations in (64) and (66) to obtain the fundamental supply constraint of the open economy, namely,

$$[\beta_1 + \gamma_1 + (\beta_{12} + \gamma_{12})\delta_1\alpha]u + (\beta_2 + \gamma_2)\Delta^2 p - (\beta_{12} + \gamma_{12})\delta_2 tb$$
$$= (\beta_0 + \gamma_0) - (\beta_{12} + \gamma_{12})z_c + z_w. \tag{67}$$

This corresponds to the unemployment–inflation trade-off in the closed economy. Now we have, instead, a three-way trade-off between unemployment, inflation, and the trade deficit. It is this trade-off that constrains the consequences of short-term monetary and fiscal policy as well as private-sector aggregate demand shocks. Thus, for example, if there is a trade deficit and rising inflation, equation (67) reveals that unemployment *must rise* if inflation is to be stabilized and the trade deficit reduced, unless there is an autonomous improvement on the trade front (z_c rises) or an exogenous fall in wage pressure (z_w falls).

Of course, (67) may be simplified by utilizing the definition of $\hat{u}$, the level of unemployment corresponding to stable inflation and balanced trade. This is determined by (67) when $\Delta^2 p = tb = 0$. Consequently (67) can be reduced to the simple form,

$$[\beta_1 + \gamma_1 + (\beta_{12} + \gamma_{12})\delta_1\alpha](u - \hat{u}) + (\beta_2 + \gamma_2)\Delta^2 p - (\beta_{12} + \gamma_{12})\delta_2 tb = 0. \tag{68}$$

So, as with the simple unemployment–inflation trade-off in the closed economy, the only way the trade-off can be improved is to reduce the equilibrium
unemployment rate $(\hat{u})$.

All this can be illustrated diagrammatically in the following way. For given
competitiveness, we can illustrate the unemployment–inflation trade-off as in
the closed-economy model in Fig. 1. Then, if competitiveness improves, both
wage and price lines shift to the left, yielding a higher stable inflation level of
unemployment as shown in Fig. 5. The story here is as follows. In order to
permit improved competitiveness, we move from u_1^* to u_2^*, and demand must
be reduced by precisely $\alpha(u_2^* - u_1^*)$ in order to keep inflation stable. This may
be achieved by the appropriate mix of monetary and fiscal policy given by (56)
and (57). (Fiscal policy is tightened relative to monetary policy.) It is clear from
this that there exists a complete range of values of c and u consistent with stable
inflation.

This range is illustrated in Fig. 6 as the upward-sloping line. Note that we
put $p - e - p^* (= -c)$ on the vertical axis, which enables us to interpret the
stable inflation curve as the non-inflationary supply curve of the economy. The
downward-sloping line reflects those combinations of unemployment and
competitiveness consistent with trade balance given by (64). The meeting point
of the two lines at A defines the level of unemployment and competitiveness
consistent with stable inflation and balanced trade $(\hat{u}, \hat{c})$. Note that if, in the
very long run, competitiveness no longer influences wage- and price-setting
$(\gamma_{12} = \beta_{12} = 0)$, then the stable inflation line becomes vertical.

If competitiveness and demand move away from $\hat{u}$ and $\hat{c}$, there are four
possible regimes depicted in Fig. 6. It is clear that it is possible to reduce the
level of unemployment consistent with stable inflation at the expense of

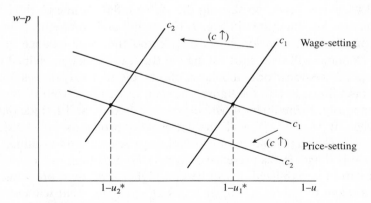

Fig. 5. *Unemployment and competitiveness.*

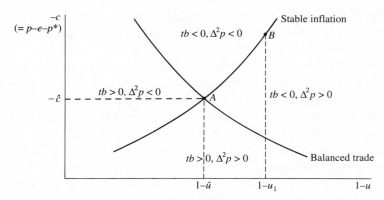

Fig. 6. *The NAIRU consistent with trade balance.*

running a trade deficit by moving to a point such as *B*. Thus, demand is expanded in the context of a tight monetary policy, thereby generating a real currency appreciation which makes imports cheaper and hence reduces inflationary pressure, counterbalancing the increased pressure arising from the expansion in economic activity. This reflects the type of policy pursued in the USA during 1983–4. The persistent trade deficit, of course, ensures that such a policy cannot be sustained indefinitely.

By way of illustration, let us finally consider the consequences of an oil shock such as hit the OECD in 1974. This has two effects. First, the rise in the price of oil is liable to worsen the trade balance at given levels of competitiveness and employment, thereby shifting the trade balance curve to the left. It will also raise the price of imports and hence exert upward pressure on wages via real wage resistance, so shifting the stable inflation line to the left. These consequences are illustrated in Fig. 7. If demand and competitiveness initially remain unchanged, inflation starts to rise and the trade balance moves into deficit. Demand will then start falling via the trade leakage. Helped on by an explicit policy response or real balance effects, the economy moves towards *A'*. On the path illustrated in the figure, the economy suffers from three problems simultaneously: rising unemployment, rising inflation, and a trade deficit; and only when it reaches *A'* will the latter two problems be cured. Higher unemployment will persist so long as real wage resistance is sustained (and for considerably longer in the presence of hysteresis). Furthermore, of course, even when inflation is stabilized, it will be at a higher level than previously, and if action is taken to reduce it, higher levels of unemployment will continue still further into the future.

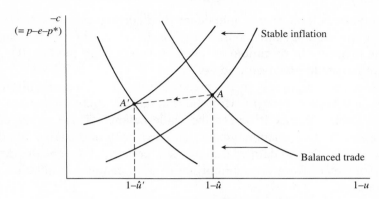

Fig. 7. *The consequences of an oil shock.*

6. Summary

We may summarize the results of this chapter as follows.

1. In a closed economy with imperfectly competitive firms and non-competitive wage determination, there is an equilibrium level of unemployment in which expectations are fulfilled. Corresponding to this is an equilibrium level of real demand.

2. Deviations from equilibrium can arise via demand shocks or real shocks, the most important of which are technology shocks and wage pressure shocks. Three aspects of the economy are important for determining the unemployment effects of these shocks. First, there is the size of the effects of economic activity on wage- and price-setting; the larger are these effects, the smaller are the unemployment consequences of any of the shocks and the more stable is the economy overall. Second, there are the hysteresis effects on wage- and price-setting; the greater are these hysteresis effects, the more persistent will be the consequences of any shock. Third, there is nominal inertia in wage- and price-setting, which is necessary for the transmission of aggregate demand shocks but tends to reduce the unemployment effects of adverse wage pressure shocks.

Corresponding to the unemployment effects of these shocks are their real wage effects. Expansionary aggregate demand shocks can generate real wage movements in either direction, whereas favourable technology shocks lead to increases in the real wage. Reductions in wage pressure, on the other hand, generally lead to falls in real wages.

3. If inflationary expectations are based on the assumption that inflation follows a random walk, then price surprises correspond to changes in inflation.

393

The equilibrium level of unemployment then corresponds to a NAIRU, and the economy faces a fundamental supply-side constraint relating changes in inflation inversely to deviations of unemployment from the NAIRU. This is the unemployment–inflation trade-off.

4. In an open economy, in the medium term, there is an infinity of levels of unemployment consistent with stable inflation, each corresponding to a different level of competitiveness and trade balance. There is, therefore, an 'equilibrium' level of unemployment consistent with both stable inflation and balanced trade. The fundamental supply-side constraint now relates deviations of unemployment from this equilibrium to both changes in inflation and the trade balance.

Notes

1. This model is a direct descendant of the models set out in Layard and Nickell (1985, 1986b, 1987) and has much in common with those described in Rowthorn (1977), Carlin and Soskice (1985, 1990), Blanchard (1986), and Blanchard and Kiyotaki (1987).
2. The serial independence of the technology shocks is assumed merely for expositional convenience. If the technology shocks were serially correlated, we could add the expected part of the shock to k and preserve the innovation as a separate entity. Without loss of generality, therefore, we simply assume that the shock is an innovation.
3. In Annex 8.1, we consider a model where the labour force is allowed to vary.
4. A more systematic treatment of the demand side is provided in the open-economy model of Sect. 4.
5. A satisfactory micro foundation for a demand function of this type is provided in Blanchard and Kiyotaki (1987). It is based on the model due to Dixit and Stiglitz (1977).
6. As in much work of this kind, we systematically ignore the problem that arises because the expectation of a log is not the log of an expectation. This is tantamount to supposing that agents have point expectations.
7. If production were exactly Cobb–Douglas, then b_2 would be $(1 - \alpha)/\alpha$. More generally, $b_2 = (1 - \alpha)/\alpha\sigma$ where α is the elasticity of output with respect to employment and σ is the elasticity of substitution between capital and labour.
8. We use deviation form because the fluctuation of the mark-up is a cyclical phenomenon; that is, it is related to demand relative to some reference level, which here we take to be the full utilization output, ($\bar{y}$).
9. Equivalent to this is the relationship between actual employment and the actual product wage, which can be written as

$$b_2\alpha(n_i - k_i) = -b_0 + b_1(y_d - \bar{y}) - (w_i - p_i) - b_2\varepsilon_i$$
$$+ [(w_i - w_i^e) + b_2\eta(p - p^e) + (b_2 - b_1)(y_d - y_d^e)]$$

This is the marginal revenue product condition, relating the marginal product of labour to the real wage. Two points are worth noting. The real product wage is not, of course, exogenous to the firm since the firm itself sets the price (p_i). Second, the relationship between the marginal product and the real wage shifts with shocks and surprises (in the square bracket) and with the level of demand (y^d). This latter effect arises only if the price mark-up on marginal cost shifts with demand (i.e. if $b_1 \neq 0$).

10.
$$\gamma_0 = \frac{(1 - \lambda)}{\lambda}c_0 - b_{01}$$
$$\gamma_1 = (1 - \lambda)c_1/\lambda - b_2\alpha, \gamma_{11} = (1 - \lambda)c_2/\lambda + b_2\alpha, \gamma_2 = (1 - \lambda)/\lambda$$
$$z_w = [(1 - \lambda)c_3\hat{z}_w + \hat{z}_{1w}]/\lambda$$

11. This procedure is not quite correct if we have expectations that arise from asymmetric information across firms as opposed to expectations that appear because decisions are taken in advance. In the former case, we have the classic islands model (e.g. Barro 1976) where each firm has its own specific information which it can use to form expectations about aggregate variables. In this case, the technique described in the text will give the correct result only if the shocks facing the firms are dominated by firm-specific elements,

for then the firm-specific information is more or less useless. If this is not the case, then some additional 'signal extraction' parameters will appear in the formulae. However, none of the substantive qualitative results are altered.

12. It is, of course, possible for demand shocks to have real effects other than via wage/price stickiness once we get away from the one-good framework; for, as Grandmont (1989) notes, demand multipliers can be induced via supply-side substitution effects. The classic example is via the real interest rate effect on labour supply, where a rise in government expenditure raises real interest rates which raises labour supply and hence output. This is an intertemporal substitution effect. Other examples of intertemporal substitution effects are provided by Kahn and Mookerjee (1988) and Jullien and Picard (1989), whereas Hart (1982) and Dixon (1988) present models that rely on intersectoral substitution. There is, however, very little evidence that such effects are important in practice.

13. In fact, all we need assume is that the inflation process has a unit root.

14. As is well known, NAIRU stands for non-accelerating inflation rate of unemployment. As is also well known, this description is incorrect, having slipped a derivative. It is the price level that is not accelerating, inflation merely being constant. Despite the initials, the NAIRU must be thought of as the level of unemployment consistent with unchanging inflation.

15. The wage gap is simply the difference between the current real wage and the real wage consistent with full employment. It is clear from our example that this concept provides no relevant information in general, and is well defined only if product markets are competitive.

16. This result is founded on the strategic interactions of the kind discussed in Bulow *et al.* (1985).

17. We shall leave the determinants of c^* deliberately vague although it should be thought of as exogenous.

18. $\sigma_{11} = \sigma_1 l_1 \omega / \Delta, \sigma_{12} = \sigma_3 l_1 / \Delta, \sigma_{13} = (\sigma_2 \omega + \sigma_3)/\Delta, \sigma_{14} = l_1(\sigma_2 \omega + \sigma_3)/\Delta,$
$\sigma_{15} = \sigma_3 l_1 \omega / \Delta, c_{11} = l_2 \sigma_1 / \Delta, c_{12} = (l_1 + \sigma_2 l_2)/\Delta, c_{13} = 1/\Delta,$
$c_{14} = l_1/\Delta, c_{15} = (l_1 + l_2 \sigma_2)\omega / \Delta, \Delta = l_1 \omega + l_2(\sigma_2 \omega + \sigma_3).$

19. We are assuming here that long-run inflation expectations, $\dot{p}^e$, do not move systematically to nullify completely any changes in fiscal and monetary policy.

20. This is particularly true given that we are conditioning on the capital stock. If we bring capital accumulation into the story, then it is feasible for there to be a persistent deficit or surplus if there are differential rates of capital accumulation and savings across different countries. There is also the possibility of introducing an intertemporal trade-off. A country could have lower unemployment today at stable inflation by running a trade deficit, at the expense of higher unemployment tomorrow, as it has to run a trade surplus in order to cover the interest on the accumulated debt. We shall, however, ignore these additional complexities.

9

Explaining Post-War Unemployment in OECD Countries

As we have already seen in Chapter 1, since 1960 there have been very large fluctuations in unemployment in many OECD economies. Furthermore, patterns of unemployment over this period have differed dramatically across countries, as the figures in Table 1 amply testify.

Two features of these data are immediately apparent. First, in every country, unemployment is higher in the 1980s than in the 1960s. Second, in the European Community (EC) group, unemployment is vastly higher in the 1980s and considerably higher in the late 1970s in comparison with the 1960s. In contrast, in the European Free Trade Association (EFTA) group and in Japan, the rise in unemployment is modest. The Oceania and North America groups are somewhere in between.

In order to set the scene for our analysis, it is worth looking briefly at the record of the OECD as a whole. In Figs. 1 and 2 we show, respectively, the OECD unemployment rate and inflation rate (GDP deflator). We see that in 1968 the OECD inflation rate started to rise quite sharply and that this was followed by the unemployment rate in 1970. Then in the early 1970s inflation really took off, as did unemployment in 1974. In 1979–80 inflation again rose sharply and unemployment shot up once more. Finally, in the early 1980s inflation fell sharply and continued falling until it reached a level last seen in the early 1960s. From the mid-1980s until 1990, unemployment fell gradually although it was still far higher than in the early 1970s. A particularly striking feature of these data is that, while inflation declined sharply after each peak, unemployment fell back only partially from its peaks in 1972, 1976, and 1983: it clearly exhibits a far greater degree of long-term persistence than does inflation.

Since the late 1960s the broad pattern of events is one in which inflation and

397

Table 1 *Unemployment in OECD countries, 1960–1990 (%)*

	1960–8	1969–73	1974–9	1980–5	1986–90
EC					
Belgium	2.3	2.4	6.3	11.3	9.5
Denmark	2.0	1.4	5.5	9.3	8.6
France	1.7	2.6	4.5	8.3	9.8
W. Germany	0.7	0.8	3.2	6.0	5.9
Ireland	5.0	5.6	7.6	12.6	16.2
Italy	3.8	4.2	4.6	6.4	7.7
Netherlands	1.2	2.0	5.1	10.1	8.8
Spain	2.4	2.7	5.3	16.6	18.7
UK	2.6	3.4	5.1	10.5	8.8
Oceania					
Australia	2.2	2.0	5.0	7.6	7.2
New Zealand	0.2	0.3	0.8	3.9	5.6
North America					
Canada	4.7	5.6	7.2	9.9	8.3
USA	4.7	4.9	6.7	8.0	5.8
Japan	1.4	1.2	1.9	2.4	2.5
EFTA					
Austria	1.6	1.1	1.5	3.0	3.4
Finland	1.8	2.3	4.4	5.1	4.3
Norway	2.0	1.7	1.8	2.6	3.5
Sweden	1.3	1.8	1.5	2.4	1.7
Switzerland	0.1	0.0	1.0	1.7	1.9

Note: Detailed sources may be found in Annex 1.6.

unemployment have moved together, although with unemployment tending to lag a year or two behind. There were three clear upward surges in both, followed by a downward drift from the early 1980s. This suggests that the OECD must have been hit by a succession of supply shocks, and these are readily identified. The first of these follows the world-wide surge in industrial militancy in the late 1960s, which is evidenced by the sharp rise in industrial conflicts to be seen in Fig. 3. The reasons underlying this were much debated at the time (see e.g. Nordhaus 1972; Wiles 1973) and continue to be discussed (e.g. Flanagan *et al.* 1983; Newell and Symons 1989). Thus, Nordhaus argued that the wage explosion of the time was generated by the rise in the general level of world prices initiated essentially by the inflationary expansion in the USA in the late 1960s. Being a demand-side explanation, however, this fails to explain the simultaneous rise in unemployment. Others, such as Wiles or, more

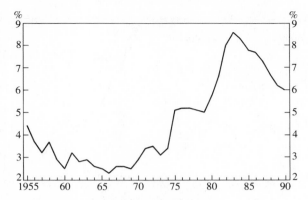

Fig. 1. *OECD unemployment rate, 1955–1990.*

The rate presented is the OECD labour-force-weighted average of the individual country rates.

Source: see Annex 1.6.

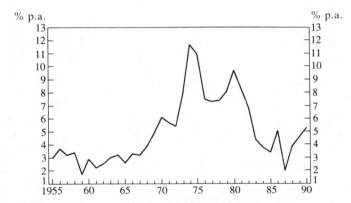

Fig. 2. *OECD inflation: changes in GDP deflator, 1955–1990.*

Sources: IMF, *International Financial Statistics*, and OECD, *Main Economic Indicators*.

recently, Newell and Symons, identify real forces in the various labour markets as the driving variables.

The subsequent shocks are, of course, the successive oil and commodity price shocks of the 1970s and 1980s, illustrated by the path of real primary commodity prices (including oil) shown in Fig. 4. There were sharp upward shifts in 1973–4 and 1979–80, followed by a dramatic downward move

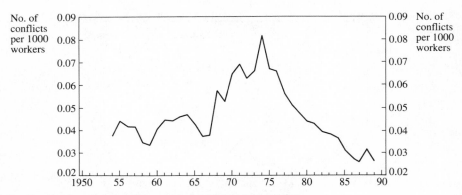

Fig. 3. *Industrial conflicts in the OECD, 1954–1989.*

Sources: ILO, *Yearbook of Labour Statistics*, and OECD, *Labour Force Statistics*.

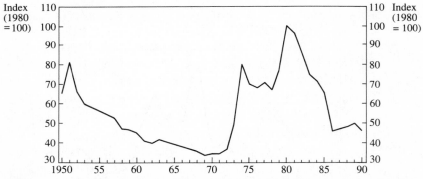

Fig. 4. *Real commodity prices (including oil), 1950–1990.*

Sources: UN, *Statistical Papers* Series M, no. 82, and *Monthly Bulletin*; IMF, *International Financial Statistics*; OECD, *Main Economic Indicators*.

culminating in the oil price collapse of 1986. In the late 1980s, real commodity prices were back at the level of the early 1960s.

The patterns of unemployment in Table 1 thus represent, at least in part, the response of each country to these shocks. It should, however, be emphasized that the size of these shocks differed widely across countries. In some countries, there was no increase in industrial militancy in 1968–9, whereas in others it was very marked. Similarly, the impact of the changes in commodity prices was much lower in commodity-rich countries with a low import–GDP ratio, such as the USA, compared with commodity-poor, very open economies, such as Ireland or Belgium.

Our first job, then, is to utilize the framework which we have developed in previous chapters to try and explain the unemployment patterns across countries. This involves setting out a version of our basic model which is suitable for this purpose, and providing estimates of the key parameters for each country. This will take up the first two sections. Then in Section 3 we look at the extent to which we can explain the overall pattern of unemployment across countries. We also see how important the key parameters of the model are in this regard. In Section 4, we focus on the parameters themselves and relate them to institutional and other features of the different economies. Thus, for example, we already know from Chapter 1 that the duration of unemployment benefits is a powerful variable in explaining cross-country differences in unemployment. Here we attempt to elucidate the reason for this by looking at how benefit duration is related to the important structural parameters of the economic system.

Section 5 presents a unified single-equation model of unemployment changes across the OECD. The idea here is to specify and estimate an equation which explains unemployment in all the OECD countries by allowing the coefficients for each country to depend systematically on institutional features. We then compare its explanatory power with individual country equations based on lagged unemployment and trends. Finally, in Section 6 we present a case-study of the British economy, focusing on the supply-side trade-offs between unemployment, inflation, and the trade balance.

1. The model

Our approach is based on Section 3 of Chapter 8. The basic model has the log-linear form

$$(1 - \beta' L)(p - w) = \beta_0 - \beta_1 u - \beta_{11} \Delta u - \beta_2 \Delta^2 p, \tag{1}$$

$$(1 - \gamma' L)(w - p) = \gamma_0 - \gamma_1 u - \gamma_{11} \Delta u - \gamma_2 \Delta^2 p + (1 - \gamma') z_w, \tag{2}$$

where $p =$ GDP deflator, $w =$ wages, $u =$ unemployment rate, $z_w =$ long-run wage pressure, and $L =$ lag operator. These equations follow from (44), (45) in Chapter 8 with two adjustments. First, we include a lagged dependent variable, both because the theory in previous chapters indicates the presence of dynamics, and because all estimated equations will have one. Second, we omit the productivity terms because they are not germane to our story, although all the estimated equations will, of course, include them.

Recall that z_w reflects all autonomous sources of wage pressure. These include industrial relations factors, the search effectiveness of the unemployed, mismatch factors, and real wage resistance factors. Commenting briefly on each, industrial relations factors are included because the strength of unions, and the extent to which this strength is utilized to raise wages, are obviously potential sources of wage pressure (see Chapters 2, 4). The search effectiveness of the unemployed and mismatch are both important because they influence the effective supply of labour at given levels of measured unemployment (see Chapters 5, 6). Finally, real wage resistance factors refer specifically to the situation where workers resist falls in their standard of living or its rate of growth. These falls may arise from an increase in the wedge between the real product wage and the real consumption wage or a slowdown in the rate of productivity growth (see Chapter 4).

2. Evidence on the parameters

In order to investigate unemployment movements in the OECD countries, we first estimate the parameters appearing in equations (1) and (2). These are based mainly on the equations in Tables A1 and A2 of the Appendix to this chapter, which we compare in Table A3 to other estimates from Bean *et al.* (1986), Newell and Symons (1985), Alogoskoufis and Manning (1988), Grubb (1986), and Grubb *et al.* (1983). It immediately becomes apparent on looking at the numbers that, for many countries, there is no overall consensus. In order to come up with a single parameter value for use in our analysis, some judgement is therefore required and our decision is explained in the Appendix. The resulting number is, perhaps, more of a 'guesstimate' than an estimate. It is also clear that we are not in a position to take account of all the particular features of each country when producing the estimates. So the whole process is bound to be somewhat rough and ready. However, it seems better to try and produce some overall picture, however broad-brush, than to give up at the outset on the grounds that it is all too difficult.

To provide estimates of the parameters, we use the following procedure.

Price equation

We start from the marginal revenue product condition written as a dynamic employment equation (see Chapter 8, n. 9 and Chapter 7, equation (21)) which has the simplified log-linear form

$$(n - k) = \lambda_0 + \lambda_1(n - k)_{-1} - \lambda_2(w - p) + \lambda_2'(w - p)_{-1}$$

$$+ \lambda_3(y_d - \bar{y}) + \lambda_4\Delta^2 w, \tag{3}$$

$$(y_d - \bar{y}) = -\alpha u, \tag{4}$$

where n = employment, k = capital stock, and $y_d - \bar{y}$ = demand index. The term in $\Delta^2 w$ reflects nominal inertia in price-setting (capturing the surprise term $w - w^e$). Equation (4) is the standard demand–unemployment relationship reflecting the production function (see Chapter 8, equation (46)). Noting that, if the labour force is l, then $l - n = u$, and (3), (4) can be transformed into the standard price equation form

$$p - w = \beta_0 + \beta'(p - w)_{-1} - \beta_1 u - \beta_{11}\Delta u - \beta_2\Delta^2 w$$

$$+ \text{productivity terms in } (k - l)$$

where

$$\beta_0 = -\lambda_0/\lambda_2, \quad \beta' = \lambda_2'/\lambda_2, \quad \beta_1 = (1 - \lambda_1 - \lambda_3\alpha)/\lambda_2, \quad \beta_{11} = \lambda_1/\lambda_2, \quad \beta_2 = \lambda_4/\lambda_2.$$

Assuming that $\Delta^2 w = \Delta^2 p$ then gives us the form of the price equation (1).

The reasons for following this rather convoluted procedure are, first, that most of the existing cross-country evidence comes in the form of estimates of equation (3), and second, that if there is a large competitive sector in the product market, then (3) is the natural—indeed, only—equation to estimate. A further point worth noting is that the hysteresis term (β_{11}) is directly related to employment inertia (λ_1), as we have already seen in Chapter 7. So we should expect such pricing hysteresis to be directly related to employment adjustment costs.

In order to estimate equation (3), we require a demand shift variable, $(y_d - \bar{y})$. We consider two alternatives. In the first, we follow a procedure used in Bean *et al.* (1986), taking deviations of GDP from potential GDP and regressing this on a series of demand factors, specifically current and lagged values of taxes, government expenditure, deviations of world trade from trend, and competitiveness; $(y_d - \bar{y})$ is then the fitted value from this regression. In the second method, we compute trend GDP by taking the fitted value from a regression of GDP on a quintic in time. We then simply use deviations of GDP from this trend, treating it as endogenous if the current value is utilized. Otherwise the variables in (3) are straightforward, although it should be emphasized that w is the gross wage including employment taxes.

Wage equation

For the wage equation we use direct estimates of equation (2), and the only problem is how to specify the wage pressure factors (z_w). Following the existing literature and bearing in mind the data constraints, we use three variables. The first is the change in the wedge between the real product wage and the real consumption wage, Δwedge. This is defined as $\Delta(t_1 + t_2 + p_c - p)$, where t_1 is the employers' labour tax rate, t_2 is the income tax rate, p_c is the consumer price index, and p is the GDP deflator. Note that this variable captures terms-of-trade shocks as well as tax shocks, and was used by Newell and Symons (1985). The second variable is the Newell–Symons 'wage explosion' dummy, XP, which takes the value 1 from 1969 to 1977. As we have seen in the introduction to this chapter, this period was one of unprecedented industrial conflict in the OECD, and Newell and Symons have found a marked increase in wage pressure in many countries during this time. However, in some countries we found that the dating used by Newell and Symons was not suitable, and we simply carried the dummy through to the end of the sample period rather than allowing it to cease in 1977. Furthermore, in Spain the starting point of the dummy is misplaced, all the evidence suggesting that the Spanish wage explosion began in 1973 with the death of Franco's prime minister, Mr Carrero-Blanco (see Dolado *et al.* 1986). Finally, we have an indicator of the search effectiveness of the unemployed. (In fact, the indicator used captures anything that makes the matching of unemployed individuals to vacancies more efficient: see Chapter 5.) Following Bean *et al.* (1986), we generate the variable by first estimating a Beveridge curve and then taking the negative of the estimated shift in the curve as a measure of search effectiveness. More specifically, we estimate

$$\log u = \varphi_0 - \varphi_1 \log v + \varphi_2 \log u_{-1} + \varphi_{31} t + \varphi_{32} t^2 + \varphi_{33} t^3,$$

where v = vacancy rate, and we take $-(\hat{\varphi}_{31} t + \hat{\varphi}_{32} t^2 + \hat{\varphi}_{33} t^3)$ as the relevant 'search' variable. The theory underlying this is discussed in Chapter 5.

Aside from this, the estimation of (2) is straightforward, although, of course, we include measures of trend productivity. The derivation of the parameters is set out in the Appendix, which covers each country in turn. Note that a bar over a parameter is the long-run coefficient; i.e., in the notation of (1) and (2), $\bar{\beta}_1 = \beta_1/(1 - \beta')$, etc.

Before reporting the results, two matters must be considered in some detail. The first of these is the use of the rate of change of inflation, $\Delta^2 p$, to capture nominal inertia. In so far as such inertia reflects nominal surprises of the form $(p - p^e)$, our procedure is clearly open to the Lucas critique. That is, we are assuming that price expectations are accurately approximated by $p^e = p_{-1} + \Delta p_{-1}$. This approximation is clearly not robust to any changes in monetary policy, for example, which lead to dramatic shifts in the inflation process. There are two points to be made on this issue. First, we do not make use of these equations to investigate the consequences of any policy changes, let alone ones that involve large changes in the monetary regime. Second, over the relevant period, the process driving inflation actually has a near unit root, so our approximation represents an accurate description of price surprises in the 1970s and 1980s. We have experimented with using fitted values from regression estimates of the inflation process to capture expectations and the results are quite consistent with those reported here. In the light of this, and given the difficulty of observing expectations, we are content with the simple approximation embodied in our use of inflation changes.

The second issue is the thorny question of the identification of the wage equation. Looking at equations (1) and (2), it is clear that, as they are written, the wage equation is not identified. Of course, (1) and (2) do not form a complete model, containing as they do three endogenous variables (w, p, u). There are, in fact, plenty of demand-side instruments available (e.g. tax rates and world trade), so there is no problem with the order condition for identification. It is the rank condition that is not satisfied, because any multiple of equation (1) can be added to equation (2) without changing its structure.

There are several points worth noting in this regard. First, the equations as currently estimated are identified in the formal sense. It might, however, be felt that the zero restrictions imposed are somewhat arbitrary and that identification is not, therefore, achieved in practice. In this case, one can only note that, if our subsequent analyses of the wage equation coefficients accord closely with prior theoretical considerations, it is unlikely that what we are analysing is complete rubbish. Second, even if our estimated wage equations are, in fact, mixtures of the true wage and price equations, our reduced-form estimates as embodied in equations (7) and (8) below, for example—and hence our explanations of unemployment patterns—remain totally unaffected.[1]

The resulting complete set of parameters is presented in Table 2, along with some derived parameters. Before discussing them in detail, some explanations are in order. For the purposes of analysing long-run secular shifts in unemployment, it is convenient to rewrite (1) and (2) in long-run form as

$$p - w = \bar{\beta}_0 - \bar{\beta}_1 u - \bar{\beta}_2 \Delta^2 p, \tag{5}$$

$$w - p = \bar{\gamma}_0 - \bar{\gamma}_1 u - \bar{\gamma}_2 \Delta^2 p + z_w. \tag{6}$$

Table 2   *Model Coefficients (Equations (1),(2))*

	Unemployment effects				Hysteresis		Nominal inertia			
	β_1	γ_1	$\bar{\beta}_1$	$\bar{\gamma}_1$	β_{11}	γ_{11}	β_2	γ_2	$\bar{\beta}_2$	$\bar{\gamma}_2$
Belgium[a]	−0.03	0.65	−0.04	4.06	2.13	0	0.10	0	0.14	0
Denmark	−0.02	0.66	−0.02	1.74	0.98	0	0	0.05	0	0.13
France	−0.18	2.22	−0.18	4.35	10.10	0.73	0.60	0.14	0.60	0.27
Germany[a]	0.58	0.55	0.58	1.01	3.58	0	0.54	0.13	0.54	0.24
Ireland[a]	0.75	0.80	1.88	1.82	4.04	0	0.46	0	1.15	0
Italy	1.04	2.07	3.35	12.94	4.45	2.51	0.69	0	2.23	0
Netherlands[a]	0.83	0.66	1.66	2.28	3.34	0.36	0.47	0	0.94	0
Spain	0.48	0.17	0.73	1.21	0.93	0	0	0.15	0	1.07
UK	0.18	0.98	0.28	0.98	0.31	0.75	0.58	0	0.91	0
Australia	0.26	0.56	0.18	0.73	1.25	0	0.13	0	0.09	0
New Zealand[a]	1.14	1.71	1.14	3.23	6.00	0	0.67	0.15	0.67	0.29
Canada	0.50	0.50	0.76	2.38	1.51	0.17	0	0.90	0	4.28
USA	3.10	0.32	3.10	0.94	−0.15	0.09	2.10	0.37	2.10	1.08
Japan	0.32	6.40	1.69	14.50	1.44	−3.69	0.15	0.01	0.79	0.02
Austria	0.63	1.43	5.73	3.11	2.30	0	0.30	0.63	2.72	1.37
Finland[a]	1.91	0.48	1.91	1.55	12.60	0.33	3.10	0.12	3.10	0.39
Norway	2.31	1.96	2.31	10.59	11.15	2.74	1.00	0.70	1.00	3.78
Sweden	1.10	2.31	1.10	12.16	14.43	0	1.61	0.68	1.61	3.57
Switzerland[a]	0.59	1.32	0.59	7.33	2.53	0	1.47	0.31	1.47	1.72

[a] In these countries, $\log u$ appears in the wage equation. The coefficient γ_1 reported here refers to the coefficient on $\log u$ divided by the average unemployment rate, 1969–85.
Note: RWR = real wage rigidity; NWR = nominal wage rigidity.

Eliminating the real wage and rearranging yields

$$u = \frac{\bar{\beta}_0 + \bar{\gamma}_0}{\bar{\beta}_1 + \bar{\gamma}_1} - \frac{\bar{\beta}_2 + \bar{\gamma}_2}{\bar{\beta}_1 + \bar{\gamma}_1}\Delta^2 p + (\bar{\beta}_1 + \bar{\gamma}_1)^{-1}z_w. \qquad (7)$$

This is the static version of equation (49) in Chapter 8, which we have already discussed at some length. The coefficient on $\Delta^2 p$ captures the long-run inflation–unemployment trade-off or nominal wage rigidity (NWR). In practice, it reflects the long-run cumulative unemployment cost of reducing inflation by one point. In fact, the term 'nominal wage rigidity' is slightly misleading, since it can be positive even if there is no nominal inertia in wage-setting but only in price-setting (i.e. if $\gamma_2 = 0$). The coefficient on z_w captures the extent to which wage pressure is converted into unemployment at constant inflation: this is known as real wage rigidity (RWR).

Table 2—*continued*

	RWR $(\bar{\beta}_1 + \bar{\gamma}_1)^{-1}$	NWR $(\bar{\beta}_2 + \bar{\gamma}_2)$RWR	H $\dfrac{\beta_{11} + \gamma_{11}}{\beta_1 + \beta_{11} + \gamma_1 + \gamma_{11}}$	Mean lag (ML) (equation (8))
Belgium	0.25	0.04	0.77	0.70
Denmark	0.58	0.08	0.60	0.45
France	0.23	0.20	0.84	2.72
Germany	0.63	0.49	0.76	2.55
Ireland	0.27	0.31	0.71	3.19
Italy	0.06	0.14	0.69	2.87
Netherlands	0.25	0.24	0.71	2.51
Spain	0.52	0.56	0.59	2.75
UK	0.77	0.70	0.48	1.36
Australia	1.10	0.10	0.60	1.08
New Zealand	0.23	0.22	0.68	1.64
Canada	0.32	1.37	0.63	1.77
USA	0.25	0.80	-0.02	1.62
Japan	0.06	0.05	-0.50	<0
Austria	0.11	0.46	0.53	<0
Finland	0.29	1.01	0.79	4.60
Norway	0.08	0.37	0.76	2.80
Sweden	0.08	0.39	0.81	1.44
Switzerland	0.13	0.41	0.57	0.41

The columns headed H and mean lag (ML), are measures of hysteresis. If we eliminate $(w - p)$ from (1) and (2) directly and rearrange, we obtain

$$u = \frac{\beta_0 + \gamma_0}{\Omega} + \frac{(\beta_{11} + \gamma_{11})}{\Omega} u_{-1} - \frac{(\beta_2 + \gamma_2)}{\Omega} \Delta^2 p + \frac{(1 - \gamma')}{\Omega} z_w$$

$$+ \frac{(\beta' - \gamma')L}{(1 - \beta'L)\Omega}(\beta_0 - \beta_1 u - \beta_{11}\Delta u - \beta_2\Delta^2 p), \tag{8}$$

where L is the lag operator and $\Omega = (\beta_1 + \gamma_1 + \beta_{11} + \gamma_{11})$. H is simply defined as $(\beta_{11} + \gamma_{11})/\Omega$, the coefficient on the lagged dependent variable if we ignore the terms arising from the wage–price lags. ML, on the other hand, is the mean lag on unemployment taking account of all the dynamics.

Turning to the actual parameters, there are a number of features worthy of comment. Real wage rigidity is very low in EFTA and Japan, and high in the EC countries and Oceania, with North America somewhere in between. Italy is, however, a notable exception in EC, as is Finland in EFTA. There is no particular pattern to nominal wage rigidity although it should be noted that in most countries nominal inertia is more prevalent in price-setting than in wage-setting. Hysteresis is a pervasive phenomenon, being absent only in Japan, the USA, and Switzerland. It is a feature of price-setting as well as wage-setting, since persistence is determined by the sluggish adjustment of factors and not only by insider or long-term unemployment effects in wage determination. Looking at the effects of economic activity or unemployment on wage and price determination, we see that these are generally much more marked in wage-setting than in price-setting (that is, $\bar{\gamma}_1 \gg \bar{\beta}_1$). In fact, the average size of this parameter in wage-setting (average $\bar{\gamma}_1 = 4.60$) is more than three times that of the corresponding price-setting parameter (average $\bar{\beta}_1 = 1.41$). This reflects the overall weakness of demand effects in pricing behaviour which is a well-known feature of much empirical work in this area (see Chapter 7).

Having obtained our parameter estimates, the next step is to make an attempt to explain the patterns of unemployment.

3. Explaining changes in unemployment

In order to check that our model is consistent with the broad movements of unemployment in each country, we undertake a number of experiments. First, we analyse the changes in unemployment from the early 1970s to the early 1980s in terms of the commodity price shocks and the RWR parameter, based on the general form of the long-run equation (7). Second, we focus on the changes in unemployment from the mid-1980s to the late 1980s in response to the favourable commodity price shock in the middle of the period, again using (7) as the basic tool. Finally, we estimate a dynamic reduced-form equation of the type specified in (8) for each country and check that the lagged dependent variable coefficient is appropriately related to the corresponding structural coefficients derived from the model parameters.

From the early 1970s to the early 1980s

Turning to the first experiment, we report in Table 3 the total change in unemployment from the early 1970s to the early 1980s and the changes in the rate of change of inflation between these two periods. In addition, we present measures of the size of the two oil shocks on each country, the real wage rigidity parameter (RWR) and the nominal wage rigidity parameter (NWR). Recall that RWR converts wage pressure into unemployment at constant inflation and NWR converts changes in inflation into unemployment. In order

Table 3 *Change in unemployment (1969–73) to (1980–85) and key explanatory factors*

	Δu	$\Delta(\Delta^2 p)$	Shock	RWR	NWR
Belgium	8.9	−0.7	7.6	0.25	0.04
Denmark	7.8	−1.0	6.3	0.58	0.08
France	5.7	−1.4	1.6	0.23	0.20
Germany	5.1	−1.3	3.4	0.63	0.49
Ireland	6.9	−3.4	8.8	0.27	0.31
Italy	2.3	−2.9	5.0	0.06	0.14
Netherlands	8.0	−1.2	7.2	0.25	0.24
Spain	13.8	−2.5	−0.1	0.52	0.56
UK	7.1	−1.9	0.7	0.77	0.70
Australia	5.6	−2.1	2.1	1.10	0.10
New Zealand	3.6	−1.2	6.3	0.23	0.22
Canada	4.3	−2.2	2.9	0.32	1.37
USA	3.1	−1.1	2.8	0.25	0.80
Japan	1.2	−1.4	5.1	0.06	0.05
Austria	1.9	−1.2	0.8	0.11	0.46
Finland	2.7	−0.9	3.7	0.29	1.01
Norway	0.9	−1.1	2.4	0.08	0.37
Sweden	0.6	−1.1	5.7	0.08	0.39
Switzerland	1.7	−0.9	−1.5	0.13	0.41

Regressions

(1) $\Delta u + (NWR)\Delta(\Delta^2 p) = 1.47 + 1.96(RWR)\text{Shock} + 11.17\text{SP}$ $R^2 = 0.70$
$\qquad\qquad\qquad\qquad\quad (4.3) \qquad\qquad\qquad (5.4)$ $N = 19$

(2) $\Delta u = 1.93 - 0.35(NWR)\Delta(\Delta^2\text{p}) + 1.90(RWR)\text{Shock} + 11.59\text{SP}$ $R^2 = 0.72$
$\qquad\qquad (0.5) \qquad\qquad (4.1) \qquad\qquad\quad (5.4)$ $N = 19$

Variables

Δu = change in unemployment rate (1980–5) − (1969–73) (percentage points)
$\Delta(\Delta^2 p)$ = change in annual increase in inflation (1980–5) − (1969–73) (percentage points).

$$\text{Shock} = \left[\sum_{73}^{81} s_{mt}\Delta\log(P_M/P)_t\right] 100.$$

s_{mt} = import share, P_M = domestic price of imports, $P = GDP$ deflator.
$RWR = (\bar{\beta}_1 + \bar{\gamma}_1)^{-1}$, $NWR = (\bar{\beta}_2 + \bar{\gamma}_2)RWR$.
SP = dummy for Spain.

Note: In these and subsequent regressions, all countries are included for which the relevant variables are available.

to measure the size of the oil shocks, we take the percentage rise in real import prices weighted by the share of imports. In the column labelled 'Shock', we show the total rise in weighted real import prices over the period 1972–81.

The first notable feature of Table 3 is the enormous variation in the size of the shocks sustained by each country. Some economies that produce hardly any primary commodities, such as Belgium, Ireland, and the Netherlands, sustain total shocks that are several times larger than those experienced by the commodity-rich countries such as Australia, Canada, Norway, and the USA. This puts their poor unemployment performance in a considerably more favourable light.

To investigate how well our estimates of real and nominal wage rigidity explain unemployment changes, consider equation (7) in difference form. In the present context we have

$$\Delta u + NWR \times \Delta(\Delta^2 p) = \gamma(RWR) \times \text{shock}. \tag{7'}$$

The parameter γ converts our measure of shock into wage pressure (so $\gamma \times \text{shock} = \Delta z_w$ in equation (7)).

In Table 3 we report this regression, the only modification being that we include a dummy for Spain (SP) to take account of the domestically generated wage explosion that occurred at the end of the Franco era at the same time as the first oil shock. The fit of the regression is good, since we explain at least 70 per cent of the change in unemployment even after having removed that part of the variation arising from the shift in the rate of change of inflation between the two periods. In regression 2 we check on the robustness of this result, by including the inflation shift as a separate regressor. Here we discover that the coefficient on the nominal wage rigidity term is negative and not significantly different from unity. Otherwise, the results are almost unchanged. Overall, therefore, our estimated parameters provide us with a good explanation of the cross-country variation in unemployment shifts up to the beginning of the 1980s.

From the mid-1980s to 1989–90

In our next experiment, we set ourselves a somewhat harder task, namely to explain the shifts in unemployment between the middle and the end of the 1980s. The reason why this is harder is, first, because the variable we are trying to explain is partly a forecast and second, because the change is outside the sample period utilized to estimate the parameters (which ended in 1986). The key numbers are presented in Table 4, the shock in this case being the sum of weighted real import price changes from 1985 to 1988. The parameters RWR

Table 4 *Change in unemployment (1983–85) to (1989–90), and key explanatory factors*

	Δu	Δ(Δ²p)	Shock	RWR	NWR
Belgium	−4.0	1.2	−9.3	0.39	0.05
Denmark	−0.4	1.0	−6.5	0.58	0.08
France	−0.3	1.8	−3.5	0.23	0.20
Germany	−2.1	1.7	−4.7	0.85	0.65
Ireland	−0.8	3.8	−5.4	0.33	0.38
Italy	0.5	1.8	−5.2	0.06	0.14
Netherlands	−3.7	2.1	−8.7	0.33	0.31
Spain	−3.0	1.7	−6.5	0.52	0.56
UK	−5.1	1.0	−3.1	1.23	1.12
Australia	−2.6	−0.3	−2.5	1.10	0.10
New Zealand	2.7	−2.9	−10.0	0.42	0.41
Canada	−3.3	2.3	−3.1	0.32	1.37
USA	−2.7	1.8	−0.3	0.25	0.80
Japan	−0.4	1.0	−6.1	0.06	0.05
Austria	−0.5	1.6	−5.1	0.11	0.46
Finland	−1.8	1.0	−5.3	0.31	1.08
Norway	2.1	1.1	0.6	0.08	0.37
Sweden	−1.1	1.1	−4.2	0.08	0.39
Switzerland	−0.8	1.7	−5.0	0.23	0.73

Regression

$\Delta u = 0.72 - 1.39(NWR)\Delta(\Delta^2 p) + 0.61(RWR)$ Shock $R^2 = 0.46$
          (3.2)   (2.4) $N = 19$

Variables

Δu = change in unemployment rate (1989–90) − (1983–5) (percentage points)

$\Delta(\Delta^2 p)$ = change in annual increase in inflation (1989–90) − (1983–5) (percentage points).

Shock = $100 \sum\limits_{86}^{88} s_m \Delta \log(P_M/P)_t$.

$RWR = (\bar\beta_1 + \bar\gamma_1)^{-1}$, $NWR = (\bar\beta_2 + \bar\gamma_2)RWR$.

Note: RWR and NWR are different from those in Tables 2 and 3 because, for those countries in which $\log u$ enters the wage equation, $\bar\gamma_1$ refers to the period 1980–90 rather than the period 1969–85. See Appendix for the relevant numbers.

and *NWR* are not the same as in Table 3 because, for those countries where $\log u$ enters the wage equation, we define γ_1 as the coefficient on $\log u$ divided by average unemployment in the 1980s. Again, note the very large variations in both unemployment changes and the size of the shock. The result is presented in Table 4 and reveals that we can explain almost half the variation in the unemployment change with the two variables. This is a reasonable perform-

411

ance, although not as good as the level of explanation achieved for the unemployment changes up to the early 1980s.

One particular feature that stands out is the much smaller coefficient on *RWR* compared with the Table 3 regressions. This simply reflects the much smaller downward shifts in unemployment (so far) consequent on the large favourable shifts in real commodity prices in the mid-1980s, compared with the very large upward movements in unemployment consequent on the unfavour-able commodity price shifts of comparable size in the 1970s. Of course, the hysteresis dynamics may not yet have had time to work through fully, but, given the time since the favourable oil shock (1985–6), it seems unlikely that this is the whole story. There definitely appears to be some form of asymmetry in response which has not been fully captured by our parameters.

The form of asymmetry consistent with this result is that real wage resistance does not work so strongly in reverse. In other words, if there is an adverse terms-of-trade shock, real wage resistance, captured by the wedge term in the wage equation, generates an increase in wage pressure and a rise in unemploy-ment at constant inflation. When the terms-of-trade shock is favourable, however, the reduction in wage pressure is smaller, per unit shock, than the corresponding increase in the adverse case. Falls in living standards are strongly resisted, but 'windfall' rises in living standards are not seen as a reason for any great moderation in wage demands. While this is a not unappealing story, it must be admitted that, at the present time, we do not have much in the way of either theory or empirical evidence to support it.

A dynamic unemployment equation

In our final experiment, we wish to check on the robustness of the hysteresis or persistence parameters. So for each country we run a reduced-form unemploy-ment equation of the form

$$u = \alpha_o + \alpha_1 u_{-1} + \alpha_{21}\Delta^2 p + \alpha_{22}\Delta^2 p_{-1} + \alpha_{31}\text{search} + \alpha_{32}\text{search}_{-1}$$
$$+ \alpha_{41}\Delta\text{wedge} + \alpha_{42}\Delta\text{wedge}_{-1} + \alpha_5 XP.$$

Then, in Table 5 we present the lagged unemployment coefficient, α_1, and the corresponding structural parameter, namely the mean lag on unemployment, *ML* (see Table 2). The regression in Table 5 reveals a fairly strong relationship between the reduced-form and structural persistence coefficients, i.e. between α_1 and *ML*.

Overall, therefore, it would appear that our simple structural model is good at explaining differences in long-run changes in unemployment across coun-tries up until the mid-1980s, but rather less good at explaining the further

Table 5 *Persistence*

	Lagged u *coefficient* (α_1)	*Structural persistence* (ML)
Belgium	0.36	0.70
Denmark	0.52	0.45
France	0.88	2.72
Germany	0.38	2.55
Ireland	1.16	3.19
Italy	0.82	2.87
Netherlands	0.80	2.51
Spain	1.11	2.75
UK	0.55	1.36
Australia	0.76	1.08
New Zealand	0.34	1.64
Canada	0.60	1.77
USA	0.62	1.62
Japan	0.46	0
Austria	0.21	0
Finland	0.78	4.60
Norway	0.28	2.80
Sweden	0.69	1.44
Switzerland	0.12	0.41

Regression

$$\alpha_1 = 0.35 + 0.14 \, ML, \qquad R^2 = 0.36, \, N = 19.$$
$$(3.1)$$

Variables

α_1 is the coefficient on u_{-1} in a regression of the form

$$u = \alpha_0 + \alpha_1 u_{-1} + \alpha_{21}\Delta^2 p + \alpha_{22}\Delta^2 p_{-1} + \alpha_{31}\text{search}$$
$$+ \alpha_{32}\text{search}_{-1} + \alpha_{41}\Delta\text{wedge} + \alpha_{42}\Delta\text{wedge}_{-1} + \alpha_4 XP.$$

The mean lag on unemployment in this equation is $1/(1 - \alpha_1)$.

ML is the mean lag on unemployment derived from the structural parameters (see Table 2).

changes until 1990. However, enough has been done to demonstrate that our estimates of the key parameters are good enough to explain a substantial fraction of the different unemployment patterns.

4. Explaining the key parameters

Having seen the important role played by the key parameters of our model in explaining patterns of unemployment movement between countries, we now attempt to explain the parameters themselves. The idea here is to relate the parameters to institutional or socio-political features of the different countries and, thereby, gain a deeper understanding of the whole process.

The six key parameters we consider are the activity or unemployment effects $(\bar{\beta}_1, \bar{\gamma}_1)$, the hysteresis coefficients $(\beta_{11}, \gamma_{11})$, and nominal inertia coefficients $(\bar{\beta}_2, \bar{\gamma}_2)$. We take these in order.

The impact of economic activity (unemployment) on price-setting $(\bar{\beta}_1)$

The main substantive empirical results noted in Chapter 7 are that the role of demand in price-setting is weak and that this weakness is particularly marked in monopolistic industries. Unfortunately, we have no comparable measures of average concentration levels across countries, so we present two rather feeble proxies in Table 6: an indicator of average firm size, and the degree of openness. As can be seen from the regressions, there is no relation between these variables and the impact of unemployment on price-setting $(\bar{\beta}_1)$. This is hardly surprising and need not disturb us unduly, because the role of this parameter in explaining unemployment differences is small relative to the role of the corresponding wage parameter $\bar{\gamma}_1$, which is typically larger and has a much higher degree of variation.

The impact of economic activity (unemployment) on wage-setting $(\bar{\gamma}_1)$

It is apparent from our previous results that the effect of unemployment on wages $(\bar{\gamma}_1)$ is a key parameter. As we have seen in previous chapters, unemployment influences wages because it reflects the disutility of job loss. (See Chapter 4, Section 5 for a complete discussion.) The impact of unemployment on wages, therefore, depends both on the extent to which the disutility of job loss influences wages, and on the extent to which unemployment accurately captures such disutility. Starting with the latter, it is clear that, for given levels of measured unemployment, the disutility of job loss is much reduced if the unemployment benefit level is high and if benefit entitlements have a long duration. Not only is the unpleasantness of unemployment thereby considerably reduced, but, because of the reduced search effectiveness of the unemployed, it becomes easier to find alternative employment, there being less competition for jobs (see Chapter 5). A second point in this context relates to the system of wage-bargaining. As noted in Chapter 2 (Section 6), if bargaining is centralized or co-ordinated, unemployment takes on a key role. If there is only one union bargain covering the entire workforce, the only alternative to employment is unemployment: in contrast to firm- or industry-level bargain-

Table 6 *Unemployment effect in the price equation*

	$\bar{\beta}_1$	Percentage of employees in large firms (PLF)	Openness M/Y
Belgium	−0.04	41.3	0.55
Denmark	−0.02	35.3	0.32
France	−0.18	49.4	0.18
Germany	0.58	60.2	0.21
Ireland	1.88	37.9	0.50
Italy	3.35	46.4	0.21
Netherlands	1.66	—	0.48
Spain	0.73	—	0.15
UK	0.28	66.3	0.24
Australia	0.18	48.6	0.17
New Zealand	1.14	—	0.27
Canada	0.76	—	0.22
USA	3.10	71.0	0.07
Japan	1.69	33.3	0.11
Austria	5.73	38.2	0.32
Finland	1.91	57.6	0.26
Norway	2.31	—	0.43
Sweden	1.10	54.1	0.26
Switzerland	0.59	—	0.33
Expected effect		−	+

Regressions

$\bar{\beta}_1 = 1.45 + 0.14\ (M/Y)$, $R^2 = 0.00,\ N = 19$.
$\quad\quad\ \ (0.10)$

$\bar{\beta}_1 = 3.19 - 2.19\ (M/Y) - 0.023\ PLF$, $R^2 = 0.03,\ N = 13$.
$\quad\quad\ \ (0.5)\quad\quad\quad (0.5)$

Variables

M/Y = imports/GDP (OECD dataset).

PLF = percentage of employees in manufacturing who work in firms that employ more than 500 people (OECD, *Employment Outlook*, 1985, Table 26).

ing, employment elsewhere is not an option. For this and a variety of other reasons discussed in Chapter 2, the aggregate level of unemployment plays a much more important role in centralized bargaining and hence will have a more powerful impact on wages.

Turning now to the extent to which the disutility of job loss influences wages, it is clear that the key factor here is the extent to which wage-bargaining in firms can be insulated from the rigours of the external labour market. This is related to the notion of insider power extensively discussed in Chapter 4. The evidence presented there indicates the possibility that such power is more easily exercised in the presence of unions and less easily exercised in the small-firm sector. In the latter, effective barriers to labour market competition are much harder to erect, since workers are dispersed and the product market is likely to be more competitive.

In Table 7 we present the relevant data. Measures of the benefit replacement ratio, the duration of benefit entitlement, and the coverage of the system capture the essential features of the benefit structure. We next present a whole group of variables which capture the institutional structure of wage-bargaining. The first ($CORP$) is an index of the degree of centralization of wage-bargaining or corporatism due to Calmfors and Driffill (1988). In the same paper, these authors argue that this is not the relevant measure, because low levels of centralization are as good as high levels of centralization in restraining wages. While we do not find this argument persuasive (see Chapter 2, Section 6), we feel that it is worth investigating, and so the second index ($CORP'$) is the adjusted index, also from Calmfors and Driffill (1988). Others, notably Tarantelli (1986), have argued that centralization is not the only relevant feature of the industrial relations system: the degree of consensus is also important, where here consensus refers essentially to a situation where the relevant interest groups broadly agree on the distribution of income. Tarantelli's own index is $TCORP$, where note that Japan, for example, has a much higher ranking than in the other indices. The next two columns ($UNCD$, $EMCD$) are indices of the extent of union and employer co-ordination in the context of wage-bargaining. (See Chapter 2 for a complete discussion.) Two further columns ($SH1$, $SH2$) capture related features of the industrial relations system and refer to measures of strike incidence during the 1960s. McCallum (1983), who constructed these series, argues that they reflect the degree of consensus in the economy, with the 1960s being chosen to ensure that these measures are exogenous to the events of the 1970s and 1980s, which we are concerned to explain. Note that all the indices that reflect bargaining institutions, with the exception of $UNCD$, $EMCD$, are ordered so that the smallest numbers refer to maximum corporatism/consensus. They should, therefore, be negatively related to the impact of unemployment on wage ($\bar{\gamma}_1$). Finally, we have unionization and the proportion of employment in small firms, both of which relate to labour market competition (negatively and positively, respectively).

The results for the full sample (where the percentage of small firms is omitted) have two important features. First, the level and duration of benefits play an important role in explaining the unemployment coefficient, particularly duration. Second, some of the measures of centralization/co-ordination are significant. The most compelling of these is the combined degree of union and employer co-ordination (equation (3)), which has a very strong effect, indicating that a move from minimum to maximum total co-ordination (from 2 to 6) suffices to raise the long-run unemployment effect on wages by 6.8. The union effect is small and insignificant. If we turn to the restricted sample, we find a significant role for the proportion of small firms.

To summarize, in explaining the impact of unemployment on wages, the role of benefit duration is clear-cut throughout, with some evidence that the proportion of small firms, the degree of inter-union and inter-employer co-ordination in wage-bargaining, and the benefit replacement rate have an effect. Among other things, this helps to explain our previous finding, in Chapter 1, that high benefit durations are strongly correlated with high levels of unemployment.

While the role of benefit durations and small firms has not been emphasized in previous work, there has been much discussion in the literature on the importance of corporatism and related variables. The seminal work in the economics literature is due to McCallum (1983) and Bruno and Sachs (1985), who respectively found that measures of strike incidence in the 1960s and an index of corporatism (due to Crouch 1985) were positively related to economic performance after the first oil shock. Both Freeman (1988*b*) and Calmfors and Driffill (1988) were critical of this work, because they thought that a high level of decentralization should also work well and, in the former case, because the whole business of corporatism indices is highly subjective. This led Freeman to utilize, not without some success, an index of wage dispersion instead.

Others have pursued the somewhat more structural approach favoured here, typically relating indices of corporatism to estimates of the $\bar{\gamma}_1$ parameter. Bean *et al.* (1986), Newell and Symons (1985, 1987*a*), and Alogoskoufis and Manning (1988) have all produced interesting results along these lines.

Hysteresis in price-setting (β_{11})

Hysteresis effects in price-setting are crucially related to employment adjustment costs (see Chapter 7) or, more generally, adjustment costs relating to any factor of production. Thus, when economic activity expands, marginal costs and hence prices will tend to rise more rapidly in the short run, before capacity and employment have fully adjusted, reverting back to their normal level only when adjustment is complete.

In Table 8 we report a number of measures which capture the extent of

Table 7 *Unemployment effects in the wage equation*

	$\bar{\gamma}_1$	Replace-ment ratio (RR)	Benefit duration (BD)	Coverage of benefits	Centralization of wage bargaining		
					CORP	CORP'	TCORP
Belgium	4.06	60	48	85	8	14	7
Denmark	1.74	90	30	73	4	2	4
France	4.35	57	45	41	11	16	9
Germany	1.01	63	48	61	6	9	2
Ireland	1.82	50	48	67	12	12	11
Italy	12.94	2	6	21	13	11	12
Netherlands	2.28	70	48	—	7	13	6
Spain	1.21	80	42	35	11	16	12
UK	0.98	36	48	73	12	12	11
Australia	0.73	39	48	—	10	17	6
New Zealand	3.23	38	48	—	9	15	8
Canada	2.38	60	6	—	17	4	7
USA	0.94	50	6	34	16	5	7
Japan	14.50	60	6	40	14	10	3
Austria	3.11	60	48	—	1	1	1
Finland	1.55	75	48	—	5	8	6
Norway	10.59	65	18	—	2	2	4
Sweden	12.16	80	14	86/70	3	3	4
Switzerland	7.33	70	12	—	15	6	3
Expected effect	—	—	—	—	—	—	—

Regressions

In no regression did *CORP'*, *SH1*, *SH2*, or *UN* show up as other than completely insignificant.

(1) $\bar{\gamma}_1 = 19.1 - 0.066RR - 0.20BD - 0.45CORP,$ $\quad\quad R^2 = 0.59, N = 19$
$\quad\quad\quad (1.6) \quad\quad (4.5) \quad\quad (2.4)$

(2) $\bar{\gamma}_1 = 13.7 - 0.046RR - 0.15BD - 0.24TCORP,$ $\quad\quad R^2 = 0.46, N = 19$
$\quad\quad\quad (0.9) \quad\quad (3.2) \quad\quad (0.8)$

(3) $\bar{\gamma}_1 = 8.79 - 0.097RR - 0.16BD + 1.70(UNCD + EMCD),$ $\quad R^2 = 0.65, N = 19$
$\quad\quad\quad (2.3) \quad\quad (4.3) \quad\quad (3.0)$

(4) $\bar{\gamma}_1 = 10.3 - 0.059RR - 0.20BD - 0.30CORP + 0.23PSF,$ $\quad R^2 = 0.73, N = 14$
$\quad\quad\quad (1.2) \quad\quad (3.9) \quad\quad (1.2) \quad\quad\quad (2.3)$

(5) $\bar{\gamma}_1 = 4.45 - 0.023RR - 0.17BD - 0.01TCORP + 0.24PSF,$ $\quad R^2 = 0.69, N = 14$
$\quad\quad\quad (0.4) \quad\quad (3.4) \quad\quad (0.1) \quad\quad\quad (2.2)$

(6) $\bar{\gamma}_1 = 3.84 - 0.082RR - 0.17BD + 1.17(UNCD + EMCD) + 0.22PSF,$ $\;R^2 = 0.76, N = 14$
$\quad\quad\quad (1.5) \quad\quad (3.8) \quad\quad (1.6) \quad\quad\quad\quad\quad (2.2)$

Variables

RR = percentage unemployment benefit replacement rates (Annex 1.3).
BD = duration for which benefits continue at a reasonable level, in months; indefinite duration = 48 mos. (Annex 1.3).

418

Co-ordination		Strike frequency		Union (UN)	% of employees in small firms (PSF)
UNCD	EMCD	SH1	SH2		
2	2	5.5	3.7	0.68	32.8
3	3	4.7	3.1	0.53	36.1
2	2	5.5	4.6	0.20	27.7
2	3	3.4	2.3	0.32	20.0
1	1	6.1	4.4	0.31	34.6
2	1	6.6	5.1	0.32	32.8
2	2	3.0	2.2	0.36	34.6
2	1	6.6	5.1	—	—
1	1	5.0	4.0	0.46	20.3
2	1	5.5	4.8	0.46	30
2	1	5.1	4.1	0.37	—
1	1	6.1	4.1	0.28	—
1	1	6.2	4.2	0.28	15.2
2	2	5.1	3.7	0.23	47.1
3	3	3.7	2.9	0.53	37
3	3	6.4	4.3	0.43	23.9
3	3	4.7	2.9	0.64	—
3	3	3.6	1.9	0.70	26
1	3	1.4	0.2	0.29	—
+	−	−	−	−	+

Coverage = percentage of unemployed receiving unemployment compensation (Annex 1.3).
CORP = corporatism: a ranking of the degree of centralization of wage bargains as measured by Calmfors and Driffill (1988: Table 3).
CORP' = adjusted corporatism ranking. Calmfors and Driffill adjusted the original ranking on the basis that low degrees of centralization in wage bargaining are better for economic performance than middle-range levels (see text) (Calmfors and Driffill, 1988: Table 11).
TCORP = index of corporatism which captures not only centralization but also the extent of consensus and the existence of formal arbitration procedures. This is due to Tarantelli (1986).
UNCD = extent of inter-union co-ordination, both formal and informal, in the process of wage-bargaining (see Ch. 1, Table 6 and Annex 1.4). '3' refers to maximum co-ordination both here and in *EMCD*.
EMCD = extent of inter-firm co-ordination, both formal and informal, in the process of wage bargaining (see Ch. 1, Table 6 and Annex 1.4).
SH1, SH2 = normalized strike indicators for the 1950s and 1960s (McCallum, 1983: Table A1).
UN = union density 1965–77 (MaCallum 1983: Table A1).
PSF = percentage of employees in manufacturing who work in firms that employ less than 100 people (OECD, *Employment Outlook*, 1985, Table 26).

419

Table 8 *Hysteresis in the price equation*

	β_{11}	% of employees with tenure < 2 years (PL2)	Severance pay (SEV)	Period of notice (NOT)
Belgium	2.13	18	1.24	1.00
Denmark	0.98	27	0.48	6.00
France	10.10	18	5.24	1.86
Germany	3.58	19	1.00	1.66
Ireland	4.04	22	0	0
Italy	4.45	13	15.86	—
Netherlands	3.34	28	—	—
Spain	0.93	—	13.56	—
UK	0.31	—	—	0.90
Australia	1.25	39	0	0
New Zealand	6.00	—	0	—
Canada	1.15	33	—	—
USA	−0.15	39	0	0
Japan	1.44	21	0	
Austria	2.30	—	0.83	3.00
Finland	12.60	28	—	—
Norway	11.15	—	12.00	3.00
Sweden	14.43	—	0	0.76
Switzerland	2.53	—	0	1.00
Expected effect		−	+	+

Regressions

$\beta_{11} = 6.29 - 0.13PL2 + 6.9FR + 10.6FN$ $R^2 = 0.94, \quad N = 12$
  (3.1)   (5.7)   (9.2)

$\log(1 + \beta_{11}) = 2.60 - 0.052PL2$ $R^2 = 0.32, \quad N = 12$
  (2.2)

$\log(1 + \beta_{11}) = 1.30 + 0.0029SEV$ $R^2 = 0.04, \quad N = 15$
  (0.8)

$\log(1 + \beta_{11}) = 1.26 + 0.041NOT$ $R^2 = 0.006, N = 12$
  (0.3)

Variables

$PL2$ = percentage of manufacturing employees with tenure of less than 2 years (Metcalf 1986: Table 4): the original source is various OECD publications.

SEV = number of months' salary given to workers as severance pay after 10 years of service (Lazear 1990: Table 1).

NOT = number of months' notice required after 10 years of service (Lazear 1990: Table 1).

employment adjustment costs, namely, the percentage of manufacturing employees with current tenure of less than two years (*PL2*) (inversely related) and measures of severance pay and periods of notice (*SEV, NOT*) taken from Lazear (1990). The regression results indicate some relationship between the tenure variable and price hysteresis once we take account of the possibility of nonlinearity, but there is no apparent correlation with the more direct measures of adjustment costs. However, these indicators of cost are unlikely to be very accurate, since they represent legal minima rather than the actual levels that are negotiated. In many cases, negotiated levels will be considerably higher, particularly in countries with strong unions.

There is no other work with which to compare our results, although a number of other authors have looked at the relationship between employment adjustment costs and unemployment. Lazear (1990) finds a significant relationship between such costs and both the employment–population ratio (negative) and unemployment (positive), using data from 23 countries over a 29-year period. On the other hand, Bentolila and Bertola (1990) find that higher firing costs have a slight tendency to increase long-run average employment levels, because the reduced rate of separations slightly offsets the reduced hiring rate.

Hysteresis in wage-setting (γ_{11})

In previous chapters (particularly 2, 3, 4), it became clear that unemployment hysteresis in the wage equation arises from either long-term unemployment or insider effects. Regarding the long-term unemployed, the dynamics are quite complicated. As unemployment rises, in the short run the proportion of long-term unemployed tends to fall because of the influx of new entrants. Since the long-term unemployed both search less intensively and are less desirable as employees, a fall in the long-term proportion increases the effective supply of labour at given levels of unemployment and hence raises the downward pressure on wages. In the long run, however, the proportion of long-term unemployed tends to rise with unemployment, thereby reversing the short-run effect. Insiders may produce hysteresis because, the higher are past levels of unemployment, the smaller are the number of insiders and hence the more upward pressure they can exert on wages without fear of losing their jobs. This positive effect of lagged unemployment on wages naturally leads to the hysteresis phenomenon.

To capture these possibilities, we present in Table 9 a measure of the long-term unemployed proportion, an index of corporatism (note that lower numbers imply more corporatism), indices of inter-union and inter-firm co-ordination in wage-setting, and the percentage of employees in small firms. The

Table 9 *Hysteresis in the wage equation*

	γ_{11}	Long-term unemployed (LTU) (%)	TCORP	UNCD	EMCD
Belgium	0	35.9	7	2	2
Denmark	0	—	4	3	3
France	0.73	30.3	9	2	2
Germany	0	21.2	2	2	3
Ireland	0	31.8	11	1	1
Italy	2.51	35.8	12	2	1
Netherlands	0.36	27.1	6	2	2
Spain	0	27.5	12	2	1
UK	0.75	24.5	11	1	1
Australia	0	21.1	6	2	1
New Zealand	0	—	8	2	1
Canada	0.17	3.5	7	1	1
USA	0.09	4.2	7	1	1
Japan	−3.69	18.8	3	2	2
Austria	0	13.3	1	3	3
Finland	0.33	12.0	6	3	3
Norway	2.74	10.8	4	3	3
Sweden	0	6.8	4	3	3
Switzerland	0	—	3	1	3
Expected effect		+	+	+	−

Regressions

(1) $\gamma_{11} = 1.07 + 0.046LTU - 0.089PSF + 0.10TCORP$ $R^2 = 0.54, N = 13$
        (1.1)   (2.1)   (0.8)

(2) $\gamma_{11} = 0.95 + 0.085LTU - 0.14PSF + 1.81UNCD - 1.09EMCD$ $R^2 = 0.76, N = 13$
        (3.2)   (4.5)   (3.0)   (2.2)

(3) $LTU = 8.97 + 0.37BD - 0.33LMP + 24.9IT$ $R^2 = 0.63, N = 16$
        (3.4)   (1.3)   (2.9)

(4) $LTU = 5.32 + 0.40BD + 28.1IT$ $R^2 = 0.58, N = 16$
        (3.7)   (3.3)

Variables
LTU   = percentage of unemployed with a duration of unemployment of more than 1 year: where possible this is measured for each country when the aggregate unemployment rate is between 5 and 7% (OECD, *Employment Outlook*, various issues).

Table 9—*continued*

% of employees in small firms (PSF)	Expend. on labour market programmes (LMP)	Replacement ratio (RR)	Benefit duration (BD)
32.8	7.4	60	48
36.1	7.9	90	30
27.7	3.9	57	45
20	10.4	63	48
34.6	5.0	50	48
32.8	0.8	2	6
34.6	2.7	70	48
—	2.1	80	42
20.3	4.6	36	48
30	2.8	39	48
—	13.1	38	48
—	4.3	60	6
15.2	2.4	50	6
47.1	5.6	60	6
37	11.3	60	48
23.9	12.9	75	48
—	9.8	65	18
26	34.6	80	14
—	3.7	70	12
—			

TCORP = Tarantelli's index of corporatism (see Table 7).
UNCD = extent of inter-union co-ordination, both formal and informal, in the process of wage bargaining (see Table 7).
EMCD = extent of inter-firm co-ordination, both formal and informal, in the process of wage bargaining (see Table 7).
PSF = percentage of employees in manufacturing who work in firms that employ less than 100 people (see Table 7).
LMP = expenditure on active labour market programmes per unemployed person as a percentage of output per person (Ch. 1, Table 5).
RR = unemployment benefit replacement ratio (see Table 7).
BD = duration for which benefits continue at a reasonable level, in months: indefinite duration = 48 months (see Table 7).

latter we see as being inversely related to insider power, since we expect such power to be exercised mainly in large establishments where a coherent group of insiders can develop. The same applies to the extent of centralization in wage bargaining. Insider power can hardly flourish if wage bargaining is completely centralized. This does not, however, apply if unions alone act in a co-ordinated fashion. This will clearly raise the power of the insiders and hence the level of hysteresis. Employer co-ordination, on the other hand, will offset this. If, for example, employers are co-ordinated but unions are not, then, unlike the employers, the insiders will not be able to co-ordinate their activities across plants and this will weaken their ability to insulate wages from external labour market conditions.

We further include some variables that might explain the long-term propor-tion, notably the benefit replacement rate, benefit duration, and a suitably normalized measure of expenditure on active labour market policies to assist the unemployed (e.g. training, direct job creation).

The regression results indicate that both long-term unemployment and insider effects may well be generating hysteresis, and that benefit duration is crucial in generating long-term unemployment. The dummy for Italy is present in order to cope with the fact that there is essentially no benefit system in Italy and, as a consequence, nearly all the unemployed are either young people or married women who do not need to rely totally on benefits. (For example, in 1983, 61.1 per cent of the unemployed in Italy were aged between 14 and 24, and 69.5 per cent were female!)

Nominal inertia in price-setting $(\bar{\beta}_2)$

The results discussed in Chapter 7 provide us with some clues as to the determinants of the $\bar{\beta}_2$ parameter. First, nominal inertia in price-setting should be negatively related to the variance of both aggregate nominal changes and firm-specific shocks; if either variance is large, future profit-maximizing prices are highly uncertain and the interval between price changes is reduced (see Ball *et al.* 1988). Second, nominal inertia should fall if general inflation is higher. This is again a consequence of the general model of price-setting intervals presented in Ball *et al.* (1988). Third, nominal inertia in price-setting is apparently higher in industries which are more concentrated (see Carlton 1986: 655). Finally, in Chapter 7, we found that prices will probably adjust less rapidly if employment adjustment costs are higher.

In order to investigate these hypotheses, we present, in Table 10, some proxies for the relevant variables. The variance of nominal shocks is captured by the average variance of nominal income changes, whereas that of firm-specific shocks is proxied by the average of the annual absolute change in the proportion of employees in the manufacturing sector. This latter is obviously a very crude measure of the variance of firm-specific shocks, but it is not possible to obtain a more disaggregated breakdown of inter-industry shifts, as in the Lilien (1982) index, that is strictly comparable across countries. By contrast, the average level of inflation, reported in Column 4, is straightforward. On the other hand, capturing the average level of concentration across countries is more or less impossible. To proxy this, we are reduced to measures reflecting firm size and the degree of openness in the economy. Finally, in Column 7 we report an (inverse) proxy for the general level of employment adjustment costs, namely the percentage of manufacturing employees with a tenure of less than 2 years.

Unfortunately, the regressions reported in Table 10 reveal no important relationships between any of the relevant variables and our measure of price inertia, β_2. While this is disappointing, there are, of course, many possible reasons for this, not least the inadequacy of both our estimated coefficients and some of the proxy variables used as regressors. Furthermore, there is more or less no other relevant cross-country evidence on this question. Most of the cross-country work has concentrated on relating variables such as inflation and the variance of shocks not to any direct measure of price inertia but to the so-called output–inflation trade-off, which is closely related to our measure of nominal wage rigidity (NWR). This, of course, depends not only on price inertia $(\bar{\beta}_2)$ but also on wage inertia $(\bar{\gamma}_2)$ and inversely on the level of activity effects $(\bar{\beta}_1 + \bar{\gamma}_1)$. Thus the cross-country correlations between this output–inflation trade-off and such variables as the variance of nominal shocks and the rate of inflation, reported in Lucas (1973), Froyen and Waud (1980), Alberro (1981) (for nominal shocks), and Ball *et al.* (1988) (for inflation), are not directly informative about the matter in hand. (See also the discussion of Ball *et al.* (1988) by Akerlof *et al.* (1988a) in the same volume.)

Nominal inertia in wage-setting $(\bar{\gamma}_2)$

The stickiness of nominal wages arises, at least in part, from the costs of negotiation, although indexation can offset this to some extent (see Chapter 2, Section 7). As with price-setting, we would expect wages to adjust more frequently in response to price changes if nominal income changes exhibit more variation. By doing so, large fluctuations in absolute and relative real wages are prevented. (See e.g. Gray 1976 on the relationship between contract length and the variance of shocks.) However, unlike for price-setting, we have some direct evidence on various features of the wage-bargaining structure in

Table 10 *Nominal inertia in the price equation*

	$\bar{\beta}_2$	Var Δlog (PY)	Relative employment shifts (mm)
Belgium	0.14	0.11	0.018
Denmark	0	0.05	0.010
France	0.60	0.05	0.014
Germany	0.54	0.08	0.013
Ireland	1.15	0.29	0.016
Italy	2.23	0.23	0.013
Netherlands	0.94	0.12	0.020
Spain	0	0.17	0.016
UK	0.91	0.21	0.017
Australia	0.09	0.14	0.024
New Zealand	0.67	0.22	0.019
Canada	0	0.11	0.024
USA	2.10	0.06	0.022
Japan	0.79	0.25	0.015
Austria	2.72	0.06	0.031
Finland	3.10	0.13	0.019
Norway	1.00	0.08	0.021
Sweden	1.61	0.05	0.026
Switzerland	1.47	0.12	0.013
Expected effect	–	–	–

Regressions

$$\bar{\beta}_2 = -0.12 + 0.84\text{var}\Delta\log(PY) + 55.9mm - 0.012\Delta p - 0.49M/Y,$$
$$\quad\quad\quad (0.2) \quad\quad\quad\quad (1.2) \quad\quad (0.1) \quad\quad (0.3)$$
$$R^2 = 0.098, \ N = 19$$

$$\bar{\beta}_2 = -0.67 + 2.13\text{var}\Delta\log(PY) + 35.2mm + 0.24\Delta p - 1.48M/Y - 0.01PL2,$$
$$\quad\quad\quad (0.4) \quad\quad\quad\quad (0.3) \quad\quad (0.9) \quad\quad (0.6) \quad\quad\quad (0.1)$$
$$R^2 = 0.22, \ \ N = 12$$

$$\bar{\beta}_2 = -2.7 + 1.44\text{var}\Delta\log(PY) + 99.0mm + 0.08\Delta p - 0.64M/Y + 0.02PLF,$$
$$\quad\quad\quad (0.4) \quad\quad\quad\quad (1.7) \quad\quad (0.9) \quad\quad (0.3) \quad\quad\quad (0.6)$$
$$R^2 = 0.36, \ \ N = 13$$

426

$\Delta p(\%)$	% of employees in large firms (PLF)	Openness M/Y	% Employees' tenure < 2 years (PL2)
4.51	41.3	0.55	18
6.64	35.3	0.32	27
6.80	49.4	0.18	18
3.76	60.2	0.21	19
6.27	37.9	0.50	22
8.49	46.4	0.21	13
4.79	—	0.48	28
9.62	—	0.15	—
7.02	66.3	0.24	—
6.19	48.6	0.17	39
7.29	—	0.27	—
5.10	—	0.22	33
4.05	71.0	0.07	39
4.76	33.3	0.11	21
4.35	38.2	0.32	—
7.30	57.6	0.26	28
3.68	—	0.43	—
5.38	54.1	0.26	—
4.12	—	0.33	—
—	+	—	—

Variables

$\text{var}\Delta\log(PY)$ = variance of the changes in log nominal GDP (OECD dataset).

mm = average annual absolute change in the proportion of employees in manufacturing (OECD dataset).

Δp = average inflation rate (GDP deflator) (OECD dataset).

PLF = percentage of employees in manufacturing working in firms with more than 500 employees (OECD, *Employment Outlook*, 1985, Table 26).

M/Y = imports as a proportion of GDP (OECD dataset).

$PL2$ = percentage of manufacturing employees with tenure of less than 2 years (see Table 8).

different countries. These refer to the length of wage contracts, the extent of indexation, and the degree of synchronization, all of which are reported in Bruno and Sachs (1985: Table 11.7) and are reproduced, with some adjustments, in Table 11. (Note that the contract-length variable is reported with the higher numbers referring to *shorter* contracts.) We would expect the extent of inertia to be directly related to the average length of wage contracts and inversely related to the extent of indexation. The role of synchronization is rather more subtle, but it is plain from the discussion in Chapter 2 (Section 7), and from the results in Jackman (1984) and Fethke and Policano (1984), that the absence of synchronized wage-setting can lead to increased inertia in the aggregate.

The results reported in Table 11 indicate that both the structure of wage contracts and the variance of nominal shocks bear some relationship to our measure of wage stickiness ($\bar{\gamma}_2$), although the degree of explanatory power is not very strong. In particular, synchronization appears to have no effect, in contrast to other measures.

One other feature of our measure of nominal inertia in wage-setting ($\bar{\gamma}_2$) is worth remarking. That is the apparent high level of this parameter in the EFTA group of countries at the bottom of the table. This was noted by Alogoskoufis and Manning (1988), who see it as a consequence of the high degree of centralization of wage-bargaining which is a general feature of most of these countries. Because wage-bargaining is centralized, the parties to the bargain readily recognize the direct impact of nominal wage increases on the future aggregate price inflation, and this leads them to moderate their response to current price inflation in order to avoid a wage–price spiral. As Flanagan *et al.* (1983: 27–8) point out, 'the relation between wage increases and price increases is more obvious to centralized bargaining institutions'.

Summary of results

In this section, we have attempted to relate our estimates of the key parameters of the basic model to such measures of the institutional or socio-political features of the different countries as are available. The following are the most important results.

Variations across countries in the impact of economic activity on price-setting were generally small, and we were unable to relate them to any available variables, although we have no sensible measure of average industrial concentration across countries. On the other hand, the large variations in unemployment effects on wages are strongly inversely related to the duration of benefits,

Table 11 *Nominal inertia in the wage equation*

	$\bar{\gamma}_2$	Length of wage contracts (LWC)	Indexation in wage contracts (IW)	Synchronization of wage contracts (SWC)	varΔlog (PY)
Belgium	0	2	2	0	0.11
Denmark	0.13	2	2	2	0.05
France	0.27	1	2	0	0.05
Germany	0.24	2	0	2	0.08
Ireland	0	2	—	—	0.29
Italy	0	0	2	2	0.23
Netherlands	0	2	2	1	0.12
Spain	1.07	1	—	—	0.17
UK	0	2	0	0	0.21
Australia	0	2	2	2	0.14
New Zealand	0.29	2	2	2	0.22
Canada	4.28	1	1	0	0.11
USA	1.08	0	1	0	0.06
Japan	0.02	2	0	2	0.25
Austria	1.37	2	0	2	0.06
Finland	0.39	1	1	1	0.13
Norway	3.78	1	1	2	0.08
Sweden	3.57	1	1	2	0.05
Switzerland	1.72	0	0	0	0.12
Expected effect	—	—	—	—	—

Regressions

$$\bar{\gamma}_2 = 3.14 - 0.68LWC - 0.42IWC + 0.21SWC - 8.13\text{var}\Delta\log(PY), \qquad R^2 = 0.33, N = 17.$$
$$\quad\;\;(1.5)\qquad(1.1)\qquad\;\;(0.5)\qquad\;(1.6)$$

$$\bar{\gamma}_2 = 3.22 - 0.50(LWC + IWC) - 8.05\text{var}\Delta\log(PY), \qquad R^2 = 0.31, N = 17.$$
$$\quad\;\;(1.9)\qquad\qquad\quad(1.7)$$

Variables

LWC = 2 if contracts generally 1 year or less,
  1 if contracts generally between 1 and 3 years,
  0 if contracts generally 3 years or more.

IWC = 2 if indexation is widespread,
  0 if there is no indexation.

SWC = 2 if wage contract renewals are more or less completely synchronized,
  1 if there is some synchronization,
  0 if there is no synchronization.

varΔlog(PY) = variance of the changes in log nominal GDP (OECD dataset).

LWC, IWC, SWC are taken from Bruno and Sachs (1985: Table 11.7), with some minor adjustments.

and directly related to the proportion of small firms in the economy. There is also a direct relation to the overall degree of inter-firm and inter-union co-ordination in wage-bargaining. As expected, hysteresis in price-setting appears to be directly related to employment adjustment costs, and unemployment hysteresis in wage-setting to the proportion of long-term unemployed, with the duration of benefits being the key variable in explaining this proportion.

Turning to nominal stickiness, we were unable to explain our estimates of nominal inertia in price-setting. In particular, we could not find any relation-ship between price inertia and either average inflation rates or the variance of nominal shocks. Nominal inertia in wage-setting, on the other hand, does seem to be related to contract length and the degree of indexation, as we might expect, and the variance of nominal shocks also appears to have some role in reducing such inertia.

In the light of these quite promising results, we next proceed to a more direct method of modelling the effect of these institutional factors on the unemploy-ment patterns of the various countries.

5. A common multi-country equation for unemployment dynamics

In order to develop a simple model of unemployment determination which can be applied to all countries, we utilize a simplified version of the general model set out in Section 2 of Chapter 8. This has the following form:

Price
(employment)
equation

$$p - w = \beta_0 + \frac{\beta_1}{\alpha}(y_d - \bar{y}) + \frac{\beta_{11}}{\alpha}\Delta(y_d - \bar{y})$$
$$- \beta_2(p - p^e) - \beta_3(k - l) \tag{9}$$

(Ch. 8, (34))

Wage equation

$$w - p = \gamma_0 - \gamma_1 u - \gamma_{11}\Delta u - \gamma_2(p - p^e)$$
$$+ \beta_3(k - l) + z_w \tag{10}$$

(Ch. 8, (37))

Demand
(Ch. 8, (35a))

$$y_d = \sigma_2(m - p) \tag{11}$$

Production
(Ch. 8, (35b))

$$(y_d - \bar{y}) = -\alpha u \tag{12}$$

Recall that $(y_d - \bar{y})$ is real demand relative to full utilization output, $k - l$ is the capital–labour force ratio, $\bar{y}$ is full utilization output, and m is the money stock. Various terms have been omitted either to keep things straightforward (e.g. terms in $y_d^e - \bar{y}$) or because suitable data are not available (e.g. productivity shocks, ε). If we suppose that money supply changes follow a random walk and that wage pressure (z_w) can be divided into anticipated and unanticipated elements ($\bar{z}_w, \varepsilon_w$ respectively), then we have

$$\Delta m = \Delta m_{-1} + \varepsilon_m, \qquad z_w = \bar{z}_w + \varepsilon_w. \tag{13}$$

In order to generate the unemployment path under rational expectations, we simply specialize our results in Chapter 8 ((39), (40a), (40b)) and obtain

$$u^* = (\gamma_0 + \beta_0 + \bar{z}_w)/(\gamma_1 + \beta_1), \tag{14}$$

the equilibrium rate, and

$$(u - u^*) = \frac{\beta_{11} + \gamma_{11}}{\beta_1 + \gamma_1 + \beta_{11} + \gamma_{11}}(u - u^*)_{-1}$$

$$- \frac{(\beta_2 + \gamma_2)\sigma_2\varepsilon_m}{\alpha(\beta_2 + \gamma_2) + \sigma_2(\beta_1 + \gamma_1 + \beta_{11} + \gamma_{11})}$$

$$+ \frac{\sigma_2\varepsilon_w}{\alpha(\beta_2 + \gamma_2) + \sigma_2(\beta_1 + \gamma_1 + \beta_{11} + \gamma_{11})}. \tag{15}$$

If we now assume that $(\beta_2 + \gamma_2)/(\beta_1 + \gamma_1 + \beta_{11} + \gamma_{11})$ is small relative to unity (note, our average estimate of this parameter across all 19 OECD countries is 0.16), (15) may be simplified using (14) and (13) to give

$$u = \frac{(\beta_{11} + \gamma_{11})u_{-1}}{\beta_1 + \gamma_1 + \beta_{11} + \gamma_{11}}$$

$$+ \left(1 - \frac{\beta_{11} + \gamma_{11}}{\beta_1 + \gamma_1 + \beta_{11} + \gamma_{11}}\right)\left(\frac{\beta_0 + \gamma_0}{\beta_1 + \gamma_1} + \frac{z_w}{\beta_1 + \gamma_1} - \frac{\beta_2 + \gamma_2}{\beta_1 + \gamma_1}\Delta^2 m\right). \tag{16}$$

This will serve as our basic model. In order to apply it to all the countries simultaneously, we must take account of the fact that the parameters are country-specific. So, if i is the country subscript and t is time, our model has the form

$$u_{it} = \omega_{0i} + \omega_{1i}u_{it-1} + (1 - \omega_{1i})\omega_{2i}z_{wit} - (1 - \omega_{1i})\omega_{2i}\omega_{3i}\Delta^2 m_{it}, \tag{17}$$

where

$$\omega_{0i} = \left(1 - \frac{\beta_{11} + \gamma_{11}}{\beta_1 + \gamma_1 + \beta_{11} + \gamma_{11}}\right)\frac{\beta_0 + \gamma_0}{\beta_1 + \gamma_1}, \qquad \omega_{1i} = \frac{\beta_{11} + \gamma_{11}}{\beta_1 + \gamma_1 + \beta_{11} + \gamma_{11}},$$

$$\omega_{2i} = (\beta_1 + \gamma_1)^{-1}, \qquad \omega_{3i} = (\beta_2 + \gamma_2).$$

Each of the ω parameters must be specified in terms of the relevant country characteristics. The constant term (ω_{0i}) we simply specify by a country dummy. The lagged dependent variable coefficient (ω_{1i}) depends crucially on the hysteresis effects ($\beta_{11} + \gamma_{11}$). As we have seen, these depend on employment adjustment costs and wage hysteresis; they are inversely related to the proportion of employees with less than two years' tenure, *PL2* (Table 8), and directly related to benefit duration, *BD* (via the long-term unemployment effect: Table 9).[2] Wage hysteresis is also related to the bargaining structure, and Table 9 indicates two possibilities. Inside power—and hence hysteresis—is lower when bargaining is centralized and is thus inversely related to the degree of corporatism. Here we use the *TCORP* measure due to Tarantelli (1986), which gives the best fit. (Note that our measures of corporatism are rankings such that *lower* numbers refer to *higher* levels of corporatism.) The alternative is to look at the extent of union and employer co-ordination in wage-bargaining (*UNCD, EMCD*), which had opposite effects: union co-ordination tends to increase the power of insiders, and hence hysteresis, whereas employer co-ordination was found to decrease it. In the light of this, we use two versions of ω_{1i}:

$$\omega_{1i} = a_1 - a_2 PL2_i + a_3 BD_i + a_4 TCORP_i$$

or

$$\omega_{1i} = a_1 - a_2 PL2_i + a_3 BD_i + a_{41} UNCD_i - a_{42} EMCD_i.$$

The coefficient specifically related to wage pressure (ω_{2i}) is inversely related to the unemployment effects ($\beta_1 + \gamma_1$). These have been most successfully related to benefit duration (*BD*) and the structure of wage bargaining (see Table 7). We use two alternatives for the latter, either *TCORP* or the sum of union and employer co-ordination (*UNCD + EMCD*), again following the results given in Table 7. So we have two versions of ω_{2i}:

$$\omega_{2i} = b_1 + b_2 BD_1 + b_3 TCORP_i$$

or

$$\omega_{2i} = b_1 + b_2 BD_i - b_{31}(UNCD_i + EMCD_i).$$

The coefficient specific to nominal shocks (ω_{3i}) reflects nominal inertia ($\beta_2 + \gamma_2$) and depends on the relevant wage-bargaining institutions, namely contract length (LWC), indexation (IWC), and synchronization (SWC) (see Table 11). These measures are all negatively related to inertia, so we may write ω_{3i} as

$$\omega_{3i} = m_1 - m_2(LWC_i + IWC_i + SWC_i).$$

As for variables capturing wage pressure and wage shocks (z_{wit}), we use the share-weighted change in real import prices ($s_m \Delta(p_m - p)$), a wage explosion dummy (XP), and a measure of the benefit replacement rate (RR). The wage explosion dummy takes the value unity after 1970, except for Spain, where it takes the value unity only after 1974 for reasons we have already discussed. The impact of this dummy is taken to be somewhat later on unemployment than on wages because of lags in the system. (Recall that in specifying the wage equation, the XP dummy takes the value unity from 1969.) Thus we have

$$z_{wit} = s_m \Delta(p_m - p)_{it-1} + c_1 XP_{it} + c_2 RR_{it}.$$

The two estimated equations for all 19 OECD countries from 1956 to 1988 are set out in Table 12. Overall, the equations look satisfactory, with the relevant variables being correctly signed and significant. But the crux of the matter lies in their ability to explain the data. Recall that we are using only four time-varying variables and a mere 12 parameters (excluding the country dummies) to explain the dramatic fluctuations in unemployment in 19 countries over some 33 years. In order to see how well the data are explained, in

Table 12 *OECD unemployment equations (19 countries, 1956–1988)*

Version 1

$u_{it} = \omega_{0i} + (0.87 - 0.022\ PL2_i + 0.020BD_i + 0.012TCORP_i)u_{it-1}$
    (61.0)   (2.8)   (4.2)   (5.9)

$- [1 - (0.87 - 0.022PL2_i + 0.020BD_i + 0.012TCORP_i)](0.25 + 0.042BD_i + 0.042TCORP_i)$
                            (2.7)   (2.5)   (2.7)

$(s_m\Delta(p_m - p)_{it-1} + 0.12XP_{it} + 0.57XP(SP)_i + 0.25RR_{it} -$
                (2.5)   (1.0)   (2.1)

$[1.94 - 0.53(LWC_i + IWC_i + SWC_i)]\Delta^2 m_{it}).$
(3.0)   (2.5)

433

Version 2

$u_{it} = \omega_{0i} + (0.87 - 0.24\ PL2_i + 0.049BD_i + 0.062UNCD_i - 0.057EMCD_i)u_{it-1}$
  (42.2) (4.9)   (7.7)   (5.0)   (6.7)

$+ [1 - (0.87 - 0.24PL2_i + 0.049BD_i + 0.062UNCD_i - 0.057EMCD_i)]$

$[0.63 + 0.15BD_i - 0.063(UNCD_i + EMCD_i)]$
(2.7) (2.7)   (2.8)

$(s_m\Delta(p_m - p)_{it-1} + 0.082XP_{it} + 0.50RR_{it} - [1.43 - 0.13(LWC_i + IWC_i + SWC_i)]\Delta^2 m_{it}).$
        (2.4)   (2.8)   (3.0)   (1.3)

Notes
  (i) t-ratios in parentheses, 19 OECD countries.
 (ii) Equations estimated by nonlinear 3SLS (SUR) in TSP 4.1A.
(iii) i = country, t = time, u = unemployment rate, $PL2$ = *proportion* of employees with job tenure of less than 2 years, BD = benefit duration *in years*, $TCORP$ = Tarantelli index of corporatism, LWC = duration of labour contracts, IWC = degree of indexation of labour contracts, SWC = synchronization of labour contracts, $EMCD$ = employer co-ordination in wage-bargaining, $UNCD$ = union co-ordination in wage bargaining. For LMP, BD, $PL2$, $TCORP$, $EMCD$, $UNCD$, see Tables 7, 9; for LWC, IWC, SWC see Table 11. s_m = share of imports, $(p_m - p)$ = real price of imports, XP = dummy taking value 1 after 1970, $XP(SP)$ = dummy taking value 1 after 1973, for Spain only, RR = benefit replacement ratio, m = narrow money stock (M1). All the time invariant variables have their means set to zero.
 (iv) Some of the variables reported in the previous tables were incomplete and were filled in on the following basis: $PL2$: $SP = IT = 13$, $NZ = AL = 39$, $UK = NL = 28$, $AU = NW = SW = SZ = FN = 28$. $LWC + IWC + SWC$: $IR = 2$, $SP = 5$.
  (v) It is important to recall that $TCORP$ is an inverse index of corporatism; i.e., high numbers mean low rank and hence a low value of corporatism. Similarly, *high* values of LWC refer to *short* contracts, so ($LWC + IWC + SWC$) is inversely related to nominal inertia.
 (vi) Sources of data: s_m, $(p_m - p)$, m: OECD dataset; RR: Emerson (1988*b*).

Table 13 we present the adjusted R^2 for each country implied by the two versions of the above model and, for comparison, the adjusted R^2 for individual country regressions containing a constant, two lags on unemployment, and a time trend (i.e. 76 parameters in total). The results indicate, first, that the structural models explain over 90 per cent of the variation in

Table 13 *Adjusted R^2 implied by model in Table 12, with comparison*

	Table 12, version 1	Table 12, version 2	Comparison model $(u_{it} = \pi_{0i} + \pi_{1i}u_{it-1} + \pi_{2i}u_{it-2} + \pi_{3i}t)$
Belgium	0.965	0.962	0.966
Denmark	0.938	0.944	0.929
France	0.988	0.988	0.985
Germany	0.909	0.929	0.918
Ireland	0.948	0.952	0.956
Italy	0.879	0.871	0.866
Netherlands	0.964	0.965	0.966
Spain	0.950	0.980	0.991
UK	0.935	0.937	0.939
Australia	0.914	0.907	0.893
New Zealand	0.905	0.915	0.908
Canada	0.889	0.880	0.826
USA	0.734	0.734	0.604
Japan	0.898	0.911	0.900
Austria	0.873	0.875	0.869
Finland	0.830	0.830	0.875
Norway	0.426	0.427	0.395
Sweden	0.597	0.566	0.602
Switzerland	0.833	0.817	0.840
Average $\bar{R}^2$	0.862	0.863	0.854

unemployment in 10 countries and under 80 per cent in only three countries (Norway, Sweden, and the USA). Relative to the country-specific autoregressions plus trend, the structural models have an adjusted R^2 at least as high as the comparison model in 9 out of 19 cases for version 1 and 11 out of 19 cases for version 2. Furthermore, they are lower by more than one percentage point in only three cases (Spain, Finland, and Sweden), with the *average* adjusted R^2 being higher in both versions than that for the country-specific autoregressions, including trends, in explaining unemployment patterns in different countries.

Having estimated these structural models of unemployment, we are in a position to compute the equilibrium path of unemployment for each country, and this we do using version 2 of Table 12, by setting $\Delta^2 m = 0$ and running a dynamic simulation starting from 1960. While this procedure is unlikely to produce results that are as accurate as those that might be obtained by a close analysis of each country, it is worth doing just to see if the numbers are sensible. So in Table 14 we set out average values of actual (u) and equilibrium (u^*) unemployment for three periods: 1960–8, 1969–79, and 1980–8.

For comparison, we also present the difference ($u - u^*$) and the change in inflation ($\Delta^2 p$) for the same periods. Recall that, if the averaging procedure enables us to ignore the unemployment dynamics, these two variables should theoretically be connected by the simple relationship

$$u - u^* = - NWR \times \Delta^2 p.$$

In fact, if we use these data combined with our estimates of nominal wage rigidity (NWR) (see Tables 2, 4), we find the regression result

$$u - u^* = 0.12 - 2.66 NWR \times \Delta^2 p, \qquad R^2 = 0.24, \ N = 57.$$
$$(0.7) \quad (4.2)$$

So, while the relationship between the two variables has a very small constant and is strongly negative, the coefficient on $NWR \times \Delta^2 p$ is uncomfortably far from its correct value of unity. This indicates that either our measure of $u - u^*$

Table 14 *Estimates of the natural rate and the unemployment–inflation trade-off*

	Actual unemployment, u			Equilibrium unemployment, u*		
	1960–8	*1969–79*	*1980–8*	*1960–8*	*1969–79*	*1980–8*
Belgium	2.34	4.53	11.07	3.77	4.82	7.04
Denmark	1.98	3.64	8.56	2.19	4.64	7.30
France	1.69	3.65	8.98	1.76	3.88	7.81
Germany	0.71	2.13	6.07	0.47	1.87	4.04
Ireland	4.99	6.72	14.12	6.08	9.13	13.09
Italy	3.82	4.37	6.87	4.31	4.94	5.42
Netherlands	1.16	3.67	9.89	1.52	4.28	7.27
Spain	2.43	4.12	17.74	4.55	9.73	14.95
UK	2.63	4.30	10.32	2.55	5.15	7.92
Australia	2.17	3.66	7.67	2.35	4.01	6.10
New Zealand	0.18	0.58	4.18	0.43	1.96	3.91
Canada	4.73	6.44	9.48	5.46	7.01	8.14
USA	4.74	5.85	7.38	5.01	5.97	6.36
Japan	1.36	1.61	2.51	1.59	1.82	2.14
Austria	1.61	1.32	3.14	0.94	0.48	2.95
Finland	1.84	3.48	5.01	1.40	2.61	4.65
Norway	2.00	1.75	2.51	2.13	2.22	2.50
Sweden	1.32	1.65	2.21	1.64	1.93	2.36
Switzerland	0.11	0.52	1.87	0.09	0.83	1.44

Table 14—*continued*

| | Annual average | | | | | |
| | 1960–8 | | 1969–79 | | 1980–8 | |
	$u - u^*$	$\Delta^2 p$	$u - u^*$	$\Delta^2 p$	$u - u^*$	$\Delta^2 p$
Belgium	− 1.42	0.29	− 0.29	0.16	4.03	− 0.33
Denmark	− 0.21	0.36	− 1.00	0.03	1.26	− 0.28
France	− 0.07	− 0.22	− 0.23	0.52	1.17	− 0.75
Germany	0.24	0.05	0.26	0.19	2.03	− 0.27
Ireland	− 1.09	0.18	− 2.41	0.80	1.03	− 1.20
Italy	− 0.49	0.22	− 0.57	1.18	1.45	− 1.00
Netherlands	− 0.36	0.39	− 0.61	0.19	2.62	− 0.39
Spain	− 2.12	0.14	− 5.61	0.48	2.79	− 0.14
UK	0.08	0.31	− 0.86	1.32	2.40	− 0.80
Australia	− 0.18	− 0.15	− 0.35	0.67	1.57	− 0.19
New Zealand	− 0.25	0.21	− 1.38	1.20	0.27	− 1.14
Canada	− 0.73	0.31	− 0.57	0.62	1.34	− 0.66
USA	− 0.27	0.31	− 0.12	0.30	1.02	− 0.53
Japan	− 0.23	0.24	− 0.21	− 0.22	0.37	− 0.24
Austria	0.67	− 0.08	0.84	0.12	0.19	− 0.29
Finland	0.44	0.30	0.87	0.36	0.36	− 0.22
Norway	− 0.13	0.39	− 0.47	0.19	0.01	− 0.39
Sweden	0.32	0.14	− 0.28	0.47	− 0.15	− 0.03
Switzerland	− 0.02	0.49	− 0.31	− 0.10	0.43	0.11

Note: u^* is generated from a dynamic simulation of model version 2 in Table 12 with $\Delta^2 m$ and the error term set to zero, beginning at 1960. The other data come from the OECD dataset.

is systematically too big, in absolute value, or our measure of *NWR* is systematically too small. The former is undoubtedly closer to the truth, because in our dynamic simulation the equation error is set to zero, which is equivalent to assuming that no part of the error is influencing the equilibrium unemployment rate u^*. In reality this is unlikely to be the case, and the true value of u^* probably tracks u rather more closely than our estimates indicate. Nevertheless, the very fact that our estimates of the deviation $(u - u^*)$ are so powerfully negatively related to $\Delta^2 p$ indicates some support in the data for our underlying framework.

6. Unemployment in Britain: a case-study of the open economy

The purpose of this section is to illustrate the use of the open-economy model of Chapter 8 (Sections 4, 5) to analyse the role of supply-side constraints in determining the pattern of unemployment in an economy.

Recall that in the open-economy model, with sticky prices, we may think of real demand (relative to full utilization output) $(y_d - \bar{y})$ and competitiveness (c) as exogenously determined on the demand side in the short run. Then, for given levels of these two variables, plus capital and labour force, the 'supply side' determines the real wage, the change in inflation, the trade balance, and the level of unemployment (and hence, of course, the level of output via the production function). In a closed economy there is a fundamental supply-side constraint, namely the unemployment–inflation trade-off. In an open economy the trade-off is three-way rather than two-way. The supply-side constraint consists of a relationship between unemployment, changes in inflation, and the trade deficit. Once any two of these are pinned down by demand-side factors, the constraint fixes the third. Furthermore, the constraint itself can be shifted only by long-run supply-side forces which influence price-setting, wage-setting, or the trade balance. Short-run shifts in monetary and fiscal policy, or other autonomous elements of demand, simply move the economy around on the fixed constraint.

In order to see this more formally, we first derive the constraint from the theoretical model in Chapter 8 and then calibrate it for the British economy and use it to analyse recent movements in the unemployment rate.

A theoretical framework

Here we produce a simplified version of the model used in the last part of Chapter 8:

Price equation
(Ch. 8, (44′))
$$p - w = \beta_0 - \beta_1 u - \beta_2 \Delta^2 p - \beta_3(k - l) \tag{18}$$

Wage equation
(Ch. 8, (45′))
$$w - p = \gamma_0 - \gamma_1 u - \gamma_2 \Delta^2 p + \gamma_{12} c + z_w + \beta_3(k - l) \tag{19}$$

Production
(Ch. 8, (64))
$$y_d - \bar{y} = -\alpha u \tag{20}$$

Trade surplus
(Ch. 8, (64))
$$\delta_2 tb = c - \delta_0 - \delta_1(y_d - \bar{y}) + z_c \tag{21}$$

Aside from the standard symbols used in this chapter, tb is the trade balance as a proportion of potential income, c is competitiveness, and z_c is a set of exogenous variables which act favourably on the trade balance. This set of equations acts as the supply side of the model, and for given levels of real demand $(y_d - \bar{y})$ and competitiveness (c) it determines real wages $(w - p)$, the change in inflation ($\Delta^2 p$), unemployment (u), and the trade balance (tb). The trade balance and unemployment are determined directly by (20) and (21), while solving out (18), (19) and using (20) gives the real wage and the change in inflation as

$$(w - p) = \frac{\beta_2\gamma_0 - \gamma_2\beta_0}{\beta_2 + \gamma_2} + \frac{\gamma_1\beta_2 - \beta_1\gamma_2}{(\beta_2 + \gamma_2)\alpha}(y_d - \bar{y}) + \frac{\gamma_{12}\beta_2}{(\beta_2 + \gamma_2)}c$$

$$+ \beta_3(k - l) + \frac{\beta_2 z_w}{\beta_2 + \gamma_2}, \tag{22}$$

$$\Delta^2 p = (\beta_2 + \gamma_2)^{-1}[(\beta_0 + \gamma_0) + \frac{1}{\alpha}(\beta_1 + \gamma_1)(y_d - \bar{y}) + \gamma_{12}c + z_w]. \tag{23}$$

To identify the fundamental supply-side constraint, we eliminate c and $(y_d - \bar{y})$ from (20), (21), (23) to obtain

$$(\beta_1 + \gamma_1 + \gamma_{12}\delta_1\alpha)u + (\beta_2 + \gamma_2)\Delta^2 p - \gamma_{12}\delta_2 tb = (\beta_0 + \gamma_0 + \gamma_{12}\delta_0) - \gamma_{12}z_c + z_w. \tag{24}$$

Hence the equilibrium rate of unemployment ($\hat{u}$), consistent with stable inflation and balanced trade, is

$$\hat{u} = \frac{(\beta_0 + \gamma_0 + \gamma_{12}\delta_0) - \gamma_{12}z_c + z_w}{\beta_1 + \gamma_1 + \gamma_{12}\delta_1\alpha}, \tag{25}$$

and we can now simplify the supply-side constraint (24) to give

$$(\beta_1 + \gamma_1 + \gamma_{12}\delta_1\alpha)(u - \hat{u}) + (\beta_2 + \gamma_2)\Delta^2 p - \gamma_{12}\delta_2 tb = 0. \tag{26}$$

As already noted in Chapter 8, this constraint is the open-economy equivalent of the unemployment–inflation trade-off in the closed economy and is obviously of profound importance, constraining the consequences of all demand-side shifts whether from the public or the private sector. Thus, for example, at the time of writing in Britain we have a trade deficit ($tb < 0$) and rising inflation ($\Delta^2 p > 0$). Equation (26) then reveals that, unless policy measures can induce a fall in the equilibrium rate ($\hat{u}$), unemployment must rise if inflation is to be stabilized and the trade deficit reduced. Our next step is to attempt to calibrate this model for the British economy in order to see how it operates in practice.

Fixing the model parameters

In order to calibrate the model, we simply estimate the basic equations. This is, of course, a very crude business, ignoring, as it does, all the multifarious complexities that are captured in the larger-scale models of the British economy utilized by HM Treasury, the Bank of England, the London Business School, and the National Institute of Economic and Social Research. So we must not expect too much of the results. However, at least by keeping things simple we can see what is going on, and so in Table 15 we present all the relevant equations. The first two equations are lifted directly from Layard and Nickell (1986*b*). Instead of estimating a price equation and a production function (equations (18), (20) in the theoretical model), we utilize a price equation and a marginal revenue product condition. This is a perfectly legitimate procedure, since the latter is a combination of the price equation and the production function which enables one to capture the dynamics of the production process (caused by adjustment costs) in a simple fashion. (See Chapter 7 for a complete discussion.)

Real demand in terms of deviations from potential output ($y_d - \bar{y}$) is a linear combination of output price competitiveness (c), the adjusted budget deficit, and the deviation of world trade from trend. Nominal inertia in price-setting is captured by changes in wage inflation ($\Delta^2 w$). The trade equation is also taken from Layard and Nickell (1986*b*), although the dependent variable has been re-normalized so that it measures the trade balance as a proportion of potential GDP. The variables that shift the relationship between the trade balance, competitiveness, and real demand include the price of UK imports relative to the world price of manufactures (both in pounds) ($p_m - p^*$) and the real value of North Sea oil production (OIL).

The wage equation is new, incorporating the long-term unemployed proportion, as in Nickell (1987), as well as a new series for the union wage mark-up which reflects union power. The long-term proportion is, itself, explained by the dynamics of unemployment, having the expected property that it falls as unemployment rises in the short run, but increases with unemployment in the long run. Note that the structure of the wage equation reflects that discussed in Chapter 4, although it does have one slightly unsatisfactory feature, namely the fact that real wage resistance is 'permanent' because of the presence of the level terms-of-trade effect. However, as noted in Chapter 4 (Section 7), disentangling short-run effects whose impact lasts for many years from long-run effects is not possible with short runs of data, so we should not be too surprised by this apparent permanent effect.

In order to generate the fundamental supply-side constraint, a few adjustments are in order. First, we must use the long-term unemployment equation to eliminate this variable from the wage equation. The proportion of long-term unemployed (LTU) is given by

$$LTU = 2.20u - 3.89\Delta u + \text{terms in } \Delta^2 u, \Delta^3 u, \text{ etc.} \qquad (27)$$

Table 15   *Equation Estimates for the UK*

Marginal revenue product condition, 1954–83

$n - k = 2.56 + 1.057(n_{-1} - k) - 0.36(n_{-2} - k) - 0.295(w - p)_{-1} + 0.067(y_d - \bar{y})$.

$\quad\quad(8.2)\quad\quad\quad(2.6)\quad\quad\quad\quad(4.9)\quad\quad\quad\quad(3.2)\quad\quad\quad\quad$ s.e. $= 0.0077$

Price equation, 1954–83

$p - w = -4.18 + 0.544(p - w)_{-1} - 0.336\Delta^2 w_{-1} - 0.242\Delta^2 w_{-1} + 0.038(y_d - \bar{y}) - 0.486(k - l)$.

$\quad\quad\quad(5.0)\quad\quad\quad\quad(4.2)\quad\quad\quad\quad(3.8)\quad\quad\quad\quad(2.1)\quad\quad\quad\quad$ s.e. $= 0.015$

Trade balance equation, 1954–83

$tb = 0.0496 + 0.430s'_m c_{-1} + 0.258s'_m(p_m - p^*)_{-1} - 0.047\,(y_d - \bar{y}) + 0.0290(IL)$.

$\quad\quad\quad(2.7)\quad\quad\quad(1.4)\quad\quad\quad\quad(2.3)\quad\quad\quad\quad(1.4)\quad\quad\quad\quad$ s.e. $= 0.012$

Wage equation, 1956–85

$w - p = 8.62 - 0.091logu + 0.193LTU + 0.0495mm + 0.20RR + 0.536s'_m(p_m - \bar{p})$

$\quad\quad\quad(4.8)\quad\quad\quad(2.7)\quad\quad\quad\quad(4.4)\quad\quad\quad\quad(1.5)\quad\quad\quad(2.9)$

$\quad\quad + 0.097s'_m\Delta(p_m - p) + 0.177um_{-1} + 0.359\Delta t + 1.07(k - l)$.

$\quad\quad\quad(0.4)\quad\quad\quad\quad\quad(2.0)\quad\quad\quad\quad(1.6)\quad\quad\quad\quad\quad\quad$ s.e. $= 0.014$

Long-term unemployment equation, 1957–85

$LTU = 0.074 + 0.496LTU_{-1} - 2.15u + 5.65u_{-1} - 2.39u_{-2}$.

$\quad\quad\quad(2.8)\quad\quad\quad(3.7)\quad\quad(5.3)\quad\quad(2.3)\quad\quad\quad\quad$ s.e. $= 0.027$

Notes

(i) $n =$ employment, $k =$ capital stock, $w =$ hourly wage including employment taxes paid by employers, $p = (1 + s'_m)\bar{p} - s'_m p_m =$ value added deflator, $\bar{p} = TFE$ deflator, $p_m =$ price of imports, $s'_m =$ share of imports in GDP, $c =$ log competitiveness $= p^* - \bar{p}, p^* =$ world price of manufactures in domestic currency, $(y_d - \bar{y}) = c + 10.76AD + 1.028WT$, $AD =$ adjusted deficit/potential GDP, $WT =$ deviation of world trade from trend, $l =$ labour force, $tb =$ trade balance (including invisibles) as a proportion of potential GDP, $OIL =$ real value of North Sea oil production in terms of output prices, $LTU =$ proportion of unemployed with duration in excess of one year, $mm =$ absolute change in the proportion of employees in production, $RR =$ replacement ratio, $um =$ union wage mark-up, $t =$ tax wedge $=$ firms' employment tax rate plus income tax rate plus excise tax rate.

(ii) t-ratios in parentheses. Current endogenous variables are instrumented in estimation.

(iii)   Sources of the equations are as follows: marginal revenue product condition: Layard and Nickell (1986*b*: Table 4); price equation: Layard and Nickell (1986*b*: Table 5, col. (1)); trade balance equation: Layard and Nickell (1986*b*: Table 7); wage and long-term unemployment equations: authors.

Sources of data: All the data are described in the appendix to Layard and Nickell (1986*b*) except *LTU*, which is taken from various issues of the *Employment Gazette*, *um*, which is taken from Layard and Nickell (1989: Annex Table 29*b*) and *u*, which is the OECD standardized rate (see Annex 1.6).

Second, when using annual data, we are never able to detect any significant nominal inertia in wage-setting. However, when using quarterly data, Layard and Nickell (1986*b*) find a significant degree of inertia (see their Table 14), and when translated into annual terms this represents an additional term of the form $-0.36\Delta^2 p$. Since the use of quarterly data probably yields more reliable results when it comes to measuring nominal stickiness, we propose simply to add this term to our wage equation. So, making this change and substituting for the long-term proportion,

$$w - p = \text{const.} - 0.36\Delta^2 p - (0.091\log u - 0.424u) - 0.75\Delta u + 0.0495mm$$
$$+ 0.20RR + 0.536s'_m(p_m - p^*) + 0.536s'_m c + 0.177um_{-1}$$
$$+ 0.359\Delta t + 1.07(k - l). \tag{28}$$

Here mm is mismatch, RR the benefit replacement ratio, s'_m the share of imports, c log competitiveness, t the tax wedge, and um the union wage mark-up; the variables are defined more fully in the notes to Table 15. To produce this equation, we have dropped terms in $\Delta^2 u$ and the minor term in $\Delta s'_m(p_m - \bar{p})$ as well as setting

$$s'_m(p_m - \bar{p}) = s'_m(p_m - p^*) + s'_m(p^* - \bar{p}) = s'_m(p_m - p^*) + s'_m c.$$

The fundamental supply constraint

Our next step is to derive the long-run supply-side constraint which corresponds to equation (24). To do this we eliminate all lags and change terms, except the changes in the tax wedge and unemployment (Δt and Δu), and then eliminate the real wage ($w - p$), real demand ($y_d - \bar{y}$), and competitiveness (c) from the wage equation (28) and the first three equations in Table 15. We end up with

$$0.091\log u + 0.054u + 1.07\Delta^2 p - 1.25tb = \text{const.} - 1.27\Delta u - 0.037OIL$$
$$+ 0.0495mm + 0.334s'_m(p_m - p^*)$$
$$+ 0.20RR + 0.177um_{-1}$$
$$+ 0.359\Delta t, \tag{29}$$

where we have assumed that, in the longer run, $\Delta^2 w = \Delta^2 p$. Equation (29) then represents the fundamental supply-side constraint on the British economy after the extensive dynamics have worked through. It differs slightly in form from (24) because of the presence of the hysteresis term in Δu on the right-hand side. Corresponding to this is the equation for the equilibrium level of unemployment $(\hat{u})$, consistent with constant inflation and balanced trade $(\Delta^2 p = tb = \Delta u = 0)$, namely

$$0.091\log\hat{u} + 0.054\hat{u} = \text{const.} - 0.037OIL + 0.0495mm + 0.334s'_m(p_m - p^*)$$

$$+ 0.20RR + 0.177um_{-1} + 0.359\Delta t. \tag{30}$$

Combining (30) and (29) gives another useful equation, corresponding to equation (26); that is,

$$0.091\log\hat{u} + 0.054\hat{u} = 0.091\log u + 0.054u + 1.27\Delta u + 1.07\Delta^2 p - 1.25tb. \tag{31}$$

Before using these equations for a detailed analysis of Britain's unemployment history, it is worth remarking on a few of their implications. The inflation–trade balance trade-off at constant unemployment indicates that, in the long run, a rise in the trade deficit of 1 per cent of potential GDP is worth just over 1 percentage point off the change in the inflation rate. Alternatively, at constant inflation it is worth around $^3/_4$ of a percentage point off unemployment in the long run, starting from a baseline unemployment rate of 6 per cent. Finally at constant trade balance a 1-percentage-point rise in unemployment from 6 per cent will reduce the change in inflation by around 1.3 percentage points. Typically, however, policy that raises unemployment tends also to improve the trade balance, thereby reducing the impact on inflation.

It will be seen from equation (30) that shifts in the equilibrium unemployment level consistent with constant inflation and balanced trade are caused both by wage pressure factors such as the international terms of trade between UK imports and manufactures $(p_m - p^*)$, and by exogenous factors influencing the trade surplus such as North Sea oil (OIL). Those variables that appear in our model include the two mentioned above along with a proxy for mismatch, namely the absolute shift in the proportion of employees in the production sector (mm), a proxy for union power, namely the union wage mark-up (um), the benefit replacement ratio (RR), and the change in the tax wedge (Δt). The direction of all these effects is fairly obvious, but, in the light of all the literature on the 'Dutch Disease', it is worth pointing out that North Sea oil generates a favourable shift on the supply side because it autonomously relaxes the trade balance constraint.

However, these are surely not the only factors involved. Autonomous sources of wage pressure can include any number of other possibilities which are hard to capture empirically because of the difficulty of finding appropriate data series reflecting the exogenous underlying causal factors. For example, there may be effects from the housing market (see Bover *et al.* 1989), from the degree of rigour with which the unemployment benefit system is operated, or from severe skill shortages in certain areas. It is also clear from equations (24) and (25) that any exogenous rise in the price mark-up on costs (the parameter β_0) will have an adverse effect on the supply constraint. Unfortunately, however, overall trends in the degree of product-market competition are extraordinarily hard to pin down. These points are important to bear in mind when we attempt to analyse long-term shifts in unemployment. An analysis that uses only the variables at our disposal is almost bound to omit many important factors and is at best, therefore, only a very crude exercise.

An analysis of long-run unemployment trends

In Fig. 5 we present the British unemployment rate from the 1950s to the present, the measure which we use being the OECD standardized rate (see Annex 1.6). For our analysis, we divide the period into six sub-periods: 1956–9, 1960–8, 1969–73, 1974–80, 1981–7, 1988–90. We then use equation (31) to generate estimates of the long-run equilibrium level of unemployment corresponding to stable inflation and zero trade deficit. To do this, we take sub-period averages of u, Δu (two periods lagged), $\Delta^2 p$ (one period lagged), and tb (two periods lagged) and solve equation (31) for each period. The idea of the lags is to take some account of the time it takes for these effects to feed through the model into unemployment. The results are presented in Table 16 and reveal that actual and equilibrium unemployment were very close until 1973, after which equilibrium unemployment rose sharply. Actual unemployment lagged behind it in the 1970s and then surged ahead of it in the early 1980s, as rising inflation and trade deficits turned to falling inflation and trade surpluses. More recently, of course, we have had a further reversal as unemployment fell

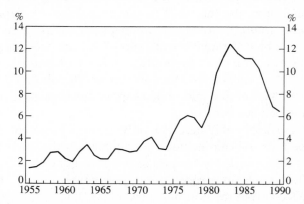

Fig. 5. *UK unemployment, 1955–1990.*

OECD standardized rate (see Annex 1.6).

Table 16 *Estimates of equilibrium unemployment* ($\hat{U}$) *in the UK based on equation (31)*

	1956–9	1960–8	1969–73	1974–80	1981–7	1988–90
u (%)	2.24	2.62	3.39	5.23	11.14	7.27
Δu (2 lags) (%)	−0.06	0.035	0.43	0.30	0.76	−0.90
$\Delta^2 p$ (1 lag) (%)	0.58	−0.11	1.00	1.51	−1.45	1.03
tb (2 lags) (%)	0.57	0.22	0.81	−1.06	1.39	−1.44
$\hat{u}$ (%)	2.2	2.5	3.6	7.3	8.7	8.7

rapidly in the late 1980s to a level below equilibrium, with inflation again rising and a large trade deficit.

The estimates of equilibrium unemployment in Table 16 give an impression of remarkable stability in the 1980s. This is perhaps a little misleading, because a more detailed look at the numbers suggests that by the mid-1980s equilibrium unemployment had risen close to 10 per cent before falling away. (The estimated value of $\hat{u}$ for 1984–6 is 9.9 per cent.) In the light of this, it is interesting to look at the situation in 1990, where we find equilibrium unemployment is around 8.3 per cent, i.e. about 2 percentage points higher than the current (1990) level of the OECD standardized rate. We shall have more to say on these numbers later, but in the meantime we consider the factors underlying the rise in equilibrium unemployment.

In order to pursue this question, we can use equation (30). We take differences of equation (30) across five adjacent time periods, and approximate $\Delta \log \hat{u}$ by $\Delta \hat{u}/\bar{u}$ where $\bar{u}$ is the current actual level of unemployment. Thus, in difference form, equation (30) becomes

$$\Delta \hat{u} = \Omega^{-1}(-0.037\Delta OIL + 0.0495\Delta mm + 0.334\Delta s'_m(p_m - p^*)$$

$$+ 0.20\Delta RR + 0.177\Delta um_{-1} + 0.359\Delta(\Delta t)), \tag{32}$$

where $\Omega = (0.091/\bar{u} + 0.054)$ and Δ refers to changes across periods. As in the previous case, we take a two-period lag on the explanatory variables in order to take some account of the dynamics. The results of this exercise are presented in Table 17. Furthermore, using these changes, we may construct a second series for $\hat{u}$ assuming that its value in the first period is 2.2 per cent. The two estimates of equilibrium unemployment are presented in Table 18. Taking the results of Table 17 at face value, we see that, from the 1950s to the early 1970s, the key factors leading to increasing equilibrium unemployment were the increasing generosity of the benefit system and the increasing power of unions, with these being offset by the continuing improvement in the international

445

Table 17 *A breakdown of changes in equilibrium unemployment in the UK based on equation (30)*

		1956–59 to 1960–68	1960–68 to 1969–73	1967–73 to 1974–80	1974–80 to 1981–87
			(percentage points)		
$-3.7\Delta OIL/\Omega$	(oil)	0	0	-0.28	-2.58
$4.95\Delta mm/\Omega$	(mismatch)	0.09	0.35	0.55	1.54
$33.4\Delta s'_m(p_m-p^*)/\Omega$	(import prices)	-0.41	-0.09	1.49	1.27
$20\Delta RR/\Omega$	(benefits)	0.34	0.59	-0.29	0.48
$17.7\Delta um_{-1}/\Omega$	(unions)	0.34	0.26	0.82	0.08
$35.9\Delta(\Delta t)/\Omega$	(tax wedge)	0.09	0	0.03	-0.32
$\Delta\hat{u}$		0.45	1.11	2.32	0.46
Δu		0.38	0.77	1.84	5.91
Ω		(3.52)	(2.74)	(1.77)	(0.87)

terms of trade. In the next period, there is a large adverse shift in the terms of trade with union power continuing to rise. In the final period North Sea oil has a powerful beneficial effect, but this is offset by the further adverse shift in the international terms of trade and the dramatic increase in our mismatch measure, reflecting the considerable industrial dislocation of that period.

However, Table 18 reveals that in the last two periods, but particularly in the 1980s, we are unable to provide complete explanations for the rise in equilibrium unemployment as estimated by our earlier method of removing the inflation, trade balance, and hysteresis (Δu) effects from the actual unemployment rate. This is surely the result of our inability to capture all the relevant exogenous factors at work, as we have already noted in the previous section. For example, there is a certain amount of evidence that skill mismatch has been a more serious problem in recent years than it was in earlier decades. In Table 19 we present some evidence on this based on the Confederation of British Industry (CBI) series on skilled and unskilled labour shortages. It is

Table 18 *Alternative estimates of equilibrium unemployment in the UK (%)*

	1956–59	1960–68	1969–73	1974–80	1981–87
u	2.24	2.62	3.39	5.23	11.14
$\hat{u}$ (Table 16)	2.2	2.5	3.6	7.3	8.7
$\hat{u}$ (Table 17)	2.2	2.7	3.8	6.1	6.6

Table 19   *Percentages of UK manufacturing firms reporting labour shortages*

	(1) % reporting shortages of skilled labour	(2) % reporting shortages of other labour	(3) Col. (1) ÷ col. (2)
1960–68	25.7	9.3	2.76
1969–73	24.4	9.0	2.71
1974–80	19.3	5.1	3.78
1981–87	8.3	1.2	6.92
1988–89	22.4	4.0	5.60

Note: CBI Industrial Trends Survey. Data weighted by size of firm.

clear that, relative to unskilled shortages, skill shortages are now considerably worse than in the late 1960s and early 1970s. Of course, in that period overall labour shortages were considerably more severe, reflecting the tighter labour market of the time. But more recently there is evidence of much more severe 'mismatch', in the sense that the skill shortages of the late 1980s are comparable with those of the 1960s, at a time when other labour shortages are relatively slight. This will generate higher wage pressure at periods of comparable overall labour market slack and hence will raise equilibrium unemployment. In addition the shift towards more decentralised bargaining (and the absence of incomes policy) has probably raised the NAIRU in the 1980s.

Another factor has worked in the opposite direction—the treatment of the unemployed. From 1986 unemployment in Britain fell dramatically, from around 11 per cent to around 6 per cent in early 1990. Furthermore, in our discussion following Table 16 we noted that there is some evidence of a fall in equilibrium unemployment over the same period, perhaps of as much as 2 percentage points. What explains these events?

There was, of course, a boom in demand—first in consumption (fuelled by deregulated credit) and then in investment. Inflation, however, was rising by only around 1 percentage point per year, held in check by a loss of competitiveness which, together with the expansion, transformed a trade surplus into a deficit equal to 4 per cent of GDP. But inflation was also held in check by important changes in the treatment of unemployed people. Under the Restart Programme, which began in 1986, unemployed people on benefit are interviewed every six months in order to ensure that they are looking for work and to provide them with a menu of help, from training to job clubs, to make it easier for them to succeed (Disney *et al.* 1991). At the same time, a much tighter test of 'availability for work' was applied to all unemployed people on benefit. The quantitative effect of these measures is discussed in Section 1 of the next chapter. But they certainly helped to reverse the 'culture of unemployment' which progressively took root in Britain in the early 1980s.

As already noted, at the time of writing (1990) the long-run NAIRU is, on our calculations, just over 8 per cent, using the OECD standardized measure of unemployment. It would be a little under 8 per cent on the UK benefit entitlement measure. In any event, on either measure it is around 2 points above the actual rate, basically because inflation is rising and would rise even faster (at given unemployment) were Britain to have the major real depreciation needed to restore trade balance. So, for inflation to be stabilized *and* the trade deficit eliminated, unemployment will have to be at least 8 per cent— indeed, even more if inflation is to fall.

7. Summary

We may summarize the results of this chapter as follows.

1. We have investigated the different patterns of unemployment across 19 OECD countries over the last three decades, using the framework set out in Chapter 8. The first step was to calibrate the basic equations, and we then found that our estimated parameters enabled us to explain unemployment movements very well until 1985 and reasonably well until 1990. We next related some of the key parameters to various economic and socio–political features of the different countries, having considerable success with the wage equation parameters but less success with those associated with price-setting. This lack of success was, in part, due to our inability to find consistent measures of product-market characteristics across our 19 countries.

2. Using these cross-section characteristics of the different countries enabled us to estimate a unified unemployment model (Table 12) whose parameters depend systematically on country-specific factors. This model provides a good explanation of the different unemployment patterns using only a very limited number of variables.

3. Finally, we have undertaken a case-study for Britain based on the open-economy model providing estimates of the three-way trade-off between unemployment, inflation, and the trade deficit and a partial explanation of Britain's unemployment performance until 1990.

4. We finish with an open question and a basic conclusion. Beginning with the former, the major open question, where further work is required, concerns the importance of product-market characteristics. Our theory suggests that a high degree of competition in product markets is an important factor in

explaining why an economy responds well to exogenous shocks. However, we have been unable to provide any evidence on this issue, one way or the other. Turning to our basic conclusion, this states that economies perform well in response to exogenous shocks under two main sets of circumstances. The first is if they have an unemployment benefit system which discourages long-term unemployment. This happens if the system offers benefits for a short duration (15 months or less). This does not necessarily mean that the system has to be very harsh. Benefits in the short term can be relatively generous, and when benefits run out the system can be constructed to ensure that a job is made available, as for example in Sweden. For we also find that active help to the unemployed reduces aggregate unemployment.

Second, economies perform well where there is a satisfactory system of wage determination. One system that works reasonably well is a competitive non-unionized labour market. But a unionized labour market can also work well if bargaining is sufficiently centrally co-ordinated—especially on the employer side.

This brings us straight to the policy issues.

Appendix: The derivation of model parameters

In this appendix, we first present in Tables A1 and A2 our own estimates of the marginal revenue product condition (equation (3)) and the wage equation (equation (2)).

We then (in Table A3) go through the countries one by one, comparing our parameter estimates with those of other authors. (NS = Newell and Symons 1985; AM = Alogoskoufis and Manning 1988; BLN = Bean, Layard, and Nickell 1986; G = Grubb 1986.) We indicate by an asterisk which source we use in the main text—in most cases it is our own estimates.

Sources to Tables A1 and A2 and UK equations. The data are based on the OECD data set, produced at the Centre for Labour Economics at the London School of Economics and described by David Grubb in Centre for Labour Economics Working Paper no. 615 with updates by Andrew Newell and Mark Walsh. The data for the UK are based on that utilized in Layard and Nickell (1986*b*) which has been updated by Paul Kong. One or two variables are new, notably the union–non-union mark-up (*um*), which is described in the Appendix to Layard and Nickell (1989: Table 29*b*), and the proportion of long-term unemployed (*LTU*) which is taken from issues of the *Employment Gazette*. The unemployment data used here differ slightly from those reported in Annex 1.6 because they are based on less recent issues of the relevant OECD publications.

Table A1 *Marginal revenue product condition, 1956–1985*
Dependent variable $(n - k)$

	$(n - k)_{-1}$	$(n - k)_{-2}$	$(w - p)$	$(w - p)_{-1}$
BE	0.64 (7.2)		−0.30 (3.3)	0.088 (1.0)
DK	0.48 (3.3)		−0.49 (2.2)	0.13 (0.4)
FR	0.74 (3.8)		−0.073 (0.8)	
GE	0.86 (8.9)		−0.079 (0.6)	−0.16 (1.1)
IR	0.85 (14.8)		−0.20 (1.7)	0.12 (1.0)
IT	0.81 (6.1)		−0.18 (1.1)	0.13 (0.9)
NL	0.85 (16.3)		−0.18 (1.7)	0.09 (0.7)
SP	0.66 (7.4)		−0.71 (3.4)	0.24 (1.2)
AL	0.35 (2.0)		−0.28 (2.1)	−0.12 (0.6)
NZ	0.84 (11.5)		−0.14 (1.8)	
CA	0.92 (7.6)		−0.61 (2.1)	0.21 (1.0)
US	0.79 (4.6)	−0.41 (2.1)		−0.20 (1.4)
JA	0.85 (13.0)		−0.59 (3.6)	0.48 (2.5)
AU	0.85 (3.4)		−0.37 (1.7)	0.33 (1.6)
FN	0.35 (2.3)		−0.046 (0.6)	
FN	0.56 (5.3)		−0.026 (0.3)	
NW	1.18 (5.8)	−0.30 (1.5)		−0.052 (1.4)
SW	0.53 (4.7)		−0.12 (1.6)	
SW	0.66 (7.5)		−0.027 (0.6)	
SZ	0.81 (12.8)		−0.32 (1.9)	

Notes: The equations are estimated by instrumental variables with $(w - p)$, $(y_d - \bar{y})$ treated as endogenous. Instruments include $(y_d - \bar{y})_{-1}$ plus current and first lag on OECD aggregate real wages, real commodity prices, and money supply shifts. For all countries except IR and NL, $(y_d - \bar{y})$ is the fitted value of the log deviations of GDP from potential GDP regressed on current and lagged taxes, government expenditure, deviations of world trade from trend, and competitiveness. For IR and NL, we take deviations of GDP from trend GDP and follow the same procedure. This is denoted as $\hat{y} - \bar{y}$ in the body of the appendix. *TP* is a measure of the technical progress coefficient in the production function and is based on the 'Solow' residual.

$(y_d - \bar{y})$	TP	$\Delta^2 w$	$\bar{R}^2$	s.e.
0.49 (2.4)	−0.08 (3.1)	0.03 (0.5)	0.9996	0.0063
0.73 (1.8)	0.27 (2.5)		0.9990	0.0108
0.49 (0.8)	−0.24 (1.6)	0.044 (0.9)	0.9998	0.0067
	0.097 (0.9)	0.13 (1.6)	0.9994	0.0110
0.21 (1.3)	−0.096 (2.8)	0.092 (1.4)	0.9988	0.0120
1.08 (0.7)	−0.06 (0.5)	0.13 (1.8)	0.9988	0.0111
0.37 (1.7)	−0.041 (1.0)	0.084 (1.1)	0.9990	0.0116
	−0.002 (0.2)		0.9993	0.0272
0.67 (1.4)	−0.29 (3.5)	0.035 (0.4)	0.9975	0.0102
	−0.009 (0.2)	0.094 (1.7)	0.9925	0.0122
−0.30 (0.3)	0.34 (1.1)		0.9921	0.0171
	−0.36 (3.1)	0.42 (2.1)	0.9921	0.0127
	−0.13 (2.1)	0.088 (1.5)	0.9998	0.0115
−0.11 (0.1)	−0.15 (0.4)	0.11 (1.0)	0.9993	0.0102
0.99 (1.6)	−0.55 (4.1)	0.086 (1.1)	0.9989	0.0116
	−0.41 (3.6)	0.14 (1.7)	0.9987	0.0130
	−0.03 (1.3)	0.052 (0.8)	0.9986	0.0094
2.04 (1.6)	−0.26 (2.7)	0.065 (1.4)	0.9989	0.0087
	−0.25 (2.5)	0.072 (1.4)	0.9988	0.0094
	−0.005 (0.0)	0.47 (3.6)	0.9975	0.0162

Table A2 *Wage equations, 1956–1985*
Dependent variable $(w - p)$

	$(w - p)_{-1}$	u or $\log u$(†)	Δu or $\Delta \log u$(†)	$\Delta^2 p$	$\Delta^2 p_{-1}$	Δwedge
BE	0.94 (5.8)	−0.045 (1.1)†		0.31 (1.0)	0.16 (0.7)	0.17 (0.6)
DK	0.62 (3.4)	−0.66 (6.3)		−0.050 (0.4)		
FR	0.49 (3.9)	−2.22 (2.3)	−0.73 (1.0)	−0.14 (1.2)		0.37 (2.0)
GE	0.46 (2.5)	−0.019 (2.3)†		−0.126 (0.6)		−0.036 (0.2)
IR	0.56 (3.6)	−0.071 (1.9)†	0.015 (0.2)†	0.13 (0.8)		0.50 (2.1)
IT	0.84 (9.8)	−2.07 (1.1)	−2.51 (1.5)	0.088 (0.4)		−0.20 (0.6)
NL	0.71 (4.5)	−0.039 (3.2)†	−0.021 (0.8)†	0.17 (0.6)		0.79 (2.2)
SP	0.86 (10.5)	−0.17 (0.6)		−0.15 (0.6)		
AL	0.23 (1.0)	−0.56 (1.5)		0.17 (0.4)		1.06 (2.0)
NZ	0.47 (2.0)	−0.0306 (2.2)†		−0.15 (0.8)		
CA	0.79 (7.6)	−0.20 (1.1)	−0.17 (0.9)	−0.50 (4.0)	−0.40 (5.8)	0.24 (1.7)
US	0.66 (4.3)	−0.32 (1.2)	−0.09 (0.4)	−0.26 (1.5)	−0.11 (0.9)	0.15 (0.9)
JA	0.56 (2.7)	−6.40 (2.0)	3.69 (1.6)	−0.0085 (0.1)		0.15 (0.6)
AU	0.54 (4.7)	−1.43 (0.9)		−0.63 (2.5)		−0.26 (0.9)
FN	0.69 (7.2)	−0.0195 (1.7)†	−0.013 (1.1)†	−0.12 (1.5)		0.58 (2.8)
NW	0.80 (4.5)	−0.61 (0.3)	−1.33 (0.9)	−0.74 (2.9)	−0.38 (1.5)	
SW	0.81 (5.6)	−2.31 (1.7)		−0.68 (1.7)		−0.00 (0)
SZ	0.82 (3.6)	−0.014 (2.3)†		−0.31 (1.4)		0.32 (1.3)

Notes: The equations are estimated by instrumental variables with u, Δu, $\Delta^2 p$ treated as endogenous. Instruments include u_{-1}, Δu_{-1}, plus current and first lag on OECD aggregate real wages, real commodity prices, and money supply shifts. For FR, IT, NL, NZ, US, JA, AU, FN, NW, and SZ, XP takes the value 0.01 for 1969–77, zero otherwise. For IR, CA, GE, XP takes the value 0.01 for 1969–end sample, zero otherwise. For SP, XP takes the value 0.01 from 1973–end sample, zero otherwise. For SW, there are two XP variables: the first takes the value 0.01 for 1969–73, zero otherwise; the second takes the value 0.01 for 1974–end sample, zero otherwise. The variables 'wedge' and 'search' are described in the chapter.

search	XP	(k − l)	(k − l)$_{-1}$	TP	$\bar{R}^2$	s.e.
9.1 (1.9)		0.42 (1.4)		−0.26 (2.4)	0.9982	0.0171
		0.37 (2.5)		0.14 (1.2)	0.9990	0.0120
−5.40 (0.6)	0.90 (1.2)	1.08 (2.1)		−0.81 (1.8)	0.9990	0.0112
	2.72 (2.0)	0.18 (1.4)		0.29 (1.1)	0.9975	0.0161
	2.9 (1.7)	0.32 (1.5)		0.064 (0.8)	0.9964	0.0203
	2.48 (1.6)	0.40 (1.6)		−0.26 (1.2)	0.9956	0.0218
	1.26 (1.0)	0.47 (2.1)		−0.04 (0.5)	0.9966	0.0235
	8.2 (2.3)	0.040 (0.9)		−0.049 (2.3)	0.9993	0.0272
		1.48 (4.1)		−0.70 (3.9)	0.9839	0.0199
−0.71 (0.7)	0.59 (0.3)	0.94 (2.5)		−0.05 (0.4)	0.9660	0.0284
−0.10 (0.0)	1.13 (1.2)	−0.10 (1.4)		0.29 (3.8)	0.9970	0.0072
−1.44 (1.0)	0.16 (0.3)		0.60 (2.5)	−0.29 (1.9)	0.9970	0.0065
−43.6 (3.3)	3.49 (2.0)	0.23 (1.1)		0.15 (0.9)	0.9993	0.0150
−14.3 (1.7)	1.11 (1.0)	−0.06 (0.3)		0.77 (2.0)	0.9986	0.0159
	0.91 (1.1)	0.42 (0.9)		−0.13 (0.3)	0.9968	0.0157
−32.9 (1.1)	5.50 (2.5)	1.36 (0.8)	−0.108 (1.6)	−0.075 (0.6)	0.9942	0.0238
	{4.05 (1.8) {1.03 (0.4)	−0.45 (1.0)		0.55 (1.6)	0.9954	0.0219
	0.05 (0.1)	0.23 (2.1)		−0.31 (1.1)	0.9936	0.0151

Parameter estimates: country-by-country comparisons

Table A3   *Country tables*

Belgium

Table A3   *Marginal revenue product condition (dependent variable $= n - k$)*

$(n-k)_{-1}$	$(w-p)$	$(w-p)_{-1}$	$(y_d - \bar{y})$	$\Delta^2 w$	Source
0.64	−0.30	0.088	0.49	0.030	Authors*
0.92	−0.19				NS
0.76	−0.21		0.54		BLN

Wage equation (dependent variable $= w - p$)

$(w-p)_{-1}$	u	Δu	$\Delta^2 p$	Δwedge	XP	search	wedge	Source
0.94	−0.045†	0	0.31	0.17	0	9.1		Authors*
0.77	−0.27			0.55	2.5			NS
1.08	−0.91	−0.06	−0.01					AM
0.93	−2.28						0.24	BLN
	−0.99							G

Coefficients: $u = -1.33(y_d - \bar{y})$ (derived from a static regresion), $\beta' = 0.29$, $\beta_1 = -0.03$, $\beta_{11} = 2.13$, $\beta_2 = 0.10$, $\gamma' = 0.84$, $\gamma_1(69\text{–}85) = 0.65$, $\gamma_1(80\text{–}90) = 0.42$, $\gamma_{11} = 0$, $\gamma_2 = 0$.

Note: † In the authors' wage equation, u is replaced by log$u$. The γ_1 coefficients are defined as $0.045/\bar{u}$ where $\bar{u}$ is the average unemployment rate for 1969–85, 1980–90 respectively. The coefficient of $\Delta^2 p$ being incorrectly signed, its coefficient is deemed to be zero. Furthermore, it is extremely difficult to obtain a Belgian real wage equation whose lagged dependent variable is much below unity, possibly because the trend productivity terms are not accurate. Since the estimated lagged dependent variable coefficient is far too high, it was reduced to 0.84 in order to make it more consistent with the NS results. In fact, this only changes $\bar{\gamma}_1$ (since γ_2 is zero), reducing it from an implausible 10.3 to a more sensible 4.06.

Denmark

Table A3—*continued   Marginal revenue product condition (dependent variable = n − k)*

$(n-k)_{-1}$	$(w-p)$	$(w-p)_{-1}$	$(y_d-\bar{y})$	$\Delta^2 w$	Source
0.48	−0.49	0.13	0.73	0	Authors*
0.26	−0.45		0.39		BLN

Wage equation (dependent variable = w − p)

$(w-p)_{-1}$	u	Δu	$\Delta^2 p$	XP	Source
0.62	−0.66	0	−0.050	0	Authors*
0.77	−0.45				BLN
0.98	−0.90	−0.37	0.37		AM

Coefficients: $u = -1.38(y_d-\bar{y})$, $\beta' = 0.26$, $\beta_1 = -0.02$, $\beta_{11} = 0.98$, $\beta_2 = 0$, $\gamma' = 0.62$, $\gamma_1 = 0.66$, $\gamma_{11} = 0$, $\gamma_2 = 0.050$.

France

Table A3—*continued   Marginal revenue product condition (dependent variable = n − k)*

$(n-k)_{-1}$	$(w-p)$	$(w-p)_{-1}$	$(y_d-\bar{y})$	$\Delta^2 w$	Source
0.74	−0.073	0	0.49	0.044	Authors*
0.90	−0.05				NS
0.72	−0.17		0.14		BLN

Wage equation (dependent variable = w − p)

$(w-p)_{-1}$	u	Δu	$\Delta^2 p$	Δwedge	XP	search	wedge	Source
0.49	−2.22	−0.73	−0.14	0.37	0.90	−5.4		Authors*
0.32	0			0.60	2.6			NS
0.61	−2.93					−2.17	0.20	BLN
0.93	−0.61	−1.67	−0.08					AM
	−1.82							G

Coefficients: $u = -1.48(y_d-\bar{y})$, $\beta' = 0$, $\beta_1 = -0.18$, $\beta_{11} = 10.1$, $\beta_2 = 0.60$, $\gamma' = 0.49$, $\gamma_1 = 2.22$, $\gamma_{11} = 0.73$, $\gamma_2 = 0.14$.

Germany

Table A3—*continued   Marginal revenue product condition (dependent variable$=n-k$)*

$(n-k)_{-1}$	$(w-p)$	$(w-p)_{-1}$	$(y_d-\bar{y})$	$\Delta^2 w$	Source
0.86	−0.079	−0.16	0	0.13	Authors*
0.88	−0.26				NS
0.36	−0.53		0.46		BLN

Wage equation (dependent variable$=w-p$)

$(w-p)_{-1}$	u	Δu	$\Delta^2 p$	Δwedge	XP	search	wedge	Source
0.46	−0.019†	0	−0.126	−0.036	2.72	0		Authors*
0.58	−0.36			0.20	1.30			NS
0.93	−3.02						−3.32	BLN
0.73	−1.36	−1.47	−0.40					AM
	−1.07							G

Coefficients: $u=-1.18(y_d-\bar{y})$, $\beta'=0$, $\beta_1=-0.58$, $\beta_{11}=3.58$, $\beta_2=0.54$, $\gamma'=0.46$, $\gamma_1(69-85)=0.55$, $\gamma_1(80-90)=0.32$, $\gamma_{11}=0$, $\gamma_2=0.126$.

Notes: To compute the price coefficients, we add the coefficients on $(w-p)$, $(w-p)_{-1}$.

† In the authors' wage equation, u is replaced by log$u$. The γ_1 coefficients are defined as $0.019/\bar{u}$, where $\bar{u}$ is the average unemployment rate of 1969–85 and 1980–90 respectively.

Ireland

Table A3—*continued   Marginal revenue product condition (dependent variable$=n-k$)*

$(n-k)_{-1}$	$(w-p)$	$(w-p)_{-1}$	$(y_d-\bar{y})$	$(\hat{y}-\bar{y})$	$\Delta^2 w$	Source
0.85	−0.20	0.12	0	0.21	0.092	Authors*
0.74	−0.09					NS
0.71	−0.30		0.25			BLN

Wage equation (dependent variable = w − p)

$(w-p)_{-1}$	u	Δu	$\Delta^2 p$	Δwedge	XP	search	wedge	Source
0.56	− 0.071†	0	0.13	0.50	2.9			Authors*
0.56	− 2.53						0.51	BLN
0.82	− 0.39	0.47	− 0.15					AM
	− 1.42							G

Coefficients: $u = -0.95(y_d - \bar{y})$, $\hat{y} - \bar{y} = -0.20\Delta u$, $\beta' = 0.60$, $\beta_1 = 0.75$, $\beta_{11} = 4.04$, $\beta_2 = 0.46$, $\gamma' = 0.56$, γ_1(69–85) = 0.80, γ_1(80–90) = 0.49, $\gamma_{11} = 0$, $\gamma_2 = 0$.

Note: † In the authors' wage equation, u is replaced by log$u$. The γ_1 coefficients are defined as $0.071/\bar{u}$ where $\bar{u}$ is the average unemployment rate for 1969–85, 1980–90 respectively. Given that the coefficient on $\Delta^2 p$ in the authors' wage equation takes the value 0.13 (wrong sign) and in *AM* it takes the value −0.15, we have compromised on zero.

Italy

Table A3—*continued*   *Marginal revenue product condition (dependent variable = n − k)*

$(n-k)_{-1}$	$(w-p)$	$(w-p)_{-1}$	$(y_d - \bar{y})$	$\Delta^2 w$	Source
0.81	− 0.182	0.125	1.08	0.125	Authors*
0.74	− 0.09				NS
0.65	− 0.13		0.10		BLN

Wage equation (dependent variable = w − p)

$(w-p)_{-1}$	u	Δu	$\Delta^2 p$	Δwedge	XP	search	wedge	Source
0.84	− 2.07	− 2.51	0.088	− 0.20	2.48			Authors*
0.80	− 1.28			0	2.90			NS
0.53	− 0.24						0.05	BLN
0.93	− 0.39	− 0.62	0.34					AM
	− 0.34							G

Coefficients: $u = -1.07(y_d - \bar{y})$, $\beta' = 0.69$, $\beta_1 = 1.04$, $\beta_{11} = 4.45$, $\beta_2 = 0.69$, $\gamma' = 0.84$, $\gamma_1 = 2.07$, $\gamma_{11} = 2.51$, $\gamma_2 = 0$.

Notes: The coefficient on $\Delta^2 p$ in the wage equation, being wrongly signed and small, is set equal to zero. The coefficient on $(y_d - \bar{y})$ in the marginal revenue product condition is set equal to zero. It has a *t*-ratio less than unity and its estimated value leads to a ludicrous price equation.

Netherlands

Table A3—*continued   Marginal revenue product condition (dependent variable = n − k)*

$(n-k)_{-1}$	$(w-p)$	$(w-p)_{-1}$	$(y_d-\bar{y})$	$(\hat{y}-\bar{y})$	$\Delta^2 w$	Source
0.85	−0.18	0.09		0.37	0.084	Authors*
0.91	−0.07					NS
0.90	−0.11		0.21			BLN

Wage equation (dependent variable = w − p)

$(w-p)_{-1}$	u	Δu	$\Delta^2 p$	Δwedge	XP	search	wedge	Source
0.71	−0.039†	−0.021†	0.17	0.79	1.3			Authors*
0.82	−0.78			0.88	3.1			NS
0.64	−0.77					−0.25	0.15	BLN
0.64	−1.83	−1.01	0.35					AM
	−2.65							G

Coefficients: $u = -1.24(y_d - \bar{y})$, $\hat{y} - \bar{y} = -0.67\Delta u$, $\beta' = 0.50$, $\beta_1 = 0.83$, $\beta_{11} = 3.34$, $\beta_2 = 0.47$, $\gamma' = 0.71$, $\gamma_1(69\text{–}85) = 0.66$, $\gamma_1(80\text{–}90) = 0.40$, $\gamma_{11}(69\text{–}85) = 0.36$, $\gamma_{11}(80\text{–}90) = 0.22$, $\gamma_2 = 0$.

Note: † In the authors' wage equation, u is replaced by $\log u$, Δu by $\Delta \log u$. The γ_1 (γ_{11}) coefficients are defined as $0.039/\bar{u}$ ($0.021/\bar{u}$) where $\bar{u}$ is the average unemployment rate for 1969–85, 1980–90 respectively. The coefficient on $\Delta^2 p$ in the wage equation is small and incorrectly signed, so it is set equal to zero.

Spain

Table A3—*continued   Marginal revenue product condition (dependent variable = n − k)*

$(n-k)_{-1}$	$(w-p)$	$(w-p)_{-1}$	$(y_d-\bar{y})$	$\Delta^2 w$	Source
0.66	−0.71	0.24			Authors*

Wage equation (dependent variable = w − p)

$(w-p)_{-1}$	u	Δu	$\Delta^2 p$	Δwedge	XP	search	wedge	Source
0.86	−0.17	0	−0.15		8.2			Authors*
0.56	−0.71	0.44	0.37					AM
	−0.49							G

Coefficients: $u = -1.24(y_d - \bar{y})$, $\beta' = 0.34$, $\beta_1 = 0.48$, $\beta_{11} = 0.93$, $\beta_2 = 0$, $\gamma' = 0.86$, $\gamma_1 = 0.17$, $\gamma_{11} = 0$, $\gamma_2 = 0.15$.

Note: $XP = 0.1$ for each year from 1973 onwards.

UK

Table A3—*continued   Marginal revenue product condition (dependent variable = n − k)*

$(n-k)_{-1}$	$(n-k)_{-2}$	$(w-p)_{-1}$	$(y_d-\bar{y})$	$\Delta^2 w$	Source
1.06	−0.36	−0.29	0.07		LN*
0.88		−0.18			NS
0.37		−0.40	0.50		BLN

Wage equation (dependent variable = w − p)

$(w-p)_{-1}$	$\log u$	LTU	$\Delta^2 p$	mm	RR	$s'_m(p_m-\bar{p})$	$\Delta s'_m(p_m-\bar{p})$	um		Δt	Source
0	−0.091	0.193	0	0.050	0.20	0.54	0.10	0.18		0.36	Authors*

$(w-p)_{-1}$	u	Δu	$\Delta^2 p$	Δwedge	XP	search	wedge	Source
0.62	−0.03			0.29	0.09			NS
0.97	−0.53					0.23	0.04	BLN
0.76	−0.26	−0.74	0.04					AM
	−1.15							G

Coefficients: Price: we have a price equation from LN of the form $p - w = 0.54\ (p-w)_{-1} - 0.34\ \Delta^2 w$ $- 0.24\ \Delta^2 w_{-1} + 0.038(y_d - \bar{y}) +$ productivity trends. If we eliminate $(y_d - \bar{y})$ between this and the LN marginal revenue product condition, we obtain, $\beta' = 0.36$, $\beta_1 = 0.18$, $\beta_{11} = 0.31$, $\beta_2 = 0.58$. Wage: $\gamma' = 0$, $\gamma_1(69–85) = 0.98$, $\gamma_1(80–90) = 0.53$, $\gamma_{11} = 0.75$, $\gamma_2 = 0$.

Note: To compute the wage coefficients, note first that we estimate
$(1 - 0.496L)LTU = 1.11u - 3.26\Delta u + 2.39\Delta u_{-1}$
or $LTU = 2.20u - 3.89\Delta u +$ terms in $\Delta^2 u$, $\Delta^3 u \ldots$
Substituting into the wage equation, we obtain unemployment terms

$$-0.091\log u + 0.424u - 0.75\Delta u \text{ or } (-\frac{0.091}{\bar{u}} + 0.424)u - 0.75\Delta u,$$

where $\bar{u} = 0.0647$ for 1969–85 and 0.0952 for 1980–90. $LTU =$ proportion of unemployed with durations over 52 weeks, $RR =$ replacement ratio, $mm =$ index of mismatch, $um =$ union power as measured by the union wage mark-up, $s'_m =$ share of imports in GDP, $(p_m - \bar{p}) =$ real import prices, $t =$ tax wedge. For further details, see Section 6 of this chapter, particularly Table 15.

Australia

Table A3—*continued Marginal revenue product condition (dependent variable $= n - k$)*

$(n-k)_{-1}$	$(w-p)$	$(w-p)_{-1}$	$(y_d-\bar{y})$	$\Delta^2 w$	Source
0.35	−0.28	−0.12	0.67	0.035	Authors*
0.49	−0.30				NS
0.43	−0.44		−0.37		BLN

Wage equation (dependent variable $= w - p$)

$(w-p)_{-1}$	u	Δu	$\Delta^2 p$	Δwedge	XP	search	wedge	Source
0.23	−0.56	0	0.17	1.06	0			Authors*
0.75	−0.27			0.57	1.9			NS
0.97	−2.77					−1.71	0.48	BLN
	−1.46							G

Coefficients: $u = -1.16(y_d - \bar{y})$, $\beta' = -0.43$, $\beta_1 = 0.26$, $\beta_{11} = 1.25$, $\beta_2 = 0.13$, $\gamma' = 0.23$, $\gamma_1 = 0.56$, $\gamma_{11} = 0$, $\gamma_2 = 0$.

Note: Since the coefficient on $\Delta^2 p$ in the authors' wage equation is incorrectly signed and small, it is set at zero.

New Zealand

Table A3—*continued Marginal revenue product condition (dependent variable $= n - k$)*

$(n-k)_{-1}$	$(w-p)$	$(w-p)_{-1}$	$(y_d-\bar{y})$	$\Delta^2 w$	Source
0.84	−0.14	0	0	0.094	Authors*

Wage equation (dependent variable $= w - p$)

$(w-p)_{-1}$	u	Δu	$\Delta^2 p$	Δwedge	XP	search	wedge	Source
0.47	−0.0306†	0	−0.15		0.59	−0.71		Authors*
0.55	−0.84					0	0.02	BLN
	−1.96							G

Coefficients: $u = -1.35(y_d - \bar{y})$, $\beta' = 0$, $\beta_1 = 1.14$, $\beta_{11} = 6.0$, $\beta_2 = 0.67$, $\gamma' = 0.47$, $\gamma_1(69\text{–}85) = 1.71$, $\gamma_{11}(80\text{–}90) = 0.65$, $\gamma_{11} = 0$, $\gamma_2 = 0.15$.

Note: † In the authors' wage equation, u is replaced by log$u$. The γ_1 coefficients are defined as $0.0306/\bar{u}$ where $\bar{u}$ is the average unemployment rate for 1969–85 and 1980–90 respectively.

Canada

Table A3—*continued* *Marginal revenue product condition (dependent variable = n − k)*

$(n-k)_{-1}$	$(w-p)$	$(w-p)_{-1}$	$(y_d - \bar{y})$	$\Delta^2 w$	Source
0.92	−0.61	0.21	−0.30	0	Authors*
0.91	−0.19				NS
0.17	−0.35		0.60		BLN

Wage equation (dependent variable = w − p)

$(w-p)_{-1}$	u	Δu	$\Delta^2 p$	Δwedge	XP	search	wedge	Source
0.79	−0.20	−0.17	−0.90	0.24	1.13	0		Authors*
0.86	−0.33			0.84	1.90			NS*
0.81	−0.94						0.14	BLN*
	−0.93							G

Coefficients: $u = -1.32(y_d - \bar{y})$, $\beta' = 0.34$, $\beta_1 = 0.50$, $\beta_{11} = 1.51$, $\beta_2 = 0$, $\gamma' = 0.79$, $\gamma_1 = 0.50$, $\gamma_{11} = 0.17$, $\gamma_2 = 0.90$.

Note: In the wage model, we raised the coefficient on unemployment (γ_1) to 0.5 to bring it more in line with the other evidence.

USA

Table A3—*continued* *Marginal revenue product condition (dependent variable = n − k)*

$(n-k)_{-1}$	$(n-k)_{-2}$	$(w-p)_{-1}$	$(y_d - \bar{y})$	$\Delta^2 w$	Source
0.79	−0.41	−0.20		0.42	Authors*
0.10		−0.63			NS
−0.28		−0.61	0.19		BLN

Wage equation (dependent variable $= w - p$)

$(w-p)_{-1}$	u	Δu	$\Delta^2 p$	Δwedge	XP	search	wedge	Source
0.66	−0.32	−0.09	−0.37	0.15	0	−1.4		Authors*
0.62	−0.11			0.43	1.0			NS
0.34	−0.05						0.07	BLN
0.98	−0.07	−0.92	−0.33					AM
	−0.94							G

Coefficients: $u = -1.62(y_d - \bar{y})$, $\beta' = 0$, $\beta_1 = 3.10$, $\beta_{11} = -0.15$, $\beta_2 = 2.10$, $\gamma' = 0.66$, $\gamma_1 = 0.32$, $\gamma_{11} = 0.09$, $\gamma_2 = 0.37$.

Japan

Table A3—*continued   Marginal revenue product condition (dependent variable $= n - k$)*

$(n-k)_{-1}$	$(w-p)$	$(w-p)_{-1}$	$(y_d - \bar{y})$	$\Delta^2 w$	Source
0.85	−0.59	0.48		0.088	Authors*
0.83	−0.15				NS
0.65	−0.36		−0.01		BLN

Wage equation (dependent variable $= w - p$)

$(w-p)_{-1}$	u	Δu	$\Delta^2 p$	Δwedge	XP	search	wedge	Source
0.56	−6.40	3.69	−0.0085	0.15	3.49	−44		Authors*
0.55	−3.22			0.18	3.40			NS
0.56	−25.4					−20.8		BLN
0.64	−1.83	−1.01	−0.35					AM
	−2.65							G

Coefficients: $u = -0.94(y_d - \bar{y})$, $\beta' = 0.81$, $\beta_1 = 0.32$, $\beta_{11} = 1.44$, $\beta_2 = 0.15$, $\gamma' = 0.56$, $\gamma_1 = 6.40$, $\gamma_{11} = -3.69$, $\gamma_2 = 0.0085$.

Austria

Table A3—*continued   Marginal revenue product condition (dependent variable = n − k)*

$(n-k)_{-1}$	$(w-p)$	$(w-p)_{-1}$	$(y_d - \bar{y})$	$\Delta^2 w$	Source
0.85	−0.37	0.33	−0.11	0.11	Authors*
0.84	−0.12				NS
0.56	−0.32		0.32		BLN

Wage equation (dependent variable = w − p)

$(w-p)_{-1}$	u	Δu	$\Delta^2 p$	Δwedge	XP	search	wedge	Source
0.54	−1.43	0	−0.63	−0.26	1.1	−14		Authors*
0.65	−0.80				2.1			NS
1.03	−2.09							BLN
0.84	−2.18	−1.51	−0.29					AM
	−1.08							G

Coefficients: $u = -1.51(y_d - \bar{y})$, $\beta' = 0.89$, $\beta_1 = 0.63$, $\beta_{11} = 2.30$, $\beta_2 = 0.30$, $\gamma' = 0.54$, $\gamma_1 = 1.43$, $\gamma_{11} = 0$, $\gamma_2 = 0.63$.

Finland

Table A3—*continued   Marginal revenue product condition (dependent variable = n − k)*

$(n-k)_{-1}$	$(w-p)$	$(w-p)_{-1}$	$(y_d - \bar{y})$	$\Delta^2 w$	Source
0.35	−0.046		0.99	0.086	Authors*
0.56	−0.026			0.14	Authors*
0.91	−0.050				NS
0.32	0.48		0.47		BLN

Wage equation (dependent variable $= w - p$ *)*

$(w-p)_{-1}$	u	Δu	$\Delta^2 p$	Δwedge	XP	search	wedge	Source
0.69	$-0.0195\dagger$	$-0.0131\dagger$	-0.12	0.58	0.91			Authors*
0.75	-0.46			0.65	2.90			NS
0.30	-2.10					-0.59	0.17	BLN
0.93	-0.61	-1.67	-0.08					AM
	-1.82							G

Coefficients: $u = -1.07(y_d - \bar{y})$, $\beta' = 0$, $\beta_1 = 1.91$, $\beta_{11} = 12.6$, $\beta_2 = 3.10$, $\gamma' = 0.69$, $\gamma_1(69\text{–}85) = 0.48$, $\gamma_1(80\text{–}90) = 0.41$, $\gamma_{11}(69\text{–}85) = 0.33$, $\gamma_{11}(80\text{–}90) = 0.28$, $\gamma_2 = 0.12$.

Notes: The price coefficients derived from either of the first two equations are unsatisfactory: to produce sensible numbers we take an average of these two equations with weights 0.65, 0.35 respectively.

$\dagger$ In the authors' wage equation, u is replaced by $\log u$, Δu by $\Delta \log u$. The $\gamma_1(\gamma_{11})$ coefficients are defined as $0.0195/\bar{u}$ $(0.0131/\bar{u})$ where $\bar{u}$ is the average unemployment rate for 1969–85 and 1980–90 respectively.

Norway

Table A3—*continued   Marginal revenue product condition (dependent variable* $= n - k$ *)*

$(n-k)_{-1}$	$(n-k)_{-2}$	$(w-p)_{-1}$	$(y_d - \bar{y})$	$\Delta^2 w$	Source
1.18	-0.30	-0.052		0.052	Authors*
-0.16		-0.08			NS
0.07		-0.18	0.39		BLN

Wage equation (dependent variable $= w - p$ *)*

$(w-p)_{-1}$	u	Δu	$\Delta^2 p$	Δwedge	XP	search	wedge	Source
0.80	-0.61	-1.33	-1.12		5.5	-33.0		Authors*
0.22	-8.38							BLN
0.86	-0.97				5.2			NS
0.83	-3.31	-4.15	-0.27					AM*
	-2.05							G

Coefficients: $u = -1.47(y_d - \bar{y})$, $\beta' = 0$, $\beta_1 = 2.31$, $\beta_{11} = 11.15$, $\beta_2 = 1.0$, $\gamma' = 0.815$, $\gamma_1 = 1.96$, $\gamma_{11} = 2.74$, $\gamma_2 = 0.70$.

Note: The wage equation coefficients are averages of the authors' equation and that estimated by AM. The reason for this is that the general evidence on unemployment effects suggests they are somewhat bigger than the authors' equation indicates. (For a full discussion see Calmfors and Nymoen 1990.)

Sweden

Table A3—*continued   Marginal revenue product condition (dependent variable = $n - k$)*

$(n-k)_{-1}$	$(w-p)$	$(w-p)_{-1}$	$(y_d-\bar{y})$	$\Delta^2 w$	Source
0.53	−0.12		2.04	0.065	Authors*
0.66	−0.027			0.072	Authors*
0.78	−0.30				NS
0.16	−0.55		−0.17		BLN

Wage equation (dependent variable = $w - p$)

$(w-p)_{-1}$	u	Δu	$\Delta^2 p$	Δwedge	XP	search	wedge	Source
0.81	−2.31	0	−0.68	0	(4.05,1.03†)	0		Authors*
0.34	−1.36			0				NS
0.03	−7.77					−9.64	0.48	BLN
0.98	−2.46	−3.80	−0.62					AM
	−3.63							G

Coefficients: $u = -1.19(y_d-\bar{y})$, $\beta' = 0$, $\beta_1 = 1.10$, $\beta_{11} = 14.43$, $\beta_2 = 1.61$, $\gamma' = 0.81$, $\gamma_1 = 2.31$, $\gamma_{11} = 0$, $\gamma_2 = 0.68$.

Notes: The price equation is the average of those appearing in the first two rows, each individually leading to a highly unsatisfactory price equation.

† XP consists of two dummies: $XP_1 = 0.01$ for 1969–73, $XP_2 = 0.01$ for 1974 onwards.

Switzerland

Table A3—*continued   Marginal revenue product condition (dependent variable = $n - k$)*

$(n-k)_{-1}$	$(w-p)$	$(y_d-\bar{y})$	$\Delta^2 w$	Source
0.81	−0.32		0.47	Authors*
0.83	−0.58			NS
0.37	−0.40	0.55		BLN

Wage equation (dependent variable $= w - p$)

$(w-p)_{-1}$	u	Δu	$\Delta^2 p$	Δwedge	XP	search	wedge	Source
0.82	-0.014†	0	-0.31	0.32	0			Authors*
0.44	-1.36			0.51	1.2			NS
0.67	-26.8						-6.46	BLN
0.93	-6.81	3.87	-0.07					AM
	-6.5							G

Coefficients: $u = -1.40(y_d - \bar{y})$, $\beta' = 0$, $\beta_1 = 0.59$, $\beta_{11} = 2.53$, $\beta_2 = 1.47$, $\gamma' = 0.82$, $\gamma_1(69\text{–}85) = 1.32$, $\gamma_1(80\text{–}90) = 0.69$, $\gamma_{11} = 0$, $\gamma_2 = 0.31$.

Note: † In the authors' wage equation, u is replaced by $\log u$. The γ_1 coefficients are defined as $0.014/\bar{u}$ where $\bar{u}$ is the average unemployment rate for 1969–85 and 1980–90 respectively.

Notes

1. For example, suppose instead of (1) and (2) we estimate

$$(1 - \beta' L)(p - w) = \beta_0 - \beta_1 u - \beta_{11} \Delta u - \beta_2 \Delta^2 p \tag{1}$$

$$\lambda(1 - \beta' L)(p - w) + (1 - \lambda)(1 - \gamma' L)(w - p) = [\lambda \beta_0 + (1 - \lambda)\gamma_0]$$

$$- [\lambda \beta_1 + (1 - \lambda)]u - [\lambda \beta_{11} + (1 - \lambda)\gamma_{11}]\Delta u - [\lambda \beta_2 + (1 - \lambda)\gamma_2]\Delta^2 p + (1 - \lambda)(1 - \gamma')z_w. \tag{2'}$$

   Then it is very simple to demonstrate that the reduced form of this model is precisely equation (8).

2. We were unable to extend the data on PSF (proportion in small firms) to all 19 countries in a satisfactory way.

Policy Implications

10

Policies to Cut Unemployment

So far we have tried to understand unemployment. The point, however, is to change it. In this chapter we reflect on the normative implications of what we have learned.

Unemployment is not determined by an optimal process of allocation. Though it does perform a vital role in the redirection of labour, its level is subject to a host of distorting influences, tending to make it higher than is economically efficient. The most obvious of these distortions are

1. the benefit system, which is subject to massive problems of moral hazard (unless administered well), and
2. the system of wage determination, where decentralized unions and employers have incentives to set wages in a way that generates involuntary unemployment, and where bargained wages create a mismatch between the pattern of labour demand and supply.

Both these systems generate negative externalities. While there may be *some* positive search externalities from unemployment (Diamond 1981; Pissarides 1990), it is hard to suppose that these are of the same order.

However, the negative distortions do not mean that unemployment is too high in every country. This depends on how much else the country has done to offset them. Policy-makers have to apply a cost–benefit approach to each possible policy option open to them in their existing circumstances. They inevitably operate in the world of the second best, and most of the forms of intervention that are proposed introduce other distortions. But even so, they may improve the welfare of millions and make an economy thrive rather than limp.

We shall begin by looking at policies directed towards the unemployed, including policies on benefits, since the lessons here are clearest. We shall go on to look at the issue of bargaining and incomes policy. Then we shall discuss the role of employment subsidies.

All these kinds of policies can help a lot. We end by discussing policies that are unlikely to do so—profit-sharing, work-sharing, early retirement, general public employment, and reduced employment protection.

1. Policies for the unemployed: benefits and active manpower policy

As we have seen, a major determinant of the level of unemployment is the search effectiveness of the unemployed. For example, consider the following simple version of our model. Pricing behaviour gives

$$p - w = \beta_0. \tag{1}$$

The target real wage increases with the ease with which unemployed people (searching with given intensity) can find employment. This is measured by the outflow from unemployment (H) divided by the number of effective job-seekers (cU).[1] But in equilibrium the outflow from unemployment (H) equals the inflow (sN), where s is the inflow rate. Thus the real wage depends on

$$\frac{H}{cU} = \frac{s}{cU/N}.$$

If target real wages depend on the logarithm of this variable, we have a wage equation,

$$w - p = \gamma_0 - \gamma_1(\log u + \log c - \log s). \tag{2}$$

Hence in general equilibrium (from adding (1) and (2)),

$$\log u = \frac{\beta_0 + \gamma_0}{\gamma_1} + \log s - \log c. \tag{3}$$

The parameters γ_0 and γ_1 will reflect a whole host of influences, including bargaining structure. But for our present purpose the key point is this: the unemployment stock depends critically on the average effectiveness of the unemployed (c) relative to the inflow rate into unemployment (s).

What can be done to improve the effectiveness of the unemployed? Broadly, there are two main avenues. The first is to take a tougher line on benefits, and the second is to offer active help in training and the provision of jobs. Benefits can be made less attractive by cutting their value, by reducing their duration, and by stiffening the work test. In our view, there are strong efficiency (missing insurance markets) and equity arguments for having a reasonable value of benefits. But indefinite benefits are not in the interest of most able-bodied individuals, nor is it reasonable that they should be made available without a clear test of willingness to work.[2]

However, many individuals do need active help in fitting themselves for work and in persuading employers of their fitness. Moreover, it is much easier to overcome the moral hazard problems of unemployment benefit when the state takes a responsibility for helping in this way. There is thus a strong efficiency and equity case for giving active help to the unemployed.

What we have in mind is the Swedish mixture, or 'employment principle' as they call it (Layard and Philpott, 1991; Jangenäs, 1985; Thalén 1988; P. Robinson 1989). This assumes that it should be normal for those who want work to have it. In other words, the proper way to acquire an income is by work rather than by a state transfer. Thus, benefits should be paid only for a transitional period. But there should be active help (and ultimately a guarantee of temporary work) to those who have difficulty getting work.

The theory of active labour market policy

This kind of approach has recently received support from the OECD (1990*b*). There are two main questions in designing such a policy: who to help, and what kind of help to provide. The model just outlined provides an important clue to the first question.

For a given inflow into unemployment, we could reduce unemployment more if we removed from unemployment someone with a long expected remaining duration of unemployment (a low expected c) rather than someone with a short remaining duration. We should always do this, if two conditions were satisfied:

1. The cost of removing the two individuals from unemployment were the same.
2. The likelihood of each individual re-entering unemployment later on were the same.

If these conditions did not hold, it would still be right to help the less effective unemployed person, provided the divergences from conditions 1 and 2 taken together were not disproportionate to the remaining durations.

So who has the highest remaining duration of unemployment? At the point of entry to unemployment, it is not always easy to tell. The majority of newly unemployed individuals have relatively short expected remaining durations, though with better diagnostic information (and research) it should become easier to make forecasts. However, in most countries people who have been unemployed for some time have much longer expected *remaining* durations than the average newly unemployed person (see Fig. 1). This provides a strong argument in favour of concentrating help on those who have already been unemployed for some time.

But then we need to consider the likely costs and likely re-entry rates to unemployment. If it is very expensive to help long-term unemployed people, and if, once helped out of unemployment, they are disproportionately likely to return, then this is not the right policy.

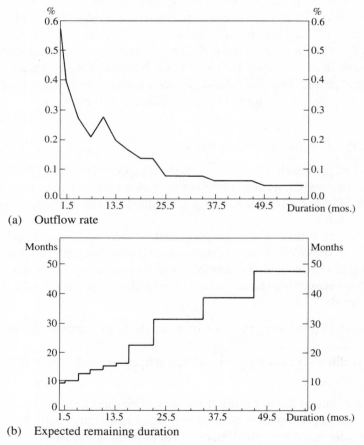

(a)   Outflow rate

(b)   Expected remaining duration

Fig. 1. *Outflow rate from unemployment and expected remaining duration, by uncompleted duration, Britain 1985.*

Sources: The data relate to registered unemployment and come from the *Employment Gazette* and from Ch. 5 above, Fig. 4.

How are we to assess these two factors? If the long-term unemployed are mostly intrinsically inadequate people, both of these problems would be acute. This is why the issue of state dependence is so important.

State dependence

In earlier chapters we provided three main facts pointing to state dependence:

1. Wage pressure increases (for given unemployment) when the proportion of long-term unemployed rises.
2. Vacancies rise (for given unemployment) when the proportion of long-term unemployed rises.
3. As the proportion of long-term unemployed has risen, the overall exit rate from unemployment has fallen sharply relative to the exit rate of newly unemployed people.

Yet with pure heterogeneity, an increase in the proportion of long-term unemployed would have no effect on the quality of the overall stock of unemployed people; hence none of these three factors would apply. We conclude that long-term unemployment as such has reduced the average effectiveness of the unemployed.

We do not know the exact reasons for this. There is a mutually reinforcing interaction between (*a*) the demoralization of the workers, following a continuous rejection, and (*b*) the stigmatizing behaviour of employers. We do not know whether employers are fully rational in their treatment of long-term unemployed people—in the sense of hiring them in proportion to their probability of effective work performance. We do know that many employers simply will not short-list any long-term unemployed people, considering the risks too high (Meager and Metcalf 1987; Winter-Ebmer 1991). There may well be some irrationality in this, based on hysteresis. After all, in a well functioning labour market, such as Europe had before 1973, there *was* generally something intrinsically wrong with a person who had been out of work for over a year. But nowadays in Europe the long-term unemployed include hundreds of thousands of people with outstanding work records; for example, in Britain the long-term unemployed (over a year) once comprised under $\frac{1}{2}$ per cent of the workforce compared with 2 per cent in 1990. It is understandable if employers' behaviour has not fully adjusted to this fact.

Equally, it is perfectly natural that a person who has been rejected over and over again does not give a very confident impression even if called for interview. And, even if recorded job search is not markedly less intensive among long-term than short-term unemployed, their tenacity is bound to be diminished. Thus occurs the vicious circle.

Types of policy

The case for intervention rests on three main pillars: first, the external cost of unemployment benefits (which could of course be removed if benefits were scrapped); second, capital market imperfections and informational asymmetries; and third, the theory of addiction (see references in Becker and Murphy 1988). Experience changes people, and the outcome of allocations that exhaust the gains from trade after a change in attitudes has occurred may not yield the same social welfare as it would if the change could be reversed.

Thus, to be specific, there is a strong case for public action to prevent long-term unemployment through appropriate use of

1. adult training,
2. recruitment subsidies,
3. public employment (as employer of last resort).

It is probably most cost-effective to apply these remedies before the onset of long-term unemployment—since the social cost of making a person employable is much greater once he is really demoralized and stigmatized.

The Swedish system is a good example of this approach. After one year's unemployment, benefit runs out and there is a legally guaranteed right to temporary work. Of course, such a guarantee can be delivered only if in the preceding half-year strenuous efforts have been made to get people into suitable training or work. In terms of public exchequer cost, such schemes may often be largely self-financing, through the reduction of benefit payments (Table 1).

The Swedish system of treating unemployed people is described at length in Layard and Philpott (1991), together with the systems in Britain, France, Germany, and the USA. This also proposes a costed Swedish-style plan for Britain. Needless to say, the cost savings to the Treasury build up substantially over time, and ultimately such schemes may well pay for themselves.

Deadweight, substitution, and displacement

Employment subsidies for unemployed people (and public employment) are often criticized, on three grounds.

1. *Deadweight.* Many of those for whom the subsidy is paid would have

been recruited anyway: money paid for those recruits is deadweight and has no effect at all.

2. *Substitution.* In addition, some of those recruited merely replace others whom the firm would have recruited instead: money paid for those recruits does ensure them preferential treatment, but does not increase total recruitment.

3. *Displacement.* Even when the firm does increase its total recruitment, this may be at the expense of jobs in other firms.

Thus the total effect of a scheme is given by

Total effect = Numbers subsidized
　　　　　　　− deadweight (in same firm)
　　　　　　　− substitution (in same firm)
　　　　　　　− displacement (in other firms).

Surveys of firms can throw some light on the first two of these items. When firms are asked about the effects of recruitment subsidies, they do indeed identify

1. those subsidized who would have been recruited anyway (deadweight);
2. those subsidized who would not have been recruited but have replaced other potential recruits (substitution);
3. the net increase in recruitment (= total recruits subsidized minus groups 1 and 2).

But this still leaves unidentified the displacement in the rest of the economy. And the whole analysis tells us little about the effect of the policy on the level of unemployment, since we do not know how quickly those who were recruited would have found work anyway.

How can we get a handle on these problems? Let us begin with displacement. Discussions of displacement normally involve a profound misconception. They assume that demand is limited, so that if someone gets a job there is one less job for others. If demand *is* limited, that is of course true, and there would be no point having any labour market policies. However, in fact, demand can easily be changed. What puts a limit on feasible demand is feasible supply. Labour market policy works only if it affects the economy's supply potential. And if it does that it cannot fail to have an effect, since in the long run the supply side rules.

The problem is to find out precisely how much a policy improves the supply potential, i.e. reduces equilibrium unemployment. If subsidies are applied that help some firms more than others, there may well be some displacement. But how can we hope to measure it? A full-blown model including the detailed market for products is well beyond the power of present-day economics. The

477

Table 1 *Public expenditure on labour market programmes in 1987 as a percentage of GDP*

	Employment services and administration	Labour market training (adults)	Special youth measures	Direct job creation and employment subsidies	Special measures for the disabled
	(1)	(2)	(3)	(4)	(5)
Australia	0.11	0.03	0.08	0.10	—
Austria	0.11	0.13	0.02	0.12	0.03
Belgium	0.17	0.08	—	0.69	0.16
Canada	0.21	0.22	0.12	0.02	—
Denmark	0.13	0.52	0.21	0.03	0.25
Finland	0.10	0.27	0.02	0.35	0.02
France	0.12	0.27	0.24	0.06	0.05
Germany	0.23	0.29	0.06	0.20	0.21
Greece	0.15	0.20	0.05	0.16	0.03
Ireland	0.17	0.56	0.40	0.32	—
Italy	0.08	0.01	0.37	—	—
Japan	0.03	0.03	—	0.10	0.01
Luxembourg	0.05	0.02	0.09	0.07	0.27
Netherlands	0.07	0.17	0.06	0.06	0.72
New Zealand	0.07	0.45	—	0.11	0.02
Norway	0.12	0.07	0.02	0.01	0.19
Portugal	0.08	0.22	0.08	0.14	0.04
Spain	0.08	0.10	0.19	0.38	0.01
Sweden	0.21	0.49	0.15	0.26	0.75
Switzerland	0.07	0.01	—	—	0.09
UK	0.16	0.11	0.27	0.31	0.04
USA	0.06	0.11	0.03	0.01	0.03

Notes: For Denmark and France, the figures refer to 1986. For Australia, Canada, Sweden, Japan, New Zealand, the UK, and the USA, the figures refer to fiscal years covering part of 1987.

Source: OECD, *Employment Outlook*, Sept. 1988, Table 3.1.

best approach is to go back to the flow equilibrium model of unemployment used earlier in this section.

This is also the only way to deal with the other problem: that we want to measure the *net* effect of the programme on the outflow from unemployment, after allowing for the fact that some of those whom the programme rescued from unemployment might have found jobs quite soon anyway—in some other firm.

Table 1—*continued*

	Subtotal: 'active' measures (cols. (1)–(5))	Unemployment compensation (6)	Early retirement for labour market reasons (7)	Subtotal: income maintenance (cols. (6)–(7))	Grand total
Australia	0.32	1.21	—	1.21	1.53
Austria	0.41	0.91	0.16	1.07	1.48
Belgium	0.10	2.42	0.83	3.25	4.35
Canada	0.57	1.68	—	1.68	2.24
Denmark	1.14	2.64	1.25	3.89	5.03
Finland	0.76	0.99	0.64	1.63	2.39
France	0.74	1.26	1.07	2.33	3.07
Germany	0.99	1.33	0.02	1.35	2.34
Greece	0.59	0.39	—	0.39	0.98
Ireland	1.45	3.66	—	3.66	5.12
Italy	0.46	0.49	0.32	0.81	1.27
Japan	0.17	0.42	—	0.42	0.59
Luxembourg	0.50	0.30	0.72	1.02	1.51
Netherlands	1.08	2.90	—	2.90	3.99
New Zealand	0.65	1.07	—	1.07	1.72
Norway	0.41	0.36	—	0.36	0.76
Portugal	0.56	0.38	—	0.38	0.94
Spain	0.76	2.50	0.04	2.54	3.30
Sweden	1.86	0.70	0.10	0.80	2.66
Switzerland	0.17	0.23	—	0.23	0.40
UK	0.89	1.66	0.02	1.68	2.57
USA	0.24	0.59	—	0.59	0.83

Evaluation: the aggregative approach

The most natural way to evaluate manpower programmes is thus as follows. We ask how the programme affected the outflow rate from unemployment and the inflow rate (other things held equal). When we know this, we know the effect of the programme upon the unemployment stock.

Let us begin with the outflow rate. The programmes have complex effects. They may take people out of unemployment; but if (like training programmes or public employment) this is only for a limited time, the subsidized individuals at some point will again compete with the remaining unemployed people for jobs. We cut through all this by simply asking, How do the programmes (X) affect the overall outflow from unemployment? For this purpose we estimate an equation of the form

$$H = V^{\alpha}(cU)^{1-\alpha},$$

where c is allowed to depend on X, as well as on other relevant variables like benefits and duration structure.[3] Once we know how the programme affects c, we know something about how it affects the unemployment rate (see equation (3)).

However, we also have to take into account the possible effect of the programmes in increasing the inflow into unemployment. This requires a parallel analysis of how the programme affects the inflow rate.

An example of the kind of outflow study discussed above is given in Disney *et al.* (1991: ch. 7). This shows in particular the major effect of the British Restart Programme in increasing the outflow rate from long-term unemployment. Under the programme, which began in 1986, all unemployed people are interviewed every six months and questioned about their efforts to find work. They are normally offered some kind of help, ranging from retraining to membership of a 'job club'. The effect has been striking.

As Chapter 9 (Fig. 5) shows, unemployment halved in Britain between 1986 and 1990. But registered vacancies did not increase and, comparing 1986 and 1990, there was not a large increase in labour shortages, as measured by the Confederation of British Industry. At the same time, wage inflation increased only slowly up to 1990. An important change has therefore been a greater effectiveness of the unemployed in filling the available vacancies. This is confirmed in Disney *et al.* (1991), where the time-series equation for outflow rates suggests that roughly the whole fall in long-term unemployment (at given vacancies) since 1986 is due to the Restart Programme. This is probably an exaggeration, since long-term unemployment also fell in Northern Ireland, which had no Restart Programme. But interestingly, in Northern Ireland long-term unemployment fell less than short-term unemployment, while in Britain long-term unemployment fell 20 per cent more than short-term unemployment. This confirms the substantial impact of Restart. Our interpretation is supported by these further facts: the low average productivity growth from 1986 onwards, as low-productivity vacancies got filled, and the rapid growth of low-paid and low-skilled employment (Layard 1990*b*).

Little comparable work on outflow rates has been done elsewhere. Edin and Holmlund (1990) have shown that in Sweden the number of people on training

480

programmes and relief work increases the ratio of hirings to unemployed people; in consequence, unemployment is reduced.

Evaluation: micro studies

Such aggregative studies should, of course, be supplemented by micro studies of individuals. But these will always be difficult to interpret. In the first place, there may or may not be offsetting general equilibrium effects of the kind discussed above. Second, the programmes may contribute to a work ethic atmosphere whose general effects cannot be picked up by comparing the achievements of those who do and do not participate in programmes (against the background of the same work ethic).

This said, it is surprising how little work has been done comparing the employment records of otherwise similar people exposed (and not exposed) to programmes. We need to know how long two otherwise identical people who enter unemployment can expect to remain unemployed (not including their time on a programme) if one of them goes on a programme and the other does not. We also want their subsequent employment records. For Sweden, Björkland (1990) summarizes six studies which are somewhat inconclusive. For the USA, most studies have concentrated on the effect on subsequent earnings rather than employment, and those that concentrate on employment tend not to concentrate on the immediate employment effect but rather on the longer term.

Cost–benefit issues

To judge the welfare effects (social present value) of a programme, we need to know more than its employment effects. We need rather to know the output benefits, the psychic benefits, and the social costs, as well as the distributional incidence. Let us comment on these briefly for the main types of programme.

1. *Tougher rules of benefit eligibility.* The real cost savings here are probably small (i.e. reduced tax wedges for those already employed). The output benefits may be considerable. But the distributional effects may be harsh.

2. *Training.* The real resource costs are large. The benefits include not only the simple output gain from lower unemployment, but also (hopefully) higher lifetime productivity for those trained. Since unemployment is one of the major sources of inequality in modern societies, there is also a major distributional gain from any reduction of unemployment that springs from increased opportunities for the unemployed, rather than from tougher benefits.

3. *Wage subsidies.* The real resource cost is small since these are essentially transfer payments—the cost is the deadweight loss from the taxes that finance the transfer. The benefits are mainly the output gain from reduced unemployment.

4. *Job creation.* The main resource cost is the supervisory labour needed. The benefits are whatever value added is produced (which in some programmes like the British Community Programme may not be very great: Normington *et al.* 1986). The benefits are likely to be much greater where the jobs are provided at regular workplaces.

Pin-point targeting

The policies we have discussed have the major merit of being targeted directly at the problem in hand. By contrast, general regional aid is often advocated on the ground that there are more unemployed in one region than another. This is a rather weak argument, for much of the expenditure generally fails to relieve unemployment at all. Instead, the policies we have been discussing aim directly at unemployment. They are thus highly regional, but are regional *as a consequence* of dealing with unemployment rather than in order imperfectly to do so. Likewise, these policies deal with skills mismatch directly where it shows up, unlike more general policies of skill training.

2. Policies on mismatch: employment subsidies and training

This brings us to the issue of whether more general action is needed to combat the mismatch across regions and across skills. We have discussed this at some length in Chapter 6, and need only summarize our conclusions here.

If there is excess supply of labour in some market, one could either stimulate demand in that sector by subsidizing employment, or reduce supply by subsidizing out-migration (i.e. physical migration or training). In the long run it does not make sense to do both. Which is appropriate depends on the externalities involved (including the distortions already embodied in the tax and benefit system). There is a strong case for subsidizing skill training (because of distortions arising from progressive taxes and capital market imperfections).[4] With regard to regions, there may be negative infrastructure externalities when people move to high-employment regions.

3. The reform of wage-bargaining and incomes policy

Bargaining systems

We turn now to the other key issue: the reform of wage-bargaining. Here Chapter 2 makes two main points. First, other things equal, unemployment is lower the lower is union coverage and the lower is union power in each bargain. This suggests the merits of limiting the power of individual unions.

But, second, for a given union coverage and union power, unemployment is lower when employers co-ordinate their wage offers at an industry or national level, and likewise when unions co-ordinate their wage claims. It is easy to see why co-ordination helps. When bargaining is decentralized, one man's wage increase is another man's price increase, as UK Prime Minister Harold Wilson once noted. So unions become more militant. At the same time, uncoordinated firms bid up wages, one against another. The result is increased inflationary pressure. By contrast, where there is a single national bargain (explicit or implicit), each man's wage increase is the *same* man's price increase. This reduces the pressure for fruitless increases in nominal wages.

So there seem to be two forms of organization that work well. One (as in the USA) has low union coverage—and preferably low union power. The other (as in Scandinavia and Austria, and to a lesser extent Germany) has high union coverage—with, again, low union power at the decentralized level but with strong national unions dealing on equal terms with employers. The choice between these is clearly political and depends also on the size of country. But economic arguments are also relevant.

The issue is really whether institutions exist which can overcome the externalities involved in decentralized wage-setting (whether by firms or by unions). The ideal here is that a consensus can develop about the going rate for the nominal wage, which can eliminate the wage–price and wage–wage spirals without requiring unemployment to perform that function. In this context there is a role for

1. an informed national debate about what rate makes sense;
2. reports by respected bodies such as Councils of Economic Advisers and research institutes;
3. national talks between employers and unions.

If the climate of opinion is responsible, a kind of implicit contract may emerge in which other bargainers follow a pattern settlement unless they face exceptional circumstances. Everyone recognizes the need for increasing flexibility in remuneration packages. But equally, it is important that most agreements stick within an accepted range of total remuneration and do not initiate a game of competitive leapfrogging.

However, this does presuppose a fairly high degree of social discipline. As Chapter 1 showed, it depends especially on the degree to which employers' associations can influence the behaviour of their members. If there is not sufficient social discipline, governments naturally consider direct inter-vention—normally called 'incomes policy'.

Conventional incomes policies

Thus, we have to consider the case for some form of government wage controls, such as a maximum permitted percentage rate of growth of wages. Incomes policies of this kind have been tried at many times and in many places.

To control inflation in the Roman Empire, the Emperor Diocletian issued a wage decree in AD 301 and those who breached it were sentenced to death. The policy was abandoned as a failure after 13 years.

In AD 1971 President Nixon introduced a three-month wage–price freeze followed by two years of less rigid controls. The policy clearly restrained inflationary pressure while it lasted, but proved unsustainable under the pressure of shortages of labour and goods (Blinder 1979).

In Britain there was a statutory incomes policy from 1972 to 1974 and a voluntary one (initially agreed with the Trades Union Congress) from 1975 to 1979. Both of these were abandoned, mainly because of union opposition. However, the second of the policies was at first remarkably successful, and helped to reduce inflation from 28 to 8 per cent in two years with no increase in unemployment. After the policy was abandoned inflation rose again. Some people said this was due to a 'catching-up effect'. But the best econometric evidence does not support the view that in Britain reductions of inflation achieved during incomes policies are automatically undone once the policies end (Wadhwani 1985).

In France an incomes policy was introduced in 1982 and inflation fell over four years from 12 to 3 per cent. The wage norms had statutory force in the public sector, and the employers' federation broadly followed the same norms.

Similarly, Belgium and Italy have, since 1982, had laws prescribing the maximum degree of wage indexation in between major renegotiations, which again implies a form of wage norm. Inflation has fallen.

Australia has a long-standing system of quasi-judicial determination of basic wage rates, above which 'overaward' payments can be negotiated. However, since 1983 the national government, in agreement with the union movement, has set the basic norm within which the system operates.

There are two main problems with fully centralized governmental incomes policies. First, they infringe the principle of free bargaining between workers and employers. Thus, many individual groups have a strong incentive to breach the norm. This is also the case, of course, where a norm has been bargained centrally between confederations of employers and unions; but individual groups are more inclined to accept a deal to which they are, at least, an indirect party. For this reason governmental incomes policies that have the support of the confederations of employers and unions are themselves more likely to last than those that are imposed. But history suggests that nearly all such policies are eventually breached. A permanent centralized incomes policy is probably infeasible.

The second problem is that a centralized incomes policy is inherently inflexible. It is bound to impose rigidity on the structure of relative wages. But the reallocation of labour may be much easier if relative wages rise where labour is scarce and vice versa. Without this, structural unemployment is likely to become worse, unless major efforts are made, as in Sweden, to promote movement of labour between industries and regions. Incomes policies sometimes try to incorporate committee mechanisms for adjusting relativities, but these cannot work as effectively as the market.

The result is that incomes policies of this kind have always been short-lived. This does not mean they have always been useless. Indeed, a temporary incomes policy is a much better way to disinflate than having a period of high unemployment. And if unemployment is above the long run NAIRU and there is hysteresis, a temporary incomes policy is an excellent way of helping unemployment to return to the NAIRU more quickly.

Tax-based incomes policies

But one would also like to achieve a permanent reduction in the NAIRU itself. If this is to be through incomes policy, it must be through some mechanism other than direct controls. This leads to the proposal for tax-based incomes policy. Under this there is a norm for the growth of nominal wages, but employers are free to pay more than the norm at the cost of a substantial financial penalty. Thus, if employers need to break the norm in order to recruit labour or avoid a strike they will do so. But all bargainers will be subject to strong disincentives to excessive settlements. Let us see more clearly how this would work.

If the free market generates excessive wage pressure, the obvious solution is to tax excessive wages. This is generally the most efficient way to deal with market failure, unless direct controls have some particular advantage. One

485

approach is through a tax on excessive wage growth; another is through a progressive tax on wage levels. For the sake of clarity, we shall discuss them in reverse order, starting with a tax on the level of wages.

Suppose that the tax is paid by firms. If a firm pays its workers a gross real wage W_i, it also has to pay the exchequer a net tax per worker of $tW_i - S$, where t is the tax rate and S a positive per-worker subsidy. Hence the firm's labour cost is

$$C_i = W_i(1 + t) - S.$$

We assume that the scheme is self-financing, so that, *ex post* in the representative firm, $C_i = W_i$.

How does this reduce wage pressure and thus unemployment? The basic mechanism is that when workers gain an extra \$1 of wages it costs the firm an extra \$$(1 + t)$. Thus the firm is more willing to resist any claim, while the workers may be more anxious about making the claim because of its greater employment effect. As on p. 101, the bargained wage W_i is that which maximizes $\beta \log(W_i - A)S_i + \log \Pi_i$. Hence the bargain fixes the wage (W_i) so that

$$\frac{\beta}{W_i - A} + \frac{\beta}{S_i} \frac{\partial S_i}{\partial C_i} \frac{\partial C_i}{\partial W_i} - \frac{N_i}{\Pi_i} \frac{\partial C_i}{\partial W_i} = 0,$$

where by the envelope theorem a rise in unit labour cost (C_i) reduces profit by N_i so that $\partial \Pi_i / \partial C_i = -N_i$.

Since the tax sets $\partial C_i / \partial W_i = 1 + t$ and *ex post* it is self-financing with $C_i = W_i$, the mark-up of the wage over outside opportunities is given by

$$\frac{W_i - A}{W_i} = \frac{1 - \alpha\kappa}{(1 + t)(\varepsilon_{SN} + \alpha\kappa/\beta)},$$

where ε_{SN} is the absolute elasticity of survival with respect to expected employment (see Chapter 2, equation (12)). The higher the tax rate, the less will wages tend to leapfrog each other. Thus equilibrium unemployment (u^*) will be lower. For, since $W_i = W = W^e$ in equilibrium,

$$u^* = \frac{1 - \alpha\kappa}{(1 + t)(\varepsilon_{SN} + \alpha\kappa/\beta)\varphi(1 - b)}.$$

For comparison, see Chapter 2, equation (20).

Alternatively, if firms set wages on the basis of efficiency considerations, the firm chooses W_i to solve

$$\min \frac{C_i}{e(W_i/W^e, u)},$$

where e is the effort function (see Chapter 3, Section 1). This requires

$$C_i \frac{e_1}{W^e} - e \frac{\mathrm{d}C_i}{\mathrm{d}W_i} = 0.$$

Thus, in equilibrium (with $C_i = W_i = W = W^e$),

$$e_1(1, u^*) = e(1, u^*)(1 + t).$$

For comparison, see Chapter 3, equation (3). Since $e_{12} < 0$ and $e_2 > 0$, the tax reduces unemployment.

Needless to say, it makes no difference whether the tax is levied on firms or workers.[5] But it must be progressive so that, when wages rise, labour cost rises faster than (net) wages do; i.e., a part of wage cost must be tax-exempt, through a positive S. A proportional tax at rate t whose proceeds were given to the Martians would have no effect.

Of course, any tax introduces some distortions, even while it offsets others. A tax on weekly earnings could have severe effects on work incentives, so the tax should be levied on hourly earnings to make it as near an ideal tax as possible.

There is however an argument for levying the tax in the form of a tax on proportional wage *growth*. Any tax is unpopular, and becomes acceptable only if its purpose is transparent. Since the aim is to reduce inflationary pressure, it seems much more natural to tax wage growth. It may even be more effective, since human responses are affected in part by perceptions and not simply by what economic calculus would dictate, given fully accurate perceptions.

A tax on wage growth is the normal form of the proposal for a tax-based incomes policy. The original proposal, by Wallich and Weintraub (1971), envisaged a variable rate of profit tax depending on whether a firm was sticking to the wage norm or not. However, in most countries many firms avoid profit tax. Moreover, Wallich and Weintraub's purpose in using the profit tax was to stop firms passing on the tax in prices. But the latter can easily be prevented at the aggregate level through a wage tax whose proceeds are distributed as a uniform per-worker subsidy. This is the scheme we propose.

Thus, the real tax per worker is $T[W_i - W_{i-1}(1 + n)] - S$, where W_i is the gross real wage and n is the norm for the growth rate of real earnings. The tax is of course expressed in nominal terms, but from the firm's point of view the general rate of inflation is exogenous. Thus the real norm (n) is the nominal norm minus expected price inflation. (One obvious possibility is to fix the nominal norm equal to expected price inflation, in which case $n = 0$.)

Let us analyse such a system. It differs from the simple tax on the wage level in that, if a firm raises its wages now (and expects the tax to continue), its wage growth next year will, other things equal, be lower. Hence it will save on future taxes, even though it pays more taxes now. In fact, the tax will only work because of discounting, and we shall discover that, if the tax rate on wage growth is T,

$$\frac{du}{dT} = \frac{du}{dt}(r - n),$$

where r is the real discount rate, n is the real norm, and du/dt is the effect of the wage level tax analysed above.

Let us analyse this for the case of efficiency wages. The firm wishes to maximize its present value. If $R(\cdot)$ is real revenue, the present value of real profit is (suppressing the subscript i for the firm)

$$PV = \sum_j (1 - r)^j \left(R_j(e_j N_j) - \frac{C_j}{e_j} e_j N_j \right),$$

where

$$C_j = W_j(1 + T) - TW_{j-1}(1 + n) - S.$$

This is maximized with respect to each period's W and each period's eN (treated as a single variable). The wage is chosen simply to minimize the cost per efficiency unit of labour (appropriately weighted). Thus, the wage in period s is chosen so that

$$\frac{\partial PV}{\partial W_s} = -(1 - r)^s \frac{e_s N_s}{e_s^2} \left(e_s(1 + T) - C_s e_{s1} \frac{1}{W_s^e} \right) + (1 - r)^{s+1} N_{s+1} T(1 + n) = 0.$$

Thus, in the steady state (with e, N constant and hence $e_{s1} = e_1$, all s) and in general equilibrium (with $C_i = W_i = W = W^e$), we have

$$e(1 + T) = e_1 + (1 - r)eT(1 + n)$$

or

$$\frac{e_1}{e} \simeq 1 + T(r - n).$$

The effect of the once-for-all tax on wage increases is thus a multiple $(r - n)$ of the effect of an equal permanent tax on the wage level. As before, we can think of the tax as shifting down the wage equation (for real labour cost) while leaving the price equation unchanged. A tax-based incomes policy requires a really stiff tax rate—if the tax is expected to last.

If we turn to wage-bargaining, it is easy to repeat the analysis, assuming a once-for-all bargain about the whole course of future wages (Jackman and Layard 1990). Once again, we find that

$$\frac{\mathrm{d}u}{\mathrm{d}T} = (r - n)\frac{\mathrm{d}u}{\mathrm{d}t}.$$

However, the analysis so far has ignored the issue of workers' effort. If wages (or wage increases) are taxed, this inevitably leads to fewer productivity bargains and lower 'effort'. There are two approaches to this problem. One is to accept this result as unavoidable, and see whether the costs of the policy exceed the benefits. In Jackman and Layard (1990) we try to compute these, and conclude that unless unemployment is very low this is unlikely to be the case.[6] The other approach is to have administrative procedures which exempt from the tax those wage increases that are based on productivity bargains (Layard and Nickell 1986*a*). On the whole, we prefer administrative simplicity and would make no exceptions.

Administrative aspects of tax-based incomes policy (TIP)

According to many people, 'the major problem with TIP is that it would be very difficult to administer' (Dornbusch and Fischer 1987: 530). Need this be true? Not at all. There are a number of basic principles.

The tax should be collected by the normal tax authorities. It should be computed on the basis of the average earnings per worker-hour in the firm. There should be no exceptions, whether for promotion, regrading, or other reasons. Thus the tax liability can be easily computed. Like other business taxes, the firm should calculate its own tax liability and pay up. The accuracy of the calculation can easily be checked by the tax authorities, provided the definition of earnings is the same as when the firm calculates the withholding income tax for its employees. To avoid an excessive number of tax returns, the tax (*and* accompanying subsidy) could be confined to firms with over, say, 100 employees. People tend to assume that existing taxes are well founded and new ones impracticable. But a TIP could be just as practicable as most existing taxes. (For further discussion see Jackman and Layard 1986.)

There are of course some distortions introduced by any tax. We have already mentioned the issue of productivity-bargaining. In addition, under our kind of TIP it pays firms to hire more unskilled workers, and to cut overtime. Firms also gain if they hive off their most skilled activities into separate companies— but this could be eliminated by imposing a joint tax liability on two or more firms that have de-merged. On balance, we believe that the benefits of the tax would in many countries outweigh the costs stemming from the distortions.

Needless to say, a policy that reduced unemployment need not *ipso facto* reduce real take-home pay. There are two forces tending to reduce pay: any terms-of-trade loss required to balance the current account, and any tendency to increased mark-ups of (value added) prices over wages. But on the other side, there is an increased tax base (and reduced unemployment benefit expenditures) from which to finance a given government expenditure ('fiscal increasing returns'). The final outcome would depend on the relative magnitudes involved (Blanchard and Summers 1987).

We have so far discussed TIP as a permanent policy. In periods of high unemployment or inflation, the argument for it on a temporary basis is even stronger. It would always be worth using incomes policy to contain a supply shock, and (in the presence of hysteresis) it would always be worth using an incomes policy to contain inflation while reducing unemployment. In this context, a TIP would always be less distorting than any other form of incomes policy.

4. Marginal employment subsidies

One can always think of any policy to reduce unemployment as shifting the feasible real wage function relative to the target real wage function. The policies we have been looking at so far work basically by reducing the target real wage function. The next policy, which has been advocated by Rehn (1982) and others, works by raising the feasible real wage. In other words, it reduces prices relative to wages.

The method is simple. Prices are a mark-up on the marginal cost of output. We therefore need to reduce the marginal cost of output, while holding wages constant. We do this by a marginal subsidy to employment, financed by an intra-marginal tax.

We shall begin by assuming that in each period marginal employment is measured from a fixed base that does not move over time. If there is a marginal employment subsidy, the marginal cost of labour is then reduced relative to the intra-marginal cost. For example, suppose there were a subsidy at rate s on the wages of all workers employed in excess of some level N_{i0}. And suppose this were financed by a tax at rate t on the wages of the N_{i0} intra-marginal workers.

We can analyse the effects first under efficiency wages and then under wage-bargaining. Under efficiency wages, in each wage-setting firm the problem is[7]

$$\max_{W_i, N_i} \Pi_i = R\left[e\left(\frac{W_i}{W^e}, u \right) N_i \right] - W_i(1 + t) N_{i0} - W_i(1 - s)(N_i - N_{i0}).$$

Wages are set according to

$$\frac{\partial \Pi_i}{\partial W_i} = R' \frac{e_1 N_i}{W^e} - (1 + t)N_{i0} - (1 - s)(N_i - N_{i0}) = 0.$$

In equilibrium the scheme is self-financing, and thus $tN_0 = s(N - N_0)$. Hence

$$R'e_1 = W.$$

Assuming for simplicity that $Y = eN$, and ignoring nominal inertia (i.e. setting $W = W^e$), this implies an aggregate *wage equation*,

$$W = e_1(1, u)\kappa.$$

This is standard. (See Chapter 3, equation (6), setting $\alpha = 1$, $W = W^e$.) But the pricing equation is altered since relative prices are a mark-up on real marginal cost $W(1 - s)/e$. Hence, again setting $W = W^e$, we have an aggregate *price equation*,

$$W = \frac{e(1,u)}{1 - s}\kappa.$$

(See Chapter 3, equation (7), setting $\alpha = 1$, $W = W^e$, for comparison.) Thus, the subsidy raises real take-home pay at given unemployment. Equilibrium unemployment falls.

The preceding discussion related to a subsidy paid relative to a fixed level of employment. If the scheme were a subsidy on employment in excess of α times last period's employment, then the firm has an intertemporal optimization problem. Equilibrium unemployment is as above except that the effective subsidy is $\hat{\delta}s$ where $\hat{\delta}$ is the real discount rate (less the growth rate of real wages).[8] This is because an increase in employment this year attracts a subsidy this year, but reduces next year's subsidy by raising the base from which next year's employment is measured. Once again, unemployment falls.

The marginal employment subsidy works equally well in a bargaining model. If unions care only about wages, the maximand is

$$\Omega_i = (W_i - A)^\beta \Pi_i,$$

where $\Pi_i = R(N_i) - W_i(1 + t)N_{i0} - W_i(1 - s)(N_i - N_{i0})$, and we require

$$\frac{\partial \log \Omega_i}{\partial W_i} = \frac{\beta}{W_i - A} - \frac{(1 + t)N_{i0} + (1 - s)(N_i - N_{i0})}{\Pi_i} = 0.$$

Hence in stationary general equilibrium, ignoring benefits and setting $\varphi = 1$,

$$u^* = \beta \frac{\Pi}{WN}.$$

If (for simplicity) $Y = N$, budget balance implies a price equation

$$W = \frac{\kappa}{1 - s},$$

and thus

$$u^* = \beta \frac{\Pi}{WN} = \beta \left(\frac{Y}{WN} - 1 \right) = \beta \left(\frac{1 - s}{\kappa} - 1 \right).$$

As the subsidy rate rises, the profit share falls and so does unemployment.

Clearly, we do not want this process to reduce post-tax profit, but this can be restored by reductions in profit tax financed by proportional taxes on workers. The latter, as we have seen, would not affect unemployment.

Empirical evidence

Marginal employment subsidies have been more discussed than practised. However, there is useful experience from Britain. In the late 1970s a marginal employment subsidy equal to almost one-third of the average wage was offered to small firms in high-unemployment areas. This was paid on all increases in employment. A control group of matched firms was established in unsubsidized areas. Employment grew by 12 per cent more in the subsidized firms. This also coincided with firms' own reports on the induced employment effect (Layard 1979).

5. Non-targeted public employment

It is sometimes suggested that, if the private sector cannot employ the whole labour force, the public sector should act as the employer of last resort. We have shown that, for the long-term unemployed, there is a case for targeted public employment and training of this kind. But the case for general public employment is much less clear.

Suppose initially that there is pure mark-up pricing (W/P independent of u). Then a given level of unemployment is always needed to make that real wage acceptable, and the mix of employment between the public and private sector is irrelevant.

At least, this is true for a closed economy. For an open economy, it is important that public services are much less import-intensive than other forms of final demand. So if public employment is expanded, the terms of trade (at a balanced current account) can improve. This will make possible a temporary fall in equilibrium unemployment.

Going further, we have normally assumed that pricing is somewhat responsive to private-sector employment. This means that an increase in public employment will not require the same fall in real wages as an increase in private employment. Thus, if public employment is increased, the real wage will rise somewhat. There will be some displacement of private employment but a net gain in total employment. Such a result depends, however, on the assumption that the taxes needed to finance public employment would be fully absorbed by labour. If this were not the case, the policy would fail, and it depends in any case on very specific assumptions about pricing behaviour and the allocation of capital between sectors.

6. Profit-sharing

We turn now to another device that has been proposed for reducing equilibrium unemployment: profit-sharing. Social reformers have often praised profit-sharing as an instrument for encouraging productivity. But more recently Weitzman (1983, 1984) has argued strongly that it will also reduce equilibrium unemployment.

Weitzman's model with long-run market-clearing

Weitzman's original argument was couched in terms of a labour market that cleared in the long run. The merit of profit-sharing was that it guaranteed stability of employment in the face of shocks. The argument was powerful and attractive. The problem with the wage system is the fragility of full employment, since, at equilibrium, firms are indifferent between employing the whole labour force or just a bit less; if demand falls at all and wages are at all rigid, they employ fewer people. If only we could find a way to ensure that at full employment firms would want to employ *more* than the whole labour force!

Weitzman had the answer: profit-sharing. If this was in place, the basic wage would be lower and this would generate excess demand for labour. Then when marginal revenue fell, firms would not cut employment, since they would still have some excess demand for labour.

Let us look at this more formally. Suppose each monopolistic competitor produces output with a concave production function $f(N_i)$. Under the wage system, the firm's equilibrium employment is given by

$$W_i = R'(N),$$

where all variables are in real terms. This is illustrated in Fig. 2(*a*). If the economy is in long-run equilibrium with an inelastic labour supply *L* spread over *F* firms, the equilibrium *real* wage *W** is given by

$$W^* = \kappa f' \left(\frac{L}{F} \right).$$

Suppose we now have a real downwards productivity shock, as shown by the line *MR'* in Fig. 2(*a*). If the wage is predetermined, employment falls. (The same would follow if we considered *W* to be fixed in nominal terms and there were a fall in nominal demand.)

We now turn to the profit-sharing system, in Fig. 2(*b*). Each worker is paid a real base wage $\underline{W}_i$ (that is below *W**) plus a share (s_i) of profits per worker. So total earnings per worker (W_i) are

$$W_i = \underline{W}_i + s_i \left(\frac{R(N_i)}{N_i} - \underline{W}_i \right).$$

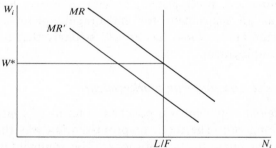

(a)   The wage system: the representative firm

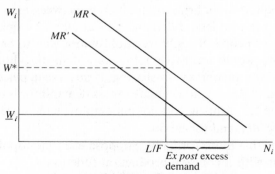

(b)   Profit-sharing: the representative firm

Fig. 2.   *The wage system and the profit-sharing system.*

Once $\underline{W}_i$ and s_i have been fixed, the firm's *ex post* desire is to maximize $(1 - s_i)(R(N_i) - \underline{W}_i N_i)$. Thus it would like to employ workers up to the level given by

$$\underline{W}_i = R'(N_i) = \kappa f'(N_i). \tag{4}$$

Since $\underline{W}_i$ is less than W^*, this level of labour demand is higher than the previous level of employment (L/F). But there are no more workers to go round, so the firm ends up employing L/F workers as before. However, it is permanently hungry for workers, and goes around with a vacuum cleaner grabbing any spare ones it can find.

But surely, one might say, even if s_i is fixed (which we shall assume), doesn't $\underline{W}_i$ rise to clear the market? The answer is No. For *ex ante*, the firm only needs to pay total remuneration $(\underline{W}_i + s_i \Pi_i)$ fractionally higher than the going rate of total remuneration (W^*) in order to get any amount of labour. It therefore selects $\underline{W}_i$ to satisfy the *ex ante* constraint

$$\underline{W}_i + s_i \Pi_i^e = W^*$$

In doing this it computes Π_i^e on the basis of an expected revenue function $R^e(N_i)$. Thus the firm faces an earnings constraint

$$\underline{W}_i + s_i \left(\frac{R^e(N_i)}{N_i} - \underline{W}_i \right) = W^*. \tag{5}$$

But this still does not tell us how to fix $\underline{W}_i$ until we know N_i. So the firm also has to make a plan for N_i. It does this so as to

$$\max R^e(N_i) - \left[\underline{W}_i + s_i \left(\frac{R^e(N_i)}{N_i} - \underline{W}_i \right) \right] N_i,$$

subject to (5). The solution for N_i is N_i^*, where

$$W^* = R^{e\prime}(N_i^*), \tag{6}$$

and the solution for $\underline{W}_i$ is given by (5) with $N_i = N_i^*$.

How on earth can we reconcile (4) and (6)? The answer is simple. Equation (4) tells us how many workers the firm would like to employ *ex post*, given $\underline{W}_i$. Equation (6) tells us how many workers the firm will plan to hire *ex ante* when it sets $\underline{W}_i$. Assuming the total labour supply is completely inelastic at L and there are F firms, each firm will end up employing L/F workers and W^* will be given by

$$W^* = R^{e\prime} \left(\frac{L}{F} \right).$$

Even so, having set $\underline{W}_i$, the firm will always be willing to hire more workers. Thus, even if the revenue function falls, employment will not fall.

The *ex ante/ex post* distinction here exactly parallels the situation of a profit-maximizing monopolist. He sets his price *ex ante* to equate expected marginal revenue and marginal cost, and this gives him his expected sales. *Ex post*, having set the price, he would like to sell much more—up to the point where marginal cost equals price (not marginal revenue). Thus, if the revenue function turns out differently from what he expected, the full adjustment is in terms of sales rather than price. In the case of profit-sharing, it is not employment that adjusts, but profits and earnings.[9]

Weitzman thinks of L as some fixed upper limit to employment. If there is profit-sharing, actual employment will almost always be equal to L. Under the wage system *equilibrium* employment will also be L, but under negative shocks actual employment will be less than L—so *average* employment will be less than L.

If the wage system is worse than the profit-sharing one, why do firms not all adopt profit-sharing? The answer is that it would not be in the interests of any one firm on its own to do so. For suppose a firm employing L/F workers at a wage W^* instead introduced a profit-sharing package $(\underline{W}_i, s_i)$ such that real labour earnings

$$W_i = \underline{W}_i + s_i \left(\frac{R(L/F)}{L/F} - \underline{W}_i \right) = W^*.$$

They would then have an *ex post* incentive to expand employment beyond L/F. But since average revenue $R(N_i)/N_i$ is falling, labour earnings would then steadily fall below W^*. The firm might promise its workers not to employ more than L/F workers. But since in a wage economy other firms would lay off workers in a downturn, the profit-sharing firm would be sorely tempted to take them on and thus dilute workers' average income. Faced with this risk, workers might not be willing to join the firm in the first place. The attraction of profit-sharing comes when *all* firms are profit-sharing. Then workers know that, since total employment is stable, the risk of a huge influx into their firm is small. The situation of excess demand for labour is in the public interest, even though it is not in the interest of any one firm.

Weitzman's analysis attracted much public attention, owing to the force of the argument and to his suggestion that profit-sharing might explain low Japanese unemployment. However, two problems were immediately apparent. First, the result depends crucially on the assumption that, after the package $(\underline{W}_i, s_i)$ has been determined, the management retains the right to determine employment (N_i). However, *it is not clear whether, once profit-sharing is introduced, workers will still leave employers with this 'right to manage'.* For an increase in employment will cut workers' individual earnings, since average revenue $(R(N_i)/N_i)$ decreases when extra workers are taken on. Thus, under profit-sharing all workers take an interest in employment, while in a wage economy (with sufficient turnover) they will not care one way or the other. Moreover, once profit-sharing is introduced, workers are bound to acquire more information about the firm and thus a greater ability to negotiate about other aspects of operations. This problem of the continuing right to manage is the central problem in any analysis of profit-sharing.

The second limitation of Weitzman's original model is that it assumed long-run market-clearing.[10] So let us see how profit-sharing would fare in our two basic non-market-clearing models of the labour market. We shall then find that profit-sharing makes no difference with efficiency wages; nor does it under wage-bargaining (at least with a Cobb–Douglas production function).

Efficiency wages

The basic problem under efficiency wages is that the workers' efficiency is determined not by the base wage $\underline{W}_i$ but by total earnings (W_i). Thus effort is

$$E_i = e\left(\frac{W_i}{W^e}, u\right)$$

where

$$W_i = \underline{W}_i + s_i\left(\frac{R(N_i)}{N_i} - \underline{W}_i\right).$$

Profit is

$$\Pi = R(E_i N_i) - W_i N_i = R(E_i N_i) - \frac{W_i}{E_i} E_i N_i.$$

Thus profit can be maximized recursively. The first step is to choose W_i to minimize

$$\frac{W_i}{e(W_i/W^e, u)}.$$

The second step is, given W_i, to choose $E_i N_i$.[11] The choice of W_i implies the usual elasticity condition,

$$\frac{e_1}{e}\frac{W_i}{W^e} = 1,$$

497

and the second step leads to the choice of N_i with

$$R'e_i = W_i$$

(i.e., marginal revenue product per worker is equal to total earnings rather than to the base wage, $\underline{W}_i$).

Thus in general equilibrium ($W_i = W = W^e$) we have our standard result that

$$e_1(1, u^*) = e(1, u^*)$$

whether or not profit-sharing is in force. Neither unemployment nor real earnings are affected by profit-sharing.

We have not so far allowed for any effect of profit-sharing *per se* upon efficiency. There is good evidence of such an effect (Estrin and Wilson 1986; Weitzman and Kruse 1990). But, as we have seen, productivity as such has no effect on equilibrium unemployment. Profit-sharing could have an effect only if it altered the marginal effect of W within the efficiency function.

Wage-bargaining

If we turn to wage-bargaining we reach similar conclusions, assuming a Cobb–Douglas production function. If we take our standard bargaining model, we can modify it to allow for bargaining not only over the base wage $\underline{W}_i$ but over the profit share s_i. Assuming that the employer will then select the level of employment, the problem is

$$\max_{\underline{W}_i, s_i} \Omega_i = \left(\underline{W}_i + s_i \frac{\Pi_i}{N_i} - A\right)^{\beta} S_i^{\beta} \Pi_i (1 - s_i),$$

subject to $N_i = N(\underline{W}_i)$. If the production function is $Y_i = N_i^{\alpha} K_i^{1-\alpha}$ and there is perfect competition ($\kappa = 1$), profit-maximizing behaviour will make

$$\frac{\Pi_i}{\underline{W}_i N_i} = \frac{1 - \alpha}{\alpha}.$$

So the problem can be written

$$\max_{\underline{W}_i, s_i} \Omega_i = \left[\underline{W}_i \left(1 + s_i \frac{1 - \alpha}{\alpha}\right) - A\right]^{\beta} S_i^{\beta} \Pi_i (1 - s_i)$$

The first-order condition for the base wage $\underline{W}_i$ is

$$\frac{\partial \log \Omega_i}{\partial \underline{W}_i} = \frac{\beta \left(1 + s_i \dfrac{1-\alpha}{\alpha}\right)}{\underline{W}_i \left(1 + s_i \dfrac{1-\alpha}{\alpha}\right) - A} + \frac{\beta}{S_i} \frac{\partial S_i}{\partial \underline{W}_i} - \frac{N_i}{\Pi_i} = 0,$$

or, multiplying by $\underline{W}_i$,

$$\frac{\beta \underline{W}_i \left(1 + s_i \dfrac{1-\alpha}{\alpha}\right)}{\underline{W}_i \left(1 + s_i \dfrac{1-\alpha}{\alpha}\right) - A} + \frac{\beta \underline{W}_i}{S_i} \frac{\partial S_i}{\partial W_i} - \frac{\underline{W}_i N_i}{\Pi_i} = 0.$$

Hence in general equilibrium (and ignoring benefits),

$$\varphi u^* = \frac{1 - \alpha}{\varepsilon_{SN} + \alpha/\beta}.$$

This is exactly the same as would have applied in the absence of profit-sharing.

The inner logic of this result can be explained by two propositions, taken together. (The propositions relate to the case where demand is known with certainty.)

1. Bargaining over profit-sharing is exactly the same as bargaining over wages and employment (with no profit share). For in a bargain over profit-sharing, the base wage ($\underline{W}_i$) determines employment ($N(\underline{W}_i)$); and given N_i, the profit share then determines total remuneration ($\underline{W}_i + s_i R(N_i)/N_i$). This important equivalence was first shown by Pohjola (1987) and subsequently by Hoel and Moene (1988).

2. Going on, we showed in the third section of Chapter 2 that, with a Cobb–Douglas production function, equilibrium unemployment was unchanged when we moved from a standard wage bargain to bargaining over wages and employment—always assuming an interior solution for this problem.

Hence, if we move from a standard wage bargain to bargaining over profit-sharing ($\underline{W}_i, s_i$), unemployment will also be unchanged.

As we said in Chapter 2, there is nothing sacrosanct about Cobb–Douglas. But the preceding analysis at least makes it clear that there is no simple presumption about how profit-sharing might affect unemployment.

Indeed, we have already been quite generous to profit-sharing. For in the certainty case, as we showed in Chapter 2, the firm will in the steady state reach a position where workers no longer care (locally) about employment. The Nash maximand is now

$$\Omega_i = (W_i - A)^\beta (R(N_i) - W_i N_i),$$

where W_i is total remuneration per worker. Under the wage system, with zero profit-share, this leads to a particular value of W_i, and firms then employ workers on the demand curve where $R'(N_i) = W_i$. This is an efficient bargain, since profit is maximized for the given value of remuneration per worker. Suppose now we introduce the possibility of profit-sharing, so that

$$W_i = \underline{W}_i + s_i(\Pi_i/N_i).$$

If s_i is chosen to be non-zero, it follows that $\underline{W}_i$ is lower than W_i. The firm then maximizes profit for a given value of $\underline{W}_i$ rather than W_i. Thus, employment lies on the demand curve at a point corresponding to $\underline{W}_i$. Since remuneration per worker exceeds W_i, the contract point is off the demand curve and thus off the contract curve. It is not efficient, since it does not maximize profit for given remuneration per worker. Any profit share greater than zero, therefore, does not maximize Ω and will not be selected. The option of profit-sharing will not be exploited because the parties can do better.

This may help to explain the extraordinarily low take-up of profit-sharing in Britain despite the tax inducements now on offer.[12] Moreover, even when tax inducements are on offer, there is the obvious danger that, if true profit-sharing does not maximize Ω, the firm and workers will devise a cosmetic scheme which looks like profit-sharing but in fact replicates what would have happened anyway; the difference is that they have in addition a nice nest-egg of taxpayers' money to divide among themselves.

Evidence from Japan and elsewhere

We have taken Weitzman's argument very seriously, as it deserves. But what evidence is there that profit-sharing works in the way he suggests? The basic force of the argument came from invoking the Japanese example. But why exactly is unemployment in Japan so low and so stable?

It is not because of any of the mechanisms Weitzman describes, as the following facts about Japan make clear (Wadhwani 1987).

1. Output is not stable. It fluctuates (about its trend) more than in most countries. It responds to monetary shocks exactly as elsewhere.
2. Nominal prices *are* affected by cost factors, and not simply by demand.
3. Excess demand for labour, as reported by firms, is rather lower than in other countries.
4. It does not appear that employment is determined in the short run by base wages. Freeman and Weitzman (1987) find that it is, when they hold output constant. But if (as appropriate) one holds capital constant, the effect found

by Weitzman and Freeman at the whole-economy level disappears (Estrin *et al.* 1987). The results of Brunello (1988) are ambiguous, in that what determines employment appears to vary between industries. But in analyses of firms, base wages have no different effect from bonus in determining employment: the number of jobs depends on total pay per worker (Brunello and Wadhwani 1991).

Having said all this, the basic fact remains that employment in Japan is stable, compared with elsewhere. What happens is roughly as follows. Only 40 per cent of Japanese workers are in the organized sector (where bonuses are paid); another 30 per cent are employees in the small-firm sector, and 30 per cent are family workers. When output fluctuates, employment in the formal sector fluctuates quite a lot. But employment in small firms varies much less (Brunello and Wadhwani 1989). This is quite simply because the flexibility of pay per worker is very high in the market-clearing small-firm sector, while it is much less high in large bonus-paying firms. Thus, Japan's stable employment record is due mainly to the wage flexibility in the small-firm sector. As a result, the total labour input (HN) fluctuates less in Japan than in other countries. On top of this, the Japanese value their human capital highly, so they use hours per worker (H) as a shock-absorber more than most other countries, further dampening fluctuations in employment (N).

In addition, the labour force (L) shrinks in recession, as 'secondary' female workers leave the labour market. This makes unemployment ($L - N$) even more stable than employment (compared with other countries).

So what does the Japanese evidence tell us about profit-sharing? Since the intermediate predictions of Weitzman's theory are not borne out, one can say either that his theory is wrong or that Japan is not a case of profit-sharing. There is a lot to be said for the latter view (Dore *et al.* 1989). While 25 per cent of remuneration is in bonus, much of this is indeed a fixed element. Thus we must probably conclude that Japan provides little evidence either for or against profit-sharing.

To understand the effects of profit-sharing, a different tack is to compare profit-sharing with non-profit-sharing firms. There is extensive evidence on the effects of profit-sharing on productivity from many countries (Weitzman and Kruse 1990). This work suggests that profit-sharing either increases productivity or has no effect. No study actually suggests that profit-sharing might hurt productivity.

There is also work on the effects of profit-sharing on employment and wages. British micro datasets fail to reveal any evidence that employment is determined by the base wage (Wadhwani and Wall 1990*b*). However, there is some suggestion that employment might be higher in profit-sharing firms (through productivity effects). On wages, the analysis of Weitzman (1987) or Jackman (1988) predicts that total remuneration would, *ceteris paribus*, be lower in profit-sharing firms. The analysis of Japanese firms in Brunello and Wadhwani (1991) strongly rejects this proposition, with the evidence suggesting the opposite.

There is also the issue of employment stability. Kruse (1987) presents US micro evidence suggesting that the statistical association between aggregate unemployment and employment at the firm level is less strong for profit-sharing firms.[13] However, Wadhwani and Wall (1990*b*) present a more formal test of this proposition in the context of a labour demand model, and find no difference in the effect of aggregate demand shocks on employment between profit-sharing and non-profit-sharing firms.

Because the productivity effect of profit-sharing is so well established, we are strong supporters of that practice. But we do not have high hopes that it will reduce unemployment.

7.   Work-sharing and early retirement

Many people believe that, to reduce unemployment, we should cut working hours and encourage early retirement. Let us review the arguments for and against these ideas.

The case for shorter working hours

The case for shorter hours runs like this. Suppose that as a nation we are going to produce a certain amount of output. This means, roughly speaking, that there is a certain total number of hours of work to be done each week. If there are unemployed people who are desperate to work, it would be much better to reduce the hours worked by each worker and increase the number of workers. This would allocate a given amount of work both more fairly and efficiently. Unwanted leisure would be reduced and valued leisure would increase (with output constant). And unemployment would fall.

The lump-of-output fallacy

There can be no doubt that, *so long as output is unaffected*, this argument is decisive. But the question is, Would output be unaffected? We cannot make that assumption: that is the 'lump-of-output' fallacy. In fact, output is a key variable in the situation. So what would happen to it?

The first step is to ask what might happen to inflation. In general, whenever unemployment is lower, inflation rises more (or falls less) than it would otherwise. This would happen whether unemployment were reduced by a general reflation (with increased output) or because hours per worker had been cut (with output fixed). So what will happen if we use shorter hours to cut unemployment? Inflation will rise more than it would otherwise. Two responses are then possible.

One could say, 'Bravo! We have cut unemployment and we are willing to accept the rising inflation.' But if this is the reaction, it would obviously have been better to cut unemployment by expanding output than by simply redistributing a given amount of work over more people. So there is no case for shorter working hours along that route.

Along the alternative route the outlook is even bleaker. In this scenario the government sees inflation rising, decides it is unacceptable, and allows unemployment to rise back to its original level (so as to control inflation). The net result of shorter working hours is then no reduction in unemployment, but a reduction in output.

Which response from the government is the more likely? If shorter working hours have no effect on the trade-off between unemployment and inflation, there is no obvious reason why they should affect the mix of unemployment and inflation that the government chooses.

Formal reasoning supports the view that hours of work (H) do not affect the NAIRU.[14] Under the efficiency wage model, we now have

$$\Pi_i = R(E_i H N_i) - \frac{W_i}{E_i} E_i H N_i,$$

where H is hours per worker (assumed exogenous), W_i is the hourly wage, and E_i is $e(W_i/W^e, u)$. The problem is recursive: first choose wages to minimize W_i/e_i, and then choose employment. The first stage leads to the standard equation for equilibrium unemployment,

$$e_1(1, u) = e(1, u),$$

independent of H. The reason is quite simply that hours do not affect the firm's desired wage mark-up, while unemployment does.

Under bargaining the same result holds. To concentrate on essentials, we can take the case where workers only value wages[15] (not employment) and there are no unemployment benefits. Thus,

$$\Omega_i = (W_i - A)^\beta \Pi_i,$$

503

with

$$A = W^e(1 - u).$$

Maximization gives

$$\frac{\partial \log \Omega_i}{\partial W_i} = \frac{\beta}{W_i - A} - \frac{HN_i}{\Pi_i} = 0.$$

Hence, as usual, in general equilibrium (with $W_i = W = W^e$),

$$u = \frac{W - A}{W} = \frac{\beta \Pi}{WHN} = \frac{1}{1/\beta\gamma}.$$

Unemployment is independent of hours, since hours do not affect the wage mark-up.

Evidence on shorter working hours

The empirical evidence also supports this view. We begin with work on wage equations. The following regression was performed by David Grubb for 19 OECD countries, 1952–82 (average coefficients and t-statistics):

$$\dot{w} = \text{const.} + 0.70\dot{p}_{-1} + 0.30\dot{w}_{-1} - 0.33(w - p)_{-1} - 1.9l + 2.0n$$
$$\quad\quad\quad\quad (3.0) \quad\quad (1.5) \quad\quad\quad (1.6) \quad (2.3)$$

$$- 0.2h + 0.2t,$$
$$(0.2) \quad (0.3)$$

where w = log nominal hourly earnings in manufacturing, p = log prices (consumption deflator), l = log labour force, n = log employment, h = log average weekly hours per worker in manufacturing, and t = time. This shows that hours per worker have no effect on the determination of hourly wages— and thus no effect on wage pressure or equilibrium unemployment.

Going on, we can look rather casually at evidence from the experience of different countries. Figure 3 shows for each country how working hours have changed, and how unemployment has changed. Average hours have fallen most in the UK, Spain, France, and the Netherlands; they have fallen least in Japan and Sweden. And what about unemployment? Unemployment has risen most in those countries where hours have fallen most. The case for shorter working hours receives no support from these statistics.

Of course, one would certainly not argue from these facts that shorter working hours have actually *caused* higher unemployment. For the comparison is not carried out with other things held constant. And to some extent, the

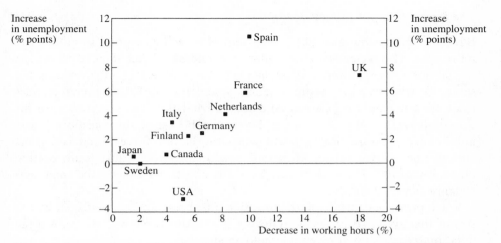

Fig. 3. *Decrease in working hours and increase in unemployment, 1975–1988.*

Average annual hours per person in employment.

Notes: Italy, 1975–83; UK, 1975–84; Netherlands, 1974–87; Spain, 1979–88.
Dependent employment for Germany and the Netherlands.

Sources: *Unemployment*: OECD, *Employment Outlook*, 1990, Table 1.A.4, and OECD, *Employment Outlook*, Sept. 1987, Table 5.7. *Hours*: OECD, *Employment Outlook*, July 1990, Statistical Annex, Table L. For UK: OECD, *Employment Outlook*, Sept. 1988, Statistical Annex, Table L.

forces that have raised unemployment in the EC countries may have also reduced working hours. However, there are two key points about the figure. First, it relates to a 13-year period, which enables us to abstract at least somewhat from the short-term cyclical factors which could tend to produce the inverse correlation observed. Second, and more important, any employment gains that were obtained from shorter working hours cannot have been great if the inverse correlation in the figures is so large. Shorter working hours certainly seem to offer little protection against unemployment, and the burden of proof is now very firmly on those who favour them.

The case for early retirement

Does more early retirement offer a better hope? Again, the case for it is clear. *If* output is unaffected, we want this output to be produced by those who most want work. If there are some in work who would not mind retiring, while others out of work are dying for a job, humanity requires that the older ones make way for those who really need the work.

The lump-of-output fallacy again

But once again, why take output as given? How will it respond to more early retirement? This depends on how inflation would be affected if more people left the labour force. If output is unchanged, the numbers of jobs remains the same; so, when workers retire, unemployment falls. Inflation therefore rises more than it would otherwise. And this is what the evidence shows. In his equations on 19 OECD countries David Grubb asked the question, 'Does inflationary pressure rise as much when the labour force is reduced (thus cutting unemployment) as when employment increases (thus again cutting unemployment)?' The answer was Yes. The effects are exactly the same and roughly as well defined.

Wage pressure depends on the unemployment rate and is unaffected by the size of the labour force. Thus, reducing the labour force will not reduce the inflationary pressure at given unemployment.

So early retirement is not an easy option either. If some workers retire and the number of jobs remains constant, inflation will increase. Once again, there are two possible responses. One is to accept the extra inflation. But then it would surely have been better to generate the extra inflation by providing more jobs than simply by shuffling the existing jobs around. Alternatively, we can surmise that the government will, in fact, choose a similar mix of inflation and unemployment to what it would have chosen otherwise. Hence unemployment will revert to its former level. But there will now be fewer jobs, because the labour force has shrunk.

On either response, we will, for a given inflation, have fewer jobs and lower output. We shall be a poorer nation.

Evidence on early retirement

Again, it is interesting to see how, comparing countries, changes in early retirement are related to changes in unemployment. This is shown in Fig. 4. The horizontal axis shows the change in the percentage of men aged 55–64 who are in the labour force. Again, the increase in early retirement has been greatest in the UK, Spain, France, and the Netherlands; it has been lowest in Japan and Sweden. Once again, the countries that have experienced more early retirement (often encouraged by government policy) are those with the biggest rise in unemployment. The causal mechanism is unclear. But the burden of proof is again surely on those who believe that more early retirement would help us avoid unemployment.

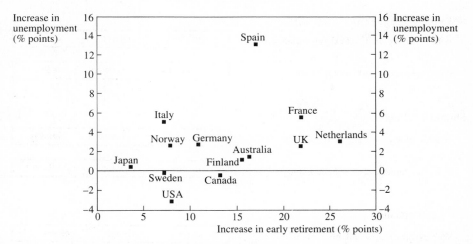

Fig. 4. *Increase in early retirement and increase in unemployment, 1975–1989.*

Increase in early retirement = fall in percentage of males aged 55–64 in labour force.

N.B.: Germany, 1975–86; Italian data for men aged 60–64.

Sources: *Unemployment*: OECD, *Employment Outlook*, July 1990, Table 1.A.4, and *Employment Outlook*, Sept. 1987, Table 5.7. *Early retirement*: OECD, *Labour Force Statistics, 1969–1989*, 1989, pt. III.

Conclusion

To many people, shorter working hours and early retirement appear to be common-sense solutions for unemployment. But they are not, because they are not based on any coherent theory of what determines unemployment. The only theory behind them is the lump-of-output theory: output is a given. In this section we have shown that output is unlikely to remain constant. The effects of the different policies are summarized in Fig. 5, but we hope that the argument is clear by now. The conclusion is that this is not the way to deal with unemployment. It may, however, be desirable on other grounds, as part of a very long-term change in patterns of life. As a country gets richer, its men (though not its women) tend to work fewer paid hours per week and fewer years per lifetime. This is fine. But it is a consequence of affluence. Let us not confuse that trend with the completely different question of how we should respond to economic misfortune. To respond to misfortune by making ourselves poorer is not common sense.[16]

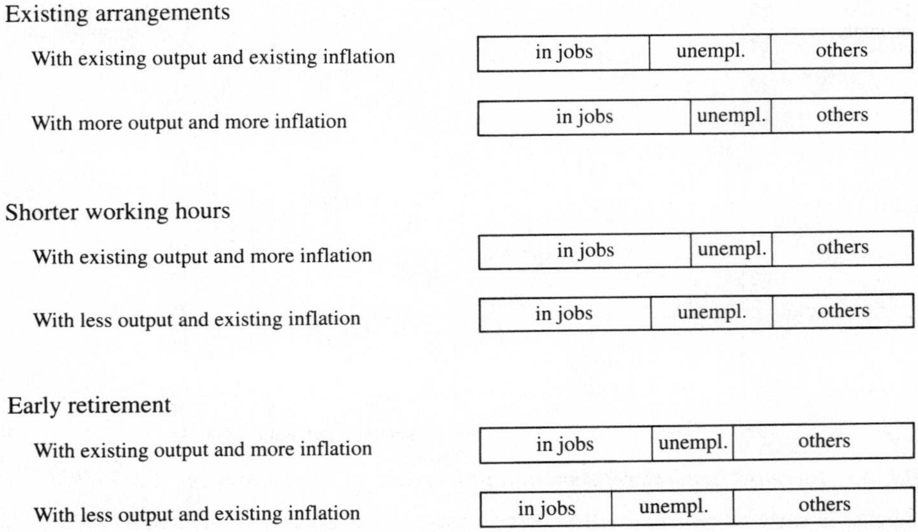

Existing arrangements

With existing output and existing inflation

in jobs	unempl.	others

With more output and more inflation

in jobs	unempl.	others

Shorter working hours

With existing output and more inflation

in jobs	unempl.	others

With less output and existing inflation

in jobs	unempl.	others

Early retirement

With existing output and more inflation

in jobs	unempl.	others

With less output and existing inflation

in jobs	unempl.	others

Fig. 5. *Economic activity with work sharing and early retirement.*

This diagram shows how the total population is divided between those in jobs, those unemployed, and those ('others') not in the labour force (including the retired).

8. Deregulation

The European countries have always had highly regulated labour markets, even when unemployment there was low. In particular, they have laws making dismissal costly to an employer. As we have seen in Chapter 5, there is no clear evidence that such laws reduce hiring more than they reduce firing. The most likely story is that they reduce both about equally, leaving the stock of unemployment unchanged but increasing its duration. This is on balance a bad thing. In addition, employment protection laws reinforce the power of insiders, tending to augment union power and thus equilibrium unemployment—at the same time increasing persistence by increasing adjustment costs (see Chapter 9). But equity arguments weigh against the total removal of these rights (Emerson 1988*a*).

9. Summary

We can now sum up our conclusions about what might reduce unemployment.

1. Unemployment will fall if unemployment benefits are of limited duration and subject to stronger job-search tests. But there is also a strong efficiency

case for active manpower policies designed to enhance the employability of unemployed people. These should include targeted adult training, quality placement services, recruitment subsidies for the hard-to-place, and (as a last resort) guaranteed temporary employment to people unemployed over a year. Without active manpower policies, harsh benefit regimes have undesirable distributional effects.

2. With regard to general subsidies towards high-unemployment groups (e.g. by skill or region), these can be justified if higher financial returns elsewhere induce few people to leave the high-unemployment group. But if migration is responsive to financial incentives, taxes/subsidies should be based on standard externality criteria—favouring subsidies to skill training, but higher taxes in congested regions.

3. Where unions are pervasive, there is a strong case for co-ordinated wage-bargaining to overcome the externalities present under a decentralized system. Where wage pressure remains excessive, a tax-based incomes policy should be considered. As a method of reducing inflation, a temporary incomes policy is far preferable to higher unemployment.

4. Marginal employment subsidies can reduce the NAIRU by reducing the mark-up of prices over wages. But they should not be taken to the point where profits and growth are imperilled.

5. General public employment is unlikely to be an important way of reducing the NAIRU.

6. Profit-sharing is also unlikely to reduce the NAIRU. There is no evidence that low Japanese unemployment is caused by the system of bonus payments in Japan.

7. Work-sharing and early retirement are also unlikely to reduce the NAIRU. But they are most effective at reducing a nation's wealth.

8. Employment protection laws increase the duration of unemployment and may increase its level by raising insider power. They require review but not abolition.

9. All the policies discussed in this chapter relate to the supply side, which in the long term dominates in determining unemployment. But in the shorter term demand is dominant. If there is significant hysteresis, then, as we show in Chapter 1, demand should ensure that unemployment is prevented from rising too far after a temporary shock—even if this means that it has to remain higher for longer.

Economies can never thrive without some unemployment. But nor can they thrive with too much of it. Prolonged unemployment diminishes people and wastes their productive power. It is not something we can just accept. Once we understand how it happens, we should act to control it.

Notes

1. As we saw in Chapter 5, H/cU is also uniquely related to the duration of vacancies, which appears to be a relevant variable for employers' wage push. The relation is unique because the matching function, $H = H(cU, V)$, is homogeneous of degree one.
2. The literature on optimum benefit structures is interesting (e.g. Baily 1978; Flemming 1978; Atkinson 1988). But it provides little guidance on policy, since the key issues in dealing with moral hazard relate to the accompanying administrative structures (Holen 1977).
3. In the long run the programmes will also have an effect by altering the duration structure of unemployment (and perhaps the quality of the unemployment inflow). The first of these can be handled by estimating duration-specific outflow equations and simulating the steady-state effect of the programmes on the unemployment stock.
4. With regard to training, the problem of 'poaching' stems essentially from capital market imperfections and workers' risk aversion, leading to firms financing general training. For the best analysis of the economics of training, see Kuratani (1973); see also Hashimoto (1981) which is easier to obtain. Regarding geographical migration, we are not opposed to specific migration subsidies to unemployed people to move (as in Sweden). This is pin-point targeting. Linked to liberalization of the housing market, it would increase gross inter-regional flows of labour without necessarily increasing net flows.
5. To analyse a tax on workers, make take-home pay (W_i) equal to $C_i(1 - t) + S$ and set $\partial \Pi_i / \partial W_i = 0$.
6. The costs can be exaggerated, since jealousy is an important feature of human psychology—see Boskin and Sheshinski (1978) and Layard (1980). Our present analysis does not allow for this.
7. We assume that if $N_i < N_{i0}$, the firm pays not only a tax $W_i t$ per worker but a fine $W_i(s + t)(N_{i0} - N_i)$.
8. Suppressing the firm-level subscript i and letting aggregate wages equal $\bar{W}$, we have

$$PV = \sum_j (1 - r)^j \left(R_j \left[e \left(\frac{W_j}{\bar{W}_j}, u_j \right) N_j \right] - (1 + t)W_j \alpha N_{j-1} - (1 - s)W_j(N_j - \alpha N_{j-1}) \right).$$

This gives an employment equation (for N_j) as follows:

$$R_j e - (1 - s)W_j - (1 - r)\alpha W_{j+1}(t + s) = 0.$$

Hence, since in stationary general equilibrium $\alpha t = (1 - \alpha)s$,

$$\kappa e = \bar{W}[(1 - s) + (1 - r)s(1 + g)],$$

where g is the growth rate of real wages. Thus the price equation is

$$\bar{W} = \frac{e(1,u)}{1 - (r - g)s}\kappa.$$

The wage equation remains unchanged.
9. The same conclusion follows in the case of monopsony. The firm fixes the wage on the basis of expected revenue. Having fixed the wage, it would always like to buy more

510

workers than it can at that wage. Thus falls in demand lead to falls in profit and no changes in employment.

10. He later also analysed profit-sharing in a non-market-clearing bargaining context (Weitzman 1987).

11. If we assume s_i fixed, the choice of W_i and N_i implies $\underline{W}_i$, using the definition of W_i.

12. If a worker receives up to 10 per cent of his pay in the form of a profit-share, one-half of that pay is tax-exempt. (as of 1990) These measures were introduced by a chancellor of the exchequer (Nigel Lawson) who not only read Weitzman's book but handed out free copies to his colleagues.

13. For a theoretical analysis showing that anything is possible, see John (1991).

14. What follows assumes H exogenous. One could also consider the case where H is endogenous and now has an upper limit.

15. It does not matter whether these are weekly or hourly, since multiplying Ω by any exogenous scalar has no effect on the first-order conditions.

16. However, a complete treatment would acknowledge that, especially in the short run, contractions in output may, by reducing imports, make possible a higher real value of domestic (relative to foreign) output—thus implying some offsetting welfare gain.

Annexes

1.1. The 'intertemporal substitution' theory of fluctuations

IF the labour market always cleared, we should have to be able to explain why more people are willing to work in booms than in slumps. The first (and most widely used) explanation is based on the notion of intertemporal substitution (Lucas and Rapping 1969). According to this, workers work harder in years when the perceived real wage or the perceived real interest rate is unusually high (making it worth working more now to consume more later).

The basic empirical problem with this is that neither the real wage nor the real interest rate is strongly pro-cyclical. And many would argue that the real wage is not far from a random walk with drift, so that the best forecast of the future real wage is the current real wage plus trend (Altonji and Ashenfelter 1980). In any case, if the theory is to fit the facts, the intertemporal elasticities of substitution must be large, which they do not appear to be (see e.g. Altonji 1986). In addition, consumption and employment move strongly together over the cycle, which, for consistency with the theory, requires non-intertemporally additive utility functions (since otherwise consumption in each period is complementary with leisure).

Thus, not surprisingly, tests of the model have been generally unfavourable (Altonji 1982; Ashenfelter 1984; Abowd and Card 1989). Perhaps the most decisive rejection comes from the work of Ham (1986), who used panel data. His key finding was that almost all the unemployed people worked far less than the estimated model predicted. Thus, the model failed to perform its main job of explaining unemployment. On aggregate time-series data on labour supply and consumption, Mankiw *et al.* (1985) also comprehensively reject the model.

One obvious shortcoming of the model is that it explains hours of work rather than employment versus non-employment. In an effort to rectify this, Hansen (1985) and Rogerson (1988) have introduced fixed costs of work which of course include the loss of unemployment benefit. Because of this, there is a reservation wage below which the hours an individual is willing to work fall discontinuously to zero. This is an important and extremely well-known fact about life. It certainly explains why, where there is a market-clearing secondary sector, not everyone is willing to work in it (see below). But, as noted above, the important fluctuations in employment originate in the primary sector, where wages exceed fixed costs. Consequently this idea helps little in understanding unemployment movements.

In any case, intertemporal substitution could only explain temporary fluctuations in employment. The notion that it could explain the persistent high unemployment of the 1930s or 1980s cannot even be contemplated.

1.2. A model of the OECD economy with endogenous commodity prices

From the point of view of any one (small) country, a rise in the relative price of oil and other commodities is an exogenous supply shock. But at the level of the OECD as a whole, it is endogenous. The relative OECD terms of trade P/P_m vary negatively with the level of OECD activity $(1 - u)$. This effect is quite marked in the short run, but weak (or zero) in the long run. The short-run and long-run relationships are shown in Fig. A1 as *SRCP* and *LRCP* respectively (for short-run and long-run commodity prices).

The relative price of commodities in turn affects the level of OECD activity consistent in the short run with stable inflation. For, from equation (3'''') in Chapter 1, with $\theta_{11} = 0$ and $\Delta\text{wedge} = s_m\Delta\log P_m/p$,

$$1 - u = 1 - u^* + \frac{1}{\theta_1}s_m\Delta\log P/P_m + \frac{1}{\theta_1}\Delta^2 p.$$

The short-run relationship is shown as *SRS* (for short-run supply) and the long-run (vertical) relationship as *LRS* (long-run supply). In the short run all points to the right of *SRS* are points of increasing inflation.

In 1973–4 world economic activity became so high that commodity prices rose to a level (such as A) where inflation was bound to rise. In 1979, the fall of the Shah of Iran induced a downwards shift in the supply of commodities. With OECD output slow to respond downwards, increasing inflation was again inevitable (as at B).

For an empirical analysis along these lines, see Cristini (1989).

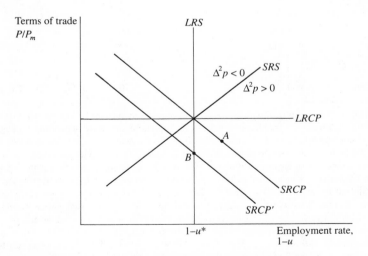

Fig. A1. *Relation of commodity prices and the OECD NAIRU.*

SCRP, LRCP refer to the determination of commodity prices; *SRS, LRS* refer to the constant-inflation supply price of output.

1.3. Unemployment benefit systems in OECD countries

Table A1 *Unemployment benefit: duration and replacement ratios: single person, 1985*

| | Maximum duration of benefits (yrs.) | Unemployment insurance | |
| | | Replacement ratio (%) | Duration (yrs.) |
	(1)	(2)	(3)
Belgium	Indef.	60	1
Denmark	2.5	90	2.5
France	3.75	57	3.75
Germany	Indef.	63	1
Ireland	Indef.	50	1.25
Italy	0.5	2	0.5
Netherlands	Indef.	70	2.5
Spain	3.5	80	0.5
UK	Indef.	36	1.0
Australia	Indef.	—	—
New Zealand	Indef.	—	—
Canada	0.5	60	0.5
USA	0.5	50	0.5
Japan	0.5	60	0.5
Austria	Indef.	60	0.6
Finland	Indef.	75	Indef.
Norway	1.5	65	1.5
Sweden	1.2	80	1.2
Switzerland	1.0	70	1.0

Notes: Col. (1): Duration of eligibility to some form of benefit paying over $120 a month. Equals sum of cols. (3) + (5) + (7), except for Sweden (see below). In Japan, 90–300 days depending on eligibility: in 1987 weighted average was 166 days (Koyo Hoken Jigyo Tokei, *Unemployment Benefit Statistics*, 1987). Col. (2): Gross benefits for a single person under 50 as % of the most relevant wage, normally gross wage. All systems pay the indicated proportion of former earnings (up to a ceiling generally exceeding average earnings), except where noted below. (In Germany data relate to benefits relative to net wage.) Gross benefits are normally taxable. *Austria*: The rate is 30–60%, depending on earnings. *Britain*: £28.45 a week. But those receiving insurance are also eligible for means-tested assistance (Supplementary Benefit) which pays their rent. Taking the relevant average rent as £10 a week gives a total equal to 36% of lower quartile weekly earnings of full-time workers (£107). *Finland*: FM70 a day indefinitely plus earnings-related additions for 21 mos. *France*: Fr40 a day plus 42% of earnings (up to 5 times average earnings). *Italy*: We do not include the Cassa Integrazione Guadagni (Wage Supplementation Fund). This pays 80% of the salary of temporary layoffs, but only about 1% of the workforce was on

Table A1—*continued*

	Supplementary insurance		Means-tested assistance	
	% of former wage (4)	Duration (yrs.) (5)	Rate (6)	Duration (yrs.) (7)
Belgium	40	$1 + \frac{1}{4}$ tenure	50% of min. wage	Indef.
Denmark	—	—	—	—
France	—	—	—	—
Germany	56	Indef.	—	—
Ireland	—	—	£28 p.w.	—
Italy	—	—	—	—
Netherlands	—	—	Dfl. 1045 p.m.	Indef.
Spain	$\{$ 70($\frac{1}{2}$yr) 60 (1yr)	1.5	80% of min. wage	1.5
UK	—	—	36% of lower quartile	Indef.
Australia	—	—	39% of $\frac{3}{4}$ ave. wage	Indef.
New Zealand	—	—	38% of $\frac{3}{4}$ ave. wage	Indef.
Canada	—	—	—	—
USA	—	—	—	—
Japan	—	—	—	—
Austria	—	—	27–54% of wage	Indef.
Finland	—	—	—	—
Norway	—	—	—	—
Sweden	—	—	30% of ave. wage[a]	0.5[a]
Switzerland	—	—	—	—

the scheme in 1988. Basic unemployment benefit was L800 per day. *Ireland*: I£39.50 p.w. plus 20–40% of earnings over £36 depending on wage (up to 1.2 × ave. earnings). Maximum is 85% of net earnings. *Japan*: 60–80% of former earnings (excl. bonus). In 1988 the weighted average was 63%. Average benefit paid per beneficiary is *ex post* equal to 35% of the *average* gross wage incl. bonus (*source*: Giorgio Brunello). *Norway*: provided for up to 1.5 years in any consecutive two calendar years. *Sweden*: UI a percentage of the former wage subject to a maximum.

[a] Sweden cols. (6) and (7) show KAS: this is flat rate equal to about 30% of average wage. *Not* means-tested; *not* available once UI expired.

Sources: Mainly US Department of Health and Social Services, *Social Security Programs Throughout the World 1985 (Reserve Report no. 60)* and Eurostat, *Definition of Registered Unemployed*, 1987, Theme 3, Series E. See also OECD, *Employment Outlook*, Sept. 1988, Tables 4.3, 4.4. *Australia*: Gregory (1986); *New Zealand*: data from NZ High Commission in London; *Norway*: Strand (1986).

Table A2   *Unemployment benefits: coverage and generosity*

	(1) % receiving benefits (1986)	(2) Expenditure on benefits per unemployed person (as % of output per worker) (1987)	(3) Expenditure on benefits per benefit recipient (as % of output per worker) (1986/7)	(4) Replacement ratio (%) (1985)
Belgium	85	18	22	60
Denmark	73	42	58	90
France	41	11	26	57
Germany	61	19	31	63
Ireland	67	15	23	50
Italy	21	4	20	2
Netherlands	—	26	—	70
Spain	35	9	—	80
UK	73	14	19	36
Australia	—	14	—	—
New Zealand	—	25	—	—
Canada	—	17	—	60
USA	34	9	26	50
Japan	40	15	36	60
Austria	—	23	—	60
Finland	—	19	—	75
Norway	—	17	—	65
Sweden	86/70	36	—	80
Switzerland	—	11	—	70

Notes: For the time–series of replacement ratios used in Ch. 9, see Emerson (1988*b*: Appendix A). His numbers were scaled to give the same numbers as we use for 1985. Col. (3) is included for rough comparison with col. (4).

Sources: Col. (1): Eurostat, Series 3c *Labour Force Survey 1986*; *Japan*: From Giorgio Brunello; *Spain*: Bentolila and Blanchard (1990); *Sweden*: Burtless (1987: Table 70) reports 86%; Standing (1988) quotes AMS, Annual Report 1985/6, p. 16 as giving 70%;. *UK*: *Employment Gazette*, Oct. 1988, p. 536, Table 1; *USA*: Burtless (1987: Table 8). (Burtless's figures for France, Germany, and UK are higher than here, especially for France, but for these countries his data represent all recipients ÷ all unemployed.) Col. (2): OECD, *Employment Outlook*, Sept. 1988, p. 86 gives expenditure on unemployment benefits as percentage of GDP in 1987. This is then divided by $u/(1-u)$ from Table 2. of Ch. 1. This gives $(BU/Y)(N/U) = B/(Y/N)$. Col. (3): col. (2) ÷ col. (1). Col. (4): Table 5 of Ch. 1.

1.4. Wage-bargaining systems in OECD countries

Note: For coverage, 'high' = 75+ per cent, 'medium' = 25–75 per cent, 'low' = under 25 per cent.

Belgium

Coverage
High.

Bargaining system
Industry-level bargains applying by law to all workers in the sector.
Firm-level bargains supplement these.

Co-ordination
Low employer co-ordination and unions divided between Socialist, Christian, and liberal.
But central tripartite agreement, 1987–8.

Minimum wage
Set by national employer–union bargain.

Incomes policy
1982: government suspends indexation, and controls on permitted indexation last to 1986.

Denmark

See Scandinavia.

France

Coverage
High.

Bargaining system
Industry-level bargains applying by law to all workers in the sector.
Most pay above this determined at employer's discretion.

Co-ordination
Employers' confederation has some influence. Unions divided between four federations.

National minimum wage
Established by law. High.

Incomes policy
June 1982: wage and price freeze for three months followed by strict public-sector pay limits, generally followed by private sector at least as regards minimum rates in each grade (as a result of informal agreements with employers' organization).

Germany

Coverage
High.

Bargaining system
Industry-level bargains in each region, frequently extended by law to all workers in the sector.
Firm-level bargains supplement these but strikes at this level illegal.

Co-ordination
Informal talks within and between national employers' organization and trade union federation. This leads to a pattern settlement generally in the metal industry in one region, broadly followed elsewhere. National industry-level union has to authorize any strike. Council of Economic Experts and the five research institutes help to create climate of opinion in favour of wage moderation.

Minimum wage
No statutory level, except via collective bargaining.

Incomes policy
1966–77: 'Concerted action'. Tripartite guidance on wage limits. Unions withdrew over 'co-determination'. Otherwise, see above. Indexation illegal.

Ireland
Similar to UK. Wage accord 1979–81.

Italy

Coverage
High.

Bargaining system
Industry-level bargains applying by law to all workers in the sector.
Firm-level bargains supplement these.

Co-ordination
Some employer co-ordination, especially regionally. Strike insurance by employers. Union confederations have variable control over their members (more in 1980s).

Minimum wage
See above.

Incomes policy
1976–8: 'historic compromise' establishing full indexation in return for presumption of low settlements and reasonable strike behaviour.
1983: agreement to alter calculation of *COL*.
1984: government proposal for reduction of permitted degree of indexation in the 'scala mobile'. Rejected by CGIL, union federation. Confirmed by plebiscite on 9 June 1985.

Netherlands

Coverage
High.

Bargaining system
Industry-level bargains applying by law to all workers in the sector.
Firm-level bargains supplement these, but at this stage strikes are outlawed.

Co-ordination
Three federations of employers and three of unions. More employer co-ordination than in Belgium. Since 1982 the Foundation of Labour, a joint employer-union organization, proposes a general framework for pay.

Minimum wage
Set by law.

Incomes policy
Tripartite incomes policy broke down in 1963. Frequent short wage freezes between 1971 and 1982.

Portugal

Coverage
High (despite very low unionization).

Bargaining system
Industry-level bargains applying by law to all workers in the sector. Unions have no strike funds.
No firm-level bargains but employers can pay at their discretion. Workers' committees in firms cannot negotiate.

Co-ordination
Three employers' confederations (for agriculture, industry, and trade). Two union confederations (Socialist and Communist). Permanent Social Concertation Council sets guidelines (since 1984).

Mediation
Government arbitration.

Minimum wage
Set by state. High relative to average earnings.

Incomes policy
1986–8: form of social contract to limit wage increases to expected inflation.

Spain

Coverage
High (despite low unionization).

Bargaining system
National tripartite framework agreement on permitted range of settlements (following 1978 Moncloa pact).
Industry-level bargains applying by law to all workers in the sector.
Firm-level bargains between firm, and workers' committee (with mainly union members) supplement these. Some large firms do not participate in industry-level bargains.

Co-ordination
Two union movements (Socialist and Communist) in competition, with some co-ordination. Employers rather weak.

Minimum wage
Set by state.

Incomes policy
See above.

UK

Coverage
High (after including workers covered by statutory Wages Councils).

Bargaining system
Some industry-level bargains.
Majority of private-sector workers covered by firm-level bargains (sometimes building on industry-level bargains).

Co-ordination
Virtually none among employers. Ditto among unions.

Minimum wage
No national minimum (but Wages Council rates have force of law).

Incomes policy
1972–4: wage freeze (for six months); £1 + 4 per cent (for six months); 5 per cent plus extra if inflation exceeded 7 per cent (which it did). Statutory.

1975–9: £6 a week (1st year); 5 per cent (2nd year); 10 per cent (3rd year); 5 per cent (4th year). Supported by TUC in first two years.

Australia

Coverage
High.

Bargaining system
National Industrial Relations Commission (present title) sets general principles for pay increases. Industry-level bargains either follow these principles or have to be endorsed by the Commission. All such bargains relate to minimum rates. However, firm-level bargains can agree 'over-award' pay increases.

Co-ordination
Employers' federation generally weaker than union federation.

Incomes policy
1983 onwards: Prices and Incomes Accord between government and unions, ratified each year by the Commission (which has power to reject it). 'No extra claims' allowed at firm level—this being a key difference from the earlier regime. Firms remain free to make voluntary 'over-award' payments, and wage drift continues at 1.5–2 per cent p.a. Policy modified substantially from 1988 with a reversion to industry-level bargaining with 'extra claims' permitted—all being subject to Commission approval.

New Zealand

Coverage
Medium.

Bargaining system
Pre-1984: similar to Australia. 1984: compulsory arbitration abolished. Though Arbitration Commission continues to register most settlements, increasing proportion of settlements are made with no Commission involvement.

Co-ordination
As Australia.

Incomes policy
1971–84: wage and price controls of some kind for most of the period.

Canada

Coverage
Medium.

Bargaining system
Firm-level bargains. More public sector bargaining than in the USA.

Co-ordination
Nil.

Minimum wage
Set by state.

Incomes policy
1975–7: wage controls.

USA

Coverage
Low.

Bargaining system
Firm-level.

Co-ordination
Nil, though some pattern bargaining within industries.

Minimum wage
Set by government (low).

Incomes policy
1971: 90-day wage freeze, and controls lasting to 1974.
1978–9: Commission on Wage and Price Stability promotes pay and price standards (essentially voluntary).

Japan

Coverage
Medium (high in large firms, low in small firms).

Bargaining system
Firm-level bargains, synchronized in Shunto (Spring offensive).

Co-ordination
Strong employer co-ordination, especially after the great inflation of 1974. Weaker union co-ordination.

Incomes policy
Nil.

Austria

Coverage
High.

Bargaining system
Industry-level agreements, which depend on approval by the union confederation.

Co-ordination
Strong guidance from tripartite Parity Commission and its bipartite Subcommittee on Wages and Prices.

Incomes policy
None, as such.

Scandinavia

Coverage
High.

Bargaining system
National bargain between trade union federation and employers' federation: one bargain in Denmark, three in Finland, Norway, and Sweden. No Swedish bargain in 1990.
Industry-level and firm-level bargains supplement these, but strikes are not allowed at firm level (because of peace agreements at higher level). National unions have to agree to local claims. LO, manual union federation, controls strike fund nationally in Sweden.

Co-ordination
Strong employers' and union federations, e.g. powerful co-ordination after 1982 Swedish devaluation.

Mediation
In Denmark and Norway this is compulsory, and there is sometimes binding arbitration.

Minimum wage
In Denmark industry-level minimum, set by state.

Incomes policies
Denmark: frequent legislative intervention setting ceiling on wage growth; 1982: wage freeze; 1983: indexation suspended; 1985–7: legal wage norms.
Finland: comprehensive tripartite incomes policy since 1968. Wage indexation opposed.
Norway: frequent social contracts mainly in the 1970s. Firm-level wage bargaining prohibited in 1978–9 and 1988.
Sweden: minimal direct intervention, though occasional guidelines.

Switzerland

Coverage
Medium.

Bargaining system
Mainly firm-level. Mainly subject to industry-wide five- to six-year peace agreements ruling out use of strikes. Multi-year settlements. Cost-of-living agreements negotiated at industry level.

Co-ordination
Strong employer co-ordination. Unions weak.

Arbitration
Important.

Sources: Blum (1981); Flanagan *et al.* (1983); Bruno and Sachs (1985); ILO (1987); OECD (1989); OECD *Country Reports*; Ashenfelter and Layard (1983); Calmfors and Driffill (1988); Calmfors (1990); Dore *et al.* (1989); Elvander (1989); Emerson (1988*b*); miscellaneous country documents; numerous conversations, especially with Guillermo de la Dehesa, Ronald Dore, David Marsden, and, above all, David Soskice.

1.5. Optimal disinflation policy with hysteresis in wage-setting[1]

We shall assume we wish to set the path of unemployment (u) to minimize

$$\int_0^\infty \tfrac{1}{2}(u^2 + \varphi\pi^2)\mathrm{e}^{-rt}\mathrm{d}t$$

$$\text{s.t.} \quad \dot{\pi} = \theta_1(u^* - u) - \theta_{11}\dot{u},$$

where π is inflation and r the real discount rate. The differential equation for unemployment is

$$\ddot{u} - r\dot{u} - \delta(u - u^*) = 0,$$

where $\delta = \dfrac{(\theta_1 + \theta_{11}r)\varphi\theta_1}{(1 + \theta_{11}^2\varphi)}$. The stable solution to this equation is

$$u - u^* = A\mathrm{e}^{\alpha t},$$

where

$$\alpha = \frac{r}{2} - \sqrt{\left(\frac{r}{2}\right)^2 + \delta} < 0.$$

The speed of approach to u^* is $-\alpha$, which is increasing in δ and

$$\text{sign}\frac{\partial\delta}{\partial\theta_{11}} = \text{sign}[r(1 - \theta_{11}^2\varphi) - 2\theta_{11}\varphi\theta_1].$$

Thus, for small r, an increase in hysteresis (θ_{11}) decreases the speed of convergence to the NAIRU.[2]

Suppose we start with inflation at an unacceptably high level. We need to go through a period of higher unemployment. Since convergence is monotonic, u goes straight to its maximal height. But the total fall in inflation is proportional to $\int(u_t - u^*)\mathrm{d}t$ (since $\int\dot{u}\mathrm{d}t = 0$). Hence slow convergence means that maximal u is low.

This analysis also applies to the case of accommodation to a temporary supply shock. Such a shock would generate a given amount of extra inflation if u were not raised. The optimal path of u to offset this extra inflation involves a smaller and more prolonged rise in u, the more hysteresis there is.

1.6. Unemployment and inflation series for each OECD country

Table A3 *Unemployment rates (%)*

	Australia	Austria	Belgium	Canada	Denmark	Finland	France
1955	0.8	2.9	4.1	4.0	4.4	0.5	2.1
1956	1.4	2.8	3.0	3.2	4.9	0.7	1.6
1957	2.0	2.6	2.4	4.3	4.6	1.8	1.2
1958	2.6	2.8	3.5	6.5	4.2	3.1	1.4
1959	2.5	2.5	4.2	5.5	3.0	2.2	1.9
1960	1.9	1.9	3.4	6.3	2.4	1.5	1.8
1961	3.5	1.5	2.6	6.5	2.1	1.2	1.5
1962	2.8	1.5	2.2	5.4	2.1	1.3	1.4
1963	2.7	1.7	1.8	5.0	2.3	1.5	1.3
1964	1.7	1.6	1.6	4.3	1.9	1.5	1.4
1965	1.5	1.6	1.8	3.6	1.7	1.4	1.5
1966	1.7	1.5	2.0	3.3	1.9	1.5	1.8
1967	1.9	1.6	2.6	3.8	1.7	2.9	1.9
1968	1.8	1.6	3.1	4.4	1.7	3.8	2.6
1969	1.8	1.6	2.3	4.4	1.7	2.8	2.3
1970	1.6	1.1	2.1	5.6	1.3	1.9	2.5
1971	1.9	1.0	2.1	6.1	1.6	2.2	2.7
1972	2.6	1.0	2.7	6.2	1.6	2.5	2.8
1973	2.3	0.9	2.7	5.5	1.0	2.3	2.7
1974	2.6	1.1	3.0	5.3	2.3	1.7	2.8
1975	4.8	1.5	5.0	6.9	5.3	2.2	4.0
1976	4.7	1.5	6.4	7.1	5.3	3.8	4.4
1977	5.6	1.4	7.4	8.0	6.4	5.8	4.9
1978	6.2	1.7	7.9	8.3	7.3	7.2	5.2
1979	6.2	1.7	8.2	7.4	6.2	5.9	5.9
1980	6.0	1.5	8.8	7.5	7.0	4.6	6.3
1981	5.7	2.1	10.8	7.5	9.2	4.8	7.3
1982	7.1	3.1	12.6	10.9	9.8	5.3	8.1
1983	9.9	3.7	12.1	11.8	10.4	5.4	8.3
1984	8.9	3.8	12.1	11.2	10.1	5.2	9.7
1985	8.2	3.6	11.3	10.4	9.0	5.0	10.2
1986	8.0	3.1	11.2	9.5	7.8	5.3	10.4
1987	8.0	3.8	11.0	8.8	7.8	5.0	10.5
1988	7.2	3.6	9.7	7.7	8.6	4.5	10.0
1989	6.1	3.2	8.1	7.5	9.3	3.4	9.4
1990	6.8	3.3	7.6	8.1	9.6	3.4	8.9

	Germany	Ireland	Italy	Japan	Nether-lands	Norway	New Zealand
1955	4.3	4.6	7.0	2.7	1.4	1.7	0.0
1956	3.5	5.3	8.6	2.5	1.0	2.0	0.0
1957	2.9	6.7	7.2	2.0	1.3	2.1	0.1
1958	3.0	6.4	6.3	2.1	2.4	3.4	0.1
1959	2.0	6.1	5.7	2.2	1.9	3.3	0.1
1960	1.1	5.6	4.4	1.7	1.2	2.4	0.1
1961	0.6	5.1	3.8	1.5	0.9	1.8	0.0
1962	0.6	4.9	3.3	1.3	0.8	2.1	0.1
1963	0.4	5.0	2.9	1.3	0.8	2.5	0.1
1964	0.4	4.7	3.2	1.2	0.7	2.2	0.1
1965	0.3	4.6	4.2	1.3	0.8	1.8	0.1
1966	0.2	4.7	4.4	1.4	1.1	1.6	0.0
1967	1.3	5.0	4.0	1.3	2.1	1.5	0.4
1968	1.5	5.3	4.2	1.2	2.0	2.1	0.7
1969	0.9	5.0	4.2	1.1	1.3	2.0	0.3
1970	0.8	5.8	3.8	1.1	1.3	1.6	0.1
1971	0.9	5.5	3.9	1.2	1.7	1.5	0.3
1972	0.8	6.2	4.5	1.4	2.9	1.7	0.5
1973	0.8	5.7	4.4	1.3	2.9	1.5	0.2
1974	1.6	5.3	3.7	1.4	3.6	1.5	0.1
1975	3.6	7.3	4.0	1.9	5.2	2.3	0.3
1976	3.7	9.0	4.6	2.0	5.5	1.8	0.4
1977	3.6	8.8	4.9	2.0	5.3	1.5	0.6
1978	3.5	8.2	4.9	2.2	5.3	1.8	1.7
1979	3.2	7.1	5.2	2.1	5.4	2.0	1.9
1980	3.0	7.3	5.2	2.0	6.0	1.6	2.7
1981	4.4	9.9	5.8	2.2	8.5	2.0	3.5
1982	6.1	11.4	6.4	2.4	11.4	2.6	3.7
1983	8.0	14.0	7.0	2.6	12.0	3.4	5.4
1984	7.1	15.5	7.0	2.7	11.8	3.1	4.6
1985	7.2	17.4	7.1	2.6	10.6	2.6	3.6
1986	6.4	17.4	7.5	2.8	9.9	2.0	4.0
1987	6.2	17.5	7.9	2.8	9.6	2.1	4.1
1988	6.2	16.7	7.9	2.5	9.2	3.2	5.6
1989	5.6	15.6	7.8	2.3	8.3	4.9	6.8
1990	5.0	14.0	7.2	2.1	7.2	5.3	7.6

Table A3 *continued*

	Spain	Sweden	Switzerland	UK (1)	UK (2)	USA
1955	2.3	1.7	1.0	1.4	—	4.3
1956	2.1	1.3	1.1	1.5	—	4.0
1957	1.8	1.6	0.7	1.9	—	4.1
1958	1.7	2.2	1.2	2.8	—	6.6
1959	1.9	1.8	0.8	2.9	—	5.3
1960	2.5	1.3	0.4	2.2	—	5.3
1961	2.5	1.1	0.2	1.9	—	6.4
1962	2.0	1.1	0.2	2.9	—	5.3
1963	2.2	1.4	0.2	3.5	—	5.5
1964	2.6	1.2	0.0	2.6	—	5.0
1965	2.5	1.0	0.0	2.2	—	4.4
1966	2.1	1.3	0.0	2.2	—	3.6
1967	2.5	1.7	0.0	3.1	—	3.7
1968	3.0	1.8	0.0	3.1	—	3.5
1969	2.6	1.5	0.0	2.9	—	3.4
1970	2.4	1.2	0.0	3.0	—	4.8
1971	3.1	2.1	0.0	3.8	2.6	5.8
1972	3.1	2.2	0.0	4.2	2.9	5.5
1973	2.5	2.0	0.0	3.1	2.0	4.8
1974	2.6	1.6	0.0	3.1	2.0	5.5
1975	3.7	1.3	0.9	4.5	3.1	8.3
1976	4.7	1.3	1.8	5.7	4.2	7.6
1977	5.2	1.5	1.2	6.1	4.4	6.9
1978	6.9	1.8	0.9	5.9	4.3	6.0
1979	8.5	1.7	0.9	5.0	4.0	5.8
1980	11.2	1.6	0.6	6.4	5.1	7.0
1981	13.9	2.1	0.6	9.8	8.1	7.5
1982	15.8	2.6	1.2	11.3	9.5	9.5
1983	17.2	2.9	2.4	12.5	10.5	9.5
1984	20.0	2.6	3.0	11.7	10.7	7.4
1985	21.4	2.4	2.4	11.2	10.9	7.1
1986	21.0	2.2	2.1	11.1	11.2	6.9
1987	20.1	1.9	1.8	10.2	10.1	6.1
1988	19.1	1.6	2.1	8.3	8.1	5.4
1989	16.9	1.4	1.8	6.9	6.3	5.2
1990	16.2	1.6	1.8	6.5	5.6	5.5

Notes: Standardized rates except for Denmark, Ireland, New Zealand, Austria, and Sweden, for which unstandardized rates are used. The standardized unemployment rates are described in 'Who are the unemployed? Measurement issues and their policy implications', OECD, *Employment Outlook*, Sept. 1987, pp. 125–41; and in C. Sorrentino, 'The Uses of the Community Labour Force Surveys for International Unemployment Comparisons', Eurostat Document no. 7 for Seminar on 12–14 Oct. 1987. Except for Italy, these numbers are very similar to the 'unemployment rate on US concepts', calculated by the US Bureau of Labor Statistics: see 'Comparative Labor Force Statistics for 10 Countries 1959–88' (mimeo).

For Italy we use the BLS numbers 'on US concepts', which exclude the considerable number of Italian people who, though registered as unemployed, have performed no active job search in the previous 4 weeks. For 1985 and earlier we multiply the BLS numbers by 7.5/6.3 to allow for the break. (See p. 2 of the document.)

For Switzerland we use registered unemployment × 3, this being the factor for 1980 shown in the 1980 Census.

For the UK we give two series: (1) a series based on OECD data and (2) the UK Department of Employment's consistent series. The analysis in Chapter 9 uses the OECD-based series.

Further details on request.

Sources: *EC*: OECD, *Economic Outlook*, Dec. 1990, Tables R18, R19 (updated using Tables 40, 41), except for Italy, Switzerland, and the UK (see Notes). Also earlier issues.

Table A4 *Inflation rate (% p.a.)*

	Australia	Austria	Belgium	Canada	Denmark	Finland	France
1955	3.2	3.1	1.5	0.6	4.8	2.9	2.1
1956	6.9	4.1	3.3	3.6	4.8	9.0	4.9
1957	0.1	4.3	4.1	2.2	1.8	7.4	6.0
1958	0.0	0.5	1.0	1.4	1.6	7.8	11.8
1959	4.5	3.6	0.4	2.0	3.8	1.3	6.3
1960	3.2	3.1	0.8	1.2	1.8	2.2	3.5
1961	1.2	4.9	1.3	1.8	4.3	5.3	3.4
1962	1.2	3.7	1.7	1.7	6.6	4.0	4.7
1963	3.7	3.5	3.0	1.7	5.8	5.1	6.4
1964	2.7	3.2	4.6	2.9	4.6	7.2	4.1
1965	2.9	5.6	5.1	3.2	7.4	5.0	2.7
1966	3.3	3.2	4.2	4.6	6.8	4.7	2.9
1967	3.1	3.2	3.1	3.7	6.0	7.4	3.2
1968	3.1	2.8	2.7	3.3	7.2	12.1	4.2
1969	4.9	2.7	4.0	4.7	6.8	4.2	6.6
1970	4.9	4.7	4.6	4.6	8.1	3.8	5.6
1971	6.3	6.2	5.7	2.0	7.9	7.6	5.8
1972	9.4	7.6	6.2	5.5	9.0	8.4	6.2
1973	14.7	8.0	7.2	9.1	10.4	14.1	7.8
1974	18.4	9.5	12.6	15.3	12.8	22.5	11.1
1975	15.1	6.5	12.1	11.4	12.8	14.5	13.4
1976	11.1	5.6	7.5	8.7	9.0	12.5	9.9
1977	7.7	5.3	7.5	7.7	8.7	10.1	9.0
1978	7.9	5.3	4.4	6.7	9.5	7.7	9.5
1979	11.0	4.1	4.5	10.6	7.6	8.4	10.4
1980	10.1	5.1	3.8	11.1	8.2	9.3	12.2
1981	10.2	6.3	4.9	10.4	10.1	11.4	11.8
1982	10.9	6.2	7.1	10.0	10.6	8.7	12.6
1983	7.5	3.7	5.9	4.8	8.2	8.6	9.5
1984	6.1	5.0	5.0	3.4	5.2	8.9	7.2
1985	7.0	3.0	5.5	3.2	5.3	5.1	5.9
1986	7.2	4.1	5.0	2.5	4.7	4.6	5.1
1987	7.7	2.6	1.9	4.3	5.1	5.2	2.9
1988	9.1	1.5	1.2	4.2	4.9	6.3	3.2
1989	7.0	2.7	2.8	4.7	4.0	5.8	3.2
1990	4.5	3.5	4.4	3.4	3.3	6.5	3.4

	Germany	Ireland	Italy	Japan	Nether-lands	Norway	New Zealand
1955	2.1	2.3	3.3	1.6	4.5	4.5	1.5
1956	3.0	2.8	4.0	5.0	3.9	7.5	3.1
1957	3.1	3.7	2.0	6.3	5.7	3.5	1.8
1958	3.4	5.8	2.4	− 1.7	1.8	0.8	1.4
1959	1.4	2.6	− 0.3	2.9	2.0	0.8	2.9
1960	2.5	0.1	2.1	6.0	2.7	1.0	2.1
1961	4.3	2.8	2.8	7.9	2.4	2.6	0.4
1962	4.1	4.4	5.8	3.6	3.5	4.8	3.6
1963	2.8	2.6	8.5	4.5	4.7	3.4	3.6
1964	3.0	9.2	6.5	4.4	8.7	4.7	4.3
1965	3.5	4.4	4.2	5.1	6.1	4.8	3.6
1966	3.6	4.3	2.2	5.0	6.0	4.0	0.7
1967	1.3	3.9	2.8	5.8	4.2	3.0	4.4
1968	1.8	4.3	1.7	5.2	4.2	4.4	4.9
1969	4.2	8.9	4.1	4.8	6.4	4.2	2.7
1970	7.6	8.9	6.9	7.3	5.6	12.8	10.2
1971	7.8	10.6	7.2	5.2	8.5	6.7	13.5
1972	5.4	13.5	6.3	5.2	9.4	5.0	10.5
1973	6.5	15.3	11.6	11.9	8.4	9.2	7.8
1974	6.8	6.1	18.5	20.6	9.3	10.3	3.1
1975	6.1	22.4	17.5	7.8	11.2	10.0	16.6
1976	3.5	21.0	18.0	6.4	8.9	7.5	17.4
1977	3.6	13.3	19.1	5.7	6.3	8.3	15.1
1978	4.1	10.5	13.9	4.6	5.2	6.4	14.2
1979	4.0	13.9	15.9	2.6	4.2	6.6	19.6
1980	4.3	14.5	20.7	2.8	5.7	14.6	13.7
1981	4.2	18.0	18.3	2.7	5.5	14.0	15.6
1982	4.7	15.6	17.9	1.8	6.0	10.2	10.9
1983	3.3	10.4	15.3	0.4	1.8	6.1	1.5
1984	2.0	7.7	10.2	1.2	1.8	6.4	8.2
1985	1.7	5.0	8.8	1.5	1.7	5.2	15.2
1986	3.1	7.3	7.6	1.8	0.7	− 1.4	17.0
1987	2.1	2.6	6.1	− 0.2	− 1.0	6.0	15.4
1988	1.5	2.2	5.9	0.4	1.6	2.9	7.9
1989	2.5	3.5	5.5	1.5	1.3	2.0	5.0
1990	3.4	3.6	6.9	1.5	3.2	4.7	4.4

Table A4—*continued*

	Spain	*Sweden*	*Switzerland*	*UK*	*USA*
1955	6.1	4.0	1.0	4.2	1.8
1956	7.2	5.6	0.8	6.4	3.1
1957	12.4	4.3	2.3	3.7	3.3
1958	10.0	3.2	5.1	4.0	1.8
1959	5.8	1.1	−0.1	1.3	2.1
1960	0.5	4.9	2.8	1.0	1.5
1961	1.8	2.9	4.1	3.3	1.0
1962	5.7	4.0	5.8	3.7	1.9
1963	8.5	1.9	4.8	2.0	1.5
1964	6.3	4.4	5.3	3.7	1.7
1965	9.4	6.0	3.8	5.1	2.0
1966	8.1	6.6	4.8	4.6	3.5
1967	7.7	5.0	4.4	3.0	2.9
1968	5.0	2.4	3.1	4.1	5.0
1969	4.4	3.4	2.6	5.4	5.1
1970	6.8	6.0	4.7	7.3	5.3
1971	8.0	7.1	9.2	9.4	5.3
1972	8.7	7.0	9.8	8.3	4.4
1973	11.8	7.0	8.1	7.1	5.5
1974	16.6	9.5	6.9	14.9	9.0
1975	16.7	14.5	7.1	27.2	9.2
1976	16.7	11.9	2.7	14.9	5.9
1977	22.8	10.5	0.3	13.9	5.7
1978	20.2	9.6	3.6	11.1	7.4
1979	16.7	7.9	2.0	14.5	8.5
1980	14.1	11.7	2.7	19.8	9.6
1981	11.2	9.5	6.9	11.7	8.9
1982	14.2	8.7	7.3	7.1	6.9
1983	11.6	9.7	3.3	4.9	3.3
1984	10.9	7.7	2.8	4.2	3.7
1985	8.6	6.8	2.7	6.0	3.2
1986	10.9	7.1	3.8	3.5	2.7
1987	5.9	5.3	2.5	4.8	3.3
1988	5.6	6.6	3.0	6.6	3.4
1989	6.3	8.0	3.3	6.8	5.0
1990	7.5	10.5	4.5	5.8	4.2

Sources: GNP/GDP deflator: OECD, *Economic Outlook*, various issues, and Centre for Economic Performance, 'OECD dataset'.

2.1. A brief note on implicit contract theory

One approach to unemployment is based on the idea that labour contracts provide workers with a form of income insurance, as well as compensation for work done. Although this literature initially generated high hopes as a tool for understanding unemployment, it has since been discovered to be inadequate in this respect (Stiglitz 1986).

The first-generation, symmetric-information models (of e.g. Azariadis 1975 and Baily 1974) delivered (real) wage rigidity and the possibility of (*ex post*) involuntary layoff unemployment. However, layoffs occurred only when they would also have occurred with *ex post* spot markets, so that the resulting unemployment was a consequence of the immobility of labour between firms rather than the contractual arrangements. Furthermore, these models tended to produce too much employment rather than too little: see Akerlof and Miyazaki (1980); Pissarides (1981*a*). The second-generation, asymmetric-information models of Grossman and Hart (1981), Hart (1983), and Grossman *et al.* (1983) managed to avoid this, but at the price of developing an implicit contract structure unrelated to anything observed in real explicit contracts.

Do these models tell us anything about unemployment? To begin with, like the basic intertemporal substitution model, they explain the input of man-hours rather than the number of heads. To explain unemployment, one therefore needs to introduce indivisibilities arising from, say, fixed costs of employment.

Second, with the exception of Grossman *et al.*, the models are generally partial equilibrium in nature. In the first-generation models what matters is the firm's relative price. Consequently all firms cannot experience bad times and make layoffs simultaneously, unless there are some price-level misperceptions of the usual sort present. Any increase in unemployment will last only as long as the misperceptions endure—there is no mechanism to explain the persistence of unemployment in the model. In Grossman *et al.* it is an increase in uncertainty rather than misperceptions that generates the increase in equilibrium unemployment, but again, it endures only so long as the increase in uncertainty.

Finally, in the asymmetric-information models a crucial role is played by the incentive-compatibility constraints which discourage the firm from dissembling over the true state of product-market conditions. However, if the firm is buffeted by a series of shocks, it can acquire a reputation for truth-telling, and the contract consequently need not be circumscribed by the need to prevent lying by the firm (see Townsend 1982).

At best, the implicit contract literature may help to explain the stylized fact that real wages fluctuate very little over the business cycle. However, it has very little that is useful to say on the causes of unemployment and its persistence.

2.2. Bargaining theory

This note sets out a simple, intuitive solution to the bargaining problem, based on the concept of a 'perfect equilibrium' from which neither party has an incentive to depart (Rubinstein 1982; Binmore *et al.* 1986; Sutton 1986).

The problem is how to divide a continuous supply of cake between two players. The players take turns to call out proposals for splitting the cake. If a proposal is accepted, the game ends; if not, no one gets anything for one period and the game proceeds to the other player's turn. There is one call per period, and both players discount the future.

Equal discount rates

In the simplest case, both players have the same discount factor (δ) per period. The game can then be represented by the first two columns of Table A5, which set out the time period and the identity of the player whose turn it is to call out a proposal. Player 1 starts the game in period 0 by calling out a proposal for splitting the cake. He calls out a number (between 0 and 1) for his own share, the remainder going to player 2. Let m be the optimal number for him to call, i.e. the number to call in period 0 which leads to his getting the highest ultimate payoff from the game.

Table A5 *Bargaining payoffs; with the same discount rates*

| Period | Caller | Payoff for player | |
		1	2
0	1	m	$1 - m$
1	2	$\delta(1 - m)$	δm
2	1	$\delta^2 m$	$\delta^2(1 - m)$

The essence of the argument is that, *if a share* m *is the optimal strategy of player 1 in period 0, it must also be the optimal strategy for either player in every subsequent round.* The reason for this is that, looking forward at each point in time, the structure of the game is identical.

If each player calls for a share m for himself in each round where he is the caller, the payoffs in each round are as shown in the final two columns of Table A5. The payoffs differ because they entail income streams starting at different points in line. Hence to compare the payoffs, we measure them in terms of permanent income streams beginning in period 0 having the same present value as the payoff. It is clear that all the payoffs attainable from period 2 onwards are dominated by those attainable in the first two rounds. Player 2 will then accept player 1's opening offer provided it exceeds the maximum he (player 2) can obtain by the best strategy *he* can play at *his* first call in period 2. His call then will also be m, but since the income stream begins one period later, its value to the player is only δm. Thus, player 1's best strategy is to call for the largest share for himself consistent with player 2 being prepared to accept it. *Hence* m *takes the maximum value satisfying the inequality* $(1 - m) \geqslant \delta m$. If m is continuous, this means that the optimal m satisfies

$$1 - m = \delta m$$

or

$$m = \frac{1}{1 + \delta}.$$

If the time period is short, so that δ is close to one, then

$$m \simeq \frac{1}{2}.$$

(To see why m cannot exceed $1/(1 + \delta)$, note that if it did $(1 - m) < \delta m$, so that each player at each round would reckon he would have a higher payoff by refusing the other player's call and proceeding to the next round. But if it is rational to refuse m in the first round, it is rational to refuse it in every subsequent round, in which case the game never finishes and the payoffs to each player are zero. Thus a value of m in excess of $1/(1 + \delta)$ cannot be an optimal strategy.)

Unequal discount rates

If the players have different discount rates, the game is no longer symmetric and the optimal calls of the two players will differ. Let the discount factors of the two players by δ_1 and δ_2 and their optimal calls be shares of m_1 and m_2 (see Table A6). Again, the structure of the game remains constant over time, and so m_1 and m_2 will be constant. *Player 1 will again want the highest-value* m_1 *to satisfy the inequality* $(1 - m_1) \geqslant \delta_2 m_2$, *but he evaluates this requirement knowing that player 2, following the same strategy, will determine* m_2 *as the highest number satisfying* $(1 - m_2) \geqslant \delta_1 m_1$. The optimal value thus satisfies

$$1 - m_1 = \delta_2 m_2,$$

$$1 - m_2 = \delta_1 m_1,$$

which can be solved to give

$$m_1 = \frac{1 - \delta_2}{1 - \delta_1 \delta_2} \qquad \left(\text{and } m_2 = \frac{1 - \delta_1}{1 - \delta_1 \delta_2} \right).$$

The actual bargain will be determined by player 1's original offer, with relative shares equal to

Table A6 *Bargaining payoffs: with different discount rates*

Period	Caller	Payoff for player 1	2
0	1	m_1	$1 - m_1$
1	2	$\delta_1(1 - m_2)$	$\delta_2 m_2$
2	1	$\delta_1^2 m_1$	$\delta_2^2(1 - m_1)$

$$\frac{m_1}{1-m_1} = \frac{1-\delta_2}{1-\delta_1}\left(\frac{1}{\delta_2}\right) \simeq \frac{r_2}{r_1},$$

where r_1, r_2 are the discount rates per period. Thus the player with the higher discount rate gets the smaller share of the surplus.

Fallback income

Now suppose that during the disagreement each party had a fallback income per period of $\bar{Y}_1$, $\bar{Y}_2$ (measured in units of cake). Then player 1 will choose m_1 so that for player 2 the present value of player 1's offer equals the present value of player 2's alternative if he rejects this offer:

$$\frac{1-m_1}{r_2} = \delta_2\frac{m_2}{r_2} + \bar{Y}_2.$$

In doing this, player 1 knows that player 2 would choose m_2, so that for player 1

$$\frac{1-m_2}{r_1} = \delta_1\frac{m_1}{r_1} + \bar{Y}_1.$$

This has the solution

$$\frac{m_1 - \bar{Y}_1}{1 - m_1 - \bar{Y}_2} \simeq \frac{r_2}{r_1}.$$

The higher the fallback, the higher the share.

The Nash maximand

It is easy to see that this solution could have been obtained by choosing m_1 to maximize

$$(m_1 - \bar{Y}_1)^{r_2/r_1}(1 - m_1 - \bar{Y}_2).$$

More generally, one can show that the perfect equilibrium of a bargaining game corresponds to the maximization of

$$(Y_1 - \bar{Y}_1)^{r_2 r_1}(Y_2 - \bar{Y}_2),$$

where Y_1, Y_2 are the present values of the bargain, subject to whatever constraints apply. These constraints need not be linear (Sutton 1986: 715–16).

Clearly, the solution depends on perfect information on both sides about the payoff to the other side. When there is imperfect information, there is not always immediate agreement as both sides grope their way forward. There may even be a wasteful delay. But this has not proved easy to model.

Bishop (1964) has a model of firm–union bargaining in which there is a sequence of actual offers (not necessarily alternating), leading up to the Nash solution. Agreement is reached without a strike. Since both sides are assumed to have full information about each other's payoffs, there is no obvious reason for the sequence of offers, since everyone must know where they will end up.

2.3. Properties of the survival function

In the main text (Chapter 2, equation (9)) the survival function S is defined. If we define $x = N_{fi}/N_i^e$ and recall that $N_i = N_i^e \tilde{\varphi}$, then (9) becomes

$$S(x) = P(\tilde{\varphi} > x) + x^{-1} E(\tilde{\varphi}\,|\,\tilde{\varphi} \leqslant x) P(\tilde{\varphi} \leqslant x).$$

Let $\tilde{\varphi}$ have a density function $h(\cdot)$ and a CDF, $H(\cdot)$, and recall that $\tilde{\varphi} \geqslant 0$ and has a unit mean. S can be written

$$S(x) = 1 - H(x) + x^{-1} \int_0^x \tilde{\varphi} h(\tilde{\varphi}) \mathrm{d}\tilde{\varphi} > 0. \tag{A1}$$

Consequently

$$S'(x) = - x^{-2} \int_0^x \tilde{\varphi} h(\tilde{\varphi}) \mathrm{d}\tilde{\varphi} < 0, \tag{A2}$$

$$S''(x) = \quad 2x^{-3} \int_0^x \tilde{\varphi} h(\tilde{\varphi}) \mathrm{d}\tilde{\varphi} - x^{-1} h(x). \tag{A3}$$

Consider first the elasticity of S with respect to N_i^e, written as ε_{SN}. This is

$$\varepsilon_{SN} = - xS'(x)/S > 0,$$

from (A1), (A2). What of the size of ε_{SN}?

$$\varepsilon_{SN} = x^{-1} \int_0^x \tilde{\varphi} h(\tilde{\varphi}) \mathrm{d}\tilde{\varphi} / (1 - H(x) + x^{-1} \int_0^x \tilde{\varphi} h(\tilde{\varphi}) \mathrm{d}\tilde{\varphi}) < 1$$

for all x. Generally, however, unless there is a severe contraction of employment, and certainly in stationary equilibrium, $x < 1$.
  Then if H is symmetric, $(1 - H(x)) > \frac{1}{2}$ and

$$x^{-1} \int_0^x \tilde{\varphi} h(\tilde{\varphi}) \mathrm{d}\tilde{\varphi} < \frac{xH(x)}{x} = H(x) < \frac{1}{2}.$$

Consequently $\varepsilon_{SN} < \frac{1}{2}$ for $x < 1$.
  Next consider, the slope of $\varepsilon_{SN}(x)$:

$$\frac{\partial \varepsilon_{SN}(x)}{\partial x} = x \left(\frac{S'(x)}{S(x)} \right)^2 - \frac{1}{S(x)} (S'(x) + xS''(x)),$$

$$= (S'(x) + h(x) - \varepsilon_{SN} S'(x))/S(x). \tag{A4}$$

So long as $x \leqslant 1$, it is easy to show that for all symmetric, single-peaked distributions,

$S'(x) + h(x) > 0$ and hence $\dfrac{\partial \varepsilon_{SN}}{\partial x} > 0$.

Now consider a robust upper bound for

$$\frac{\partial \varepsilon_{SN}(x)}{\partial x} = \varepsilon'_{SN}$$

From (A2), (A4),

$$\varepsilon'_{SN} = x^{-1}(\varepsilon_{SN})^2 - x^{-1}\varepsilon_{SN} + \frac{h(x)}{S(x)} < \frac{h(x)}{S(x)}$$

Evaluating this expression at a stationary equilibrium, $x = 1 - \delta$, where δ is the rate of voluntary quitting. The data suggest that $1 - \delta$ satisfies $0.7 < 1 - \delta < 0.9$. Furthermore, the data suggest that survival probabilities are unlikely to fall below 0.75 in most firms (see Chapter 2, Table 4). Assuming that H is symmetric, these suggest that $\varepsilon_{SN} < \frac{1}{2}$, $x^{-1} < (0.7)^{-1}$, $(S(x))^{-1} < 1.33$. Assuming further that H is single-peaked, the maximum possible value for $h(x)$ arises if H is uniformly distributed from 0.9 to 1.1 (recall that 0.9 is the maximum value of x), in which case $h(x) = 5$. Using these numbers, we have

$$\varepsilon'_{SN} < 5 \times 1.33 = 6.7.$$

2.4. Effect of employment measures upon wage-bargaining in corporatist economies

Suppose that compensating government employment (N_C) is set at

$$N_C = \lambda(L - N_P - N_G), \tag{A5}$$

where N_G excludes compensating employment. This, it is argued, will raise unemployment by encouraging unions to push harder on wages because the resulting job loss will be reduced by a fraction λ (Calmfors and Horn 1985).

To see how this could work, suppose a feasible real wage relation that slopes down because of diminishing marginal productivity. This is shown as PP in Fig. A2 and includes in employment any exogenous public employment. With no compensatory employment the union chooses an interior point Q. If we now allow compensatory public employment, we move to a relation PP'. Provided Q is sufficiently close to full employment, the government's policy must reduce employment, since the negative substitution affect outweighs the positive expansion effect.

However, this argument does not take into account the financing of the government expenditure. It is unrealistic to suppose that a centralized union would not realize that extra government expenditure had to be financed out of higher taxes. In this case the government budget constraint requires

$$\text{const.} + N_G + N_C = t(N_P + N_G + N_C). \tag{A6}$$

We wish to investigate the effect of a change in $\log W$ on $\log V = \log[W(1 - t) (N_P + N_G + N_C)]$. This is given by

$$\frac{\partial \log V}{\partial \log W} = 1 - \frac{1}{1 - t}\frac{\partial t}{\partial \log W} + \frac{1}{N}\left(\frac{\partial N_P}{\partial \log W} + \frac{\partial N_C}{\partial \log W}\right).$$

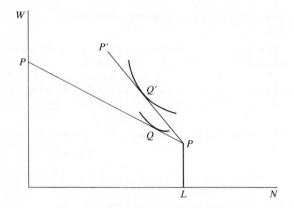

Fig. A2. *Effects of government response function.*

To evaluate this, we note that from (A5)

$$\frac{\partial N_C}{\partial \log W} = -\lambda \frac{\partial N_P}{\partial \log W},$$

and, combining (A5) and (A6),

$$\frac{\partial t}{\partial \log W} = -\frac{t + \lambda(1-t)}{N} \frac{\partial N_P}{\partial \log W}.$$

Hence

$$\frac{\partial \log V}{\partial \log W} = 1 + \frac{1}{N}\frac{\partial N_P}{\partial \log W}\left(\frac{t + \lambda(1-t)}{1-t} + 1 - \lambda\right)$$

$$= 1 + \frac{N_P}{N}\frac{\partial \log N_P}{\partial \log W}\frac{1}{1-t}.$$

This is independent of λ. Thus we see that the whole externality has been internalized.

Another criticism of the model is that, if the government perceived that compensatory public employment was self-defeating, it would surely abandon the policy. One is in any case struck by the high employment levels in countries which do pursue compensatory policies. This is probably due more to the detailed structure of the policies (see Chapter 10). The aggregative implications are probably unimportant.

3.1. Efficiency wages and bargaining combined

Clearly, it is likely that when firms bargain with workers they are also influenced by efficiency wage considerations. We want to check that in this case equilibrium unemployment is higher than it would be if wages were set either by (*a*) bargaining with no efficiency considerations, or (*b*) efficiency considerations with no bargaining. We can also check that in this case the elasticity of effort with respect to wages will be less than unity.

For simplicity, we assume that the union cares only about wages. The bargain then chooses W_i to maximize

$$\Omega_i = (W_i - A)^\beta \{ R \left[N_i e \left(\frac{W_i}{W^e}, u \right) \right] - W_i N_i \},$$

subject to the firm's employment decision given by

$$\frac{\partial \Pi_i}{\partial N_i} = R'e - W_i = 0. \tag{A7}$$

Maximizing Ω_i gives

$$\frac{\partial \log \Omega_i}{\partial W_i} = \frac{\beta}{W_i - A} + \frac{1}{\Pi_i} \left(R'N_i \frac{e_1}{W^e} - N_i + (R'e - W_i) \frac{\partial N_i}{\partial W_i} \right). \tag{A8}$$

Hence from (A7) and (A8),

$$\frac{\partial \log \Omega_i}{\partial \log W_i} = \frac{\beta W_i}{W_i - A} + \frac{N_i W_i}{\Pi_i} \left(\frac{e_1 W_i}{e W^e} - 1 \right) = 0.$$

Firms are now pushed to pay higher wages than they would like, so that the elasticity of effort with respect to wages is less than one. (The bracketed term is negative.)

In general equilibrium, if $A = W^e(1 - u)$, we set $W_i = W = W^e$ and obtain

$$u^* = \beta \frac{\Pi}{NW} \left(1 - \frac{e_1}{e} \right)^{-1}, \tag{A9}$$

where e_1/e is the elasticity of effort with respect to relative wages. Assuming our standard Cobb–Douglas case, Π/NW is constant. We can now compare this outcome first with the case of pure bargaining without efficiency considerations. With pure bargaining,

$$u^* = \beta \frac{\Pi}{NW} < \beta \frac{\Pi}{NW} \left(1 - \frac{e_1}{e} \right)^{-1},$$

since $(1 - e_1/e)$ is positive and less than one. Thus, with no efficiency wage considerations unemployment would be lower.

Equally, if there were only efficiency wage considerations and no bargaining, we should have $\beta = 0$ and unemployment determined by

$$e(1,u) - e_1(1,u) = 0.$$

It is easy to show that, as β rises, the total effect on u in equation (A9) is positive.[3] Thus, unemployment rises as union bargaining strength rises.

4.1. Wage determination in a turnover model

Firm i has capital (K_i) and available job slots (N_i^*), where

$$N_i^* = K_i v \qquad (A10)$$

with v constant. Production (Y) satisfies

$$Y_i = N_i(K_i/N_i^*)^{1-\alpha} \qquad (N_i \leqslant N_i^*).$$

The total number of accessions per period is $a(W_{it}/A_t)(N_i^* - N_{it})$, where $N_i^* - N_{it}$ is the number of vacancies and a is the rate of accessions per vacancy, which depends on the ratio of wages to outside opportunities. The firm thus chooses the wage path

$$\max\Sigma \frac{1}{(1+r)^t}(P_{it}N_{it}v^{-(1-\alpha)} - W_{it}N_{it})$$

$$\text{s.t. } N_{it} - N_{it-1} - a(W_{it}/A_t)(N_i^* - N_{it}) + sN_{it} = 0 \qquad (N_{it} \leqslant N_i^*), \qquad (A11)$$

where s is the exogenous separation rate. The first-order conditions for an interior solution are

$$\frac{1}{(1+r)^t}(P_{it}v^{-(1-\alpha)} - W_{it}) - \mu_{it}(1 + a + s) + \mu_{it+1} = 0, \qquad (A12)$$

$$-\frac{N_{it}}{(1+r)^t} + \frac{\mu_{it}a'}{A_t}(N_i^* - N_{it}) = 0, \qquad (A13)$$

where μ_{it} is the multiplier associated with the employment constraint. Defining

$$\eta_a = \frac{a'W_{it}}{aA_t},$$

in stationary equilibrium, wages satisfy

$$W_i = \frac{P_i(K_i/N_i^*)^{1-\alpha}s\eta_a}{s(1+\eta_\alpha) + a(W_i/A) + r}. \qquad (A14)$$

Noting that A is given by equation (6) in Chapter 4. Taking log differentials of (A14) yields equations (13), (14) in that chapter.

4.2. A model of wages and employment in a two-stage bargaining framework

Here we follow the two-stage bargaining model due to Manning (1987), described in Section 4 of Chapter 4. Suppose the union and firm contributions to the Nash bargain are given by

$$U - \bar{U} = N(W - A), \qquad \Pi - \bar{\Pi} = (EN)^\alpha - WN, \qquad (A15)$$

where effort (E) satisfies

$$E = (W/A - 1)^\lambda \qquad (\lambda < 1) \qquad (A16)$$

and the notation is standard. In the union utility function, it is assumed that effort has been substituted out. Note that this will imply that any other variables which enter the effort function will also enter union utility and this will ensure that they are not able to assist in identification. In the second stage of the bargain, employment solves

$$\max_{N} \beta_n \log[N(W - A)] + \log[(EN)^\alpha - WN],$$

where β_n is union power in the employment bargain. From the first-order condition, N satisfies

$$\omega_n E^\alpha N^{\alpha - 1} = W, \qquad \omega_n = \frac{\beta_n + \alpha}{\beta_n + 1}. \qquad (A17)$$

In the first stage, wages solve

$$\max_{W} \beta_w \log[N(W - A)] + \log[(EN)^\alpha - WN]$$

subject to (A17) where β_w is union power in the wage bargain. Using (A16), (A17), this objective reduces to an equivalent form (dropping constants) of

$$\max_{W} [\alpha\lambda(1 + \beta_n) + \beta_n(1 - \alpha)]\log(W - A) - (\alpha + \beta_n)\log W.$$

The first-order condition then yields

$$a(1 - \lambda)W = \omega_w A, \qquad \omega_w = \frac{\beta_w + \alpha}{\beta_w + 1}. \qquad (A18)$$

Making use of (A16), we thus have structural employment and wage equations of the form

$$(1 - \alpha)n = \log\omega_n + \alpha\lambda\log(W - A) - \alpha\lambda a - w, \qquad (A19)$$

$$w = \log\omega_w + a - \log\alpha(1 - \lambda); \qquad (A20)$$

or, using (A18) to eliminate $\log(W - A)$, (A19) can be written

$$(1 - \alpha)n = \log\omega_n + \alpha\lambda\log\left(1 - \frac{\alpha(1 - \lambda)}{\omega_w}\right) - \alpha\lambda a - (1 - \alpha\lambda)w. \qquad (A21)$$

In order to proceed, it is convenient to linearize the term in ω_w, so suppose we may write

$$\log\left(1 - \frac{\alpha(1 - \lambda)}{\omega_w}\right) = \alpha_0 + \alpha_1\log\omega_w.$$

Then (A21) becomes

$$n = \frac{\alpha\lambda\alpha_0}{1 - \alpha} + \frac{1}{1 - \alpha}\log\omega_n + \frac{\alpha\lambda\alpha_1}{1 - \alpha}\log\omega_w - \frac{\alpha\lambda}{1 - \alpha}a - \frac{(1 - \alpha\lambda)}{1 - \alpha}w. \qquad (A22)$$

From now on we treat (A20), (A22) as our structural model in w and n. Suppose we have two observed variables x_1, x_2, which determine union power (we could have n variables, but this would add nothing of interest), and suppose that ω_n, ω_w satisfy

$$\log\omega_n = q_0 + q_1x_1 + q_2x_2, \tag{A23}$$

$$\log\omega_w = p_0 + p_1x_1 + p_2x_2. \tag{A24}$$

Then the reduced-form equations for wages and employment can be written as

$$n = a_0 + a_1x_1 + a_2x_2 + a_3a, \tag{A25}$$

$$w = b_0 + b_1x_1 + b_2x_2 + b_3a, \tag{A26}$$

where

$$a_1 = \frac{q_1 + p_1[\alpha\lambda\alpha_1 - (1 - \alpha\lambda)]}{1 - \alpha}, \qquad a_2 = \frac{q_2 + p_2[\alpha\lambda\gamma_1 - (1 - \alpha\lambda)]}{1 - \alpha},$$

$$a_3 = -\frac{1}{1 - \alpha}, \qquad b_1 = p_1, \qquad b_2 = p_2, \qquad b_3 = 1.$$

We are now in a position to investigate the restrictions implied by various hypotheses of interest.

1. Efficiency wages absent: $\lambda = 0$. From the definitions of the reduced-form coefficients, this implies *no restrictions*.
2. Efficient bargaining: $\beta_n = \beta_w$, which implies $p_1 = q_1$, $p_2 = q_2$. It is clear that this implies the single restriction $a_1/b_1 = a_2/b_2$.
3. Right to manage, i.e. bargain on the demand curve: $\beta_n = 0$, which implies $\omega_n = \alpha$ or $q_1 = q_2 = 0$. This again implies the single restriction $a_1/b_1 = a_2/b_2$.
4. Efficiency wages absent *and* efficient bargaining: $\lambda = 0$, $\beta_n = \beta_w$, which implies $\lambda = 0$, $p_1 = q_1$, $p_2 = q_2$. The restrictions implied are $a_1 = 0$, $a_2 = 0$.
5. Efficiency wages absent *and* right to manage: $\lambda = 0$, $\beta_n = 0$, which implies $\lambda = 0$, $q_1 = 0$, $q_2 = 0$. The restrictions implied are $a_1/b_1 = a_2/b_2 = a_3/b_3$. These results imply that (*a*) the absence of efficiency wages cannot be tested; (*b*) in the presence of efficiency wages, it is not possible to discriminate between efficient bargaining and right to manage; (*c*) in the absence of efficiency wages, it is possible to discriminate between efficient bargaining and right to manage.

5.1. Unemployment stocks and flows: selected countries

Table A7 *Unemployment stocks and flows: selected countries*

	Unemployment rate (%) (U/N)	Inflow rate (% per mo.) (S/N)	Steady-state average duration (mos.) (U/S)
Australia			
1978	6.6	1.4	4.7
1979	6.6	1.3	4.9
1980	6.4	1.2	5.2
1981	6.0	1.2	5.0
1982	7.6	1.6	4.8
1983	11.0	1.3	8.4
1984	9.8	1.5	6.6
1985	8.9	1.5	6.1
1986	8.7	1.5	5.8
1987	8.7	1.5	5.9
1988	7.8	1.4	5.6
Austria			
1973	1.0	0.1	7.2
1974	1.1	0.1	10.1
1975	1.7	0.2	8.2
1976	1.8	0.2	9.6
1977	1.6	0.2	8.6
1978	2.1	0.2	9.3
1979	2.1	0.2	10.2
1980	1.9	0.2	10.2
1981	2.6	0.3	9.5
1982	3.6	0.4	8.6
1983	4.3	0.5	9.5
1984	4.0	0.5	7.9
1985	3.7	0.6	6.6
1986	3.2	0.7	4.5
1987	4.0	—	—
1988	3.7	—	—
Belgium			
1983	13.8	0.5	27
1984	13.8	0.4	34
1985	12.7	0.3	43
1986	12.6	0.3	37
1987	11.1	0.2	54
1988	10.7	0.2	61
Canada			
1976	7.6	2.5	3.1
1977	8.7	2.7	3.3
1978	9.1	2.7	3.4
1979	8.0	2.6	3.1
1980	8.1	2.6	3.1
1981	8.1	2.8	2.9
1982	12.2	3.4	3.6
1983	13.4	3.2	4.2
1984	12.6	3.3	3.9

Table A7—*continued*

	Unemployment rate (%) (U/N)	Inflow rate (% per mo.) (S/N)	Steady-state average duration (mos.) (U/S)
1985	11.6	3.0	3.7
1986	10.5	3.0	3.5
1987	9.6	2.8	3.5
1988	8.3	2.6	3.2
1989	8.1	2.6	3.1
Denmark			
1983	11.6	0.7	17
1984	11.2	0.8	15
1985	9.9	0.7	15
1986	8.5	0.7	12
1987	8.5	0.9	9
1988	9.4	0.8	11
Finland			
1982	5.6	1.1	5.1
1983	5.7	1.1	5.1
1984	5.5	1.3	4.2
1985	5.5	1.0	5.5
1986	5.6	1.2	4.6
1987	5.3	1.1	4.9
France			
1968	2.7	0.4	6.6
1969	2.4	0.4	6.4
1970	2.6	0.5	5.5
1971	2.8	0.4	6.7
1972	2.9	0.5	6.3
1973	2.8	0.4	6.7
1974	2.9	0.5	5.9
1975	4.2	0.6	7.6
1976	4.6	0.4	10.6
1977	5.2	0.4	11.7
1978	5.5	0.5	11.1
1979	6.3	0.5	13.8
1980	6.7	0.5	14.2
1981	7.9	0.5	15.1
1982	8.8	0.6	13.7
1983	9.1	0.5	19.4
1984	10.7	0.5	20.6
1985	11.4	0.5	22.9
1986	11.6	0.6	19.0
1987	11.7	0.6	18.5
1988	11.1	0.6	21.1
1989	10.6	0.7	15.5
Germany			
1983	8.0	0.6	15.3
1984	7.6	0.5	14.1
1985	7.8	0.5	15.3
1986	6.8	0.4	18.1
1987	6.6	0.4	17.3
1988	6.6	0.4	16.3

545

Table A7—*continued*

	Unemployment rate (%) (U/N)	Inflow rate (% per mo.) (S/N)	Steady-state average duration (mos.) (U/S)
Ireland			
1983	16.3	1.2	13.5
1984	18.3	1.0	18.7
1985	21.1	0.6	32.8
1986	21.1	0.8	27.2
1987	21.2	0.5	41.7
1988	20.0	0.7	30.4
Italy			
1983	7.5	0.21	36.4
1984	7.5	0.18	42.0
1985	7.6	0.19	39.7
1986	8.1	0.18	45.0
1987	8.6	0.23	38.0
1988	8.6	0.24	35.9
Japan			
1977	2.0	0.50	4.1
1978	2.2	0.47	4.8
1979	2.1	0.38	5.7
1980	2.0	0.38	5.3
1981	2.2	0.59	3.8
1982	2.5	0.46	5.3
1983	2.7	0.54	5.0
1984	2.8	0.42	6.6
1985	2.7	0.45	5.9
1986	2.9	0.49	5.8
1987	2.9	0.43	6.8
1988	2.6	0.47	5.4
Netherlands			
1987	10.6	0.56	18.8
1988	10.1	0.42	25.2
Norway			
1978	1.8	0.78	2.4
1979	2.0	0.84	2.4
1980	1.6	0.65	2.5
1981	2.0	0.85	2.4
1982	2.7	0.87	3.1
1983	3.5	0.99	3.6
1984	3.2	0.80	4.0
1985	2.7	0.87	3.1
1986	2.0	0.77	2.7
1987	2.1	0.75	2.9
1988	3.3	1.1	3.0
Spain			
1977	5.5	0.38	14
1978	7.4	0.52	14
1979	9.3	0.47	20
1980	12.6	0.53	24
1981	16.1	0.55	29
1982	16.8	0.44	39

Table A7—*continued*

	Unemployment rate (%) (U/N)	Inflow rate (% per mo.) (S/N)	Steady-state average duration (mos.) (U/S)
1983	18.5	0.48	38
1984	25.0	0.57	44
1985	27.2	0.67	41
1986	26.6	0.64	41
1987	25.2	0.28	89
1988	23.6	0.23	105
Sweden			
1971	2.1	0.81	2.7
1972	2.2	0.74	3.1
1973	2.0	0.67	3.0
1974	1.6	0.61	2.6
1975	1.3	0.50	2.7
1976	1.3	0.50	2.6
1977	1.5	0.53	2.9
1978	1.8	0.62	3.0
1979	1.7	0.60	2.9
1980	1.6	0.55	3.0
1981	2.1	0.63	3.4
1982	2.7	0.70	3.8
1983	3.0	0.79	3.8
1984	2.7	0.69	3.9
1985	2.5	0.67	3.7
1986	2.2	0.59	3.8
1987	1.9	0.69	3.5
1988	1.6	0.49	3.3

Notes and sources: see Table 1 of chapter 5.

5.2. The reservation wage: the dynamic programming approach

The reservation wage is selected to maximize the unemployed individual's expected present value (V_U), i.e. the expected present value of someone who is currently unemployed but will not be so for ever.

This expected present value is shown in equation (A27) below and is derived as follows. In this period the individual is unemployed and will be paid B. Next period he may or may not be unemployed. He has a chance p of hearing of a job paying above W_c and a chance λ of getting it if he applies. Hence his chances of getting a job (if he uses the W_c cut-off) is $p(W_c)\lambda$. His chance of remaining unemployed is $1 - p(W_c)\lambda$.

If he gets a job, his present value is the expected present value (V_E) of a person employed at the average wage above W_c. If he is still unemployed in the following period, the model assumes that nothing will have changed and his present value is the same as now, V_U. In practice, of course, a person's probability of getting a job may decline the longer he has been unemployed. Thus, in our notation λ would become $\lambda(t)$ with $\lambda' < 0$. In this note, for expositional purposes, we ignore this point, and assume that the probability of getting a job is constant. Then the present value of the unemployed person is

$$V_U = \frac{1}{1+r}[B + \lambda p V_E + (1 - \lambda p)V_U], \tag{A27}$$

where for convenience we assume the income is paid at the end of 'the period' and evaluate the present value at the beginning of the period. The unemployed person chooses W_c to maximize V_U.

But first we need to know what V_E is. It is shown in equation (A28). If the person gets a job, he can expect to be paid the average wage in all jobs paying above W_c, i.e. $\bar{W}(W_c)$. However, the following period he may lose the job, with probability s, and end up again unemployed. His present value will then again be V_U, since he will use the same reservation wage to deal with unemployment if he finds himself unemployed a second time. However, there is a good chance $(1 - s)$ that he will remain employed and his present value will then remain V_E. So

$$V_E = \frac{1}{1+r}[\bar{W}(W_c) + sV_U + (1 - s)V_E]. \tag{A28}$$

Combining (A27) and (A28) and noting that $p = p(W_c)$, we find that

$$V_U = \frac{(r + s)B + p(W_c)\lambda\bar{W}(W_c)}{r[r + s + p(W_c)\lambda]}. \tag{A29}$$

Note that the expected wage ($\bar{W}$) rises with the reservation wage, while the probability of applying (p) falls. It is this trade-off that determines the choice of reservation wage.

To find the reservation wage, we could use (A29) to find $\partial V_U/\partial W_c$ and set it to zero. However, a simpler approach comes from the inner logic of the problem. If the person just accepts a job at the reservation wage, he must by doing so be exactly as well off as if he remained unemployed. Hence $V_U = V_{W_c}$. But the present value of someone employed at the reservation wage is, by the same logic as (A28),

$$V_{W_c} = \frac{1}{1+r}[W_c + sV_U + (1 - s)V_{W_c}].$$

So

$$V_{W_c} = \frac{1}{r+s}(W_c + sV_U) = V_U.$$

It follows that

$$W_c = rV_U. \tag{A30}$$

The reservation wage equals the expected permanent income stream of an unemployed person.

From (A29) and (A30), we have the implicit function for the reservation wage which we derived earlier:

$$W_c = B + \frac{\lambda}{r+s}p(W_c)[\bar{W}(W_c) - W_c].$$

5.3. Allowing for employed job-seekers

Flows through the labour market in Britain in the year to April 1985 were roughly as follows[4]

E	Total engagements	6.8m
	of which:	
	Engagements of people already in work	2.5m
	Engagements from the education sector	0.6m
H	Engagements of unemployed people	3.7m

The corresponding stocks were

U	Unemployed job-seekers	2.8m
J	Employed job-seekers	1.3m
V	Vacancies	0.5m

The average durations implied by these figures (stock/flow) are roughly

Unemployed job search	9 mos.
Employed job search	6 mos.
Vacancies	$3\frac{1}{2}$ wks.

Thus, to model the outflow from unemployment, we should in principle allow for job competition between the employed and the unemployed. The total number of hirings (E) per period depends on the number of vacancies and on the number of 'effective' job-seekers, ($cU + c'J$), where c' is the effectiveness of employed job-seekers. Hence the 'hiring function' is

$$E = f(\overset{+}{V}, \overset{+}{cU + c'J}).$$

So the ease of job-finding per effective job-seeker ($E/(cU + c'J)$) depends positively on the ratio of vacancies to effective job-seekers:

$$\frac{E}{cU + c'J} = f\left(\underset{+}{\frac{V}{cU + c'J}}, 1\right).$$

But the ease of job-finding must (by definition) be the same for an effective job-seeker whether he is employed or unemployed. Hence

$$\frac{H}{cU} = \frac{E - H}{c'J} = \frac{E}{cU + c'J} = f\left(\underset{+}{\frac{V}{cU + c'J}}, 1\right).$$

Each of these variables is in turn related to the duration of vacancies (V/E), since the hiring function can also be written

$$\frac{E}{V} = f\left(1, \underset{+}{\frac{cU + c'J}{V}}\right).$$

Hence the exit rate for effective unemployed job-seekers is directly related to the duration of vacancies:

$$\frac{H}{cU} = g\left(\frac{V}{E}\right).$$

This relationship can be estimated without requiring any data on employed job-seekers (or their effectiveness).

The relationship has a further advantage in countries like Britain, where we have no time-series data on total vacancies but only on vacancies registered at government Job Centres. Provided the duration of Job Centre vacancies is proportional to the duration of all vacancies, it is an adequate proxy for the duration of all vacancies. (The two national surveys of vacancies in 1977 and 1988 confirm this assumption.) Thus, in Jackman *et al.* (1989) we attempt to estimate the above equation. In the present text, however, it is expositionally clearer to estimate equation (16) in Chapter 5, where the vacancy series is an estimate of total vacancies obtained by multiplying registered vacancies by the ratio of total engagements to engagements of the unemployed. Readers will be reassured to know that the results of Jackman *et al.* (1989) are broadly consistent with those reported in Section 5 of Chapter 5.

6.1. Mismatch and substitution between types of labour

The curvature of the real wage frontier depends on the elasticity of substitution in demand between different types of labour.[5] Using a CES production function of the form

$$Y^\rho = \varphi \Sigma \alpha_i N_i^\rho \qquad (\Sigma \alpha_i = 1, \rho - 1 = -1/\sigma; \sigma \geq 0, \sigma \neq 1),$$

we obtain a price function[6]

$$AP = \Sigma \alpha_i^\sigma W_i^{-(\sigma-1)}.$$

where $A = \varphi^{-\sigma}{}_\kappa - (\sigma - 1)$

Setting the price level at unity, the price function gives us a feasible real wage frontier:

$$A = \Sigma \alpha_i^\sigma W_i^{-(\sigma-1)}.$$

If the wage functions are, as before,

$$W_i = \beta_i u_i^{-\gamma_1},$$

the unemployment frontier is now

$$A = \Sigma \alpha_i^\sigma \beta_i^{-(\sigma-1)} u_i^{\gamma_1(\sigma-1)}.$$

Using empirically relevant magnitudes such as $\gamma_1 \simeq 0.1$ (see below) and $0 < \sigma < 10$, this is a concave function in the u_is.

To find the aggregate unemployment rate, we multiply by $u^{-\gamma_1(\sigma-1)}/A$ to obtain

$$u^{-\gamma_1(\sigma-1)} = \frac{1}{A} \Sigma \alpha_i \alpha_i^{\sigma-1} \beta_i^{-(\sigma-1)} \left(\frac{u_i}{u}\right)^{\gamma_1(\sigma-1)}.$$

If α_i, β_i, u_i/u, and L_i/L are approximately independent,[7] then

$$\log u \simeq \frac{1}{2}[1 - \gamma_1(\sigma - 1)]\mathrm{var}\frac{u_i}{u} + \mathrm{const.}$$

Mismatch is now

$$MM = \frac{1}{2}[1 - \gamma_1(\sigma - 1)]\mathrm{var}\frac{u_i}{u}.$$

8.1. A 'disequilibrium' framework

The purpose of this annex is to give some idea of the consequences of allowing 'disequilibrium' phenomena into the demand side of our model. This relates to the style of analysis exemplified by Sneessens and Drèze (1986) and by Lambert (1988), where some firms do not—indeed, cannot—necessarily supply what is demanded at the predetermined price when demand is revealed. In addition, we drop the assumption of a fixed labour force. Thus it is an extension of the basic model set out in Section 1 of Chapter 8. We do not attempt, here, to provide a comprehensive formal discussion, but merely to give some flavour of the implications of this type of analysis.

In order to ensure that firms cannot necessarily supply what is demanded, we replace our standard production function given in equation (1) of Chapter 8 by

$$y_i = \min(x_n + n_i, x_k + k_i), \tag{A31}$$

where the variables are in logs and the labour and capital coefficients (x_n, x_k) are fixed over the period under consideration. Suppose now that there are random differences in the environment of each firm which ensure that some firms are constrained by their (predetermined) capital stock whereas others are not. For example, we might suppose that there are random differences across firms in the allocation of demand, which last for some time but have an overall mean of zero.

In aggregate, we may now define full utilization output $(\bar{y})$ by

$$\bar{y} = x_n + l, \tag{A32}$$

which replaces equation (3) of Chapter 8. Furthermore, following the notions used by Sneessens and Drèze (1986), we define the 'Keynesian' demand for labour (n_d) and the potential demand for labour (n_p) by

$$n_d = y_d - x_n = (y_d - \bar{y}) + l, \tag{A33}$$

$$n_p = x_k - x_n + k. \tag{A34}$$

n_d is thus the demand for labour if no firms are 'capital-constrained', and n_p is the maximum possible demand for labour given the current capital stock. We now propose that actual aggregate employment is given, in unlogged form, by

$$N = F(N_d, N_p), \tag{A35}$$

where $1 > F_1 > 0, 1 > F_2 > 0, N < N_d, N < N_p$, F is homogeneous of degree one. The idea underlying this formulation is that of 'smoothing by aggregation'. Because of the fixed-coefficients technology and the random variations in demand, some firms are constrained by demand and some by their capital stock. Aggregate employment, therefore, does not respond fully to changes in aggregate demand, as in our standard model. Lambert (1988) demonstrates that, if the random variations across firms follow a particular distribution, F may be closely approximated by a CES function. Many examples of the use of this particular framework are in Drèze and Bean (1991).

In order to introduce dynamic adjustment, we now make the further assumption that the capital stock always adjusts to make potential employment equal to Keynesian employment in the long run. Thus, those firms that are capital-constrained will eventually invest until their capital shortage disappears, whereas those that have too much capital will allow it to depreciate until they can just satisfy demand. We could, of course, allow a more complex investment function. Thus, we might have profits influencing the speed at which investment closes the gap, for example, but here we ignore such complications. We may write the adjustment process in log form as

$$n_p = A(L)n_d \qquad (A(1) = 1), \tag{A36}$$

where L is the lag operator and $A(L)$ is a lag polynomial. From (A33) we thus have

$$n_p = A(L)(y_d - \bar{y} + l),$$

and hence employment is given by

$$N = F\{\exp(y_d - \bar{y} + l), \exp[A(L)(y_d - \bar{y} + l)]\}. \tag{A37}$$

By homogeneity, (A37) may be rewritten as

$$N = \exp(y_d - \bar{y} + l)F\{1, \exp[(A(L) - 1)(y_d - \bar{y} + l)]\}$$

or

$$u = -(y_d - \bar{y}) - \log F\{1, \exp[(A(L) - 1)(y_d - \bar{y} + l)]\}, \tag{A38}$$

recalling that $u = l - n$. Since $A(1) = 1$, the expression $[(A(L) - 1)(y_d - \bar{y} + l)]$ can be written entirely in first differences, and if we linearize (A38), we obtain

$$u = -(y_d - \bar{y}) + \sum_{i=0}^{m} \omega_i(\Delta(y_d - \bar{y})_{-i} + \Delta l_{-i}). \tag{A39}$$

The difference terms on the right-hand side are the consequence of firms' inability to supply what is demanded in the short run. The faster demand (relative to $\bar{y}$) or the labour force is increasing, the higher is unemployment at any given *level* of demand, essentially because capital fails to adjust instantly and *ex post* substitution is ruled out. These effects are, of course, absent in the models discussed in the main body of Chapter 8 (see e.g. equation (26)).

Turning next to pricing behaviour, here we may simply suppose that we have an additional effect which reflects the fact that prices will tend to rise as more firms are constrained. This is clearly somewhat arbitrary. However, if we were to aggregate over the optimal prices for constrained and unconstrained firms, we would certainly obtain something along these lines, since prices would be higher for constrained firms and the aggregate price level would rise as more firms became constrained. Taking an equation of the form given in Chapter 8's equation (27) as our baseline, this suggests that we add a term in $(n_d - n_p)$ which captures the extent of demand relative to capacity, and hence measures the overall level of capital constraint. This suggests a price equation of the form

$$p - w = \beta_0 + \beta_1(y_d - \bar{y}) + \beta_{11}(n_d - n_p) - \beta_{21}(p - p^e)$$
$$- \beta_{22}(w - w^e) - x_n, \tag{A40}$$

where x_n captures trend productivity. From (A33), (A36), we have

$$n_d - n_p = (1 - A(L))(y_d - \bar{y} + l),$$

and hence (A40) can be rewritten as

$$p - w = \beta_0 + \beta_1(y_d - \bar{y}) + \beta_{11}\Sigma a_i[\Delta(y_d - \bar{y})_{-i} + \Delta l_{-i}]$$
$$- \beta_{21}(p - p^e) - \beta_{22}(w - w^e) - x_n. \tag{A41}$$

The additional terms in the price equation are demand hysteresis and population growth effects, which arise from the fact that the slow adjustment of capital to demand puts upward pressure on prices in the short run.

Finally, we consider the implications for wage-setting, and here the key difference arises from the possibility of labour force growth. If we look at equation (16) in Chapter 8, we see that the possibility of 'insider' effects in wage-setting introduces a term in lagged employment. If this is taken into account, then in the aggregate wage equation we have an additional positive term in labour force growth, which reflects the fact that new unemployed entrants to the labour force add to the number of outsiders among the unemployed and thus reduce the wage-reducing effect of any given level of unemployment.

To summarize, allowing for the possibility of short-run capital constraints and labour force growth means that, first, supply tends to lag behind demand; second, there is additional hysteresis in the price equation; and third, an increase in population growth may add to inflationary pressure on the price front if absolute demand keeps pace with the rising labour force (i.e. if $y_d - \bar{y}$ remains unchanged) and on the wage front if there are insider hysteresis effects in wage-setting. In particular, therefore, we see that the possibility of capital shortage does not change the overall structure of the model, but it could well substantially increase the degree of persistence in the economy arising from hysteresis in price-setting.

Notes

1. We are grateful to Charles Bean for this analysis.
2. The magnitudes are of the order $r = 0.05$; $\varphi, \theta_1 = 1$. Hence if θ_{11} is (rather than zero) anything larger than 0.025, δ is higher. θ_{11} typically is of the order of unity.
3. Note that, differentiating (A9), we have

$$\frac{\partial \log u^*}{\partial \log \beta} \left(1 - \frac{1}{(1 - e_1/e)} \frac{\partial (e_1/e)}{\partial \log u^*} \right) = 1,$$

and since

$$\frac{\partial e_1/e}{\partial u} < 0,$$

this immediately reveals that $\partial \log u^* / \partial \log \beta > 0$.

4. *Sources*: total engagements: Jackman *et al.* (1989: 387); engagements of people already in work: *General Household Survey*, 1985: Table 6.31; engagements of people from outside the labour force (the number reaching the age of 16 (*Employment Gazette*, July 1985: 261) less school-leavers included in the inflow to unemployment (*Employment Gazette*)): this calculation assumes that the number of 16-year-olds who did not enter the labour force equals the number of people over 16 who entered employment from outside the labour force; engagements of unemployed people (total engagements less the other two categories of engagements): this approximately equals the outflow for unemployment, some of which may enter employment after a period out of labour force; unemployed job-seekers: *Labour Force Survey*, 1985; employed job-seekers: Burgess (1989b: 27); vacancies: *Employment Gazette* on the assumption that registered vacancies are one-third of all vacancies, as shown by Surveys in 1977, 1982, and 1988 (*Employment Gazette*, November 1978: 1284–8), Hedges (1983), and Smith (1988).
5. This reflects the elasticity of substitution in production or the elasticity of substitution in consumption between different products.
6. Under monopolistic competition with demand elasticity η, and P normalized to unity,

$$W_i = \frac{\partial Y}{\partial N_i} \kappa = \varphi \alpha_i \left(\frac{N_i}{Y} \right)^{-1/\sigma} \kappa.$$

By Euler's theorem,

$$1 = \sum_i \frac{\partial Y}{\partial N_i} \frac{N_i}{Y} = \kappa^{-1+\sigma} \varphi^\sigma \sum_i W_i \left(\frac{W_i}{\alpha_i} \right)^{-\sigma}.$$

7. If $\Sigma \alpha_i = 1$ and α_i, x_i, y_i, and z_i are independent, then $\Sigma \alpha_i x_i y_i z_i = \bar{x} \bar{y} \bar{z}$. Hence if α_i, β_i, and u_i are independent, equation (5) of Ch. 6 implies

$$u^{-\gamma_1(\sigma - 1)} = \frac{1}{A} \Sigma \alpha_i \alpha_i^{\sigma - 1} \Sigma \alpha_i \beta_i^{-(\sigma - 1)} \Sigma \alpha_i \left(\frac{u_i}{u} \right)^{\gamma_1(\sigma - 1)}$$

or

$$u^{-\gamma_1(\sigma - 1)} = \Sigma \alpha_i \left(\frac{u_i}{u} \right)^{\gamma_1(\sigma - 1)} \times \text{const.}$$

Going on, if we assume $(\alpha_i - L_i/L)$ independent of u_i/u, we obtain

$$u^{-\gamma_1(\sigma-1)} = \Sigma \frac{L_i}{L} \left(\frac{u_i}{u}\right)^{\gamma_1(\sigma-1)} \times \text{const.}$$

Taking logarithms of this equation, and making use of the expansion,

$$\Sigma \frac{L_i}{L} \left(\frac{u_i}{u}\right)^{\gamma_1(\sigma-1)} \simeq 1 + \frac{1}{2}[\gamma_1(\sigma-1)-1]\gamma_1(\sigma-1)\text{var}\frac{u_i}{u},$$

we have

$$-\gamma_1(\sigma-1)\log u \simeq -\frac{1}{2}[1-\gamma_1(\sigma-1)]\gamma_1(\sigma-1)\text{var}\frac{u_i}{u} + \text{const.}$$

Discussion Questions

Chapter 1

1. Consider the following statements:
   (i) Changes in inflation depend on the level of unemployment.
   (ii) Inflation depends on financial factors and in particular on the growth of national spending in nominal terms.
   What truth, if any, is there in either view?
2. 'Unemployment is high because real wages are too high.' Discuss.
3. Consider a wholly unionized economy. It is argued that, 'if each wage is set by a voluntary contract between a firm and its union, the outcome must be efficient.' Is this logically correct? Might it be preferable to have a single national bargain between the employers' federation and the union federation? If so, why?
4. 'If there are no unions, there is no reason why there should be involuntary unemployment.' Discuss.
5. 'Productivity growth can have no effect on unemployment.' Discuss. Is the same true of changes in taxes and the terms of trade?
6. 'If unemployed people look harder for work, this cannot affect the number of jobs.' Discuss.
7. 'There are always some jobs available, so unemployment cannot be due to job rationing.' Discuss.
8. How would you explain the different unemployment rates in different countries?
9. What policies, if any, would reduce unemployment? Even if they would, would they be desirable in some overall sense?

Chapter 2

1. In an individual union bargain, what factors affect the resulting level of wages and why? How, in a world of decentralized unions, do these same factors affect the level of unemployment?
2. (i) Why might the number of insiders have an effect on wage pressure?
   (ii) Suppose that natural wastage could accommodate all variations in employment: would the number of insiders still have an effect? If not, would this mean that insider power was irrelevant as an explanation of unemployment?
3. What is meant by real wage resistance? What mechanisms could explain it? Is it likely to persist in the very long run?
4. What could explain why so few bargains specify the number of workers to be employed?

556

5. Does featherbedding create jobs?
6. Why is it difficult to reduce wage inflation without increasing unemployment, even when agents know all about the state of the economy?

Chapter 3

1. 'Efficiency wages require that effort cannot be observed.' Discuss.
2. Does the pattern of inter-industry wages in the USA provide convincing evidence in favour of the efficiency wage theory?
3. Does efficiency wage theory help to explain why a productivity downturn might increase unemployment?

Chapter 4

1. Why are wages higher in large firms?
2. Is the evidence on union mark-ups consistent with the view that unions contribute significantly to European unemployment?
3. What light do micro-level wage equations throw on the sources of hysteresis in unemployment behaviour (in particular, on the role of insider and outsider forces)?
4. 'Wages must rise faster in higher-productivity growth industries.' Discuss.

Chapter 5

1. 'Most workers would take any job paying more than unemployment benefits.' Discuss.
2. What does the evidence suggest about the effect of unemployment benefit on the duration of unemployment?
3. Does long-term unemployment reduce a person's chances of getting a job?
4. Why in so many countries has the Beveridge curve (u/v curve) shifted out?

Chapter 6

1. Why are there persistent differences in unemployment rates between age-groups, between skill groups, and between regions?
2. 'Unemployment has risen because the unemployed have become less well matched to the available jobs.' Develop a mismatch index to investigate this proposition. What light does it shed on the proposition?
3. 'Regional mismatch is a problem because wages respond to local unemployment, with the response increasing at lower levels of unemployment.'
   (i) Why would this create a problem?
   (ii) Would things be better if regional wages depended on employment in a leading sector, or in the whole economy?
   (iii) What is the evidence on actual regional wage behaviour?
4. 'It is absurd to subsidize the employment of unskilled workers since (although their unemployment rate is high) such a subsidy will simply discourage training.' Discuss.

5. 'Changes in the structure of demand cannot help explain either short-run fluctuations in unemployment or, indeed, the long-run level of unemployment.' Discuss.

Chapter 7

1. 'Roberts *et al.* have found in time series data for 20 two-digit US industries over 1958–83 that the adjustment of nominal prices to nominal labour and materials costs takes place extremely rapidly. This provides strong evidence that the menu cost approach is on the wrong track, and that the key issues concern the stickiness of both wages and materials costs, not final goods prices.'* Discuss.
2. It is often asserted that prices are more responsive to changes in costs than to changes in demand. Suggest why this might be the case.
3. It is still commonplace in models of pricing behaviour to have prices responding in a partial fashion to changes in wages; i.e., $p_{it} = \beta p_{it-1} + (1 - \beta)w_{it} +$ other terms. Explain why this is unlikely to be a stable (fixed-parameter) model of firm behaviour.
4. Assess the interaction between costs of changing prices and costs of changing output.
5. How does product-market structure influence industry pricing behaviour?

Chapter 8

1. According to most empirical macroeconomic models, a demand expansion is followed by a rise in output and employment and a rise in the real wage. Yet it is often asserted that unemployment is high because real wages are too high. Explain.
2. 'Imperfect competition may have important implications for relative prices, but there is no reason why it should exert any effect on unemployment.' Discuss.
3. 'In the mid-1980s, the US economy staged a significant demand-led expansion without any noticeable impact on inflation. The NAIRU model is, therefore, not applicable to the United States.' Discuss.
4. 'Natural rate models assume market-clearing and, consequently, are useless for understanding highly unionized economies.' Discuss.
5. Suppose the long-term unemployed exert no influence on wage determination: what are the implications for the behaviour of the economy in general, and of unemployment in particular?
6. Suppose a country in which inflation is endemic fixes, permanently, its exchange rate with a country whose inflation rate is permanently low. Will this change the equilibrium unemployment rate in the former country?

---

* R. J. Gordon (1990), 'What is New-Keynesian Economics?' *Journal of Economic Literature*, 28: 1115–71, referring to J. M. Roberts, D. J. Stockton, and C. S. Struckmeyer (1989), 'An Evaluation of the Sources of Aggregate Price Rigidity', Washington DC: Board of Governors of the Federal Reserve System, Division of Research and Statistics, Economic Activity Section, Working Paper no. 99.

Chapter 9

1. Bruno and Sachs found that countries with a high degree of nominal wage rigidity performed well after the first oil shock in the mid-1970s. Yet Friedman had previously recommended indexation as a policy for enhancing the stability of an economy. Was Friedman wrong?
2. It is often asserted that unions create unemployment. Yet some of the most highly unionized countries have very low unemployment rates. Explain.
3. How important are labour market institutions in explaining cross-country differences in unemployment?
4. 'A characteristic of low-unemployment countries is the fact that they have a relatively low duration of unemployment benefit availability.' Discuss.
5. The responsiveness of wages to labour market conditions is a key parameter that varies dramatically across countries. Is this parameter an immutable consequence of the social structure of each country, or can it be changed in a systematic way by policy action?
6. Unemployment exhibits a great deal of persistence. Why?

Chapter 10

1. 'Money spent on active labour market policy mainly reallocates the existing number of jobs. The costs outweigh the benefits.' Discuss.
2. 'In a unionized economy, a move towards more centralized bargaining would only increase union power and thus increase unemployment.' Discuss.
3. 'A tax-based incomes policy would introduce more distortions than those it was designed to offset.' Discuss.
4. Would marginal employment subsidies reduce unemployment?
5. 'By making pay more flexible, profit-sharing would reduce average unemployment.' Discuss.
6. Why is unemployment in Japan so low and so stable?
7. 'Reductions in hours would not affect unemployment but would reduce output. The same is true of early retirement schemes.' Discuss.
8. 'Employment protection protects employment.' Discuss.
9. Any other suggestions.

List of Symbols

—   not available

Variables

P	price of value added
P_c	price of consumption
P_m	price of imports
W	wage rate including employers' taxes
Z	'push factors' affecting wages
L	labour force
N	employment
K	capital
Y	output
F	number of firms
t_1	tax rate on wages, paid by employer
t_2	tax rate on wages, paid by worker
t_3	indirect tax rate
E	effort (also written $e(\cdot)$)
Π	profit
Ω	maximand in Nash bargain
A	alternative expected income (if disemployed)
U	unemployed (number)
u	unemployment rate, U/L
u^*	NAIRU
u_s^*	short-run NAIRU
c	search effectiveness *or* log competitiveness
V	vacancies (number)
v	vacancy rate, V/N
H	hirings, number per period
h	hiring rate, H/U
S	separations, number per period
s	separation rate, S/N

Where other uses occur, this is made clear. For the first ten variables, the logarithm is denoted by the use of lower-case letters.

Main Symbols

Key recurring parameters come from the following relations

Prices: $\quad\quad p - w = \beta_0 - \beta_1 u - \beta_{11}\Delta u - \beta_2 \Delta^2 p.$

Wages: $\quad\quad w - p = \gamma_0 - \gamma_1 u - \gamma_{11}\Delta u - \gamma_2 \Delta^2 p + z.$

Production: $\quad y = \alpha n + (1 - \alpha)k.$

Demand: $\quad\quad y_{di} = -\eta(p_i - p) + y_d - f. \quad\quad (\kappa = 1 - 1/\eta)$

Estimation

Throughout the book, we omit equation diagnostics. In general, all regression equations have serially uncorrelated errors and stable parameters. Figures in brackets are normally t-statistics.

Statistics

All figures are individually rounded and therefore do not necessarily add up.

Germany

Throughout the book 'Germany' refers to 'West Germany'.

List of Tables

(Multi-country, except where shown)

Chapter 1

1 Percentage of labour force unemployed, 1979 and 1990   6
2 Percentage of labour force unemployed, by age and sex   7
3 Unemployment by skill: flow and duration, Britain, USA   45
4 Variance of relative unemployment rates, Britain, 1974–1985   48
5 Unemployment experience of different countries, and treatment of the
  unemployed   51
6 Collective bargaining in different countries   52
7 Real and nominal wage rigidity   58

Chapter 2

1 Percentage of workers unionized, 1970–1986   88
2 Percentage of workers covered by collective agreements, Britain   89
3 Workers covered by collective bargaining analysed by level of bargain,
  Britain   89
4 Layoffs and employment adjustment, USA, UK   93
5 Percentage of union establishments for which each item is generally
  bargained over, Britain   94
6 Percentage of workers involved in strikes per year, 1950s–1980s   98
7 Schematic analysis of unemployment   138

Chapter 3

1 The stylized facts: which efficiency wage theories do they support? 166

Chapter 4

1 Correlations of log manufacturing wages among countries   180
2 Factors influencing pay settlements, Britain, 1979–1984   182
3 Factors influencing the level of pay in the most recent settlement, Britain 187
4 Estimates of λ, the weight attached to firm-specific factors in wage
  determination   188

List of Tables

Chapter 5

1	Unemployment rates and flows	222
2	Unemployment duration and flows, USA	223
3	Unemployment durations and flows, Britain	224
4	Exit rates per month from unemployment, by duration, USA, Australia	228
5	Search intensity by duration of unemployment, Britain	236
6	Search intensity, USA	237
7	Methods of job search by unemployed men, Britain	238
8	Methods of job search, USA	239
9	How jobs were found, Britain, USA	240
10	Number of job applications, males, Britain, USA	241
11	Percentage of employees currently engaged in on-the-job search, by status 12 months earlier, Britain	245
12	Savings of the unemployed, Britain	247
13	Jobs taken by the unemployed, Britain, USA	248
14	Overall exit rate and exit rate of new entrants, Britain, 1969–1988	264
15	The unemployed stock, by reasons for unemployment, USA, 1974–1989	270
16	The unemployed by reasons for unemployment, USA	271
17	The unemployed by main reason for unemployment, Britain	271
A1	Number of job applications, Britain	277
A2	Search intensity in Britain, by week of interview	278
A3	Search intensity in Britain, by week of interview	279
A4	Job acceptances and refusal by the unemployed, Britain	280
A5	How the unemployed found jobs, Britain	280
A6	Savings and debts of the unemployed who returned to work within nine months of start of unemployment, Britain	281
A7	Jobs taken by the unemployed, Britain	281

Chapter 6

1	Unemployment by occupation	287
2	Dispersion of occupational unemployment rates, 1973–1987	290
3	Unemployment by occupation, inflow and duration, Britain, USA	291
4	Unemployment rate by highest educational level	292
5	Unemployment by region, Britain, USA	293
6	Dispersion of regional unemployment rates, 1974–1987	294
7	Regional turbulence indices, 1960s to 1980s	297
8	Unemployment by industry, age, race and sex, Britain, USA	299
9	Dispersion of industrial unemployment rates, 1973–1987	300
10	Industrial turbulence indices, 1950s to 1980s	301
11	Non-manual wages relative to manual wages, 1970–1986	317
12	Unemployment rates and registered vacancy rates by occupation, region and industry, Britain	327
13	U/V mismatch, Britain, 1963–1988	328
14	Differences between occupations in vacancy flows and stocks, Britain	330

List of Tables

Chapter 9

1	Unemployment in OECD countries, 1960–1990	398
2	Model coefficients	406
3	Change in unemployment (1969–1973) to (1980–1985), and key explanatory factors	409
4	Change in unemployment (1983–1985) to (1989–1990), and key explanatory factors	411
5	Persistence	413
6	Unemployment effect in the price equation	415
7	Unemployment effects in the wage equation	418
8	Hysteresis in the price equation	420
9	Hysteresis in the wage equation	422
10	Nominal inertia in the price equation	426
11	Nominal inertia in the wage equation	429
12	OECD unemployment equations, 1956–1988	433
13	Adjusted R^2 implied by model in Table 12	435
14	Estimates of the natural rate and the unemployment–inflation tradeoff	436
15	Equation estimates for the UK	441
16	Estimates of equilibrium unemployment in the UK	445
17	A breakdown of changes in equilibrium unemployment in the UK	446
18	Alternative estimates of equilibrium unemployment in the UK	446
19	Percentages of UK manufacturing firms reporting labour shortages	447
A1	Marginal revenue product condition, 1956–1985	450
A2	Wage equations, 1956–1985	452
A3	Country tables	454

Chapter 10

1	Public expenditure on labour market programmes as a percentage of GDP	478

Annex 1.3

A1	Unemployment benefit, duration and replacement ratios (single person)	514
A2	Unemployment benefits, coverage and generosity	516

Annex 1.6

A3	Unemployment rates in each OECD country, 1955–1990	526
A4	Inflation rates in each OECD country, 1955–1990	530

Annex 2.2

A5	Bargaining payoffs, with the same discount rates	534
A6	Bargaining payoffs, with different discount rates	535

Annex 5.1

A7	Unemployment stocks and flows	544

List of Figures

Chapter 1

1	Unemployment, EC, USA, EFTA, and Japan, 1960–1990	2
2	Unemployment since the 19th century, UK, USA	3
3	Industrial conflicts in the OECD, 1954–1989	4
4	Real commodity prices, 1950–1990	5
5	Unemployment–inflation trade-off in the OECD, 1967–1990	9
6	Unemployment and inflation	14
7	Aggregate supply and demand	17
8	With normal-cost pricing, real wage pressure raises unemployment but not real wages	19
9	Centralized versus decentralized bargaining	30
10	The terms of trade and the NAIRU	33
11	Vacancy rates and unemployment rates, various countries, 1960s to 1980s	36
12	Proportion of unemployed people leaving unemployment within next 3 months, by existing duration of unemployment	40
13	Maximum duration of benefit (1985) and percentage of unemployed out of work for over a year (1983–1988)	41
14	Unemployment in a two-sector model	43

Chapter 2

1	Bargaining over wages and employment	113
2	Bargaining over wages and employment and over wages only, the general equilibrium comparison under Cobb–Douglas	117
3	The firm's choice of effort	123
4	A world with good and bad jobs	126
5	Centralized versus decentralized bargaining	131

Chapter 3

1	The efficient wage	152
2	Determination of effort when it is observable	159
3	Industrial wages in the USA and Japan, 1982	166
4	Wage differentials over time, USA, 1923 and 1984	167
5	Effect of a fall in productivity upon unemployment	170

List of Figures

Chapter 5

1	The pool of unemployment	221
2	Unemployment inflow and outflow, Britain, 1968–1988	221
3	Inflow rates and duration of unemployment, USA, Britain, 1962–1989	225
4	The experience of unemployment, Britain	
	(a) Proportion of a cohort still unemployed	226
	(b) Proportion of cohort leaving in each quarter	226
	(c) Outflow rates per quarter at each duration	226
5	The reservation wage when B or λ fall discretely at duration T	251
6	Male unemployment, male monthly outflows, and vacancies, Britain, 1967–1989	257
7	Percentage of unemployed people with given duration leaving unemployment within next quarter, males, Britain, 1968–1988	260
8	Percentage of unemployed people with given duration leaving unemployment within the next quarter, males, Britain, 1979–1987	261
9	Quarterly outflow rate, effectiveness index ($\hat{c}$) and V/U ratio, Britain, 1969–1988	262
10	Unemployment, monthly hires and vacancies, USA, 1968–1981	267

Chapter 6

1	Fluctuations in mismatch and turbulence, Britain, 1963–1990	296
2	Industrial turbulence index, UK, USA, 1900–1990	298
3	Employment and wages in a single sector, labour force given	302
4	Employment and wages in a single sector, labour force endogenous, zero-migration equilibrium	304
5	Introductory presentation of mismatch and the NAIRU	307
6	The unemployment frontier (wages responding to own sector unemployment)	309
7	The unemployment frontier (wages responding to leading sector unemployment)	313
8	Skilled and unskilled labour markets, L_1, L_2 fixed (W_1 flexible, $\bar{W}_2$ rigid)	318
9	Skilled and unskilled labour markets, L_1, L_2 variable (W_1, W_2 flexible)	320
10	The U/V curve of a group	325

Chapter 7

1	An optimal Ss pricing rule	355

Chapter 8

1	The unemployment–inflation tradeoff	380
2	The unemployment–inflation tradeoff with concave unemployment effects	381
3	The short-run NAIRU	383
4	A rise in wage pressure	383

List of Figures

5   Unemployment and competitiveness   391
6   The NAIRU consistent with trade balance   392
7   The consequences of an oil shock   393

Chapter 9

1   OECD unemployment rate, 1955–1990   399
2   OECD inflation, 1955–1990   399
3   Industrial conflicts in the OECD, 1954–1989   400
4   Real commodity prices, 1950–1990   400
5   UK unemployment, 1955–1990   444

Chapter 10

1   Outflow rate from unemployment, and expected remaining duration, by
    uncompleted duration, Britain   474
2   The wage system and profit-sharing system   494
3   Decrease in working hours and increase in unemployment, selected coun-
    tries, 1975–1988   505
4   Increase in early retirement and increase in unemployment, selected
    countries, 1975–1989   507
5   Economic activity with work-sharing and early retirement   508

Annex 1.2

A1 Relation of commodity prices and the OECD NAIRU   513

Annex 2.4

A2 Effects of government response function   539

References

Abowd, J. M. and Ashenfelter, O. (1981), 'Anticipated Unemployment, Temporary Layoffs, and Compensating Wage Differentials', in S. Rosen (ed.), *Studies in Labor Markets*, Chicago: University of Chicago Press.

Abowd, J. M. and Zellner, A. (1985), 'Estimating Gross Labor-Force Flows', *Journal of Business and Economic Statistics*, 3(3): 254–83.

Abowd, J. M. and Card, D. M. (1989), 'On the covariance structure of earnings and hours changes', *Econometrica*, 57: 411–46.

Abraham, K. G. and Katz, L. F. (1986), 'Cyclical Unemployment: Sectoral Shifts or Aggregate Disturbances?', *Journal of Political Economy*, 94(3), pt. 1: 507–22.

Addison, J. J. and Hirsch, B. T. (1989), 'Union Effects on Productivity, Profits and Growth: Has the Long Run Arrived?', *Journal of Labor Economics*, 7(1): 72–105.

Aizcorbe, A. M. (1990), 'Procyclical Labor Productivity, Increasing Returns to Labor, and Labor Hoarding in US Auto Assembly Plant Employment', Bureau of Labor Statistics, mimeo.

Akerlof, G. A. (1982), 'Labor Contracts as Partial Gift Exchange', *Quarterly Journal of Economics*, 97(4): 543–69.

Akerlof, G. A. (1984), 'Gift Exchange and Efficiency-Wage Theory: Four Views', *American Economic Review*, 74(2): 79–83.

Akerlof, G. A. and Katz, L. F. (1989), 'Workers' Trust Funds and the Logic of Wage Profiles', *Quarterly Journal of Economics*, 104(3): 525–36.

Akerlof, G. A. and Main, B. G. M. (1980), 'Unemployment Spells and Unemployment Experience', *American Economic Review*, 70(5): 885–93.

Akerlof, G. A. and Miyazaki, H. (1980), 'The Implicit Contract Theory of Unemployment meets the Wage Bill Argument', *Review of Economic Studies*, 47(2): 321–38.

Akerlof, G. A. and Yellen, J. L. (1985), 'A Near-Rational Model of the Business Cycle, with Wage and Price Inertia', *Quarterly Journal of Economics*, 100, suppl.: 823–38.

Akerlof, G. A. and Yellen, J. L. (1990), 'The Fair Wage-Effort Hypothesis and Unemployment', *Quarterly Journal of Economics*, 105(2): 255–83.

Akerlof, G. A., Rose, A. and Yellen, J. (1988*a*), 'Discussion of Ball *et al.* 1988', *Brookings Papers on Economic Activity*, 1: 66–75.

Akerlof, G. A., Rose, A. and Yellen, J. L. (1988*b*), 'Job Switching and Job Satisfaction in the US Labor Market', *Brookings Papers on Economic Activity*, 2: 495–582.

Alberro, J. (1981), 'The Lucas Hypothesis on the Phillips Curve: Further International Evidence', *Journal of Monetary Economics*, 7(2): 239–50.

Alchian, A. A. (1969), 'Information Costs, Pricing, and Resource Utilization', *Western Economic Journal*, 7(2): 109–28. Reprinted in E. S. Phelps *et al.*, *Microeconomic Foundations of Employment and Inflation Theory*, New York: W. W. Norton, 1970.

References

Alogoskoufis, G. S. (1983), 'The Labour Market in an Equilibrium Business Cycle Model', *Journal of Monetary Economics*, 11(1): 117–28.

Alogoskoufis, G. and Manning, A. (1988), 'On the Persistence of Unemployment', *Economic Policy*, no. 7: 427–69.

Alogoskoufis, G. S. and Manning, A. (1991), 'Tests of Alternative Wage Employment Bargaining Models with Application to the UK Aggregate Labour Market', *European Economic Review*, 35: 23–37.

Altonji, J. G. (1982), 'The Intertemporal Substitution Model of Labour Market Fluctuations: An Empirical Analysis', *Review of Economic Studies*, 49(5): 783–824.

Altonji, J. G. (1986), 'Intertemporal Substitution in Labor Supply: Evidence from Micro Data', *Journal of Political Economy*, 94(3): S176–S215.

Altonji, J. G. and Ashenfelter, O. (1980), 'Wage Movements and the Labour Market Equilibrium Hypothesis', *Economica*, 47: 217–45.

Andrews, M. and Harrison, A. (1989), 'Testing for Efficient Contracts in Unionised Labour Markets', University of Manchester Department of Economics, Discussion Paper no. ES 21.

Archibald, G. C. (1969), 'The Phillips Curve and the Distribution of Unemployment', *American Economic Review*, 59(2): 124–34.

Argyle, M. (1987), *The Psychology of Happiness*, London: Methuen.

Ashenfelter, O. (1984), 'Macroeconomic Analyses and Microeconomic Analyses of Labor Supply', in K. Brunner and A. Meltzer (eds.), *Essays on Macroeconomic Implications of Financial and Labor Markets and Political Processes, Carnegie–Rochester Conference Series on Public Policy*, xxii, pp. 117–55.

Ashenfelter, O. C. and Layard, R. (1983), 'Incomes Policy and Wage Differences', *Economica*, 50: 127–43.

Ashenfelter, O. and Layard, R. (eds.) (1986), *Handbook of Labor Economics*, Amsterdam: North-Holland.

Atkinson, A. B. (1970), 'On the Measurement of Inequality', *Journal of Economic Theory*, 2(3): 244–63.

Atkinson, A. B. (1988), 'The Economics of Unemployment Insurance', Presidential Address to the Econometric Society, mimeo.

Atkinson, A. B. and Micklewright, J. (1991), 'Unemployment Compensation and Labor Market Transitions: A Critical Review', *Journal of Economic Literature* 29(4).

Atkinson, A. B., Gomulka, J., Micklewright, J. and Rau, N. (1984), 'Unemployment Benefit Duration and Incentives in Britain: How Robust Is the Evidence?', *Journal of Public Economics*, 23(1/2): 3–26.

Azariades, C. (1975), 'Implicit Contracts and Underemployment Equilibria', *Journal of Political Economy*, 83(6): 1183–1202.

Baily, M. N. (1974), 'Wages and Employment under Uncertain Demand', *Review of Economic Studies*, 41(1): 37–50.

Baily, M. N. (1978), 'Some Aspects of Optimal Unemployment Insurance', *Journal of Public Economics*, 10(3): 379–402.

Baily, M. N. and Tobin, J. (1977), 'Macroeconomic Effects of Selective Public Employment and Wage Subsidies', *Brookings Papers on Economic Activity*, 2: 511–41.

References

Ball, L. and Cecchetti, S. G. (1988), 'Imperfect Information and Staggered Price Setting', *American Economic Review*, 78(5): 999–1018.

Ball, L. and Romer, D. (1989), 'The Equilibrium and Optimal Timing of Price Changes', *Review of Economic Studies*, 56(2): 179–98.

Ball, L. and Romer, D. (1990), 'Real Rigidities and the Non-Neutrality of Money', *Review of Economic Studies*, 57(2): 183–203.

Ball, L., Mankiw, N. G. and Romer, D. (1988), 'The New Keynesian Economics and the Output–Inflation Trade-Off', *Brookings Papers on Economic Activity*, 1: 1–65.

Banks, M. and Jackson, P. (1982), 'Unemployment and the Rise of Minor Psychiatric Disorders in Young People', *Psychological Medicine*, 12: 789–98.

Bannock, G. and Daly, M. (1990), 'Size Distribution of UK Firms', Department of Employment, *Employment Gazette*, 98(5): 255–8.

Barro, R. J. (1976), 'Rational Expectations and the Role of Monetary Policy', *Journal of Monetary Economics*, 2(1): 1–32.

Barro, R. J. and Grossman, H. I. (1971), 'A General Disequilibrium Model of Income and Employment', *American Economic Review*, 61(1): 82–93.

Barron, J. M., Bishop, J. and Dunkelberg, W. C. (1985), 'Employer Search: The Interviewing and Hiring of New Employees', *Review of Economics and Statistics*, 67(1): 43–52.

Bean, C. R. and Turnbull, P. J. (1988), 'Employment in the British Coal Industry: A Test of the Labour Demand Model', *Economic Journal*, 98: 1092–1104.

Bean, C. R., Layard, R. and Nickell, S. J. (1986), 'The Rise in Unemployment: A Multi-Country Study', *Economica*, 53: S1–S22. Reprinted in Bean *et al.* (1987).

Bean, C. R., Layard, R. and Nickell, S. J. (eds.) (1987), *The Rise in Unemployment*, Oxford: Basil Blackwell.

Becker, G. S. and Murphy, K. M. (1988), 'A Theory of Rational Addiction', *Journal of Political Economy*, 96(4): 675–700.

Beenstock, M. *et al.* (1985), 'A Medium Term Macroeconomic Model of the UK Economy, 1950–82', City University Business School, London, mimeo.

Bell, L. A. and Freeman, R. B. (1985), 'Does a Flexible Industry Wage Structure Increase Employment? The US Experience', NBER Working Paper no. 1604, Cambridge, Mass.

Benabou, R. (1989), 'Optimal Price Dynamics and Speculation with a Storable Good', *Econometrica*, 57(1): 41–80.

Bentolila, S. and Bertola, G. (1990), 'Firing Costs and Labour Demand: How Bad is Eurosclerosis?' *Review of Economic Studies*, 57(3): 381–402.

Bentolila, S. and Blanchard, O. J. (1990), 'Spanish Unemployment', *Economic Policy*, no. 10: 234–81.

Berg, G. J. van den (1990a), 'Nonstationarity in Job Search Theory', *Review of Economic Studies*, 57(2): 255–77.

Berg, G. J. van den (1990b), 'Search Behaviour, Transitions to Non-Participation and the Duration of Unemployment', *Economic Journal*, 100: 842–65.

Berndt, E. R., Friedlaender, A. F. and Chiang, J. S.-E. W. (1990), 'Interdependent Pricing and Markup Behavior: An Empirical Analysis of GM, Ford and Chrysler', NBER Working Paper no. 3396, Cambridge, Mass.

Beveridge, W. H. (1942), *Social Insurance and Allied Services*, Cmd. 6404, London: HMSO.

References

Bhaskar, V. (1988), 'Pricing and Employment in the UK: An Open Economy Model', Nuffield College, Oxford mimeo.

Bils, M. (1987), 'The Cyclical Behavior of Marginal Cost and Price', *American Economic Review*, 77(5): 838–55.

Bils, M. (1989), 'Pricing in a Customer Market', *Quarterly Journal of Economics*, 104(4): 699–718.

Binmore, K., Rubinstein, A. and Wolinsky, A. (1986), 'The Nash Bargaining Solution in Economic Modeling', *RAND Journal of Economics*, 17(2): 176–88.

Bishop, R. L. (1964), 'A Zeuthen–Hicks Theory of Bargaining', *Econometrica*, 32(3): 410–17.

Björklund, A. (1990), 'Evaluations of Swedish Labor Market Policy', Swedish Institute for Social Research, University of Stockholm. *Finnish Economic Papers*, 3(1).

Blackaby, F., Bladen-Hovell, R. C. and Symons, E. (1990), 'Unemployment Duration and Wage Determination in the UK: Evidence from the FES 1980–86', University of Manchester Department of Economics, Discussion Paper no. 68.

Blanchard, O. J. (1983), 'Price Asynchronization and Price Level Inertia', in R. Dornbusch and M. H. Simonsen (eds.), *Inflation, Debt, and Indexation*, Cambridge, Mass.: MIT Press.

Blanchard, O. J. (1986), 'The Wage Price Spiral', *Quarterly Journal of Economics*, 101(3): 543–65.

Blanchard, O. J. (1987), 'Aggregate and Individual Price Adjustment', *Brookings Papers on Economic Activity*, 1: 57–109.

Blanchard, O. J. and Diamond, P. A. (1989a), 'The Beveridge Curve', *Brookings Papers on Economic Activity*, 1: 1–60.

Blanchard, O. J. and Diamond, P. A. (1989b), 'Beveridge and Phillips Curves', MIT, mimeo.

Blanchard, O. J. and Diamond, P. A. (1990), 'Ranking, Unemployment Duration, and Wages', MIT Department of Economics, Working Paper no. 546.

Blanchard, O. J. and Fischer, S. (1989), *Lectures on Macroeconomics*, Cambridge, Mass.: MIT Press.

Blanchard, O. J. and Kiyotaki, N. (1987), 'Monopolistic Competition and the Effects of Aggregate Demand', *American Economic Review*, 77(4): 647–66.

Blanchard, O. J. and Summers, L. H. (1986), 'Hysteresis and the European Unemployment Problem', in S. Fischer (ed.), *NBER Macroeconomics Annual 1986*, Cambridge, Mass.: MIT Press.

Blanchard, O. J. and Summers, L. H. (1987), 'Fiscal Increasing Returns, Hysteresis, Real Wages, and Unemployment', *European Economic Review*, 31(3): 543–60.

Blanchflower, D. (1989), 'Fear, Unemployment and Pay Flexibility', London School of Economics Centre for Labour Economics, Discussion Paper no. 344.

Blanchflower, D. and Freeman, R. (1990), 'Going Different Ways: Unionism in the US and other Advanced OECD Countries', London School of Economics Centre for Economic Performance, Discussion Paper no. 5.

Blanchflower, D. G and Oswald, A. J. (1988a), 'Internal and External Influences upon Pay Settlements', *British Journal of Industrial Relations*, 26(3): 363–70.

Blanchflower, D. G. and Oswald, A. J. (1988b), 'The Economic Effects of Britain's Trade Unions', *Economic Report*, Employment Institute, September.

571

References

Blanchflower, D. G. and Oswald, A. J. (1990), 'The Wage Curve', *Scandinavian Journal of Economics*, 92(2): 215–35.

Blanchflower, D., Millward, N. and Oswald, A. (1989), 'Unionisation and Employment Behaviour', London School of Economics Centre for Labour Economics, Discussion Paper no. 339.

Blanchflower, D. G., Oswald, A. J. and Garrett, M. D. (1990), 'Insider Power in Wage Determination', *Economica*, 57: 143–70.

Blau, D. M. and Robins, P. K. (1990), 'Job Search Outcomes for the Employed and Unemployed', *Journal of Political Economy*, 98(3): 637–55.

Blaug, M., Layard, R. and Woodhall, M. (1969), *The Causes of Graduate Unemployment in India*, London: Allen Lane, Penguin Books.

Blinder, A. S. (1979), *Economic Policy and the Great Stagflation*, New York: Academic Press.

Blum, A. A. (ed.) (1981), *International Handbook of Industrial Relations*, London: Aldwych Press.

Boskin, M. J. and Sheshinski, E. (1978), 'Optimal Redistributive Taxation when Individual Welfare Depends upon Relative Income', *Quarterly Journal of Economics*, 92(4): 589–601.

Bover, O., Muellbauer, J. and Murphy, A. (1989), 'Housing, Wages and UK Labour Markets', *Oxford Bulletin of Economics and Statistics*, 51(2): 97–136.

Brack, J. (1987), 'Price Adjustment within a Framework of Symmetric Oligopoly: An Analysis of Pricing in 380 US Manufacturing Industries, 1958–71', *International Journal of Industrial Organization*, 5(3): 289–302.

Brickman, P. and Campbell, D. T. (1971), 'Hedonic Relativism and Planning the Good Society', in M. H. Appley (ed.), *Adaptation Level Theory*, New York: Academic Press.

Brown, C. (1980), 'Equalizing Differences in the Labor Market', *Quarterly Journal of Economics*, 94(1): 113–34.

Brown, C. and Medoff, J. (1989), 'The Employer Size–Wage Effect', *Journal of Political Economy*, 97(5): 1027–59.

Brown, J. N. and Ashenfelter, O. (1986), 'Testing the Efficiency of Employment Contracts', *Journal of Political Economy*, 94(3): S40–S87.

Brown, W. and Wadhwani, S. (1990), 'The Economic Effects of Industrial Relations Legislation since 1979', *National Institute Economic Review*, no. 131: 57–70.

Brunello, G. (1988), 'Bonuses, Profits and Employment in Japan: A Reappraisal Based on Panel Data', Osaka University, mimeo.

Brunello, G. (1990), 'Hysteresis and "The Japanese Unemployment Problem": A Preliminary Investigation', *Oxford Economic Papers*, 42(3): 483–500.

Brunello, G. and Wadhwani, S. (1989), 'The Determinants of Wage Flexibility in Japan: Some Lessons from a Comparison with the UK Using Micro Data', London School of Economics Centre for Labour Economics, Discussion Paper no. 362.

Brunello, G. and Wadhwani, S. (1991), 'The Effects of Profit-Sharing on Wages, Employment and Productivity in Japan', London School of Economics Centre for Economic Performance, mimeo.

Bruno, M. and Sachs, J. D. (1985), *Economics of Worldwide Stagflation*, Oxford: Basil Blackwell.

Budd, A., Levine, P. and Smith, P. (1988), 'Unemployment, Vacancies and the Long-Term Unemployed', *Economic Journal*, 98: 1071–91.

Bulow, J. I., Geanakoplos, J. D. and Klemperer, P. D. (1985), 'Multimarket Oligopoly: Strategic Substitutes and Complements', *Journal of Political Economy*, 93(3): 488–511.

Burchell, B. (1990), 'The Effects of Labour Market Position, Job Insecurity and Unemployment on Psychological Health', ESRC Social Change and Economic Life Initiative Working Paper no. 19.

Burda, M. (1988), 'Monopolistic Competition, Costs of Adjustment, and the Behaviour of European Manufacturing Employment', INSEAD, Fontainebleu, mimeo.

Burdett, K. (1979), 'Search, Leisure and Individual Labor Supply', in S. A. Lippman and J. J. McCall (eds.), *Studies in the Economics of Search*, Amsterdam: North-Holland.

Burgess, S. M. (1989*a*), 'Unemployment Flows and Turnover in Britain: Some Facts', University of Bristol Department of Economics, Discussion Paper no. 88/22.

Burgess, S. M. (1989*b*), 'A Model of Competition between Unemployed and Employed Job Searchers: An Application to the Unemployment Outflow Rate in Britain', University of Bristol, mimeo.

Burtless, G. (1987), 'Jobless Pay and High European Unemployment' in R. Z. Lawrence and C. Schultze (eds.), *Barriers to European Growth: A Transatlantic View*, Washington DC: Brookings Institution.

Butters, G. R. (1977), 'Equilibrium Distributions of Sales and Advertising Prices', *Review of Economic Studies*, 44(3): 465–91.

Cahill, J. and Ingram, P. (1987), *Changes in Working Practices in British Manufacturing Industry in the 1980s: A Study of Employee Concessions Made during Wage Negotiations*, London: CBI.

Calmfors, L. (ed.) (1990), *Wage Formation and Macroeconomic Policy in the Nordic Countries*, Oxford: Oxford University Press.

Calmfors, L. and Driffill, J. (1988), 'Centralisation of Wage Bargaining and Macroeconomic Performance', *Economic Policy*, no. 6: 13–61.

Calmfors, L. and Horn, H. (1985), 'Classical Unemployment, Accommodation Policies and the Adjustment of Real Wages', *Scandinavian Journal of Economics*, 87(2): 234–61.

Calmfors, L. and Nymoen, R. (1990), 'Real Wage Adjustment and Employment Policies in the Nordic Countries', *Economic Policy*, no. 11: 397–448.

Cannan, E. (1946), *Wealth: A Brief Explanation of the Causes of Economic Welfare*, 3rd edn., London: Staples Press.

Caplin, A. S. (1985), 'The Variability of Aggregate Demand with (S,s) Inventory Policies', *Econometrica*, 53(6): 1395–1409.

Caplin, A. S. and Spulber, D. F. (1987), 'Menu Costs and the Neutrality of Money', *Quarterly Journal of Economics*, 102(4): 703–25.

Card, D. (1986), 'Efficient Contracts with Costly Adjustment: Short-run Employment Determination for Airline Mechanics', *American Economic Review*, 76(5): 1045–71.

Card, D. (1988), 'Unexpected Inflation, Real Wages and Employment Determination in Union Contracts', Princeton University Industrial Relations Section, Working Paper no. 232.

References

Card, D. (1989), 'Deregulation and Labor Earnings in the Airline Industry', Princeton University Industrial Relations Section, Working Paper no. 247.

Carlin, W. and Soskice, D. (1985), 'Real Wages, Unemployment, International Competitiveness and Inflation: A Framework for Analysing Closed and Open Economies', University College, Oxford, mimeo.

Carlin, W. and Soskice, D. (1990), *Macroeconomics and the Wage Bargain: A Modern Approach to Employment, Inflation, and the Exchange Rate*, Oxford: Oxford University Press.

Carlton, D. W. (1985), 'Delivery Lags as a Determinant of Demand', University of Chicago Graduate School of Business, mimeo.

Carlton, D. W. (1986), 'The Rigidity of Prices', *American Economic Review*, 76(4): 637–58.

Carlton, D. W. (1989), 'The Theory and the Facts of How Markets Clear: Is Industrial Organization Valuable for Understanding Macroeconomics?', in R. Schmalensee and R. D. Willig (eds.), *Handbook of Industrial Organization*, i, Amsterdam: North-Holland.

Carruth, A. A. and Oswald, A. J. (1988), 'Testing for Multiple Natural Rates of Unemployment in the British Economy: A Preliminary Investigation', in R. Cross (ed.), *Unemployment, Hysteresis and the Natural Rate Hypothesis*, Oxford: Basil Blackwell.

Carruth, A. A. and Oswald, A. J. (1989), *Pay Determination and Industrial Prosperity*, Oxford: Clarendon Press.

Carruth, A. A., Oswald, A. J. and Findlay, L. (1986), 'A Test of a Model of Trade Union Behaviour: The Coal and Steel Industries in Britain', *Oxford Bulletin of Economics and Statistics*, 48(1): 1–18.

Chatterjee, S. and Cooper, R. (1989), 'Multiplicity of Equilibria and Fluctuations in Dynamic Imperfectly Competitive Economies', *American Economic Review*, 79(2): 353–7.

Chowdhury, G. and Nickell, S. J. (1985), 'Hourly Earnings in the United States: Another Look at Unionization, Schooling, Sickness, and Unemployment Using PSID Data', *Journal of Labor Economics*, 3(1): 38–69.

Christofides, L. N. and Oswald, A. J. (1989), 'Real Wage Determination in Collective Bargaining Agreements', NBER Working Paper no. 3188, Cambridge, Mass.

Clark, A. and Oswald, A. J. (1989), 'An Empirical Study of Union Preferences', London School of Economics Centre for Labour Economics, Discussion Paper no. 352.

Clark, K. B. and Summers, L. H. (1979), 'Labor Market Dynamics and Unemployment: A Reconsideration', *Brookings Papers on Economic Activity*, 1: 13–60.

Coe, D. and Gagliardi, F. (1985), 'Nominal Wage Determination in Ten OECD Countries', OECD Economics and Statistics Department, Working Paper no. 19.

Cooper, H. (1989), *The West Midlands Labour Market*, Department of Employment, London: HMSO.

Coutts, K., Godley, W. and Nordhaus, W. (1978), *Industrial Pricing in the United Kingdom*, Cambridge: Cambridge University Press.

Cox, D. R. (1972), 'Regression Models and Life-Tables', *Journal of the Royal Statistical Society*, B, 34(2): 187–202.

574

References

Cristini, A. (1989), *OECD Activity and Commodity Prices*, Lincoln College, Oxford, unpublished D.Phil. thesis.

Crouch, C. (1985), 'Conditions for Trade Union Restraint', in L. N. Lindberg, and C. S. Maier (eds.), *The Politics of Inflation and Economic Stagflation*, Washington, DC: Brookings Institution.

Daniel, W. W. (1981), *The Unemployed Flow: Stage 1*, interim report, London: Policy Studies Institute.

Daniel, W. W. (1983), 'How the Unemployed Fare after They Find New Jobs', *Policy Studies*, 3(4): 246–60.

Daniel, W. W. (1990), *The Unemployed Flow*, London: Policy Studies Institute.

Daniel, W. W. and Millward, N. (1983), *Workplace Industrial Relations in Britain: The DE/PSI/SSRC Survey*, London: Heinemann Educational Books.

Daniel, W. W. and Stilgoe, E. (1978), *The Impact of Employment Protection Laws*, London: Policy Studies Institute.

Davis, S. J. and Haltiwanger, J. (1990), 'Gross Job Creation and Destruction: Microeconomic Evidence and Macroeconomic Implications', University of Chicago Graduate School of Business and University of Maryland Department of Economics, mimeo.

Department of Employment (DE) (1988), *Employment for the 1990s*, London: HMSO.

Diamond, P. A. (1981), 'Mobility Costs, Frictional Unemployment, and Efficiency', *Journal of Political Economy*, 89(4): 798–812.

Dickens, W. T. and Katz, L. F. (1987), 'Inter-Industry Wage Differences and Industry Characteristics', in K. Lang and J. S. Leonard (eds.), *Unemployment and the Structure of Labor Markets*, New York: Basil Blackwell.

Dickens, W. T. and Lang, K. (1988), 'The Re-emergence of Segmented Labour Market Theory', *American Economic Review*, 78(2): 129–34.

Dickens, W. T., Katz, L. F., Lang, K. and Summers, L. H. (1989), 'Employee Crime and the Monitoring Puzzle', *Journal of Labor Economics*, 7(3): 331–47.

Disney, R., Belman, L., Carruth, A., Franz, W., Jackman, R., Layard, R., Lehmann, H. and Philpott, J. (1991), *Helping the Unemployed: Active Labour Market Policies in Britain and Germany*, London: Anglo-German Foundation.

Dixit, A. K. and Stiglitz, J. E. (1977), 'Monopolistic Competition and Optimum Product Diversity', *American Economic Review*, 67(3): 297–308.

Dixon, H. (1988), 'Unions, Oligopoly and the Natural Range of Unemployment', *Economic Journal*, 98: 1127–47.

Dolado, J. J., Malo de Molina, J. L. and Zabalza, A. (1986), 'Spanish Industrial Unemployment: Some Explanatory Factors', *Economica*, 53: S313–S334. Reprinted in Bean *et al.* (1987).

Domowitz, I., Hubbard, R. G. and Petersen, B. C. (1986*a*), 'Business Cycles and the Relationship between Concentration and Price–Cost Margins', *RAND Journal of Economics*, 17(1): 1–17.

Domowitz, I., Hubbard, R. G. and Petersen, B. C. (1986*b*), 'The Intertemporal Stability of the Concentrations–Margins Relationship', *Journal of Industrial Economics*, 35(1): 13–34.

Donovan Report (1968), Royal Commission on Trade Unions and Employers' Associations 1965–8, *Report*, London: HMSO.

References

Dore, R., Bounine-Cabalé, J. and Tapiola, K. (1989), *Japan at Work: Markets, Management and Flexibility*, Paris: OECD.

Dornbusch, R. and Fischer, S. (1987), *Macroeconomics*, 4th edn., New York: McGraw-Hill.

Drèze, J. H. and Bean, C. R. (1991), *Europe's Unemployment Problem*, Cambridge, Mass.: MIT Press.

Duncan, G. J. and Holmlund, B. (1983), 'Was Adam Smith Right After All? Another Test of the Theory of Compensating Wage Differentials', *Journal of Labor Economics*, 1(4): 366–79.

Edwin, P.-A. and Holmlund, B. (1990), 'Unemployment, Vacancies, and Labour Market Programmes: Swedish Evidence', Uppsala University, Department of Economics Working Paper no. 1990: 3.

Ehrenberg, R. G. and Jakubson, G. H. (1988), *Advance Notice Provisions in Plant Closing Legislation*, Ithaca, NY: Cornell University/W. E. Upjohn Institute for Employment Research.

Ehrenberg, R. G. and Schwartz, J. L. (1986), 'Public-Sector Labor Markets', in O. Ashenfelter and R. Layard (eds.), *Handbook of Labor Economics*, ii, Amsterdam: North-Holland.

Eichenbaum, M. and Singleton, K. J. (1986), 'Do Equilibrium Real Business Cycle Theories Explain Postwar US Business Cycles?', in S. Fischer (ed.), *NBER Macroeconomics Annual 1986*, Cambridge, Mass.: MIT Press.

Elvander, N. (1989), 'Incomes Policies in the Nordic Countries', mimeo.

Emerson, M. (1988a), 'Regulation or Deregulation of the Labour Market: Policy Regimes for the Recruitment and Dismissal of Employees in the Industrialised Countries', *European Economic Review*, 32(4): 775–817.

Emerson, M. (1988b), *What Model for Europe?*, Cambridge, Mass.: MIT Press.

Encaoua, D. and Geroski, P. (1986), 'Price Dynamics and Competition in Five OECD Countries', *OECD Economic Studies*, 6: 47–74.

Erens, R. and Hedges, B. (1990), *Surveys of Incomes In and Out of Work*, London: SCPR.

Estrin, S. and Wilson, N. (1986), 'The Micro-Economic Effects of Profit-Sharing: The British Experience', London School of Economics Centre for Labour Economics, Discussion Paper no. 247.

Estrin, S., Grout, P. and Wadhwani, S. (1987), 'Profit Sharing and Employee Share Ownership', *Economic Policy*, no. 4: 13–52.

Farber, H. S. (1986), 'The Analysis of Union Behavior', in O. Ashenfelter and R. Layard (eds.), *Handbook of Labor Economics*, ii, Amsterdam: North-Holland.

Fehr, E. (1990), 'Cooperation, Harassment, and Involuntary Unemployment: Comment', *American Economic Review*, 80(3): 624–30.

Feinstein, C. H. (1972), *National Income, Expenditure and Output of the United Kingdom 1855–1965*, Cambridge: Cambridge University Press.

Feldstein, M. S. (1975), 'The Importance of Temporary Layoffs,' *Brookings Papers on Economic Activity*, 3: 725–44.

Feldstein, M. S. (1976), 'Temporary Layoffs in the Theory of Unemployment', *Journal of Political Economy*, 84(5): 937–57.

References

Feldstein, M. S. and Ellwood, D. T. (1982), 'Teenage Unemployment: What Is the Problem?', in R. B. Freeman and D. A. Wise (eds.), *The Youth Labor Market Problem*, Chicago: University of Chicago Press.

Fethke, G. and Policano, A. (1984), 'Wage Contingencies, the Pattern of Negotiation and Aggregate Implications of Alternative Contract Structures', *Journal of Monetary Economics*, 14(2): 151–70.

Fischer, S. (1977), 'Long-Term Contracts, Rational Expectations, and the Optimal Money Supply Rule', *Journal of Political Economy*, 85(1): 191–205.

Flaig, G. and Steiner, V. (1990), 'Markup Differentials, Cost Flexibility, and Capacity Utilization in West German Manufacturing', Augsburg University, Volkswirtschaftliche Diskussionreiche, no. 40.

Flanagan, R. J. (1987), 'Efficiency and Equality in Swedish Labor Markets', in B. P. Bosworth and A. M. Rivlin (eds.), *The Swedish Economy*, Washington, DC: Brookings Institution.

Flanagan, R. J., Soskice, D. W. and Ulman, L. (1983), *Unionism, Economic Stabilization, and Incomes Policy: European Experience*, Washington DC: Brookings Institution.

Flemming, J. S. (1978), 'Aspects of Optimal Unemployment Insurance: Search, Leisure, Saving and Capital Market Imperfections', *Journal of Public Economics*, 10(3): 403–25.

Flinn, C. J. and Heckman, J. J. (1982), 'New Methods for Analyzing Structural Models of Labor Force Dynamics', *Journal of Econometrics*, 18(1): 115–68.

Flinn, C. J. and Heckman, J. J. (1983), 'Are Unemployment and Out of the Labor Force Behaviorally Distinct States?', *Journal of Labor Economics*, 1(1): 28–42.

Frank, R. H. (1985), *Choosing the Right Pond: Human Behavior and the Quest for Status*, New York: Oxford University Press.

Franz, W. (1987), 'Hysteresis, Persistence, and the NAIRU: An Empirical Analysis for the Federal Republic of Germany', in R. Layard and L. Calmfors (eds.), *The Fight against Unemployment*, Cambridge, Mass.: MIT Press.

Freeman, R. B. (1986), 'Demand for Education,' in O. Ashenfelter and R. Layard (eds.), *Handbook of Labor Economics*, i, Amsterdam: North-Holland.

Freeman, R. B. (1988*a*), 'Evaluating the European View the United States Has No Unemployment Problem', *American Economic Review*, 78(2): 294–9.

Freeman, R. B. (1988*b*), 'Labour Market Institutions and Economic Performance', *Economic Policy*, no. 6: 64–78.

Freeman, R. B. and Bloom, D. (1986), 'The Youth Labour Market Problem: Age or Generational Crowding', in *OECD Employment Outlook 1986*, Paris: OECD.

Freeman, R. B. and Katz, L. (1987), 'Industrial Wage and Employment Determination in an Open Economy', Harvard University, mimeo.

Freeman, R. B. and Medoff, J. L. (1984), *What Do Unions Do?*, New York: Basic Books.

Freeman, R. and Pelletier, J. (1990), 'The Impact of Industrial Relations Legislation on British Union Density', *British Journal of Industrial Relations*, 28(2): 141–64.

Freeman, R. B. and Weitzman, M. L. (1987), 'Bonuses and Employment in Japan', *Journal of the Japanese and International Economies*, 1(2): 168–94.

Friedman, M. (1968), 'The Role of Monetary Policy', *American Economic Review*, 58: 1–17.

References

Froyen, R. T. and Waud, R. N. (1980), 'Further International Evidence on Output–Inflation Tradeoffs', *American Economic Review*, 70(3): 409–21.

Garman, A. and Redmond, G. (1990), 'The Changing Characteristics of Unemployed Men', Department of Employment, *Employment Gazette*, 98(9): 470–4.

Gennard, J. (1981), 'The Effects of Strike Activity on Households', *British Journal of Industrial Relations*, 19(3): 327–44.

Gennard, J. (1982), 'The Financial Costs and Returns of Strikes', *British Journal of Industrial Relations*, 20(2): 247–56.

Gibbons, R. and Katz, L. F. (1989), 'Does Unmeasured Ability Explain Inter-Industry Wage Differences?', MIT Department of Economics, Working Paper no. 543.

Gordon, R. J. (1982), 'Why US Wage and Employment Behaviour Differs from that in Britain and Japan', *Economic Journal*, 92: 13–44.

Grandmont, J. M. (1989), 'Keynesian Issues and Economic Theory', CEPREMAP Discussion Paper no. 8907, Paris.

Gray, J. A. (1976), 'Wage Indexation: A Macroeconomic Approach', *Journal of Monetary Economics*, 2(2): 221–35.

Greenwood, M. (1985), 'Human Migration: Theory, Models and Empirical Studies', *Journal of Regional Sciences*, 25: 521–44.

Gregory, M., Lobban, P. and Thomson, A. (1985), 'Wage Settlements in Manufacturing, 1979–84: Evidence from the CBI Pay Databank', *British Journal of Industrial Relations*, 23(3): 339–57.

Gregory, M., Lobban, P. and Thomson, A. (1987), 'Pay Settlements in Manufacturing Industry, 1979–84: A Micro-Data Study of the Impact of Product and Labour Market Pressures', *Oxford Bulletin of Economics and Statistics*, 49(1): 129–50.

Gregory, R. G. (1986), 'Wages Policy and Unemployment in Australia', *Economica*, 53: S53–S74. Reprinted in Bean *et al.* (1987).

Griffin, G. (1990), *The Bristol Labour Market*, Bristol: Employment Service.

Grossman, S. J. and Hart, O. D. (1981), 'Implicit Contracts, Moral Hazard, and Unemployment', *American Economic Review*, 71(2): 301–7.

Grossman, S. J., Hart, O. D. and Maskin, E. S. (1983), 'Unemployment with Observable Aggregate Shocks', *Journal of Political Economy*, 91(6): 907–28.

Grubb, D. (1984), 'The OECD Data Set', London School of Economics Centre for Labour Economics, Working Paper no. 615.

Grubb, D. (1986), 'Topics in the OECD Phillips Curve', *Economic Journal*, 96: 55–79.

Grubb, D., Jackman, R. and Layard, R. (1982), 'Causes of the Current Stagflation', *Review of Economic Studies*, 49(5): 707–30.

Grubb, D., Jackman, R. and Layard, R. (1983), 'Wage Rigidity and Unemployment in OECD Countries', *European Economic Review*, 21(1/2): 11–39.

Hall, R. E. (1970), 'Why Is the Unemployment Rate So High at Full Employment?', *Brookings Papers on Economic Activity*, 3: 369–402.

Hall, R. E. (1972), 'Turnover in the Labor Force', *Brookings Papers on Economic Activity*, 3: 709–56.

Hall, R. E. (1977), 'An Aspect of the Economic Role of Unemployment', in G. C. Harcourt (ed.), *The Microeconomic Foundations of Macroeconomics*, London: Macmillan.

References

Hall, R. E. (1982), 'The Importance of Lifetime Jobs in the US Economy', *American Economic Review*, 72(4): 716–24.

Hall, R. E. (1988*a*), 'Substitution over Time in Work and Consumption', NBER Working Paper no. 2789, Cambridge, Mass.

Hall, R. E. (1988*b*), 'The Relation between Price and Marginal Cost in US Industry', *Journal of Political Economy*, 96(5): 921–47.

Ham, J. C. (1986), 'Testing whether Unemployment Represents Intertemporal Labour Supply Behaviour', *Review of Economic Studies*, 53(4): 559–78.

Ham, J. C. and Rea, S. A., Jr (1987), 'Unemployment Insurance and Male Unemployment Duration in Canada', *Journal of Labor Economics*, 5(3): 325–53.

Hamermesh, D. S. (1977), 'Economic Aspects of Job Satisfaction', in O. C. Ashenfelter and W. E. Oates (eds.), *Essays in Labor Market Analysis*, New York: John Wiley.

Hamermesh, D. S. (1986), 'The Demand for Labor in the Long Run', in O. Ashenfelter and R. Layard (eds.), *Handbook of Labor Economics*, i, Amsterdam: North-Holland.

Hansen, G. D. (1985), 'Indivisible Labor and the Business Cycle', *Journal of Monetary Economics*, 16(3): 309–27.

Harris, J. R. and Todaro, M. P. (1970), 'Migration Unemployment and Development: A Two-Sector Analysis', *American Economic Review*, 60(1): 126–42.

Hart, O. D. (1982), 'A Model of Imperfect Competition with Keynesian Features', *Quarterly Journal of Economics*, 97(1): 109–38.

Hart, O. D. (1983), 'Optimal Labour Contracts under Asymmetric Information: An Introduction', *Review of Economic Studies*, 50(1): 3–35.

Hashimoto, M. (1981), 'Firm-Specific Human Capital as a Shared Investment', *American Economic Review*, 71(3): 475–82.

Hay, D. A. and Liu, S. (1990), 'Incentives for Workers in Chinese Manufacturing Enterprises, 1980–87', Oxford University Institute of Economics and Statistics, mimeo.

Heady, P. and Smyth, M. (1989), *Living Standards during Unemployment*, i, London: HMSO.

Heckman, J. J. (1979), 'Sample Selection Bias as a Specification Error', *Econometrica*, 47(1): 153–61.

Heckman, J. J. and Singer, B. (1984), 'A Method for Minimizing the Impact of Distributional Assumptions in Econometric Models for Duration Data', *Econometrica*, 52(2): 271–320.

Hedges, B. (1983), *Surveys of Employers' Recruitment Practices 1982*, London: SCPR.

Hendricks, W. E. and Kahn, L. M. (1983), 'Cost-of-Living Clauses in Union Contracts: Determinants and Effects', *Industrial and Labor Relations Review*, 36(3): 447–60.

Hoel, M. and Moene, K. O. (1988), 'Profit Sharing, Unions and Investments', *Scandinavian Journal of Economics*, 90(4): 493–525.

Holen, A. (1977), 'Effects of Unemployment Insurance Entitlement on Duration and Job Search Outcome', *Industrial and Labor Relations Review*, 30(4): 445–50.

Holmlund, B. and Zetterberg, J. (1989), 'Insider Effects in Wage Determination: Evidence from Five Countries', Uppsala University, mimeo.

Holt, C. C. and David, M. H. (1966), 'The Concept of Job Vacancies in a Dynamic Theory of the Labor Market', in *The Measurement and Interpretation of Job Vacancies*, New York: NBER and Columbia University Press.

References

Holzer, H. J. and Montgomery, E. B. (1990), 'Asymmetries and Rigidities in Wage Adjustments by Firms', NBER Working Paper no. 3274, Cambridge, Mass.

Holzer, H. J., Katz, L. F. and Krueger, A. B. (1988), 'Job Queues and Wages: New Evidence on the Minimum Wage and Inter-Industry Wage Structure', NBER Working Paper no. 2561, Cambridge, Mass.

ILO (International Labour Office) (1987), *World Labor Report*, iii, *Incomes from Work: Between Equity and Efficiency*, Geneva: ILO.

IMS (Institute of Manpower Studies) (1981), 'Redundancy Provisions Survey', *Manpower Commentary*, no. 13.

Jackman, R. (1984), 'Money Wage Rigidity in an Economy with Rational Trade Unions', in G. Hutchinson and J. Treble (eds.), *Recent Advances in Labour Economics*, London: Croom Helm.

Jackman, R. (1985), 'Counterinflationary Policy in a Unionised Economy with Nonsynchronised Wage Setting', *Scandinavian Journal of Economics*, 87(2): 357–78.

Jackman, R. (1988), 'Profit-Sharing in a Unionised Economy with Imperfect Competition', *International Journal of Industrial Organisation*, 6(1): 47–57.

Jackman, R. (1990), 'Wage Formation in the Nordic Countries Viewed from an International Perspective', in L. Calmfors (ed.), *Wage Formation and Macroeconomic Policy in the Nordic Countries*, Oxford: Oxford University Press.

Jackman, R. and Layard, R. (1982), 'An Inflation Tax', *Fiscal Studies*, 3(1): 47–59.

Jackman, R. and Layard, R. (1986), 'Is TIP Administratively Feasible?', in D. C. Colander (ed.), *Incentive-Based Incomes Policy*, Cambridge, Mass.: Ballinger.

Jackman, R. and Layard, R. (1987), 'Innovative Supply-Side Policies to Reduce Unemployment', in P. Minford (ed.), *Monetarism and Macroeconomics*, London: Institute of Economic Affairs.

Jackman, R. and Layard, R. (1990), 'The Real Effects of Tax-Based Incomes Policy', *Scandinavian Journal of Economics*, 92(2): 309–24.

Jackman, R. and Layard, R. (1991), 'Does Long-term Unemployment Reduce a Person's Chance of a Job? A Time-Series Test', *Economica*, 58 (229): 93–106.

Jackman, R. and Roper, S. (1987), 'Structural Unemployment', *Oxford Bulletin of Economics and Statistics*, 49(1): 9–36.

Jackman, R., Layard, R. and Pissarides, C. A. (1984), 'On Vacancies', London School of Economics Centre for Labour Economics, Discussion Paper no. 165. Revised.

Jackman, R. *et al.* (1986), 'A Job Guarantee for Long-Term Unemployed', London: Employment Institute. Reprinted in Shields (1989).

Jackman, R., Layard, R. and Savouri, S. (1987), 'Labour Market Mismatch and the Equilibrium Level of Unemployment', London School of Economics Centre for Labour Economics, Working Paper no. 1009.

Jackman, R., Layard, R. and Pissarides, C. A. (1989), 'On Vacancies', *Oxford Bulletin of Economics and Statistics*, 51(4): 377–94.

Jackman, R., Pissarides, C. and Savouri, S. (1990), 'Labour Market Policies and Unemployment in the OECD', *Economic Policy*, no. 11: 449–90.

Jackman, R., Layard, R. and Savouri, S. (1991), 'Mismatch: A Framework for Thought', in F. Padoa Schioppa (ed.), *Mismatch and Labour Mobility*, CEPR. Cambridge: Cambridge University Press.

References

Jangenäs, B. (1985), *The Swedish Approach to Labor Market Policy*, Stockholm: Swedish Institute.

John, Andrew (1991), 'Employment Fluctuations in a Share Economy', *Oxford Economic Papers*, 43 (1)

Johnson, G. E. (1990), 'Work Rules, Featherbedding and Pareto-Optimal Union–Management Bargaining', *Journal of Labor Economics*, 8(1), pt. 2: S237–S259.

Johnson, G. E. and Blakemore, A. (1979), 'The Potential Impact of Employment Policy on the Unemployment Rate Consistent with Nonaccelerating Inflation', *American Economic Review*, 69(2): 119–23.

Johnson, G. E. and Layard, R. (1986), 'The Natural Rate of Unemployment: Explanation and Policy', in O. Ashenfelter and R. Layard (eds.), *Handbook of Labor Economics*, ii, Amsterdam: North-Holland.

Jones, S. R. G. (1989), 'Job Search Methods, Intensity and Effects', *Oxford Bulletin of Economics and Statistics*, 51(3): 277–96.

Jullien, B. and Picard, P. (1989), 'Efficiency Wage and Macroeconomic Policy: A Dynamic Model with Rational Expectations', CEPREMAP, Paris, mimeo.

Kahn, C. and Mookherjee, D. (1988). 'A Competitive Efficiency Wage Model with Keynesian Features', *Quarterly Journal of Economics*, 103(4): 609–45.

Kahneman, D., Knetsch, J. L. and Thaler, R. (1986), 'Fairness as a Constraint on Profit Seeking: Entitlements in the Market', *American Economic Review*, 76(4): 728–41.

Katz, L. F. (1986*a*), 'Layoffs, Recall and the Duration of Unemployment', NBER Working Paper no. 1825, Cambridge, Mass.

Katz, L. F. (1986*b*), 'Efficiency Wage Theories: A Partial Evaluation', in S. Fischer (ed.), *NBER Macroeconomics Annual 1986*, Cambridge, Mass.: MIT Press.

Katz, L. F. and Meyer, B. D. (1988), 'The Impact of the Potential Duration of Unemployment Benefits on the Duration of Unemployment', Harvard University and NBER/Northwestern University and NBER, mimeo.

Kaufman, R. T. (1984), 'On Wage Stickiness in Britain's Competitive Sector', *British Journal of Industrial Relations*, 22(1): 101–12.

Kennan, J. (1986), 'The Economics of Strikes', in O. Ashenfelter and R. Layard (eds.), *Handbook of Labor Economics*, ii, Amsterdam: North-Holland.

Kennan, J. and Wilson, R. (1989), 'Strategic Bargaining Models and Interpretation of Strike Data', *Journal of Applied Econometrics*, 4, suppl.: S87–S130.

Knoester, A. and Windt, N. van der (1987), 'Real Wages and Taxation in Ten OECD Countries', *Oxford Bulletin of Economics and Statistics*, 49(1): 151–69.

Krueger, A. and Summers, L. (1986), 'Efficiency Wages and the Wage Structure', NBER Working Paper no. 1952, Cambridge, Mass.

Krueger, A. B. and Summers, L. H. (1987), 'Reflections on the Inter-Industry Wage Structure', in K. Lang and J. S. Leonard (eds.), *Unemployment and the Structure of Labor Markets*, New York: Basil Blackwell.

Krueger, A. B. and Summers, L. H. (1988), 'Efficiency Wages and the Inter-Industry Wage Structure', *Econometrica*, 56(2): 259–93.

Kruse, P. (1987), 'Profit-Sharing and Employment Variability: Microeconomic Evidence', Harvard University, mimeo.

Kuratani, M. (1973), 'A Theory of Teaching, Earnings, and Employment: An Application to Japan', Columbia University, unpublished Ph.D dissertation.

References

Kydland, F. E. and Prescott, E. C. (1982), 'Time to Build and Aggregate Fluctuations', *Econometrica*, 50(6): 1345–70.

Lambert, J.-P. (1988), *Disequilibrium Macroeconomic Models: Theory and Estimation of Rationing Models using Business Survey Data*, Cambridge: Cambridge University Press.

Lancaster, T. (1979), 'Econometric Methods for the Duration of Unemployment', *Econometrica*, 47(4): 939–56.

Lancaster, T. and Chesher, A. (1983), 'An Econometric Analysis of Reservation Wages', *Econometrica*, 51(6): 1661–76.

Lancaster, T. and Nickell, S. (1980), 'The Analysis of Re-Employment Probabilities for the Unemployed', *Journal of the Royal Statistical Society*, A, 143, pt. 2: 141–52.

Lang, K. and Leonard, J. S. (eds.) (1987), *Unemployment and the Structure of Labor Markets*, New York: Basil Blackwell.

Layard, R. (1979), 'The Costs and Benefits of Selective Employment Policies: The British Case', *British Journal of Industrial Relations*, 17(2): 187–204.

Layard, R. (1980), 'Human Satisfactions and Public Policy', *Economic Journal*, 90(360): 737–50.

Layard, R. (1982), 'Youth Unemployment in Britain and the United States Compared', in R. B. Freeman and D. A. Wise (eds.), *The Youth Labor Market Problem: Its Nature, Causes and Consequences*, Chicago: Chicago University Press.

Layard, R. (1986), *How to Beat Unemployment*, Oxford: Oxford University Press.

Layard, R. (1990a), 'Wage Bargaining and Incomes Policy: Possible Lessons for Eastern Europe', in S. Commander (ed.), *Managing Inflation in Socialist Economies in Transition*, World Bank, forthcoming.

Layard, R. (1990b), 'Understanding Unemployment', London School of Economics Centre for Economic Performance, Discussion Paper no. 4.

Layard, R. and Mincer, J. (eds.) (1985), 'Trends in Women's Work, Education, and Family Building', *Journal of Labour Economics*, 3(1), pt. 2: S(i)–S397.

Layard, R. and Nickell, S. J. (1980), 'The Case for Subsidizing Extra Jobs', *Economic Journal*, 90: 51–73.

Layard, R. and Nickell, S. J. (1985), 'The Causes of British Unemployment', *National Institute Economic Review*, no. 111: 62–85.

Layard, R. and Nickell, S. J. (1986a), 'An Incomes Policy to Help the Unemployed', London: Employment Institute. Reprinted in Shields (1989).

Layard, R. and Nickell, S. J. (1986b), 'Unemployment in Britain', *Economica*, 53: S121–S169. Reprinted in Bean *et al.* (1987).

Layard, R. and Nickell, S. J. (1987), 'The Labour Market', in R. Dornbusch and R. Layard (eds.), *The Performance of the British Economy*, Oxford: Oxford University Press.

Layard, R. and Nickell, S. J. (1989), 'The Thatcher Miracle?', London School of Economics Centre for Labour Economics, Discussion Paper no. 343. Shorter version in *American Economic Review*, 79(2): 215–19.

Layard, R. and Nickell, S. J. (1990), 'Is Unemployment Lower if Unions Bargain over Employment?', *Quarterly Journal of Economics*, 105(3): 773–87.

Layard, R., Jackman, R. and Philpott, J. (1991), *A Stop to Unemployment*, mimeo.

Layard, R., Metcalf, D. and Nickell, S. J. (1978a), 'The Effect of Collective Bargaining on Relative and Absolute Wages', *British Journal of Industrial Relations*, 16(3): 287–302.

Layard, R., Piachaud, D. and Stewart, M. (1978*b*), *The Causes of Poverty*, Royal Commission on the Distribution of Income and Wealth, Background Paper no. 5, London: HMSO.

Lazear, E. P. (1986), 'Retirement from the Labor Force,' in O. Ashenfelter and R. Layard (eds.), *Handbook of Labor Economics*, i, Amsterdam: North-Holland.

Lazear, E. P. (1989), 'Pay Equality and Industrial Policies', *Journal of Political Economy*, 97(3): 561–80.

Lazear, E. P. (1990), 'Job Security Provisions and Employment', *Quarterly Journal of Economics*, 105(3): 699–726.

Lebergott, S. (1957), 'Annual Estimates of Unemployment in the United States, 1900–1950', in *The Measurement and Behavior of Unemployment: A Conference of the Universities–National Bureau Committee for Economic Research*, Princeton: Princeton University Press.

Leibenstein, H. (1963), *Economic Backwardness and Economic Growth*, New York: John Wiley.

Leonard, J. S. (1987), 'In the Wrong Place at the Wrong Time: The Extent of Frictional and Structural Unemployment', in K. Lang and J. S. Leonard (eds.), *Unemployment and The Structure of Labor Markets*, New York: Basil Blackwell.

Leontief, W. (1946), 'The Pure Theory of the Guaranteed Annual Wage Contract', *Journal of Political Economy*, 54(1): 76–9.

Lester, R. (1952), 'A Range Theory of Wage Differentials', *Industrial and Labor Relations Review*, 5(4): 483–500.

Lester, R. (1967), 'Pay Differentials by Size of Establishment', *Industrial Relations*, 7(1): 57–67.

Levine, D. (1988), 'Tests of Efficiency Wage and Rent-Sharing Theories: The Pay–Productivity Relation', University of California at Berkeley, mimeo.

Lewis, H. G. (1963), *Unionism and Relative Wages in the United States*, Chicago: University of Chicago Press.

Lewis, H. G. (1986), 'Union Relative Wage Effects', in O. Ashenfelter and R. Layard (eds.), *Handbook of Labor Economics*, ii, Amsterdam: North-Holland.

Lilien, D. M. (1982), 'Sectoral Shifts and Cyclical Unemployment', *Journal of Political Economy*, 90(4): 777–93.

Lilien, D. M. and Hall, R. E. (1986), 'Cyclical Fluctuations in the Labor Market', in O. Ashenfelter and R. Layard (eds.), *Handbook of Labor Economics*, ii, Amsterdam: North-Holland.

Lindbeck, A. and Snower, D. J. (1988), 'Cooperation, Harassment, and Involuntary Unemployment: An Insider–Outsider Approach', *American Economic Review*, 78(1): 167–88.

Lindbeck, A. and Snower, D. J. (1989), *The Insider–Outsider Theory of Employment and Unemployment*, Cambridge, Mass.: MIT Press.

Lipman, M. and McGraw, W. R. (1988), 'Employee Theft: A $40 Billion Industry', *Annals of the American Academy of Political and Social Science*, 498: 51–9.

Lipsey, R. G. (1960), 'The Relation between Unemployment and the Rate of Change of Money Wage Rates in the United Kingdom 1862–1957: A Further Analysis', *Economica*, n.s., 27: 1–31.

References

Lucas, R. E., Jr (1972), 'Expectations and the Neutrality of Money', *Journal of Economic Theory*, 4(2): 103–24.

Lucas, R. E., Jr (1973), 'Some International Evidence on Output–Inflation Tradeoffs', *American Economic Review*, 63(3): 326–34.

Lucas, R. E., Jr (1977), 'Hedonic Wage Equations and Psychic Wages in the Returns to Schooling', *American Economic Review*, 67(4): 549–58.

Lucas, R. E., Jr and Rapping, L. A. (1969), 'Real Wages, Employment, and Inflation', *Journal of Political Economy*, 77(5): 721–54.

Lynch, L. M. (1983), 'Job Search and Youth Unemployment', in C. A. Greenhalgh, P. R. G. Layard and A. J. Oswald (eds.), *The Causes of Unemployment*, Oxford: Clarendon Press.

Machin, S. and Wadhwani, S. (1991a), 'The Effects of Unions on Investment and Innovation: Evidence from WIRS', *Economic Journal*, 101(2): 324–330.

Machin, S. and Wadhwani, S. (1991b), 'The Effects of Unions on Organisational Change and Employment', *Economic Journal*, 101(4): July.

MacKay, D. I., Boddy, D., Brock, J., Diack, J. A. and Jones, N. (1971), *Labour Markets under Different Employment Conditions*, London: George Allen & Unwin.

MaCurdy, T. E. and Pencavel, J. H. (1986), 'Testing between competing Models of Wage and Employment Determination in Unionised Markets', *Journal of Political Economy*, 94(3), pt. 2: S3–S39.

Main, B. G. M. (1981), 'The Length of Employment and Unemployment in Great Britain', *Scottish Journal of Political Economy*, 28: 14–164.

Malinvaud, E. (1977), *The Theory of Unemployment Reconsidered*, Oxford: Basil Blackwell.

Mankiw, N. G. (1985), 'Small Menu Costs and Large Business Cycles: A Macroeconomic Model of Monopoly', *Quarterly Journal of Economics*, 100(2): 529–37.

Mankiw, N. G., Rotemberg, J. J. and Summers, L. H. (1985), 'Intertemporal Substitution in Macroeconomics', *Quarterly Journal of Economics*, 100(1): 225–51.

Manning, A. (1987), 'An Integration of Trade Union Models in a Sequential Bargaining Framework', *Economic Journal*, 97: 121–39.

Manning, A. (1990), 'Imperfect Competition, Multiple Equilibria and Unemployment Policy', *Economic Journal*, 100, suppl.: 151–62.

Marston, S. T. (1976), 'Employment Instability and High Unemployment Rates', *Brookings Papers on Economic Activity*, 1: 169–203.

McCallum, J. (1983), 'Inflation and Social Consensus in the Seventies', *Economic Journal*, 93: 784–805.

McCormick, B. (1990), 'A Theory of Signalling during Job Search, Employment Efficiency, and "Stigmatized" Jobs', *Review of Economic Studies*, 57(2): 299–313.

McCormick, B. (1991), *Unemployment structure and the unemployment puzzle*, Employment Institute.

McDonald, I. M. and Solow, R. M. (1981), 'Wage Bargaining and Employment', *American Economic Review*, 71(5): 896–908.

McDonald, I. M. and Solow, R. M. (1985), 'Wages and Employment in a Segmented Labor Market', *Quarterly Journal of Economics*, 100(4): 1115–41.

Meadows, P., Cooper, H. and Bartholomew, R. (1988), *The London Labor Market*, London: HMSO.

References

Meager, N. and Metcalf, H. (1987), 'Recruitment of the Long Term Unemployed', Institute of Manpower Studies, IMS Report no. 138.

Metcalf, D. (1984a), 'An Analysis of the Redundancy Payments Act', London School of Economic Centre for Labour Economics, Working Paper no. 606.

Metcalf, D. (1984b), 'On Redundancies: Can Employment Subsidies Avert Them? How Do Local Labour Markets Respond to Them?', London School of Economics Centre for Labour Economics, Working Paper no. 640.

Metcalf, D. (1986), 'Labour Market Flexibility and Jobs: A Survey of Evidence from OECD Countries with Special Reference to Great Britain and Europe', London School of Economics Centre for Labour Economics, Working Paper no. 870.

Metcalf, D. (1989), 'Water Notes Dry Up: The Impact of the Donovan Reform Proposals and Thatcherism At Work on Labour Productivity in British Manufacturing Industry', *British Journal of Industrial Relations*, 27(1): 1–31.

Metcalf, D. (1990), 'Labour Legislation 1980–1990: Philosophy and Impact', London School of Economics Centre for Economic Performance, Working Paper no. 12.

Meyer, B. D. (1990), 'Unemployment Insurance and Unemployment Spells', *Econometrica*, 58(4): 757–82.

Millward, N. and Stevens, M. (1986), *British Workplace Industrial Relations 1980–1984: The DE/ESRC/PSI/ACAS Surveys*, Aldershot: Gower Press.

Minford, P. (1983), 'Labour Market Equilibrium in an Open Economy', *Oxford Economic Papers*, 35, suppl. 207–44.

Modigliani, F., Padoa Schioppa, F. and Rossi, N. (1986), 'Aggregate Unemployment in Italy, 1960–1983', *Economica*, 53: S245–S273. Reprinted in Bean *et al.* (1987).

Mortensen, D. T. (1970), 'A Theory of Wage and Employment Dynamics', in E. S. Phelps *et al.*, *Microeconomic Foundations of Employment and Inflation Theory*, New York: W. W. Norton.

Mortensen, D. T. (1977), 'Unemployment Insurance and Job Search Decisions', *Industrial and Labor Relations Review*, 30(4): 505–17.

Mortensen, D. T. (1986), 'Job Search and Labor Market Analysis', in O. Ashenfelter and R. Layard (eds.), *Handbook of Labor Economics*, ii, Amsterdam: North-Holland.

Mortensen, D. T. (1987), 'A Structural Model of UI Benefit Effects on the Incidence and Duration of Unemployment', Northwestern University, mimeo.

Moylan, S. and Davies, R. (1981), 'The Flexibility of the Unemployed', Department of Employment, *Employment Gazette*, 89(1): 29–33.

Moylan, S., Millar, J, and Davies, R. (1982), 'Unemployment—The Year After', Department of Employment, *Employment Gazette*, 90(8): 334–40.

Moylan, S., Millar, J. and Davies, R. (1984), 'For Richer, for Poorer?', DHSS Research Report no. 11.

Murphy, K. M. and Topel, R. H. (1987), 'Unemployment, Risk, and Earnings: Testing for Equalizing Wage Differences in the Labor Market', in K. Lang and J. S. Leonard (eds.), *Unemployment and the Structure of Labor Markets*, New York: Basil Blackwell.

Murphy, K. M., Shleifer, A. and Vishny, R. (1987), 'The Big Push', Chicago Business School, mimeo.

References

Narendranathan, W. and Nickell, S. (1985), 'Modelling the Process of Job Search', *Journal of Econometrics*, 28(1): 29–49.

Narendranathan, W., Nickell, S. and Stern, J. (1985), 'Unemployment Benefits Revisited', *Economic Journal*, 95: 307–29.

Nash, J. F., Jr (1950), 'The Bargaining Problem', *Econometrica*, 18(2): 155–62.

Nash, J. F., Jr (1953), 'Two-Person Cooperative Games', *Econometrica*, 21(1): 128–40.

Newell, A. and Symons, J. S. V. (1985), 'Wages and Unemployment in OECD Countries', London School of Economics Centre for Labour Economics, Discussion Paper no. 219.

Newell, A. and Symons, J. S. V. (1987a), 'Corporatism, Laissez-Faire and the Rise in Unemployment', *European Economic Review*, 31(3): 567–601.

Newell, A. and Symons, J. S. V. (1987b), 'The Phillips Curve Is a Real Wage Equation', London School of Economics Centre for Labour Economics, Working Paper no. 1038.

Newell, A. and Symons, J. S. V. (1989), 'The Passing of the Golden Age', London School of Economics Centre for Labour Economics, Discussion Paper no. 347.

Nickell, S. J. (1979a), 'The Effect of Unemployment and Related Benefits on the Duration of Unemployment', *Economic Journal*, 89: 34–49.

Nickell, S. J. (1979b), 'Estimating the Probability of Leaving Unemployment', *Econometrica*, 47(5): 1249–66.

Nickell, S. J. (1981), 'Biases in Dynamic Models with Fixed Effects', *Econometrica*, 49(6): 1417–26.

Nickell, S. J. (1982), 'The Determinants of Equilibrium Unemployment in Britain', *Economic Journal*, 92: 555–75.

Nickell, S. J. (1984), 'A Review of *Unemployment: Cause and Cure* by Patrick Minford [*et al.*]', *Economic Journal*, 94: 946–53.

Nickell, S. J. (1986), 'Dynamic Models of Labour Demand', in O. Ashenfelter and R. Layard (eds.), *Handbook of Labor Economics*, i, Amsterdam: North-Holland.

Nickell, S. J. (1987), 'Why is Wage Inflation in Britain So High?', *Oxford Bulletin of Economics and Statistics*, 49(1): 103–28.

Nickell, S. J. and Kong, P. (1988), 'An Investigation into the Power of Insiders in Wage Determination', University of Oxford Institute of Economics and Statistics, Applied Economics Discussion Paper no. 49.

Nickell, S. J. and Wadhwani, S. (1990a), 'Employment Determination in British Industry: Investigations using Micro-Data', London School of Economics Centre for Labour Economics, Working Paper no. 1096R.

Nickell, S. J. and Wadhwani, S. (1990b), 'Insider Forces and Wage Determination', *Economic Journal*, 100: 496–509.

Nickell, S. J., Wadhwani, S. and Wall, M. (1989), 'Unions and Productivity Growth in Britain, 1974–86: Evidence from UK Company Accounts Data', London School of Economics Centre for Labour Economics, Discussion Paper no. 353.

Nordhaus, W. (1972), 'The Worldwide Wage Explosion', *Brookings Papers on Economic Activity*, 2: 431–64.

Normington, D., Brodie, H. and Munro, J. (1986), *Value for Money in the Community Programme*, London: Department of Employment, Manpower Services Commission.

References

OECD (1988), *Measures to Assist the Long-Term Unemployed: Recent Experience in Some OECD Countries*, Paris: OECD.

OECD (1989), *Economies in Transition*, Paris: OECD.

OECD (1990*a*), *OECD Employment Outlook*, Paris: OECD.

OECD (1990*b*), *Labour Market Policies for the 1990s*, Paris: OECD.

Oi, W. Y. (1962), 'Labor as a Quasi-Fixed Factor', *Journal of Political Economy*, 70(6): 538–55.

Okun, A. (1981), *Prices and Quantities: A Macroeconomic Analysis*, Washington, DC: Brookings Institution.

O'Neill, J. (1985), 'The Trend in the Male–Female Wage Gap in the United States', *Journal of Labor Economics*, 3(1), suppl.: S91–S116.

Oswald, A. J. (1986), 'Unemployment Insurance and Labor Contracts under Asymmetric Information: Theory and Facts', *American Economic Review*, 76(3): 365–77.

Oswald, A. J. (1987), 'Efficient Contracts Are on the Labour Demand Curve: Theory and Facts', London School of Economics Centre for Labour Economics, Discussion Paper no. 284.

Oswald, A. J. and Turnbull, P. J. (1985), 'Pay and Employment Determination in Britain: What Are Labour "Contracts" Really Like?', *Oxford Review of Economic Policy*, 1(2): 80–97.

Padoa-Schioppa, F. (1990), 'Union Wage Setting and Taxation', *Oxford Bulletin of Economics and Statistics*, 52(2): 143–67.

Pencavel, J. H. (1972), 'Wages, Specific Training and Labor Turnover in U.S. Manufacturing Industries', *International Economic Review*, 13(1).

Phelps, E. S. (1972), *Inflation Policy and Unemployment Theory: The Cost–Benefit Approach to Monetary Planning*, New York: W. W. Norton.

Phelps, E. S. (1978), 'Disinflation without Recession: Adaptive Guideposts and Monetary Policy', *Weltwirtschaftliches Archiv*, 114(4): 783–809.

Phillips, A. W. (1958), 'The Relation between Unemployment and the Rate of Change of Money Wage Rates in the United Kingdom, 1861–1957', *Economica*, n.s. 25: 283–99.

Philpott, J. (1990), 'A Solution to Long-Term Unemployment: The Job Guarantee', London: Employment Institute.

Pissarides, C. A. (1979), 'Job Matchings with State Employment Agencies and Random Search', *Economic Journal*, 89: 818–33.

Pissarides, C. A. (1981*a*), 'Contract Theory, Temporary Layoffs, and Unemployment: A Critical Assessment', in D. Currie, D. Peel, and W. Peters (eds.), *Microeconomic Analysis*, London: Croom Helm.

Pissarides, C. A. (1981*b*), 'Staying on at School in England and Wales', *Economica*, 48: 345–63.

Pissarides, C. A. (1982), 'From School to University: The Demand for Education in Britain', *Economic Journal*, 92: 654–67.

Pissarides, C. A. (1986), 'Unemployment and Vacancies in Britain', *Economic Policy*, no. 3: 499–559.

Pissarides, C. A. (1990), *Equilibrium Unemployment Theory*, Oxford: Basil Blackwell.

Pissarides, C. A. and McMaster, I. F. (1984), 'Regional Migration, Wages and

Unemployment: Empirical Evidence and Implications for Policy', London School of Economics Centre for Labour Economics, Discussion Paper no. 204.

Pissarides, C. A. and Moghadam, R. (1990), 'Relative Wage Flexibility in Four Countries', in L. Calmfors (ed.), *Wage Formation and Macroeconomic Policy in the Nordic Countries*, Oxford: Oxford University Press.

Pissarides, C. A. and Wadsworth, J. (1989), 'Unemployment and the Inter-Regional Mobility of Labour', *Economic Journal*, 99: 739–55.

Podgursky, M. (1986), 'Unions, Establishment Size, and Intra-Industry Threat Effects', *Industrial and Labour Relations Review*, 39(2): 277–84.

Pohjola, M. (1987), 'Profit-Sharing, Collective Bargaining and Employment', *Journal of Institutional and Theoretical Economics*, 143(2): 334–42.

Poterba, J. M. and Summers, L. H. (1986), 'Reporting Errors and Labor Market Dynamics', *Econometrica*, 54(6): 1319–38.

Prentice, R. L. and Gloeckler, L. A. (1978), 'Regression Analysis of Grouped Survival Data with Application to Breast Cancer Data', *Biometrics*, 34(1): 57–67.

Pugel, T. A. (1980), 'Profitability, Concentration and the Interindustry Variation in Wages', *Review of Economics and Statistics*, 62(2): 248–53.

Raff, D. M. G. (1988), 'Wage Determination Theory and the Five-Dollar Day at Ford', *Journal of Economic History*, 48(2): 387–99.

Raff, D. M. G. and Summers, L. H. (1987), 'Did Henry Ford Pay Efficiency Wages?' *Journal of Labor Economics*, 5(4), pt. 2: 557–86.

Ramey, V. (1988), 'Nonconvex Costs and the Behaviour of Inventories', University of California at San Diego, Department of Economics, mimeo.

Ravenscraft, D. J. (1983), 'Structure–Profit Relationships at the Line of Business and Industry Level', *Review of Economics and Statistics*, 65(1): 22–31.

Rees, A. (1973), *The Economics of Work and Pay*, New York: Harper & Row.

Rehn, G. (1982), 'Anti-Inflationary Expansion Policies (with Special Reference to Marginal Employment Premiums)', Swedish Institute for Social Research, Occasional Papers no. 4/1982.

Ridder, G. (1987), 'The Sensitivity of Duration Models to Misspecified Unobserved Heterogeneity and Duration Dependence', University of Amsterdam Department of Actuarial Science and Econometrics, mimeo.

Ridder, G. (1990), 'The Non-Parametric Identification of Generalised Accelerated Failure–Time Models', *Review of Economic Studies*, 57(2): 167–81.

Ridder, G. and Gorter, K. (1986), 'Unemployment Benefits and Search Behaviour: An Empirical Investigation', University of Amsterdam, Faculty of Actuarial Science and Econometrics, Report no. AE11/86.

Roberts, K. (1989), 'The Theory of Union Behaviour: Labour Hoarding and Endogenous Hysteresis', London School of Economics, STICERD Discussion Paper no. TE/89/209.

Robinson, C. (1989), 'The Joint Determination of Union Status and Union Wage Effects: Some Tests of Alternative Models', *Journal of Political Economy*, 97(3): 639–67.

Robinson, P. (1988), 'Why Are the Long Term Unemployed Locked Out of the Labour Market, And What Can Be Done about It?', Campaign for Work, *Research Report*, 1(2).

References

Robinson, P. (1989), 'What Can Britain Learn from Sweden's Commitment to Full Employment?', Campaign for Work, *Research Report*, (1)3.

Robinson, P. (1991), *Full Employment in Britain in the 1990s*, Avebury/Gower: Campaign for Work.

Rogerson, R. (1988), 'Indivisible Labor, Lotteries and Equilibrium', *Journal of Monetary Economics*, 21(1): 3–16.

Rose, N. L. (1987), 'Labor Rent Sharing and Regulation: Evidence from the Trucking Industry', *Journal of Political Economy*, 95(6): 1146–78.

Rosén, Å. (1989), 'Bargaining over Effort', London School of Economics Centre for Labour Economics, Discussion Paper no. 351.

Rosen, S. (1986), 'The Theory of Equalizing Differences', in O. Ashenfelter and R. Layard (eds.), *Handbook of Labor Economics*, i, Amsterdam: North-Holland.

Rosenfeld, C. (1975), 'Job Seeking Methods Used by American Workers', *Monthly Labor Review*, 98(8): 39–42.

Rosenfeld, C. (1977), 'Job Search of the Unemployed', *Monthly Labor Review*, 100(5): 39–43.

Rotemberg, J. J. (1982), 'Sticky Prices in the United States', *Journal of Political Economy*, 90(6): 1187–1211.

Rotemberg, J. J. and Saloner, G. (1986), 'A Supergame-Theoretic Model of Price Wars during Booms', *American Economic Review*, 76(3): 390–407.

Rotemberg, J. J. and Woodford, M. (1989), 'Oligopolistic Pricing and the Effects of Aggregate Demand on Economic Activity', NBER Working Paper no. 3206, Cambridge, Mass.

Rowthorn, R. E. (1977), 'Conflict, Inflation and Money', *Cambridge Journal of Economics*, 1(3): 215–39.

Rubinstein, A. (1982), 'Perfect Equilibrium in a Bargaining Model', *Econometrica*, 50(1): 97–109.

Salter, W. E. G. (1966), *Productivity and Technical Change*, 2nd edn., Cambridge: Cambridge University Press.

Sargent, T. J. (1978), 'Estimation of Dynamic Labor Demand Schedules under Rational Expectations', *Journal of Political Economy*, 86(6): 1009–44.

Savouri, S. (1989), 'Regional Data', London School of Economics Centre for Labour Economics, Working Paper no. 1135.

Schmalensee, R. (1989), 'Inter-Industry Studies of Structure and Performance', in R. Schmalensee and R. D. Willig (eds.), *Handbook of Industrial Organization*, ii, Amsterdam: North-Holland.

Schmitt, J. (1990a), 'Mismatch by Skill and Education in Britain, 1974–86', London School of Economics Centre for Economic Performance, Working Paper no. 49.

Schmitt, J. (1990b), 'Unemployment by Skill Level in Britain, 1974–86', London School of Economics Centre for Economic Performance, Working Paper no. 47.

Shah, A. (1984), 'Job Attributes and the Size of the Union/Non-union Wage Differential', *Economica*, 51: 437–46.

Shapiro, C. and Stiglitz, J. E. (1984), 'Equilibrium Unemployment as a Worker Discipline Device', *American Economic Review*, 74(3): 433–44.

Sheshinski, E. and Weiss, Y. (1977), 'Inflation and Costs of Price Adjustments', *Review of Economic Studies*, 44(2): 287–303.

Sheshinski, E. and Weiss, Y. (1983), 'Optimum Pricing Policy under Stochastic Inflation', *Review of Economic Studies*, 50(3): 513–29.

Shields, J. (ed.) (1989), *Making the Economy Work*, London: Macmillan, in association with the Employment Institute.

Sims, C. A. (1988), 'Comments and Discussion', *Brookings Papers on Economic Activity*, 1: 75–9.

Slichter, S. H. (1950), 'Notes on the Structure of Wages', *Review of Economics and Statistics*, 32(1): 80–91.

Slichter, S. H., Healy, J. J. and Livernash, R. E. (1960), *The Impact of Collective Bargaining on Management*, Washington, DC: Brookings Institution.

Smith, A. (1976), *An Inquiry into the Nature and Causes of the Wealth of Nations* (first published 1776), ed. R. H. Campbell, A. S. Skinner, and W. B. Todd, Oxford: Clarendon Press.

Smith, E. (1988), 'Vacancies and Recruitment in Great Britain', Department of Employment, *Employment Gazette*, 96(4): 211–13.

Sneessens, H. R. and Drèze, J. H. (1986), 'A Discussion of Belgian Unemployment, Combining Traditional Concepts and Disequilibrium Economics', *Economica*, 53: S89–S119. Reprinted in Bean *et al.* (1987).

Solow, R. M. (1969), *Price Expectations and the Behavior of the Price Level*, Manchester: Manchester University Press.

Solow, R. M. (1979), 'Another Possible Source of Wage Stickiness', *Journal of Macroeconomics*, 1(1): 79–82.

Staiger, D. (1990), 'Why Do Union Contracts Exclude Unemployment?', MIT, mimeo.

Standing, G. (1988), *Unemployment and Labour Market Flexibility*, Geneva: International Labour Office.

Stern, J. (1983), 'Who Becomes Unemployed?', Department of Employment, *Employment Gazette*, 91(1): 21–3.

Stewart, M. B. (1983), 'Relative Earnings and Individual Union Membership in the United Kingdom', *Economica*, n.s., 50: 111–25.

Stewart, M. B. (1987), 'Collective Bargaining Arrangements, Closed Shops and Relative Pay', *Economic Journal*, 97: 140–56.

Stewart, M. B. (1990), 'Union Wage Differentials, Product Market Influences and the Division of Rents', *Economic Journal*, 100: 1122–37.

Stiglitz, J. E. (1984), 'Price Rigidities and Market Structure', *American Economic Review*, 74(2): 350–5.

Stiglitz, J. E. (1986), 'Theories of Wage Rigidity', in K. J. Koford, J. L. Butkiewicz, and J. B. Miller (eds.), *Keynes' Economic Legacy*, New York: Praeger.

Stouffer, S. A., Suchman, E. A., deVaney, L. C., Star, S. A. and Williams, R. M., Jr (1949a), *The American Soldier: Adjustment during Army Life*, i, Princeton: Princeton University Press.

Stouffer, S. A., Lumsdaine, A. A., Lumsdaine, M. H., Williams, R. M., Jr, Smith, M. B., Jarvis, I. L., Star, S. A. and Cottrell, L. S., Jr (1949b), *The American Soldier: Combat and its Aftermath*, ii, Princeton: Princeton University Press.

Strand, J. (1986), 'En Vurdering av Ordningen for Okonomisk Stotte til Permitterte Arbeidstakere i Norge', Norwegian Department of Labour, mimeo.

Summers, L. H. (1988), 'Relative Wages, Efficiency Wages, and Keynesian Unemployment', *American Economic Review*, 78(2): 383–8.

References

Sutton, J. (1986), 'Non-Cooperative Bargaining Theory: An Introduction', *Review of Economic Studies*, 53(5): 709–24.

Symons, E. and Walker, I. (1988), 'Union/Non-Union Wage Differentials, 1979–1984: Evidence from the UK Family Expenditure Survey', Keele University, mimeo.

Tarantelli, E. (1986), 'The Regulation of Inflation and Unemployment', *Industrial Relations*, 25(1): 1–15.

Taylor, J. B. (1979), 'Staggered Wage Setting in a Macro Model', *American Economic Review*, 69(2): 108–13.

Taylor, J. B. (1980), 'Aggregate Dynamics and Staggered Contracts', *Journal of Political Economy*, 88(1): 1–23.

Taylor, J. B. (1983), 'Union Wage Settlements during a Disinflation', *American Economic Review*, 73(5): 981–93.

Thalén, I. (1988), 'Swedish Labour Market Policy', London: Campaign for Work.

Thomson, A. W. J., Mulvey, C. and Farbman, M. (1977), 'Bargaining Structure and Relative Earnings in Great Britain', *British Journal of Industrial Relations*, 15(2): 176–91.

Tinsley, P. A. (1971), 'A Variable Adjustment Model of Labor Demand', *International Economic Review*, 12(3): 482–510.

Tobin, J. (1972), 'Inflation and Unemployment', *American Economic Review*, 62(1): 1–18.

Topel, R. H. (1983), 'On Layoffs and Unemployment Insurance', *American Economic Review*, 73(4): 541–59.

Towers, B. (1989), 'Running the Gauntlet: British Trade Unions under Thatcher, 1979–1988', *Industrial and Labor Relations Review*, 42(2): 163–88.

Townsend, R. M. (1982), 'Optimal Multiperiod Contracts and the Gain from Enduring Relationships under Private Information', *Journal of Political Economy*, 90(6): 1166–86.

Tsiddon, D. (1987), 'On the Stubbornness of Sticky Prices', Columbia University, mimeo.

Vroman, W. (1984), 'Wage Contract Settlements in US Manufacturing', *Review of Economics and Statistics*, 66(4): 661–5.

Wadhwani, S. (1985), 'Wage Inflation in the United Kingdom', *Economica*, 52: 195–207.

Wadhwani, S. (1987), 'The Macroeconomic Implications of Profit Sharing: Some Empirical Evidence', *Economic Journal*, 97, suppl: 171–83.

Wadhwani, S. and Wall, M. (1990*a*), 'A Direct Test of the Efficiency Wage Model Using UK Micro-Data', London School of Economics Centre for Labour Economics, Working Paper no. 1022, revised.

Wadhwani, S. and Wall, M. (1990*b*), 'The Effects of Profit-Sharing on Employment, Wages, Stock Returns and Productivity: Evidence from Micro-Data', *Economic Journal*, 100: 1–17.

Wallich, H. C. and Weintraub, S. (1971), 'A Tax-Based Incomes Policy', *Journal of Economic Issues*, 5(2): 1–19.

Warr, P. (1987), *Work, Unemployment and Mental Health*, Oxford: Clarendon Press.

References

Weiss, A. (1980), 'Job Queues and Layoffs in Labor Markets with Flexible Wages', *Journal of Political Economy*, 88(3): 526–38.

Weiss, L. W. (1966), 'Concentration and Labor Earnings', *American Economic Review*, 56(1): 96–117.

Weitzman, M. L. (1983), 'Some Macroeconomic Implications of Alternative Compensation Systems', *Economic Journal*, 93: 763–83.

Weitzman, M. L. (1984), *The Share Economy*, Cambridge, Mass.: Harvard University Press.

Weitzman, M. L. (1987), 'Steady State Unemployment under Profit Sharing', *Economic Journal*, 97: 86–105.

Weitzman, M. L. and Kruse, D. L. (1990), 'Profit Sharing and Productivity', in A. S. Blinder (ed.), *Paying for Productivity: A Look at the Evidence*, Washington, DC: Brookings Institution.

West, K. D. (1988), 'Evidence from Seven Countries on Whether Inventories Smooth Aggregate Output', NBER Working Paper no. 2664, Cambridge, Mass.

White, M. (1983), *Long-term Unemployment and Labour Markets*, London: Policy Studies Institute.

Wiles, P. (1973), 'Cost Inflation and the State of Economic Theory', *Economic Journal*, 83: 377–98.

Winter-Ebmer, R. (1991), 'Some Micro Evidence on Unemployment Persistence', *Oxford Bulletin of Economics and Statistics*, 53(1).

Wolpin, K. I. (1987), 'Estimating a Structural Search Model: The Transition from School to Work', *Econometrica*, 55(4): 801–17.

Wood, D. (1982), *DHSS Cohort Study of Unemployed Men*, DHSS Working Paper no. 1, London: HMSO.

Yellen, J. L. (1984), 'Efficiency Wage Models of Unemployment', *American Economic Review Papers and Proceedings*, 74(2): 200–5.

Yoon, B. J. (1981), 'A Model of Unemployment Duration with Variable Search Intensity', *Review of Economics and Statistics*, 63(4): 599–609.

Zabalza, A. and Tzannatos, Z. (1985), *Women and Equal Pay: The Effects of Legislation on Female Employment and Wages in Britain*, Cambridge: Cambridge University Press.

Zeuthen, F. (1930), *Problems of Monopoly and Economic Warfare*, London: Routledge.

Index of Names

Abowd, J. M. 282 n., 512
Abraham, K. G. 329, 333 n.
Aizcorbe, A. M. 340
Akerlof, G. A. 155, 157, 158, 172 n., 242, 234, 333 n., 350, 425, 533
Alberro, J. 425
Alogoskoufis, G. S. xv, 193, 194, 200, 204, 212, 373, 402, 417, 428, 449, 454–66 passim
Altonji, J. G. 512
Andrews, M. 193, 194
Archibald, G. C. 333 n.
Argyle, M. 108
Armstrong, M. xv
Ashenfelter, O. xv, 144 n., 193, 512, 524
Atkinson, A. B. 52, 255, 333 n., 510 n.
Azariadis, C. 533

Baily, M. N. 333 n., 533
Ball, L. 142, 340, 354, 356, 358 n., 424, 425
Banks, M. 259
Bannock, G. 284 n.
Barro, R. J. 22, 395 n.
Barron, J. M. 242, 358 n.
Bean, C. R. xv, 193, 194, 200, 210, 402, 403, 404, 449, 454–66 passim, 552, 554 n.
Becker, G. S. 476
Beenstock, M. 211
Bell, L. A. 188, 208
Benabou, R. 355
Bentolila, S. 268, 343, 421, 516 n.
Berg, G. J. van den 251, 252, 255, 256
Berndt, E. R. 340, 341
Bertola, G. 268, 343, 421

Beveridge, Lord 62
Bhaskar, V. 385
Bils, M. 340, 358 n.
Binmore, K. 99, 533
Bishop, R. L. 536
Björklund, A. 78 n., 481
Blackaby, F. 199
Blakemore, A. 333 n.
Blanchard, O. J. xv, 109, 140, 141, 142, 148 n., 184, 202, 206, 234, 260, 265, 268, 326, 329, 352, 353, 356, 358 n., 365, 375, 395 n., 490, 516 n.
Blanchflower, D. 144 n., 187, 195, 199, 209, 315
Blau, D. M. 242
Blaug, M. 305
Blinder, A. S. 62, 484
Bloom, D. 302
Blum, A. A. 524
Blundell, R. xv
Boskin, M. J. 510 n.
Brack, J. 339
Brickman, P. 108
Britton, A. xv
Brown, C. 178, 190, 191, 193
Brown, J. N. 144 n.
Brown, W. 97
Brunello, G. 187, 188 n., 189, 199, 200, 202, 208, 501, 502, 515 n., 516 n.
Bruno, M. 129, 212, 417, 428, 429 n., 524, 559
Budd, A. 283 n.
Bulow, J. I. 396 n.
Burchell, B. 259
Burda, M. 343
Burgess, S. M. 554 n.

Burtless, G. 516 n.
Butters, G. R. 234

Cahill, J. 198
Calmfors, L. 136, 149 n., 210, 211, 214 n., 416, 417, 419 n., 524, 538
Campbell, D. T. 108
Caplin, A. S. 142, 355, 356, 358 n.
Card, D. xv, 192, 193, 195, 512
Carlin, W. 388, 395 n.
Carlton, D. W. 339, 356, 424
Carruth, A. A. 191, 193, 370
Cecchetti, S. G. 142, 354
Chatterjee, S. 370
Chesher, A. 252
Chowdhury, G. 196, 248
Christofides, L. N. 199
Clark, A. 144 n.
Clark, K. B. 245, 248 n., 270
Coe, D. 204
Cooper, H. 244, 248, 370
Coutts, K. 339
Cox, D. R. 254
Cristini, A. 513
Crouch, C. 129, 417

Daly, M. 284 n.
Daniel, W. W. 94 n., 240, 242, 245, 247, 248, 258
David, M. H. 284 n.
Davies, G. xv
Davies, R. 283 n.
Davis, S. J. 93 n.
Dehesa, G. de la 524
Diamond, P. A. xv, 234, 260, 265, 266, 267, 326, 329, 471
Dickens, W. T. 155, 164, 166 n., 167, 179, 191
Disney, R. 447, 480
Dixit, A. K. 131, 395 n.
Dixon, H. 396 n.
Domowitz, I. 341
Dore, R. 501, 524
Dornbusch, R. xv, 489
Drèze, J. H. 551, 552
Driffill, J. 136, 416, 417, 419 n.
Duncan, G. J. 178–9

Edin, P.-A. 480
Ehrenberg, R. G. 144 n.
Eichenbaum, M. 377
Ellwood, D. T. 270

Elvander, N. 524
Emerson, M. 39, 95, 97, 257, 434, 508, 516 n., 524
Encaoua, D. 339, 356
Erens, R. 243, 245, 248, 249, 269, 272, 277 n., 279 n., 280 n., 281 n., 284 n.
Estrin, S. 498, 501

Farber, H. S. 90
Feinstein, C. H. 3
Feldstein, M. S. 145 n., 270
Fethke, G. xv, 428
Fischer, S. 140, 141, 142, 356, 358 n., 489
Flaig, G. 340, 345
Flanagan, R. J. 398, 428, 524
Flemming, J. S. 510 n.
Flinn, C. J. 270
Frank, R. H. 161
Franz, W. 204, 283 n.
Freeman, R. B. xv, 84, 87, 89 n., 97, 144 n., 148 n., 188, 190, 195, 208, 209, 302, 417, 500–1
Friedman, M. 77 n., 559
Froyen, R. T. 425

Gagliardi, F. 204
Garman, A. 247
Gennard, J. 145 n.
Geroski, P. 339, 356
Gibbons, R. 177, 214 n.
Gordon, R. J. 558 n.
Gorter, K. 255
Grandmont, J. M. 396 n.
Gray, J. A. 425
Gregory, M. 187, 515 n.
Griffin, G. 244, 248
Gross, R. xv
Grossman, S. J. 22, 91, 533
Grubb, D. xv, 139, 169, 172 n., 201, 308, 379, 402, 449, 454–66 *passim*, 504, 506

Hall, R. E. 92, 169, 201, 234, 282 n., 305, 345, 358 n.
Haltiwanger, J. 93 n.
Ham, J. C. 256, 512
Hamermesh, D. S. 311
Hansen, G. D. 512
Harris, J. R. 305
Harrison, A. 193, 194
Hart, O. D. 91, 396 n., 533
Hashimoto, M. 510 n.
Hay, D. A. 188 n.

Heady, P. 247, 259
Heckman, J. J. 196, 253, 254, 270
Hedges, B. 243, 245, 248, 249, 269, 272, 277 n., 279 n., 280 n., 281 n., 284 n., 554 n.
Hoel, M. xv, 499
Holen, A. 510 n.
Holmlund, B. 178–9, 188, 202, 480
Holt, C. C. 284 n.
Holzer, H. J. 155, 179, 209
Horn, H. 149 n., 538

Ingram, P. 198

Jackman, R. 37 n., 140, 148 n., 225 n., 257 n., 260 n., 261 n., 262 n., 264 n., 265, 297 n., 326, 329, 428, 489, 502, 550, 554 n.
Jackson, P. 259
Jakubson, G. H. 144 n.
Jangenäs, B. 473
John, A. 511 n.
Johnson, G. E. xv, 3, 93 n., 96, 169, 172 n., 317, 333 n.
Jones, S. R. G. 283 n.
Jullien, B. 396 n.

Kahn, C. 396 n.
Kahneman, D. 161
Katz, L. F. xv, 46 n., 155, 164, 166 n., 167, 177, 179, 188, 191, 209, 214 n., 227, 255, 329
Kaufman, R. T. 157, 164
Kennan, J. 99
Keynes, J. M. 140
Kiyotaki, N. 395 n.
Knoester, A. 210
Kong, P. xv, 188, 189, 200, 208, 449
Kreuger, A. B. xv, 164, 165, 166 n., 167 n., 175, 176, 177, 178, 179, 180 n., 192
Kruse, P. 498, 501, 502
Kuratani, M. 510 n.
Kydland, F. E. 377

Lambert, J.-P. 551, 552
Lancaster, T. 252, 253, 254, 255
Lawson, N. 511 n.
Layard, R. 1, 3, 78 n., 89, 93 n., 118, 168, 169, 172 n., 197, 211, 214 n., 258 n., 260, 261 n., 262 n., 264 n., 265, 284 n., 311, 314, 317, 395 n., 440,

441 n., 442, 449, 454–66 *passim*, 473, 480, 489, 492, 510 n., 524
Lazear, E. P. 155, 333 n., 420 n., 421
Lehmann, H. xv
Leibenstein, H. 172 n.
Leonard, J. S. 92, 93 n.
Leontief, W. 91
Lester, R. 174, 190
Levine, D. 164
Lewis, H. G. 138, 195, 198
Lilien, D. M. 92, 284 n., 329, 333 n.
Lindbeck, A. 97, 144 n., 146 n., 202
Lipman, M. 156
Lipsey, R. G. 307, 333 n., 381
Liu, S. 188 n.
Lucas, R. E. 20, 377, 404, 425, 512
Lynch, L. M. 252

McCallum, J. 416, 417, 419 n.
McCormick, B. 238, 249
McDonald, I. M. 91, 96, 112, 114, 115
McGraw, W. R. 155
Machin, S. 128, 198, 199
McKay, D. I. 165, 174
MaCurdy, T. E. 144 n., 193
Malinvaud, E. 22
Mankiw, N. G. xv, 350, 512
Manning, A. xv, 193, 194, 200, 204, 212, 370, 402, 417, 428, 449, 454–66 *passim*, 541
Marsden, D. 524
Marston, S. T. 284 n.
Meadows, P. 244, 248
Meager, N. 246, 475
Medoff, J. L. 84, 87, 89 n., 97, 148 n., 190, 191, 195
Metcalf, D. 95, 97, 246, 420 n., 475
Meyer, B. D. 254, 255, 256
Micklewright, J. 52
Millward, N. 78 n., 89 n., 92, 94 n.
Mincer, J. 89
Minford, P. xv, 128, 211
Miyazaki, H. 533
Modigliani, F. 210
Moene, K. O. 499
Moghadam, R. 214 n.
Montgomery, E. B. 209
Mookherjee, D. 396 n.
Mortenson, D. T. 214 n., 251, 252
Moylan, S. 240 n., 245, 283 n.
Murphy, K. M. 176–7, 370, 476

Narendranathan, W. 250, 252, 255, 256, 284 n.
Nash, J. F. 100
Newell, A. 200, 398, 399, 402, 404, 417, 449, 454–66 *passim*
Nickell, S. J. 93 n., 118, 128, 146 n., 187, 188, 189, 193, 195–200 *passim*, 202, 204, 208, 211, 214 n., 248, 250, 252, 253, 254, 255, 304, 342, 358, 395 n., 440, 441 n., 442, 449, 455–66 *passim*, 489
Nixon, R. 67, 484
Nordhaus, W. 398
Normington, D. 482

Oi, W. Y. 358 n.
Okun, A. 337, 354
O'Neill, J. 88
Oswald, A. J. xv, 91, 92, 93, 94, 144 n., 145 n., 187, 191, 195, 199, 315, 370

Padoa-Schioppa, F. 210
Pelletier, J. 97
Pencavel, J. H. 144 n., 164, 179, 193
Phelps, E. S. 140
Phillips, A. W. 199
Philpott, J. 473
Picard, P. 396 n.
Pissarides, C. A. xv, 214 n., 262, 282 n., 316, 471, 533
Podgursky, M. 197
Pohjola, M. 499
Policano, A. 428
Poterba, J. M. 282 n.
Prentice, R. L. 254
Prescott, E. C. 377
Pugel, T. A. 191

Raff, D. M. G. 167
Ramey, V. 340
Rapping, L. A. 512
Ravenscraft, D. J. 191
Rea, S. A. 256
Redmond, G. 247
Rees, A. 358 n.
Rehn, G. 490
Ridder, G. 253, 255
Roberts, J. M. 558
Roberts, K. 145 n.
Robertson, D. 210
Robins, P. K. 242
Robinson, C. 196

Robinson, P. 259, 473
Rogerson, R. 512
Romer, D. 340, 354, 358 n.
Roper, S. 297 n., 326
Rose, N. L. 192
Rosen, S. 174, 214 n.
Rosenfeld, C. 240 n., 241 n., 283 n.
Rotemberg, J. J. 340, 343
Rowthorn, R. E. 395 n.
Rubin, M. xv
Rubinstein, A. 533

Sachs, J. D. 129, 212, 417, 428, 429 n., 524, 559
Sadler, M. xv
Saloner, G. 340
Salter, W. E. G. 206, 207
Sargent, T. J. 358 n.
Savouri, S. xv, 315
Schmalensee, R. 191
Schmitt, J. xv, 297 n.
Shah, A. 214 n.
Shapiro, C. 158, 162
Sheshinski, E. 355, 510 n.
Sims, C. A. 343
Sinclair, P. xv
Singer, B. 253, 254
Singleton, K. J. 377
Slichter, S. H. 165, 174
Smith, A. 174
Smith, E. 282 n., 554 n.
Smyth, M. 247, 259
Sneessens, H. R. 551
Snower, D. J. 97, 144 n., 146 n., 202
Solow, R. M. xv, 91, 96, 112, 114, 115, 139, 172 n.
Sorrentino, C. 529 n.
Soskice, D. xv, 388, 395 n., 524
Spulber, D. F. 142, 355, 356
Staiger, D. 92
Standing, G. 516 n.
Stanton, D. xv
Steiner, V. 340, 345
Stern, J. 269
Stevens, M. 78 n., 89 n., 92, 94 n.
Stewart, M. B. 191, 195, 214 n.
Stiglitz, J. E. 131, 158, 162, 340, 395 n., 533
Stilgoe, E. 258
Stouffer, S. A. 158
Strand, J. 515 n.
Struckmeyer, C. S. 558 n.

Summers, L. H. xv, 109, 148 n., 155, 164, 165, 166 n., 167 n., 172 n., 175, 176, 177, 178, 179, 184, 192, 202, 206, 245, 248 n., 270, 282 n., 365, 375, 490
Sutton, J. 533, 536
Symons, E. 214 n.
Symons, J. S. V. xv, 200, 210, 211, 398, 399, 402, 404, 417, 449, 454–66 *passim*

Tarantelli, E. 416, 419 n., 423 n., 432
Taylor, J. B. 139, 140, 353
Thalén, I. 473
Tinsley, P. A. 358 n.
Tobin, J. 235, 282 n., 333 n.
Todaro, M. P. 305
Topel, R. H. 145 n., 176–7
Towers, B. 97
Townsend, R. M. 533
Tsiddon, D. 356
Turnbull, P. J. 93, 94, 193, 194
Tzannatos, Z. 88

Wadhwani, S. xv, 62, 97, 128, 164, 169, 187, 188 n., 189, 193, 195, 197, 198, 199, 200, 202, 204, 208, 484, 500, 501, 502
Wadsworth, J. 316
Walker, I. 214 n.
Wall, M. 164, 501, 502

Wallich, H. C. 487
Walsh, M. xv, 449
Warr, P. 259
Waud, R. N. 425
Weibull, W. 254
Weintraub, S. 487
Weiss, A. 172 n.
Weiss, Y. 355
Weitzman, M. L. xv, 71, 72, 493, 496, 497, 498, 500–1, 502, 511 n.
West, K. D. 340
White, M. 242
Wiles, P. 398
Wilson, H. 483
Wilson, N. 498
Wilson, R. 99
Wint, N. van der 210
Winter-Ebmer, R. 283 n., 475
Wolpin, K. I. 252
Wood, D. 243
Woodford, M. 340

Yellen, J. L. 333 n., 350
Yoon, B. J. 252

Zabalza, A. 88
Zellner, A. 282 n.
Zetterberg, J. 188, 202

Index of Subjects

ability
  appropriate controls 178
  differences 212
  uncertainty about 177
  unmeasured 175, 176
adaptation theory 108
addiction theory 476
adjustment
  capital 553
  price 356
  wage 186; asymmetries 208
adjustment costs
  employment 206, 339, 348, 358 n., 372,
    373; convex 337, 342–4; pricing
    hysteresis directly related to 403,
    417, 421, 430, 432; quadratic 346
  price 346, 348, 349–50; convex 351;
    fixed 354–6
age-groups
  differences between skill groups,
    regions and 310, 311, 331, 557;
    causes 44–8 passim; young people 7,
    269, 285, 297–9
  increase in relative size 302
  migration between 300
aggregation 366–9, 551
agreements 483–4, 518, 519, 536
  collective 53, 85, 87; percentage of
    workers covered by 89
  contractual 358 n.
  cost-of-living 524
  one-off severance pay specified by 95
  peace 97, 523
  redundancy 91
  tripartite 517, 520

America, North, see Canada; United
  States
arbitration 97, 419, 521, 523, 524
asymmetries
  adjustment 208
  information 476, 533
attitudes 216, 476
Australia 291, 410, 460, 521
  benefits 52
  dispersions 290, 294, 295, 299
  exit rates 228
  occupations 288, 290
  quasi-judicial determination of basic
    wages 54, 68, 484
  relative pay 89
Austria 288, 329, 463, 529 n.
  corporatism 129
  employment exchanges 283 n.
  low unemployment 31, 83
  unions: bargaining 83, 86;
    centralized 53; high coverage 66, 83,
    483, 523

baby boom 297, 302
bargaining, see wage-bargaining
baseline hazard 253, 254, 256
Belgium 48, 316, 317, 401, 410, 454
  unions 517
  wage indexation laws 68, 484
benefits 5, 39, 63, 416, 447–8, 476, 503,
  557
  administration 243
  costs 129, 130
  coverage and generosity 365, 516
  effects 211

exogenous 27, 107
expenditures 490
job search and 216, 243, 244, 254–6
levels 276, 414
real 101; exogenous 107
regulations 260
supplementary 95
systems 3, 200, 443, 445, 449, 471,
   514–16
utility of 119, 146–7 nn.
see also cost–benefit analysis; duration
   of benefits; replacement ratios
Beveridge curve 286, 404
shifts 38, 47, 268, 332, 557
BMW 136, 149 n.
bonding 154–6, 162–3, 170
booms 8, 20, 21, 52
collusion between oligopolistic
   firms 340
delivery lags 339
more people willing to work 512
price mark-up reduced 370
world 34
Bristol 244, 248, 249
Britain 7, 77 n., 437–48, 529 n.
benefits 244, 514 n.;
   administration 243, 258;
   duration 52
dispersion 290, 299
duration of unemployment 221, 227,
   257, 260, 261, 276; outflow and 474
early retirement 506
employers 42
employment exchanges 63, 283 n.
exit rate 264
fluctuations 1
government 136
hours of work 504
incomes policy 67, 484
industries 298, 310, 327
inflows 225, 266–7, 284 n., 291
job search 220, 224, 235–6, 242–4;
   acceptances 280; applications 241,
   277; choosiness 247–8;
   intensity 278–9; jobs taken 281;
   methods 237–8, 239, 240;
   on-the-job 245; vacancies 268,
   282 n., 327, 328, 330, 480, 549–50
layoffs 92, 93–4
long-term unemployed 475, 476
marginal employment subsidies 492
marginal revenue 459

mismatch 289, 291, 293–5 *passim*, 305,
   310, 315–16, 331
morale 259
number of workers in smaller
   establishments 274
profit-sharing 500
reason for unemployment 271–2
relative unemployment 47, 48
replacement ratio 38, 52
savings of the unemployed 247, 281
severance pay 95
small firms 200
turbulence 294, 295, 296, 297, 329
unions 212; bargaining 90, 121, 129,
   144 n., 520–1; collective
   agreements 89; coverage 87, 196,
   197, 520; insider weight 189;
   largest 91; power 84, 97, 127;
   settlements 90
wages 140–1, 195, 204, 214 n., 520;
   determination 188; insider
   effects 209; manufacturing 180; and
   mobility 316–17; and profits 191;
   regional 313–15; real, rise 128;
   settlements 182, 187
see also CBI; England; Scotland;
   Ireland, Northern; Wales;
   Workplace Industrial Relations
   Survey
British Community Programme 482
budget
constraint 133, 320, 538
cuts 60
deficit 440
business cycles 269, 350, 533
real 285, 373; equilibrium 21
shocks the dominant cause of 377
unemployment variation between 1–4

Canada 256, 410, 461
dispersions 290, 294, 299
manufacturing wages 180
negative unemployment effects 199
occupations 288, 290
unions and bargaining 54, 90, 521–2;
   and strikes 99
capital 26, 395 n., 438, 500
accumulation 396 n.
adjustment of 553
allocation 493
constraint 553
exogenous 107

capital (*cont.*):
    fixed 27; costs 146 n.
    insiders relative to 104, 105
    installed 189
    intensity 167, 171, 192, 273, 342
    force ratio 431
    quasi-rent of 132
    ratio of: to labour 96, 167, 273; to
        planned output 385
    shortage 552, 553
    unused 274
    see also capital markets; capital stock
capital markets 246
    imperfect 144 n., 155, 163, 476, 482,
        510 n.
capital stock 273, 364, 403
    conditioning on 396 n.
    predetermined 368, 369, 551, 552
CBI (Confederation of British
        Industries) 99, 330 n., 446–7, 480
    Databank Survey 181, 182, 187, 198,
        199
CES functions
    production 300, 311, 550, 552
    utility 149 n., 266, 333 n.
changes in inflation 51, 55, 389–90,
        404–5, 408, 410, 436
    annual 77 n., 409
    effect on mark-up of prices over
        wages 56
    increased 19–21 *passim*, 24, 390,
        397–8, 445, 447, 503; annual 411;
        unanticipated 211
    supply side and 438–9
    unemployment and 15–16, 556
China 188
choosiness
    employer 257
    unemployed 247–9
Chrysler 340, 341
closed economies 180, 362–70, 393, 438,
        439, 492
Cobb–Douglas production function 31,
        206, 215 n., 308, 499
    and bargaining 116, 117–18, 122,
        144 n., 498, 499; constant elasticity
        demand 102, 120, 152; efficiency
        wages 497, 540; function and profit
        share 103; long-run unemployment
        107; monopolistic competition 131
collective bargaining, *see*
    wage-bargaining

commodity prices 17, 18, 34
    endogenous 513
    long-run 503
    real 400, 412, 450 n.
    shocks 4, 33, 408
compensating differentials 178–9, 214 n.,
        305
competition
    imperfect 30, 558
    jobs 34, 233, 365, 414, 549
    labour market, barriers to 416
    monopolistic 131, 150, 554 n.
    perfect 124, 320, 498
    price 192
    product market 110, 186, 189, 356,
        357, 444; increased, reducing profit
        mark-up 71; perfect 320;
        reduction 369
    vacancies 234, 251
competitive sector 191–2
competitiveness 386, 388, 394, 403, 442,
        450 n.
    demand and 389, 390, 391–2, 438
    imperfect 393
    international 102, 384–5
    long-run expected level 387
    loss 33, 148 n.; inflation held in check
        by 447
    output price 440
    product market 24, 26–7, 102–7
        passim, 132, 181, 212, 213, 341, 403,
        416; aggregate wage affected by 105;
        increase 121; index 153, 308, 338;
        real product wages determined by
        degree of 107
conflicts 4, 398, 400
    see also militancy; turbulence
congestion 323, 324, 332, 509
consumer price index 134, 385
consumption 246–7, 447, 512, 554 n.
contract curve 113, 115, 144 n., 194
contracts 96, 117, 138, 197, 533
    see also wage contracts
co-ordination, employer/union 50, 55,
        416–19, 422–4, 432, 434 n., 517–24
        passim
    central 449
corporatism 29–31, 129–37, 416, 417,
        421
    Tarantelli's index (TCORP) 418, 419,
        422–3, 432, 433, 434 n.
corporatist economies 538–9

cost–benefit analysis 64, 471, 481–2
costs 303, 444, 558, 559
  efficiency 91
  fixed capital 146 n.
  higher wage 275
  hiring 154, 170, 342–3
  job search 233, 238, 235, 250
  'menu' 343
  nominal prices affected by 72
  per unit of effort 23
  social 319, 321
  stock-out 340
  unemployment benefits 476
  see also adjustment costs; labour costs;
    marginal costs
Current Population Surveys 175, 176,
  177, 282 n.

deadweight 65, 476–7
debts 247, 281, 396 n.
decision-making 90
deficits
  budget 440
  trade 390, 392, 438, 443, 447, 448;
    large 445; zero 444
deflation 18, 19, 382
delivery 338, 343, 363
demand 204–5, 370–1, 386–9, 438
  aggregate 16, 217, 552; on
    employment 139; nominal 138;
    real 145 n.
  allocation of 551
  boom in 447
  changes in structure 558
  effect on prices 337, 338, 339–41, 342,
    346, 357
  elastic 148 n., 322, 362–4
  exogenous shifts 306
  expanded 392
  expected 366
  fluctuations 363, 339
  management 74–5
  nominal 75, 86, 146 n., 494
  output 345
  product 120
  real 384, 393, 431, 440, 442
  relative to capital 86
  unemployment relationship 374, 378,
    403
  see also demand curve; demand
    elasticity; demand function; demand
    shocks; labour demand

demand curve 23, 113–14, 116, 117, 125,
  148 n.
  product 26
  right to manage on 543
demand elasticity 23, 196
  labour 136, 137
  monopolistic competition with 554 n.
  prices 338, 339, 340, 350, 353, 362;
    adjustment costs 356;
    open-economy model 385
  product 120, 146 n., 181, 214 n.
  real wage 148 n.
demand function 127, 149 n., 302, 341,
  395 n.
demand shocks 56, 60–1, 361, 379, 380,
  396 n.
  aggregate 341, 390, 393; cycles
    predominantly generated by 376,
    377
  exogenous 367
  persistence after 142
  potential for increase in
    employment 342
  supply and 16–18
  wage and price stickiness important
    for 375
demographic factors 331
demoralization 75, 257, 259, 475, 476
  and stigmatizing effects 220, 233
Denmark 210, 455, 529 n.
  high replacement ratios 52
  unions 87, 523
  wages 317
Department of Employment 136, 221,
  244, 248, 283 n.
  see also *Employment Gazette*
depreciation 33, 387, 448
deregulation 192, 508
devaluation 523
DHSS (Department of Health and Social
  Security) 236, 284 n.
discount rates 163, 172 n., 233, 284 n.,
  305, 349
  bargaining and 99, 100, 101
  British cohort study (1987) 250–1
  conditional expectations and 250
  high 235
  real 488, 524
  unequal 535–6
discrimination 254, 256, 258
disequilibrium 44, 45, 46, 551–3
disinflation 50, 77 n., 524–5

dismissal 267, 269
  unfair 257, 258
dispersion 290, 291, 294, 295, 299, 309
displacement 64–5, 183, 477
disputes 97, 197
disruption 158, 163
distortions 66
  benefit system 61–2, 471, 482
  tax 70, 482, 487, 489, 559
  wage determination system 61–2, 471
disturbances 10, 21, 44, 75, 109
disutility 162, 414, 415
Donovan Committee (1968) 136
downturns 266, 276, 291, 293, 297, 496
  turbulence and industrial mismatch
    increase 295
DSS (Department of Social
    Security) 283 n.
duration of benefits 50, 55, 59, 200,
    214–15 nn., 258
  disutility of job loss and 414
  indefinite 423, 473
  limited 5, 40, 62, 508
  low 559
  OECD countries 49, 401, 416–18
    passim, 423, 424, 434 n.; hysteresis
    and 430, 432; maximum 41, 514;
    unemployment effects on wages
    inversely related to 428
  open-ended 51–2, 61
  reducing 472
  short 449
  unconditional 62
duration of unemployment 39–41, 45,
    211, 422 n., 459 n., 549
  determinants 250–5, 256–66
  effect of unemployment benefit 557
  effectiveness of the unemployed 168
  increased, secular risk associated
    with 46
  job search and 220–5; distribution of
    spell lengths 225–30
  limited 52
  motorized transport factor 248
  occupation 291
  OECD countries, steady-state
    average 544, 545, 546, 547
  remaining, long expected 473, 474
'Dutch Disease' 443
dynamic optimization 344, 346
dynamic programming approach 547–8

early retirement 73–4, 502, 508, 559
  case for 505
  evidence 506–7
earnings 494, 496, 497
  constraint 495
  elasticity of entrants 316
  manual workers 198
  real, cut in 247–8
  see also wages
EC (European Community)
  benefits 51, 63–4
  budget cuts 60
  inflation 10
  inter-industry co-ordination 54
  real wage rigidity 57, 407
  unemployment rate 1, 5, 48, 222, 397,
    398
  unions 31
  working hours 505
  see also *Labour Force Survey*
education 66, 288, 292, 303, 549
efficiency wages 31, 43, 133, 150–72, 194,
    195, 284 n., 302, 488
  and bargaining combined 539–40
  basic problem 497–8
  and effort 557
  hours of work 503
  incentive to pay 305
  leapfrogging and 56, 70
  market-clearing and 11, 21, 22–5, 29
  wage dispersion and 230
  wage-setting and 490
effort 22, 119–20, 151, 542
  disutility 162
  efficiency wages and 557
  individual 159–61
  lower, taxed wages and 489
  marginal variations 156
effort function 160, 161, 194
EFTA (European Free Trade
    Association) countries
  benefit replacement ratio 52
  nominal inertia in wage-setting 428
  unemployment 2, 5, 48, 61, 397, 398
  union membership 53
  wage rigidity 58, 407
  see also Austria; Norway; Portugal;
    Sweden; Switzerland
elasticities 78 n., 276, 497
  absolute 73, 102, 104, 119, 131
  accessions 185

employment 26, 322
exit rates 39
expected unemployment duration 253, 255
insurance benefits 255
job security 181
labour supply 374
long-run 262
output 395 n.
price of exports 135
standard constant 152, 204
substitution 107, 137, 311, 333 n., 395 n., 554 n.; and efficient bargaining 118; intertemporal 512
survival 26, 102, 104, 486, 537
unemployment 315
unit income, of imports 148 n.
wages 153, 122, 161, 163, 164; real 30; unemployment 315; short-run 373
see also demand elasticity
employers 44, 132–3, 329, 483, 485, 556
choosiness 257
discrimination 242, 256, 258
former 243
last resort 492
national bargain between unions and 129–34
recruitment practices 216; screening 39, 249, 258
stigmatizing behaviour 475
subsidizing 235, 318
taxes 317
see also co-ordination, employer/union
employment 149 n., 205, 304, 421, 497, 512
aggregate 552
aggregate demand, impact of changes in 139
bargaining 91–5, 112–18, 193–5, 541–3
behaviour 336–58; dynamic 350–1
equilibrium 496
exit rate 145 n.
fluctuations 72, 93 n., 139, 501
full 131, 136
lagged 29
measures 538–9
non-inflationary 32, 33
primary/secondary sector 43–4
principle 53
public 492–3, 539; temporary 63–4
rate 8–9, 14, 19, 30, 33, 66

real wages and 130, 132, 133, 134
share of, downward drift 305
stability of, guaranteed by profit-sharing 493
stabilization 186
subsidies 318, 476, 482
taxes on 318, 319, 403
Employment Acts (1980 and 1982) 197
employment exchanges 63, 235, 283 n.
Employment Gazette 92, 93 n., 224–5 nn., 257 n., 474 n.
and average weekly earnings 236 n.
and long-term unemployed 449
and reasons for unemployment 271 n.
and turbulence 297 n., 301 n.
and unemployment by region 293 n.
and vacancies 327–8 nn.
employment protection 261, 262, 559
laws 74, 257–8, 509
Employment Protection Act (1975) 257
endogeneity problems 177, 178, 196
enforced idleness 239
engagements 549, 554 n.
England
North 45, 285, 305
South 312
EOPP survey (1980) 242
Equal Pay Act 88
equilibrium unemployment 20, 27, 31, 496, 539
concept 8, 10
employment protection laws augmenting 508
falling 477, 486, 491, 493
general 106–7
high, leapfrogging and 25, 156
labour market institutions and 276
OECD countries 436, 437, 439, 443–6 *passim*
shocks and 337
unaffected by labour force size 73
unemployment–inflation trade-off 391
vacancies and 154
wage pressure and 32, 219, 388; exogenous 368–9
wage-setting and 14, 105, 106–8 *passim*, 147 n., 151–2, 372
wedge influence 210
see also NAIRU
Euler
equation 347

Euler (*cont.*):
 theorem 554 n.
Europe
 inflation 18
 labour market 475
 unemployment: high 64, 139, 307;
  zero 64
 unions: loss of legal rights 83;
  membership 87; power 84
Eurostat Review 317 n.
exchange rate 33, 384, 387
exit rates 228, 252, 256, 259–65, 475
 directly related to duration of
  vacancies 550
 elasticity 39
 see also outflow
exogenous factors 286, 389, 446
 demand 362
 prices 338
 trade surplus 443
 wage determination 366
expenditures 482
 benefits 490, 516
 job search 243
 labour market
  policies/programmes 49, 51, 423,
  424
 transfer 65
'expense-preference' 161
externalities 66, 321, 539
 benefit 334 n.
 congestion 323, 332
 infrastructure 482
 positive search 61, 471

factors of production 348, 357, 417
 see also capital; labour
Fair Wages Resolution 87
fallbacks 99–100, 133, 536
featherbedding 84–5, 118–25, 127–8, 212,
 557
Finland 188, 214 n., 329, 435, 463–4
 benefits 514 n.
 duration of unemployment 222 n., 224,
  288
 real wage rigidity 407
 unions 87, 523
firms
 characteristics 189–92
 large 190–1, 207, 212, 557
 oligopolistic 340
 pricing behaviour 362–4; and

 employment behaviour 336–58
 small 200, 417, 423, 430, 467 n.
 two-stage bargaining framework 541–3
fiscal policy 372, 374, 375, 379, 388, 389
 short-run shifts 438
 short-term 390
flows, *see* inflow; outflow
fluctuations 1, 16–19, 397, 433
 caused by exogenous shifts 329
 intertemporal substitution theory 21,
  512
 long-frequency 2
 mismatch 297
 short-run 558
Ford 136, 149 n., 167, 340, 341
France 48, 326, 455, 476
 early retirement 506
 hours of work 504
 incomes policy 67, 484, 518
 strikes 55
 unions 88, 517
 wages 180, 316, 317, 518

GDP 16, 100, 314, 403, 427, 450 n.
 benefits percentage 516 n.
 imports 415 n., 441 n.
 labour market programme expenditure
  percentage 478
 trade balance 440
 trade deficit percentage 443, 447
GDP deflator 362, 401, 404, 409
 inflation 8, 9, 397, 399, 427
 prices relative to 32, 134–5, 385
General Health Questionnaire 259
General Household Survey 45, 287, 290,
 291
General Motors 340, 341
Germany 46, 48, 188, 340, 456, 476
 benefits 514 n.
 labour market policy 53
 mismatch 287, 289, 317, 326;
  dispersion 290, 294, 299
 strikes 54
 unions 66, 67, 87, 88, 483, 518
 wages 180, 204, 317, 518
gift exchange 157, 166, 167
GNP 64, 148 n., 151, 155
GNP/GDP deflator 532
government 149 n., 182 n., 522
 arbitration 519
 budget constraint 133, 320, 538–9
 expenditure 396 n., 403, 450 n., 538

regulation 192
training schemes 272
unions and 135–6, 521

heterogeneity 253, 259, 263–6, 475
hiring 267, 274–5, 282 n., 318, 481, 496
  differential costs of vacancies 166
  discouraging 257, 258
  costs 154, 170, 343
  decisions 234
  and firing 342–3
  needs 273
  rate 268, 421
hiring function 217–19, 256, 260, 266,
    325–6, 549
  long-run 268
Holland, *see* Netherlands
homogeneity 256, 551, 552
hours of work
  endogenous 511 n.
  exogenous 503, 511 n.
  overtime 358 n.
  reduced 73
  shorter 502, 504–5, 508
human capital 87, 175, 256
  firm-specific 45, 98
  Japanese value of 72, 501
  standard model 304
hyperinflation 378
hysteresis 59, 258, 261, 412, 414, 442
  demand 553
  incomes policies 485, 490, 509
  inflation in Europe 18
  insiders and 28–9, 34, 109–11, 143,
    201, 204, 213, 557
  NAIRU and 68, 485, 525
  partial 336
  price equation 420
  price-setting 337, 342, 356, 372, 407,
    408, 417–21; changes in activity 361;
    employment adjustment costs 344,
    348, 349, 350, 403, 430, 432; shocks
    persistence 374, 377, 393
  real wage resistance 210, 392
  role: inflationary pressure 382–3; wage
    and price equations 389
  short-term 10
  strong 74
  wage equations 380, 381
  wage-setting 201–2, 361, 372, 407, 408,
    421–4, 430, 432; habit
    persistence 373; optimal

disinflation 525; shocks
  persistence 374, 377, 393

IFF Research Limited 330 n.
ILO (International Labour
    Organization) 7, 98, 288, 524
  and dispersions 290, 299
  and fluctuations in mismatch and
    turbulence 297
  and industrial conflicts (OECD) 4
  and industrial wages (US and
    Japan) 166
IMF (International Monetary
    Fund) 5 n., 399 n.
imports 415, 442, 511 n.
  cheap 390
  prices 12, 31–4, 59, 409, 459 n.;
    raised 392; real 210, 385–6, 410;
    UK 440, 443
IMS (Institute of Manpower Studies) 95
incentives 133, 335 n., 340, 487
  financial 216, 324
income 61, 145 n.
  fallback 99–100, 133, 536
  growth 56
  marginal utility 112
incomes policies
  absence of, and raised NAIRU 447
  conventional 67–8, 484–5
  OECD countries 517–23 *passim*
  tax-based (TIP) 68–70, 485–90, 559
indexation 55, 68, 142
  full 519
  laws prescribing maximum degree 484
  nominal inertia and 211, 213, 425,
    428, 429, 433
  suspended 523
India 305
indifference curve 113, 114, 115
indivisibilities 533
industrial relations 416
Industrial Relations Act (1971) 257
industry 47, 48
  heavy 46
  unemployment by 298, 305, 310, 327
  wage premia 179
industry-switchers 176, 177–8
inflation 8-10, 64, 139, 396 n., 508, 558
  acceptable level 75
  aggregate 343, 355
  average 425, 427, 430
  constant 406, 412, 443

inflation (*cont.*):
  exogenous 487
  expected 343, 386, 387, 520
  high 74, 525
  nominal inertia and 60, 348–9, 356,
    357
  OECD countries 530–2
  relation between unemployment
    and 14
  shocks and: commodity price 4;
    demand/supply 17
  stable 12–13, 23, 106, 391–4 *passim*,
    444, 513
  stochastic 355
  wage 141, 440, 480, 557
  see also changes in inflation; deflation;
    disinflation; hyperinflation;
    inflationary pressure; NAIRU;
    reflation; stagflation; trade-offs
inflationary pressure, 71, 111, 392, 487,
  506
  control 67
  development 8
  population growth 553
  restrained 484
  short-run 382
inflow 218–25 *passim*, 276, 282 n., 284 n.,
  291, 472
  manpower programmes 480
  occupations 330
  OECD countries 544, 545, 546, 547
  psychological health 259
  race differences 299
  stable 263
  U/V curve 266–72
  young people 297
information 235, 238, 246
  acquisition 233
informational asymmetries 476, 533
infrastructure 66, 482
innovations 345, 395 n.
insiders 86, 106, 109, 112, 114, 205,
  214 n.
  asymmetric effects 208–9
  hysteresis 34, 203, 204, 213, 421
  insider–outsider models 144 n., 206–7
  jobs at stake 212
  power 28–9, 83, 111, 416, 424, 432
  relative to capital 104, 105
  survival 103, 181, 202
  union model with 181–4

wages 364, 365, 368, 421, 553, 556,
  557
  weight 185–9, 200
interest rate 386, 387, 396 n., 512
intervention 65, 67, 471, 476, 484, 523
interviews 239, 259, 280, 283 n., 475
inventories 340, 358 n., 363
inverse Mills (IM) ratio 196
Ireland, Northern 480
Ireland, Republic of 289, 401, 410,
  456–7, 529 n.
  benefits 515 n.
  persistent high unemployment 306
  wage-bargaining 518
IS-LM system 362
isoprit curves 114
Italy 7, 457, 529 n.
  benefits 424, 514 n.
  high regional unemployment 46, 285,
    289, 295, 305–6
  unions 57, 88
  wages 317, 407, 518; indexation 68,
    484, 519

Japan 67, 397, 416, 462, 522
  absence of hysteresis 408
  benefits 52, 514 n., 515 n.
  early retirement 506
  low unemployment 2, 5, 48, 224, 559;
    profit-sharing and 72–3, 496, 500–2,
    509
  regional differences 289, 295
  wages 199, 200, 209, 212, 407;
    industrial 165, 166; insider
    weight 188, 189; manufacturing 180
  working hours 73, 504
job applications/finding, *see* job search
job loss 93, 144 n., 538
  disutility 414, 415
  exogenous 177
  higher wages leading to 25
  less risk of 86, 117
  psychological impact 259
job search 12, 34–42, 53, 75, 554 n.
  applications 179, 258, 283 n.;
    numbers 240–1, 276, 277;
    travel-to-work effect 248, 249
  choosiness 247
  competition 233
  costs 233, 235, 238, 250
  ease 549

effectiveness 233, 237, 257, 264, 402, 472; influences 216–17; outsiders 41
employed job-seekers 549–50
factors affecting 38–41
hours spent 283 n.
information 236–40, 245
intensity 236, 237, 250, 278–9
journey-to-work times 249
leavers 269
locations 249
methods 239
mobility 262
movement, job-to-job 244–5
obstacles 242
offers/acceptances 242, 243, 280
on-the-job 231–3, 235, 245, 246, 250
probability 227
reason for not 243–4
refusals 243, 280
rejection 282 n., 475
screening 258
theory 230–5
see also duration of unemployment; hiring function
jobs
  bad 85, 125–9
  creation 306, 482
  good 125–9, 143
  opportunities 303
  personal service 269
  primary sector 44
  productive 273
  queues 168, 170, 179
  rationing 11, 22, 42, 66, 250, 556
  satisfaction 249
  security 138
  slots 184, 185
  tenure 269, 421, 425, 432
  transfer 305
  see also job loss; job search

Korea 180

labour 144 n., 157, 273, 304, 311, 488
  contracts 533
  direct 45
  elasticity of substitution between capital and 395 n.
  heterogeneous 163, 253
  hoarding 339
  homogeneous 163

immobility 533
intensity 103, 104, 105
lesser power of 118
marginal product 342
migration 305
mismatch and substitution 550–1
movement 485
quality, unobserved 175–8
ratio of capital to 96
reallocation of 68
share of 135; raised 107
shortages 446–7, 480, 484
skilled 22, 42, 168, 318–19, 322, 329
taxes 363
turnover 59
see also labour costs; labour demand; labour force; labour market
labour costs 32, 69, 274, 358 n., 486, 487
  exogenous changes 209
  future 363
  minimizing 154
  past 109
  real 75, 108, 210, 213
labour demand 160, 194, 495, 502
  elasticity 137
  excess 72, 493, 500
  'Keynesian' 551
  limited 64
  mismatch between labour supply and 310, 321, 471; persistent imbalance 285, 286
  shifts 45, 46, 175; exogenous 329
labour demand curve 20, 193, 194
labour demand function 321, 341, 351, 373
labour force 125, 144 n., 317–18, 395 n., 506
  constant/fixed 106, 551
  endogenous 299, 303–7, 321, 322–4
  exogenous 300–4, 322
  growth 553
  OECD countries 8, 403, 438
  re-entrants 270
  relative 286
  response to wage differentials 324
  shrinkage, in recession 72, 501
  see also labour supply
Labour Force Survey 6, 327 n.
  and flows 45 n., 291 n., 298 n.
  and job search 237, 244, 245, 272, 283 n.

labour market 18, 217, 259, 276, 549
  bad conditions 267
  casual 138
  competitive 174–81, 190, 206
  continuously in balance 21
  demand 216
  equilibrium 14, 43, 71
  external 416, 424
  low-unemployment 47
  manual 44, 125
  market-clearing 71, 72, 168, 493, 512
  non-clearing 12, 22–31, 163
  policies 53, 61, 63, 424, 473–5, 477
  programmes 423, 478–9
  regional 314
  'secondary' female workers 501
  secondary sector 11
  skilled 318; and unskilled 320
  spending 55
  steady states in, comparing 263
  Swedish 64
  theory of employment and 8
  unionized 449
  US 88
  variables 193, 194, 399
  wages 370, 447, 559
  well-functioning, long-term
    unemployed in 475
labour supply 126, 141, 255, 302, 421,
    512
  effective excess, raising 34
  inelastic 494
  long-run 306
  mismatch between labour demand
    and 310, 471; persistent
    imbalance 285, 286
  price of 97, 98, 158, 250
  real interest rate effect on 396 n.
  reduced 42, 65
labour supply equation 21
labour supply function 373, 380
layoffs 25, 91–2, 111, 112, 143
  criteria 93–5
  risk of 28
  temporary 114, 514 n.
  voluntary 533
leading sector 312–13, 315, 324
leapfrogging 27, 69, 75, 152, 156, 484
  inducing 56
  preventing 25, 67, 150
Leeds 241, 249, 259
LIFO (last-in, first-out) 93, 94, 95, 144 n.

linearity 201, 266
living standards 31, 60, 74, 388, 412
  potential, changes in 33
  reduced 34, 209, 210
London 98, 244, 248
long-term unemployment 200, 204,
    282 n.
  case for targeted public
    employment 492
  demoralization arising from 75, 220,
    257
  exit probabilities 263
  growth 262
  less damaging to manual workers'
    prospects 246
  OECD countries 49, 422, 430, 440–1,
    449, 459
  policies 64, 474–6, 480
  reduced 65
  search effectiveness: application
    rate 241; interviews 258–9, 283 n.;
    obstacles 242; reduced by 217, 237,
    238, 264, 276
  used as a screening device 39
Lucas supply curve 21

McDonald–Solow efficiency
  conditions 112, 114, 115, 116, 144 n.
management 84–5, 97, 161
  effort set by 121, 122, 198
  personnel 164, 170
  rights 91, 495, 497
manning levels 95, 118–19, 121, 143, 198
manpower policies 51, 62–5, 472–92, 509
manual workers 125, 287
  earnings 198, 314, 316
  job search 234, 242, 246, 269
  number of unemployed men 8, 44
marginal costs 340–1, 345, 353–4, 356,
    370, 490
  expected 363, 371, 496
  long-run 344, 348, 372
  marginal revenue equal to 338
  price mark-up on 22, 71, 339, 342,
    357, 369, 385, 395 n., 491
  short-run 344, 348, 372, 417
marginal revenue 338, 345, 493, 496
marginal revenue product 102, 120, 205,
    351, 395 n., 498
  fall 71
  labour 341, 342
  OECD countries 440, 441, 450, 454–65

market-clearing 75, 369, 501, 558
efficiency wages 11, 150, 168, 170
manual labour 125
secondary sector 42, 85, 512
wages 21, 24
Weitzman's theory 71, 72, 493–7
market failure 69, 485
market power 191, 192
mark-ups
price 376, 384, 395 n., 492; on
marginal cost 71, 338, 340–1, 357,
369, 376, 491; on wages 13, 19, 339,
340, 364, 367, 370, 385, 490
wage 115–16, 118, 156, 161, 197,
214 n.; alternative income 102; key
to understanding
unemployment 117; over outside
opportunities 26–7, 104, 105, 486;
over prices 75; union 32, 126, 138,
442, 443, 557; union–non-union
195–9, 212, 449; on value added
prices 368
means-tested assistance 515
mediation 519, 523
mental health 259
Michigan Panel Study 259
Midlands, West 244, 248–9
migration 299–300, 316, 324
discouraging 65
equilibrium 199
failure to keep pace with labour
demand 45–6
high-unemployment areas: into 66;
from 305
steady-state 306–7
subsidies 317, 319, 482
zero 303–4, 319–20, 322–3, 335 n.
militancy 60, 197, 400
greater 4, 17, 61, 483; world-wide 398
mismatch 285–335, 402, 442–3, 459 n.,
557
causes 44–6
increase 4, 38
labour demand/supply 61, 471
policies 65
relation to NAIRU 46–8
skills 65, 446–7, 482
types of labour 550–1
U/V 47–8, 217, 257, 261, 324–31
mobility 285, 313–17, 331
monetary policy 374, 375, 378, 388, 389,
405

aggregate 379
short-run shifts 438
short-term 390
money
growth 60
illusion 20
spent 278, 279
supply 372, 450 n., 452 n.
monopolies 20, 22, 71, 355, 414, 493
product market 27
see also competition
monopsony 153, 163, 214 n., 510 n.
moral hazard 95, 155, 162, 170, 473
benefits and 62, 510 n.
morale 258, 259
motivation 151–3, 157, 160, 161, 170,
216
adverse effect of prolonged
unemployment 258, 259
effect of wages 164
loss of 254, 256
MSC (Manpower Services
Commission) 242, 249
multiple equilibria 369–70

NAIRU (non-accelerating-inflation rate
of unemployment) 15–17 *passim*, 28,
50, 57, 106, 389, 394, 396 n., 525,
558
consistent with trade balance 392
hours of work and 503
incomes policies and 70, 447
long-run 10–11, 18, 33, 68, 75, 213,
448, 485
OECD 513
profit-sharing and 72
reducing 509; incomes policies 70
relation of mismatch to 46–8, 307–13,
315
search effectiveness and 216
short-run 41, 77 n., 111, 146 n.
unemployment–inflation trade-off
and 377–84
Nash bargaining 193, 194, 541
maximand 100, 101, 108, 119, 499, 536
National Labour Relations Act 144 n.
National Survey of Engagements and
Vacancies 272, 284 n.
natural wastage 25, 27, 111, 112, 556
Netherlands 48, 317, 329, 410, 458
benefits 255
early retirement 503

Netherlands (*cont.*):
  hours of work 504
  unions 54, 87, 519
New Earnings Survey 314
new entrants 264, 267, 306
New Zealand 52, 54, 289, 460, 515 n.,
    529 n.
  compulsory arbitration 97, 521
nominal inertia 15–16, 56, 57, 186, 356,
    361, 363, 372, 414, 432
  capturing, rate of change of
    inflation 404
  contract structure 55
  cycles generated by demand shocks
    allied to 376, 377
  labour demand unaffected by 20
  in price equation 426
  price-setting 16, 21, 75, 336, 375, 379,
    393, 403, 408, 424–5, 440;
    adjustment costs 337, 342, 344,
    347–51 *passim*, 357, 358 n.
  unions and 86, 138–42, 143
  in wage equation 429
  wage-setting 16, 75, 211–12, 213, 375,
    379, 393, 425–8, 442
non-market-clearing 155, 511 n., 197
non-union wage models 184–5
Nordic countries, *see* Scandinavia
norms 67–8, 69, 484, 485, 523
Norway 188, 210, 224, 329, 435
  benefits 515 n.
  shocks 410
  unions 523
  wages 83, 180
notice 420, 421

occupations 47, 48, 247–8, 305, 310,
    326–31
  differences 285, 286–9, 291, 303;
    between age-groups and 44; most
    important 8
  inter-industry wage relativities 167
  skilled 306–7
Oceania 397, 398, 407
  see also Australia; New Zealand
OECD countries
  adjusted R^2 434–5
  benefits 41, 49, 514–16
  collective bargaining 50–1
  dispersion 294–5, 299
  early retirement 507

incomes policies 517, 518, 519, 520,
    521, 522
industrial conflicts 4
industrial differences 294–7
inflation 18, 377–8, 506, 530–2;
    wage 141
labour market policy/programmes 473,
    478–9
NAIRU 513
oil shock 392
strikes 98
terms of trade 33
treatment of unemployed 49
turbulence 296–7, 300
turnover rate 222
unemployment 36–7, 47, 49, 222, 292,
    526–9; duration 222; explaining
    changes in 408–13; regional 294–5,
    296–7; stocks and flows 544–7
unemployment–inflation trade-off 8–9
unionized workers 88
vacancy rates 36–7
wages: bargaining systems 517–24
    passim; inflation 141; rigidity 58–9,
    60
wedge effects 210
working hours 505–6
see also Australia; Austria; Belgium;
    Britain; Canada; Denmark; Finland;
    France; Ireland, Republic of; Italy;
    Japan; Netherlands; Norway;
    Portugal; Spain; Sweden;
    Switzerland; United States
oil 46
  North Sea 440, 443, 446
oil shocks 63, 377, 399, 408–10, 417, 559
  consequences 392–3
  favourable 412
  impact 58–9
  inflation following 18
Okun's law 148 n., 337
open economies 134–5, 389–92, 394, 401,
    437–8, 492
  model 384–9
outflow 218–21 *passim*, 226–7, 234,
    256–62 *passim*, 265, 268, 472, 480
  explaining 250
  weighted average of unemployment
    and vacancies 266, 267
output 169, 172 n., 274, 321, 333 n., 345,
    366, 438, 508

changes 149 n.
  constant, increased leisure with 502
  demand and 136–7, 389
  dependent on effort 151
  effort-bargaining and 124
  expected price 183
  fall in 60
  fluctuating 72, 500
  full utilization 431, 551
  limited by non-skilled labour
    shortages 42
  lump-of-output theory 502–5, 506, 507
  marginal cost, reducing 490
  national 34
  planned 363, 364, 385
  potential 440
  price surprises and 21, 377
  raising 318–19
  relative wages and 164
  supply price 513
  value added 152, 338, 362, 386
outside opportunities 26, 27, 104, 105,
  486
outsiders 53, 83, 84, 213
  hysteresis 34, 557
  search effectiveness 41
overmanning 83, 118
overtime hours 358 n.

pay settlements 199, 519, 520
  factors influencing 181, 182, 187
payoffs 536
payroll taxes 210
performance
  economic 417, 419
  unemployment 410, 448
  wages related to 188
  work 475
persistence 18–19, 143, 276, 307, 413,
  559
  causes, in the aftermath of shocks 216
  determination 408
  efficiency wages and 168–70
  endogenous sources 139
  habit 373
  insider power 111
  long-term 397
  medium-term 83, 142
  open-ended benefits and 61
  shocks 377
  unions and 85–6

Phillips curve 15, 21, 49, 56, 59, 379, 381
piece-rate workers 191
pin-point targeting 65, 66, 482
placements 63, 509
'poaching' 66, 510 n.
policy implications 317–24
Policy Studies Institute 247
population 331
  growth 306; effects 553
Portugal 54, 60, 88, 519–20
present value 547, 548
price 22, 137, 152, 212, 213
  behaviour 338–9
  changing 142
  competition 192
  determination 408
  dynamic 346–9
  and employment 341
  expectations 139, 405
  index 209
  inflation 236 n.
  law of one 156–7
  nominal 72, 204, 308, 500
  output 186
  predetermined 387, 551
  profit-maximizing 424
  relative 32
  rigidity 343, 356
  rises 8
  staggering 337
  surprises 21, 374, 376, 377, 378
  see also commodity prices; imports;
    mark-ups; price equation; price
    function; price-setting; pricing
price equation 23, 47, 402–3, 430, 438,
  440, 441, 459 n., 510 n., 553
  country-specific parameters and 56, 60
  generalized 370–1
  unemployment effect in 415
price function 308, 550
price-setting 142, 345, 370, 376, 384–5,
  448
  competitiveness, impact of 386, 388,
    389
  economic activity (unemployment),
    impact of 414, 428
  hysteresis 337, 356, 372, 373, 374, 377,
    408, 430, 553
  influences 438
  nominal inertia 20, 75, 375, 393, 403,
    406, 440

price-setting (*cont.*):
  real product wage determined by 24
  staggered 21, 351–4
  wage-setting and 12–14
pricing 19, 47, 205, 366, 493
  behaviour 130, 219, 336–58, 362–4,
    472, 552, 558
  mark-up 376
  nominal inertia 21
  optimal 354–6
primary sector 42, 43–4, 249, 250
probabilities 229, 232, 254, 265, 274
  exit 230, 250, 252, 263, 273
  failing to obtain a job 201
  job-finding 200, 218, 233, 234, 282 n.,
    547–8
  selection 251
  survival 100–1, 102, 103, 181, 202, 252
product markets 22, 168, 191–2, 448, 558
  imperfect 115
  see also competition; competitiveness
production 204, 205, 337, 366, 430, 438
  elasticity of substitution 554 n.
  labour intensity 26
  variance 339–40
production function 137, 181, 333 n.,
    369, 438, 440, 551
  employment determined by 364, 367;
    and output 387, 389
  see also CES functions; Cobb–Douglas
    production function
productivity 21, 31, 124, 169, 302, 557
  fall 170
  growth 32, 34, 52, 84, 172 n., 369, 402,
    556
  individual, in different jobs 230
  marginal 70, 538
  no impact on unemployment 5, 152
  overmanning and 118
  and profitability 186–7
  profit-sharing and 71, 73, 493, 498,
    501
  raising 212
  slowdown 377
  standard marginal 341, 342
  total factor 171, 208
  trend 186, 214 n., 368, 369, 385, 404,
    553
  unions and 148 n.
  wages and 183, 184, 198, 199;
    bargains 489; correlation 163;
    effect 204–9; influence 364; and

profitability 186–7, 189
  worker-vacancy match important
    for 249
profitability 161, 167, 171, 181, 189
  productivity and 186–7
profits 24, 154, 157, 339, 356, 486
  differentiating 152
  effort-bargaining and 124
  exogenous forces 161
  expected 273, 274
  falls in demand and 511 n.
  lagged 161
  maximizing 20, 22, 23, 102–3, 150,
    151, 338, 341, 363, 497; discounted
    value 172 n.; short-run 385
  operating 101
  optimal 350
  real 346
  share of 147, 386, 492; relative 119,
    120; *see also* profit-sharing
  steady-state 153
  wages and, link between 191
profit-sharing 71–2, 493–502, 509, 511 n.
psychological ill-health 259
public employment 492–3, 539
  exogenous 538
  temporary 63–4
public expenditure 478–9

quit rates 153, 166, 172 n., 179, 202
  exogenous 103, 107
  reducing 24
  wage differences and 171

race 7, 285, 298–9, 310, 322, 331
Ramsey-type equation 321, 323
real wages 342, 369, 438, 512, 533, 550
  aggregate 450 n., 452 n.
  employment, relation to 341
  equilibrium 494
  fall in, effort-bargaining and 124
  flexibility 14, 15
  high 383, 556, 558
  impact of shocks 375–6, 380
  price-setting 19
  product 404
  relation to unemployment 19–21, 382
  resistance 107–9, 209–11, 213, 392,
    402, 412, 440
  rigidity 57–8, 59, 379, 406–7, 408–12,
    533
secondary sector 43

substantial rise 128
target 472
recession 34, 198, 208, 241, 276
labour force shrinkage 72, 501
recruitment 153–4, 216, 273, 365, 477
and retention 163–4
subsidies 63
redundancies 91, 94, 181, 257, 267
payments 144 n.
Redundancy Payments Act (1965) 257
reflation 503
refusals 243, 280
regions 311, 326–8, 557
aid 482
differences: occupations, groups and 7,
47, 285, 289–94, 303, 331, 557
labour mobility 315–16
wage behaviour 313–15
regulations 257
rejection 282 n., 475
rents 24, 28, 179, 191, 214 n.
product-market 27, 104, 132
quasi- 27, 189
regulatory 192
rent-sharing 161, 192
replacement ratios 27, 55, 183, 186, 200
EFTA countries 52
exogenous 107, 109–10, 117
motivation influenced by 258
OECD countries 49–50, 416, 418, 433,
434 n., 442–3, 459 n., 516; impact on
unemployment 211; single
person 514
rising 61
search effectiveness affected by 38–9
reservation wages 42, 43, 231–3, 246,
250–2, 255
dynamic programming
approach 547–8
Restart programme 52, 447, 480
restrictive practices 128, 198
retention 153, 157, 163, 164
retirement 246, 306
early 73–4, 502, 505, 506–7, 508, 559
retraining 63
revenue function 184, 495, 496
rights
legal, against unfair dismissal 257
management 91, 495, 497
voting 114
work 63–4, 96, 476

sales 208, 339, 496
savings 246, 247, 281, 396 n.
Scandinavia
employer co-ordination 55
firm-level strikes 54
insider weight 188, 189
low unemployment 31, 85
unions 53, 66, 85, 86, 129, 189, 483
see also Denmark; Finland; Norway;
Sweden
school-leavers 259
Scotland 293, 327
SCPR (Social and Community Planning
Research) 236 n., 238, 240, 241, 244,
283 n.
screening 39, 249, 258
search/search effectiveness, *see* job search
secondary sector 11, 42–4, 85, 249, 250,
512
self-employment 42
sequestration 198
settlements, *see* pay settlements
severance pay 95, 145 n., 420, 421
sex groups 285, 298, 310, 311, 322
differences 299
unequal numbers 217
Sheffield 241, 249
shirking 158, 161–3, 166
shocks 3, 48, 139, 409, 411, 533
adverse 62, 169, 202
commodity price 4, 33–4, 399–400, 408
demand 16–18, 21, 206; nominal 11
deterministically staggered 354
exogenous 336, 367, 371, 449, 513
firm-specific 355, 356, 424–5
fiscal policy 372, 375
monetary 500
money supply 372
negative 496
nominal 140, 428, 430, 432
nominal inertia role in explaining 141
persistence after 85, 109, 168, 171, 216
price 336; import 31, 60
productivity 206, 371, 431, 494
response to 368, 370, 374–7
structural 285, 331
supply 17–18, 56, 142, 398;
exogenous 513; inflationary 75;
NAIRU response 57; persistence
after 168, 171
technology 362, 371, 372, 376–8
passim, 393, 395 n.

shocks (*cont.*):
  temporary 333 n., 509
  terms-of-trade 32, 169, 412
  vacancy–unemployment ratio a
    measure of 268
  wage 58, 337, 361, 433
  wage pressure 372, 375, 376, 384, 393
  see also demand shocks; oil shocks
short-spell unemployed 236 n., 237, 238
Shunto 212, 522
skills
  formation 323
  groups 311, 316, 318, 557
  requirements 179
slumps 8, 512
small firms 200, 416, 417, 423, 430,
  467 n.
social contracts 520, 523
social pressure 40
Solow condition 122, 151, 156, 184
Solow residual 450 n.
Spain 1, 7, 59, 409, 434 n., 458
  dispersion 299
  early retirement 506
  high replacement ratios 52
  hours of work 04
  occupations 289, 290
  wage-bargaining 88, 520
  wage explosion 404, 410
stability 559
stagflation 384
standard of living, *see* living standards
state dependence 263–5, 475–6
stigmatization 258, 475, 476
strikes 51, 54–5, 87, 96–9 *passim*, 133,
  524
  behaviour 519
  firm-level 53–4
  fund 523
  illegal 92
  income 101
  insurance by employers 518
subsidies 319, 320–1, 323, 324, 509
  employment 65–6, 69, 476, 482, 557;
    marginal 70–1, 74, 490–2, 559
  migration 319, 334 n.
  recruitment 63
substitution 64–5, 477, 550–1
  effects 396 n.
  intertemporal 21, 512, 533
  negative 538
supplementary insurance 515

supply 367, 477
  aggregate 16
  constraint 438, 439, 442–4
  factors 304
  function 341
  long-run 513
  policies 74
  shocks 398
  short-run 513
  see also labour supply
surpluses 438, 443, 444, 447
surprises 403, 404
  price 21, 345, 374, 378; shocks
    and 376, 377
  wage 374, 377
survival
  chances 28
  elasticity 104
  probability 100–1, 102, 103, 181, 202,
    252
survival curve 225–6
survival function 537–8
Sweden 79 n., 188, 224, 435, 465, 529 n.
  benefits 40, 52, 53, 449, 476, 515 n.
  dispersion rate 299
  early retirement 506
  'employment principle' 473
  hours of work 504
  manpower policy 63, 64
  mismatch 288, 289, 290, 329, 331
  movement of labour 485, 510 n.
  training programmes 480–1
  unions 83, 87, 149 n., 523
  wages 180, 210, 214 n.
Switzerland 54, 97, 465–6, 524, 529 n.
  absence of hysteresis 408
synchronization 211, 213, 428, 429, 433,
  434 n.

Tarantelli's index of corporatism, *see*
  TCORP
taxes 71, 209, 320–3 *passim*, 493
  concessions 324
  distortions 65, 70, 482
  effect on unemployment 5, 31–2,
    107–9
  higher, in congested regions 509
  inducements 500
  intra-marginal 490
  lagged 403, 450 n.
  lump-sum 318
  penalties 324

product wages and 211
profit 487, 492
subsidies 331, 332
support for unemployed financed
by 144 n.
uniform 66
wage growth 69
see also wedge
Taylor expansion 346
TCORP (Tarantelli's index of
corporatism) 416, 418, 419, 422,
423, 432–4 *passim*
technical progress 107, 184, 204, 213,
450 n.
technology
constant-return 362
shocks 362, 371, 372, 376–8 *passim*,
393, 395 n.
teenagers 245
see also young people
temporary work 63–4, 476
terms of trade 107–9, 440, 490, 492, 556
adverse shift in 169
international 443, 445–6
OECD countries 33
shock 412
threat effect 148 n., 158, 163, 165, 166,
167
time delays 351–4
TIP, *see* incomes policies
tort actions 198
trade balance 388, 393, 394, 401, 438–41
passim,
adverse 390
depreciation needed to restore 448
equilibrium 389
see also deficits; surpluses; trade-offs
trade-offs 140, 396 n.
output–inflation 425
real wages–employment 132, 133, 134,
135
trade balance–inflation 390, 443
unemployment–inflation 9, 391, 394,
436, 439; deterioration 61;
long-run 406; and NAIRU 361,
377–84; and trade deficit 390, 438,
448
Trade Union Act (1984) 197
training 63, 66, 557
costs 305, 481; amortized 319
subsidizing 482, 509
travel-to-work 48, 249, 289, 310

trends 440 n., 444–8, 450 n.
TUC (Trades Union Congress) 67,
144 n., 484, 521
turbulence 46, 295–7, 300, 301, 329,
333 n.
degree of, in regions 291, 293–4
frictional unemployment and 207
increase 295–7
turnover 101, 115, 146 n., 249, 294, 303
insider falls owing to 114
occupations with high rate of 288, 305
relation between inflow and 222, 224
exogenous 153
wage determination 541

UK, *see* Britain
unemployment 138
'culture' of 448
difference between countries 44, 48–61,
559
effect 199–204
frictional 207
history 60–1
long-run secular shifts 405
macroeconomics 361–96
mismatch 285–335
policies to cut 471–511
reasons for 269–72
regional 200
re-entry to 270, 245
urban 305
voluntary/involuntary 41–4
zero 64
see also dispersion; duration of
unemployment; equilibrium
unemployment; fluctuations; inflow;
layoffs; long-term unemployment;
NAIRU; outflow; persistence
unemployment insurance 95, 145 n.
unemployment–vacancy
relationship 35–8, 324–31
see also Beveridge Curve
unfair dismissal 257, 258
union power 96–9, 101, 104, 184–6
passim, 189, 483, 542, 543
change in 127
decreasing 200
equilibrium unemployment an
increasing function of 107
fall in 127, 128
impact of, on effort 147 n.
increased 110, 116, 117, 121, 445, 559

union power (*cont.*):
  and increased unemployment rate 305
  rise and fall (Europe) 84
  wages and 212, 443, 459 n.
  weak 150
unionization 88, 170, 171, 449, 558, 559
unions 11, 29–31, 75, 366, 369, 556
  centralized 130
  co-ordination 416–19 *passim*, 422, 423,
    432, 434 n.
  coverage 51, 85, 128–9, 137, 143,
    148 n., 167, 189, 196, 197, 483;
    density and 87–90
  decentralized 61, 471
  effect of 193–9
  higher rents for 191
  mark-ups 557
  membership 3–4, 53, 87
  militancy 17, 483
  objectives 100–1
  'overaward' payments 68
  strength 34, 402, 421
  see also insiders; threat effect; TUC;
    union power; unionization;
    wage-bargaining
United States 1–6 *passim*, 32, 38, 61,
    77 n., 481
  absence of hysteresis 408
  average unemployment 48
  benefits 5, 40, 476; duration 52, 62
  boom and decline 46
  Bureau of Labor Statistics 240, 297 n.,
    301 n.
  duration of unemployment 222–8
    passim, 235–43 *passim*, 248, 255,
    259, 266–72 *passim*, 276, 282 n.,
    283 n.; flow and 45
  efficiency considerations 25
  hiring-and-firing costs 343
  inflationary expansion 398
  long-term unemployed 39
  low import–GDP ratio 401
  marginal costs 340
  mismatch 286–95 *passim*, 298, 299,
    302, 315, 329
  policy 392
  prices 558
  shocks 60
  surveys 6, 247
  unemployment insurance funds 95,
    145 n.
  unions 31; coverage 66, 482, 522

wages 180, 188–97 *passim*, 209, 212,
    214 n.; bargaining and unions 54,
    67, 83–98 *passim*, 114, 129, 139,
    144 n., 522; industrial 165, 166, 167,
    557
  working hours 73
utility 122, 159, 161, 177, 186, 257
  functions 512, 542
  leisure 250
  value 121

vacancies 4, 11, 154, 184, 201, 541
  compulsory notification 63
  duration 329–31, 510 n., 549, 550
  flows 330
  ineffective fillers of 213
  level of, unemployment rise relative
    to 4, 39
  long-term unemployed and 475
  lower 170
  reducing 24
  registered 480, 554 n.
  well-paid 42
  see also job search; mismatch;
    unemployment–vacancy relationship
value added 13, 212, 490
  output 152, 338, 362, 386
  prices 362, 368
variables
  aggregate 314
  endogenous 405, 450 n., 452 n.
  exogenous 252, 368, 438, 443
  wage pressure 219, 385
voluntary quits 103, 267, 276

wage-bargaining 22, 29, 31, 199, 385,
    498–500
  centralized 84, 85, 137, 143, 213,
    415–19 *passim*, 424, 559; versus
    decentralized 30; wages more
    responsive to unemployment under
    200
  collective 25, 50, 55, 84, 87–8, 125, 128
  concession 116
  co-ordinated 51, 417, 419, 430, 434 n.,
    449
  in corporatist economies, effect of
    employment measures 538–9
  decentralized 129–37, 204, 447
  effort 121, 124, 125, 198
  free 68, 485
  industry-level 136–8

payoffs 534–5
power 100
reducing unemployment by 71
right-to-manage 194
structure 61, 374, 425, 432
systems 414, 483–4, 517–24
theory 86–100, 533–6
two-stage framework 541–3
unions and 21, 25–8, 53–5, 83–149,
    167, 193–5, 275; co-ordination 51,
    417, 430, 449; outside and inside
    factors 181, 189, 212; reforming
    66–7; structure 374
wage behaviour 173–215, 219
    regional (Britain) 313–15
wage contracts 61, 140, 142
    durations 211, 212, 213, 429, 433,
        434 n.
    flexibility 51, 55
    staggered, nominal inertia induced
        by 141
    synchronization 211, 213, 428, 429,
        433, 434 n.
    voluntary 556
wage determination 3, 173–215, 364–6,
        384, 471
    long-term unemployment and 408, 558
    non-competitive 361, 393
    policies 74
    turnover model 541
wage equation 315, 430, 438, 441,
        452–66 *passim*, 491, 542
    aggregate 106, 162
wage explosion 410, 433
    Newell–Symons 404
wage function 302, 307, 308, 311, 321–2
wage pressure 31–5 *passim*, 217, 219,
        312, 372, 385–90 *passim*
    downward 381
    excess 150, 509
    exogenous 368, 386
    explaining 54
    factors 314
    fuelled by fall in unemployment 10,
        143
    increased 213, 379, 475;
        consequences 383–4
    insider effect 556
    long-run 401
    OECD countries 406, 410, 431–3
        passim, 443, 447
    reduced 41, 69, 486

shocks 375, 376, 384, 393
taxes to discourage 324
union strength and 305
wage push 14, 57, 59–60, 118, 302–4
    passim
wage rigidity
    nominal 406, 408–9, 410, 411, 425,
        436–7, 559
    real 57–8, 59, 379, 406–12, 533
wages 47, 304, 309, 334 n., 415, 500, 501,
        540
    adjustment 207
    aggregate 105–6, 510 n.
    average 308
    claims 8
    and conditions 230
    consumption 31, 32, 385, 402, 404
    controls 67
    council 520
    differentials 324
    dispersion 417
    distribution 252
    and effort 119–21
    elasticity 153, 322, 373
    elasticity of employment 104
    equilibrium 104
    firm-level 102
    flexibility 59, 188, 311, 322
    high 214 n.
    higher 156–8 *passim*, 190, 273, 275,
        303, 304; reducing absenteeism 164
    indexation 68
    industry premia 179
    inflation 52, 440
    insider 366
    minimum 517–20 *passim*, 522, 523
    money 138, 140, 141, 143
    non-market-clearing 197
    occupational 316–17
    primary sector 44; job rationing
        and 249–50
    product 386
    relative 68; rigidity 485
    shocks 361
    skilled labour 318
    spirals: wage–price 8, 12–13, 67, 162;
        wage–wage 13, 67
    structure 164–8, 333 n.
    surprises 374, 377
    see also efficiency wages; leapfrogging;
        mark-ups; real wages; reservation
        wages; wage-bargaining; wage

wages (*cont.*):
    behaviour; wage contracts; wage
    determination; wage equation; wage
    explosion; wage function; wage
    pressure; wage push; wage rigidity;
    wage-setting
wage-setting 12–14, 19–22 *passim*, 337,
    370, 490–1
  behaviour 105, 159, 384
  competitiveness and 386, 388, 389
  decentralized 66, 483
  by firms 274–6
  highly corporatist 5
  hysteresis 202, 372, 374, 377, 408,
    421–4, 553; optimal disinflation
    policy 524–5
  impact of economic activity
    (unemployment) 414–17
  nominal inertia in 20, 75, 211–13
    passim, 375, 430, 442
  productivity and 186–7, 204, 205, 207
  supply-side forces and 438
  unions and 53
Wages Councils 87
Wald test 262
Wales 293, 327
wedge 66, 209–10, 219, 412, 442, 443
  effect on wage pressure 33, 34

product wage/consumption wage 385,
    404
reduced 481
WEGs (wage employment
    guarantees) 145 n.
welfare 70, 320, 333 n., 335 n., 476,
    511 n.
  effect of system 62
willingness to work 11, 161, 473, 512
women 7, 217, 272, 282 n., 507
  married 271, 424
  relative pay of men and 89
work ethic 262, 481
working conditions 178, 179, 190, 212
working hours 73, 502, 503, 504–5, 508
  endogenous 511 n.
  exogenous 511 n.
  overtime 358 n.
Workplace Industrial Relations
    Survey 89, 187 n., 191, 198, 199
work-sharing 73–4, 502–5

young people 271, 282 n., 285, 297, 424
  much more likely to be unemployed 7,
    269
Yugoslavia 180

Index compiled by Frank Pert

DATE DUE

FEB 11 1993			
APR 03 1994			
NOV 0 5 1995			
MAR 28 1996			
FEB 0 9 2000			
NOV 2 9 2003			
			Printed in USA